THE WRITINGS OF RABASH

ESSAYS

Volume Three

LAITMAN
KABBALAH
PUBLISHERS

Rav Baruch Shalom Halevi Ashlag

The Writings of RABASH
Volume Three—Essays

Copyright © 2023 by Michael Laitman All rights reserved
Published by Laitman Kabbalah Publishers

Contact Information
E-mail: info@kabbalah.info
Web site: www.kabbalah.info
Toll free in USA and Canada: 1-866-LAITMAN

1057 Steeles Avenue West, Suite 532, Toronto, ON, M2R 3X1, Canada

No part of this book may be used or reproduced in any manner without written permission of the publisher, except in the case of brief quotations embodied in critical articles or reviews.

ISBN: 978-1-77228-140-8

Translation: Rinah Shalom, Chaim Ratz
Translation Assistance: Mickey Cohen, Moshe Eisenberg
Content Editing: Noga Bar Noye
Editing and Proofreading: Mary Pennock, Mary Miesem
Internal Design: Gill Zahavi
Cover Design: Baruch Khovov/Inna Smirnova
Executive Editor: Chaim Ratz
Printing and Post Production: Uri Laitman

SECOND EDITION: SEPTEMBER 2023

Table of Contents

Tav-Shin-Mem-Zayin (1986 - 1987)

The Good Who Does Good, to the Bad and to the Good 9
The Importance of Recognition of Evil 13
All of Israel Have a Part in the Next World 30
It Is Forbidden to Hear a Good Thing from a Bad Person 39
What Is the Advantage in the Work More than in the Reward? 46
The Importance of Faith that Is Always Present 74
The Miracle of Hanukkah 82
The Difference between Mercy and Truth and Untrue Mercy 94
One's Greatness Depends on the Measure of One's
Faith in the Future 113
What Is the Substance of Slander and Against Whom Is It? 129
Purim, and the Commandment: Until He Does Not Know 147
What Is Half a Shekel in the Work - 1 155
Why the Festival of Matzot Is Called Passover 181
The Connection between Passover, Matza, and Maror 192
Two Discernments in Holiness 207
The Work of the General Public and the Work of the Individual 214
The Meaning of the Strict Prohibition to
Teach Idol Worshippers the Torah 222
What Is Preparation for Reception of the Torah? 243
What Are Revealed and Concealed in the Work of the Creator? 253
What Is Man's Private Possession? 265
What Are Dirty Hands in the Work of the Creator? 274
What Is the Gift that a Person Asks of the Creator? 282

Peace After a Dispute Is More Important than
Having No Disputes At All 293
What Is Unfounded Hatred in the Work? 319
What Is Heaviness of the Head in the Work? 328
What Is a Light Commandment? 338
What Are "Blessing" and "Curse" in the Work? 346
What Is Do Not Add and Do Not Take Away in the Work? 354
What Is "According to the Sorrow, So Is the Reward"? 365
What Is a War Over Authority in the Work - 1 375
What Is Making a Covenant in the Work? 392

Tav-Shin-Mem-Het (1987 - 1988)

Why Life Is Divided into Two Discernments 401
What Is the Extent of *Teshuva* [Repentance]? 411
What It Means that the Name of the Creator is "Truth" 416
What Is the Prayer for Help and for Forgiveness in the Work? 424
What Is, "When Israel Are in Exile, the *Shechina* Is
With Them," in the Work? 430
What Is the Difference between a Field and a Man of
the Field, in the Work? 448
What Is the Importance of the Groom, that His
Iniquities Are Forgiven? 454
What Does It Mean that One Who Prays Should
Explain His Words Properly? 463
What Does It Mean that the Righteous Suffers Afflictions? 468
What Are the Four Qualities of Those Who Go to the
Seminary, in the Work? 478
What Are the Two Discernments before *Lishma*? 486
What Are Torah and Work in the Way of the Creator? 492
What Is "the People's Shepherd Is the Whole People" in the Work? .. 521
The Need for Love of Friends 527
What Is "There Is No Blessing in an Empty Place" in the Work? 532
What Is the Foundation on which *Kedusha* [Holiness] Is Built? ... 545
The Main Difference between a Beastly Soul and a Godly Soul 591
When Is One Considered "a Worker of the Creator" in the Work? ... 602
What Are Silver, Gold, Israel, Rest of Nations, in the Work? 614
What Is the Reward in the Work of Bestowal? 634
What Does It Mean that the Torah Was Given Out of
the Darkness in the Work? 642
What Are Merits and Iniquities of a Righteous in the Work? 650
What Beginning in *Lo Lishma* Means in the Work 658

The Concealed Things Belong to the Lord,
and the Revealed Things Belong to Us 669
What Is the Preparation on the Eve of Shabbat, in the Work? 680
What Is the Difference between Law and Judgment in the Work? 690
What Is, "The Creator Does Not Tolerate the Proud," in the Work? .. 699
What Is, His Guidance Is Concealed and Revealed? 710
How to Recognize One Who Serves God from One
Who Does Not Serve Him 721
What to Look For in the Assembly of Friends...................................... 731
What Is the Work of Man that Is Attributed to
the Creator, in the Work? 742
What Are the Two Actions During a Descent?..................................... 757
What Is the Difference between General and Individual
in the Work of the Creator? 765
What Are Day and Night in the Work?... 775
What Is the Help in the Work that One Should Ask of the Creator?..... 784

Tav-Shin-Mem-Zayin

(1986 - 1987)

The Good Who Does Good, to the Bad and to the Good

Article No. 1, Tav-Shin-Mem-Zayin, 1986-87

We say, "And all believe," etc., "the Good who does good, to the bad and to the good." We should understand this in the work, meaning those who want to draw near the Creator, and who regard this as "good," meaning that this is all that they expect—to be rewarded with *Dvekut* [adhesion] with the Creator. Therefore, why should we interpret here "to the bad and to the good"? That is, why are they regarded as "bad" if we are speaking of a person who wants to reach the good, which he regards as *Dvekut* with the Creator? And accordingly, what do we regard as the degree of "good"?

To understand this, we first need to bring in the purpose of creation, which we know is about "doing good to His creations." Accordingly, it means that when we say, "And all believe," etc., "the Good who does good," it means, as our sages said, that "the conduct of the Good is to do good." And yet, we believe that He does good to the bad and to the good, meaning that the bad, too, will receive the delight and pleasure.

According to the simple meaning, we should say that "bad" are those people who do bad to others, meaning that they are concerned only with their own well-being and not to bestow. "Good" are those people who like to do good to others; these are the people who are called "good." For this reason, we should interpret "the Good, who does good to the bad and to the good" to mean that bad people, who are immersed in self-love, will also receive delight and pleasure.

According to the rule we learn—that there was a restriction and concealment on the vessels of reception in order to receive, that the light will not shine again in this place and it will remain a space devoid of light, and that restriction is called *Tzimtzum Aleph* [first restriction], which will never be revoked, but only *Tzimtzum Bet* [second restriction] will be revoked, but one who receives in order to receive will never receive—so how can "does good to the bad and to the good" be true? After all, they do not have vessels to receive the upper abundance, called "to do good to His creations."

Baal HaSulam once said that there are two types of *Kelim* [vessels] in a person: 1) vessels of bestowal, 2) vessels of reception, which Kabbalah calls *Kelim de Panim* [anterior *Kelim*], which are vessels of bestowal, and *Kelim de Achoraim* [posterior vessels], which are vessels of reception. The vessels of bestowal are called "good vessels," and there are people who can correct themselves only with vessels of bestowal. This means that only with vessels of bestowal can they direct their intention to be in order to bestow, and not more. Others are rewarded with a higher degree, meaning that they can aim in order to bestow with vessels of reception, too.

According to the above, we should interpret the meaning of "Good, who does good to the bad and to the good," to mean that a person should believe that the Creator gives help from above, as our sages said, "He who comes to purify is aided." Therefore, when they ask of the Creator to give him the strength to be able to direct his actions to be in order to bestow, to ask for a complete prayer, meaning that the Creator will help him have the power to overcome in order to bestow even over his vessels of reception, too, so they will be in order to bestow, this is called "to the bad," meaning to the vessels of reception. And "to the good" means vessels of bestowal. Both of them should have the intention for the Creator.

Now we can understand why it can be said of a person who wishes for the Creator to bring him closer to His work, so he can aim his work for the Creator, that they are called "bad." According to the above, it will mean that those who want the vessels of reception—which are called "bad *Kelim*"—to also draw near to the Creator, we call them "bad." It follows that when we speak of bad *Kelim* that will be corrected in order to bestow it is a higher degree than the "good," since "good" means that he wants the Creator to give him the power to prevail over them and aim in order to bestow.

And regarding the evil inclination and good inclination, Baal HaSulam once said that *Yetzer* [inclination] comes from the word *Tziur* [depiction]. Therefore, sometimes the inclination means that a person receives a good depiction about keeping Torah and *Mitzvot* [commandments] for the Creator, meaning that he begins to feel the delight and pleasure that he will have by being rewarded with adhering to the Creator and adhering to the root that has created all creations, meaning that the Creator's intention was to do good to His creations.

At that time, this depiction gives one a great yearning to leave all corporeal matters because he feels that they are all inconsequential and will be cancelled. He says about every corporeal matter he examines that it is not worth wasting his life in order to obtain it. Rather, he feels that it is worthwhile to give up everything in order to achieve *Dvekut* with the Creator, and to have connection with all the souls that were in this world and were rewarded with the life of the next world, and he will be rewarded with entering the seminaries, as it is in *The Zohar*, "the seminary of Rashbi," "the seminary of Matat." It follows that the good depiction he has received about spirituality causes him to depart from bodily pleasures and approach pleasures of the souls, since he longs, as our sages said, for "You will see your world in your life, and your end in the life of the next world" (see "Introduction to the Study of the Ten Sefirot," Item 89). This is the good inclination.

Sometimes a person receives a bad depiction, meaning he receives a depiction that if he takes upon himself to work only for the Creator and not for his own benefit, and that all his work will be dedicated to the Creator, he receives depictions as though he is lost from the world, which is filled with the joy of life, and he is leaving his entire family, with whom he was always together, and he suddenly leaves them. All the yearnings he wanted to obtain, and thought that he had obtained some, and some he did not, now, all at once, he loses everything and feels as though the whole world has grown dark for him. He cannot find in himself any desire or craving to have the ability to overcome all the depictions he is now receiving about the corporeal world.

Moreover, a person is surprised that he has never attributed such importance to the corporeal world as he does now, and he already agreed many times to work devotedly so that everything will be to benefit the Creator and not for his own benefit. However, he never felt such taste in the corporeal life as it seems to him now, in such a state where he received such bad depictions about spirituality, and good depictions about corporeality. This is called "the evil inclination."

According to the above, we should interpret what is written in "And for a sin that we sinned before You coercively and willingly," and afterwards we say, "for a sin that we sinned before You with the evil inclination." Everyone asks, "Was the previous 'for a sin' about the good inclination and not about the evil inclination? After all, transgressions come only from the evil inclination."

By this we should interpret what we have taken upon ourselves: to hear the bad depictions it tells us about spirituality. That is, on the one hand, we are immersed in all the corporeal sins, and in addition, we receive from it bad depictions about spirituality, and we can interpret "for a sin that we sinned before You with the evil inclination" as bad depictions about spirituality.

The Importance of Recognition of Evil

Article No. 2, Tav-Shin-Mem-Zayin, 1986-87

It is written in *The Zohar*, *Beresheet Bet* (Items 218-219 in the *Sulam* [Ladder] commentary): "'Let the water under the heavens gather unto one place, and let the dry land be seen.' 'Let the water ... gather' is the Torah, which is called 'water.' 'Unto one place' means Israel. It is also written, 'Let the water ... gather unto one place,' where water means Torah, and 'one place' means Israel, the recipients of the Torah. Conversely, the nations of the world did not wish to receive the Torah, hence the land remained desolate and dry. The Torah is the settling of the world, and in it, it exists. The nations of the world, who did not receive it, remained desolate and dry."

We should understand the words of *The Zohar*, which interprets about the whole, meaning about Israel and the nations of the world. But how does it interpret the individuals, meaning Israel and the nations of the world in one body? It is known that *The Zohar* says that "each person is a small world in and of itself," and includes within it all seventy nations, as well as Israel.

It is written in *Pirkei Avot* (Chapter 4, Mishnah 21): "Rabbi Yaakov says, 'This world is like a corridor to the next world. Prepare yourself in the corridor so you may enter the living room.'" It is clear that you cannot correct something in which you find no flaw. Since when instructing in the work of the Creator, they are educated by way of wholeness, meaning that since there are many individuals in the collective, and each one is different from the others, as our sages said (*Midrash Rabbah* 21, Sanhedrin 38), "As their faces are not the same, so their views are not the same."

Therefore, the collective must be guided in a manner that the education is suitable for everyone, meaning that every person will have a grip on Torah and *Mitzvot* [commandments]. It is as our sages said (*Minchot* 99), "Rabbi Ami said, 'We learn from the words of Rabbi Yosi that even if one has learned only one chapter of the morning prayer and one chapter of the evening prayer, he has kept the *Mitzva* [commandment], 'This book of Torah shall not move from your lips.' Rabbi Yohanan said in the name of Rabbi Shimon Bar Yochai, 'Even if a person reads only the Shema reading morning and evening, he has kept, 'This book shall not move.' This must not be said to uneducated people.' And Raba said, 'It is a *Mitzva* to say it to uneducated people.'"

We see from this that there are many measures to keeping Torah with respect to the public. This is so deliberately, since no person is like another. Therefore, one must not be forced to keep, "This book of Torah shall not move from your lips," but rather each according to his ability. And since the whole collective is regarded as one body, it follows that in general, each one joins into the collective. It follows that there is much Torah in the whole public together, meaning that much Torah is learned in general. Thus, he is keeping by reading the Shema reading morning and evening, and in the eyes of Rabbi Shimon Bar Yochai he has done his duty of "And you shall contemplate Him day and night."

This is an innovation that Rabbi Shimon Bar Yochai, of whom it was said (*Berachot* 35), "Many have done as Rabbi Ishmael and succeeded, and many have done as Rashbi but did not succeed. Rabbi Ishmael says, 'since it is written, 'And you shall gather your grain,' what do we learn from this? Since it was said, 'This book of Torah shall not move from your lips,' the words can be understood literally. 'And you shall gather your grain,' deal with them as is customary,' the words of Rabbi Ishmael. Rashbi says, 'It is possible for one to plow at the time of plowing, sow at the time of sowing, and harvest at the time of harvesting, thresh at the time of threshing, and spread at the time of the wind. The Torah, what shall become of it?'"

We should understand why Rabbi Yohanan says in the name of Rashbi (*Masechet Makkot* 99): "Even if a person reads only the Shema reading morning and evening, he has kept, 'This book of Torah shall not move from your lips.'" However, we should explain that the general public, says Rashbi, may keep the verse, "shall not move," by reading morning and evening, but to the individuals he says, "It is possible for one to plow at the time of plowing ... The Torah, what shall become of it?"

For this reason we must always distinguish between the general public and the individuals. We can also interpret that the general public is called "landlords," and individuals, meaning people who belong to the individuals, are regarded as having the view of Torah.

The meaning of "view of landlords" is that normally, one who buys a house, it is said that that house belongs to this or that person, meaning that this house belongs to none other than specifically that person. Even if he buys a small object, it is the same, meaning that when we ask one another, "To whom does this object belong?" It belongs to so and so, who has acquired it through the labor he has given for the object, so the object will be his, and the person's name is given to the object.

It is likewise in the work of the Creator. When a person makes an effort and wants reward for his labor, it follows that the reward he wants to receive is named after him, and he wants to acquire the reward of this world and the reward of the next world. It follows that everything comes into his own authority, that he is the landlord of all those things that he acquires through his labor.

These people are called "the view of landlords" because the reason that they understand is not to do anything except for their own good, meaning that they will be the owners of the things they can obtain through labor. If they do not see that they can obtain some benefit for themselves, they have no strength to work and exert, unless they see that there is room to gain something for their own authority, which is called "self-love." This is called "general public," who are regarded as landlords.

But the individuals are called "the view of Torah." This means that all those people who belong to the individuals have the view of Torah, since they want to cancel their own selves so they will have no existence in and of themselves because they do not want to merit a name. That is, they do not want to own anything because they want to exit self-love and not care for their own selves in any way, but only annul before the Creator. This is all they want—to cancel their own authority. They want there to be only one domain, the domain of the Creator. That is, they do not want there to be two domains, but only the domain of the Singular One.

When they read the Shema reading, they aim, when they say, "Hear O Israel, the Lord our God, the Lord is One," that there will be only one authority in the world, and want to cancel their own authority, and there will be only one Creator. This is called "the view of Torah." It is as our sages said (*Berachot* 63), "Words of Torah come true only in one who puts himself to death over it." This means that he puts his self to death, meaning his self-love.

This means that the individuals and the view of Torah are the same thing. That is, it is about achieving *Dvekut*, called "equivalence of form," and cancellation of self-love, and his only aim is to annul before Him. As long as one feels that he is still immersed in self-love although he keeps Torah and *Mitzvot* in every detail, he cannot see himself as whole in his work, saying that it is complete work, since he sees that in everything he does he still wants everything to go into his own authority, called "the view of landlords," and he does not care that he has two authorities. But he takes to heart that he has two authorities. At that time he can pray a true prayer, from the bottom of his heart, that the Creator will deliver him from his own authority and admit him into the authority of the

Creator. That is, he will feel that there is only one authority in the world and everything is annulled before Him. Because of it there is specific education to the general public and specific education to the individuals.

However, we should understand why the general public is educated through wholeness, meaning that there is wholeness in everything they do, as was said that even Rashbi, who is more meticulous than Rabbi Ishmael, asks, "It is possible for one to plow at the time of plowing... The Torah, what shall become of it?" Still, he says, "Even if a person reads only the Shema reading morning and evening, he has kept, 'This book of Torah shall not move from your lips'" meaning as though he has kept the verse, "And you shall contemplate Him day and night."

However, since the general public must have a grip on Torah and *Mitzvot*, and we see that there is a law in nature that one cannot do anything unless he sees progress in his work, and since the general public has the view of landlords, if they are told that there is the view of Torah they will not even understand what is being said to them.

It is as though someone speaks only Hebrew, and if he is spoken to in English he will certainly not understand a single word. Likewise, the view of landlords, who understand only the language of self-love, will certainly not understand another language, meaning the language of bestowal.

Therefore, in order to have a grip on Torah and *Mitzvot*, which is necessary for the benefit of the general public, as it was said that there is wholeness in the public through the quantity, if they are told that there is no wholeness in their work they will stop keeping Torah and *Mitzvot*. But it is not a lie that they are not told the truth, since any grip on Torah and *Mitzvot* is a great thing because penny by penny joins into a great amount, for Israel are responsible for one another. Thus, any work that anyone gives joins into the work of each and every one in the public.

It is as Baal HaSulam said, that there are two who are strong—strong in quantity and strong in quality. The strong in quality is a lion, and the strong in quantity is locust, and both have power that is hard to overcome. Therefore, we need the general public, who are strong in quality [quantity]. For this reason, we say that when we pray, even if we do not know the meaning of the words, it is still very important because the holy words have great power that shines as surrounding for a person although he does not feel it internally.

However, if a person sees the words that he is saying and knows a little bit about the meaning of the words, and sees that the body does not agree to what he is saying, then he is not told, "This has nothing to do with you; do not take into consideration the alien thoughts that the body is telling you, and you do not agree with what the body argues." Rather, in the end, all will be well. That is, "only when you say the words that our sages have arranged, that we need to say the full order of prayers and litanies, you need not mind all that, meaning you should not consider what the body is saying—that you are telling lies. That is, what you are uttering is all lies, meaning you are asking for something, but in truth, you yourself have no regard for the request you are making."

For example, you are saying, "Return us, our Father, to Your law." However, you are not even thinking about what you are asking because your lack, which you feel you need, is for respect and money and so forth. Thus, it is making true arguments. At that time he is told, "You need not mind the arguments of the body. Rather, it is not making its argument so that you will ask for repentance, but in order to fail you, so you will not pray. This is why it comes to you and makes the argument of a righteous. However, these are alien thoughts that you must not take into consideration whatsoever."

The reason he is taught to advance in a manner that everything he does is in wholeness is that a person cannot work in something in which he sees no progress. It is similar to arrangements made in corporeal matters. For example, when a person begins to study carpentry and sees that he is not progressing in his profession, he is told, "carpentry is not for you; go learn another trade." If he does not succeed in the next profession, he is told, "You cannot continue this because you are not making any progress in these studies." Rather, he cannot be a professional worker but only a simple one.

It is likewise here in the work of the Creator. When we want him to continue in the work because in spirituality, everything we do is regarded as wholeness from the perspective of the general public, we must not mention any flaw in his work. Rather, he is told, "Everything you do is perfect because penny by penny joins into a great amount and no act in spirituality is lost. Rather, at the time of the end of correction, all the acts will be corrected."

It follows that he is not lied to, but that for him this is sufficient work because he cannot work in the way of individuals, where one is taught to walk on the path of criticism, meaning can he really keep what he is asking, meaning are his mouth and heart the same in what he asks of the Creator, or that he sees that the body disagrees with what he is asking, and he must always see his true state.

We find the reason for the two conducts in our sages (*Ketubot* 17), in the dispute between the house of Shammai and the house of Hillel regarding "How to dance before the bride." The house of Shammai say, "The bride as she is," meaning to say the truth whatever it is. The house of Hillel say, "a handsome and virtuous bride." The house of Shammai said to the house of Hillel, "If she is lame or blind, is she told, "a handsome and virtuous bride"? (RASHI interpreted that virtuous means that a thread of grace is stretched over her.) But the Torah said, "stay far from false words." The house of Hillel said to the house of Shammai, "According to you, one who has made a bad bargain in the market, will he praise him or condemn him in his eyes? He will praise him in his eyes." From here our sages said, "One's view should always be mingled with the people." RASHI interpreted that one's view should be mingled with the people, to do according to each man's wish.

This requires clarification: If a person who is not so proficient, for example, in real-estate or diamonds, takes with him a professional in these matters, and if that taker wants to buy an apartment or a diamond that he likes, and the person he took with him as a professional sees that they are not good, is it better if he does not tell him the truth, that this is a bad deal? Can we say this? According to RASHI's interpretation, who interprets, "One's view should always be mingled with the people, to do according to each man's wish," meaning if he wants a bad deal he should tell him, "Yes, it is a good deal"?

Instead, we should say that there is a difference because before a person has made a bad deal, and he can still fix it, meaning not to close the bad deal, of course he should be told the truth. But if he has already closed the deal and cannot fix it, it is forbidden to tell him the truth because what will he gain by knowing the truth? He will only suffer pointlessly.

At that time it can be said, as RASHI interpreted, "to do according to each man's wish." This means that the desire of each person is to feel pleasure. Therefore, if he suffers because he is told the truth, he must not be told the truth, for this is not his wish, as man's wish is to enjoy life, for this was the purpose of creation. For this reason, if he is told the truth, he will suffer. But if he has still not made the purchase he should be told the truth because he will be happy since now that he knows the truth he will not make the bad deal but will make a good deal, as he advises him, and will pay the required price for the good deal.

The same applies here, concerning the work of the Creator. People who belong to the general public, who won't, or cannot understand any other language but the language of self-love, if they are told that their work is incomplete, which is similar to what our sage said, "one who makes a bad deal," meaning that he cannot fix it, he must not be told it is a bad deal. Rather, "He should praise it in his eye." This is so because as RASHI explained about what our sages said, "Therefore, one's view should always be mingled with the people," meaning to do according to each man's wish. This means that if a person desires only self-love he should be told, "This work, that you are working *Lo Lishma* [not for Her sake], is good and virtuous work. But how can two opposite things be said at the same time, meaning that your work is *Lo Lishma* but it is still good and perfect work?

However, he begins to understand by himself that he cannot work *Lishma* [for Her sake], but like the general public, who work only *Lo Lishma*. For this reason, he says, "I am no worse than the general public." And regarding what is written in all the places—that a person must work *Lishma*—this work was given only to a chosen few in the generation and not to the general public, since the work *Lishma* is hard work. Hence, it follows that he is guided according to his wish.

However, people who belong to the individuals, who have an inner drive and are dissatisfied with the work of the general public because they have a penchant for the truth and cannot understand contrasts, but rather tell themselves, "Either I am serving the Creator or I am serving myself." That is, he is uncompromising and says, "Either I am entirely for the benefit of the Creator and not for my own benefit, or I am for my own benefit and not for the benefit of the Creator. It is as our sages said (*Sukkah* 45), "All who combine work for the Creator and another thing are uprooted from the world." This means that if he wants to work to benefit the Creator, but also a little for his own benefit, he is uprooted from the eternal world.

Therefore, when one's desire is to see the truth, he is guided to criticize his actions, meaning if his mouth and heart are the same in what he says. If they are not then he should exert to be able to aim for the Creator. At that time it is to the contrary, meaning that the body makes him understand that he should know that he is above ordinary people and not equal to the rest of the people, who belong to the general public, while he belongs to the chosen few in the generation who ascend on degrees.

If the Creator does not help him with his request as soon as he asks, he immediately becomes angry and says, "Other people, who are from the type that belongs to the general public, when they ask You to satisfy their wishes, that You will grant them corporeal needs, meaning desires of self-love, I can understand it if they are not worthy of You granting their wishes. But when I ask You only spiritual wishes, meaning for Your benefit, because what do I want?

To work for You, to serve only You, and I am not asking anything for myself, so why are You not answering me right away, especially since I have been asking You for a long time that I want to work for You except my body does not allow me to work and I am asking for Your help, so why aren't You helping me?"

It follows that he comes with real complaints. We should understand why he is not answered. The reason is simple: he is arguing that he is right. The question is, in what is he right? He will say that normally, when someone wants to do something good to another, the beneficiary listens to the giver. For this reason, here, in the work of the Creator, when he wants to work for the Creator, it follows that the Creator is the recipient of the benefit, and the person is the giver. This is why he is angry with the Creator for not listening to him.

However, in the work of the Creator, it is the opposite of what the person thinks, since it is similar to what our sages said about matrimony funds (*Kidushin*, p 7a), that the rule about one who marries a woman, the writing says, "And he placed it in her hand," meaning that the husband must give the matrimony funds. However, if he is an important person, if she gives the matrimony funds and he sanctifies [weds] her, then she is sanctified [wedded]. The reason is that with an important person, his pleasure of receiving from her is regarded as actual giving.

It therefore follows that when a person wants to give everything to the Creator, he is regarded as a receiver. That is, if the Creator accepts his work it will be regarded that the person is the receiver, and not that the person is the giver, as the person thinks.

Therefore, when a person wants to give something to the Creator, it is considered that the Creator is giving to the person. At that time it is seen above if that person is worthy of being given the pleasure, meaning that the Creator will receive from him. This is why his prayer is not granted immediately, as the person thinks, that he is the giver. As for the giver of the gifts, no conditions are required of the giver. On the contrary, the receiver might have to meet the conditions that the giver requires.

For this reason, as with an important person, the giver is regarded as a receiver, and the important person can set conditions to the giver, or he will not receive from him. Likewise, in the work of the Creator, the Creator requires that the person will give Him certain things in his work in order to bestow, or else the Creator will not want to receive from the person what the person wants to give Him. For this reason, a person must make many requests of the Creator, so He will want to receive from the person.

Only once the Creator sees that a person is fit and worthy of the Creator's receiving from him what he wants to give Him, the Creator gives him the help so he can do everything in order to bestow. Prior to this he does not receive help in a way that a person can see directly that the Creator is helping him. Rather, the help a person receives until he is fit to do everything in order to bestow, and until then, although without the Creator's help there is nothing, but a person is unable to see this directly.

For this reason, a person who wants the Creator to help him be able to observe, as our sages said (Avot 2:12), "All your works will be for the Creator," must first feel the importance of the Creator so as to understand His giving, as was said about an important person. At that time he will know that what he wants to give, he should think that now he is going to receive from the Creator because with an important person, "By the pleasure he receives from him, the giving is considered receiving."

Therefore, a person must first appreciate the importance of the Creator and seek advice how to obtain the greatness of the Creator. This means that all the Mitzvot he performs will be with the aim to thereby obtain the greatness and importance of the Creator.

It is similar to what is written in *The Zohar* about the verse, "Her husband is known at the gates." *The Zohar* says, "Each according to what he assumes in his heart," for only then, according to the importance and greatness of the Creator that he assumes in his heart, he begins to feel that he wants to give all his works only to benefit the Creator. It is so because he wants to receive pleasure from the Creator's reception from him what he wants to give Him, as was said about an important person.

And since the quality of reception of pleasure is imprinted in man, when one feels the importance and greatness of the Creator, since there is pleasure in an important person receiving from him, the desire naturally awakens in a person to want to do everything to benefit the Creator. That is, he wants to give everything he has to the Creator because of the pleasure he feels while giving to the Creator.

However, this is not regarded as "bestowing in order to receive." Rather, bestowing in order to receive means that it is like commerce, where the taker gives money to the seller. It follows that the taker is giving to the seller so that the seller will give him some reward in return for his giving.

It follows that there are two things here: 1) the money that the customer gives, 2) the seller who gives him some object in return. Conversely, with the work of the Creator the smaller one gives the greater one some object and does not want anything in return. Rather, there is a single act here. Therefore, we should distinguish two intentions in the same act here, meaning the object that the person gives to the important person.

We should discern two opposite intentions here: 1) the giver, and the giver intends to receive pleasure from the giving, 2) the receiver of the object, who is an important person, and whose intention is to bestow pleasure upon the giver. It follows that the giver is called "receiver," and the receiver is called "giver."

As was said above, this pleasure that a person enjoys bestowing upon the Creator, is because of the importance. The thing is that since we were given the matter of correction, called "equivalence of form," called *Dvekut*, as our sages said about the verse, "and to cleave unto Him," we should say that it means, "as He is merciful" and enjoys giving to the creatures, "so you are merciful," meaning enjoying giving to the Creator. It turns out that when he bestows upon the Creator and does not enjoy, there is a flaw in the equivalence of form.

Rather, precisely if he enjoys giving to the Creator it can be said that there is equivalence of form here. However, how can one come to such a degree where he enjoys giving to the Creator? This can happen only when he feels the greatness and importance of the Creator. At that time there is natural joy, as with an important person. By this one can receive pleasure from bestowal because this bestowal gives him pleasure, and in a place of reception a person can work.

However, this brings up the question, "How does one come to feel the greatness of the Creator?" Baal HaSulam said about this that there is a matter of faith above reason. That is, he gave a depiction that sometimes a person feels that this man is above all others and has the most valuable qualities in the world. As for wisdom, he is the wisest man on Earth. This is the first discernment.

The second discernment is that he does not feel his greatness and importance, but believes in him above reason—that he has all the qualities in the world. If his faith is one hundred percent, it is as though he has achieved it by knowing.

There are two discernments to make concerning faith above reason:

1. He has no way of obtaining his importance and greatness, and therefore believes that he is the most important person in the world.

2. He does have a way to attain and feel his importance and greatness, but because of his honor, so there will not be a flaw in his investigating the truth. It is like a person who asks someone for a loan and promises that he will repay him in time, and the lender investigates if he is a trustworthy person. Sometimes the borrower hears about it. It follows that the borrower was also blemished by this, as he is the most important person in the world. It follows that because of the honor, he believes above reason, even though he has another way.

Accordingly, it follows that if one wants specifically "Because of God's honor, conceal the matter," he wants to believe in the Creator even though he has a way by which to attain and know the importance of the Creator. Still, he waives the sparks in his body that tell him: "Why do you need to go above reason where you can attain everything within reason?" This degree applies to those who have already been rewarded with some spirituality, who have a way by which to attain the greatness of the Creator, and still want to go above reason.

However, the same applies in the work that is the preparation to enter true spirituality. That is, when he takes upon himself to believe in the importance of the Creator above reason, he must take upon himself that he wants to go specifically with faith above reason. Even though he was given the reason to see the greatness of the Creator within reason, he prefers faith above reason due to "because of the honor of the Creator, conceal the matter."

This is regarded as wanting to go above reason. Precisely then he becomes a *Kli* [vessel] that is fit to receive spirituality, since he has no concern at all for himself, but all his intentions are only to bestow upon the Creator. For this reason there is no longer fear that should he be given some illumination it will go into the vessels of reception, since he is always trying to exit self-love.

Baal HaSulam said that as the will to receive wants only to receive and not bestow, even where it is told to work above reason it is only regarded as bestowing and not receiving because a person suffers where he has to go above reason. The evidence of this is that since the body is always concerned with receiving delight and pleasure in everything it does, and since if a person must work above reason, the body is dissatisfied with it, therefore, when a person is taught to go above reason he begins the work of bestowal. It therefore follows that when one prefers to go by way of above reason it is safeguarding that he will walk on the right path, which is the route for achieving *Dvekut* with the Creator.

According to the above, we should always remember the meaning of "above reason," that one should first know that he is going to take upon himself the discernment of above reason, to depict what is within reason, meaning what his reason tells him, for which it is worthwhile to work for the Creator. Also, one should depict in which way, under this or that condition, he would agree to work in order to bestow.

And we see in nature that when the small one serves the great one, he has delight and pleasure, for we see that there are people who pay in order to be able to serve the great one. And when one knows and feels the greatness of an important person he does not need to strain himself for the body to want to serve him, because of it the Creator has placed in nature the existence of pleasure in serving a great one, and he annuls before him as a candle before a torch. However, this is so specifically when the body feels his greatness and importance. For this reason we must always think how to obtain the greatness and importance of the Creator.

Now we come to explain the words of *The Zohar* when it interprets the verse, "Let the water ... gather unto one place, and let the dry land be seen." According to what we explained above regarding the general public and individuals, the general public has the "view of landlords," called "self-love," meaning that they want to receive everything into their own authority. This means that although they believe in the Creator, that He is the Landlord of the world and everything is called by His name, still, when they engage in Torah and *Mitzvot* they want to draw out into their own authority reward from the Creator in return for the labor in Torah and *Mitzvot*. This is called "taking from authority to authority," meaning taking out from the singular authority to the public authority. It is considered that they want there to be two authorities—the authority of men and the authority of the Creator.

But the individuals belong to the "view of Torah," which is cancellation of the authority, as our sages said (*Berachot* 63b), "Words of Torah come true only in one who puts himself to death over it," as it was said, "This is the law, should a man die in a tent." The meaning is that one cancels one's self, meaning self-love, and wants to do everything only for the Creator, meaning that there will be only one authority in the world, the authority of the Singular One.

At that time he can be rewarded with the Torah because then he is in a state of equivalence of form, called *Dvekut* with the Creator. And then he is named "Israel," meaning that he is rewarded with all his thoughts, words, and actions being directly

Yashar-El [straight to the Creator] because all their aspirations are only to achieve bestowal, called "equivalence of form," since he annuls himself before the Creator, which is called "the singular authority" and not two authorities—that they also have a desire for self-love.

However, since there is a rule that they are many, since the view of the majority has a great power to rule over the individual, and since the general public feel themselves as whole concerning the work of the Creator, the view of the majority also reaches the individual. And although the individual does not want to assume the method of the general public, they still weaken the individual so he will not feel its absence so much, and the individual is weakened in his work.

That is, the body says to him, "It's true that you are not complete in the work for the Creator, but it's not so terrible that you should regret it and make a heartfelt prayer for it. That is, that you must say that if you are not rewarded with the degree of bestowing contentment upon the Creator you say about it, 'My death is preferable to me than my life.' You are not obligated to do this. After all, you see that the general public takes the path of landlords. True, it would be better if you could do everything in order to bestow, but you must ask the Creator to help you. And if you still did not receive help from the Creator you are so worried that you say, 'My death is preferable for me than my life.' But this is not so terrible; look at the general public."

By this the individual surrenders to the general public. That is, it weakens him from doing things he can do until he obtains help from the Creator, who will give him that strength so he can do everything in order to bestow, as the individual demands.

And when a person begins to receive wholeness from the general public, a person can no longer see the truth because for every deficiency he elicits by himself he immediately finds for himself an excuse that justifies him to an extent that he no longer feels that now he is controlled by the general public.

Therefore, in order to be in a state where the work is revealed before him, and to not be drawn after the control of the collective, *The Zohar* comes and advises us to focus everything we do in Torah and *Mitzvot* in one place. That is, we must come to have only one place, meaning one authority, and not two authorities.

At that time he can say, "Hear, O Israel, the Lord our God, the Lord is One." It is as was written above, the "view of Torah." Otherwise, meaning in the view of landlords, there must be two authorities: 1) the authority of the Creator, 2) man's authority. When a person examines his work he sees that he has no connection to *Dvekut* with the Creator, called "equivalence of form," so naturally, he is separated from the Life of Lives and is similar to the nations of the world, who would not receive the Torah. The Torah should be interpreted as the "view of the Torah." Rather, they want the view of landlords, and from that there cannot be existence to the world. By seeing and examining himself he can see his true state in the ways of the Creator and will not be taken after the wholeness of the general public, who want to ordain the view of landlords.

It is as *The Zohar* says, "Let the water ... gather unto one place." Water, which is the Torah, will gather unto one place, meaning that the two authorities that there are in the world will be one authority, which is called "the view of Torah." As *The Zohar* ends, "The Torah is the settling of the world, and in it, it exists. And the nations of the world, who did not receive it, remained desolate and dry."

All of Israel Have a Part in the Next World

Article No. 3, Tav-Shin-Mem-Zayin, 1986-87

It is written in *The Zohar*, Noah (Item 2): "Come and see: 'All of Israel have a part in the next world.' It asks, 'What is the reason?' It says, 'Because they keep the covenant on which the world stands, as it is written, 'If My covenant is not day and night, I have not appointed the ordinances of heaven and earth.'' Therefore, Israel—who are keeping the covenant because they have taken it upon themselves—have a part in the next world."

We should understand, since first he says, "All of Israel have a part," meaning that anyone who is called by the name, "Israel," without any preconditions, has a part in the next world. But afterwards he interprets that not all of Israel. Rather, he sets conditions, that only those who are keeping the covenant. He brings evidence from the verse, that it refers to the keepers of the covenant, by what is written, "If My covenant is not day and night, I have not appointed the ordinances of heaven and earth." We should also understand that the verse, "If My covenant is not day and night," refers to the covenant.

It is written in *Pesachim* (p 68b): "Rabbi Elazar said, 'Were it not for the Torah, heaven and earth would not exist,' as it was said, 'If My covenant is not day and night, I have not appointed the ordinances of heaven and earth.'" RASHI interprets "If My covenant is not day and night" to mean the study of Torah, of which it is written, "And you shall contemplate it day and night." Therefore, it means that the covenant is called 'Torah.' And here *The Zohar* interprets that a covenant is circumcision, which keeps the covenant.

Concerning Abraham's making of the covenant, as it is written, "And made the covenant with him," our sages explained that the Creator helped the making of the covenant for he could not make the covenant alone. Rather, the Creator helped him. We should understand what it means in the work that he could not make the covenant without the Creator's help.

It is written concerning Abraham and Avimelech, "And the two of them made a covenant." Baal HaSulam asked, "If two people understand that it is worthwhile for them to love each other, why should they make a covenant? How does an act of seemingly signing a contract help? What does it give us?" Then he said, "It gives us that when we make a covenant we mean that since it is possible that something might separate them, they are making a covenant now, so that just as now they understand that there is love and equivalence between them, this covenant will persist even if afterwards things will come that should separate them. Still, the connection they are establishing now will be permanent. Accordingly, we should say that if afterwards things will come that should separate them, we should say that each one should go above reason and say that they will not notice what they see within reason, but go above reason. Only in this way can the covenant hold and there will be no separation between them.

It therefore follows that whether we say that the covenant is the Torah or that the covenant is circumcision, it does not mean that only this gives the covenant with the Creator, that his covenant with the Creator will not part, meaning that his heart will be whole with the Creator. Rather, both the Torah and circumcision come to keep the making of the covenant, where a person's heart must be whole with the Creator, and cling to Him with a stake that will never fall, as it is written, "If My covenant is not day and night, I have not appointed the ordinances of heaven and earth." This is so because the matter of the creation of heaven and earth was with the intention to do good to His creations, and the creatures cannot receive the delight and pleasure without equivalence of form, meaning that all his actions will be in order to bestow. Otherwise there will be separation between the creatures and the Creator.

This is why we were given two covenants—the circumcision and the covenant of the Torah—by which we can come to make a covenant with the Creator with faith above reason and will be able to do everything in order to bestow.

This is the meaning of "If My covenant is not," meaning If I did not create the counsels by which to achieve equivalence of form, it would not be possible to receive the delight and pleasure, which is the whole purpose of creation, to do good to His creations. And if I did not prepare the ways by which to achieve equivalence of form, I would not need to create heaven and earth for they would not be able to receive any benefit from creation, and the whole of creation would be pointless because there would not be anyone who could enjoy it. On this covenant—that he made the covenant of the stake that will never fall—Abraham needed His help. This is the meaning of the Creator having to help him. And this is the meaning of "And made a covenant with him," meaning that the Creator helped him be able to go above reason.

There are three discernments to make in the work above reason:

1. He does not feel any lack in his work, so as to have a need to go above reason.

2. He feels his deficiency, but he is as a female, meaning as feeble as a female, having no strength to overcome and go above reason.

3. He is regarded as a male. This means that he has the strength to overcome and go above reason.

1) For example, when a person wants to rise before dawn and is woken up, sometimes the person hears but does not pay attention

and keeps sleeping. At that time there is no one who feels his deficiency because he immediately fell asleep and therefore had no time to think of his deficiency. For this reason, he is still not regarded as a human being, where it is possible to distinguish between male and female. Adam [man/human] comes from the words *Ish Adama* [man of the earth], meaning that he is tilling the land so as to yield crops and fruits to sustain people.

This can be said only of one who feels his deficiency, who begins to work and correct his deficiency. However, when one does not feel his deficiency, there is no one to speak of. That is, even if you tell him his deficiency he will not hear because he has many excuses for everything. Naturally, he has no room for prayer that the Creator will help him have the ability to come out of the obstructions coming to him.

2) When he is woken up he begins to think, "It's true that I said to my friend to wake me up but when I said to my friend that I wanted to get up before dawn it was because I had some desire to get up and study; I craved the pleasure I would receive from the Torah. And even if I did not think that I would find great pleasure in studying Torah, I nevertheless did not have the suffering of having to get out of bed and give up the pleasure of rest. When I spoke to my friend about waking me up I was thinking only of the pleasure I could derive from studying Torah; this is why I asked him. But now that I am lying under the blanket, and if there is rain and wind outside, I certainly feel pleasure in the rest. But now I have to get up. How do I know that I will receive greater pleasure from learning Torah? For this reason, it is better for me to 'Sit and do nothing,' for certainty is preferable to doubt, since the rest certainly gives me pleasure, while studying Torah does not shine as pleasurable to me."

However, afterward, thoughts come to him: "We learned that we have to go above reason, meaning not regard the amount of pleasure I will have and that this will be my gauge. Rather, we have to work for the Creator. So why am I calculating for myself, meaning how much I will gain from this? Instead, I should be calculating if the act I am doing is keeping the commandment of the Creator and He enjoys my heeding Him. And why do I have thoughts of self-love? But what can I do now, since I cannot overcome my thoughts?"

It follows that he is regarded as a servant of the Creator, who wants to overcome the alien thoughts, meaning that these thoughts are alien to the path of Torah. This is regarded as being a female, meaning that he is as feeble as a female, that he lacks the strength to overcome.

3) He is as a male, meaning has the strength to overcome. That is, when he is woken up, if thoughts come to him—"Why should you get up from the rest you are enjoying? You probably think that when you get out of bed and go study you will enjoy more than you are enjoying now, but how do you know that this is so?" It promptly advises him to test if this is so. But then it tells him: "What flavor are you now tasting in the study, that you are hoping to receive later?" and he immediately gets such flavors that the world grows dark on him, meaning that depictions of concealment come to him, which hide from him the vitality in the Torah. Then the body asks him: "Tell me, are these the states you long for?"

If he is a man, called "man of war," he tells his body: "Everything you say is true. That is, according to your view, you are right. However, the foundation on which I am building the engagement in Torah and *Mitzvot* [commandments] is above reason. This means that reason mandates that the will to receive delight and pleasure will determine whether or not it is worth working for, and above reason means that he is working in order to bestow. That is, the will to receive does not need to agree to it, but the desire to bestow determines.

This means that if he believes that the work he wants to do now will bring contentment to the Creator, he is promptly willing to do it, without any delays. And although the body claims the opposite, he still has the power to overcome it. This is called "male."

However, after a person has completed these three discernments in the work—1) when he still does not feel his deficiency so as to ask the Creator to help him, 2) that he does feel his deficiency but has no strength to overcome, which is called "a female," and 3) when he is a male, a man of war, meaning that he can overcome his deficiency—he comes to a state of Shabbat, meaning rest from his work. This is called "You shall work six days, but on the seventh day you shall rest."

By this we can interpret, "These are the generations of Noah, a righteous man." Noah is regarded as *Naicha* [Aramaic: "rest"], as it is written in *The Zohar*. This is why he is called "righteous," since there is rest in him. *The Zohar* says, "Where there is work, there is *Sitra Achra* [other side]. Hence, naturally, one who is righteous cannot have work. It is as Baal HaSulam said, that where *Kedusha* [holiness] shines, a person is annulled as a candle before a torch, and it cannot be said there that the body has work because the *Kedusha* is the source of delight and pleasure.

However, when a person has some grip of the *Sitra Achra*, it clothes man with self-love, called "receiving in order to receive," and on this there was a *Tzimtzum* [restriction] and concealment and *Kedusha* cannot be revealed there. Only concealment is on this place, meaning that the delight and pleasure do not shine there, but to the contrary.

And saying, "For they are our lives and the length of our days, and we contemplate them day and night," or when we say, "They are nicer than gold, than much fine gold, and sweeter than honey and the drippings of the honeycomb," this is when a person has proper *Kelim* [vessels] for it, which are called "vessels of bestowal." This gives us equivalence of form, at which time the reception of pleasures is in order to bestow. Otherwise, meaning if the light and abundance illuminated in vessels of reception, the receivers would become more remote from the Creator. The purpose is that we must cling to the Creator, as it is written, "And you who cleave unto the Lord your God are alive every one of you this day."

It therefore follows that one who is righteous, there is no room there for the *Sitra Achra*, but there is a place of rest for the spirit [contentment]. This is the meaning of Shabbat, as it is written, "for in it He ceased and rested," as due to the sanctity of Shabbat there is no room for work now.

However, our sages said (*Avoda Zarah* 3a), "The Creator said to them: 'Fools, he who toiled on the eve of Shabbat shall eat on Shabbat. He who did not toil on the eve of Shabbat, from where will he eat on Shabbat?'"

This means that one who toiled, meaning had labor and toil with the *Sitra Achra*, who obstructed him from going on the path of *Lishma*, that is, during the work he felt that he could not overcome the evil in him, it is because he was still not rewarded with entering *Kedusha*. However, he believes that as soon as he enters *Kedusha* the *Sitra Achra* will be canceled as a candle before a torch and he will have no contact with the *Sitra Achra*. It follows that he knows he is missing one thing—for the Creator to help him and let him attain some *Kedusha*, and then everything will be fine.

For this reason, during the labor and the work he prays from the bottom of the heart that the Creator will help him. At that time he feels that without help from the Creator he will not attain a thing. This feeling that he has, that the Creator can help him, makes a *Kli* [vessel] in a person to receive the help from the Creator because a deficiency is called a *Kli* to receive filling. For this reason, the faith that he has in the Creator, that, as it is written, "You hear the prayer of every mouth," makes the *Kli* to receive the help.

By this we will understand the matter of "He who did not toil on the eve of Shabbat," meaning who did not work with himself to work in order to bestow and see that he cannot win alone, without the Creator's help, naturally, he has no room for prayer, which is the *Kli* to receive His help. Since the rule is that there is no light without a *Kli*, we need preparation so as to have what to eat on Shabbat, for the six workdays are the preparation to receive the light of Shabbat, and Shabbat is considered the abundance extended to fill the empty *Kelim* awaiting His help.

It is as it is written, "The light in it reforms him," as it is written about Shabbat, "All the judgments are impregnated by her, and none other govern all the worlds but her" (*Kegavna* on the night of

Shabbat). Thus, since after the labor with the *Sitra Achra*, when they feel the deficiency, called *Kli*, they can receive the Shabbat, called "ceasing" and "rest."

Now we can understand what we asked. He says there, "All of Israel have a part in the next world," without any conditions. Afterward, he says it is specifically those who kept the covenant, and not all of Israel.

We should interpret the world *Ysrael* [Israel] to mean *Yashar-El* [straight to the Creator]. This means that in everything he does, he wants his work to be directly to the Creator and not for his own benefit. It is as we explained about the verse, "And there shall be no foreign God in you, and you will not bow to a strange God."

Our sages said (*Shabbat* 105b), "Which is the foreign God in man's body? It is the evil inclination."

We should understand this. After all, the good inclination is also in a man's body, as it is written (*Zohar, Lech Lecha*, Item 86), "'For we are brothers,' meaning the evil inclination and the good inclination are close to each other. One stands to one's right and the other stands to one's left. The evil inclination on the left, and the good inclination on the right."

Thus, we see that the good inclination is also in man's body. Therefore, what does it mean that they said that the evil inclination is in man's body? We should interpret this according to our way: The evil inclination is concerned with, and aspires for everything that it does to enter his body, that the intention will be entirely for his own benefit, which is regarded as "into his own body." Conversely, the good inclination strives that all his actions will be outside his body. This is considered that his whole aspiration is to come to doing all his works for the Creator and not for his own benefit. By this we can interpret the word Israel to mean *Yashar-El*—that all his actions will be only for the Creator.

Similarly, it is presented in the interpretation of our sages (*Yerushalmi* 9a): "Rabbi Levi said, 'The heart and the eye are two mediators of sin, as it is written, (Proverbs), 'Give Me your heart,

My son, And let your eyes delight in My ways,' said the Creator. If you give Me your heart and eyes I will know that you are Mine.'"

This means that when we say, "Who chooses His people, Israel," when is one regarded as belonging to the people of the Creator? It is when a person places his eyes and heart there, meaning that everything he looks at and what the heart craves, he tries to make it all in favor of the Creator and not for his own benefit. This is called "You are Mine," meaning "You belong to Me." Then he is included in His people *Yashar-El*.

Accordingly, we should interpret "All of Israel have a part in the next world," and afterwards he interprets who is regarded as Israel and says that only one who keeps the covenant on which the world exists is called Israel. Otherwise, meaning who does not keep the covenant by which the world exists does not belong to Israel but to the nations of the world.

And what is the covenant by which the world exists? It is that he makes a covenant with the Creator that all his works will be only to benefit the Creator. This is called "in order to bestow," for specifically by this there will be existence to the world. This means that the world was created in order to do good to His creations, and as long as there is no equivalence of form, the delight and pleasure cannot clothe in the creatures.

It follows that the whole creation of the world, which was in order to do good to His creations, was in vain because there is no one to receive the delight and pleasure. However, through the covenant with the Creator the creatures will be fit to receive the delight and pleasure.

In order to achieve the covenant, there is the Torah and the circumcision, meaning that in everything we do we must intend that by this we will be rewarded with making a covenant with the Creator forever. Especially, we must believe that the Creator hears the prayer of every mouth, and by this we will be saved.

It Is Forbidden to Hear a Good Thing from a Bad Person

Article No. 4, Tav-Shin-Mem-Zayin, 1986-87

It is written (Genesis 13:8-9), "And Abram said to Lot, 'Please let there be no strife between you and me, or between my herdsmen and your herdsmen, for we are brothers. Is not the whole land before you? Please part from me: if to the left, then I will go to the right; and if to the right, then I will go to the left.'"

We should understand why he says "For we are brothers," since they were not brothers.

The Zohar (*Lech Lecha*, Item 86) interprets this as follows: "'For we are brothers,' meaning the evil inclination and the good inclination are close to one another. One stands to the right of a person and the other to his left. That is, the evil inclination stands to his left, and the good inclination to his right." Accordingly, "for we are brothers" means that we are speaking of one body and the quarrel is between the good inclination and the evil inclination, which are called brothers.

This is perplexing. The good inclination tells the evil inclination, "If to the left," meaning you are telling me to take the path of the left, which is the path of the evil inclination, for it is always on the left, as it is written in *The Zohar* that the evil inclination is to his left. The good inclination tells him: "I will not go by your way. Rather, I will go by the way of the right, the way of the good inclination, which is always on the right. We can understand this. But when it says, "If to the right," meaning that if the evil inclination goes to the right, which is the path of the good inclination, why does the good inclination tell it, "Then I will go to the left," meaning that the good inclination will go by the way of the left, which is the path of the evil inclination? This is difficult to understand.

Baal HaSulam asked why is it that when Jacob had an argument with Laban, it is written (Genesis 31:43), "And Laban replied and said to Jacob, 'The daughters are my daughters, and the children are my children, and the flocks are my flocks, and all that you see is mine.'" That is, Wicked Laban argued that everything is his, meaning that Jacob had no possessions and everything belonged to wicked Laban.

But why is it written (Genesis 33:9), when Jacob gave the presents to Esau, "And Esau said, 'I have a lot, my brother. Let what is yours be yours.'" He did not want to receive from him everything he wanted to give him. But Laban claims the opposite—that everything is his.

He said that here there is an order of work—how to behave in the work with the evil inclination when it comes to a person with its just arguments in order to obstruct a person from achieving *Dvekut* [adhesion] with the Creator.

"Laban said" means that it comes with the argument of a righteous. It tells him, when a person wants to pray and wishes to prolong his prayer a little, or another example, when he wants to go study at the seminary, a person had in mind to be as strong as a lion and overcome his laziness. The evil inclination comes and argues, "It is true that you want to overcome, to do the will of your Father in heaven, as it is written (*Avot*, Chapter 5), "Yehuda Ben Tima says, 'Be as fierce as a leopard, as light as an eagle, running like a gazelle, and as strong as a lion to do the will of your Father in heaven.'

"However, I know that you have no desire to do the will of your Father in heaven. I know the truth—that you are working only for self-love and you have no love for the Creator that you can say that the fact that you are going to do something now is for the Creator. Rather, you are working only for me, for the *Sitra Achra* [other side], and not for *Kedusha* [sanctity/holiness].

"Thus, what is this overcoming? That is, if you are working for me then I advise you to sit calmly and enjoy, since everything you want to do is for me. Therefore, I have pity on you so you will not make great efforts, and enjoy the rest." This is what Laban said. That is, he dressed in a white *Talit* [prayer shawl], meaning he said, "The daughters are my daughters ... and all that you see is mine."

Jacob countered him: "It is not so. I am working for the Creator. Therefore it is worthwhile for me to overcome my laziness and do the Creator's will. I do not want to listen to your argument—the argument of a righteous that you are making."

Wicked Esau was the opposite. When Jacob came to him and wanted to give him his possession of Torah and *Mitzvot* [commandments], Esau told him, "I have a lot." That is, "I have a lot of Torah and *Mitzvot* from other people, who are all working for me and not for the Creator. But you are righteous; you are not working for me but for the Creator. Therefore, I have no part in your Torah and work. This is why I do not want to receive it and admit it into my authority. Rather, a righteous, and you are working only for the Creator."

Baal HaSulam asked about it: Which of them made a true argument, Laban or Esau? He said that in truth, both said the truth—what is good for the *Sitra Achra*, that they obstruct a person from achieving wholeness. The difference is in their arguments: whether it comes before the act or after the act. That is, prior to the act, when a person wants to overcome and do something in *Kedusha* to benefit the Creator, the evil inclination dresses in the argument of a righteous and tells him: "You cannot do anything for *Kedusha*. Rather, everything you do is for me." This is called "All that you see is mine." That is, you are doing everything for the *Sitra Achra*. In that case, it is better for you to sit and do nothing. Why exert to overcome your laziness? By this it subdues a person so as not to engage in Torah and *Mitzvot*. This is Laban's argument.

Esau's argument is after the act. That is, if one finally overcomes Laban's argument and follows the path of Jacob, Esau comes to him and says: "You see what a mighty man of war you are? You are not like your friends. They are lazy and you are a man! There is no one like you!" This puts him into the lust of pride, of which our sages said (*Sotah* 5b), "Rav Hasda said, 'Mar Ukva said, 'Any man in whom there is crassness of spirit, the Creator said, 'He and I cannot dwell in the world.''"

For this reason, Jacob counters him and argues, "This is wrong! Everything I did was only for you," meaning for his own benefit, which is a will to receive that belongs to the *Sitra Achra*. "Now I must begin the work anew so it will all be for the Creator and not for you. But until now I have been working only for you." This is what Jacob gave to Esau as a gift and Esau would not receive from him and argued to the contrary, that Jacob was righteous and worked only for the Creator and not for his own benefit.

Now we can interpret what we asked, "How can it be said that the good inclination said to the evil inclination, 'If you take the right path, I will take to the left.'" After all the path of the left belongs to the *Sitra Achra* and not to the side of *Kedusha*. According to the above we can interpret that the good inclination said to the evil inclination: "You should know that you cannot deceive me because I know one thing—that you want to obstruct me from achieving the degree of a servant of the Creator, meaning that all my thoughts will be in order to bestow. And you, due to your role, are trying to leave me in self-love. Therefore, how can I listen to your right, meaning when you come to me and clothe in the argument of a righteous, namely advise me to be righteous and work for the Creator. This cannot be since it is not your role. You probably want to fail my achieving the goal with your counsels. For this reason, when you come with the argument of the right, called Laban, what should

I do? Anything but listen to you, and do the complete opposite of your opinion." This is why it is written, "and if to the right, then I will go to the left."

Accordingly, a person should always be alert not to fall into the net of the evil inclination that comes to him with the argument of a righteous, and not listen to it. Although it makes us understand that we are not going on the straight path, since what we want to do now is a *Mitzva* [commandment] that comes through transgression, by these words it ties us and we fall into the trap and the net, as it wants to control us with the justness of its words.

It is said in the name of the Baal Shem Tov that to know whether it is the advice of the evil inclination we must scrutinize: If what it says requires labor, it belongs to the good inclination. But if listening to it will cause you not to need to labor, it is the sign of the evil inclination. By this we can discern if this is the advice of the good inclination or the evil inclination.

For example: If a thought comes to him that not every person should rise before dawn, that this work belongs to people whose Torah is their craft, and not just any Jew can equal wise disciples, who must keep, "And he will contemplate His law day and night," but just a Jew. It also brings evidence from the words of our sages to justify its argument, from what Rabbi Yohanan said in the name of Rabbi Shimon Bar Yochai (*Minchot* 99): "Even if a person reads only the *Shema* reading morning and evening, he has kept, 'This book of Torah shall not move from your lips.'" Thus, it argues before him: "It is better for you to get up in the morning like everyone else and not be tired the rest of the day. Then you will be able to pray with more intention than you will be able to pray if you rise before dawn."

It is known from all the books of *Hassidut* that prayer is the most important, since in prayer, a person thinks of nothing but that the Creator will hear his prayer. The prayer is when we can aim more easily and feel before whom we stand. It is not so when studying Torah, although it is written, "Learning Torah is equal to all of them."

It is also interpreted that the meaning is that the Torah brings one importance and greatness of the Creator. It follows that the Torah is only a remedy that brings a person the ability to pray and feel the words "before whom you stand," which is a remedy by which to achieve *Dvekut* [adhesion]. When a person prays to the Creator he can know with whom he speaks and in what manner he is speaking with the Creator. At that time he can annul before the Creator, and this is the most important—that he will annul his own authority. He needs to come to feel that there is nothing in the world but the Creator, and a person wants to adhere to Him and annul his own authority.

Our sages said even more: All the good deeds that a person does, both Torah and other things in *Kedusha*, a person can see if they are in order according to his feeling during prayer. It follows that prayer is the most important. "If you rise before dawn it will all be ruined. So what are you gaining?" Clearly, it is arguing the argument of a righteous.

At that time a person can scrutinize: If he listens to its argument and it will give him more work then he can know it is the argument of the good inclination. If he listens to its advice and it will give him less work, it is a sign that now the evil inclination speaks to him, but clothed in the argument of a righteous. By this it traps him in the net it has set up for him by speaking to him the words of the righteous. In truth, we always need a guide who knows how to lead a person, so as to tell between truth and falsehood, since one cannot scrutinize alone.

Accordingly, when the evil inclination comes with an argument of a righteous, wanting to advise a person how he can enter *Kedusha*, we can interpret what our sages said (*Baba Batra* 98a), "Anyone who boasts with a *Talit* of a wise disciple, but is not a wise disciple, is not admitted into the presence of the Creator."

We should understand why it is such a grave sin to boast with the mantle of a wise disciple, meaning to regard the clothing of a wise disciple so highly as to boast of it. After all, he did not commit such a grave transgression worthy of such a harsh punishment as not to be admitted into the presence of the Creator. It implies that we are speaking of a person who is worthy of being in the presence of the Creator, but this sin of boasting with a garment of a wise disciple deserves such a harsh punishment.

We should interpret that it means that the evil inclination comes to a person and boasts of the *Talit* of a wise disciple, meaning speaks to a person like a wise disciple speaking to an uneducated person and advising him to be a wise disciple. It is as Baal HaSulam asked, "What is a wise disciple? Why do we not say simply, 'wise?'" It implies we should know that wise means the Creator, whose desire is to bestow upon His creatures. One who learns from the Creator this quality of being a giver is called "wise disciple," meaning that he has learned from the Creator to be a giver.

Now we can interpret that the evil inclination comes to a person and advises him how to achieve *Dvekut* with the Creator, meaning to be in the presence of the Creator, but he is not really a wise disciple, namely that the aim of the evil inclination is not to bring him to *Dvekut*, but on the contrary—to separation—and it is speaking like a wise disciple because it wants to set a trap for him to divert him from the right path.

If a person does not notice who is speaking to him—the good or the evil inclination—and only hears that it is speaking with the *Talit* of a wise disciple, it takes pride in it, meaning lets him understand the importance of a wise disciple while conspiring to divert him to another path, to disparity of form. At that time one is told that he should know that if he listens to its advice, one who listens to its advice will not be admitted into the presence of the Creator, but to the contrary.

Therefore, one must be very careful and know with whom he speaks. He should not mind what he is saying, meaning that even if it says good things, he must still not listen to it. It follows that from an indecent person it is forbidden to hear even decent words.

What Is the Advantage in the Work More than in the Reward?

Article No. 5, Tav-Shin-Mem-Zayin, 1986-87

RASHI interprets the verse, "And the Lord appeared to him": "He opened the tent door to see if there were any passers by to let them into his house. At midday, the Creator took out the sun from its sheath, not to trouble him with guests. And since He saw him regretting that guests were not coming, He brought him angels in the similitude of people."

We should understand 1) why he says, "And since He saw him regretting that guests were not coming, He brought him angels in the similitude of people." Did the Creator not know in advance that he would regret not having guests? Thus, why did He take out the sun from its sheath? 2) Did the Creator have no other way to send him guests other than by deceit, meaning that he deceived him into thinking that they were people? After all, He could easily put the sun back in its sheath and people would be able to come to him as guests.

Our sages said (in the *Midrash*) that Abraham said, "Before I was circumcised, passers by would come to me. Now that I have been circumcised they are not coming to me." The Creator said to him: "Before you were circumcised, uncircumcised would come to you. Now, I and My entourage come to you."

This, too, is perplexing: 1) What is the answer to the question he asked, "Why are guests not coming now?" So He told him: "Before, uncircumcised would come to you. Now, I and My entourage." But He did not reply why guests were not coming. 2) What is the question, "Why are they not coming?" It is simple: because it is midday. This is why guests cannot come. 3) In general, what is the reply that the Creator gave him, as if now you are in a greater and more important state than before, when uncircumcised would come? After all, our sages said, "Greeting guests is greater than greeting the *Shechina* [Divinity]." Accordingly, Abraham's complaint is just, since Abraham understood that once he had circumcised himself, he must certainly reach a higher degree, but he sees that it is not so. Rather, he suffered a descent; he had lost a great thing, meaning greeting guests.

However, we should understand why greeting guests is greater than greeting the *Shechina*. Our sages said (*Shavuot* 35b), "Rav Yehuda said, 'Rav said, 'Greeting guests is greater than greeting the *Shechina*.''" "Greater" means it is more important.

However, in the reality of this world we see that the important things in the world are only in a chosen few and not in ordinary people. It is only a handful of people. But things that are less valuable are found in more people than important things. Accordingly, the rule should have been that many people will be rewarded with greeting the *Shechina*, and a few with greeting guests.

However, in reality we see the opposite: There are more people who are greeting guests than people who have been rewarded with greeting the *Shechina*. It is so much so that we cannot even know how many there are in the world who have been rewarded with greeting the *Shechina*. Moreover, we must believe that there is such a thing in the world, that they have been rewarded with greeting the *Shechina*, although we do not know who they are. But our sages said (*Sukkah* 45), "There is not a generation without thirty-six righteous." But who knows them?

Instead, we must believe that they exist in the world, and it was said about them that greeting guests is more important than greeting the *Shechina*. But according to reason, it should have been the opposite, as it is in reality, that important things are more difficult to find than things that are not so important.

Likewise, we should understand what our sages said (*Berachot* 8a), "He who enjoys his labor is greater than fear of heaven." This implies that one who enjoys his labor has no fear of heaven. And if the intention is that one who enjoys his labor has fear of heaven, why is it so remarkable? Of course one who has fear of heaven—and in addition has the merit of enjoying his labor—is more important. However, we should say that the intention is that one who has only one thing—only labor—is more important than fear of heaven. We need to understand this, too, for it is contrary to reality.

We see that in reality, many people enjoy their labor. However, we do not see many people with fear of heaven. And if those who enjoy their labor were more important than those who have fear of heaven, there should have been many more people with fear of heaven, and people who enjoy their labor should have been a small part of the public.

To understand the above said, we will interpret this according to the work, as this path brings one to enter the King's palace, and it is called "the path of Torah." This pertains specifically to servants of the Creator and not to the view of landlords, as we have said in previous articles.

However, we should understand what is the work that He has given to man, and in which he must toil, as our sages said (*Megillah* 6b), "I labored and did not find, do not believe. I did not labor and found, do not believe. I labored and found, believe." However, we should understand why we need this labor.

We should interpret once again what we said in the previous articles, that it is known that the purpose of creation was that the Creator created creation because of His desire to do good to His creations. It is as they said (*Beresheet Rabbah*, Chapter 8) concerning man's creation: "The angels said to Him: 'What is man that You remember him, and the son of man that You should visit him? Why do You need this trouble?' The Creator said to them, 'Then what are sheep and oxen for?' What is this like? It is like a King who had a tower filled with great abundance, but no guests. What pleasure has the king that he has abundance? Promptly, they said to Him, 'O Lord, our Lord, how great is Your name in all the earth! Do that which pleases You.'"

However, accordingly, why are the creatures not receiving the delight and pleasure that He wanted to give to the creatures? The answer is known—He has given us Torah and *Mitzvot* [commandments] so we will not have the bread of shame, for by observing Torah and *Mitzvot* we will be able to receive the delight and pleasure and we will not feel in it the bread of shame.

However, accordingly, this is perplexing, since there is a clear *Mishnah* [treatise] (*Avot*, Chapter 1, 3) that says as follows, "He would say, 'Be not as slaves who are serving the rav in order to receive reward. Rather, be as slaves who are serving the rav in order not to receive reward.'" Thus, how is it permitted to labor and exert in Torah and *Mitzvot* so we can receive reward for the labor, for only in this way we will receive the delight and pleasure without shame?

According to what is explained in the "Introduction to the Study of the Ten Sefirot," the meaning is that since we have been imprinted with a desire to receive pleasure, which is called "self-love," and we have no understanding of love of others, but when we are told that we must do something for another our body promptly asks, "What will we get out of working for others?" For this reason, when we are told to observe Torah and *Mitzvot*, our body asks, "What is this work for you?" That is, what will we gain from this? We have to exert in Torah and *Mitzvot* for this. Therefore, it is told that by this it will be happy in this world and will also have the next world. That is, it is impossible to work without reward. It follows that we teach the general public to observe Torah and *Mitzvot* in order to receive reward; otherwise, no one will want to engage in Torah and *Mitzvot*.

Maimonides (*Hilchot Teshuva*, Chapter 10) writes, "Our sages said, 'One should always engage in Torah, even if *Lo Lishma* [not for Her sake], since from *Lo Lishma* he will come to *Lishma* [for Her sake]. Therefore, when teaching little ones, women, and uneducated people, they are taught to work only out of fear and in order to receive reward. Until they gain knowledge and acquire much wisdom, they are taught that secret little-by-little and are accustomed to the matter calmly.'"

Thus, it is clear from the words of Maimonides that there is a difference between the general public and individuals. That is, it is possible to reveal the path of the Creator only to individuals, meaning the path to the Creator's palace, meaning the way by which they can achieve *Dvekut* [adhesion] with the Creator, as it is written, "And to cleave unto Him," meaning that he achieves equivalence of form. This is the meaning of what our sages said, "As He is merciful, so you are merciful."

This is the difference between the view of Torah and the view of landlords. The view of a landlord is that in everything he does, he knows that he must profit and receive all the profits into his own authority, meaning he feels that he has his own authority and that he controls his possessions.

Conversely, the view of Torah is that he has no authority of his own. It is as our sages said (*Berachot* 63), "Rish Lakish said, 'How do we know that words of Torah come true only in one who puts himself to death over it? It was said, 'This is the Torah [law], should a man die in a tent.''"

However, we should understand the words of our sages in what they said, "The Torah exists only in one who puts himself to death over it."

1) Why do I need this death? Why should one put himself to death in order for the Torah to exist in him?

2) What is the measure of death that we need for this? It cannot be said that it is actual death, for it is written, "For they are our lives and the length of our days," which is the opposite of death.

3) We also cannot say that needing much time to study Torah and to understand it is called "death." After all, we see that even those who exert only in secular studies and not in holy words, but rather want to get a PhD in some science, they, too, sit day and night and study. And we also see that there are those who have already received their PhD, and still continue to study to become professors. Also, there are people who have already become professors but do not stop studying. They want to put all their energy and vigor into research and become world famous scientists. Still, it is not said about them that the wisdom does not exist in them, but that they must die, as our sages said that the Torah does not exist. This means that secular studies do not have such conditions. Thus, what is the meaning of "The Torah exists only in one who puts himself to death over it"? What is this death?

4) We should also understand what our sages said, "The Torah exists only..." what is this existence? If we interpret that existence means that he should know and remember what he has learned, that this is regarded as the Torah existing, should one put himself to death over this? It follows that one who was born talented, with an acute mind and perfect memory, memorizing everything that he has learned, there remains the question why he needs to put himself to death so the Torah will exist in him.

To understand the above, we should reiterate what we have begun to clarify regarding the purpose of creation, which is in order to benefit His creations. As he explains there ("Introduction to the Study of the Ten Sefirot"), since all the creatures are called "creatures" because something new was created here, which did not exist prior to the creation of the worlds, namely a lack and craving to receive delight and pleasure, since the measure of delight from the pleasure depends on the measure of craving and coveting of the matter, to that extent he can enjoy. Likewise, one who is not hungry cannot enjoy the meal he is given.

However, here, through the desire to receive pleasure that was imprinted in the creatures, it caused separation and disparity of form between the Creator and the creatures, and it is known that disparity of form separates into two in spirituality. To the extent of the difference between them, they also become remote from one another. For this reason, the creatures were separated from the Creator and became two authorities, where man says that he, too, is the host and not the guest, and has his own authority.

However, we should know that this will to receive is the evil that exists in the world, as is explained there ("Introduction to the Study of the Ten Sefirot"). That is, all the thefts, murders, and wars in the world, as well as all the bad qualities such as anger and pride derive from this will to receive, which wants with all its might to satisfy its self-love. Wherever it sees that it can derive pleasure, it is immediately ready and willing to be filled with it.

Even laziness, when a person does nothing, is also due to self-love. Now he chooses to do nothing because now he feels that the body craves to receive pleasure from rest. For this reason, he relinquishes other pleasures because at the moment, it sees and thinks that it will give him more pleasure than other things. That is, lazy means that he derives excessive pleasure from rest. However, all these fall into self-love, which is the evil from which the entire world suffers.

In order to correct this evil, which is called "evil inclination" and causes us separation, and for which we cannot receive the delight and pleasure that the Creator wants to give us, it is if we exit self-love and cancel our own authority, and our desire will be only to bestow contentment upon the Creator. This is called "cancelling the authority," since we are not concerned with our own pleasure and contentment, but desire only to benefit the Creator and not ourselves.

At that time a person comes to feel with what he can delight the Creator. That is, what a person can say that will bring contentment to the Creator, since nothing is missing in the King's palace. At that time a person finds one thing that he can say will bring contentment to the Creator, since the purpose of creation was to delight His creatures. For this reason, a person searches how to derive pleasure, in order to delight the Creator.

By wanting to give contentment to the Creator, he elicits a new thing: He really does enjoy. Otherwise, it is regarded as lying. That is, he makes room for the Creator to carry out His will, His desire for the creatures to enjoy. And if he does not enjoy and says that he is enjoying then he is lying to the Creator. In truth, he really does receive delight and pleasure, but the whole difference is in the intention, meaning that the pleasure he receives is because the Creator wants it. For himself, even though he desires and craves pleasures, he overcomes his desire, goes against it, and does not want to receive. This is called "receiving in order to bestow."

By this we see that although in terms of the act they are the same, meaning that both enjoy, there is still a difference in the intention. One who enjoys because of self-love follows the counsel of the evil inclination, and one who, due to self-love, relinquishes the pleasure and enjoys because of the commandment of the Creator, that He desires to do good, and this is why he receives the pleasure, that person is regarded as following the counsel of the good inclination.

Similarly, we find in the words of our sages (*Nazir* 13): "Rabbah Bar Hana said, 'Rabbi Yohanan said, 'Why is it written, 'For the ways of the Lord are straight, the righteous will walk and the transgressors will fail?' There is an allegory of two people who were roasting their lambs. One did it for the purpose of *Mitzva* [commandment/good deed] and the other for crass eating. The one who ate it for a *Mitzva* is 'the righteous will walk.' The one who ate for crass eating is 'the transgressors will fail.' Rish Lakish said to him, 'Do you call this one wicked? True, it is not a first rate *Mitzva*, but he did indeed perform the *Pesach* offering.'""

This means that there is a difference in the intention, although in the act, they are the same. Rish Lakish says "He is not regarded as wicked because in any case, he did perform a *Mitzva*, but it is not first rate." We can interpret this that specifically concerning *Mitzva* we say that it is regarded as a *Mitzva*, but not a first rate one. This is why our sages said (*Nazir* 23b), "Rav Yehuda said, 'Rav said, 'One should always engage in Torah and *Mitzvot* even *Lo Lishma* [not for Her sake], because from *Lo Lishma* he will come to *Lishma* [for Her sake].'"

However, concerning permission, there is certainly a difference between receiving the pleasure because it is the commandment of the Creator, who wants to do good to His creations. Otherwise, meaning due to self-love, he would relinquish the pleasure. It follows that the main thing is the intention. But concerning a *Mitzva*, we say that even if he does not have the intention it is still considered a *Mitzva*. (It is as said above, that concerning the general public, they are taught to observe Torah and *Mitzvot Lo Lishma*, as Maimonides says.)

Accordingly, we should interpret the matter of a person having to put himself to death. We asked, "What is the meaning of death?" Now we will understand that death means annulment of one's own authority. He says that there is no authority in the world but the Creator's. This is called "singular authority." This is the meaning of our saying, "Hear, O Israel, the Lord our God, the Lord is one," meaning that there is only one authority in the world, and he cancels his self-love.

By this we can interpret what the ARI says, that we must take upon ourselves devotion while saying the Shema Israel, that the intention is to annul self-love. Afterward, we can say, "And you shall love the Lord your God with all your heart and with all your soul and with all your might," since his own reality does not exist with respect to himself because all this thoughts are for the Creator. This is called "putting himself to death over it."

Now we can understand why the Torah exists only in one who puts himself to death over it. We asked, "What does it mean to observe the Torah, that without putting oneself to death over it the Torah cannot exist?" We should interpret that observing refers to what the Torah has promised us, meaning as it is written, "For they are our lives and the length of our days," and as it is written, "They are more desirable than gold, than much fine gold, and sweeter than honey and the drippings of the honeycomb," and other such promises that the Torah has promised us.

This is as was said above, that all those things are included in the purpose of creation, called "His desire to do good to His creations." All this cannot come to the creatures for the above reason, which is the matter of disparity of form from the Creator, who desires to bestow, while the creatures want to receive into their own domain, which is called "separation" in spirituality, and from which derives the matter of the bread of shame.

Therefore, there must be concealment, meaning that the upper abundance included in the purpose of creation cannot shine. The reason is to give room for choice. It follows from this that we see in the world concealment of the face. This is what King David said (Psalms 73), "Behold, these wicked and those who are always at ease have obtained riches."

However, when a person has already come to a state of "putting himself to death over it," meaning that he puts his self to death, which is self-love, and he has no concern for himself but worries only about increasing the glory of heaven above, as it is written, "May His great name grow and be sanctified." At that time, when one wants to bestow contentment upon the Creator, it is regarded as "and to cleave unto Him; as He is merciful, so you are merciful." At that time we can be rewarded with all those things that the Torah has promised us; then they come true.

By this we can understand the words of our sages, who said, "The Torah exists only in one who puts himself to death over it." It follows that the meaning of "The Torah exists only," which He promised us, is only after he has put his self to death over it.

Now we will explain what we asked about what our sages said, "I labored and did not find." We asked, "Why do I need this labor?" However, there is a famous question about this, since finding comes only when there is no preparation. That is, it just happened to a person that he found something, but without preparation. But here in the Torah there is a condition before the finding, that it takes great labor to obtain the find. Accordingly, it should have said, "I labored and acquired."

Baal HaSulam interpreted that it means that if a person has labors in Torah first, he is rewarded with the Creator's favor and the Creator gives him the Torah as a gift. This is the meaning of "I labored and found."

By the above-said we can understand why the Creator does not want to give the Torah as a gift before a person has labored. And also, what is the labor? The answer is as it is said ("Introduction to the Study of the Ten Sefirot"), that since man was created with a will to receive for himself, he therefore becomes separated from the Creator. In order to adhere to the Creator he must be in equivalence of form, "As He is merciful, so you are merciful." Otherwise, if he receives true pleasure from the Torah, he will be farther from the Creator.

Therefore, when one wants to come into a state where "All your actions are for the Creator," the will to receive in the body resists it. This is the real labor that the creatures have because they must go against the nature with which they were born. It follows that the labor is that we need to go against nature. But why do we need the labor? It is in order to come to "and to cleave unto Him," so there will be one authority.

It follows that we should discern between the general public and individuals. That is, the general public is taught and educated to work *Lo Lishma*, which is in order to receive reward. They are called "servants who serve the rav in order to receive reward."

But the individuals are told, "Be as servants who are serving the rav not in order to receive reward, and let the fear of heaven be upon you." *The Zohar* interprets ("Introduction of the Book of Zohar," Item 191), "Fear, which is the most important, is that one should fear one's Master because He is great and ruling." It teaches us that "There are three manners in the fear of God, only one of which is considered real fear: 1) Fear of the Creator and keeping His *Mitzvot* so his sons may live and he will be kept from bodily punishment or a punishment to one's money. This is a fear of punishments in this world. 2) When fearing punishments of Hell, as well.

"Those two are not real fear, for he does not keep the fear because of the commandment of the Creator, but because of his own benefit. It follows that his own benefit is the root, and fear is a derived branch of his own benefit.

"3) Rather, the fear that is the most important is for one to fear one's Master because He is great," because He is the root.

It therefore follows that the labor applies primarily to people who wish to go by the path of individuals, which is the view of Torah, which is about annulment of plural authority, and want there to be only one authority.

That is, the general public, as said in the words of *The Zohar*, want the reward of both this world and the next world. But individuals, who annul their authorities and care only about delighting the Creator, their whole intention is the work and the labor, and not the reward, for they want to serve the rav not in order to receive reward. It follows that neither this world nor the next world matter to them; their sole desire is the work.

When they are craving work, they are certain that they are not deceiving themselves that they are working for the Creator. But the minute they are looking at the reward, although he can say that he aims for the Creator, who knows if this is really so? Therefore, the only precious thing they have is room for work in order not to receive reward at all.

According to the above, we can understand the words of our sages, who said in the *Midrash* that Abraham said, "'Before I was circumcised, passers by would come to me. Now that I have been circumcised they are not coming to me.' The Creator said to him: 'Before you were circumcised, uncircumcised would come to you. Now, I and My entourage come to you.'"

We asked, What is the answer to his question why he cannot keep the *Mitzva* of greeting guests? The answer is that now he has a higher degree, which is greeting the *Shechina* [Divinity]. This is why He said to him: "Now, I and My entourage come to you."

But previously he had a higher degree, which is greeting guests, and hospitality is greater than greeting the *Shechina*. Thus, what is the Creator's answer?

However, we should understand this, too. This is the opposite of common sense, since normally, it is a great privilege to people if an important person comes to them. According to the person's importance, so is the value of the preparation to greet him, such as if the greatest man in his town should come to him, or the greatest in the country, or the greatest in the world.

But here we are saying that he was rewarded with greeting the *Shechina*, which is something that cannot even be evaluated. We cannot even know what it means to greet the *Shechina*, as is explained in all the books, that a person cannot attain it unless he has been granted with it. And who is granted with it, certainly the greatest righteous in the generation. And we cannot even attain who are those righteous, unless by faith, when we believe that there are such people. It was said about this that greeting guests is greater than this.

Certainly, there are answers to this in the literal meaning, but we will interpret this in the work. There is the matter of labor in the Torah and knowing the Torah. Labor in the Torah is that since man wants to serve the Creator not in order to receive reward, he looks only at the labor. If he begins to think about knowing the Torah it will seem like he is expecting a reward, for we must believe that no reward is greater than knowing the Torah, as it is written in *The Zohar*, "For the whole of the Torah is the names of the Creator." Also, a complete man is one who has been rewarded with "The Torah and the Creator and Israel are one." Therefore, indeed, greeting the *Shechina* is very important because the purpose is for man to achieve this degree.

But to come to greet the *Shechina* requires prior preparation, for one to be fit for it. In the words of our sages, this is called "As

He is merciful, so you are merciful." This is the interpretation of the verse, "and to cleave unto Him, cleave unto His attributes." It means, as explained in the book *Matan Torah* [*The Giving of the Torah*], that only by a person working in love of others can he achieve *Dvekut* [adhesion] with the Creator. There are many names to this: "Instilling of the *Shechina*," "attainment the Torah," "greeting the *Shechina*," etc.

The main preparation, which is called "labor," is that one must prepare oneself to annul one's authority, meaning one's self. We can call this hospitality [greeting guests], meaning that he cancels the view of landlords and craves the view of Torah, which is called "annulling of authority." Naturally, he becomes the guest of the Creator, who is the Host of the entire world.

And since there are ups and downs about it, meaning that many times the body makes him see that he, too, is a host, meaning that he is allowed to do what he wants and he is not subjugated to the Host, who is the Creator. Naturally, he wants to do whatever he wants. But later, a person overcomes the body's thoughts and desires and accepts that he is the guest and the Creator is the Host, and a person has no authority; he is only a passing guest in this world.

This matter, namely these ascents and descents, repeat themselves. It follows that from time to time a person always lets guests into his body. That is, a person always walks around with thoughts that he is the guest. We can call this "greeting guests," where each time he lets into his body thoughts of guests. However, this is a great labor because it is against the body's nature.

Afterward, he is rewarded with the reward called "greeting the *Shechina*." For this reason, in order for one not to deceive himself that he is not concerned about the reward, called "in order to receive reward," but wants to work not in order to receive reward, for this reason a person's greatness is seen if he says, "greeting guests is greater than greeting the *Shechina*." Then, a clear awareness is carved and becomes evident in a person that he is not looking at the reward, but at the work and labor, that he has something with which to serve the Creator, and this is all he wants.

We can understand it through an allegory: Two men who were great friends loved each other dearly. Once, one of them needed 5,000 dollars urgently. He said to his friend: "I need a big favor from you, to lend me this sum, and I know that you don't have that kind of money, but I know that you have relatives and friends, and you can borrow from twenty people—from each one 250 dollars, and then you will have the money I need. In two weeks, God willing, I'll pay you back."

That person did not know what to do. Now he had to go to twenty people to borrow money from them with the promise he would pay them back in two weeks. "What if he does not have the money to pay back in time as he has promised me? What will I do? How will I be able to look in their faces, since I did not keep my promise to them?"

Afterward, he thinks differently: "He is my friends and certainly loves me, for if he did not know for certain that he will be able to pay back in time he would not make me feel bad." After that he gets another thought: "It's true that he would not ask for the loan if he did not know for certain that he would have the money to give me, but perhaps he made a mistake, meaning that the places from which the thought he would get this sum, his calculation was not very accurate, so what will happen if he does not pay me in time?" Subsequently, another thought comes to him: "Since he loves me as much as I love him, I have to say that he has thought several times before asking me for the loan." These thoughts continue back and forth.

In the end he decides above reason, meaning although his reason leaves him in doubt if he will meet the payback time, but he goes with faith above reason and tells himself: "Since we have love of friends, I want to do my friend a favor, for by this I can show the love I have for him."

But when he gave him the $5,000 dollars, his friend took out of his pocket two checks that he had to receive from the government, one to be paid in a week, and the other in two weeks. In that state, the person faced a dilemma:

1. He tells his friend, "Why didn't you show me the two checks when you asked me for the loan? Only now that I have brought you the money you are showing me?" The friend asks, "What is the difference?" So he tells him, "I haven't been able to sleep for two nights thinking what will I do if you cannot pay back in time? Now it is as though a load has been taken off my back because now I'm sure I can be a decent person in the eyes of those twenty people from whom I borrowed."

2. He tells him: "Why did you show me these checks? If you hadn't shown them to me now, I would have two whole weeks to work on love of friends above reason, and I would have a great gain in love of friends, which I regard as a great thing. By showing me the checks now, it's as though you have robbed me of work."

By the above allegory we can understand the words of the *Midrash*, that after Abraham was rewarded with making a covenant with the Creator, as it is written, "And made the covenant with Him," he was rewarded with greeting the *Shechina*, and then he was rewarded with permanent faith in the Creator, without ascents and descents. He saw the reward for his work and felt that now he could not labor. He thought that now all his work was in order to receive, which is self-love, and longed for work, since here he could know for certain that his intention was not to receive reward, but that he wants to work not in order to receive reward. But now, after he was circumcised, he has no ascents or descents and no room for overcoming in the work.

Therefore, he complained to the Creator and said to Him: "Before I was circumcised, passers by would come to me." That is, previously, I saw that I was transgressing the words of Torah and not keeping them as one should keep the law of the Creator, but then I overcame. "Returning" ["passers by" is written in Hebrew as passing and returning] means that I have repented. Afterward, they pass by again, meaning that I had another descent from my state.

Subsequently, I overcame my state and repented, which is called "returning," and so on and so forth.

It follows that I feel that I am doing something for You. But now that I have been circumcised and rewarded with making a covenant with You, I am not doing anything for You, but I long to do some service for You, so I will be able to say that it is not in order to receive reward. But this has vanished from me. This means that Abraham had a just argument.

However, the Creator replied to him: "Before you were circumcised, uncircumcised would come to you." Nonetheless, you were uncircumcised. Even though you had some ascents in the work, you were still uncircumcised. But now you have been rewarded with greeting the *Shechina*. This is why the Creator said to him: "Now, I and My entourage come to you. So why are you angry at Me?"

Now we should know the truth, meaning whose argument is more truthful. The answer is that both are true, as said in the allegory. That is, the lender, after the borrower showed him the two $5,000 checks, since the borrower did not want his friend to be tormented by the possibility that he might not be able to pay him in time.

And the lender is angry at his friend because he had lost room for work. That is, had his friend not shown him from where he could pay, he would have work the whole two weeks—working in himself that he needs to adhere to love of friends and believe in my friend that he thought several times before asking me something, so that it would not pain me in any way. At the same time, the body always brings him evidence to the contrary, since it wants to install in my heart hatred of friends. Naturally, I would have ascents and descents. But then I would enjoy working with myself.

But now, by wanting to do me a favor, I lost. We see from this allegory that both are correct. That is, by each one claiming that he wanted to show his love, the love is established forever.

It is the same here: The Creator showed Abraham the love by coming to him by making the covenant between them, as it is written, "And made the covenant with him." Likewise, by complaining to the

Creator, Abraham showed his love for Him, that he wanted to serve Him not in order to receive reward, and that this is why Abraham longed for work called "hospitality," as we explained concerning greeting guests.

Now we will clarify what we asked about what RASHI interpreted, "At midday, the Creator brought out the sun from its sheath, not to trouble him with guests. And since He saw him regretting that guests were not coming, He brought him angels in the similitude of people." We asked, "Did the Creator not know that he would regret not having guests? If so, why did He take the sun out from its sheath?" We also asked, "Why did He have to send him angels in the similitude of people, for it seems as though there is deception here? He could have simply put the sun back in its sheath, so people could be able to come to Him."

We should understand the meaning of taking the sun out from its sheath in the work. The light of the Creator is called "day" or "sun." A "sheath" is like the sheath that covers a sword. When he wants to say that the light of the Creator is covered, he says that the sun is covered in the sheath and is unfelt.

During the work, meaning before a person exits his self-love, he must work in concealment. That is, although he still does not feel any taste in Torah or prayer, he should exert in Torah and prayer, and not say, "When I feel the taste of Torah and prayer I will pray and study." Rather, if a person does not think of himself, but wants to serve the King, then he does not care what taste he feels. Instead, he should say, "Now I am keeping the commandment of the Creator and I want to bring Him contentment by keeping His commandments, and not consider myself, but only consider what will bring the Creator more contentment."

However, when the Creator sees that he is already fit to receive everything in order to bestow, a person is rewarded with the revelation of the face of the Creator. This is called "taking the sun out from its sheath," when the concealment of the face of the Creator is removed from him, and instead His face becomes revealed.

It is as our sages said (*Avot*, Chapter 6), "Rabbi Meir says, 'Anyone who engages in Torah *Lishma* is rewarded with many things and the secrets of Torah are revealed to him.'" This means that if he engages *Lishma*, meaning not for his own benefit, but his intention in keeping the Torah and *Mitzvot* is only for the Creator, by this he becomes fit to receive the abundance because there is equivalence of form here, called *Dvekut*, meaning that as the Creator wants to bestow upon the creatures, man wants to bestow upon the Creator.

At that time, the concealment is removed from his place because the concealment was only due to the correction of the bread of shame. But now that he has come to a degree where he wants to bestow, there is no more room for shame because everything he receives now is not for his own benefit, but because the Creator wants it. Thus, naturally, he is rewarded with greeting the *Shechina*. This is called "taking the sun out from its sheath," meaning taking out the upper abundance from the concealment it had been in until now.

According to the above, there is no room for asking why the Creator took the sun out from its sheath if the Creator knew in advance that Abraham would regret not having guests, called "passers by," meaning ascents and descents, since He did not place the sun in its sheath. That is, He made the concealment only so that man could come to aim to bestow upon the Creator.

That is, even though he does not see any reward in this work he is doing, to achieve Torah *Lishma*, and not to receive reward, but now that Abraham has achieved this there is certainly no room for concealment. Instead, the concealment is removed from the place that belongs to the Creator, as it is written, "In every place where I mention My name, I will come to you and bless you" (Exodus 20:21).

The question is about "where I mention." It should have said that if a person mentions the name of the Creator, "I will come to you and bless you." What is, "I will mention"? It means that the Creator will mention His own name.

We should interpret that if a person annuls himself as we explained about the view of Torah, meaning follows "puts himself to death over it," which is annulment of the authority so there is only the singular authority here—that of the Creator—then the Creator can say, "In every place where I mention." Why can I mention My name? It is because man has canceled that place for the Creator. At that time, "I will come to you and bless you" comes true. For this reason, he comes to a state where the Creator took the sun out from its sheath, which is the greeting of the *Shechina*.

Naturally, there is no room here for the question about the Creator saw that he regretted, He placed the sun back in its sheath, since this contradicts the goal. The purpose of creation is as is written, "And let them make Me a Temple that I may dwell among them," and not depart. As long as there is a place of equivalence of form, meaning a desire to bestow, the Creator, too, brings Himself to that place. Only in a place of sin—when falling to the vessels of reception in order to receive due to some sin—the abundance departs due to the iniquities. This is called "the ruin of the Temple."

This is why He could not give him a state of greeting guests, for that state is still not *Kedusha* [holiness], for there are ascents and descents there. Instead, He sent him angels, which is complete *Kedusha*, for it could no longer be differently, as he has already made the everlasting covenant with the Creator. However, in the similitude of people, meaning that he must discover the situation, that it is only a façade, meaning that he will be able to criticize himself—whether he is aiming for the reward, namely greeting the *Shechina*, or craving to serve the rav not in order to receive reward.

At that time, if he delights in having been rewarded with guests, although he later discovers that they are angels, but his criticism of himself—that he wanted to see if he was deceiving himself and was thinking of the reward and not of the work—he already received from being happy that he could greet guests again, meaning have room for work. At that time it was clear to him that he was working not in order to receive reward.

It is as Baal HaSulam explained people's question about the verse, "And He said, 'Do not reach out your hand to the youth, and do not do anything to him, for now I know that you are God fearing.'" The question is, "Did the Creator not know this before the test?"

He said that the meaning of "for now I know" is that you know that you are God fearing. That is, Abraham wanted to know if he was on the path of only for the Creator and he himself did not merit a name. For this reason, the Creator sent him a test, so that Abraham would know that he can endure the test, for then he would not fear extending upper abundance downward, for now it was clear to him that he will not blemish the upper abundance because he saw that his only wish was to bestow, and nothing for himself, which is called "receiving in order to bestow."

According to the above, we should interpret what we asked about what our sages said, "Greater is one who enjoys his labor more than fear of heaven." We asked, "How can this be?"

It is known that there is labor in the Torah and there is the study of Torah. Study of Torah is called that which the Torah teaches us—to keep the commandments of the Creator in act and in intention. It is as we see that there are two blessings: 1) "Blessed are you, O Lord ... to engage in words of Torah"; 2) "Blessed are you, O Lord, who teaches Torah to His people, Israel."

This means that if we thank the Creator for allowing us to engage in words of Torah, it pertains to the labor—that we can engage, which is the engagement in Torah. Also, we thank the Creator for studying Torah, meaning that we have been rewarded with the Creator teaching us. This is called "knowledge of the Torah"—what the Torah teaches us.

We need both labor and knowledge. This is the meaning of what we learn, that there is no light without a *Kli* [vessel], meaning that there is no filling without a lack. Similarly, a person cannot enjoy rest if he did not previously have toil and labor.

However, here, in the work of the Creator, there are two discernments in the lack: The first is that he craves pleasures. This is the first discernment in the *Kli*, called "deficiency," meaning that he feels deficient of this pleasure. The second is that there is a condition to satisfying his deficiency: He must pay for the pleasure. For example, in corporeality, if a person walks into a store and sees something nice that he wants to buy, it follows that now a desire for this something has awakened in him.

The second deficiency is that there is a lack that he wants to receive the object, but he is not given without something in return. Rather, he must pay the owner, and then he is given the object. The fact that he must pay is regarded as labor. This is regarded as a deficiency, since a person thinks that if he were given without pay then he would not be deficient, meaning he would not have the money to pay for the object, which is the reward required of him, and would not be able to give.

It turns out that now he has two deficiencies: 1) He wants that thing. 2) He cannot pay for it.

Thus, the craving for it caused an even greater deficiency because now he knows that he cannot give what is asked in return for the object. It turns out that here, in the work of the Creator, one whose soul yearns to cling to the Creator, a deficiency is born in him. But who causes him that lack of craving for the Creator? This comes from above.

This is called an "awakening from above," when a person is summoned to enter *Kedusha*, as it is written, "You will be holy, for I the Lord am holy." All of a sudden, a person begins to feel that he is far from the Creator, meaning where previously he used to be preoccupied with other needs, and now he sees that all he needs is spirituality.

Afterward, he begins to think, "What is the real reason that I do not have spirituality?" At that time he comes to a resolution that it is only due to absence of equivalence of form, as in, "as He is merciful, so you are merciful."

It follows that the first deficiency is that he feels that he is deficient of spirituality. This is the first deficiency. Now he needs to work on equivalence of form but he sees that he cannot, and this is the second deficiency. It is as our sages said, "Man's inclination overcomes him every day, and if the Creator did not help him, he would not be able to overcome it" (*Sukkah* 52).

However, this second lack, too, comes from above. That is, the Creator has deliberately made man unable to overcome it (for the reason we already discussed) unless with His help. It follows that that deficiency comes from above, as well. It turns out that the labor is primarily in the second lack, which is regarded as not being able to pay the price required for studying Torah.

That is, there is a high price to being rewarded with the Torah, namely equivalence of form, so there will not be the bread of shame. This is the meaning of what we interpreted concerning the words of our sages, "The Torah exists only in one who puts himself to death over it," and this is the real labor. It is for this deficiency that the filling comes and fills this lack. This is the greeting of the *Shechina*, or the secrets of Torah, etc.

Especially, here begins the real division between labor and the reward, meaning that some want to labor without reward, and want to be among the workers who serve the Rav in order not to be rewarded, or who work in order to receive reward, meaning the reward for the labor. That is, they look at what they can gain by the labor, which is called Torah, in the sense that the whole Torah is the names of the Creator. This is called "And you will know that I am the Lord your God."

It is as our sages said (*Berachot* 38a), "When I take you out I will do something so you will know that I am the One who brought you out of Egypt" (as said in Article No. 13, *Tav-Shin-Mem-Vav*). I said there that the intention is that the Creator, besides delivering them from the *Klipa* [shell/peel] of Egypt, made it so they would be rewarded with knowing the Creator, as in, "The Torah, Israel, and the Creator are one."

We need to understand the difference between labor in the Torah and knowing the Torah, meaning that he wants only to serve the Rav not in order to be rewarded, without the pay, called "knowledge of the Torah." Since the Creator's wish is to reveal the Torah, as it is written, "The Lord desires, for His righteousness He will extol and magnify the Torah," at that time a person says, "I agree to labor several hours in the Torah so that I may know the Torah. And when there is a desire to reward me for my labor, I agree that the reward will be given to another. That is, I will labor in the Torah, and another will receive the reward, meaning the knowledge of the Torah that should be revealed by the labor that he has given."

This is true labor because he wants only the labor and not the reward, although the reward is very important to him. Still, he gives it up because he wants to serve the Rav not in order to receive reward. And because the Creator's wish is that the Torah will be revealed to His creatures, he wants his friend to be rewarded with the knowledge of the Torah, while he wants to continue exerting in the Torah. This is a true exertion because he craves the knowledge of the Torah, as is evident from the fact that only he is making the effort, and not his friend. However, because he wants his work to be for the Creator, he wants to stay in a state of labor.

However, there are people who walk on the path of "Be as servants serving the Rav in order to receive reward." Because of this, their wish is only the knowledge of the Torah and not the labor. According to what our sages said (*Midrash Rabbah*, portion, "This Is the Blessing"), "The Creator said to Israel, 'All the wisdom and all the Torah are easy. Anyone who fears Me and carries out the words of Torah, all the wisdom and all the Torah are in his heart.'"

In order to attain the reward without labor, and since though fear of heaven it is possible to receive the wisdom and the Torah easily, without any effort—as said in the *Midrash*—they want to be fearing heaven, in order to receive the reward, called "wisdom" and "Torah." It follows that his fear of heaven is founded on self-love, meaning he is serving the Creator in order to receive reward, called *Lo Lishma*, but in order to receive reward. This is called "the view of landlords." It is as Maimonides says, "Until they gain much knowledge and grow wiser, they are taught to engage in Torah and *Mitzvot Lo Lishma*, but in order to receive reward."

Now we can interpret what we asked about what our sages said, "He who enjoys his labor is greater than fear of heaven." We asked, "How can such a thing be?" According to the above, we can interpret that fear of heaven means that he wants to receive the wisdom and the Torah easily and effortlessly. That is, he expects the reward, not the labor. He does not want to serve the Rav not in order to be rewarded. Rather, he wants the reward and not the service, called "labor." This is called *Lo Lishma*, which is in order to receive reward.

It is not so with one who enjoys his labor, which is the labor in the Torah, and does not think of the reward, but rather that through the labor he will be rewarded with a *Kli*, which is a place where the *Shechina* can clothe because there is equivalence of form between the light and the *Kli*, and he wants only to bring contentment to his Maker and not to himself, as said above (concerning having guests being greater than greeting the *Shechina*). Of course, this degree of one who enjoys his labor is greater than fear of heaven. In fear of heaven, his intention is *Lo Lishma*, but one who enjoys his labor thinks only *Lishma*, meaning he has no other aim but to bestow.

However, we could ask about the *Midrash* that says that the Creator said to Israel, "The whole wisdom and the whole Torah are easy: Anyone who fears Me, all the wisdom and all the Torah are in his heart." According to the above, this is called *Lo Lishma*, so how can he be granted wisdom and Torah? The Creator says that through the fear they can be rewarded with wisdom and Torah.

We can interpret this the same as when I asked about the question people ask about the verse (Numbers 31:1-3): "And the Lord spoke to Moses, saying, 'Avenge the vengeance for the sons of Israel on the Midianites...' And Moses spoke to the people, saying, '...Go against Midian to execute the Lord's vengeance on Midian.'"

The question is, why did Moses change what the Creator had told him? The Creator said, "Avenge the vengeance for the sons of Israel," and Moses said to the people, "the Lord's vengeance on Midian."

The thing is that the Creator created the world with the aim of benefiting His creatures, meaning that the creatures will receive delight and pleasure. In order not to have unpleasantness, called "bread of shame," about the pleasures that the creatures will receive, there was a correction that the receivers will not receive the delight and pleasure from the Creator except on condition that they can receive in order to bestow. This is called *Dvekut*, equivalence of form.

This is as our sages said (*Hagigah* 7): "As I for free, so you are for free." That is, as I want to give you delight and pleasure without any reward, but I rather want you to have contentment, likewise, you are for free, meaning the work you do for Me will be for free, without any reward for your work. This is called equivalence of form.

For this reason, we can interpret that the Creator says to Israel, "It is easy: All the wisdom and all the Torah are in his heart." However, man should say, "I do not want to the pleasure You want to give me," which is as it is called, "For this is your life and the length of your days," and "They are more desirable than gold, yes, than much fine gold; sweeter also than honey and the drippings of the honeycomb." He gives all of this up although his soul craves these good things. Still, since all those things come into vessels of self-love, and self-love separates him from the Creator due to disparity of form, and he wants equivalence of form, therefore he gives them up.

However, precisely those who want equivalence of form and to be among those who serve the rav not in order to be rewarded, they are the people who have a *Kli* in which to instill the upper light. There are several names to this: "Instilling of the *Shechina*," "greeting the *Shechina*," "the secrets of Torah," or "the light of Torah," for then the purpose of creation to do good to His creations will come true.

According to the above, we can interpret what our sages said about the verse, "Greater is one who enjoys his labor more than fear of heaven." It is written about fear of heaven, "Happy is he who fears the Lord," while concerning one who enjoys his labor, it is written, "If you eat from the labor of your own hands, happy and delighted are you, happy in this world and delighted in the next world." Concerning fear of heaven, it is not written about it, "and delighted are you."

We should interpret this world as the time of work, while the next world is called "the time of reward" that he is destined to receive after the work, as it is written, "To do them today and receive the reward for them tomorrow." Therefore, concerning fear of heaven, the reward is the main thing for him, that he will later be rewarded easily with wisdom and Torah, which is called "the next world." This is the good he expects to be awarded later. This is why it is written about it once, since it is written about it only "happy are you," meaning the reward in the next world, this is what he expects. This world is called "the time of labor." He is not happy in this, and each day he stands and waits, "When will I be rewarded with the reward called 'wisdom' and 'Torah'?"

But one who enjoys his labor is happy during the work, as this is all he wants. He wants to serve the Rav not in order to be rewarded. It follows that he enjoys in this world, called "to do them today," and he is also rewarded with the next world, called "to receive the reward for them tomorrow."

Accordingly, we can interpret what we asked about what our sages said, "I have labored and found." Labor [finding] is without any preparation. It should have said, "I labored and acquired," meaning that the labor was a preparation for acquiring, but finding is something that comes absentmindedly. According to the above, it may be so since while the labor is the goal because he wants to serve the rav not in order to be rewarded, and as I said above, he agrees that knowledge in the Torah—that will be revealed after his labor—his friend will be rewarded with it, and since the Torah is revealed only after the labor, which is regarded as light and *Kli*, meaning deficiency and filling. But now that he is giving the *Kli* and the lack, he agrees that his friend will be rewarded with the filling.

It therefore turns out that during the work he is not thinking about the reward at all. Thus, his labor was not preparation for finding, which is knowing the Torah, for this was not the intention while he was working. Rather, he longed to be among the servants who are serving the rav not in order to be rewarded. Accordingly, the labor was not a preparation for the acquisition. Also, the Torah is called "possession" (*Avot*, Chapter 6). This is why they said, "I labored and found," since he was rewarded with knowing the Torah, which came to him absentmindedly, without any preparation for it, hence it is called "finding."

According to the above, which we said about Abraham, that even after he was rewarded with greeting the *Shechina* he still longed to have guests because he wanted it to be clear that his intention was not the reward but to serve the rav not in order to receive reward. Now we will understand what Baal HaSulam explained about people's question about the verse, "And Israel feared," and then "and they believed," which would mean that they would not believe before they saw. He explained that it means that even after they were rewarded with seeing, they craved faith.

And as said above, the advantage in work over expectation for reward is evident.

The Importance of Faith that Is Always Present

Article No. 6, Tav-Shin-Mem-Zayin, 1986-87

The *Zohar* asks (*Vayetze*, Item 75), "Rabbi Yehuda said, 'Since the Creator promised him, 'Behold, I am with you and will keep you wherever you go,' why did he not believe, but said, 'If God is with me'? He replies, 'Jacob said, 'I dreamt a dream.' And as for dreams, some are true and some are not true. If it comes true, I will know that the dream was true.' This is why he said, 'If God is with me,' as I dreamt, and 'Then the Lord shall be a God unto me.'"

We need to understand the above question, as well as the answer, in the work, as far as it concerns us. Also, what is a dream and what is the promise that the Creator made, and what is the condition that Jacob said, "If God is with me then the Lord shall be a God unto me," then he will keep the vow.

To explain all this in the work, we should begin with the purpose of creation, which the Creator created in order to do good to His creations. It is considered that the Creator promised to give the creatures abundance. We should certainly understand this, that He promised abundance to the creatures—it certainly means that He would give to people only the abundance suitable for people.

For example, we see what is good for cats: When they catch mice and eat them, this is their abundance. We cannot say that this abundance, which He gives to vermin and insects, He should give to people. The same applies to the speaking, called "human." In them, too, there are those who know nothing more than what the still, vegetative, and animate know as good. Certainly, animals, for example, were given the abundance that is good for them. And should we give them other abundance, it would be bad because they do not have the *Kelim* [vessels] to feel any taste in it. It is likewise with the vegetative and with the still. That is, within the speaking we should discern the still, vegetative, and animate.

This is as it is written in the "Introduction to the Book of Zohar" (Item 33): "And you must know that any contentment of our Maker from bestowing upon His creatures depends on the extent to which the creatures feel that He is the giver, and the one who delights them. Then He takes great pleasure in them, as a father playing with his beloved son, to the degree that the son feels and recognizes the greatness and exaltedness of his father, and his father shows him all the treasures he has prepared for him."

Accordingly, we can see that the purpose of creation of doing good to His creations is that they will achieve the revelation of Godliness. There was no intent for corporeal pleasures because all the corporeal pleasures from which the creatures are nourished before they obtain vessels of bestowal are only, as it is written in *The Zohar*, a frail light of sparks of *Kedusha* [holiness] that fell among the *Klipot* [shells/peels]. This is all of their vitality. But the primary delight and pleasure are clothed in Torah and *Mitzvot* [commandments/good deeds].

However, in order for the pleasure that the Creator wishes to impart upon the creatures to be complete, the correction of *Tzimtzum* [restriction] took place, namely the concealment on the delight and pleasure that exist in Torah and *Mitzvot*. (It is so that the world will exist, so they can receive the pleasure and enjoy, in the meantime, from the frail illumination that fell among the *Klipot* and on which the world feeds.)

Through the concealment there is room for man to accustom himself that everything he does will be for the Creator because he wants to serve the King without anything in return, since he is keeping Torah and *Mitzvot* without any appearance of light, which is called "the true delight and pleasure."

Once he has become accustomed to keeping his intent only to bestow, then, when he receives the delight and pleasure, there will not be any bread of shame in it because he will not be receiving the delight and pleasure for his own benefit. For himself, he will be willing to give up the pleasures. But since he wants to please the Creator and sees that the Creator lacks only one thing—that He can carry out His goal, meaning that the creatures will receive from Him—for this reason he now receives the abundance, to please the Creator, for the Creator can receive only this from the lower ones: that they will receive from Him delight and pleasure. And since the Creator wants to delight the creatures, the creatures must delight the Creator, too. This is called "equivalence of form."

However, it takes great labor to achieve equivalence of form, which means that all the actions are done for the Creator, since it is against nature. Since man is created with a will to receive pleasure for himself, called "will to receive for himself," and a person is told that he must cancel this will to receive and acquire a new *Kli* [vessel], called "desire to bestow," so not every person is rewarded with being able to acquire these *Kelim*, which are fit to contain the upper light.

In order for one to have a desire to bestow, our sages said (*Kidushin* 30), "I have created the evil inclination; I have created for it the spice of Torah." Thus, precisely by the Torah he can achieve vessels of bestowal.

Also, there is a saying by our sages (*Sukkah* 52): "Rabbi Shimon Ben Levi said, 'Man's inclination overcomes him every day and seeks to put him to death, as it was said, 'The wicked watches the righteous and seeks to put him to death.' Were it not for the Creator's help, he would not overcome it, as it was said, 'The Lord will not leave him in its hand,' referring to this will to receive, since it is separated from the Creator, as it is known that in spirituality, disparity of form separates the spiritual and divides it in two.'"

It is explained in the "Introduction to the Book of Zohar" (Item 10) that "Indeed, first we must understand the meaning of the existence of *Tuma'a* [impurity] and *Klipot*. Know that this is the great will to receive, which we said, and which He placed (the will to receive) in the system of the impure worlds *ABYA*. Because of it, they have become separated from the Creator and from all the worlds of *Kedusha* [holiness]. For this reason, the *Klipot* are called 'dead,' as it is written, 'sacrifices of the dead.' And the wicked that follow them, as our sages said, 'The wicked, in their lives, are called 'dead,'" since the will to receive imprinted in them in oppositeness of form to His Holiness separates them from the Life of Lives, and they are far from Him from one end to the other. It is so because He has no interest in reception, but only in bestowal, whereas the *Klipot* want none of bestowal, but only to receive for themselves, for their own delight, and there is no greater oppositeness than this."

According to the above, in order for a person to have equivalence of form so he may receive the delight and pleasure from the Creator, one is required to great exertion and much help from above so he can defeat the evil in him, which is the will to receive, and to be able to use it with the aim to bestow. There are many people who are not rewarded with it, and for those who are rewarded with it, it is truly a miracle.

Now we should explain what we asked about what is written about Jacob, what it comes to teach us of the way of the Creator in that the Torah tells us his dream and the vow he made, and that the vow was on condition in that he said, "If God is with me."

It is written, "And Jacob arose from his sleep... and took the stone he had placed under his head." It is known that a stone is called *Malchut*, and *Malchut* is called "faith." That is, when a person wants to understand, and understanding is called "head" [mind], he takes this understanding in his mind and places it under his head. This means that he places faith in the head and places his understanding and knowledge under his head. It follows that afterwards the order is that faith is above and reason is below.

This is called "faith above reason." Accordingly, we can interpret what is written, "And he took one of the stones of the place and put it under his head." It is written, "and [Jacob] set it up as a headstone," meaning that he had made faith above reason his state. *Matzeva* [headstone] comes from the word *Matzav* [state], meaning that the state that he wants to build the structure of *Kedusha* will be in faith above reason. This is the meaning of the words, "Then Jacob made a vow, saying, 'If God is with me... then the Lord will be a God unto me.'"

The Zohar asked about it: "Why did he not believe but said, "If God is with me"? It replies that Jacob said, "I dreamt a dream. And as for dreams, some are true and some are not true. If it comes true I will know that the dream was true."

We should interpret the meaning of this world and the next world in the work. This world is like a dream. That is, however we solve it, so it exists. It is as our sages said (*Berachot* 55), "All the dreams follow the mouth," as was said, "As he solved it for us, so it was." In the literal meaning, this is difficult to understand that however people solve it, so it comes true. Accordingly, why should I torment myself over a bad dream? There is a simple advice: He can go to people who are his friends and they will certainly resolve the dream favorably, as our sages said, "All the dreams follow the mouth," and there is no doubt that there are explanations in the literal.

We will interpret this in the work. The Creator created the world in order to do good to His creations. In order not to have shame in the delight and pleasure, man is in this world, which is a place of work where he can obtain vessels of bestowal by which to receive everything in order to bestow. By this there is no room for shame here because he is receiving everything because of a *Mitzva* [commandment].

This is the meaning of what *The Zohar* says, "The Creator promised Jacob abundance." However, He spoke to him by way of a dream, meaning in this world, which is like a dream. That is, according to how a person solves it, meaning if a person goes according to the view of Torah (as it is written in Article No. 5, *Tav-Shin-Mem-Zayin*), it follows that he gives a good solution to what the Creator promised, in that He has created with the world with the intention to do good to His creations. But this promise is a dream, meaning that by a person solving the promise to do good, which is what the Creator wants to bestow, he will give the solution: As the Creator is the giver, likewise, man can work only in order to bestow.

This is regarded as the promise that the Creator promised, to do good, being if a person also provides the solution, namely to do good. This is as our sages said, "As He is merciful, so you are merciful."

But if a person does not offer the solution to the dream, but what the Creator promised, which is to do good to His creations, and he wants the opposite, meaning he wants to receive in order to receive, it follows that he solves it negatively. That is, the good that the Creator wants to give cannot be upheld because he did not prepare the suitable *Kelim* for the delight and pleasure to able to enter them, meaning that there will not be separation between them, as it is known that disparity of form separates the spiritual in two.

Now we can understand why the dream follows the solution. The meaning is that the Creator's promise to do good to His creations depends on man's work in this world, where this world is like a dream, and everything depends on its solution, on how it is solved. That is, if the solution in this world is for the better, meaning if all of a person's actions are to do good, meaning to bestow, then the promise that the Creator promised, to do good, will come true. If the solution follows the evil inclination then the dream, which is the work in this world—that the Creator will give the abundance—cannot come true.

Accordingly, we can understand what our sages said, "All the dreams follow the mouth." It means that if a person speaks good things with his mouth, meaning that he always says that we should do good deeds, that everything is for the Creator and not for his own sake, then the good dream comes true. That is, he is rewarded, as our sages said (*Berachot* 17), with "You will see your world in your life, and your end in the life of the next world."

But if his mouth solves badly and he says that he must care for his own benefit, it is a bad dream because he solved the dream negatively. It follows that the Creator gave His promise to give the delight and pleasure as a dream, meaning within this world, which is like a dream.

Now we can understand the condition and the vow, and the importance of the vow, what greatness there is in the vow, where he said, "If the Lord keeps everything that He has promised me," what a great thing he will do then, as it is written, "This stone, which I have set up as a headstone, will be God's house."

Accordingly, the verse, "And he took from the stones of the place" means that he took the stones, meaning the understandings and concepts and views of the place, where each one has his own view. According to everyone's understanding, he should walk in the path of the Creator only where the intellect dictates, and not go against reason, saying that this is why we were given reason—so we will understand what we are doing. However, he saw that although each one has a different intellect, he saw that the Creator, by creating the creatures with a nature of wanting to receive, there is really only one view here, namely self-love, except each one elicits his self-love with a special intellect. But they are equal in that they are only will to receive and nothing more. It is as it is written, "And he took the stone," one stone.

That is, he placed reason, called "stone," under his head, and took faith into his head, with reason being below faith. The vow was that "If God is with me," meaning if he is rewarded with greeting the *Shechina* [Divinity], as it is written, "Then the Lord shall be a God unto me." And still, I will not take this as the basis, but my whole structure of God's house will be on faith above reason. This is the meaning of what is written, "This stone, which I have set up as a headstone, will be God's house."

Now we will understand the importance of the vow that he said, "If God helps me solve it positively," meaning that he will acquire the appropriate vessels of bestowal where the upper abundance clothes, this is called "greeting the *Shechina*." However, he still wants to use only the stone he had taken in the beginning and which he made into a headstone, meaning the stone that was below his head. And then the vow was that although he would be rewarded with "God is with me and the Lord shall be a God unto me," that stone, which I have placed as a headstone, will be the house of God. That is, he wants to stay in faith even though he has all the revelations. It follows that faith applies both in *Katnut* [infancy/smallness] and in *Gadlut* [adulthood/greatness]. From here we see the importance of faith, for the vow was that even in *Gadlut* he would not move from faith.

The Miracle of Hanukkah

Article No. 7, Tav-Shin-Mem-Zayin, 1986-87

In the Hanukkah poem, we say, "Greeks," etc., "and from the one remnant of the jars, a miracle was made for the roses. Sons of *Bina* [understanding], eight days, established song and chanting." The interpreters ask, "Why did they make the days of Hanukkah eight?" After all, they had oil for one night, and the miracle was that it burned seven more days. Therefore, according to the miracle, they should have set it only for seven days."

They explained that since there remained on the first night from the oil that was needed for the first night, so the miracle on the first night was that not all the oil burned, but rather some of the oil burned and the rest remained seven more days.

This means that their finding the oil jar that was sealed with the seal of the High Priest is not regarded as a miracle, although it was a miracle that the Greeks did not see the oil jar. Instead, he regards a miracle as that which was unnatural, and that which was done above nature is regarded as a miracle, since the oil jar was in the world but they did not see it.

This is not so with the oil. Of the measure required for lighting during one night, only a small part of the oil burned. That small part, which was blessed, burned longer. This was unnatural. That is, it is not according to nature to burn longer than predicted. It follows that what was left of the first night, the fact that not all the oil burned, this is called "a miracle," since this did not exist in the world.

We should interpret in the work the meaning of the Greeks, the oil jar, and the eight days of Hanukkah—that they established specifically eight days. That is, what do the eight days imply? In other words, why was it not nine or ten days, but rather the miracle lasted only eight days? In the literal Torah, it is said in the name of Rokach that the reason why the miracle lasted only eight days and not longer was because the place of the olives, from which the oil is brought, was four days' walk there, and four days' walk back, thus eight days. This answers why the miracle did not last longer than eight days.

It is known that our work, in which we need to exert in every way, is only to achieve equivalence of form, called *Dvekut* [adhesion]. Only then is it possible to achieve the purpose of creation—to do good to His creations—meaning to revelation.

But before the creatures obtain the *Kelim* [vessels] of equivalence of form, the purpose of creation cannot be revealed to everyone. Rather, it is concealed and we must merely believe that it is with the intention to do good.

What was revealed to everyone contradicts the good, since each one always feels deficiency in his life, and always lives with grievances against the upper guidance. He finds it difficult to say that he is enjoying his life and say all day long, "Blessed is the Lord." That is, I am grateful to You for dealing with me benevolently.

Instead, a person's life is always full of lacks and pains. He always sees that there is no meaning to his life, when he begins to think about life's purpose, namely the benefits he gains while suffering the war of life.

This means that only when he tastes some pleasure, the pleasure intoxicates him and he loses his mind and reason and forgets to think about life's purpose. But when the pleasure in which he is immersed departs from him, for whatever reason, he immediately begins to ponder life's purpose.

Only when one has nothing with which to nourish his body, meaning when he does not feel pleasure, he immediately begins to think about life's purpose. That is, a person asks himself "What is the meaning of my life? For what purpose was I born in the world? Was creation made so there would be creatures that suffer torments and pains in the world?"

That state causes one to begin to contemplate life's purpose—what is it and what is it for. This is regarded as a person raising his head from the currents of life, where all the creatures are, and they have no time to think about what they are. Rather, they go with the flow where the water goes. And there is no one who can see the end, meaning where the flow of life is leading.

Only he, because the lack of pleasure causes him to raise his head up in order to look at life's purpose, at that time he sees and hears as though a clarion from above tells him that the world was created with the intention to do good to His creations. But in order to taste that benefit, he is told by books and authors that there are conditions in order to achieve that good, called "the purpose of creation." The Creator demands that they first meet these conditions, or He will not want to give them the delight and pleasure.

However, it is not that He requires these conditions, meaning that the Creator's demands of man are for the sake of the Creator, and if the creatures do not abide by these conditions He will not want to give to them. With flesh and blood, if we want the seller to give us something then the seller sets the conditions for the customer, which, if he meets them, the seller will agree to give, but the conditions are in favor of the seller.

Conversely, the Creator is not deficient or needs the lower ones to meet the conditions required of them, as it is written, "If he is right, what will he give you?" Rather, these conditions that the Creator sets before them are for man's sake.

We can see that this is like a person telling his friend, "I want to give you much silver and gold, but you must meet one condition or you will not receive anything from me." His friend asks: "What is it you require that I will give you so that you will give me the silver and gold?" So he tells him, "Bring me large and small sacks so you can fill them with silver and gold. But you must know that for my part, there are no limitations on how much you will take. Rather, the amount of silver and gold depends on your limits. That is, as many *Kelim* [vessels] as you will bring me I will fill, not more and not less, but exactly that. This is the condition I am setting before you. Certainly, there is no doubt that the conditions that his friend requires are not for the sake of the giver, but everything is for the sake of the receiver.

Here, in the work of the Creator, where one must meet the demands that the Creator demands, they are only for man's sake. However, a person thinks that they are for the sake of the Creator. And since man was created with a will to receive, he cannot understand anything of what needs to be done unless he sees that it is to his own benefit. But here he is told that the Creator wants us to work for Him and not for our own benefit. For this reason, the body resists these works. This is our work—we must go against our nature. This is called "work."

But when one works and feels the reward he is receiving from the work—that it is for his own sake—he does not feel that this is called "work," meaning that he wants to be rid of the work, since this, too, exists in man's nature: He does not want to eat the bread of shame because our root is not receiving or deficient.

For this reason, when one feels that he is receiving something without anything in return, there is the bread of shame there and he is ashamed to receive. Therefore, a person does not resent having to work. Rather, one can regret being paid less than he thinks he is worth.

It follows that if a person knows he will be rewarded for his work, this is not considered "work." But in the work of the Creator, it is regarded as work because he is required to work without any reward, which is called "working not in order to receive reward." This is not in our nature, which is why this is called "work." This is why our body resists these works and always has grievances with the Creator for giving us such hard work that we must work against our nature.

Thus, what do we need in order to be able to work in order to bestow? It is one thing: If we believe that although we do not see it right away, since our bodies do not show us the truth, if we exert to believe that working in order to bestow is in our favor, since that we need these sacks, as said in the allegory, that the sacks we are preparing are all of our *Kelim* for reception of the delight and pleasure, it follows that all the work that is with the aim to bestow makes part of the *Kli* [vessel] that is fit to receive the abundance. Also, every effort joins into the complete amount until we have a complete *Kli* fit for reception of the light.

However, it is difficult to believe and tell ourselves that what He gives is our vessels of reception to receive in it the delight and pleasure that are in the purpose of creation to do good to His creations.

Accordingly, we can interpret the matter of the governance of the Greeks, which is the opposite of the way of Judaism. The matter of the Greeks is that we must go only within reason in both mind and heart. Naturally, when Israel wanted to go above reason and not consider what the outer mind necessitates, they could not.

This is called *the war against the Greeks*. This is when the real work begins, namely that the people of Israel wanted to mount the track that leads to *Dvekut* [adhesion] with the Creator. This path is called "faith above reason." The Greeks wanted to control the body so it will not relinquish anything unless the reason agrees to it. Once this prevailed, and once that prevailed, and this caused one to have ascents and descents.

This, the reason, is the reason and the cause. That is, once a person has decided that he must go with faith above reason, as a result, an awakening from above comes to him and he begins to feel a good taste in the work of the Creator. At that time, it is human nature, since he loves to rest, for this reason he says, "Thank God that now I do not have to work with myself and assume the work of the Creator in the form of faith. Rather, now I feel good and my reason agrees to take upon itself to engage in Torah and Mitzvot [commandments] since now I feel contentment."

He accepts this awakening as a basis and a foundation for the work of the Creator. That is, the basis of the flavor that he feels now, on this he builds his entire Judaism. It therefore follows that now he is blemishing the faith and says, "It is a shame that this awakening did not come to me right away, when I began the work. Then, I would not have to go above reason, meaning against the view of the body. Rather, I would need to believe what is received from books and from authors—that we must assume the burden of the kingdom of heaven although the body disagrees that this is good for me, and to believe that only in this state, when the body disagrees, is the best way for me."

In other words, he believes above reason that only the path of working with mind and heart is good for him, meaning that then he will find the happiness that the Creator has prepared for him. It is very hard to believe this. But now he does not need to believe that this is so. Rather, he feels that indeed, observing Torah and Mitzvot will bring him happiness, since he feels that this is so, and he does not need to believe it.

It turns out that this is the real reason that later causes his descent, since his foundation is built on pleasure rather than on bestowal. If he remains with this foundation, he will never achieve Dvekut with the Creator because as long as he is on this path, everything will fall into the Klipot [shells/peels] of the will to receive for himself.

Baal HaSulam said that when a person receives feeling and reason from above, when the body, too, begins to say that it is worthwhile to engage in Torah and work, one should be careful and say that he does not take this feeling and reason as a basis and foundation, "as the reason why I have decided that now it is worthwhile to work, since the body agrees to this work because of the pleasure I am receiving."

Instead, he should say, "Now I see that this path, which is above reason, is a true path, since I see that it has granted me with being favored in the eyes of the Creator, that He is bringing me closer. For this reason, now I am fond of the *Kedusha* [sanctity/holiness], as well, and I feel the importance of the *Kedusha*—that it is worthwhile to work only for the sake of the Creator. For this reason, what should I do now? Brace myself and walk only on this path called 'faith above reason,' for by this I will be rewarded with permanent *Dvekut* with the Creator."

It thus follows that specifically by being granted some good taste in the work, from this they took support for the path of faith. It follows that the basis of the faith grows stronger through the delight and pleasure that he now feels in the work.

Now we will explain the miracle of Hanukkah, as well, that they defeated the Greeks, meaning that they were rewarded with faith and felt good taste in this work, and did not go and take the delight and pleasure as a basis and foundation for work within reason, which is regarded as Greeks. On the contrary, they said that being rewarded with good taste in the work is a testimony that the path of faith is the true path, unlike the view of the Greeks.

Had they gone by the way of the Greeks, meaning that delight and pleasure would henceforth be their basis and foundation, that this would be their support to sustain their work, they would immediately descend from their degree, as this is the main reason why a person suffers a descent from his state. This is to his benefit, so he will not fall into the *Klipa* [shell/peel] of the Greeks. It follows that this descent is a great correction. Otherwise, everything he adds would only build the *Klipa* of the Greeks.

Therefore, there are two ways when coming to that state called an "ascent":

1) To say that now he is liberated from the burden of faith. That is, until now he suffered because each time he had to assume the burden of the kingdom of heaven, the body always resisted it.

For example, when one must rise before dawn to go to his regular lessons, as soon as he opens his eyes and wants to get up, the body promptly comes and asks, "But you are enjoying the rest, you are lying in bed, and you must give up this pleasure!"

This can be as is done in commerce. That is, we relinquish the pleasure of money in order to obtain something that will bring us a pleasure that we need more. In other words, we will receive greater pleasure than money.

It is known that the value of every pleasure is measured by the need. For example, a person loves rest, but relinquishes rest for money. A person loves money but relinquishes it in favor of eating and drinking, etc. A person loves to eat and drink, but sometimes he avoids it if he knows it is bad for his health. It follows that he has relinquished eating and drinking in order to obtain health.

For this reason, the body asks the person, when he wants to rise before dawn to serve the Creator, telling him: "What do you think you will gain now if you relinquish the rest?" When he tells it, "I want to gain the next world by observing the King's commandment," the body replies, "Fine, you can get up in the morning like all other people. Why are you rushing to rise sooner than others? You have the whole day to observe Torah and *Mitzvot*!"

At that time the person says to his body: "Know that there is the world in general, called 'ordinary people,' and there are people who do not go with the flow, but want to be exceptional. That is, they want to be rewarded with the goal for which they were created, which is called '*Dvekut* with the Creator,' '*Torah Lishma* [for Her sake].' Our sages said that we can be awarded this by learning Torah after midnight, as explained in *The Zohar*, and this is also accepted among those who want to obtain anything in their lives."

At that time the body comes with strong arguments and says to him: "You'd be right if this were as you say, that you have a lofty goal in your life, and you want me to assist you in your role. But, you see how much work and efforts you have put into this work in order to come to work *Lishma*, and you see that you have not moved an inch, meaning to have more desire to work in bestowal. If you calculate honestly, you will see the opposite—that you regressed by ten degrees! That is, now you have a greater will to receive than before you began the work on bestowal. Therefore, you see that you are not exceptional. You are like everyone else! Therefore, it is better if you enjoy the rest of staying in bed, and don't tell me nonsense, that you are better than everyone else."

With these arguments, which are true arguments, meaning that reasonably speaking, he calculates and sees that it is one hundred percent correct and there is nothing to reply to it. At that time, he does not always manage to overcome with faith above reason and tell the body: "Although you are correct with your arguments and common sense dictates following your way, I will go above reason."

This is a lot of work because at that time a person suffers bodily torments as the body pricks him with slandering the work above reason. For this reason, when some awakening comes to him and he begins to feel some flavor in Torah and *Mitzvot*, when he feels a little bit of an ascent, he says, "Thank God I don't have to go by the path of faith above reason, but that reason, too, says it is worthwhile to observe Torah and *Mitzvot*." And as soon as he blemishes faith, saying, "Now I am relieved from the burden of faith," this is the reason that he soon suffers a descent from his state because he has blemished the faith.

2) The second way is to say, "Now I see that the real way is to go above reason and not take feeling delight and pleasure as a basis on which to take upon myself henceforth to engage in Torah and *Mitzvot*. Rather, I want to work without any basis of delight and pleasure, since the idea is to work in order to bring contentment to the Creator. Therefore, how can I rely on the basis of delight and pleasure to build my Judaism? Thus, what should I do when I feel good taste in the work?"

At that time he should say what Baal HaSulam said, that *he can receive his good feeling not as a basis, but as a testimony*. That is, he should say, "Now I see that the path of above reason is the real way by which the Creator wants to be served. And the evidence of this is that I see that He has brought me closer by removing His concealment from me and I have been granted feeling His kindness and mercy—that He wants to bestow delight and pleasure upon the creatures, for this is the purpose of creation."

However, in order not to come to separation by receiving from Him delight and pleasure, since reception of pleasure is in disparity of form from Him, this is why He has made the *Tzimtzum* [restriction] and concealment. But when we go by faith above reason, the body has no contact, but to the contrary, the body resists the work above reason. But now that I have gone above reason, He has removed from me some of His concealment. Thus, henceforth I will grow stronger and walk only in the path of faith above reason.

By this he will not fall into the trap of self-reception, called "separation from *Kedusha*." On the contrary, now he will begin to work more forcefully with mind and heart, and the Creator will not throw him once again into the bottomless pit called "receiving in order to receive." Rather, he will remain in a state of ascent. Moreover, he will ascend to a degree of greater revelation because he is not blemishing the faith, which is the keeping that one will not fall into the vessels of reception.

It therefore follows that in a state of ascent he has two ways. But how can a person win and walk in the path of the people of Israel and not in the path of the Greeks, which let him see that within reason they will be greater servants because reason agrees with this path more than with the path of faith?

Baal HaSulam explained the quarrel between the herdsmen of Abram's cattle and the herdsmen of Lot's cattle (Genesis 13:7). He said that "cattle" means possessions. Abram's possession was only faith. This is the meaning of the word *Av-Ram* [Abram (High Father)], meaning that the father in heaven is high, above reason. "Herdsmen" means that he was sustaining only the possession of his faith. That is, he always sought sustenance—how he could sustain the faith so it has power and might, and not fail in the reason.

This is not so with the herdsmen of Lot's cattle. *The Zohar* says that Lot comes from the [Aramaic] word *eltlatia*, meaning "curse." That is, the herdsmen of Lot's cattle were sustaining the possession of knowing and receiving. From this there cannot come a blessing, only a curse, for it is the opposite of bestowal, while blessing is only where one engages in bestowal.

In other words, the *Kelim* with which we can receive the upper abundance are specifically *Kelim* that give. With these *Kelim* we can receive. But with *Kelim* that want to receive, the upper abundance cannot enter due to oppositeness of form. Now we can understand the two ways that a person has when he has received some ascent in spirituality.

Yet, with what can we decide toward the good, called "faith," meaning to be in the state of "the herdsmen of Abram's cattle"? Baal HaSulam said in the name of The Baal Shem Tov that when one can do two opposite things and he cannot decide between them, the advice is to choose that which demands of him more effort. This is what he should choose for himself, since where there is labor, where the body disagrees, this is certainly *Kedusha*. He should hurry and do this, and take upon himself to do. It follows that here, too, he has two ways: 1) the way of faith, 2) the way of knowledge.

He should choose for himself the way of faith since the body does not agree to this, as it is toward *Kedusha*, meaning toward the desire to bestow, while the body wants the exact opposite. Therefore, it turns out that what is the determining factor? It is that the body rejects and regards the matter is redundant and superfluous. That is, he has no need for this and does not know why it is required in the first place. For this reason, it always wants to get rid of this matter of faith.

It therefore follows that the miracle that happens to a person, that he can decide for the side of *Kedusha*, is not a matter of intellect. Rather, it is something that the body deems redundant, which is the labor. The body loathes it and regards the whole matter of labor as redundant. But precisely from this redundancy, meaning what a person leaves and does not want or crave, from here comes to him the miracle remaining in *Kedusha*.

This is the meaning of "From the one remnant of the jars, a miracle was made for the roses." A jar is as it is written, that Rabbi Meir purified the vermin with one hundred and fifty flavors. It means that in every thing there are views both ways. With what can we scrutinize? It is with what remains, meaning with what the body deems redundant, what it regards as nothing. This is faith above reason, and only by this can we be saved from falling into the trap of the *Klipot*.

This is the meaning of the jar of oil that they found, which was sealed by the seal of the High Priest. A *Kohen* [priest] is called *Hesed* [mercy/grace]. "High" means *Hesed* that became *Hochma*, meaning abundance of *Hassadim*, called "Priest." The priest is the quality of *Hesed*, and *Hesed* indicates faith above reason. This is the meaning of Abraham, the quality of *Hesed*, being the father of faith.

The Greeks cannot see faith because they see only through reason, and not above reason. Therefore, when they walked above reason, the Greeks could not govern them. This is the meaning of the Greeks not seeing the oil jar.

And concerning the miracle that it burned eight days, it is an indication that it illuminated the *Hassadim* in *Bina*. From *Bina* to *Malchut* there are eight *Sefirot*, but *Hochma* of *Hochma* did not illuminate. This is why they established it as eight days, since it illuminated only in eight, as it is written, "Sons of *Bina* [understanding], eight days, established song and chanting."

The Difference between Mercy and Truth and Untrue Mercy

Article No. 8, Tav-Shin-Mem-Zayin, 1986-87

It is written, "[Jacob] called his son , Joseph, ...and deal with me *Hesed* [mercy] and truth."

The interpreters ask, "Why did he call specifically Joseph and said to him, 'Deal with me mercy and truth.'" RASHI interpreted about "mercy and truth": Mercy that one does with the dead is true mercy, for he does not expect a reward in return." RASHI interprets the verse: "I give you one portion more than your brothers," "since you trouble yourself with my burial."

RASHI's words contradict what is written here. He explains "giving you one portion more than your brothers" that it is because he troubles himself with my burial. Thus, this is not true mercy, since he is paying him for his effort by giving him one portion more than his brothers. Concerning "true mercy," RASHI interprets that he does not give him anything for his effort to bring him to the

Land of Israel, as he says, "For the mercy that one does with the dead is that he does not expect a reward in return."

Our sages said about the verse, "And he commanded Joseph saying, 'Your father commanded before his death,'" that they changed the matter because of peace, since Jacob did not command this, for Joseph was not suspicious in his eyes. Although our sages' interpretation answers the question that we did not find that Jacob commanded the above before his death, this can still be implied. That is, by intimation, he did command him prior to his demise, but not explicitly, actually telling him; this did not happen.

To understand the above, we must first repeat what we already said many times, namely what is the purpose of creation. We learned that it is to do good to His creations. However, in order not to have the bread of shame, it was set up so that by this the shame upon reception of the delight and pleasure would be cancelled. This matter is called "to aim in order to bestow" upon receiving the pleasure.

At that time, because the receiver does not intend for his own benefit, but rather, all that he receives is because he wishes to please the Creator, as this was His will, for He wants to do good, by this the shame was removed. For this reason, the lights departed from the *Kelim* [vessels] when the intention to bestow departs from them. In the upper *Partzufim*, this is called *Hizdakchut* of the *Masach*, and by this they have no *Ohr Hozer* [Reflected Light].

Ohr Hozer means that the lower one wants to return the joy to the upper one. This means that as the upper light comes to the lower one in order to do good to His creations, the lower one now returns the pleasure to the upper one. That is, the lower one wants to delight the upper one by receiving the abundance from the upper one.

Likewise, for this reason the *Klipot* [shells/peels] were born, whose quality is the will to receive only for themselves. The good and the bad that we feel in our world also extends from this reason. All the corruptions and corrections revolve only around this point called "desire to receive pleasure."

If the vessel of reception remains as it emerged—receiving in order to receive—it would cause shame due to disparity of form. For this reason, there was the correction called "in order to bestow." This matter, meaning turning the will to receive into working in order to bestow, is all the work that the lower ones have. In the upper worlds, this matter is called "departure of lights" or "expansion of lights."

That is, the aim to bestow is what moves all the worlds. In other words, if the lower one has the power of bestowal, he receives the upper abundance. Moreover, the measure of the abundance that the lower one receives depends on the measure of bestowal that the lower one has.

We learned that the thicker one is, and the more he can overcome and give *Ohr Hozer*, the higher the degree he receives. In other words, everything depends on the measure of bestowal that the lower one can give.

We already said that this will to receive is the only thing that is regarded as a new creation and is called a *Kli* [vessel], in which the upper abundance is poured. From this extends that the lower creatures should discern four discernments in their will to receive: 1) the general public, which follows the ambition to receive delight and pleasure because they want to please themselves, 2) those who do bestow delight and pleasure upon others.

However, in this, too, there are two discernments to make: 1) If they bestow delight and pleasure upon others but receive money for this, it is not regarded as bestowing upon others. Rather, it is called a "barter," where each one trades what he has and the other one gives him what he has in return.

For example, a person who has a restaurant or a hotel and gives people a place to sleep or eat and drink. No one will say that this person engages in bestowal, since he receives money for his work. Moreover, he assesses the price—how much money he should take in return for what he gives.

Or, for example, waiters, who are serving guests. Although they are not receiving anything from the guests, still, no one will say that the waiters engage in bestowal because the hotel manager pays them for serving the guests.

2) When engaging in bestowal, as said above, meaning giving people food and drink and a place to sleep, but without any monetary reward. Only he knows that by trying to do good to others he is buying for himself a good name and the whole town will know that he is a person who should be respected because he is giving his energy and money for the needs of the collective. That person has acquired a reputation as a good person, a merciful, hospitable person, etc. And although he does this for respect, no one will say that the things he does are all for himself, meaning because he wants respect.

It is customary that if a person behaves in this way, meaning works for the sake of the collective, it is regarded that he is working for the sake of the collective not in order to receive reward. Indeed, everyone respects him for his righteousness and integrity.

This discernment in the work of the Creator is called "bestowing in order to receive." This means that the first discernment is called "receiving in order to receive." But this discernment, when he does not want money for his work, is called "bestowing, but in order to receive." This is called *Lo Lishma* [not for Her sake]. That is, the act is bestowal, meaning that he gives of his strength and wealth for sacred purposes, but he wants a reward. This is why it is called "bestowing in order to receive," and this is called the "second discernment."

The third discernment is that he does not want any reward for the exertion he makes in strength and money. That is, he works in concealment between man and man, and between man and God, and he says to the Creator, "I am grateful to You for giving me the desire and craving to do something to please You. This is my entire reward in life—that I have been privileged with serving You. In return, I ask that You will give me the reward of more desire and craving to have no foreign thoughts to do something for myself. Rather, my only wish is to work for the sake of the Creator. I think that there is nothing more important in the world that a person can expect to be rewarded with in life, which will make him happy in the world. The whole world works for wealth; everybody wants to achieve it. But they do not know what happiness is.

"However, in this, everyone is equal—they want to be happy. And I do know what happiness is. If one can be rewarded with serving the King and not think of one's own benefit, but of the benefit of the King, that person is the happiest in the world. How do I know this? Since this is what I feel. Well, what reward do I want? Only this." This is why he says, "Lord, grant me works for the sake of the Creator." It is as our sages said (*Avot*, Chapter 4): The reward for a *Mitzva* [commandment]: *Mitzva*. For this reason, this is the reward that I expect. This discernment is called "bestowing in order to bestow," and this is regarded as *Lishma* [for Her sake].

The fourth discernment is that he can already say, "I want to receive delight and pleasure not necessarily from bestowing. Rather, I want to receive delight and pleasure from actually receiving, since he has already achieved the degree of "bestowing in order to bestow" and is not concerned with his own benefit. For this reason, he begins to think, "What can I say that will please the Creator? After all, He does not need to be given anything because the whole world is His, as it is written, 'and if he is right, what will he give You?'"

This thought makes him begin to think about the purpose of creation. He sees that it is written that the purpose of creation is to do good to His creations. That is, the Creator wants to impart upon the creatures delight and pleasure. For this reason, he says to the Creator, "Give me delight and pleasure. I do not want this because I want to delight myself. Rather, I want to delight myself because You enjoy our delight. It is only with this intention that I ask You to give me delight and pleasure. That is, I have no desire whatsoever to benefit myself. Rather, everything I think and do is only to please You."

When a person wants to exit the state of "the general public," which receives in order to receive, the order is that he enters the second state, called "bestowing in order to receive," which is called

Lo Lishma. This is so because the act is of bestowal, but he hopes to be rewarded by performing acts of bestowal.

In this, too, there are two discernments: 1) He wants people to reward him, so it seems as though he is doing good deeds, to the extent that people compel him by giving him respect and so forth. It follows that it seems as though he is observing Torah and *Mitzvot* [commandments] because people are commanding him to observe, and it is not the Creator who obligates. 2) He is working in concealment and does not want any reward from people. He does not show them the work that he does, and naturally, they are giving him nothing in return. Instead, he wants the Creator to pay him for observing Torah and *Mitzvot*.

Here there is a big difference between the state of *Lo Lishma*. In that state, the Creator is the one who commands to observe Torah and *Mitzvot*, and it is not people who compel him to observe Torah and *Mitzvot*. This is why that person is called a "servant of the Creator," since all his work is only to observe the commandments of the Creator, which He has commanded us. However, he wants reward for his work, that the Creator will pay his reward and not people.

However, our sages said (*Pesachim* 50b), "One should always engage in Torah and *Mitzvot*, even if *Lo Lishma*, since from *Lo Lishma* we come to *Lishma* [for Her sake]." In the work *Lo Lishma*, by which a person wants to come to the degree of *Lishma*, in that state, this is where one needs extra caution and much understanding, and special guidance how to exit the state of *Lo Lishma* and arrive at *Lishma*.

This place is very complicated because one cannot scrutinize the truth, meaning which is true and which is false, as it is human nature not to see any faults in oneself because a person is close to himself. For this reason, he is biased, and "Bribery blinds the eyes of the wise."

Moreover, even if he sees the truth—that he is marching on the wrong path and must change his way, meaning to come out of self-love—the *Klipa* [shell/peel] of Egypt controls the body. A person can come out of that control only with help from above, as our sages said, "Man's inclination overcomes him every day, and were it not for the Creator's help, he would not be able to overcome it." Therefore, the work begins primarily in the second state, called *Lo Lishma*.

It therefore follows that the work with the body, when it resists and does not let one work, is primarily when one is working in concealment and does not expect any reward from people, but works only for the Creator. Because He has commanded us to observe Torah and *Mitzvot*, he wants to do His will, and this is his reason for observing Torah and *Mitzvot*.

The only thing he lacks is that he expects a reward for this. That is, he sees that he cannot work not in order to receive reward, but only if he promises to his body that it will receive some reward for its labor. To the extent that the body believes this—that it will receive reward—to that extent he can observe Torah and *Mitzvot*. But when he doubts the reward, he has no fuel for work.

In such a state, when a person yearns to be a servant of the Creator in order not to receive reward, the body protests with all its might and does not give him rest when he says to it: "I want to observe Torah and *Mitzvot* without any reward. I want to observe the *Mitzva* [commandment] of faith," meaning believe in the greatness of the Creator although the body does not feel the greatness and importance of the Creator—that it is worthwhile to obey Him and observe His commandments in every detail.

"By this I am serving Him and I imagine that if the greatest in the generation were here to serve, and he would not let just anyone serve him but has chosen a handful of people, and I am among them, how happy would I be then? So why here, with serving the Creator, I cannot work without any reward and I expect to be given something in return for the service?"

This is so because there I see a person whom everyone respects and tell me how great he is. I can grasp the greatness that they say about him. In that case, I serve him because of his importance. But with the Creator, we need to *believe* in his greatness and importance, and especially, believe that He is good and does good, since the body does not want to believe but to see with its own eyes that this is so.

For this reason, sometimes one overcomes and has partial faith, meaning to give Him small portions. However, he does not have the strength to believe in whole faith, as it is written in the "Introduction to The Study of the Ten Sefirot" (Item 14).

Now we can understand why a person cannot advance in the work of bestowal. That is, where he does not see a reward for his work, he has no fuel and the body slacks in its work.

We should say that this is only for lack of faith. When a person knows this, meaning when he knows the reason that causes him to weaken it so he does not have the strength to work, there is hope that he will be able to correct himself in a way that he will be healthy and strong and will be able to go to work.

But when he does not know the real reason for his weakness, he could listen to several people advising him on how to become better. However, nothing will help him because each one tells him what they understand according to their views with respect to healing him. Temporarily, he receives a medicine from them and begins to think that they understand something, or he would not heed their advice.

Moreover, it is easier to believe that they know what they are saying because they themselves think that they are great experts, and the medicines they prescribe do not risk his life, of self-love.

For this reason, anyone who feels some weakness in the work goes to them. They give them medicines, which are pacifiers. That is, when one feels some pain in the work of the Creator, when he sees that he is far from the truth and does not want to deceive himself, for this reason he goes to seek some cure to heal his weakness in the work.

When he takes the medicines they give, it is real remedy for the time being. That is, the pains he had have gone away thanks to their cure, and now he is not in pain for not walking on the path of truth.

That is, through the medicine that he received from them he no longer has a demand for the truth. It follows that the medicines that he received from them are pacifiers, meaning not to feel the pain.

This is similar to a person with a headache who takes painkillers. The pills do not cure him; they only calm his pain. It is likewise with our matter: All the counsels he receives from the advisors that belong to the general public cannot be counsels to perform acts of bestowal. They are merely painkillers but do not heal the illness, which is the main reason for his weakness.

But when he has learned the cause of the illness, meaning that the reason is only that he lacks faith, to believe in the greatness and importance of the Creator. *The Zohar* calls this "*Shechina* [Divinity] in the dust," and our work is to raise the *Shechina* from the dust. This gives us a different order in the work of the Creator.

This means that one should know that there are actions and intentions, and we were given the observance of Torah and *Mitzvot* in word and in action. However, all of them, both Torah and *Mitzvot*, have an intention, too, meaning to aim what I want in return for observing Torah and *Mitzvot*, meaning what I must intend while observing Torah and *Mitzvot*.

Primarily, he should know for whose sake he must observe them. That is, it cannot be said of people in the general public that they should have intentions because they will come from *Lo Lishma* to *Lishma*, and the actions alone will do. For this reason, they cannot be obligated to keep intentions.

Rather, as they observe Torah and *Mitzvot* in action, which applies to *Mitzvot* dependent on words or actions, the intention is not important then, for even if they have no intention, but rather they aim that now they are observing what the Creator has commanded them to do, this is enough for them for *Lo Lishma*.

But when a person wants to achieve *Lishma*, meaning he wants to observe Torah and *Mitzvot* not in order to be rewarded, but rather wants to bring contentment to the Creator, to achieve this there is the matter of intention. That is, this *Mitzva* I am observing, with what intention am I doing this?

It is known that it is impossible to work without reward. Thus, how can it be said to a person that it is worthwhile to work not in order to receive reward? After all, he needs a reward. There is only one thing that can be said to him: He will be rewarded with serving the King, and there is no greater pleasure than serving the King. Then, according to the importance of the King, so he will enjoy. That is, the measurement of the pleasure from serving the King depends on the importance of the King, on the extent to which he appreciates Him.

But since the *Shechina* is in exile and in the dust, it is said in *The Zohar* that one should aim to raise the *Shechina* from the dust. Dust means lowliness, which a person tramples with his feet. This means that in every thing a person does in observing Torah and *Mitzvot*, he should intend that by this he will be rewarded with "raising the *Shechina* from the dust." It means that he wants reward for his labor in Torah and *Mitzvot*, to feel that he is serving a great King.

That is, during the labor he feels that for spirituality, when he wants to work in order to bestow, at that time he tastes the taste of dust during his work. This is so because there is a great concealment on spirituality—that we neither see nor feel the importance of the matter. From this all the obstacles come to him.

But if the Creator were to remove the concealment from him and he would feel the importance of the King, this would be his entire reward that he wishes for himself in life. This is so because he wants to serve the King, as it is written that we say in the prayer, "And ... came to Zion," "Blessed is He our God, who has created us for His glory."

A person wants to be able to thank the Creator for creating him for His glory, meaning to serve the Creator. This means that a person will agree with all of his organs, and that his "mouth and heart will be the same," in that he gives thanks to the Creator for creating man in His glory and for not creating man for his own benefit, but that His will and yearning will be only to bestow contentment upon the Creator.

A person should have this intention in everything he does: Thanks to this deed he is doing, the Creator will give him the intention that all his actions will be only in order to bestow, that He will cancel his desire for self-love, since he sees that he cannot exit its control and is in exile among the "nations of the world" in his body.

It is known that *The Zohar* says that every person is a small world. It was also said that there are seventy nations in the world, as well as the people of Israel. Also, within each person there are the seventy nations, as well as Israel, and the Israel in him is in exile under the rule of the seventy nations within him.

This is as our sages said, "He who comes to purify is aided" (*Shabbat* 104b). We should interpret the word "comes." We can say that "comes" is the act he is doing. He wants to do it *Lishma* but he cannot because he is in exile under the rule of the nations of the world. "Aided from above" means that the Creator redeems him from the exile among the nations who governed him.

It turns out that when a person performs an act, and wants the act to be *Lishma*, and not because of self-love, meaning to receive some reward for the act, namely a reward in this world or the next world. Primarily, he wants something for his action. However, he wants the Creator to give him complete satisfaction from the act he does and to feel that he is the happiest person in the world now, in that he is serving the King.

But if he receives anything else besides the service that he does, it blemishes the service for the King. The evidence of this is that he wants something more. But what he can demand is why he has no inspiration and true sensation when he is speaking to the King.

For example, he is asking the King that when he blesses for pleasures and says, "Blessed are You O Lord, who brings bread out of the earth," why does he not have the manners to be standing with fear and trepidation as one stands before the King? Rather, he speaks to the Creator and has no emotion, no feeling with Whom he speaks.

This pains him. But since he is incapable of correcting himself, he asks the Creator to help him and give him some revelation, so he will feel before Whom he stands: before the King of Kings. So why does he not feel it?

It was said about it in *The Zohar*, "He who comes to purify is aided." It asks, "With what?" and it replies, "With a holy soul." That is, he is given abundance from above, called *Neshama* [soul], which helps him have the ability to come out of the governance of self-love and enter *Kedusha* [holiness], meaning that all of his thoughts will be only to bestow contentment upon the Creator.

Through the soul he obtains, the concealment and restriction are removed and he feels the greatness of the Creator. At that time, the body surrenders to the light of the Creator "as a candle before a torch," and he feels that he has come out from enslavement to freedom. That is, while he wanted to work only for the Creator, the questions of the nations of the world in his body promptly came and asked, "How can you give up the existence of the body and have no thought at all in its favor, and instead devote all the efforts and the senses only to be able to find ways to bring contentment to the Creator?"

Their questions are even worse because a person does not think that these thoughts belong to the people of Israel, but that they are thoughts of the seventy nations. However, a person thinks that they are his thoughts, that he is asking himself these questions, and how can a person fight against himself?

Baal HaSulam said that one should know that these thoughts and desires are foreign to the Jewish spirit. They do not pertain to Israel itself, but rather come from thoughts of the general nations of the world, which enter the personal nations of the world that exist in every person. When one believes that this is so—that they are not his—then one can fight with another body. But when he thinks that these foreign thoughts are his own, a person cannot fight against himself.

Thus, there is no other way but to ask the Creator to help us come out of this bitter exile only with His help, as was said in *The*

Zohar, that the help that comes from above is that he is given a soul. Through the soul, which shows the revelation of His greatness, only then does the body surrender.

By this we can interpret what is written about the exodus from Egypt (in the Passover Haggadah [story]): "And in all the gods of Egypt I will do judgments. I am the Lord; I am He, and not the messenger. I am the Lord; it is I and not another."

This comes to say that only the Creator can help one out of one's enslavement in the exile in Pharaoh King of Egypt, who is keeping him from exiting self-love and doing only works that benefit his self-love, and he has no way by which to do something for the sake of the Creator. At that time comes the Creator's help.

However, Baal HaSulam said, "When can one say that he cannot do anything for the Creator? It is precisely when he has done everything he could. That is, he has already tried every advice in the world that he thought could help him, yet these counsels did not help him. This is when he can say wholeheartedly, "If the Creator does not help me, I am lost. As far as the work of the lower ones, in terms of what they can do, I have done everything and it did not help."

It is like a person who had a sick man at home. What does he do? He goes to the doctor and says that the doctor will be a good messenger of the Creator and the sick will be well. But if the sick has not yet healed, normally, he goes to a professor. He says that he will certainly be a good messenger of the Creator and will heal the sick. If the professor also cannot help, they make a conference of professors, perhaps together, but consulting, they will be able to find a remedy for the sick.

But if that, too, does not help, then normally we say to the Creator: "Dear Lord, if You do not help me, no one can help me. We have been to all the great doctors, who are Your messengers, and none could help me. I have no one else to ask but You, that You will help me." Then, when he is healed, he says that only the Creator Himself helped him and not a messenger.

This is what is written in the Passover Haggadah [story], that the exodus from Egypt was done by the Creator Himself and not by a messenger. It is as they said, "And in all the gods of Egypt I will do judgments. I am the Lord; I am He, and not the messenger. I am the Lord, and not another."

In other words, when a person has done all the counsels and tactics, which are as messengers such as the above mentioned doctors, but they did not help, then a person can pray from the bottom of the heart because he has nowhere to turn to for help, as he has already done all the counsels he could think of.

This is the beginning of the matter of "the children of Israel sighed from the work, and they cried out, and their cry went up to God from the work." We explained what it means that their cries were from the work. "From the work" means after they had done all that they could in the work that pertained to them, and saw that no help was coming from here after all the work, for this reason, their cry was from the bottom of the heart. That is, they saw that no messenger could help them but the Creator Himself, as it is written, "I am He, and not a messenger." This is when they were redeemed and came out of Egypt.

By this we will understand what the holy ARI said, that prior to the exodus from Israel, the people of Israel were in forty-nine gates of *Tuma'a* [impurity], and then the King of Kings appeared to them and redeemed them. The question is, why did He wait until that time when they were in utter lowliness?

According to the above we should understand that when they saw their true, lowly state, that they have regressed and could not advance to the side of *Kedusha*, they understood that no messenger could help them, as with the allegory about the doctors. Then they cried out only to the Creator to help them. This is why it is written, "I am He, and not the messenger."

The meaning of He Himself redeeming them and delivering them from exile means that they attained that there are no messengers in the world, but the Creator does everything. This is as it is written in

The Zohar, "He who comes to purify is aided. It says, 'With what is he aided? With a holy soul.'" That is, he receives the revelation of His Godliness, called *Neshama*. By this he attains his root, and then a person annuls as a candle before a torch, after he has obtained the *Neshama*, for then he feels that it is a part of God above.

Now we can understand what we asked, "Why did He call specifically to Joseph and not to the rest of his brothers to tell them as he said to Joseph: "Deal with me mercy and truth." RASHI interprets that the mercy we do with the dead is true mercy, for he expects no reward.

Here there is a contradiction to the words of RASHI in that he interprets the verse, "And I give you one portion more than your brothers." He said, "Because you toil with my burial." This is perplexing with regard to what he says, that Jacob said to Joseph to deal with him true mercy, since he expects no reward. After all, he is paying him for the trouble by giving him one portion more than to his brothers.

Here is an intimation of the order of the work from beginning to end. Jacob commanded his son Joseph: 1) Deal true mercy. This is so because the beginning of the work is that we must achieve *Lishma*, which is called "bestowing in order to bestow," and we demand no reward for the work. This is the meaning of what RASHI interprets, that the mercy we do with the dead is that he expects no reward; they only do mercy, meaning acts of bestowing in order to bestow without expecting a reward.

By this he wants to imply that it is because "The wicked in their lives are called dead" (*Berachot* 18b). Also, in the "Introduction of the Book of Zohar" he says why "The wicked in their lives are called dead." It is because they are immersed in self-love, called "will to receive only for themselves." By this they are separated from the Life of Lives, hence they are called "dead." This is the discernment that we said is called "receiving in order to receive."

And since man was created with a desire to receive that comes from the impure *ABYA*, as is written in the "Introduction to the

Book of Zohar" (Item 11), therefore, one should try to deal true mercy with his body, which is called "dead." In other words, he should guide it into performing acts of bestowal in order to bestow, which is called "true mercy" that he does with his body, which is called "dead." It should come to the degree of performing acts of bestowal, and the dead will not expect any reward. When he achieves this degree, it is regarded as having attained the third degree, called "bestowing in order to bestow," which is *Lishma*. This is the meaning of "He called his son Joseph and commanded him to deal with him true mercy."

Afterwards comes the fourth degree, called "receiving in order to bestow." That is, after he has come to the degree of *Lishma* in vessels of bestowal, he guides it that it should receive, except only what it has the strength to receive with the aim to bestow. This is what RASHI interprets about the verse, "I give you one portion more than to your brothers," since you trouble yourself with my burial." This shows wholeness, for afterwards he can receive in order to bestow.

This is the meaning of what we asked, why he called his son Joseph. It could be said that he wanted to imply to him what is written, "And He commanded Joseph saying, 'Your father had commanded before his death.'" Our sages interpreted that we did not find that Jacob said this to him. They explained that the matter was changed because of peace.

We should say that by commanding Joseph to deal true mercy, the aim was that he would engage only in bestowal and not for his own sake. It therefore implies that he would have no hatred for the brothers, for one who marches on the path of bestowal and does not worry about self-love, it cannot be said that he hates those who hurt him.

Now we can understand the difference between true mercy, and untrue mercy. We explained that in the work, mercy that one does with the dead is called "true mercy" because he expects no reward. This means that a person performs acts of bestowal, meaning Torah and *Mitzvot*, and they are *Mitzvot* that are only from our sages [*De Rabanan*] or from the customs of Israel, which are generally called "620 *Mitzvot*," which are called *Keter*, as explained in the book *A Sage's Fruit*.

The body is called "dead" because it extends from the impure ABYA, hence it is called "wicked" and "dead," for it is separated from the Life of Lives. We are told that the mercy he does with the body should be true, meaning that the intention will truly be as the act, meaning that the aim, too, will be to bestow. If the aim is not to bestow, this mercy is not regarded as true.

If this mercy is not true, it does not correct his dead, which was called "wicked" because of his will to receive, by which the body received two appellations: "wicked" and "dead." In order to correct it, there should be a correction where it goes completely opposite from where it went thus far, as it was walking on the path of reception and not of bestowal.

It follows that if this mercy is not true mercy, but has a different intention from the act of mercy that he does, as a result, the body receives no fundamental correction. And although there is the matter of "from *Lo Lishma* we come to *Lishma*," it is only by passing through, meaning that it is impossible to achieve true mercy before we pass through the first stage, called "untrue mercy."

However, the most important is to come to the truth, that the mercy will be true mercy, and not only that on the outside we see that it is mercy, meaning what is revealed, but what is covered, namely the aim, we cannot see what a person has in his heart. Perhaps, within the heart, where there is the intention on the act, he has calculated that by the mercy that he does he will receive some reward, which is called "bestowing in order to receive."

We can interpret this as was said, "Go humbly with the Lord your God." "Go humbly" means that a person cannot see what the person thinks about the act, for the aim is concealed and the other does not know his friend's thoughts. Then the writing says, "Go humbly." That which is in your heart, try to make it be with the

Lord your God, meaning to bestow, such as what is revealed. This is called "his mouth and heart are the same."

For this reason, we should make two discernments: 1) untrue mercy, which is *Lo Lishma*, meaning bestowing in order to receive, 2) true mercy, which is *Lishma*, meaning bestowing in order to bestow.

Indeed, there is the main discernment, which is the purpose of creation—for the lower one to receive delight and pleasure, but with the aim to bestow. That discernment, too, is implied in what was said, "And deal with me mercy and truth," meaning that this mercy will bring him to the truth. "Truth" means as it is written in *The Study of the Ten Sefirot* (Part 13, Item 17): "The seventh correction of the thirteen corrections of *Dikna* is 'truth,' called by the name 'two holy apples,' which are the two *Panim* [faces]."

He interprets there (in *Ohr Pnimi*) that when attaining the seventh correction, called "truth," we see that His guidance with the creatures is indeed a guidance of good and doing good. That is, the guidance that was previously only in faith, now they have been rewarded with attainment and feeling that this is truly so. At that time they receive the good in the form of receiving in order to bestow. This is the purpose of creation—for the creatures to receive the delight and pleasure, for this realizes the purpose of creation.

Now we can interpret the verse "The Lord is near to all who call upon Him, to all who call upon Him in truth" in two ways, too.

1) "The Lord is near" means that He hears the prayer of all "who call upon Him in truth." That is, they feel when they are exerting in acts of bestowal, yet see that they are far from the intention to bestow. This means that they see the truth—that there is a great distance between the act and the intention, that they cannot exit the intention of self-love. They pray to the Creator to deliver them from this enslavement, and this is all they want and crave. This is the only salvation they expect.

They believe that as long as one is in self-love, he is separated from the Life of Lives. The verse says about this: "The Lord is near to all who call upon Him." The Lord will give them the truth, meaning that they will be able to deal true mercy and will not settle for dealing untrue mercy, meaning *Lo Lishma*. And since it is a prayer for the truth, the Creator helps them and they receive from him the quality of truth.

2) They want to be rewarded with the quality of truth, which is the seventh correction of the thirteen corrections of *Dikna*. Through this correction, He is revealed to the created beings and indeed everyone sees that the Creator leads His world with a guidance of good and doing good. This is called "revealed *Hassadim* [mercies]," when the Creator's mercies are revealed to all—that they are true.

One's Greatness Depends on the Measure of One's Faith in the Future

Article No. 9, Tav-Shin-Mem-Zayin, 1986-87

It is written in *The Zohar* (*BeShalach*, Item 216): "'Then shall Moses ... sing.' It should have said, 'Sang.' And it replies, 'But this thing depends on the future, when he complemented for that time and complemented for the future, when Israel are destined to praise this singing in the future.' 'This singing' is in female form [in Hebrew], but it should have said, 'This song,' in male form [in Hebrew]. And it replies, 'This singing is that the queen praises the King.' Rabbi Yehuda said, 'Thus, if it is the singing of the queen to the King, why does it say, 'Moses and the children of Israel'? After all, the queen should have been the one who is praising.' It replies, 'Happy are Moses and Israel, for they know how to properly praise the King for the queen.'"

We should understand the answer that he gives about what is written in future tense, that it refers to the future. What does it come to teach us in the work? We should also understand about the answer he is giving, why it writes "singing" in female form, which interprets the intention to *Malchut*, meaning that *Malchut* is praising the King, about which Rabbi Yehuda asked. Thus, if he is referring to *Malchut*, why does it say, "Moses and the children of Israel"? For this reason, he must interpret that his intention is Moses and Israel, who know how to praise the King for the *Malchut*. We should also understand the meaning of Moses and Israel having to praise the King for the *Malchut*, and why they do not have to praise the King for themselves, but for *Malchut*.

It is known that Moses is called "the faithful shepherd." Baal HaSulam interpreted that Moses was providing Israel with faith, and faith is called *Malchut* [kingship]. In other words, he instilled fear of heaven, called "kingdom of heaven," into the people of Israel. This is why Moses is called "the faithful shepherd," after the faith. It is written about it, "And they believed in the Lord and in his servant, Moses," meaning for Moses instilling in them faith in the Creator.

It is known that one cannot live from negativity, but from positivity. This is so because "nourishment" refers to what a person receives and *enjoys receiving*. This comes to us from the purpose of creation, called "His desire to do good to His creations." Therefore, a person must receive delight and pleasure so as to have something with which to delight one's body. This is called "positivity," meaning a filling. And with this filling, he satisfies his needs.

But a person also needs a lack. Otherwise, there is no place in which the light of life can enter. A lack is called "a *Kli*" [a vessel]. This means that if one has no *Kelim* [vessels], he cannot receive anything. A lack is called "a desire," meaning that he has a desire for something and he feels that he is lacking this thing and wishes to satisfy the need. To the extent that he feels its absence and to the extent that he needs to satisfy his need, this is the measure of his lack. In other words, a great lack or a small lack depends on the measure of one's sense of necessity to satisfy that need.

This means that if a person comes to feel that he is lacking something, and he feels that feeling in his every organ, yet he does not have a strong desire to satisfy his need, there are many reasons why he does not have such a great desire to satisfy his need.

1. He told his friends what he needs, and he feels the necessity for it. However, the friends made him see that what he needs is unattainable. So his friends influenced him with their views that he must accept his situation. They weakened his strength to overcome so he can prevail over the obstacles on his way to obtaining what he wants. In consequence, the need and craving weakened, too, since he sees that he will never obtain what he wants. For this reason, meaning because he sees that it is utterly impossible that he will ever be able to satisfy his need, this is the reason why he does not obtain his goal—it causes him to lessen his lack. It turns out that his great desire has waned due to despair.

2. Sometimes he does not even tell his friends what he wants; he only hears from friends speaking with each other. He hears that they have already given up, and that affects him, too. In other words, their despair affects him and he loses the enthusiasm that he had for achieving *Dvekut* [adhesion] as soon as possible. Thus, he loses that willpower.

3. Sometimes one thinks for himself without any slander from the outside, but sees that each time he wishes to draw near to *Kedusha* [holiness], when he begins to analyze, he realizes the opposite, that he is regressing instead of moving forward. And this causes him to lose his strength for the work.

It turns out that then he collapses under his load. He has nothing from which to receive sustenance because he sees only negativity and darkness. Thus, he loses the spirit of life that he had when he seemingly had some livelihood, called "sustaining his soul." Now he feels spiritually dead, meaning he cannot make a single movement in the work, just as if he were actually dead.

This means that even though now he sees the truth, meaning the recognition of evil, it is negative, and from this, one cannot receive any livelihood, since *provision of the body is specifically from positivity*. Therefore, one must walk on the right line for two reasons: 1) to keep his desire from waning when he hears slander, 2) to receive vitality, which is specifically from positivity, meaning that it is positive, that there is a matter of wholeness here.

However, it is difficult to understand how, when he criticizes his work-order and sees that his being immersed in self-love is the truth, how can he be told to walk on the right line, which is called "wholeness"? After all, as far as he can see, when he judges honestly, it is a total lie.

It is known that general and particular are equal. This means that the individual follows the same order that applies to the collective. In regard to the collective, it was given to us to believe in the coming of the Messiah (in the prayer, "I Believe"), "I believe in the coming of the Messiah. And though he may be delayed, I await his arrival still."

Hence, one must never give up and say, "I see that I cannot obtain *Dvekut* [adhesion] with the Creator." This is considered that he exits the exile among the nations of the world, called "self-love," and comes under the authority of *Kedusha* [holiness], and comes to correct the root of his soul and cling to the Life of Lives.

It follows that if one believes in the general redemption, he should believe that redemption will come to him in particular. Hence, one should receive wholeness for himself with respect to the future, in a way that one should depict for himself the measure of goodness, pleasure, and joy that he will receive when all his needs are satisfied. This certainly gives him emotional satisfaction and energy to work to obtain this goal that he hopes to achieve.

It turns out that first one must depict for himself what he is hoping for—that it will make him happy and joyful if he obtains what he anticipates. However, first one should thoroughly know the goal he wants to obtain. If one does not pay close attention and much scrutiny to what he expects from his life, meaning that he should tell himself, "Now I have decided what I want, after analyzing the joy in life that can be obtained in the world."

One's Greatness Depends on the Measure of One's Faith in the Future

If he has the opportunity to obtain this, he will have the strength and wisdom to say, "Now I can thank the Creator for creating His world." Now he can wholeheartedly say, "Blessed is He who said, 'Let there be the world,' since I feel the delight and pleasure, that it is truly worthwhile for me and for all creations to receive this delight and pleasure that I have now received from the purpose of creation, called 'His desire to do good to His creations.'"

And although he is still far from obtaining the goal, if he nonetheless knows for certain from what he can receive his future happiness, it is as it is written (*Avot*, Chapter 6), "Rabbi Meir says, 'Anyone who engages in Torah *Lishma* [for Her sake] is rewarded with a great many things. Moreover, the whole world is worthwhile for him. He is let into the secrets of the Torah and he becomes like an everlasting spring.'"

When he pays attention to this—to what he can achieve—meaning when he feels the importance of the goal and depicts for himself the happiness he will achieve, the joy that he will experience when he attains it are unimaginable.

Thus, to the extent that he believes in the importance of the goal, and to the extent that he believes that "Though he may be delayed, I await his arrival still," he can receive the filling of the light of life from the future goal. It is known that there is inner light and there is surrounding light. Baal HaSulam interpreted "inner light" as referring to what one receives in the present, and "surrounding light" as the light that is destined to shine, but which one has not yet attained. However, the surrounding light shines, to an extent, in the present, to the extent of his confidence that he will attain it.

He said that this is like a person who bought merchandise from the market. Since many people brought this merchandise to the market, it had little value. All the merchants wanted to sell the merchandise at any price, but there were no buyers because everyone was afraid to buy, perhaps it might grow even cheaper.

Then one man bought all the merchandise for a very low price. When he came home and told them what happened in the market, they all laughed at him: "What did you do? Of course all the merchants wanted to sell all the merchandise they had in stock. This will only make everything cheaper, and as a result, you will lose all your money."

But he insisted, saying, "Now I am happier than ever, since I will profit from this merchandise not as before, when I knew I could get twenty percent profit from the merchandise. Instead, I'll make a five hundred percent profit. However, I will not sell it now. I will store it and I will take it to the market in three years, for by then this merchandise will not be found here in the country, and I will get the price that I want."

It turns out that if he calculates how much he has earned in the present, meaning this year, then he has nothing. This is considered that he has nothing in the present with which to be happy.

This is an allegory about the inner light, which shines in the present. However, the surrounding light, called "light that shines specifically in the future," shines in the present, too, to the extent of his belief that in the future he will receive the full reward he hopes for, and then his joy will be complete. Now he is receiving joy and high spirits from what he will receive in the future.

This explains the above allegory, that this merchant was ridiculed by everyone for buying the merchandise in the market precisely when it was irrelevant, when no one wanted to buy it. Yet, he bought it as something that others left because it was worthless, and now he is delighted because he is one hundred percent sure that in three years this merchandise will not be found anywhere and then he will get rich. And so, he enjoys in the present what will happen in the future.

It follows that to the extent that he believes that it will come to him—and does not despair about the future—as it is written, "Though he may be delayed, I await his arrival still," he can enjoy in the present what will come in the future.

Thus, when a person is told that even though he walked on the left line—meaning criticized and saw that he was in utter baseness—and he sees this truth, since he does not wish to deceive himself and justify his thoughts and actions, but seeks the truth and does not care if the truth is bitter, yet he wishes to reach the goal for which he was born, but because of all this truth he cannot go on living, since it is impossible to live without pleasure, called "vitality" and "life." To live, one needs light, which revives a person. By living, it is possible to work and to reach the goal. For this reason, he must then shift to the right line, called "wholeness."

However, this wholeness—from which he now receives the liveliness that sustains his body—should be built on a basis of truth. This brings up the question, "How can he receive wholeness when he sees the truth, that he is in the lowest state, immersed in self-love from head to toe and without a spark of bestowal?"

To that he should say, "Everything I see is true." However, it is so from the perspective of the inner light. This means that in the present, he is in lowliness and has nothing from which to receive joy and life. But from the perspective of the surrounding light, which is the future, he believes that "Though he may be delayed, I await his arrival still."

It turns out that through the surrounding light that shines in relation to the future, he can draw it so it will shine in the present. And to the extent of the faith and confidence that he has in the coming of the Messiah on the personal level, he can draw vitality and joy so it will shine in the present.

It follows that now that he is walking on the right line to receive wholeness, it is the real truth, since the surrounding light shines in the present. And besides, it is a path of truth, and since by believing in the coming of the Messiah on the personal level, it is a great remedy that through the commandment of faith, the future will draw nearer to the present in him. This means that the surrounding light will be internal. This is considered that the light actually dresses in the present. It is called "the surrounding will become internal."

Thus, from here—meaning from faith, from believing that in the end he will reach the goal, even though reason shows him each time that he is retreating from the goal and not advancing—he overcomes and goes above reason. And then faith itself accumulates each time in the form of "penny by penny joins into a great amount," until he is rewarded with permanent whole faith, which is the attainment of the light of *Hassadim* in illumination of *Hochma*, as it is written in the *Sulam* commentary.

Now we can understand what we asked about why *The Zohar* explains that this is why it is written, "Shall ... sing," in future tense. By that, it implies that Israel are destined to praise this singing in the future. What does that come to teach us in the work? In matters of work, we should know what we have now, in the present, and know what we must do. Thus, what can we learn about what the future holds?

As we explained, we must walk on the right line, which is wholeness, and receive vitality from it, because it is impossible to live from negativity. Hence, there is advice to feel wholeness from what will be in the future. This is the meaning of what the righteous call, "singing in the future." In other words, now—in the present—they are singing about what they will receive in the future. This means that to the extent that they picture the delight and pleasure they will receive in the future, they can feel it in the present, provided they have faith that there is a future, meaning that in the future everyone will be corrected.

This is something one can already be thankful for in the present. To the extent that he feels it, this is the measure of the praise that he can give in the present. And besides receiving life in the present from positivity, he gains from the goal in general being important for him because he must picture for himself the delight and pleasure in store for the creatures to receive.

And each time he contemplates the matter, he gradually sees a bit more of what he can receive in the future, meaning what has been prepared for us by the purpose of creation. And although he sees that in his current state he is miles away from the goal, this depends on the measure of his faith in the goal, as in the example of the allegory above. This follows the rule, "All that is certain to be collected is deemed collected" (*Yevamot* 38).

With the above, we can understand what *The Zohar* explains—that the reason why it writes "Shall ... sing," in future tense, is to imply that Israel are destined to praise this singing in the future. This is so because we must know this, so we can receive joy and vitality in the present from what will be in the future. By this we can sing in the present as if now we were receiving all the delight and pleasure.

This is regarded as being able to receive illumination from a surrounding. In other words, the surrounding shines in the internal from afar, meaning that although a person is still far from obtaining the delight and pleasure, he can still draw illumination from the Surrounding Light also in the present.

Now we will explain what we asked about *The Zohar* explaining why he writes, "This singing" in female form [in Hebrew]. It is because Moses and Israel know how to properly praise the King for the queen. And we asked, "Why do Moses and Israel not praise the King for themselves?"

First, we must understand why we have to praise the King. In corporeality, we understand that a flesh and blood king needs honors, to be respected. He enjoys the praises that the people give him. But with regard to the Creator, why does He need us to praise Him and sing before Him chants and songs?

It is a known rule that everything we say in regard to the Creator is only by way of "By Your actions we know You." However, there is no attainment in Him, Himself, whatsoever. Rather, all we speak of relates to the attainment of the lower ones.

This is the reason why one must praise and thank the Creator, for by this one can measure and assume the greatness and importance of the giving that the Creator has given him. To that extent, one can test how much importance and greatness of the King he feels.

The purpose of creation is to do good to His creations, meaning for the creatures to enjoy Him. And by the measure of the greatness of the Giver, there is meaning and pleasure in giving, that they give Him in order to delight. And when one tries to give thanks, he already has reason for considering and scrutinizing the giving: what he received and from whom he received, meaning the greatness of the giving and the greatness of the giver.

It follows that one's gratitude should not be because the upper one will enjoy it, but so that the lower one will enjoy it. Otherwise, it is similar to the allegory that Baal HaSulam said about the verse, "Who has not taken My name in vain."

He asked, "What does it mean that a person takes in vain? Does it mean that he was given a soul from above in vain?" He said that it is similar to a child being given a bag of gold coins. He is delighted about the coins because they look so nice and are lovely to look at. But the child is incapable of assessing the value of the gold coins.

From this we can understand that the gratitude and praise that we give to the Creator are only to benefit the creatures, meaning that we have something by which to praise the King. This means that when one tries to praise the Creator, this is the time when he is capable of feeling the importance of the gift and the importance of the giver of the gift. For this reason, what one should mind most is the praise that one gives to the King. This enables him to be given every time anew. Otherwise, if one cannot appreciate the King's gift, one cannot be given anything because he falls under the definition of "Who is a fool? He who loses what he is given" (*Hagigah* 4a).

And what is the reason that a fool loses what he is given? This is simple: He is a fool. He does not appreciate the importance of the matter, so he does not pay attention to keeping the gift that he has been given. For this reason, the extent of the importance of the gift is his keeping of it. Thus, he can be in a state of constant ascension because it is evident that he does not lose what he is given, for he appreciates it.

It follows from the above that one may have many descents because he does not appreciate the gift of the King. In other words, he cannot appreciate the measure of importance of the nearing—that he has been given from above a desire and a thought that it is worthwhile to be a servant of the Creator.

And since he did not appreciate the importance of the matter, meaning the calling that he was given—to enter and serve the King—he might even corrupt, if he serves the King without knowing how to keep himself from blemishing something. In that state, a person is thrown back to a place of garbage and waste.

In that state, he sustains himself on the same waste that cats and dogs search to sustain themselves, and he, too, searches for provision for his body in that place. He does not see that he can find provision elsewhere. Meaning, during the descent, those things that he said were waste and unfit as food for humans—but are suitable as food only for animals—he himself chases that provision and has no desire for human food because he finds it completely tasteless.

For this reason, the stability of the states of ascent depends primarily on the importance of the matter. This is why it depends mainly on the praise and gratitude he gives to being accepted from above. This is so because the praises themselves that he gives to the Creator enhance His importance and esteem. This is why we are commanded to think very seriously about praising.

There are three discernments in regard to praising:

1. The measure of the giving. This means that the importance of the gift is according to the measure of praise and gratitude that one gives for the gift.

2. The greatness of the giver, meaning if the giver is an important person. For example, if the king gives a present to someone, the gift may be a very small thing but it will still be very important. In other words, the measure of the praise and gratitude does not take the greatness of the gift into account, but rather measures the greatness of the giver. Meaning, the same person might give to two people, but to one, the giver is more important and he recognizes the importance and greatness of the giver. Thus, he will be more grateful than the other, who does not recognize the importance of the giver to the same extent.

3. The greatness of the giver, regardless of whether he gives or not. Sometimes, the king is so important in the eyes of a person, that the person has a strong desire to merely speak to the king, but not because he wishes to speak to the king so the king will give him something. He doesn't want anything, but his whole pleasure is in having the privilege of speaking to the king.

However, it is impolite to come to the king without some request, so he is searching for some request that the king may grant. In other words, he says that he wants to come to the king so the king will give him something, but in truth, he says that he wants the king to give him something only on the outside. In his heart, he does not want anything from the king. Just having the ability to speak to the king is enough for him and it does not matter to him if the king has given him something or not.

When people on the outside see that he did not receive a thing from the king, and look at him as he is walking out of the king's house delighted and elated, they laugh at him. They tell him, "What a fool you are! How mindless are you? You can see for yourself that you are leaving as empty-handed as you came in. You walked into the king to ask for something of the king, yet you walked out empty-handed, so why the joy?"

We can understand this if while a person prays to the Creator to give him something, we can discern about it, 1) that one prays to the Creator to give him what he demands of the Creator. If He accepts his demand for the prayer to be granted, when he receives what he wants, he is willing to thank the Creator. And the extent of salvation that he received from the Creator is the extent of his joy, high spirits, praise, and gratitude. In other words, *everything is measured by the degree of salvation he has received from the Creator.*

2) The measure of the greatness of the Giver. In other words, to the extent that he believes in the greatness of the Creator, this is what determines for him what he receives from the Creator. That is, even though in the eyes of the receiver it is a small thing, he still received something from the Creator. Thus, he can already be

happy and praise and thank the Creator, since it is the giver who is important to him, as in the above-mentioned allegory.

3) The greatness of the giver without giving. He, too, has great importance. In other words, the king is so important in his eyes that he does not want anything from the king, but will consider it great fortune if he can speak even a few words with the king. And the reason why he comes in with some request is only superficial, since one cannot come before the king without some request. Yet, he did not come for the king to grant his request. The reason he said he was asking for something was only for the external ones, who do not understand that speaking to the king is the most valuable giving, but the external ones do not understand it.

When we speak of a single body, we should say that "external ones" are the thoughts that come to a person from the outside world, meaning those who have no concept of the internality, and have no tools to understand that the internality of the king is what counts. Rather, they value the king only by what extends from the king to them, which is called "the externality of the king." But they have no clue of the internality of the king, meaning the king himself and not what extends from the king outward.

Hence, these thoughts mock a person when he says, "Since I just spoke to the king, it does not matter if the king is granting my wish." Rather, his only wish is the internality of the king, not what extends from him.

Therefore, if a person prays to the Creator and does not see that the Creator has given him something—since what matters to him is the internality of the king—he can be happy and rejoice in having been rewarded with speaking to the king. Yet, external thoughts within him wish to revoke that joy in him because they consider only the vessels of reception—what he has received from the king in his vessels of reception, while he tells them, "I am delighted and joyful, and I praise and thank the king simply for having given me the chance to speak with him. This is enough for me."

Moreover, he says to his external ones, "Know that I want nothing from the king except to praise him and thank him. By this I adhere to the king because I want to bestow upon him by praising him. I have nothing else to give him. It follows that now I am considered 'a servant of the Creator,' and not 'a servant of myself.' For this reason, I cannot hear your telling me, 'What have you gained?'"

"For example, all year long you engaged in Torah and in prayer, keeping all the Mitzvot [commandments], but you are still standing on the same degree as a year ago or two ago. Thus, why the joy that you praise the Creator and say, 'This is my gain, that I spoke to the Creator many times, and what else do I need?' In other words, if the king had given me something, I might have received it in order to receive. But now that I have nothing in my hand, I am happy and thank the Creator because my intention in the work was only to bestow."

However, since in that state a person is telling the truth, he faces strong resistance from the external ones, who cannot tolerate one who is walking on the path of truth, if his only aim is to bestow. In that state, he has a great war, and they wish to shatter his joy. They make him think that the opposite is true—that what they are telling him is the path of truth, and that he is deceiving himself thinking that he is right.

In this world, a lie usually succeeds. For this reason, he needs great strengthening, and to tell them, "I am walking on the path of truth, and now I want to hear no criticism. If there is truth in your words, I ask that you will come to me with your complaints, to show me the truth, when *I* decide it is time for criticism. Only at that time will I be willing to listen to your views."

It therefore follows that in order for one to have joy in the work of the Creator, all he needs is faith. In other words, when he believes in the greatness of the Creator, he does not need the King to give him anything. Simply being able to speak to the King is all he wants, meaning to speak to the Creator, as mentioned in the third discernment of giving praise.

If he pays more attention to praising the King, then high inspiration will come to him by itself because he does not want anything from the King. This is similar to the *Sefira Bina*. It is known that at its end, *Hochma* does not wish to receive the light of *Hochma*, but *Hochma* wishes to bestow upon the Emanator as the Emanator bestows upon *Hochma*. And she wants equivalence of form.

In that state, the abundance, called "light of *Hassadim*," after the *Kli*, comes by itself. This means that the receiver wishes to engage in *Hesed* [grace/mercy], hence the abundance is called "light of *Hassadim*" [plural of *Hesed*]. It is similar here. When a person wants nothing of the King except to bestow upon the King, and pays attention to what He thinks, an inspiration from above comes upon him by itself when he engages in singing and praising of the King, to the extent that he has prepared himself.

Now we can understand the matter of Moses and Israel singing and praising the King for the queen, and not the queen herself. It is known that everything we say about the upper worlds is only in relation to the souls, that *Malchut* is called "the collective soul of Israel" or "the assembly of Israel." It is explained in *The Study of the Ten Sefirot* (Part 16), that the soul of Adam HaRishon came out from the interior of the worlds *Beria*, *Yetzira*, and *Assiya*, from which he received *Nefesh*, *Ruach*, *Neshama*. And they all came out from *Malchut de* [of] *Atzilut*, called *Shechina* [Divinity]. And *Zeir Anpin*, who gives to the *Malchut*, is called "King."

Since *Malchut* is the receiver for the souls, it follows that *Malchut* cannot receive abundance for the people of Israel because they are still unfit—having no vessels of bestowal. Otherwise, it will all go to the *Sitra Achra* [other side], who are called "dead," since there is reception in order to receive in them, which is called "separation and remoteness from the Creator," who is called "the Life of Lives." This is why they are called "dead."

In *The Zohar*, it is considered that a person must be concerned about the sorrow of the *Shechina*, meaning sorrow at not being able to receive abundance for her children, who are the people of Israel.

She is called "the assembly of Israel" because she assembles within her the abundance that she should give to Israel. Therefore, when the people of Israel engage in equivalence of form, there is room for *Malchut* to receive the upper abundance from the King, who is called "the Giver," ZA, so as to give to the people of Israel.

This is called "*Malchut*, who is called 'the Queen,' praising the King for the abundance she has received from Him." Likewise, when she cannot receive abundance for Israel from the King, it is called "the sorrow of the *Shechina*." And when she *can* receive abundance, she is called "The mother of the sons is happy," and she praises the King.

Yet, all the sorrow and joy relate only to the whole of Israel. This is why *The Zohar* says that Moses and Israel say the song, meaning praise the king for the queen. It means that the reason why Moses and Israel praise the king is for the queen, which means that they have established themselves to praise the King, since what the King was to give to Moses and Israel was not for themselves, but for *Malchut*. In other words, they cannot tolerate the sorrow of the *Shechina*, which is why they engage in equivalence of form, so that *Malchut* can bestow. This is why it says, "Happy are Moses and Israel, for they know how to properly praise the King for the queen."

What Is the Substance of Slander and Against Whom Is It?

Article No. 10, Tav-Shin-Mem-Zayin, 1986-87

It is written in *The Zohar* (*Metzora*, Item 4), "Come and see, with the slander that the serpent said to the woman, he caused the woman and the man to be sentenced to death, them, and the whole world. It is written about slander, 'And their tongue, a sharp sword.' For this reason, 'Beware the sword,' meaning slander. 'Wrath brings the punishments of the sword.' What is, 'Wrath brings the punishments of the sword'? It is the sword for the Creator, as we learned that the Creator has a sword with which He judges the wicked. It is written about it, 'The Lord has a sword full of blood,' 'And My sword shall eat flesh,' which is the *Malchut* from the side of *Din* [judgment] in her. Hence, 'Beware the sword, for wrath brings the punishments of the sword, that you may know there is judgment.'

"It writes *Din*, but it means, 'That you may know that thus it is judged,' that anyone with a sword in his tongue who speaks slander, the sword that consumes everything is ready for him—the *Malchut* in the form of the *Din* in her. It is written about it, 'This shall be the law of the leper.' *Malchut*, which is called 'this,' sentences the leper because he slandered, for afflictions come for slander." Thus far its words.

This needs to be understood, since *The Zohar* says that for anyone with a sword in his tongue, meaning who slanders, the sword that consumes everything is ready for him—the *Malchut* in the form of *Din* in her. And we learn this from what is written about the serpent, who slandered the woman. However, there the slander was about the Creator; how is this a proof between man and man, that it should be so grave as to cause death, as it explains about the verse, "And their tongue, a sharp sword," about slander between man and man?

In other words, there is the same measure and severity of iniquity of slander between man and man as in slander between man and the Creator. Is it possible that one who slanders his friend will be similar to one who slanders the Creator?

When slandering the Creator, we can understand that it causes death, since by slandering the Creator he becomes separate from the Creator. For this reason, since he is separated from the Life of Lives, he is considered dead. But why should it cause death when the slander is between man and man?

The Zohar says that afflictions come for slander. Our sages said (*Arachin* 15b), "In the West they say: The talk of a third kills three: It kills the one who tells, the one who receives, and the one about whom it is said." RASHI interprets "The talk of a third" as gossip, which is the third between man and man, revealing to him a secret. Also there, Rabbi Yohanan said in the name of Rabbi Yosi Ben Zimra: "Anyone who slanders, it is as though he denies the tenet." And Rav Chisda said, "Mr. Ukva said, 'Anyone who slanders, the Creator says, "He and I cannot dwell in the world."'"

Also, we should understand the severity of the prohibition on slander, to the point that it is as though one has denied the tenet, or according to what Mr. Ukva says, that the Creator says, "He and I cannot dwell in the world." It means that if we say, for example, that if Reuben said something bad to Shimon about Levi, that he did something bad, the Creator cannot dwell in the world, due to Reuben's slander about Levi. But with other transgressions that Reuben might have committed, the Creator can dwell in the world with him. Thus, if this is such a grave matter, then we should understand what makes slander so bad.

We will interpret this in the work. In the essay "The Giving of the Torah," he explains the great importance of the commandment, "Love thy friend as thyself." "Rabbi Akiva says, 'This is the great rule of the Torah.' This statement of our sages demands explanation. The word *Klal* (collective/rule) indicates a sum of details that, when put together, form the above collective. Thus, when he says about the commandment, 'Love thy friend as thyself,' that it is a great *Klal* in the Torah, we must understand that the rest of the 612 commandments in the Torah, with all their interpretations, are no more or no less than the sum of the details inserted and contained in that single commandment, 'Love thy friend as thyself.'

"This is quite perplexing, because you can say this regarding *Mitzvot* [commandments] between man and man, but how can that single *Mitzva* [commandment] contain all the *Mitzvot* between man and God, which are the essence and the vast majority of its laws?

"He also writes there about a convert who came before Hillel (*Shabbat* 31) and told him: 'Teach me the whole of the Torah while I am standing on one leg.' And he replied: 'That which you hate, do not do unto your friend (the translation of 'Love thy friend as thyself'), and the rest is commentary; go study.'

"Here before us is a clear law, that in all 612 commandments and in all the writings in the Torah there is none that is preferred to the commandment, 'Love thy friend as thyself' ... since he specifically says, 'the rest is commentary; go study.' This means that the rest of the Torah is interpretations of that one commandment, that the commandment to love your friend as yourself could not be completed were it not for them."

We should understand why, when the convert told him in the holy tongue [Hebrew], "Teach me the whole of the Torah while I am standing on one leg," Hillel did not reply to him in the holy tongue, but replied to him in the language of translation [Aramaic] and told him, "That which you hate, do not do unto your friend."

We should also understand that in the Torah, it is written, "Love thy friend as thyself," which is a positive *Mitzva* [commandment to perform some action], but Hillel spoke in a negative term [commandment to avoid some action], for he told him, "That which you hate, do not do unto your friend," which is negative phrasing.

In the essay "The Giving of the Torah," he explains the greatness and importance of the rule, "Love thy friend as thyself," since the purpose of creation is to do good to His creations, and for the creatures to feel delight and pleasure without any lacks. There is a rule that *any branch wishes to resemble its root*. Since our root is the Creator, who created all the creatures, He has no deficiencies or needs to receive anything from anyone.

Therefore, when the creatures receive from someone, they, too, feel ashamed of their benefactors. Thus, for the creatures not to be ashamed while receiving delight and pleasure from the Creator, the matter of *Tzimtzum* [restriction] was set up in the upper worlds. This causes the upper abundance to be hidden from us, so we do not feel the good that He has hidden in the Torah and *Mitzvot* that the Creator has given us.

We are made to believe that the corporeal pleasures that we see before us, feeling its virtue and benefit, and the whole world, meaning that all the creatures in this world devotedly chase after pleasures to obtain them. Still, there is but a tiny light in them, a very small illumination compared to what can be obtained by keeping Torah and *Mitzvot*. It is written about it in *The Zohar* that the *Kedusha* [holiness] sustains the *Klipot* [shells]. This means that if *Kedusha* did not give sustenance to the *Klipot*, they would not be able to exist.

There is a reason why the *Klipot* should exist, since in the end, everything will be corrected and will enter the *Kedusha*. This was given for the creatures to correct, for by having the concept of time for them, there can be two topics within the same topic, even though they are in contrast. It is written about it ("Introduction to The Book of Zohar," Item 25), "For this reason, there are two systems, '*Kedusha* [holiness],' and the 'Impure *ABYA*,' which are opposite to one another. Thus, how can the *Kedusha* correct them?"

This is not so with man, who is created in this world. Since there is a matter of time, they (two systems) are in one person, but one at a time. And then there is a way for *Kedusha* to correct the impurity. This is so because until thirteen years of age, a person attains the will to receive that is in the system of impurity. Afterward, through engagement in Torah, he begins to obtain *Nefesh de* [of] *Kedusha*, and then he is sustained by the system of the worlds of *Kedusha*.

Yet, all the abundance that the *Klipot* have, which they receive from the *Kedusha*, is but a tiny light that fell because of the breaking of the vessels and through the sin of the tree of knowledge, by which the impure *ABYA* were made. And yet, we should believe, imagine, and observe how all the creatures chase that tiny light with all their might, and none of them says, "I will settle for what I have acquired." Instead, each always wishes to add to what he has, as our sages said, "One who has one hundred wants two hundred."

And the reason why there was no wholeness in them is because there was no wholeness in them to begin with. But in spirituality, the upper light is dressed in everything spiritual. Hence, when a person attains some illumination of spirituality, he cannot tell if it is a small or a great degree, since in the spiritual, even the degree of *Nefesh de Nefesh*, which is a part of the *Kedusha*—and like the rest of *Kedusha*, it is wholeness—there is wholeness in even a part of it. This is so because the discernments of "great" or "small" in the upper light are according to the value of the receiver.

In other words, it depends on the level to which the receiver is capable of obtaining the greatness and importance of the light. But there is no change at all in the light itself, as it is written, "I the Lord (*HaVaYaH*), do not change" (as explained in the "Preface to the Wisdom of Kabbalah," Item 63).

Accordingly, the question arises, "Why does the whole world chase the tiny light that shines in corporeal pleasures, while for spiritual pleasures, which hold the majority of delight and pleasure, we do not see anyone wishing to make such great efforts, as they make for corporeality?" However, corporeal pleasures are in the impure *ABYA*. There were no restriction or concealment on them, and purposely so, or the world would not exist, since it is impossible to live without pleasure.

Also, it extends from the purpose of creation to do good to His creations. Hence, without pleasure there is no existence to the world. It turns out that the pleasures *had* to be disclosed in them. This is not so with additions, meaning with receiving delight and pleasure for more than sustaining the body, which is the real pleasure. On that, there were restriction and concealment so they would not see the light of life that is clothed in Torah and *Mitzvot*, before a person accustoms himself to working in order to bestow, called "equivalence of form." This is so because *had the light that is clothed in Torah and Mitzvot been revealed, there would be no room for choice.*

In other words, where the light is revealed, the pleasure that one would feel in keeping Torah and *Mitzvot* would be in the form of self-reception. Thus, he would not be able to say that he is keeping Torah and *Mitzvot* because of the commandment of the Creator. Rather, he would have to keep Torah and *Mitzvot* because of the pleasure that he feels in them. While a person feels pleasure in some transgressions, he can calculate that the pleasure is only a tiny light compared to the real taste in Torah and *Mitzvot* and how it is difficult to overcome the lust, and that the greater the desire, the harder it is to endure the test.

It turns out that while the immensity of the pleasure in Torah and *Mitzvot* is revealed, a person cannot say, "I am doing this *Mitzva* [commandment] because it is the Creator's will," meaning that he wants to give pleasure to the Creator by keeping His *Mitzvot* [commandments]. After all, without the Creator's commandment, he would still keep Torah and *Mitzvot* because of self-love, and not because he wants to give to the Creator.

This is the reason for the placement of the restriction and the concealment on Torah and *Mitzvot*. And this is why the whole world chases corporeal pleasures, while having no energy for the pleasures in Torah and *Mitzvot* because the pleasure is not revealed for the above-mentioned reason.

It therefore follows that regarding faith, we must assume the importance there is in Torah and *Mitzvot*, and, in general, believe in the Creator—that He watches over the creatures. This means that one cannot say that he is not keeping Torah and *Mitzvot* because he does not feel the Creator's guidance, how He gives abundance to the creatures, since here, too, he must believe, even though he does not feel it.

This is so because if he felt that His guidance is benevolent, there would be no question of faith there anymore. But why did the Creator make it so we would serve Him with faith? Would it not be better if we could serve in a state of knowing?

The answer is—as Baal HaSulam said it—that one shouldn't think that the fact that the Creator wants us to serve Him with faith is because He cannot shine to us in the form of knowing. Rather, the Creator knows that faith is a more successful way for us to reach the goal, called "*Dvekut* [adhesion] with the Creator," which is equivalence of form. By that, we will have the power to receive the good while being without the "bread of shame," meaning without shame. This is so because the only reason we will want to receive delight and pleasure from the Creator is that we will know that the Creator will derive pleasure from it. And since we wish to bestow upon the Creator, we wish to receive delight and pleasure from Him.

Thus, we see that the main work we must do, to achieve the purpose for which the world was created—to do good to His creations—is to qualify ourselves to acquire vessels of bestowal. This is the correction for making the King's gift complete, so they will feel no shame upon reception of the pleasures. And all the evil in us removes us from the good that we are destined to receive.

We were given the remedy of Torah and *Mitzvot* so as to achieve those *Kelim*. This is the meaning of what our sages said (*Kidushin* 30), "The Creator says, 'I have created the evil inclination; I have created for it the spice of Torah,' by which he will lose all the sparks of self-love within him and will be rewarded with his desire being only to bestow contentment upon his Maker."

In the essay "The Giving of the Torah" (Item 13), he says, "There are two parts in the Torah: 1) *Mitzvot* [commandments] between man and God, 2) *Mitzvot* between man and man. And both aim for the same thing—to bring the creature to the final goal of *Dvekut* with Him.

"Furthermore, even the practical side in both of them is really one and the same. ... Toward those who keep Torah and *Mitzvot Lishma*, there is no difference between the two parts of the Torah, even on the practical side. This is because before one accomplishes it, one is compelled to feel any act of bestowal—either toward another person or toward the Creator—as emptiness beyond conception...

"Since this is the case, it is reasonable to think that the part of the Torah that deals with man's relationship with his friend is better capable of bringing one to the desired goal. This is because the work in *Mitzvot* between man and God is fixed and specific and is not demanding, one becomes easily accustomed to it, and everything that is done out of habit is no longer useful. But the *Mitzvot* between man and man are changing and irregular, and demands surround him wherever he may turn. Hence, their cure is much more certain and their aim is closer."

Now we understand why Rabbi Akiva said about the verse, "Love thy friend as thyself," that it is "the great rule of the Torah." It is because the important thing is to be rewarded with *Dvekut* with the Creator, which is called "a vessel of bestowal," meaning equivalence of form. This is why the remedy of Torah and *Mitzvot* was given, so that through it we would be able to exit self-love and reach love of others, as stage one is the love between a person and his friend, and then we can achieve the love of the Creator.

Now we can understand what we asked above, why when the convert came to Hillel and told him, "Teach me the whole of the Torah while I am standing on one leg," Hillel did not reply to him in the holy tongue, as he asked, "Teach me the whole of the Torah while I am standing on one leg," but replied to him in the language of translation [Aramaic], "That which you hate, do not do unto your friend" (the translation of "Love thy friend as thyself"). And there is more to understand, since in the Torah, it is written, "Love thy friend as thyself," which is a positive *Mitzva* [commandment to perform some action], while he replied to the convert in a negative tongue, "Do not do," since he told him, "That which you hate, do not do unto your friend."

According to what he explains about the importance of the *Mitzva*, "Love thy friend as thyself," in his explanation of the words of Rabbi Akiva, who said that "Love thy friend as thyself" is the great rule of the Torah, that specifically this *Mitzva* has the power to bring one the remedy for reaching the love of the Creator, for this reason, when the convert came to Hillel and told him, "Teach me the whole of the Torah while I'm standing on one leg," he wished to tell him the rule, "Love thy friend as thyself," as it is written in the Torah. However, he wished to explain to him the grave iniquity called "slander," which is even graver than the *Mitzva*, "Love thy friend as thyself."

The *Mitzva*, "Love thy friend as thyself" gives one the power to overcome and exit self-love. By exiting self-love, he can achieve the love of the Creator.

It follows that if he does not engage in the *Mitzva*, "Love thy friend as thyself," he is in a state of "sit and do nothing." He did not progress in coming out of the domination of self-love, but did not regress, either. In other words, although he did not give love to others, he also did not relapse and did nothing to evoke hatred of others.

Yet, if he slanders his friend, by that, he relapses. Not only does he not engage in love of others, he does the opposite—engages in actions that cause hatred of others by slandering his friend.

Naturally, one does not slander one he loves, for it separates the hearts. Therefore, we do not wish to slander one that we love so as not to spoil the love between us, since slander inflicts hatred.

It therefore follows that the severity of the iniquity of slander is that love of others yields love of the Creator, and hatred of others yields hatred of the Creator, and there is nothing worse in the world than that which yields hatred of the Creator. But when a person sins with other transgressions and cannot overcome his will to receive because he is immersed in self-love, it still does not make him hate the Creator. This is why it is written about the rest of the transgressions, "I am the Lord, who dwells with them in the midst of their impurity." But in regards to slander, by this action he becomes hateful of the Creator, as it is the very opposite act of love of others.

Now we can understand the words of Rabbi Yohanan in the name of Rabbi Yosi Ben Zimra: "Anyone who slanders, it is as though he denies the tenet." Can it be that slander would make one deny the tenet? However, since it causes him to hate the Creator, he denies the very purpose of creation—to do good. And we see that one who does good to another and gives him more delight and pleasure each time, certainly loves him. But when a person slanders, it makes him hate the Creator. Thus, this person denies the very purpose of creation—to do good.

Now we can also understand what we asked about what Rav Hasda said in the name of Mr. Ukva: "Anyone who slanders, the Creator says, 'He and I cannot dwell in the world.'" Is it possible that slander could cause the Creator not to dwell in the world with him?

As we said above, one who slanders becomes hateful of the Creator. As in corporeality, a person can be in a house with many people and yet be indifferent to whether they are good people or not. But when he sees his hater there, he immediately runs away from there, for he cannot be in a single room with a hater. Similarly, we say that one who becomes hateful of the Creator, the Creator cannot be with him in the world.

We could ask, "But one who steals something from his friend also causes his friend to hate, since when the one from whom it was stolen finds out that he stole, he will see that he is his hater?" Or, we could say that even if he never knows who stole from him, the thief himself—instead of engaging in love of others—engages in an opposite act, in hatred of others, by which he becomes more immersed in self-love. And yet, they do not say that stealing is as bad as slander. Also, it means that robbing is not as grave as slander, too.

The answer should be that one who engages in stealing or robbing does not rob or steal because of hatred. The reason is that he has love for money or for important artifacts, and this is why he steals or robs, not because of hate. But with slander, it is not because of some fancy, but only out of hatred.

It is as Rish Lakish said (*Arachin* 15), "Rish Lakish said, 'Why is it written, 'If the serpent bites without whispering, there is no advantage to the one with the tongue?' In the future, all the animals will come to the serpent and tell him, 'The lion preys and eats; a wolf preys and eats. But you, what pleasure have you?' He tells them, 'And what is the advantage of the one with the tongue?'"

RASHI interprets, "'A lion preys and eats,' all who harm people derive pleasure. The lion preys and eats. He eats of what is alive. And if a wolf preys, it kills first and then eats. It has pleasure. But you, what is your pleasure in biting people? The serpent replied, 'And what is the advantage of the one with the tongue? One who slanders, what joy does he have? Similarly, when I bite, I get no pleasure.'"

With the above said, we can see that there is a difference between harming people because one derives pleasure, such as the lion and the wolf, who have no desire to harm because they hate people, but because of desire, since they take pleasure in people. Thus, the reason why they harm others is only out of desire.

This is not so with slander. One does not receive any reward for it, but it is an act that causes hatred of people. And according to the rule, "Love thy friend as thyself," where from love of man one comes to love of the Creator, it follows that from hatred of people one can come to hatred of the Creator.

Similarly, we find these words (*Berachot* 17a): "'The fear of the Lord is the beginning of wisdom; a good understanding have all they that do them.' It did not say, 'That do,' but 'That do them,' they who do *Lishma* [for Her sake] and not they who do *Lo Lishma* [not for Her sake]. And anyone who does *Lo Lishma*, it is better for him to not be born. In the *Tosfot*, he asks, 'And if the sayer should say, 'Rav Yehuda said, 'Rav said, 'One should always engage in Torah and *Mitzvot*, even in *Lo Lishma*, for out of *Lo Lishma* he will come to *Lishma*.''' We should say, 'Here we are dealing with one who is learning only in order to annoy his friends, and there it was about one who is learning in order to be respected.'"

We should understand the answer of the *Tosfot*, when he says that we should distinguish between *Lo Lishma* in order to annoy and *Lo Lishma* in order to be respected, meaning to call him "a rabbi" and so on. We should understand it according to the rule that Rabbi Akiva said, "Love thy friend as thyself is the great rule of the Torah." By what he explains in the essay "The Giving of the Torah," it is because through this *Mitzva* [commandment] he will acquire love of others, and from this he will later come to love of the Creator.

It therefore follows that one should try to exit self-love, and then he will be able to engage in Torah and *Mitzvot Lishma*, meaning in order to bestow and not for his own benefit. This is done by keeping Torah and *Mitzvot*. Thus, *as long as he does not exit self-love, he cannot engage in Lishma. And although he engages in self-love, there is power in keeping Torah and Mitzvot in order to exit self-love and from that to subsequently come to love of the Creator, at which time he will do everything in order to bestow.*

Achieving *Lishma* is possible only when he engages in Torah and *Mitzvot* in order to be respected. That is, he is learning but he still cannot work for the sake of others, since he hasn't acquired the quality of love of others. Hence, engagement in Torah and *Mitzvot* will help him achieve the quality of love of others.

But when he learns in order to annoy, which is an opposite act from love of others, keeping Torah and *Mitzvot* for the hatred of others, in order to annoy, how can two opposites be in the same carrier? Meaning, it is said that the Torah assists in achieving love of others when one performs an act of bestowal—although the intention is to receive a prerogative, the Torah assists him toward the intention of obtaining the desire to bestow, as well. But here he engages in the very opposite, in hatred of others. How can this cause love of others?

It is as we said about the distinction between a thief or a robber, and a slanderer. Thieves and robbers love money, gold, and other important things. They have no personal dealings with the individual himself. In other words, thieves and robbers have no thought or consideration of the person himself, but their thoughts are focused on where they can get more money more easily, and with greater difficulty for the police to expose them as the thieves or robbers. But they never think of the person himself.

With slander, however, one has no consideration of the act itself when he slanders. Rather, his only thought is to humiliate his friend in the eyes of people. Thus, the only thought is one of hatred. It is a rule that one does not slander one he loves. Hence, it is specifically slander that causes hatred of others, which subsequently leads to hatred of the Creator. For this reason, slander is a very grave iniquity, which actually brings destruction of the world.

Now we will explain the measure of slander—how and how much is considered slander, whether a word or a sentence that is said about one's friend is already considered slander. We find this measure in Hillel's answer to the convert, "That which you hate, do not do unto your friend." This means that with any word that you want to say about your friends, observe and consider if you would hate it if this was said about you. In other words, if you would derive no pleasure from these words, "Do not do unto your friend."

Thus, when one wishes to say something about one's friend, he should immediately think, "If this were said about me, would I hate that word?" "Do not do unto your friend," as Hillel said to the convert. From here we should learn the measure of slander that is forbidden to say.

And with the above said, we can understand why Hillel spoke to the convert in the language of translation and not in the holy tongue [Hebrew], just as to the convert, who told him [in Hebrew], "Teach me the whole of the Torah while I am standing on one leg." Instead, he spoke in the language of translation, meaning that what he told him was, "That which you hate, do not do unto your friend" [in Aramaic], the translation of "Love thy friend as thyself."

First, we should understand what the language of translation implies to us. The Ari said (*The Study of the Ten Sefirot*, Part 15, p 1765), "'And the Lord God caused a deep sleep' is translation in *Gematria* [*Tardema* (sleep) = *Targum* (translation)], and it is considered *Achoraim* [posterior]." This means that the holy tongue [Hebrew] is called *Panim* [anterior] and the translation [Aramaic] is called *Achoraim* [posterior].

Panim means something that illuminates or something whole. *Achor* [back] means something that is not illuminating or is incomplete. In the holy tongue, which is called *Panim*, it writes, "Love thy friend as thyself," which is wholeness, since through love of man one achieves the love of the Creator, which is the completion of the goal, for one should achieve *Dvekut* [adhesion], as it is written, "And to cleave unto Him."

But the translation of "Love thy friend as thyself" that Hillel told him, "That which you hate, do not do unto your friend," we should say that it relates to slander, which is about negation, that slander is forbidden because it brings hatred, and from this, one might come to hatred of the Creator. However, this is still not considered wholeness because by not slandering, one still does not achieve love of others, and from love of others he will reach wholeness, called *Dvekut* with the Creator.

However, this is why slander is worse, since not only does he not engage in love of others, he does the opposite—engages in hatred of others. For this reason, when teaching the general public to begin the work, they are first taught how to not spoil and harm the public. This is called "avoiding." Otherwise, you are harming the public by doing things to harm.

This is why Hillel said to the convert who came to him only the translation of "Love thy friend as thyself": 1) Because it is more harmful when slandering, for it causes hatred, which is the opposite of love of others. 2) Because it is easier to keep, for this is only in "sit and do not do." But "Love thy friend" is "Rise up and do," when one should take action to sustain the love of friends.

However, afterwards there are exceptions: people who each wish to be a servant of the Creator personally. A person is told that the matter of "Love thy friend," which is the rule that Rabbi Akiva said—as above-mentioned, that love of others can bring him to achieve love of the Creator—is the main goal: that one will have vessels of bestowal and that in these vessels he will be able to receive delight and pleasure, which is the purpose of creation, to do good to His creation.

Two methods in education extend from this:

1. Focusing the learning on not slandering because this is the worst iniquity.

2. Focusing the education on "Love thy friend," since this will bring man to love others, and from love of others he will come to love of the Creator, and from love of the Creator he can then receive the purpose of creation—to do good to His creations. This is because he will already have the suitable vessels for receiving the upper abundance, as he will have vessels of bestowal, which he has obtained by love of others. And then there will be no room for slander.

Concerning slander, *The Zohar* says that the serpent's slandering to the woman caused death to the world. It says there that the sword that consumes everything is ready for anyone with a sword in his tongue, meaning who slanders. And *The Zohar* concludes, "As it is written, 'This will be the law of the leper,' as for afflictions come for slander." It follows that he began with death and ended with afflictions, which means that only afflictions come and not death.

Certainly, there are explanations for the literal meaning. But in the work, we should interpret that afflictions and death are one and the same. In other words, the purpose of the work is to achieve *Dvekut* with the Creator, to adhere to the Life of Lives. By this we will have suitable vessels for reception of the delight and pleasure that is found in the purpose of creation, to do good to His creations. Through slander, he becomes a hater of the Creator, and there is no greater separation than this. Certainly, by that he becomes separated from the Life of Lives.

It follows that where he should have received delight and pleasure from the Creator, he receives the opposite. In other words, instead of pleasure, it becomes affliction [in Hebrew "pleasure" and "affliction" contain the same letters]. This is the meaning that through slander, afflictions come instead of pleasures. This is the meaning of "The wicked, in their lives, are called 'dead,'" since they are separated from the Life of Lives. It follows that in the work, death and afflictions are the same.

In other words, if one adheres to the Life of Lives, he receives abundance from Him. And if it is to the contrary and he becomes separated from Him, then he is full of afflictions where he should have been filled with pleasures.

With the above-said, we can interpret what they said (*Arachin* 15), "In the West they say: The talk of a third kills three: It kills the one who tells, the one who receives, and the one about whom it is said." We know the words of our sages, "The Torah, Israel, and the Creator are one." It means, as explained in the book *A Sage's Fruit* (Part One, p 65), that Israel is one who wishes to adhere to the Creator. He achieves this through the 613 *Mitzvot* [commandments] of the Torah, at which time he is rewarded with the Torah, which is the names of the Creator. And then everything becomes one. It turns out that one who slanders causes the killing of three: 1) the one who tells, 2) the one who receives, 3) the one about whom it is said.

The three discernments are to be made between man and man.

However, between man and the Creator there is also the matter of slander, as mentioned concerning "The Torah, Israel, and the Creator are one." When a person comes and looks in the Torah, he sees all those good things that the Creator has promised us in keeping the Torah. For example, it is written, "For this is your life," and it is also written, "They are more desirable than gold, yes, than much fine gold; sweeter also than honey and the drippings of the honeycomb," and other such verses. If a person is not rewarded and does not feel it, this is called "slandering the Creator."

It follows that three discernments should be made here: 1) the slanderer, 2) the Torah, 3) the Creator.

When a person looks in the Torah, if he is not rewarded, he does not see the delight and pleasure clothed in the holy Torah, and stops learning the Torah because he says he found no meaning in it. Thus, in speaking of the Torah, he is slandering the Creator.

It follows that he blemishes three things: the Torah, Israel, and the Creator. Where one should exert to make the unification of "Are one"—that they will all shine, meaning that the discernment of Israel will obtain the unification that the whole Torah is the names of the Creator—he causes separation in that, through slander.

A person must believe above reason that what the Torah promises us is true, and the only fault is in us—that we are still unfit to receive the delight and pleasure, called "the hidden light" or "the flavors of Torah and *Mitzvot*," as it is written in *The Zohar* that the whole Torah is the names of the Creator.

To achieve this, we need vessels of bestowal—to have equivalence of form between the light and the *Kli* [vessel]. Achieving vessels of bestowal is done by love of friends. It is as Rabbi Akiva said, "Love thy friend as thyself is the great rule of the Torah," for through it we achieve love of others, and through love of others we arrive at love of the Creator and the love of Torah. The Torah is called "a gift," and gifts are given to loved ones. The opposite of this is slander, which causes hatred of people and hatred of the Creator, as we said above.

Now we can understand what our sages said about slander, "The talk of a third kills three: It kills the one who tells, the one who receives, and the one about whom it is said." RASHI interprets that out of hatred they provoke one another and kill each other. We can understand that this applies between man and man; but how does this apply between man and the Creator?

When a person looks in the Torah and tells the Torah that he does not see or feel the delight and pleasure that the Creator said that He is giving to the people of Israel, he is slandering the Creator. There are three things here: the telling person, the receiver, meaning the Torah, and the one of whom it is said, meaning the Creator. Since when a person engages in love of others, he obtains the love of the Creator and the love of Torah, in that state, the Creator imparts upon him life, as it is written, "For with You is the source of life." This is from the side of *Dvekut* [adhesion], as it is written, "And you who cleave."

In that state, one is rewarded with the law of life. But through slander, the life from the Creator, which he should have received, is withheld from him. Thus, 1) the life from the Torah—where he should have sensed the Torah of life—is withheld from him, 2) he himself becomes lifeless, which is considered that he is killed, and 3) life stops in three places. And through the love of others, life flows from two places and he is the receiver of the life.

Purim, and the Commandment: Until He Does Not Know

Article No. 11, Tav-Shin-Mem-Zayin, 1986-87

Our sages said (*Megillah* 7), "On Purim, one must drink until he does not know the cursed Haman from the blessed Mordechai." However, it is impossible to come to a state of not knowing before one is in a state of knowing. Afterward, it is possible to say that we should achieve a higher degree, called "not knowing." Certainly, this is a higher degree than knowing, since we are instructed to observe this only on Purim and not all year long, as our sages said, "On Purim, one must," and not throughout the year.

Accordingly, we should understand the meaning of knowing and not knowing. We should also understand the commandment in the Torah to read the portion, *Zachor* [Remember]. The *Magen Avraham* wrote (*Orach Chaim*, Mark 685), "I should explain the custom, for because of whom is it written in the Torah that they should read specifically on this Shabbat [Saturday]? The sages determined that it is this Shabbat because many people come to the synagogue. And it is close to Purim in order to attach the story of Amalek with the story of Haman."

This means that "Remember that which Amalek had done to you" always applies. However, they determined that it should be read on Shabbat before Purim in order to attach the story about Amalek to the story of Haman. Also, what does the attachment of "Remember" to Purim teach us in the work?

In order to understand all the above, we should first understand the purpose of creation. From this we will know what is "between the cursed Haman and the blessed Mordechai," and what is "cannot tell between the cursed Haman and the blessed Mordechai."

It is known that the purpose of creation is to do good to His creations. In order for the good that the Creator gives to be complete, that upon reception they will not feel any unpleasantness, since there is a rule that every branch wants to resemble its root, and the root of the creatures is His desire to give to the creatures, when the creatures receive from Him, they feel shame, as it is opposite from the root.

For this reason, there was a correction called "restriction and concealment" on the original vessel of reception, which is—as it was initially created—receiving in order to receive. It was done by correction, meaning that in this *Kli* [vessel], there is already control over her through the establishing of the restriction so the upper abundance does not come to the *Kli* called "will to receive." The *Kelim* [vessels] of this kind remained in a state called "vacant space without light," and she remained in the dark.

Only when they can place an intention to bestow on this *Kli*, which is called "receiving," meaning although he has a great desire and craving to receive the abundance, still, if he is not sure if what he receives from the Creator will be due to *Mitzva* [good deed], which is because the Creator wants to give, as it was said, He wants to do good to His creations, he is willing to relinquish the delight that he receives from the Creator. Instead, he wants to receive delight and pleasure only because of the purpose of creation.

Now we can know the difference between the cursed Haman and the blessed Mordechai. The way of Righteous Mordechai is to work only in order to bestow upon the Creator, which is called "bestowing." By this we can later come to the degree of wholeness, when he comes to a degree where he can already say to the Creator, "I want You to give me delight and pleasure because I want to observe Your desire: to give to the creatures delight and pleasure. Now I am ready to receive the delight and pleasure because I know that I do not want this due to self-love, but in order to bestow."

Now, with the aim to bestow, reception of the King's gift is in wholeness. That is, there is no shame there because the reception is because of his desire to assist the Creator, for the purpose of creation to be revealed, so everyone will know that the purpose of creation is to do good to His creations.

Since our sages said (*Kiddushin* 40b), "If he performs one *Mitzva* [good deed/correction], happy is he, for he has sentenced himself and the entire world to the side of merit." Therefore, since he is in a state where he has no concern for self-love but rather for love of others, it follows that by wanting to receive delight and pleasure from the Creator, he wants to keep the love of others between man and God, and between man and man.

This is as it is written in *The Zohar* ("Introduction of the Book of Zohar," Item 67): "'And to say to Zion, "You are My people."' ...Do not pronounce 'You are My people [*Ami*]' with a *Patach* in the *Ayin*, but "You are with Me [*Imi*]," with a *Hirik* in the *Ayin*, which means partnering with Me. ...Happy are they who exert in the Torah."

Although there it speaks of between man and the Creator, but the matter of interpretation of a partner can also be applied between man and man, since this implies that later, the whole world will receive the side of merit. It follows that he did good between man and man by causing the entire world to receive the delight and pleasure that exist in the purpose of creation.

It follows that he has become a partner of the Creator in that through him will come the assistance by which everyone will achieve the purpose of creation. Thus, he has become a partner of the Creator, as it is written, "I started creation by wanting to give delight and pleasure, and Israel exert to realize the goal by making *Kelim* [vessels] that are fit to receive the upper abundance without any flaw, called 'bread of shame.' Rather, even when they receive the delight and pleasure, they will not lose the *Dvekut* [adhesion], called 'equivalence of form,' for this was the reason for the *Tzimtzum* [restriction]."

This is regarded as knowing the path of Mordechai, which is a path that brings blessing to the entire world, as it was said above, "If he merits, he sentences himself and the entire world to the side of merit." This is called "the blessed Mordechai."

Conversely, Haman's way is not to look at the correction of the *Tzimtzum* that was placed on the vessels of reception. Rather, he says, "Since the Creator created the world in order to do good to His creations, and we see that in our nature there is a desire to receive delight and pleasure, then why did the Creator create this desire if not to use it? Did He instead create in us a desire and craving to receive pleasure and said not to use it but be tormented by it?"

It therefore follows that this is the opposite way. It is said that He created the world in order to do good to His creations. By Righteous Mordechai saying not to use this desire, it means that He has created the world in order to do bad to His creations. So, it would probably be better not to create the will to receive delight and pleasure altogether then to create a desire and craving to receive delight, and then say not to use it but to torment oneself and remain devoid of pleasure.

Therefore, how is it possible to agree with Mordechai's way and say that it is forbidden to use the *Kelim* that want to enjoy? After all, this is the real *Kli* [vessel] that the Creator created. Even Mordechai admits that the Creator created the desire to receive delight and pleasure in the world. Therefore, Haman argues that Mordechai's way is not the path of truth.

Especially, he has many supporters for his way. The whole world says that the real way in the world is as Haman says. It is as it is written (Esther 3): "All the king's servants, who are at the king's gate, kneel and bow to Haman, for so the king commanded for him."

This means that Haman made them see that thus the king commanded. That is, Haman claimed that since the king, meaning the Creator, created the will to receive, He must want us to receive and enjoy. And all the king's servants kneeled, meaning surrendered to Haman's view because he argued that this will to receive—which Mordechai says not to use—is incorrect because the Creator did not create it in vain, but rather to be used. And Mordechai says "No," as it is written, "And Mordechai did not kneel and did not bow." This is the meaning of what is written, "And the king's servants, who are at the king's gate, said to Mordechai: 'Why are you defying the king's commandment?'"

Baal HaSulam said about this that it means that the king's servants said to Mordechai: "Haman is telling us that his going in his way and not in Mordechai's way is because this is the path of truth." This is the meaning of their asking Mordechai, "Why are you defying the king's commandment?" meaning the Creator, for Haman said that so the king had commanded him, meaning the King of Kings.

This means that since the will to receive and to crave for self-love is the King of all Kings, He has created this force in the creatures. This is why the whole world supports Haman's view and mind.

Also, Haman's view was written in the Torah, as our sages said (*Hulin* 139b), "Haman (manna) [in Hebrew: "from" is spelled the same as Haman] from the Torah, where is it from? Have you eaten off the tree from which I have commanded you not to eat?"

Eating from the tree of knowledge is explained in the introduction to the book *Panim Meirot*. It explains there (Item 18) that *Adam HaRishon* was completely separated from the *Sitra Achra*, "And it has already been explained that *Adam HaRishon* did not have the *Gadlut* of reception in his structure whatsoever, which extends from the vacant space. Rather, he extended entirely from the system of *Kedusha* [sanctity], which is about bestowal." It is written in *The Zohar* (*Kedoshim*) that "*Adam HaRishon* did not have anything from this world. This is why the tree of knowledge was forbidden for him, like his root and the entire system of *Kedusha*, which are separated from the *Sitra Achra* due to their disparity of form." It follows that Haman means using the big will to receive in order to receive, for this was the whole of the serpent's advice.

It is also written there that he said to the serpent, "God had eaten from this tree and created the world. That is, He looked at this in the form of 'The end of the act is in the preliminary thought,' and this is why He created the world." This is the meaning of the serpent's argument that eating from the tree of knowledge is God's commandment.

So why did the Creator command *Adam HaRishon* not to eat? To this, the serpent gave Adam and Eve a good answer. Essentially, he means to observe the Creator's commandment by advising them to eat from the tree of knowledge. This is also the issue here in the Book of Esther, where it is written, "And all the king's servants who are at the king's gate kneel and bow to Haman." It is so because so the king had commanded him.

By this we will understand that "cursed Haman" means that Haman's way is a cursed path, meaning a path of a curse. This is as it is written (Genesis 3), "And the Lord God said unto the serpent: 'Because you did this, cursed are you more than all beasts.' ...To the woman He said, 'I will greatly multiply Your sadness.' ...And to the man He said, 'Because you have ... eaten from the tree ... Cursed is the earth because of you.'"

According to the above, we understand that the man should reach the degree of "knowing." Meaning, what is the big difference between "cursed Haman" and "blessed Mordechai"? It is the difference between life and death, since Mordechai's way brings life, and one is rewarded with adhering to the Life of Lives, but Haman's way, he already knows, brings curse to the world, for all the death in the world is caused by "Have you eaten off the tree from which I have commanded you not to eat?"

It is about this that the writing says "cursed." This matter applies until the end of correction, that one should be careful not to fall into the path of Haman. At the end of correction, all the will to receive will be corrected in order to bestow, and then death will be swallowed up forever. It is as *The Zohar* says, "At the end of correction, SAM will be a holy angel."

Now we can understand the attachment of blotting out Amalek when we read, "Remember what Amalek had done to you." Specifically, when we know everything that Amalek had done to us, which is the death that he caused to the world by his control—not to walk in the path of bestowal, to adhere to the Life of Lives—then we try to obliterate him from the face of the earth. Otherwise, before a person achieves the degree of knowing what Haman and Amalek did to us, a person does not crave to obliterate him.

It follows that specifically when one has reached the degree of knowing the cursed Haman from the blessed Mordechai, it is possible to blot out Amalek. For this reason, before Purim, which is the time when we should reach the degree, "until he does not know," we must reach the degree of knowing, and only then can we blot out Amalek.

In other words, when a person wants to observe, "Blot out the memory of Amalek," it is a sign that he has already been rewarded with knowing. Otherwise, a person cannot blot out Amalek. Rather, he is still immersed in the *Klipa* [shell/peel] of Amalek and does not want to keep, "Blot out the memory of Amalek."

Now we will explain what our sages said, "On Purim, one must drink until he does not know the cursed Haman from the blessed Mordechai." We asked, "What is the *Gadlut* [greatness/adulthood] that only on Purim can we do such a thing, meaning until "he does not know"? The holy ARI says (*The Study of the Ten Sefirot*, Part 16, Item 220), "Therefore, in the future, all the special days will be canceled except for the Book of Esther. The reason is that there has never been such a great miracle, not on Shabbats and not on good days, when there was such illumination even after the departure of the *Mochin* from the female, except in the days of Purim. In this respect, there is a great advantage to Purim over the rest of the days, even over Shabbats and good days."

In the commentary *Ohr Pnimi*, he interprets there that before the end of correction it is impossible to correct all the sparks and *Kelim* that broke, but only the 288 sparks from the 320 sparks can be sorted and brought into *Kedusha* [sanctity]. Yet, this, too, will be sorted gradually, leaving 32 sparks out of all the sparks which must not be sorted. This is called the "stony heart." Only by sorting the 288 sparks, when they are completely sorted, the stony heart will be sorted by itself, as well, as in, "And I will remove the stony heart from your flesh, and I will give you a heart of flesh. At that time, death will be swallowed up forever, all the bad will be corrected into good, and darkness will shine as light."

Since these lights of Purim are a similitude of the end of correction, for they illuminated only thanks to the miracle, for this reason, all the special days are cancelled besides Purim, for it belongs to the end of correction. Then, when all the bad is corrected, there will be no difference between "the cursed Haman and the blessed Mordechai," and Haman, too, will be corrected into good.

What Is Half a Shekel in the Work - 1

Article No. 12, Tav-Shin-Mem-Zayin, 1986-87

The verse says, "When you take a census of the children of Israel to number them, each one of them shall give a ransom for his soul to the Lord, when you number them, and there shall be no plague among them when you count them. This is what they shall give: half a shekel in the shekel of holiness. The rich shall not pay more and the poor shall not pay less than half a shekel, to make atonement for your souls."

In order to understand this in the work, we must first present what our sages said (*Nida* 31b), "Our sages said, 'There are three partners in a person: the Creator, his father, and his mother. His father sows the white; his mother sows the red, and the Creator places in him a spirit and a soul.'" It is known that all of our work is only to achieve *Dvekut* [adhesion] with the Creator, called "equivalence of form," since we were born with a desire to receive delight and pleasure for self-love. This is the opposite of the Creator, whose wish is to bestow upon His creatures.

It is also known that disparity of form creates separation. When the creatures are separated from the Life of Lives, they are called "dead." For this reason, there was a correction that is known as

Tzimtzum [restriction] and concealment, to such an extent that we must work on faith, to believe in the Creator and in reward and punishment. However, all the concealments are only so as to have the ability to engage in Torah and *Mitzvot* [commandments] in order to bestow and not for our own sake.

If the delight and pleasure were revealed, and Providence were revealed—that the Creator behaves benevolently with His creatures as good and as doing good, it would be utterly impossible for the creatures to work and observe Torah and *Mitzvot* in order to bestow. Instead, they would have to work in order to receive, for they would have no way to overcome the pleasures they would feel in Torah and *Mitzvot*.

But once the concealment has been established, and the delight and pleasure in Torah and *Mitzvot* are not revealed, in order for the world to exist, so they would have some vitality and feel pleasure in their lives, we were given light and pleasure clothed in corporeal pleasures, as *The Zohar* says. But we must believe that this is only a very thin light, called "thin light," which was given to the *Klipot* [shells/peels] so they can exist and sustain man before he is rewarded with receiving other *Kelim* [vessels], called "vessels of bestowal," for only in those *Kelim* is it possible for the upper light to appear.

Therefore, the beginning of man's work is to believe above reason concerning everything he sees and feels, that it is only a concealment that was placed deliberately for man's sake. But the truth is not as he sees and feels, so he should tell himself: "The have eyes and do not see, ears, and do not hear."

This means that only through this work, by overcoming the mind and heart, can he be rewarded with vessels of bestowal, for specifically with these *Kelim* he can see and feel the Creator's guidance as benevolent.

However, what can one do when he sees that it is not easy to overcome self-love, and to have the ability to come to the degree of bestowal in mind and heart? In that state, when a person begins to feel that there is evil in him, and he wants to exit the evil's control, but feels that he cannot exit its control and that it is not so easy, but probably requires great exertion to obtain vessels of bestowal, he is willing to exert but does not know in what way he can arrange his way so as to clearly know that this is the right way that will bring him to the King's palace, meaning to be rewarded with *Dvekut* with the Creator, as it is written (Deuteronomy 30), "To love the Lord your God, to hear unto His voice, and to cling unto Him, for He is your life."

The order is that first he must divide his work into two opposite ways. That is, there is a way where one must walk on a path of wholeness, and although he sees that he is full of flaws, there is still happiness: He is happy that he is not deficient. It is as our sages said, "Who is rich? He who is happy with his lot" (*Avot* 4:1). This depends on the extent to which he appreciates the importance of the King.

That is, he examines the measure of his desire to cling to the Creator, meaning that it is worthwhile to relinquish himself and annul before Him. This is as it is written in the book *Matan Torah* (*The Giving of the Torah*) (p 129), where he presents the following allegory: "The soul is an illumination that extends from His essence. This illumination has parted from the Creator by the Creator clothing it in a desire to receive, for that thought of creation to delight His creatures created in every soul a desire to receive pleasure. Yet, the disparity of form of the will to receive separated that illumination from His essence and made it a separate part from Him."

When a person believes this, that his soul comes from His essence, but was separated from the Creator and became an authority of its own with creation, meaning through the will to receive installed in her, he gives the following allegory about it: "Now the soul is just like an organ that was cut off and separated from the body. Although prior to the separation, the organ and the rest of the body were one, exchanging thoughts and feelings, after the organ was cut off from the body they became two authorities. Now one does not know the thoughts of the other. This is all the more so once the soul clothed in a body of this world—all the ties it had prior to her separating from His essence have stopped."

Therefore, when a person sees how important is his engagement in Torah and *Mitzvot*—that the Creator has given to us to observe His commandments, for by keeping what He has commanded to us we have the privilege of keeping contact with the Creator. And although he still does not feel this privilege, for lack of importance, since we see that in corporeality, when a person enjoys his life, how much time during the day does he enjoy the corporeality? He is limited in receiving pleasure. Instead, he has certain times when he enjoys, such as when he eats and drinks and sleeps and sees nice things or listens to singing and good music. However, he cannot eat, drink, look, and listen all day long. Rather, he settles for what he has and feels wholeness in the corporeal life, and does not say, "If I cannot enjoy all those things today, I give them up." The reason is the importance of corporeality.

It therefore follows that if a person pays attention to the importance of the King, he will have complete satisfaction in being given the Torah and *Mitzvot* to observe as much as he can. Even if, for example, he has the privilege of speaking with a great king with whom not anyone is permitted to come and speak. Rather, it requires much persuasion among the king's confidants to let him speak a few words with the king. How elated that person would be when he sees that many people are not permitted to approach the king, or are even told that the king is here in town and there are people who can speak with the king.

He sees that there are people in the world who do not know that there is a King in the world, and only a very small group of people in the world were given the thought and desire to believe that there is a King in the world. Even those who were informed about the King do not know that it is possible to speak with Him. But that person was given knowledge from above that he can come in and speak with the King, meaning that he can believe.

We can understand this with an allegory. A person who comes to drink water is told, "Go, come in and speak with the King. Tell him, 'I thank You for letting me drink,' and say the blessing 'Blessed are You, O Lord…'" In other words, he thanks and says to Him: "I thank You for 'everything that is made by His word.'" It follows that if he believes that he is speaking with the King, as it is written, "The whole earth is full of His glory," what elation a person feels when he believes that he is speaking with the King for only a moment.

The excitement from standing and speaking with the King for even a moment should give complete satisfaction so he will have vitality and joy throughout the day. Although he does not see the King, we were given the belief that "the whole earth is full of His glory," and we were also given the belief that "You hear the prayer of every mouth."

Baal HaSulam said about that, "*every* mouth," means even the mouth of the lowliest person. The Creator hears everyone! It follows that according to one's faith when he is speaking with the Creator, meaning whether he thanks Him or asks Him for something, the Creator hears everything. That person, if he walks in this path, can be happy all day long because he feels contentment from speaking to the King.

Especially during the prayer, it does not even matter if he does not know the meaning of the words because his praying and uttering what is written in the prayer book, a person should know that this is the order that the ministers of the King have arranged, that when entering the King's place, these are the words to be said. Therefore, it makes no difference if he knows what he is saying or not, for it is not man who has made this prayer or this thanksgiving, for this is the order for everyone, as anyone who comes in to speak to the King, they arranged it and not he.

Indeed, what a person asks is not written in the prayers or in the thanksgivings that he says. Rather, the prayers that a person says are written and inscribed in man's heart. That is, a person asks not what is written in the prayer book, but what is written in his own heart. It therefore follows that although everyone prays with the same prayer book, each one demands and prays that He will satisfy the deficiency in his heart.

It is as it is written in the blessing for the new month: "Life, that the Lord will fulfill our heart's wishes for the best." This means that after all the prayers we say in the blessing for the new month, which our sages have set up, we conclude with our own prayer, meaning what the heart prays, and say that the Creator will fulfill our heart's wishes for the best.

We should understand why we say that the Lord will fulfill our heart's wishes for the best. Why do we add "our heart's wishes for the best"? We understand that man's heart, what he asks and prays for, comes from his heart. But who knows if the heart yearns for good things? The heart could ask for bad things. For this reason, we were given the addition "our heart's wishes for the best." Conversely, when our sages established the prayers, their heart was completely with the Creator. Certainly, all their prayers are good prayers. But we are not so, hence we must add "for the best."

It therefore follows that one should rejoice in having been rewarded with speaking a few words with the King. This is called "right line," meaning the path of the right, which is called "wholeness." This means that he does not feel in himself any lack.

By this we can interpret what our sages said, "There are three partners in a person: His father sows the white." His father is called "male," meaning complete. But the mother is called "female," deficient. This is why they said, "His father sows the white," from the color "white," meaning that it is spotless there, completely white, without any deficiency.

This is as our sages said (*Yotze* 16), "Every turn you turn will be only through the right." This means that the order of the beginning of the work should be in the right, meaning in wholeness, when a person sees no deficiency in himself. Naturally, at that time it is possible to praise the King for giving him wholeness, and then it can be said, "the blessed cling to the Blessed."

But when a person feels deficient, our sages said "The cursed does not cling to the blessed." For this reason, in such a state he is separated. Therefore, a man must walk on the right line, called "wholeness," from which a person receives life, when he is adhered to some extent to the Life of Lives. But a person, as long as he lives, can see whether his deeds are good or bad and correct them.

If a person dies, meaning has no vitality, nothing from which to receive life, he cannot correct his actions because at that time he is considered dead. And with all of his vitality, it is possible that if he could escape the life he is in while in this world, and die a physical death, or at least, if he could take a sleeping pill so he could sleep for at least three months, if he were to see such a sleeping pill and could receive vitality from it, but what can he do if in the meantime he wants nothing but to sleep? And if he must do something, when he remembers that soon he will have time to sleep, from this he receives his vitality for the time being.

For this reason, a person must make the first basis in his work the walk on the right line, the line of wholeness, without any deficiency in mind or heart. Baal HaSulam said about what is written in the Book of Esther, "And Mordechai knew all that was done, and Mordechai tore up his clothes and wore sack and ashes and went out and cried a great and bitter cry, and came up to the king's gate, for it is forbidden to come into the king wearing sackcloth."

The Even Ezra interprets there that it is the way of the degrading of the kingship. He said a commentary on this, that when a person engages in Torah and *Mitzvot*, or when he prays, it is regarded as standing at the King's gate. At that time, if a person looks at himself and wants to see if he is OK, meaning if he is not transgressing the King's commandment, through this act the King is degraded, by Him seeing that there are people, of whom he is one, who do not want to recognize the greatness of the King. They do not want to take upon themselves the King's authority. On the contrary, they have the power to say that they do not recognize the King's kingship.

Rather, the King's glory is that everyone recognizes the importance of the King and everyone wants to serve Him with their hearts and souls. It is beautiful to see how they are all standing and praising the King, how He cares about the well-being of all the people in the country. This is the meaning of "It is forbidden to come into the King's gate wearing sackcloth," which is a dirty garment.

Rather, when coming into the King's gate, one should be dressed with clothes that befit sitting at the King's gate. Otherwise, when he is sitting wearing sackcloth, it is a sign that he is not happy with the King, but is rather sitting and mourning what he is missing in life and has no peace of mind. It follows that he sits and mourns, and he is in contempt of the King for the King not having mercy on him and not satisfying his wish.

Instead, when one engages in Torah and *Mitzvot*, he should believe above reason that what he has is very important, and that he is unworthy of more, but should be content with little and be happy with his lot, that despite the small amount that He has given him, he has a grip on spirituality, meaning small in quality and small in quantity.

From everything, a person should be happy, meaning with any extent of grip on spirituality that he may have. He believes that he was given this from above, that this, too, is not "my strength and the might of my hand." Naturally, he can adhere to the Creator to the extent called "the blessed clings to the blessed."

This is the meaning of what our sages said (*Shabbat* 30), "The *Shechina* [Divinity] is present only through the joy of *Mitzva* [good deed/commandment]," as it was said, "And now, take me a musician, and he was as a playing musician and the hand of the Lord shall be upon him." Rav Yehuda said, "So it is with words of the law." That is, *Dvekut* [adhesion] must be equivalence of form. It follows that when a person feels that he is cursed, there is no place for *Dvekut*. We should interpret why Rav Yehuda said, "So it is with the words of the law." It is known that *Halacha* [law] is called *Hakalah* [the bride], which pertains to the acceptance of the Kingdom of Heaven.

That is, the acceptance of the Kingdom of Heaven, which is above reason, is called "the joy of *Mitzva*."

And there is a higher degree, called "the instilling of the *Shechina*," and it all comes through joy. Otherwise, it turns out that it is specifically the blessed who cling to the blessed. But if he feels that he is cursed, he cannot cling to the blessed. Naturally, in that state he remains lifeless.

It therefore follows that when we say, "Blessed are You, O Lord, who hears a prayer," it means that we are thanking the Creator for hearing the prayer. But when a person is deficient, for otherwise he has no room for prayer, he is in a state of "cursed." Thus, how can he have *Dvekut* with the Creator during the prayer? Moreover, if he is deficient, what is he thanking Him for?

The answer to this is that by believing that He hears the prayer, we already have joy because He will certainly save us. It follows he already has joy about the prayer, for even when he is confident, he must work above reason that the Creator will help him and he will be able to immediately be rewarded with *Dvekut*, since the confidence itself gives him wholeness and he is already called "blessed," and as said above, the blessed cling to the blessed.

However, precisely when a person asks the Creator to bring him closer, the evil inclination comes and lets him understand that the Creator is not hearing his prayer. It does not let him trust in the Creator's help, and brings him several proofs and says, "Look back and see how many times you have already prayed and thought that the Creator was helping you, only to later remain bare and destitute? This happens to you every time, and each time you say, 'Now the Creator is certainly hearing me and I'll be permanently adhered to spirituality.' You tell me, what happens afterwards? You fell again into the place of lowliness and sank into greater self-love than before you prayed. Therefore, why are you now so sure that now the Creator will hear you that you are already so thankful to the Creator that you say, 'Blessed are You, O Lord, Who hears a prayer'?"

What can a person reply to the body when it brings him evidence from the past that his prayer was not granted? Based on what does a person want to tell it that this is not so, but that I believe above reason that now I am certain that the Creator will answer my prayer?

The answer is that since the whole foundation is built on above reason, and man must observe this *Mitzva*, therefore, the evidence from the past that you are bringing me—that my prayer was not granted and this is why there is no reason to trust in the Creator that my prayer will be accepted this time—you bring me evidence from the past in order to weaken my power of faith.

But I am telling you that specifically now I can say that I believe and trust above reason because you bring evidence only from within reason. I thank you very much for the questions you are asking me and for the proofs, for you are giving me a place on which to build the above reason. Therefore, now I am continuing with great joy for the opportunity to observe the *Mitzva* of faith and confidence above reason.

It therefore follows that from the same place where the body comes to weaken him from the joy that he has from the prayer, and his confidence that the Creator will now answer his prayer, a person needs to bring the power for faith above reason. That is, on the place of reason there is now an opportunity to place the above reason. If the reason did not bring him the opposite, how could he say that he is going above it?

Therefore, a person must always say that each time, he is given descents from above so as to have room to go above reason, so in any case, the body cannot weaken the faith and confidence that he has during the prayer when the body resists his thanking the Creator and saying, "Blessed are You, O Lord, Who hears a prayer." The body argues, "How do you know that the Creator will answer your prayer that you are thanking Him?"

It cannot be said that he is thankful to the Creator for answering others. He thanks Him for this and says to Him: "Blessed are You," when a person normally blesses for what he has obtained by himself, and not that he is thankful for others. And in general, how does one know what is in the heart of one's friend?

Rather, a person thanks the Creator for himself, and also says to the body, "Thank you for coming to me with correct arguments, since now I have room to work above reason." This is called "right line," "wholeness," and this is the main road on which a person must walk. From here a person draws vitality, for then he is on the degree of "blessed." This is called "The blessed clings to the blessed."

However, a person cannot walk on one leg, called "right leg," which is wholeness. He also needs another leg, which is the left leg. "Left" means something that requires correction, where there is a deficiency that needs to be corrected. It is as our sages said (*Sotah* 47), "Our sages said, 'The left should always reject, and the right brings closer.'"

We should interpret this according to our way that "right" is when he works in a way of "the right brings closer," meaning that it brings him closer to *Kedusha* [sanctity/holiness]. He looks and sees how he is close to spirituality, and with every portion, when he sees that he is close to *Kedusha*, even if by a tiny grip, he is happy and thanks the Creator for it, and does not look at the negative.

"The left rejects" is when he is walking on the left leg. At that time he is looking only at the rejections, how much he is rejected and removed from *Kedusha* in both quantity and quality. This means that these two ways are completely opposite to one another, from one end to the other. For this reason, right is called *Hesed* [mercy], as it is known that the right line is mercy, and it is also called "day," as it is written, "In the day, the Lord commands His mercy."

The thing is that one who walks on the "right" looks only at the mercy that the Creator is doing with everyone, and how he himself is receiving mercy from the Creator. He thanks the Creator for all the receptions of mercy, and naturally lives in a day that is all good, for when he feels the mercies that the Creator is doing with him, he rejoices and has something for which to thank the Creator.

However, when he wants to walk on the left leg, too, concerning the "left," we learned that the left rejects. This means that when he criticizes his actions—if something requires correction—this is the time to see only rejections: how he is repelled from spirituality and all his thoughts, words, and actions are immersed in self-love. He does not see any possibility that he will be able to exit the body's control, which controls him with all its might.

Moreover, as soon as he begins to think that it is not worthwhile to remain in a state of reception, the body promptly comes to him with stronger arguments than the body usually said when he did not want to obey it but wanted to work in order to bestow, since now the body has become shrewder and asks more poignant questions.

He asks himself: "How come before I started to work harder and with greater effort in the holy work the body was not that clever, and now that I have begun to do the holy work I understood that the good side of a person should be smarter and more clever, and more energetic because I have engaged in holy work?"

According to the rule, "A *Mitzva* [good deed/commandment] induces a *Mitzva*," I understood that the body grows weaker. That is, the arguments it had thus far ceased and it had no strength to argue because the *Kedusha* was strengthened by the good deeds that I was doing all the time in holy work. But now I see the opposite: The body has become smarter and presents stronger and more sensible arguments.

But what despairs him most is that it says it would be better for him to stop this work called "working in order to bestow," and be like the rest of the people, without looking to be extraordinary, meaning to return to the normal state. That is, it is enough for us to observe Torah and *Mitzvot* without intentions, and we need to give all our energy to observing Torah and *Mitzvot* more meticulously, since this is easier than the aim to bestow.

Especially, I see that compared to those who want to be extraordinary, ordinary people engage more meticulously with Torah and *Mitzvot* than other people, and this awards them titles.

One is called "righteous," another is called *Hassid* [pious], and another is called "A very important person." So why should he walk into the path of for the Creator instead of for his own benefit?

In that state, a person needs great mercy in order not to escape the campaign. One has no way out of this situation unless through faith above reason, and to say that the body has now become very clever because it is given from above a sensation of what is reason so it will now be possible for him to go above reason.

"Reason" means reason that comes from an external mind. Externality is the original will to receive, in which there is no bestowal. The "inner reason" is reason that dresses in the inner *Kelim* [vessels], which is *Bina*, whose origin is bestowal and who has no reception in her whatsoever. For this reason, the external mind does not understand that there is a reality of a desire to bestow. Hence, when a person awakens to do something in order to bestow, it immediately stands against him like an experienced warrior and begins to subdue a person with great craftiness.

Do not be surprised, since the verse says that the evil inclination is called an "old and foolish king." So why do we say that it is clever? We should ask a different question about this: "How can it be said that an angel, who is spiritual, is a fool, as it is written in *The Zohar* about the verse, 'For He will command His angels to you to guard you in all your ways'?" It interprets "His angels" to mean two angels: the good inclination and the evil inclination. If the evil inclination is called an "angel," how can it be a fool? We must interpret that an angel is named after the action, as it is written (Judges 13), "And the angel of the Lord said unto him, 'Why do you ask for my name, for it is wondrous?'"

This means that the name of the angel changes according to the mission it was sent to do. It follows that the action determines its name.

Accordingly, we should say that the evil inclination is called a "fool" because it tries to make man do foolish things, and they make people fools with great cleverness. Therefore, when a person begins to overcome and does not want to listen to it, it must show the person more cleverly that it is right. And when a person overcomes the arguments of the evil inclination, the evil inclination must come to him with even cleverer arguments, so that one cannot defeat it unless through faith above reason and to say that reason is meaningless and that he is going above reason.

However, if a person overcomes the external reason, which is making just arguments, he gains that each time, his faith grows to a higher degree than what he had prior to the coming of the evil inclination with its reasoning that it is not worthwhile to exit self-love. Because the reason of the evil inclination grows each time, one has no other choice—if he wants to remain in *Kedusha*—but to draw upon himself greater faith. That is, each time he becomes more needy of the Creator to help him be saved from his evil. This means that one should not pray that the foreign thoughts will die but that they will repent.

This is done specifically by receiving help from above in the form of faith above reason. It follows that he is not asking the Creator that the thoughts will die so he will not have to overcome the thoughts, but rather to settle for the faith he has in the Creator, that to the extent of the faith he has before the evil inclination came with its correct arguments, and which could not be answered without the help of the Creator, he receives the strength to go above reason.

But one who is not walking on the path of truth, whose work is based entirely on a foundation of mind and heart, asks the Creator to take these thoughts away from him so they will not disrupt his work. It follows that he remains in his degree and cannot advance, since he has no need to advance. Instead, he wants to remain in the current state permanently, this is all he expects, and he has no need for greatness.

Although he wants higher degrees than the rest of the people, meaning, if he is a wise disciple and knows that there are people who are not nearly at his level, and of course he wants to be at the top in the work, for this reason he wants to rise to a higher level than where he feels he is right now. However, this is all in excess; it is not necessity. One who prays for surplus, his prayer cannot be from the bottom of the heart because he knows that his situation is not so bad. He sees that there are people who are worse than he, and he needs it only as a surplus.

The rule is that "There is no light without a *Kli* [vessel]," and a *Kli* means a lack and a need that he must satisfy. Surplus, however, is not regarded as a lack in spirituality, and for this reason a person stays where he is and cannot move at all.

However, it is not so for one who wishes to walk on the path of truth, who wants to work in mind and heart. When the body comes to him and begins to attack him over why he wants to veer off from the common way, that everyone works in order to receive, and after each time he overcomes it, it comes to him with stronger arguments, in that state he does not ask the Creator to take away its arguments, but rather asks the Creator to repent on all those arguments that the wicked one is presenting, meaning that the Creator will give him the strength to go above reason.

It follows that his asking the Creator to give him more strength is not because of surplus, but simply that he wants to be a Jew who believes in the Creator, and it brings him thoughts that slander the path of the Creator and everything related to *Kedusha*. That is, whenever he wants to do something in order to bestow, it immediately comes to him with the arguments of the wicked, who mock the servants of the Creator, as it is written, "Not to us, O Lord, not to us, but to Your name give glory, for why should the nations say..."

Therefore, the reason that each time he wants greater powers from above is necessity: He is asking for help to be saved from death, to enter life, for "The wicked in their lives are called 'dead.'" And since it wants to put him in the camp of the wicked with its arguments, it follows that he is not asking the Creator's help so He will give him luxuries, but simply for his soul, so he will not be wicked.

It therefore follows that a person always benefits from the questions of the wicked by giving him a need to ask the Creator to grant his heart's wishes favorably, meaning to be good and not bad. Such a prayer is called a "prayer from the bottom of the heart." It is received above immediately since it is regarded as a "prayer of the poor," as it is written in *The Zohar* about the verse, "A prayer for the poor when he is weak," where it says that the prayer of the poor delays all the prayers since its prayer is received before all other prayers.

The reason is that to him, this is not luxury, but he simply wants to live and not be as one who is dead, for the wicked in their lives are called "dead." This is the meaning of what is written, "The Lord is near to all who call upon Him in truth."

We should interpret that the Lord is near to save those who seek, who want to walk on the path of truth called "for the sake of the Creator."

That is, they see that they cannot overcome self-love and work in order to bestow, and ask the Creator to help them overcome the body. That is, they ask the Creator for only one thing—to be able to do something for the Creator, to be able to say wholeheartedly, "Blessed is our God, who has created us for His glory," and not for the sake of the body.

Now we can understand what our sages said, "There are three partners in a person: the Creator, his father, and his mother. His father gives the white."

"White" is called the "right line," which is regarded as white, meaning that there is no stain or flaw there, but only wholeness. However, as said above, the wholeness is from the perspective of importance. That is, he sees that he has faults, but how does he know that he has faults? It comes from his mother, who is called "left line," meaning that she is in the form of "the left rejects," which is regarded as *Nukva* [female], a deficiency.

When he examines his spiritual state, he sees that he does not have all the desirable intentions, meaning that they will all be in order to bestow. Rather, he sees how he is immersed in self-love. Moreover, he sees that it is impossible for a person to come out of this control, but only the Creator can deliver him from exile, as it was in the redemption from Egypt. It is written about it, "I the Lord," and our sages explained, "I and not a messenger." That is, only the Creator can deliver the enslavement of self-love, called "the land of Egypt," for *Eretz* [land] comes from the [Hebrew] word *Ratzon* [desire]. In other words, the will to receive wants only to restrain the *Kedusha*, and this is called "the land of Egypt."

For this reason, once he has started with the right line, which is wholeness, and he should certainly thank and praise the King for giving him wholeness in the importance, as it is written, "Therefore, we must thank You and praise and be grateful to Your name. Happy are we; how fortunate we are. We are happy when we rise and in the evening in synagogues and in seminaries" (prior to reading the "Shema of Offerings").

Afterward, we move to the left line, called "deficiency." Meaning, it is called "mother," female, who indicates lacks, meaning the real measure of his rejection from the desire to bestow. That is, he sees how each time he wants to place the intention to bestow on the act, the body repels him and he cannot overcome it.

In that state, there is room for prayer to the Creator to help him overcome. Subsequently, he returns to the right line and says that he has wholeness and a great privilege, at least with regard to actions. Although the service he is doing for the King is out of an intention for self-love, called *Lo Lishma* [not for Her sake], this service is still very important to him because whatever the case may be, he is serving the King in his actions.

And since the King is important to him, he can be happy with the small grip that he has on *Kedusha*. It follows that through the left line, he now receives a way to overcome in the right, and say that he is happy that he can appreciate the little grip he has on *Kedusha*. That is, before he came to the left line, he thought that he really did have wholeness, but it was incomplete wholeness.

Therefore, naturally, I have something for which to praise the King. But now that the left line has let him see that he is remote from wholeness, it follows that now he should be sad and not happy. Still, he braces himself and says, "Since the King is very important, therefore, although I have only a small grip on spirituality, it is still important to me."

It therefore follows that the left line always causes him to observe the greatness and importance of the Creator, or he will have nothing with which to praise the King, for there is nothing more important in spirituality than to have something for which to be thankful. Hence, the right line causes the left line to grow bigger in him each time, and the left line forces the right line to grow, and by this, the lines grow. When they come to a certain measure that it is clear that these two lines are opposite from one another, the Creator gives the soul, and then he comes out from the exile. This is called "He who comes to purify is aided," as in the words of *The Zohar*, that he is given a soul, and this is the help he receives from the Creator.

Now we will explain what we asked about the half shekel and what it implies to us in the work. We should interpret "When you count the heads." When one wants to be a head in *Kedusha* and not a tail, it is as we say on the eve of the new year [*Rosh Hashanah*], "May we be the head and not the tail." A tail means that he himself has no opinion, but he follows the majority without any criticism over what he does, meaning that he wants to be independent and understand for himself the purpose of his actions. Certainly, after the work, we receive reward. But what reward does he expect in return for his work? Is it true what he has heard from his tutors, who explained to him that it is better to relinquish rest—both bodily rest and the rest of the intellect—and engage in Torah and *Mitzvot*, for by this he will receive reward? Why is this a reward? They gave him many examples of reward, that it is certainly worthwhile to make an effort in order to be rewarded with this reward. Or, there is a higher and more sublime reward. They showed him examples of reward only suitable to his being a beginner in the work. If he were shown a higher reward than the one they said to him, he would not understand the benefit of the reward due to the smallness of his mind. Therefore, now he must scrutinize and see if this is really the reward that he had heard from them, or should he go and ask what is really the reward he should receive in return for his work?

Moreover, now he wants to know what is really the exertion that he needs to make, and what is this matter of exertion, meaning if observing Torah and *Mitzvot* in practice is enough in and of itself or is an intention required, too. That is, do I also need to know why I am doing the act, and not because I am doing these actions because I see that there are others who are doing, and they are the leaders of the people so I want to do as they do. Rather, I want to know if it is possible to know the aim of Torah and *Mitzvot*, or is there no one in the world who has a clue what are Torah and *Mitzvot*, more understanding, more feeling than little children when they assume the burden of Torah and *Mitzvot*. That is, although the children grow up, become famous in the greatness of the Torah, this is only with respect to the revealed Torah. That is, they have more knowledge of how and in what way the revealed actions should be done. But in the actual greatness of Torah and *Mitzvot* they add nothing.

This means that all the greatness is only in the externality of the Torah and *Mitzvot*, but to have something internal, no one in the world has a clue.

Or, perhaps there are people for whom the internality that is in the Torah and *Mitzvot* was added. He wants to know its interior, meaning what special intention there is in each and every *Mitzva* [commandment]. He heard or saw what is written in *The Zohar* (presented in the *Sulam* commentary, Part 1), which says that the *Mitzvot* in the Torah are called in *The Zohar* by the name "613 deposits," and they are also called "613 counsels." The difference between them is that in everything there is anterior and posterior. A preparation for something is called "posterior," and attainment of the matter is called "anterior."

Likewise, in Torah and *Mitzvot* there is "we will do" and "we will hear," as our sages wrote (*Shabbat* 88), "Doers of His word, to listen to the voice of His words. In the beginning, they do, and afterwards, they hear. The *Mitzvot* are called by the name '613 counsels,' and they are the posterior. When one is rewarded with hearing the voice of His word, the 613 *Mitzvot* become deposits, from the word 'deposit.' This is so because there are 613 *Mitzvot*, and in each *Mitzva* the light of a special degree is deposited, corresponding to a unique organ in the 613 organs and tendons of the soul and the body."

By this we can interpret "When you count the heads of the children of Israel." That is, when you awaken to be the head and not the tail, as was written above, the children of Israel, when he wants to understand what is *Yashar-El* [straight to the Creator] by their numbers, meaning the *Mitzvot* as deposits. It is written about it, "Each of them shall give a ransom for his soul when you count them." Counting means calculating, counting how much he knows about the intention of Torah and *Mitzvot*, and the measure of his nearing the Creator by observing Torah and *Mitzvot*. At that time he can fall into despair and escape from the war. This is called a "flaw." To correct this, the children of Israel were blessed first, and then Israel are blessed once more in the end, and there was no flaw in them. It is as it is written (*Ki Tissa*, Item 2), "Come and see; they established that there is no blessing above for something that is counted. It follows that in the beginning, Israel are blessed when receiving the ransom. Afterward, Israel are blessed again."

(And in Item 3) It asks, "Why is a plague [also "flaw"] appearing because of the count?" It replies, "It is because there is no blessing in what is counted. And since the blessing disappears, the *Sitra Achra* is on it." We should understand why there is no blessing on something that is counted. According to what we explained above, that the blessed cling to the blessed, for this reason, when a person begins to enter the left line, to examine if he already understands everything with his reason, meaning if he already feels that he is progressing in the work, and if he really has faith and confidence that the Creator will help him be rewarded with spirituality and will not remain in his lowliness, during the criticism, opposite thoughts and calculations come to him, from what he would like to see. That is, when he begins to contemplate if the effort he has made in order to be rewarded with some spirituality is worthwhile, and if he is walking on the path of truth, then he can see the truth better than the rest of the people. He sees his real situation, that he is actually far from *Kedusha*, and he begins to doubt the beginning. That is, he has exerted in vain because now he sees according to his reason that it is a shame to waste time for nothing.

In other words, before he began to walk on the path of truth, he had better thoughts about spirituality. He was not so materialistic, meaning he did not find such good tastes in corporeal things. But now that he has begun the work of bestowal, he has received more lust for corporeal lusts because he finds more pleasure in them.

It follows that according to this calculation, he doubts the beginning. That is, now he has greater regret for his current work, called "bestowal," that he has left the previous work. He was satisfied with actions and felt utterly complete because he knew that the act was the most important, and there is no need to reflect on the intention. He also had assistance from our sages, who said, "It is not the learning that is the most important, but the act," and in actions, he was complete. Naturally, he did everything gladly because he felt that he was a complete person. Should the Creator punish him, he understands that perhaps he deserves the punishment because he did not put a lot of efforts into the commandment, "Reprove your neighbor," as our sages said, "Anyone who can protest and does not protest is punished for it" (*Shabbat* 54). It is only in this that he feels that he has been lazy with this *Mitzva*.

This is what he always thought. But now that he has begun to work on the way of in order to bestow, he sees the evil that exists in him more than ever. Therefore, why should he continue in this way. For this reason, now he is in a state of "cursed," and "The cursed does not cling to the blessed." It follows that now he is regarded as dead because he has parted from the Life of Lives, and this is regarded as death, called "plague."

By this we can interpret the reason why there is no blessing in something that is counted, and "since the blessing disappears, the *Sitra Achra* is on it" and it can harm. Something that counted is regarded as a person beginning to count the gains he has made in spirituality. At that time he sees the opposite; he feels that he has only lost. The *Sitra Achra* always brings him proof that it is better for him to escape the campaign and he regrets every day that he has exerted in vain, for this path is not for him. It therefore follows that the person cannot do anything in the right way. It follows that on the left line, called "counting," there is danger of death.

If one can be in one line, meaning walking on the path he walked on before he chose to work in order to bestow, when he knew that only actions were required, and not intentions, for a person is not demanded from above to work with intentions, unless he can observe the *Mitzvot*, this is really wholeness for him and he need not think about intentions. However, from this he will never reach the truth, for the truth is that every act should be for the sake of the Creator.

It is likewise, in a state of counting, when he is going to calculate if he has gained from the exertion he has put thus far into the work of the Creator, and wants to see the truth. There is great danger here because when he sees that he is not progressing in the work, he might regress from the work and come to a state called "pondering the beginning."

For this reason, *The Zohar* says that there was a correction there "that they did not count before all of that ransom was collected and counted. It follows that first, Israel are blessed when receiving the ransom, and then Israel are blessed again. It follows that Israel were blessed in the beginning and in the end, and there was no plague in them."

By what is said in the words of *The Zohar*, we can understand the advice that we can give when wanting to walk on the path toward being rewarded with *Dvekut* with the Creator. According to the rule that there is no light without a *Kli* because there is no filling without a lack, and a lack means a need, and the need must be from the bottom of the heart, to feel what he needs as necessity and not as luxury, when a person feels a lack, he is in a state of "cursed," and the cursed does not cling to the blessed. In a state of blessed, a person feels that he has wholeness and no lacks at all. Otherwise, he is not regarded as whole. But if he is in wholeness and has no lack, then he has no need—called a *Kli*—for the Creator to satisfy.

To this comes the answer that Israel were blessed before the count and after the count, and for this reason there could not be a plague in Israel. The thing is that blessing means that the order of man's admission to the work begins with the right. That is, he should appreciate the service he is giving to the Creator by observing the commandments of the Creator. To the extent that he appreciates the greatness of the Creator, he rejoices in being rewarded with doing what the Creator commanded.

This matter of appreciating the great one is in our nature. We see that it is regarded as a great honor, if there is someone who is the greatest in the generation and people regard him as an important person. Everyone wants to serve him.

However, the satisfaction in the service depends on the greatness and importance that the world attributes to this great person. It follows that when one feels and depicts to himself that he is serving the Creator, he feels that he is blessed, and then comes the rule that the blessed clings to the blessed.

It follows that in such a state a person feels himself as the happiest in the world. This is the time when he needs to thank the Creator for giving him the little service that he served Him. It follows that in that state he is adhered to the Creator because there is joy in him, as our sages said, "The *Shechina* [Divinity] is present only out of joy." Yet, at the same time, he still does not have a *Kli* so as to have a need for the Creator to truly bring him closer, meaning that his intention will be only to bestow, called *Lishma* [for Her sake]. And in order to achieve *Lishma*, a person must have a desire and need. But on the right line, where he feels wholeness, there is no place for a lack.

Therefore, he must switch to the left line, regarded as counting and calculating, to see with his own mind if he really wants to be a servant of the Creator and not serving himself. That is, in everything he does, he has no other thought but his own benefit. At that time, he sees the truth, meaning the left rejects. He sees that he is unable to do anything for the Creator.

To the extent that he felt wholeness in the right and felt good about himself, delighted that he was serving the Creator, to that extent he feels bad about himself when he sees that he is in a state of remoteness from the work of the Creator. That is, now everything is black, to the point where he has no hope of emerging from this control. At that time he can pray, and then he is in a state called "cursed," "dead," "wicked," for he sees that he cannot work for the sake of the Creator.

In order not to have a flaw, since regarding something that is counted, there is not a righteous man on earth who does good and does not sin, he always finds flaws. He must shift to the right line, and then he needs additional overcoming in greatness of the Creator so as to be able to say that he is happy that he has some grip on the work of the Creator, since it is a very important thing to serve the King. For this reason, although it is a tiny grip, still, with respect to importance, I regarded it as a great thing. The fact that the grip on *Kedusha* has now become smaller is because of the left line, for he saw that he was in utter lowliness. Hence, now it is difficult for him to say the opposite—that he has wholeness. But the truth is that when he says he has wholeness, it is only because of the importance of the greatness of the King, according to the rule that when something is of very high quality, even a small amount of the great quality is more important than a great amount of the low quality.

It therefore turns out that each time, he must increase the right by way of above reason, and always say that as much as he assumes the greatness and importance of the Creator, and that it is worthwhile to be thankful for a small amount, he should glorify and praise the King even more for letting him serve Him just a little. It is as it is written (in *The Soul of Every Living Being*), "We do not thank You enough, the Lord our God."

It turns out that by returning to the right line, where there is work in wholeness, called "blessed," and then returning once again to counting and calculating, and then above reason once again, where there is no place for intellectual calculations, this is called "blessing before the count, and blessing after the count." This is the correction that there will be no flaw in them, that he will not remain in lowliness and will despair and escape the campaign forever.

This is the meaning of "half a shekel in the shekel of holiness." It means that the work of holiness, to weigh the work, to give half the work called "right," which is blessed, as ransom to the Creator, saying that now he is working entirely for the Creator and he has no lack in him, so naturally, I can praise and thank the Creator, and I feel that I am blessed, clinging to the blessed, this is the ransom that he will not remain in the lowliness of the left, called "cursed" and is regarded as separation from the Creator.

The other half of the work is in the left. This is as *The Zohar* says, that there must be a blessing prior to the counting. This means that before a person walks on the left line, called "counting," he must be in a state of "right," called "blessed." Afterward it is repeated, and naturally there will be no flaw when they count them, meaning when he wants to be rewarded with the *Mitzvot* being for him as 613 deposits. This is the meaning of what is written, "The rich shall not pay more and the poor shall not pay less than the half shekel."

"Rich" means "right"—one who is walking on the path of wholeness without lacking anything. Rather, he is delighted with whatever he has. This is why it is said, "The rich shall not pay more than half a shekel." That is, that he will not walk on the right all the time, but should also shift to the left, called "counting" and "calculating."

"The poor shall not pay less." "Poor" means that he has nothing, for when he begins to count and calculate his work, whether it is for the sake of the Creator or for his own sake, he sees that he has nothing with which to say that he is doing this for the sake of the

Creator. This is why it is said that the poor shall not pay much less than half. That is, he must shift to the right, which is blessing and wholeness. However, the work should be balanced. These two lines should be equal so that each of them will increase the other.

This is the meaning of what is written, "to atone for your souls." Specifically by those two, which are opposite to one another, atonement comes, the soul comes out of the control of the exile, where the nations of the world control Israel with the power of self-love. By this they will be rewarded with a head of *Kedusha*, and will not be as a tail.

This is the meaning of what is written, "There are three partners in a person ... His father sows the white." That is, from the right side, called "his father," "male," and male is regarded as wholeness, and wholeness is regarded as white, without any dirt. The mother is called *Nukva* [female]. She sows the red. Here we see a place of danger that we must correct.

Afterward, the Creator gives the soul, since out of the two above lines emerges a *Kli* suitable to receive the flow of abundance. At that time we can say that it is regarded as "He who comes to purify." This comes after he walks on the two above-mentioned two lines, and then "He is aided with a holy soul."

Why the Festival of Matzot Is Called Passover

Article No. 13, Tav-Shin-Mem-Zayin, 1986-87

There is a question: Why do we call the good day, which is called in the Torah "Festival of *Matzot* [unleavened bread]," "Passover" (*Kedushat Levi*, Bo). The answer is because it is written, "I am for my Beloved and my Beloved is for me." That is, we praise the Creator and the Creator praises Israel. This is why this good day is called in the Torah, the "Festival of *Matzot*." It is as though the Creator praises Israel, meaning that Israel and I call the good day by the name "Passover," as it is written, "And you shall say, 'It is a Passover offering to the Lord, who passed over the houses of the children of Israel in Egypt when He smote the Egyptians, and spared our homes.'"

We likewise find in the war of Midian (Numbers 31:2-3), "And the Lord spoke to Moses saying, 'Avenge the vengeance for the children of Israel on the Midianites.' And Moses spoke to the people, saying, 'Bring out men from among you for an army, that they may go against Midian to execute the Lord's vengeance on Midian.'" We should understand why the Creator said to Moses that the war against Midian is the vengeance of the children of Israel, and Moses said to the people the opposite of what the Creator had told him: He said that the war against Midian was the Lord's vengeance. We should explain this in the same manner: The Creator praised Israel, that it is the vengeance of the children of Israel, and Moses praised the Creator before Israel. This is why he changed what the Creator had said to him.

However, we should also understand what does it mean that the Creator praises Israel and the people of Israel praise the Creator. Are we speaking of flesh and blood people, where each one respects the other? Can you imagine that the Creator needs to be respected? I already said an allegory about this: It is like a man walking into a hen-house, and since he heard what our sages said (*Shabbat* 113a), "Rabbi Yochanan called his garments 'My honorers'" (meaning that when a person wears dignified clothes he is respected). For this reason, since he wants the hens to respect him, he wears nice clothes. Clearly, anyone who sees him doing this will laugh at him because what honor can one receive from hens?

Accordingly, how can we say that the Creator wants us to respect and praise Him? Evidently, the Creator is not even similar to our allegory, since the distance between a human and a hen is only one degree, for chickens are animals and we are regarded as speaking, but it is all corporeality. But what distance is there between us and the Creator that you can say that the Creator is impressed by our praise, and that this is why Moses changed the words of the Creator, who said, "Avenge the vengeance of the children of Israel," and he said to Israel, "the Lord's vengeance"?

To understand the above, we must remember the purpose of creation, which—as our sages said—is to do good to His creations. In order for the benefit that He wishes to impart upon the creatures to be complete, meaning so that there will be no shame in it, there was a correction called "concealment." Accordingly, while a person is still unable to do all his work in order to bestow, only when he corrects his actions and exits self-love, to that extent he exits the darkness and enters the light. This is called "coming out from darkness to light," for then all of his receptions are only because he wants to impart pleasure upon the Creator by helping Him carry out His goal, which is unbounded bestowal, meaning a gift without any shame upon reception of the pleasure from the Creator.

By this we will understand why the Creator praises Israel. That is, the Creator wants to do good to His creations; this is why He praises Israel, for the intention is to benefit Israel. From this, the will to receive was created in the creatures, who want to receive in order to receive. This is regarded as wanting to receive because of self-love, since due to the will to receive that the Creator created in the creatures, they crave to receive abundance in order to satisfy the need that the craving causes them, which is why they receive. This is called "in order to receive."

However, from this extends separation due to disparity of form. For this reason, the people of Israel take upon themselves the *Tzimtzum* [restriction]—not to receive delight and pleasure despite their craving. Nevertheless, they do not want to receive unless they know that they can aim to receive the pleasure in order to bestow. This means that since He desires to give, this is why they receive the abundance. But as far as their own benefit, they relinquish the pleasures. It follows that the people of Israel are praising the Creator. That is, they relinquish their own will and engage only in praising the King, meaning that which the King wants, they do.

This is why Moses changed what the Creator had said, "Avenge the vengeance of Israel." The Creator said what Israel should do only for Israel's benefit, but Moses changed what the Creator had told him, but this is not regarded as deviating from the purpose of benefiting His creations. Rather, the reason for the change was also to do good. Additionally, it was not because it is impossible for Israel to receive the benefit of delight and pleasure unless they aim their actions only to benefit the Creator. This is regarded as all their actions being only because of the praise of the Creator, meaning due to the fear of sublimity, which is because of the greatness and importance of the King.

However, we should understand why the praise of the Creator is called "Passover," after the Creator's passing over. It is also written, "and you shall eat it in haste; it is the Lord's Passover." RASHI interprets that the offering is called Passover after the passing over, and the passing over is that the Creator skipped over the houses of Israel from among the houses of the Egyptians. He would jump from Egyptian to Egyptian, and Israel in the middle escaped.

We should understand the meaning of skipping and passing over in the work. It is known that the essence of our work is to achieve *Dvekut* [adhesion] with the Creator, which is equivalence of form, by which we receive *Kelim* [vessels] that are suitable for reception of the abundance. It is also known that our *Kelim* come from the breaking of the vessels. The breaking of the vessels means that we want to use the vessels of reception in order to receive, and this is regarded as separation from the Creator. This occurred in the upper worlds, and also through the sin of the tree of knowledge, when the *Kelim* fell into the *Klipot* [shells/peels], and we must elevate them because we come from their *Kelim*. By working with our desires to receive—which come from there—in order to bestow, we correct each time a piece of these *Kelim*, which are in the *Klipot*, and raise them to *Kedusha* [holiness/sanctity] by wanting to work only with the aim to bestow contentment upon the Creator.

Each time and each day, pieces of the *Klipot*—called "in order to receive"—are sorted. They are corrected so they can be used in order to bestow. The order is that a piece is elevated to *Kedusha*, and then we come down to a state of reception once again, and even forget that there is the matter of bestowal. But then we receive an ascent once more, take the part of the will to receive in us, overcome it, and correct it to work in order to bestow. This repeats itself each time until we acquire a certain measure of reception that has received the correction of bestowal. To that extent, there will be room for the upper abundance to enter. This *Kli* [vessel] is made by adding all the ascents that one had into one *Kli*, as it is written, "Penny by penny joins into a great amount" (*Sotah* 8).

Why the Festival of Matzot Is Called Passover

By this we can interpret what we asked about Passover, that our sages said, "He would jump from Egyptian to Egyptian, and Israel in the middle escaped." This means that every descent is called "Egyptian," meaning he receives everything for self-love. "Israel in the middle" is an ascent, when he overcomes and does everything in order to bestow and not for his own sake. That state is called "Israel." But afterwards he descends once more. It follows that he descends once more into being an Egyptian, and so on and so forth. "And Israel ... escaped" means that he escaped from the Egyptians and became Israel.

In order for a person to have a complete *Kli* that can receive within it upper abundance, the Creator jumps from Egyptian to Egyptian, meaning He takes into account only the Israel that is between each two Egyptians and joins them into a great amount. It is as though there is no interruption between Israel and Israel. Skips over the Egyptian means that it is as though the Egyptian does not exist in reality. For this reason, all the Israelites are joined into a great amount until he has a complete *Kli*.

Accordingly, we should interpret what is written there, that He skipped over the houses of Israel and only the Egyptians were killed. It is as RASHI interprets, He passed over, meaning jumped from Egyptian to Egyptian, and Israel in the middle escaped. This means that all the Egyptians were killed, and only the Israelite, who were in the middle, in between the Egyptians, stayed alive. The literal meaning is that all the descents that are between the ascents were erased, and only ascents remained.

This is as though they never had descents, since they were erased. This is the meaning of the Egyptians being killed. Hence, now it is possible for all their ascents to connect and become one state.

There are many discernments in the will to receive that was corrected into working in order to bestow and become one complete *Kli* for reception of the light of redemption, called the "exodus from Egypt," when they were liberated from the exile in Egypt, enslaved to self-love, called the "*Klipa* of Egypt," as it is written, "and He brought out His people, Israel, from among them, to eternal freedom."

Had the descents remained, there would be interruptions between each two ascents due to the descent in the middle. But when the descents disappear we should look only at the ascents, and then we can speak of the *Kli* that will be fit to receive the light of redemption.

For this reason, we should learn that one should not focus on the descents, when he always falls from his spiritual state. Rather, he should focus on the ascents. Therefore, when he sees that he is in a state of lowliness, he must not despair. Instead, he must overcome above reason and rise again. He must not look at the past and say, "Since until now I thought that I had already understood that it is not worthwhile to focus on self-love," still he sees that he soon suffers a descent. Therefore, a person asks, "What's the point of ascending if I must keep falling? What do I gain by this?"

To this comes the answer: "And the children of Israel sighed from the work, and their cry rose up to the Lord." That is, there was an awakening from below. Then the Creator killed the Egyptians and the Israelites remained and joined into a great amount, meaning because of all the ascents that they had one at a time, they had a big *Kli* in which to receive the abundance.

It therefore follows that no good deed of a person is lost. For this reason, we must not say, "How do the ascents help me if I lose them right away?" This would be true if he could hang on to them henceforth and not descend. But it was said about this, "Who will climb up the mountain of the Lord?" This is one discernment.

The other discernment is "And who will rise in the place of His holiness?" To this comes the answer, "He who is of clean hands and a pure heart," meaning one who has been rewarded with clean hands and has no more self-love in him, but his only intention is to bestow. "A pure heart" means that his heart is with the Creator, that faith is fixed in his heart. These people have no descent in the degrees of lowliness, but all their ascents and descents are in spiritual degrees. Since we should attain complete degrees, called NRNHY de Nefesh and NRNHY de Ruach, their ascents and descents are all in the King's palace, and not outside the King's palace, and they are not thrown down to the place of darkness and the shadow of death.

However, at the same time we must know that no ascent is lost. Rather, "penny by penny joins into a great amount." For this reason, a person should be happy when he feels that spirituality is desirable to him and he wishes to come as close as possible to the Creator. He considers it a great privilege that an awakening from above has suddenly come to him, and he begins to look at self-love as loathsome and not worth living for, and yearns only for spirituality.

Yet, one should know that he should not say, "When I have an awakening from above, I will begin to do the holy work." Rather, the fact that a person remembers that there is spirituality, even if he has no desire for it, he should already be thankful to the Creator for knowing that there is spirituality in the work, though he has no desire for the work.

This is similar to a great king who comes to town but not all the people are told about it. Only a handful of people are informed, and not all of them are permitted to enter, but only a chosen few, and they, too, require much persuasion among the ministers in order to receive the permit to enter.

And this person was informed only that the king has come, but he was not given an entry permit. How is that person thankful to those who notified him?

It is likewise here. He is aware that there is a King in the world, but he was not yet permitted to enter and serve the King. That is, he knows and believes to some extent that there is a Creator to the world, but he has not been granted permission to leave his work and work for the sake of the King. That is, he has not received from above a desire to leave his corporeal engagements and engage in spirituality. That person should be delighted with this knowledge, meaning that he has some faith in the Creator.

If a person appreciates this knowledge although he cannot overcome and engage in serving the Creator, still, the joy from remembering that there is a King in the world can lift him from his lowliness, admit him into the work, and give him a desire to overcome his body. This is so precisely if a person pays attention and values this awareness.

This extends from the root, as our sages said, the *Shechina* [Divinity] is present only out of joy of *Mitzva* [good deed/commandment]" (*Shabbat* 30). This means that the joy he has while performing the *Mitzva* causes him *Dvekut* with the Creator, as said above, "The blessed clings to the blessed," since joy is a result of wholeness.

Since he values the Giver, His importance and greatness, and there is a rule that if the giver of the gift is an important person, even if he gives a small gift, it is still regarded as a great thing. For this reason, from the awareness that he believes that he was notified from above that the King is in town, although he was not permitted to come in and speak with the King, since it is evident that he values the knowledge that the King exists, he is immediately permitted to enter and serve the King. Because they see that he values the King, they treat him with consideration and give him strength to overcome the thoughts and desires of the body.

Accordingly, we can praise joy. That is, because of the joy of being inspired by the importance of the King, he is given from above an illumination that is placed on the *Kli* of joy, which he has given from below as an awakening from below. This causes an awakening from above, and he is given permission, meaning a desire and craving to overcome the thoughts of the body.

It therefore follows that Passover is named after the Creator's passing over the houses of Israel and leaving each and every one from Israel alive. It is known that there is no absence in spirituality, for the smallest discernment in Israel remained alive, and nothing was lost. Because the Creator saved Israel, this good day is called Passover, after the Creator's deeds.

And regarding what we asked about the praise, how can it be said that the Creator wants to be praised and is He impressed by the praise of flesh and blood, there are two answers to this: 1) With respect to the goal, that His desire is to do good to His creations, meaning that all the delight and pleasure that the people of Israel receive, while they receive them, they aim to benefit the Creator, meaning that the Creator will enjoy this because He wants the creatures to receive delight and pleasure. And since they want equivalence of form, when they engage in Torah and Mitzvot, it is only because they want to bestow upon the Creator and not for their own benefit. This is regarded as the people of Israel praising the Creator, that because of the greatness and importance of the Creator, we try to please Him.

The Creator praising Israel means that He wants to give delight and pleasure, which is the purpose of creation, and He also wants that there will be no shame upon receiving the delight and pleasure. For this reason, He wants them to work in order to bestow. It follows that His praising Israel means that the people of Israel relinquish self-love and want to work only in order to bestow.

For this reason, He always focuses on their merit, meaning He counts the works that they do in order to bestow, so that He will be able to bestow abundance and there will be no flaw of shame. He does not speak of what they do in order to receive; He wants to erase this from the face of the Earth, as said in the clarification on the name, "Passover," that He passed over, meaning killed the Egyptians that were between Israel and Israel, and spared the Israel in between. Naturally, He could have focused only on the merit of Israel, meaning on the ascents that they had, which is the merit of Israel, meaning the awakening from below that they did then in baking the Matzot [unleavened bread].

This is why the festival of Matzot and the people of Israel were written in the Torah, since the Creator focused on the merit of Israel while baking Matzot for the sake of the Creator, and did not focus on other things. This is called that the Egyptians who were there, He killed, meaning obliterated them as though they weren't in reality. By this, all of Israel joined into one big degree, which was whole, becoming a *Kli* to receive the abundance. This is regarded as the people of Israel calling that good day "Passover."

Now we can understand the second reason why the people of Israel named it in praise of the Creator. The first reason is His desire to do good to His creations, and their not wanting to receive because of self-love. Therefore, they receive the delight and pleasure because He wants us to receive. This is called "in order to bestow," and this is in praise of the Creator.

The second reason that we praise the Creator is that He did not regard the descents and focused only on the ascents. This is regarded as passing over, where He took all the ascents into account and erased the descents from the face of the Earth. This is the praise of Passover, and this is regarded as speaking in praise of the Creator.

We should understand why it is written, "And you shall eat it in haste; it is the Lord's Passover." Why Passover is called "haste"? According to what RASHI interprets, Passover is called "haste" because the Creator jumped and passed over from Egyptian to Egyptian, and Israel in the middle, escaped. We see that skipping to the end means that He rushed the end, as though it was not yet time. Since he rushed himself, this is why Passover is called "haste." It is as though he had to hurry so that the Egyptians who were among the Israelites would not awaken, as it was still not their time to be corrected. This is why He rushed Himself and saved what He could save. That is, only Israel received correction and not the Egyptians. This is why it is called "haste."

However, it is written concerning the end of correction (Isaiah 52:12), "For you will not go out in haste, nor will you not flee, for the Lord will go before you, and the God of Israel will be your rear guard. Behold, My servant will be enlightened, He will be high and lifted up and greatly exalted." The ARI interprets that this will be at the end of correction, when even *SAM* becomes a holy angel, and the stony heart, which was forbidden to sort prior to the end of correction and remained in the *Klipot*, it, too, will then be sorted into *Kedusha*.

This is the meaning of "very good." "Good" is the angel of life. "Very" is the angel of death, and it, too, will be a holy angel. This is called "Death will be swallowed up forever." This is how the ARI interprets.

Indeed, we can interpret what is written, "For you will not go out in haste, nor will flee," not as it was in the land of Egypt, when redemption was in haste and He jumped from Egyptian to Egyptian, and Israel in the middle escaped, since He had to obliterate the Egyptians and only the people of Israel remained alive.

But at the end of correction, when the Egyptians will also be corrected, there will be no need to be in haste because there will be no need to jump from Egyptian to Egyptian with Israel in the middle remaining in *Kedusha*. Rather, all the Egyptians will receive their correction from the Whole One. Therefore, there will be no need to hurry, meaning jump, but all the discernments that were in the *Klipot* will be corrected, as it is written, "And I will remove the heart of stone from your flesh, and I will give you a heart of flesh."

Therefore, a person should be happy. Through the joy he can come out of the state of lowliness that he is in. If a person asks, "What is there to rejoice about when he sees that he is in lowliness and has no desire to engage in Torah and *Mitzvot*?" He should receive his joy from the fact that he nonetheless knows that there is a King in the world. From this awareness alone he can be happy, as in the above allegory, that he was informed that the king came to town, and this gives him strength to ascend.

The Connection between Passover, Matza, and Maror

Article No. 14, Tav-Shin-Mem-Zayin, 1986-87

It is written in the Haggadah [Passover story]: "Thus did Hillel in the time of the Temple: He would bind together Passover [lamb], *Matza*, and *Maror* [bitter herb] and eat them together, to observe what was said, 'They shall eat it with *Matza* and bitter herbs.'"

We should understand this in the work. What does the connection between those three things that he would eat together imply?

To understand the meaning of the Passover offering at the time of the exodus from Egypt, when they came out from the enslavement they were under in Egypt, we should first understand the meaning of the exile in Egypt—from what did they suffer there.

Concerning the *Maror*, it is written in the Haggadah, "This *Maror* we are eating, what is it for? For the lives of our fathers in Egypt were made bitter by the Egyptians, as it was said, 'And they made their lives bitter with hard work ... which they made them do hard labor.'"

The Connection between Passover, Matza, and Maror

We should understand what "And they made their lives bitter with hard work" means. What is it in the work of the Creator? It is known that the work of the Creator is when we work for the sake of the Creator, when we are rewarded with adhering to the Life of Lives. Precisely when we work in order to bestow, this is the time to receive the delight and pleasure that the Creator created in order to do good to His creations. This means that the salvation of the Lord comes into the vessels of bestowal.

We should make two discernments concerning the entrance of the abundance into the vessels of bestowal: 1) The abundance comes in order to create vessels of bestowal. 2) The light that comes once he has vessels of bestowal.

This means that when one wants to walk on the path of bestowing contentment upon one's Maker and not for one's own sake, the body resists with all its might and does not let him make any movement. It takes away from him all the motivation and strength that he had in order to do things for the Creator.

When a person sees the truth as it really is, when he sees how immersed he is in self-love and there is not a spark in his body that will let him do anything in order to bestow, in that state a person has already achieved the truth, meaning he has come to the recognition of evil. At that time he has no way to help himself, and there is only one advice: to cry out to the Creator to help him, as it is written, "And the children of Israel sighed from the work, and they cried out, and their cry rose up to God from the work."

This is the meaning of what was said, "He who comes to purify is aided." *The Zohar* asks, "With what?" It replies, "With a holy soul."

It follows that the meaning of "And they made their lives bitter" means that they did not let them work in order to bestow, which yields *Dvekut* [adhesion] with the Life of Lives. Instead, the *Klipa* [shell/peel] of Egypt and Pharaoh governed the children of Israel with their governance of self-love so they could not do anything against the Egyptians' will. This was the exile—that they wanted to come out of this exile but could not.

Accordingly, the meaning of what is written, "And the children of Israel sighed from the work," which work are we speaking of? It means that it is from the work of the Creator, that this is called "hard work," since it was difficult for them to work in order to bestow because the Egyptians and Pharaoh, King of Egypt, installed in them their thoughts and wishes.

In other words, since the *Klipa* of Egypt is primarily self-love, the Egyptians ruled over the people of Israel so that the people of Israel, too, would walk in their way, called "self-love." It was difficult for Israel to overcome these thoughts. This is the meaning of what is written, "And the children of Israel sighed from the work."

That is, while they were walking on the path of the Egyptians, which is in order to receive, the body gave them fuel and it was not hard for them to do the work of the Creator. It is known that the Egyptians were servants of the Creator, as our sages wrote about what is written (*Tanchuma, Beshalach*), "And he took six hundred carriages": "(And should you ask) From where did Egypt have livestock, for it was said, 'And all the livestock of Egypt died,' it was from those who fear the word of the Lord, as it is written, 'The one among the servants of Pharaoh who feared the word of the Lord made his servants and his livestock flee into the houses.'" From here they said, "He who fears the word of the Lord will cause Israel's failure."

RASHI concludes from this: "Rabbi Shimon would say, 'The purest among the Egyptians, kill; the best among the snakes, smash its brains.'" It therefore follows that the hard work that they had was work in the field, for a field is the holy *Shechina* [Divinity], as it is known that *Malchut* is called a "field."

It was difficult for them to take upon themselves the burden of the kingdom of heaven in order to bestow, but the Egyptians wanted them to do the holy work in order to receive. They let them think that this is called "He who fears the word of the Lord."

However, from here, from this discernment, came Israel's failure, meaning to those who are *Yashar-El* [straight to the Creator]. They wanted all their work to be only for their own sake, and from this emerged the failure.

That is, the failure was primarily when the Egyptians spoke to Israel in the language of fearing the Creator. From this language emerge all of Israel's failures. Had the Egyptians spoke the language of the secular, the people of Israel would have fled from their influence for sure if they had come to them with their thoughts and wishes.

Now we can interpret what is written (Exodus), "And the Egyptians enslaved Israel *BaPerech* [with hard work]." Our sages said, *bePeh Rach* [with a soft mouth]. We should understand the meaning of "soft mouth" in the work of the Creator.

As was said above, the Egyptians spoke with thoughts and desires that we must serve the Creator, but in order to receive. This is called a "soft mouth." That is, the body agrees more to do the holy work with the intention to receive, and there is no need to aim to bestow.

It follows that with these words they caused Israel to have hard work while assuming the burden of the kingdom of heaven, and for this reason, everyone in Israel said that the holy work, in order to bestow, is very difficult.

For this reason, the Egyptians imparted upon them thoughts that it is better to work in order to receive, that in this way they would see that each day they are progressing in good deeds. But in the work in the form of Israel, they see for themselves that it is difficult. And the evidence of this is that they see no progress in the work.

It follows that a "soft mouth" means that they make Israel think that if they follow their way it is easier work. This is called "soft," meaning that it is easier to advance in the holy work.

With these complaints, the Egyptians made their lives bitter with hard work, for they would always explain to Israel that the work of Israel is called "hard work" and it is not for them.

"With *Homer* [mortar]" means that the Egyptians explained to Israel the *Humra* [severity] of bestowal, whereas in the work of Egypt, they will always be white, meaning they will feel no darkness in the work and the body will agree to this work. This is called "*Levenim* [bricks]," meaning that the work of Egypt is always regarded as *Levanim* [white], without any stains or dirt, but they will always be perfect. By this they made it really difficult for Israel to work for the Creator.

In other words, the hard work extended from the Egyptians always telling them about the *Homer* [severity] in the work of bestowal, and the *Levanim* [whiteness] that there is in this work and the fear of the Egyptians.

It was said that from the one who feared the Lord extended Israel's failure. This means that from this extended to them the hard work in the field, meaning in the kingdom of heaven that they wanted to take upon themselves but could not.

It is from here that Rabbi Shimon says of "He who fears the word of the Lord": "The purest among the Egyptians, kill; the best among the snakes, smash its brains." We should interpret the words of Rabbi Shimon, "The purest among the Egyptians, kill."

That is, what the Egyptians say is pure, kill, since our sages said, "He who comes to kill you, kill him first." In other words, that which the Egyptians tell you is pure, that this path is fit to walk in, know that he wishes to kill you from spiritual life. Therefore, kill these thoughts.

"The best among the snakes, smash its brains" means that if the snake, which is the evil in man, advises you that this path is good for you, and makes you clearly see in the way that the serpent came to Eve, do not argue with it, but smash its brains. That is, all the intellect that it explains, smash that intellect. In other words, we must go above reason.

Now we will explain the meaning of the *Matza* [Passover's unleavened bread]. In the work, we should interpret the word *Matza* from the word *Meriva* [strife], for the "Massah and Meriva, and for the quarrel of the children of Israel, and for their trying the Lord, saying, 'Is the Lord among us, or not'" (Exodus 17:7).

The translation [into Aramaic] says about *Meriva*, "The *Matza* [strife] is because the children of Israel strove." It follows that *Matza* comes from the word "strife," meaning that the people of Israel had a quarrel with the Creator over why He made it so difficult to work in order to bestow, and why, even though they try to come out of Egypt's governance, not only are they not advancing, they see that they are even regressing.

In other words, they were tasting bitterness in the work, which caused them to quarrel with the Creator, and a strife is called *Matza*. We see that over such a complaint, the people of Israel quarreled with Moses, meaning when they saw that when they began to work for the sake of the Creator they had become worse, as it is written (Exodus 5:21), "And they said to them, 'May the Lord look upon you and judge, for you have made our scent odious in Pharaoh's eyes.'"

These complaints that they said to Moses, Moses said to the Creator, as it is written, "And Moses returned to the Lord and said, 'O Lord, why have You brought harm to this people? Why did You send me? Ever since I came to Pharaoh to speak in Your name, he has done harm to this people, and You have not delivered Your people at all.'"

We should interpret their complaints to Moses. When they said, "Will see and judge," it means that they quarreled with Moses, since Moses told them to believe in the Creator, so they went out of the body's control. Pharaoh King of Egypt controls the body, and he afflicts the *Kedusha* [sanctity/holiness]. They began to work in mind and heart and saw that the body, which is Pharaoh, began to govern them. That is, everything they wanted to do in the work of the Creator, the body resists it vigorously.

Before they began to walk in Moses' way, they had strength in the work. But now, everything they do, the body loathes. This is the meaning of what is written about Moses, "for you have made our scent odious in Pharaoh's eyes." In other words, our body loathes our spirit in the work of the Creator once we begin the path of bestowal.

Afterward, Moses went to the Creator with the complaints of Israel, who quarreled with Moses over bringing them the message from the Creator. It is written about it, "And Moses returned to the Lord and said, 'Why have You brought harm to this people? Why did You send me'" (meaning what are the complaints)? He said, "Ever since I came to Pharaoh to speak in Your name, he has done harm to this people, and You have not delivered Your people at all."

"Ever since I came to the children of Israel" means to their bodies, which are called "Pharaoh." "To speak in Your name" means that everyone will begin to work for the sake of the Creator. This is the meaning of "in Your name." It stands to reason that since everyone wants only the truth, for is there anyone who is a fool and wants to walk on the path of falsehood? Rather, indeed everyone wants the truth, as always when knowing that someone is lying, no one wants to listen to him.

But here they said, "Why is it that when Moses came and told them to walk on the path of truth, the body, which is called 'Pharaoh,' makes our scent odious when we begin this work?"

For this reason, they had grievances against the Creator over becoming worse now than before Moses came to them as the Creator's messenger. He wanted to deliver them from exile, so why are they seeing now that they are going deeper into exile, that Pharaoh controls the body more forcefully and with more intellect, making them understand each time with a different argument? It follows that Israel's situation prior to Moses' coming to them as a messenger of the Creator was better in the work. Now, however, they see that their bodies, which are regarded as "Pharaoh," have complete control over the children of Israel.

That is, where there should have been high spirits from knowing that they are walking on the path of truth, the opposite occurred. In the eyes of the body, which is called "Pharaoh," what spirit did they have? It is written about it, "for you have made our scent odious in Pharaoh's eyes." The body was telling them, "What spirit is there in the work of bestowal?"

Making the scent odious means a bad smell that is impossible to tolerate. This means that they could not stand this mindset and wanted to escape the way one runs from stench. That is, instead of the work on the path of truth bringing high spirits so that a person will want to stay forever in that mindset, the opposite occurred here. From the work of bestowal, they received a mindset of stench, meaning that they wanted to escape that mindset and could not stand it for even a minute. It is as was said to Moses, "for you have made our scent odious."

Moses brought Israel's grievances to the Creator and asked Him, "Why have You sent me?" The Creator replied to Moses, as it is written, "And the Lord said to Moses, 'Now you will see that which I will do to Pharaoh, for with a mighty hand he will send them.'" The answer to why He has made the work of bestowal so hard was that He wanted the mighty hand to be revealed, as it is written, "for with a mighty hand he will send them, and with a mighty hand he will drive them out of his land."

In which way is a mighty hand necessary? It is precisely when the other party resists with all its might. Then it can be said that we must use a mighty hand. But if the other party is weak, it cannot be said that it requires a mighty hand to deal with it. It is as the allegory that Baal HaSulam said, that normally, when two people are disputed, sometimes they move into a fist fight. The one who sees that he cannot overcome the other takes a knife against him. When the other one sees that he has a knife, he takes a pistol, and when that one sees he has a pistol, he takes a rifle, and so forth, until the other one takes a machine gun, and if he has a machine gun, the other one takes a tank. However, we have never heard that if someone takes a stick and wants to hit with it, the other one takes a tank to fight the one who took the stick.

It is likewise in the work. It cannot be said that we must go against Pharaoh with a mighty hand if Pharaoh does not resist very strongly. And since the Creator wanted to show him a mighty hand here, the Creator had to harden Pharaoh's heart, as it is written, "for I have hardened his heart, and the heart of his servants, that I may set these tokens of Mine within him."

However, we should understand why it is written that the Creator hardened Pharaoh's heart because the Creator wanted to set those tokens so that the name of the Creator would become known. Is the Creator deficient? Does he need others to know that He can set tokens and signs? Also, what does it imply to us in the work that we should know this for generations?

According to what Baal HaSulam said about the question that Abraham asked after the Creator promised him (Genesis 15:7), "And He said to him, 'to give you the land to inherit it.'" He asked, "How will I know that I will inherit it?" "And He said to Abram: 'Know for certain that your descendants will be strangers in a land that is not theirs, and they will be enslaved and afflicted four hundred years. ... And afterward they will come out with many possessions.'"

He asked, What is the answer to Abram's question, "How will I know that I will inherit it," meaning what is the meaning of what the Creator replied to him?

Answer: "Know for certain that your descendants will be strangers ... and they will be afflicted. ...And afterward they will come out with many possessions." He asked, "The text implies that the answer was satisfactory, since Abram did not ask further, and we see that Abram's way was to argue with the Creator, as in the case of the people of Sodom when the Creator said to Abram, 'The outcry of Sodom and Gomorrah is indeed great.'"

But here, when He told him, "Know for certain," he was pleased with the reply.

He said that since Abraham saw the magnitude of the inheritance that He had promised to his sons, Abraham thought according to the rule that there is no light without a *Kli* [vessel], meaning there is no lack without a filling. He did not see that the children of Israel would need such high degrees and attainments in the upper worlds, which is why he asked the Creator, "How will I know that I will inherit it," since they haven't the *Kelim* [vessels] or the need for the great inheritance that You are showing me that You will give to my sons; they haven't the need.

To this, the Creator replied to him, "I will give them a need for the lights, just as I will give them the lights." In other words, the Creator will give them both the lights and the *Kelim*. Do not think that I bestow only the abundance. Rather, I bestow upon them both the need, which is called *Kli*, and the abundance. This is called "lack and filling."

By the people of Israel being in exile in Egypt four hundred years, which is a complete degree of four *Behinot* [discernments], by being in exile in a land that is not theirs, meaning that the Egyptians will impart Israel with a desire for self-reception, a desire that does not belong to *Kedusha*, which is called *Eretz* [land], from the word *Ratzon* [desire], and their wanting to escape that desire, when I make them unable to come out of that governance by themselves and see that only the Creator can help them, and they will have no other choice but to ask Me for help, it is as our sages said, "He who comes to purify is aided." And *The Zohar* says that the help is that they are given a holy soul. By the many prayers when they seek the Creator's assistance, they will receive a higher degree each time, and by this they will have a need to ask of the Creator. This will cause them to ask of the Creator and receive a higher degree, after which I will be able to give them the inheritance.

Thus, the Creator deliberately made them unable to overcome, so they would have *Kelim*.

It follows that the hardening of the heart was done to Pharaoh in order to make room for a need for the upper lights. If they did not have hard work, they would not have the need for the great lights.

One who is going to fight against someone, with the hand or with a stick, the other has no need to use a tank or a cannon against him. For this reason, in order for the lower ones to have a need to receive great lights, they must be faced with strong *Klipot* [shells/peels], which a person must draw great lights in order to break.

Otherwise, he would be content with little. It follows that Pharaoh's hardening of the heart causes them to draw great lights.

By this we will understand what we asked, "Did He set the tokens in order for the nations to know that the Creator can do miracles and wonders? That is, did He make the hardening of the heart in order to be respected? Does the Creator have grievances against His creations, meaning does something against the will of the creatures? After all, the whole purpose of creation is to do good to His creations, and here it turns out the opposite, that He made the hardening of the heart to the creatures so everyone would see His greatness, that He is almighty.

Now we can understand this simply. Pharaoh and Egypt refer to the governance of the will to receive that is in the creatures. In order for the creatures to need to receive the high degrees that the Creator has prepared for them, and our sages said that by their being unable to overcome their will to receive, they will awaken to *Dvekut* with the Creator, which came to them by merit of the patriarchs, to whom the Creator promised that their children would be rewarded with the delight and pleasure that He has prepared for the creatures, for this reason, He made the hardening of the heart, so that they would need to ask the Creator to help them. His help comes, as *The Zohar* says, by bestowing upon them a holy soul.

It follows that all the overcoming is that they draw a little bit of illumination from above. By this they will eventually have *Kelim*, meaning a need for the inheritance that the Creator promised to the forefathers. It therefore follows that the verse, "that I may set these tokens of Mine" is not for the sake of the Creator, but for the sake of the creatures. It means that through the hardening of the heart that He does to Pharaoh, where the body becomes more assertive each time and does not let a person work in order to bestow, but since man yearns for *Dvekut* with the Creator, he must try to make greater efforts each time or he will not be able to defeat it. And in order to receive greater powers, the only counsel is to pray to the Creator, for only He can give him the required forces.

The forces of the Creator are as said above: The spiritual force that the Creator gives him each time is called a "soul," the "light of Torah." This means that each time, he receives the "letters of the Torah" according to the overcoming that he needs to perform. This is called "that I may set these tokens of Mine." Meaning, in order for the letters of the Torah to reveal to Israel, He must create in them a need. This is the meaning of the Creator giving the hardening of the heart for the sake of the creatures.

Accordingly, we can understand what we said above, that we need upper abundance for the making of the *Kelim*, meaning to have *Kelim* fit to receive the upper light. This assistance is regarded as the light coming to make *Kelim* of *Kedusha*, which will want to work in order to bestow, as in, "He who comes to purify is aided."

Once he has obtained the *Kelim* that want to bestow upon the Creator, the abundance comes as abundance and not in order to make *Kelim*.

In that respect, when he has a desire for the Creator, he no longer needs the hardening of the heart in order to receive the light of the Torah, since according to the rule, when a person works for his own sake, a different thought comes to him—that from here, too, from this pleasure, called "the pleasure of rest," you should not deny yourself. It follows that the pleasure of rest causes him not to have a need for higher degrees. Instead, he is content with less. This is why the Creator had to give the hardening of the heart, meaning that he sees that he cannot do anything for the Creator, that as long as he has not qualified his *Kelim* to work in order to bestow and he is still in self-love, they give him satisfaction in the little bit of work for the sake of the Creator with which he was rewarded. Since he feels that he is working for the Creator, he is satisfied and cannot yearn for higher degrees. It follows that there was no room for the revealing of the letters of the Torah.

For this reason, each time he receives some help from above and then descends from his degree once more and wants to enter the *Kedusha*, he must receive help once more. It is as it is written about

Pharaoh in the plague of the hail: "And Pharaoh sent and called for Moses, 'The Lord is the righteous one, and I and my people are the wicked.'" Afterward, it is written, "Come unto Pharaoh, for I have hardened his heart that I may set these tokens of Mine within him."

That order continues until he corrects his *Kelim* that belong to his degree, and then begins the order of the coming of the lights.

However, when he has been rewarded with *Kelim* of *Kedusha* and wants only to bestow upon his Maker, he does not say, "Now I am saying that I have already given you a lot and now I want to rest a little bit because I need to receive for my own sake, too." Instead, one who has only the desire to bestow does not need to be given hardening of the heart, as when he is making the vessels of bestowal, since he has no interest in this. One who has been rewarded with the desire to bestow wants only to bestow upon the Creator.

It therefore follows that when a person has only the desire to bestow and he wants to bring contentment to the Creator, he begins to think what the Creator needs that he can give to the Creator, which He does not have. Therefore, he decides that the Creator has no lacks except that He has created the world with the intention to do good to His creations, for the creatures to receive from Him the delight and pleasure. For this reason, he asks the Creator to give him the delight and pleasure because this can be said that He needs—for the lower ones to receive from Him the great lights that have been prepared for the creatures. From this we can say that the Creator enjoys.

But if the lower ones are unable to receive the light of Torah, called "letters of the Torah," it is as though there is a lack above. This is the meaning of what our sages said (Sanhedrin 46), "When a person regrets, what does the *Shechina* [Divinity] say? 'My head is heavy; my arm is heavy.'" Thus, when is there contentment above? Only when the creatures have delight and pleasure.

For this reason, at that time there is no room for hardening of the heart. Rather, the time when hardening of the heart must be given from above is only for the purpose of making vessels of bestowal so that one can receive delight and pleasure, which is in order to "set these tokens of Mine." We should interpret that this refers to letters, for letters are called *Kelim*. That is, in order for a person to have a need, called *Kelim*, there needs to be a hardening of the heart, as it is written, "that I may set these tokens of Mine." But once he has the *Kelim*, there is no more a need for the hardening of the heart.

Now we can understand what we asked about the connection between Passover, *Matza*, and *Maror* [bitter herb], as Hillel did at the time when the Temple stood, and said it was to keep what was said, "they shall eat it with unleavened bread and bitter herbs."

We asked what this implies in the work of the Creator. According to the above, it follows that the essence of the purpose of the work is to achieve *Dvekut* with the Creator. Because of the disparity of form within us due to the will to receive that was imprinted in us, the creatures became removed from the Creator. This is mainly what we must correct.

However, the question is, "How do we correct this, since equivalence of form is about bestowing and not receiving, and how can we go against nature, since the body has its own nature?" The answer is through the power of Torah and *Mitzvot*.

If the creatures were to receive the force of bestowal easily, they would settle for this, since they would feel that they are already giving and they would have no need to reveal the letters of the Torah, as was said, "that I may set these tokens of Mine," for the Creator wants to reveal to them the Torah as the names of the Creator.

But from where will they take the need for this? After all, once they have prevailed over the will to receive and want only to bestow upon the Creator, they already have *Dvekut*. What else do they need? Also, it is known that there is no light without a *Kli*, and no filling without a lack. So, what did the Creator do? He gave the hardening of the heart so that a person will not be able to overcome the evil in him by himself, but will need help from the Creator, as was said, "He who comes to purify is aided with a holy soul."

Concerning the soul, it is written in the book *A Sage's Fruit: Letters of Baal HaSulam*: "There are five discernments in the soul, and they are called NRNHY. In the NRNHY, we make two discernments: 1) lights, 2) *Kelim*. We obtain the *Kelim* of the NRNHY by observing the

613 *Mitzvot* [commandments] of the Torah, and the seven *Mitzvot* of our great sages. The lights of *NRNHY* are the essence of the Torah, and the light clothed in the Torah is *Ein Sof* [infinity]. It follows that the Torah and the soul are one, but the Creator is *Ein Sof* who is clothed in the light of the Torah that exists in the above-mentioned 620 *Mitzvot*. This is the meaning of what our sages said, 'The whole of the Torah is the names of the Creator.' This means that the Creator is the whole, and the 620 names are pieces and parts. These parts are according to the steps and degrees of the soul, which does not receive its light at once, but gradually, one at a time."

From this we see that the Creator has made it so that man will not be able to overcome the evil by himself, but will need the Creator's help. But there is a state of in-between, meaning that this causes one to taste bitterness in the work because the body does not let him work in order to bestow. This causes him to quarrel with the Creator over why He has created a body that is so bad that he is utterly incapable of exiting the governance of evil, called "will to receive for himself." When all the *Kelim* that a person needs to complement himself are completed, so as to have a *Kli* in which to hold the blessing, he begins to feel the salvation of the Creator, meaning that he feels on himself the nearing of the Creator.

By this we will understand the connection between *Matza*, *Maror*, and the Passover offering. Through *Matza* and *Maror* he obtains the real need for the letters of the Torah. That is, only through *Matza* and *Maror* does a need for the Creator's help form within him, and His help is through the soul, regarded as "The Torah and the Creator are one," as was said in the book *A Sage's Fruit*.

When he has the need, the Creator brings a person closer, and this is called "the Passover offering," when the Creator passes over all of his flaws and brings him closer to be rewarded with the purpose of creation.

Two Discernments in Holiness

Article No. 15, Tav-Shin-Mem-Zayin, 1986-87

There is *Kedusha* [sanctity/holiness] above and there is *Kedusha* below, as it is written, "You will be holy." Thus, there is *Kedusha* below, meaning that the creatures should be holy. Afterward it is written, "For I the Lord your God am holy." This is the *Kedusha* above.

This is the reason why there should be *Kedusha* below. Because He is holy above, he wants below to be holy too. Our sages said (*Torat Kohanim*), "You will be holy; you will be chaste, for I am holy." That is, "If you sanctify yourselves, I will regard you as though you have sanctified Me."

This seems difficult to understand, since it implies as though there is no *Kedusha* above. Yet, since the Creator wants to be holy, He says, "If you sanctify yourselves, I will regard you as though you have sanctified Me." We should understand this. The literal meaning seems to mean that since the Creator is holy, He says that the creatures should also be holy, as it is written, "You will be holy, for I the Lord your God am holy."

The words of our sages imply that the lower ones should be holy and sanctify Him, as they said about what is written, "for I the Lord your God am holy." That is, "If you sanctify yourselves, I will regard you as though you have sanctified Me." It is as though the reason we should be holy is so that there will be *Kedusha* above.

Our sages also said (*Kedoshim Rabbah* 24:9), "You will be holy. Can he be like Me? The text explains, 'for I am holy.' My holiness is higher than your holiness." This, too, is difficult to understand. Can you imagine that Israel will be like the Creator? Is this even conceivable?

To understand the above, we must understand the meaning of what was said about "You will be holy, you will be chaste." That is, from what should one abstain? We should also understand why a person should abstain. The text seems to mean that a person should abstain because "I am holy."

But that, too, we should understand. We can understand that the Creator is holy, but why is the fact that the Creator is holy a reason for a person to also be holy? Can a person resemble the Creator? Is this possible? And if it is, we must understand what it means that a person is obligated to be as holy as the Creator.

Also, it seems as though this is the main thing that a person needs to be. Otherwise, it seems that he is the opposite of *Kedusha*, *Tuma'a* [impurity], as though there is nothing in between, a middle between *Kedusha* and *Tuma'a*. And we should also understand what is *Tuma'a* in the work and what is *Kedusha* in the work.

We should interpret all those matters in one direction, meaning to return to the purpose of creation, what it is, what is the root of the corruptions, and what are the corrections that we must correct in order to fully realize the purpose of creation—for the creatures to receive the delight and pleasure that the Creator wants to give them, since His desire is to do good to His creations.

It is known that the desire to do good created a desire to receive and a yearning to receive the good that He wants to give. That desire to receive is called the "root of the creatures." From this desire, many discernments later expanded in this will to receive. That is, when it first emerged and was revealed, and received on this discernment, that state was called the "world of *Ein Sof* [infinity]."

This means that this will to receive did not put a stop on the upper light, but received the delight and pleasure in this *Kli* [vessel]. For this reason, a correction was made not to receive the abundance in order to receive but in order to bestow. By this, they would not feel any shame upon the reception of the pleasures.

It therefore follows that in the world of *Ein Sof* there was only one desire. Only afterward—after the correction of the *Tzimtzum* [restriction] was done, that something should be received only to the extent that it is possible to aim to bestow—that desire divided into many discernments. It is so because when *Malchut* received with the *Kli* we attribute to the Creator, for He has made something new, existence from absence, called "yearning to receive pleasures," *Malchut* could receive everything that the Creator wanted to give, since He has created a desire to receive to the extent that He desired to give.

Naturally, *Malchut* could receive all the abundance that the Creator wishes to give. This is why this is regarded as one desire. It is known that the light is indivisible, but rather all the divisions we discern in the lights are only from the perspective of the receivers. For this reason, since there was only one discernment in the receiving *Kli*, it was regarded as one light, since one *Kli* is discerned as one desire.

But after the correction of the *Tzimtzum*, we must place over the will to receive the aim to bestow. Since we attribute the matter of bestowal to the creatures, the *Kelim* that the creatures must create certainly cannot be completed at once.

For this reason, each time we should take a part of the will to receive and correct it into working in order to bestow. This is why the general will to receive that was created was divided into several pieces. According to the measure of the intention to bestow that is placed on them, to that extent the desire receives the light that befits this desire, which is corrected with the intention to bestow.

It therefore follows that when we interpret "You will be holy, you will be chaste," we asked, From what should one abstain? We must say that one should abstain from self-love, meaning from self-reception, and engage only in bestowal because "I am holy."

That is, it is in order for you to be able to receive the delight and pleasure. The benefit that you will receive will be without any shame if you are in the form of "desire to bestow." This will bring you equivalence of form, as our sages said, "As He is merciful, so you are merciful." This is the meaning of "You will be holy." You will be as a desire to bestow. "For I am holy," for I, too, only bestow. This is why we need equivalence of form, called *Dvekut* [adhesion].

Now we can understand what we asked. Here it implies that the reason for "You will be holy" is that the Creator is holy. Therefore, what does it mean that our sages said, "for I am holy," meaning that "If you sanctify yourselves, I will regard you as though you have sanctified Me?" This implies the opposite, that you must be holy so as to seemingly sanctify Me. In general, it is difficult to grasp that the people of Israel should sanctify the Creator. What does it mean?

We always say, "Blessed are You, O Lord, who sanctifies Israel and the times," "Blessed are You, O Lord, who sanctifies Israel and the day of remembrance." We also say in the *Kiddush* [blessing in the beginning of Shabbat (the Sabbath)], "For You have chosen us and sanctified us from among all the nations." Thus, what does it mean, "as though you have sanctified Me?"

It means that the Creator needs us to give Him something for His benefit, since He seemingly needs our *Kedusha*, and He cannot obtain this unless through us. Can it be said that He needs the creatures to give Him something?

As we explained, "holy" means bestowing. In order for the creatures to have *Kelim* to receive His abundance, there must be equivalence of form. That is, the creatures, too, must want only to bestow and not to receive. Otherwise, it will not be apparent that the Creator is bestowing upon them.

This is why the Creator said that "If you sanctify yourselves," meaning abstain from self-reception, and engage only in work of bestowal, called *Kedusha*, "I will regard you as though you have sanctified Me." That is, by engaging in bestowal, you made Me able to bestow abundance upon you.

It therefore follows that the Creator needing the creatures to sanctify Him by sanctifying themselves refers to the revelation that the Creator is the giver. Otherwise, He will have to remain concealed from the creatures. Then, He will not be able to give them abundance because by receiving the abundance they will fall into a *Kli* of self-reception, an excess.

In other words, previously, they received corporeal delight and pleasure into the vessels of reception. But when He bestows upon them the upper abundance, which is the real pleasure, they will certainly be real receivers, as we know that the light makes the *Kli*. That is, the pleasure causes coveting, as our sages said, "The eye sees and the heart covets."

Now we can understand that the Creator needing the creatures to sanctify themselves is for the creatures' benefit. That is, by working in order to bestow, the Creator will be able to give them abundance and they will remain in bestowal and not in self-love, which creates separation in spirituality.

This is the meaning of the words, "I will regard you as though you have sanctified Me." In other words, by this, you have made it revealed to all that I am holy, bestowing delight and pleasure upon the entire world, for bestowing means holy.

Now we can understand what we asked about what our sages said, "You will be holy. Can he be like Me? The text explains, 'for I am holy.' My holiness is higher than your holiness." We asked, Can anyone think that the sanctity of Israel is similar to the sanctity of the Creator?

And according to the above said, we should interpret that since the Creator said, "You will be holy," it means that you will abstain from vessels of reception and work only with vessels of bestowal. "Can he be like Me?" meaning like the Creator, who does not use vessels of reception because from whom would He receive? Instead, everything we can say about the Creator is only from what we receive from Him, as it is written, "By Your actions, we know You."

For this reason, the Creator says, "Do not think of being like Me," that you will stay as bestowing in order to bestow, which is the meaning of "Can he be like Me?" In other words, as I give and do not receive anything, you, too, will remain bestowing in order to bestow.

He said about this, "No! you should achieve a state of receivers, actual reception! You must use your vessels of reception. It is only the intention that should be in order to bestow, since the purpose of creation was to do good to His creations, for the creatures to receive delight and pleasure." This is the meaning of what is written, "My holiness is higher than your holiness."

It therefore follows that we should discern between the *Kedusha* of above and the *Kedusha* of below. Although it is written, "You will be holy, for I the Lord your God am holy," which we interpreted to mean that you will work only in order to bestow, just as I am the giver, it is as our sages wrote, "As He is merciful, so you be merciful."

Still, there is a difference between the *Kedusha* of above and the *Kedusha* of below. The *Kedusha* of above is all to bestow. There is no reception there at all. But the *Kedusha* of below is not so. Rather, the wholeness is precisely when you do use the vessels of reception. The *Kedusha* is over the intention! In other words, the requirement of the creatures to be holy, meaning giving and not receiving, refers primarily to the intention that they will work in order to bestow.

However, in the order of the work we should discern between *Katnut* [infancy/smallness] of *Kedusha* and *Gadlut* [adulthood/greatness] of *Kedusha*. The order of the work is that we go from light to heavy. Therefore, we must begin with working so that the actions will be in bestowal in order to bestow. This is regarded as all the *Mitzvot* [commandments] he performs will be with the aim not to receive reward or anything in return for keeping Torah and *Mitzvot*. Rather, it will all be *Lishma* [for Her sake] and not for his own sake. This is called "bestowing in order to bestow."

Afterward comes the *Gadlut*, when we begin to work with vessels of reception in order to bestow. This is regarded as the creatures saying, "We want to receive delight and pleasure because this is His will, for He has created the world in order to delight His creatures." It follows that we should discern two kinds of *Kedusha*: 1) *Kedusha* of above, which is all to bestow and not to receive at all, 2) *Kedusha* of below, which is to receive in action, but the intention is to bestow.

The Work of the General Public and the Work of the Individual

Article No. 16, Tav-Shin-Mem-Zayin, 1986-87

It is written in *The Zohar* (*Emor*, Item 58): "Come and see, when a person is born, a force from above is not appointed over him until he is circumcised. Once he is circumcised, the spirit awakens upon him, meaning the light of *Nefesh* from above. When he is rewarded with engaging in Torah, he is a complete man, whole in everything, for he has been rewarded with the light of *Haya*. But when a beast is born, as soon as it is born, the power it has in the end, it has when it is born. This is why it is written, 'When an ox or a sheep or a goat is born.'"

We should understand this differentiation between beast and man, and what it teaches us in the work. First, we must understand what is "man" in the work and what is "beast" in the work. What is "man"? Our sages said (*Berachot* 6) about what was said, "In the end of the matter, all having been heard, fear God and keep His commandments, for this is the whole of man." What is "for this is the whole of man"? Rabbi Elazar said, "The Creator said, 'The whole world was not created but for this.'" In other words, the whole world was created for the fear of the Creator. This is the meaning of what he said, "for this is the whole of man." It follows that "man" is one who has fear of the Creator, and one who does not have fear of the Creator is not called "man."

This also explains what they said (*Yevamot* 61), "Thus would Rabbi Shimon Ben Yochai say, that it was said, 'And you are My sheep, the sheep of My pasture. You are man. You are called 'man,' and the idol-worshippers are not called 'man.'" We should also interpret that by "man," he is referring to one who has fear of heaven (although in terms of the judgment, he is not important. Rather, he is from an impure one; although a person has only the degree of a beast, he is still defiled in the tent. Nonetheless, in the work, we learn within one man the discernments of Israel and the seventy nations, as *The Zohar* says that every person is a small world. For this reason, with respect to practical *Mitzvot* [commandments], called "the revealed part," we learn everything separately, meaning a gentile and Israel separately, meaning we learn everything as separate bodies. This is why the rule is that the graves of idol-worshippers are not defiled in a tent, since it is written about *Tuma'a* [impurity], "Should a man die in a tent." This is why idol-worshippers are not defiled in a tent.)

It therefore follows that one who has fear of the Creator is called "man," and one who has no fear of the Creator is considered a "beast," and not a man. However, we should understand the measure of the fear of the Creator, since there are many discernments in this.

The Zohar ("Introduction of The Book of Zohar," Item 190) writes, "Fear is interpreted in three discernments, two of which do not contain a proper root, and one is the root of fear. There is a person who fears the Creator so that his sons will live and not die, or fears a bodily punishment, or a punishment to one's money. Hence, he always fears Him. It follows that the fear he fears of the Creator is not placed as the root, for his own benefit is the root, and the fear is the result of it.

And there is a person who fears the Creator because he fears the punishment of that world and the punishment of Hell. Those two kinds of fear—fear of punishment in this world and fear of punishment in the next world—are not the essence of fear and its root. The fear that is the essence is that one should fear one's Master because He is great and ruling."

According to the worlds of *The Zohar*, the essence of the fear of the Creator is because the Creator is great and ruling. This is what compels us to observe His *Mitzvot* [commandments], since this is regarded as working not in order to receive reward, meaning not for one's own sake—so he will receive some reward for his work. Rather, the work itself is the reward because he feels it is a great privilege that he sees that he was given a thought and desire to serve the King, and regards the great gift he has been given from above as a fortune.

It therefore follows that a "man" is one who walks on the path where all his actions will be with the aim for the Creator and not for his own sake. But one who does not have the intention, but only the act, while this is a great thing, without the intention it is regarded as a "beast," as it is written (Proverbs 19:2), "Also, a soul without knowledge is not good." "Without knowledge" means that "knowledge" means intention, as it is written, "You grant man knowledge."

This is perplexing, since the path of truth is to go above reason, so (why) do we pray to be given reason? Baal HaSulam said that knowledge of *Kedusha* [holiness/sanctity] is called *Dvekut* [adhesion], "equivalence of form." Accordingly, we should interpret "without knowledge" to mean "a soul without *Dvekut*," but in a state of "beast," not walking on the path of being rewarded through the power of Torah and *Mitzvot* to come to a state where he can aim in order to bestow. He is called "a beast without knowledge," without equivalence of form. This means that in everything he does, he has no other intention but his own benefit. This is called a "beast," and he is not regarded as "You are called 'man,' and not the idol-worshippers."

Now we will explain what we asked—what does the difference between the birth of a beast and the birth of a man imply to us. *The Zohar* brings evidence to its words—that a newborn beast has the same strength in the end as it has when it is born—with the verse, "An ox or a sheep or a goat that is born," that a day old ox is called an ox, since it is not written, "A calf that is born." And concerning the work, this is (what) comes to teach us to know the order of development of man and beast.

First, when speaking of the work, we must know what is birth. That is, according to the rule that we learn about differentiating beast from man, it all applies to the same body. Because a person consists of seventy nations, he therefore consists of all that exists in the world, since according to what *The Zohar* says, man is a whole world. Therefore, we should know what is birth.

It is known that when we speak of a person, we mainly speak of the mind and the heart. We attribute the thoughts to the mind, and we attribute the desires to the heart. Therefore, when he has in his mind and heart thoughts and desires that pertain to the beast, this is regarded as the birth of a beast. But if the mind and the heart have thoughts and desires that pertain to "man," this is regarded as the birth of a man. By this we discern between man and beast.

However, externally, in corporeality, we see that there are big changes in a beast from the day it is born. After some time, it develops in length, width, and height. However, the main difference for which they said that there are no differences in a beast from the day it is born to the end—that it has the same strength—refers to its internality. This comes to imply to us the order of the work. Saying "A beast that is born" means that from this basis he begins to build the building in which he will dwell his entire life.

Saying, "A beast that is born" means that the basis with which he builds his work in Torah and *Mitzvot* is on the state of a beast, called "action without intention." He wants to continue in this way his entire life, for he thinks that this is the true path, that it is enough for those who want to walk on the path of the Creator to give all their energy and strength to observing Torah and *Mitzvot* meticulously, and aim, while working, to observe the commandment of the Creator, and what else do I need?

Primarily, a person who is born as a beast claims that he brings evidence to his correctness from the general public of Israel and how they behave, meaning on what foundation they rely. You will certainly see that they are going by the way of a beast. That is, if they observe Torah and *Mitzvot*, and even take upon themselves some additional restrictions to the *Mitzvot* that we were given, then everyone feels whole and sees no flaw in themselves that should be corrected. As evidence, they bring the words of our sages (*Berachot* 45): "Go see what the people do." That is, when in doubt, go see what the general public is doing.

Indeed, he is correct. One who is born as a beast belongs to the general public and should do as the public does. This is as Maimonides writes in his interpretation on the words of our sages, "One should always engage in Torah, even *Lo Lishma* [not for Her sake], since from *Lo Lishma* he will come to *Lishma* [for Her sake]. Therefore, when teaching children, women, and uneducated people, they are taught only to work out of fear and in order to receive reward. Until they gain more knowledge and acquire much wisdom, they are taught that secret bit by bit, and are accustomed to this matter with ease until they attain Him and serve Him with love" ("Laws of Repentance," Chapter 10).

Clearly, it is only just that one who wishes to follow the general public produces for himself evidence from the general public. But this applies to one who is born as a beast, for whom *The Zohar* says that the power he will have in the end, he has on the day when he is born. This is why it is said, "A day old calf is called an 'ox.'" This means that until the end, he will not have more knowledge of *Kedusha* than he had at birth, when he began to work as a beast.

However, we should understand the words of Maimonides when he says, "until they gain more knowledge and acquire much wisdom." The question is, "How can we know that they have already gained more knowledge and have acquired much wisdom?" Moreover, what is the measure of knowledge that is regarded as having acquired much knowledge? And also, what is the measure of much wisdom, from which onward it is permitted to reveal to them the meaning of *Lishma*, called "not in order to receive reward"?

According to the above, when a "man" is born means when thoughts and desires that a person should be a man come into his mind. A "man" means one who wants to walk on the path of fearing the Creator, meaning that all his actions will be for the Creator, in order to bestow, and not for himself, as a beast, who has no sensation of the other. Instead, he specifically wants to work in order to bestow.

Although he has not yet been rewarded with this, "being born" means that he has begun to walk on the basis of "man," meaning that he wants to build his work on the basis of fear of the Creator, called "man," and a beginning is called "birth."

This is the time when a person comes and says that he wants to be a man because now he is born with the discernment of "man" in his mind and heart. This is called "until they gain more knowledge and acquire much wisdom," meaning until wisdom and knowledge are born in their hearts, that it is not worth living a life of a beast, called *Lo Lishma*, as was written above, "Also, a soul without knowledge is not good." At that time it is permitted to reveal to him the matter of *Lishma*, called "fearing the Creator," and not that he engages in Torah and *Mitzvot* because he fears for his own benefit. But before the discernment of "man" comes to him, he must not be told, as in the words of Maimonides.

By this we will interpret what *The Zohar* tells us, that there is a difference between one who is born as a beast, where as soon as he is born, meaning in the beginning of his work, he immediately has the wholeness he will obtain afterwards, meaning the same mind he had received when he was born. This pertains to the foundation—that he began to work as a beast, called "self-benefit," and everything he will build afterwards will be on the basis of self-love, and he will acquire no additions. Externally, he will grow as beasts grow after they are born—in length, width, and height. But a beast does not grow internally. That is, in terms of its mind, there is no difference between the day it is born and after it has grown over several years, since the beast remains with the mind.

The same applies to a person whose foundation and basis of the work is that of a beast, which is *Lo Lishma*. Here, too, there is no difference in the internality, which is the mind. Although he certainly grows externally, meaning that over time he has acquired and collected much Torah and many *Mitzvot*, internally, he has remained on the same degree. And the mind, which is the interior, did not undergo any change at its end.

This is why *The Zohar* says, "A man who is born, no force from above is appointed over him until he is circumcised. Once he is circumcised, he receives the light of *Nefesh*, until he is rewarded with obtaining the light of *Haya* because he was rewarded with these four degrees that are from the four worlds *ABYA*."

It therefore follows that there is work that belongs to the general public, which is *Lo Lishma*, and is called a "beast." We must not say that we should work *Lishma* because such people will not understand anyway, since they were born a beast and they cannot understand otherwise. Therefore, they must be taught only *Lo Lishma*.

According to the above, we can interpret what our sages said (*Avoda Zarah* 19), "Raba said, 'One should always learn Torah where his heart desires.'" RASHI interpreted that "where his heart desires" means that his teacher should teach only the *Masechet* [chapter in the Mishnah/Talmud] that he asks of him, for if he teaches him a different *Masechet*, it will not be, for his heart is with his desire.

This is so because if he is born as a beast, meaning if the mind and heart understand that they must go according to the general public, based entirely on *Lo Lishma*, it is impossible to make him see that we should work in order to bestow. It is as RASHI interpreted, "If he teaches him a different *Masechet*, it will not be, for his heart is with his desire." For this reason, he will make up many excuses why he cannot be as a "man," called "fearing the Creator," which is in order to bestow. It is as Maimonides wrote, "One should not say, 'I am observing the *Mitzvot* of the Torah in order to receive the blessings written in it, or in order to be awarded with the life of the next world.' Only uneducated people, women, and children serve the Creator in this manner, for they are taught to work out of fear until they gain more knowledge and serve Him with love."

We explained that the meaning of "until they gain more knowledge" is until he is born in the discernment of a man, meaning until thoughts and desires that he should work the true work, meaning in order to bestow, come to his mind. It is as Maimonides writes, that we must serve the Creator only in order to bestow upon the Creator, as he phrased it, "He does the truth because it is the truth," for "truth" means *Lishma* and not for one's own sake. He says that this truth must not be revealed to the general public because they will not understand it, as RASHI interpreted, "for his heart is with his desire," hence he cannot understand otherwise.

However, when he is born as a man, when thoughts and desires of being a man appear in his mind and heart, when he understands he needs to walk on the path of truth, although he still cannot walk, since he was born just now, meaning that now he has begun this work. Although he understands he must achieve it, meaning to do everything in order to bestow, though when he is born he has nothing, as *The Zohar* says, "When a person is born, a force from above is not appointed over him until he is circumcised."

This means that when he begins to walk on a line of bestowal, called "giving birth," he always sees the opposite value. In other words, he sees that after all his exertion, he has made no progress. Rather, he always sees that he has regressed.

This order, meaning the state of concealment that he feels, continues until he is rewarded with circumcising himself. Afterward, he goes forward until he obtains the four degrees called *Haya, Neshama, Ruach, Nefesh*. This is the difference between the general public and the individual, such as the difference in corporeality between man and beast.

The Meaning of the Strict Prohibition to Teach Idol Worshippers the Torah

Article No. 17, Tav-Shin-Mem-Zayin, 1986-87

Our sages said (*Hagigah* 13), "Rav Ami said, 'Words of Torah are not to be given to idol worshippers, as it is written, 'He has not done so with any nation and did not did not make ordinances known to them.' In the Sanhedrin (59), Rabbi Yohanan said, 'An idol worshipper who engages in Torah must die, as it is written, 'Moses commanded us a law, an inheritance.' The inheritance is for us and not for them.'"

The Gemara asks, "Rabbi Meir would say, 'How so? After all, even an idol worshipper who engages in the Torah is as the high priest, as it is written, 'If a man does them, he shall live by them.' It did not say, 'priests,' 'Levites,' or 'Israelis,' but 'man.' This means that even an idol worshipper who engages in Torah is as the high priest.'"

The Meaning of the Strict Prohibition to Teach Idol Worshippers the Torah

We should understand it in the work, according to the rule that in the work we learn the whole Torah in one person. *The Zohar* says that each person is a small world in and of itself. This means that he consists of all seventy nations of the world. Thus, what is "Israel" and what are "idol worshippers" within the person himself?

Another question about the words of Rabbi Meir is that he brings evidence from the verse, "If a man does them, he shall live by them." After all, Rabbi Shimon says, "a man refers to Israel," and he brings as evidence the verse, "You are called 'man,' and not the nations of the world." Thus, how does Rabbi Meir bring evidence from the word "man" as referring to idol worshippers? The *Tosfot* wishes to explain in the Sanhedrin that there is a difference between "man" and "the man."

RASHI interprets that there should not be misunderstandings about Rabbi Shimon, who says, "Man means Israel." It is simple, he does not differ from Rabbi Shimon—that a man means specifically Israel. Also, we should understand the great disparity between Rabbi Yohanan and Rabbi Meir, where Rabbi Yohanan says, "An idol worshipper who engages in Torah must die," and to Rabbi Meir he seems not like an ordinary person from Israel, but as the high priest. Can it be that he will be greater than an ordinary person from Israel?

The Zohar says (*Aharei*, p 103, and in the *Sulam* Commentary, Item 289), "Rabbi Elazar asked Rabbi Shimon, his father. It is written, 'He has not done so with any nation.' However, we should ask that since it is written, 'He declares His words unto Jacob,' why does it say, 'His statutes and His ordinances unto Israel'?"

This is a double meaning! And since the Torah is the hidden, high, and precious one, His very Name, the whole of Torah is therefore hidden and revealed, meaning that in it, there is hidden and literal in His Name.

Hence, Israel are in two degrees: concealed and revealed. We learned that three are the degrees that connect to one another: 1) the Creator, 2) the Torah, 3) Israel. This is why it is written, "He declares His words unto Jacob, His statutes and His ordinances unto Israel." They are two degrees—one is revealed: the degree of Jacob, and one is concealed: the degree of Israel.

What does the text imply by that? He replies, "Anyone who is circumcised and inscribed in the holy name is given into the revealed things in the Torah." This is the meaning of what is written, "He declares His words unto Jacob."

However, "His statutes and His ordinances unto Israel" is at a higher degree. Hence, "His statutes and His ordinances unto Israel" are the secrets of the Torah. The laws of the Torah and the secrets of the Torah need not be disclosed except to those at a properly higher degree. And as Israel is so, meaning that they disclose the Torah only to one who is at a high degree, it is all the more so for idol-worshipping nations.

In Item 303, it is written, "Come and see that the first thing in the Torah that is given to infants is the alphabet. This is something that the people in the world cannot come to wish and conceive in their understanding." To understand the above-said, we first need to know what Israel is, and what is an idol-worshipper in the work.

Our sages said about the verse (*Shabbat* 105b), "There shall not be a strange God within you, nor will you bow before a strange God." What is the strange God in man's body? It is the evil inclination. This means that an idol-worshipper is called "the evil inclination." It follows that when speaking of a single body, then idol-worshipping, which is called "a foreign God" or "a strange God," is entirely within man. Accordingly, we should discern the idol-worshipping in the person himself, which is the evil inclination, and the discernment of Israel, which is the good inclination.

However, we should understand why this inclination, which tempts one to delight himself and enjoy life, is called "evil." After all, it tells a person, "If you listen to me, you will enjoy life." Thus, why is it called "evil inclination" or "a strange God"? Also, what is the connection between idolatry and the evil inclination, and why is it called "Godliness" and praised and bowed to as one serves idolatry?

The Meaning of the Strict Prohibition to Teach Idol Worshippers the Torah

It is known that there are two kings in the world: 1) The King of All Kings, 2) an old and foolish king, meaning the evil inclination. It is also called "two authorities": 1) the authority of the Creator, 2) the authority of man.

Our sages said that when a person is born, he is born immediately with the evil inclination, as it is written, "Sin crouches at the door." In *The Zohar*, it means that as soon as one comes out of the womb, the evil inclination comes to him. In the work, we should interpret that immediately, from the day one is born, he works and serves the evil inclination within him with his heart and soul.

However, it is known that the evil inclination is only the will to receive within us, as explained in the "Introduction of The Book of Zohar." And as soon as one is born, his only purpose is to serve the will to receive. This means that all his senses focus on how to serve the old and foolish king. Also, one bows before him, and bowing means that he subjugates his reason and his mind before him.

This means that sometimes he hears that one should serve the King of All Kings, and at times, the mind and heart resolve that the reason we are born is not to serve the will to receive. And yet, he subjugates that view and says, "Although my reason shows me that it is not worthwhile to toil and serve the will to receive my whole life, but that it is worthwhile to serve the Creator, I go above reason. In other words, the body tells me, 'Drop everything you have received from books and from authors—that you must serve the Creator. Rather, as then, so now, do not defy the will to receive but serve it with your heart and soul.'"

It follows that one bows before the will to receive because subjugating the reason is called "bowing." And this is considered that a person is serving a strange God who is a stranger to *Kedusha* [holiness]. He is also called "a foreign God," for he is a foreigner to *Kedusha*.

At that time, the person who serves him is called a "foreigner" or an "idol-worshipper," and this is the strange God in a man's body. In other words, the strange God is not something on the outside—that he is serving something outside his own body. There is a thought that this is actually considered that he is committing idolatry. Rather, by serving and working for his body, which is called "the will to receive," inside man's body, it is regarded as committing idolatry, and that person is called a "foreigner" or an "idol-worshipper."

This is so because he has no connection to *Kedusha* [holiness/sanctity], since *Kadosh* [holy] means the Creator, as it is written, "You shall be holy, for I the Lord am holy." It means, "You shall abstain" (as said in Article No. 16, *Tav-Shin-Mem-Zayin*). Since the Creator is the giver, to have *Dvekut* [adhesion] with Him, called "equivalence of form," a person should be a giver, too, and *this* is called *Kedusha* [holiness].

It therefore follows that one who serves and works for the will to receive creates an object, meaning that it is his God. He wishes to serve only it with his heart and soul, and in everything he does, even an act of bestowal, he does not even consider the act of bestowal, except according to the benefit that his will to receive will derive from it. He does not divert his focus from it but clings to his faith that this is all that must be served.

Even though his mind resolves that it is not worthwhile to serve it, he still does not have the power to betray his God, whom he has been serving since the day he was born. This is why it is called "faith," since he is serving his will to receive above reason. And there is no reason in the world that can detach and separate him from the adhesion that he is attached to it from the day he was born. This is called "a gentile" or "a foreigner."

Israel means the opposite of a strange God, meaning *Yashar El* [straight to God]. This means that his sole intention is for everything to be straight to the Creator. In other words, his only thought and desire is to come directly to *Dvekut* with the Creator, and he does not want to listen to the voice of the will to receive. He says that the name that was given to the will to receive, "evil inclination," suits it because it only inflicts harm upon him.

In other words, the more he tries to satisfy its wish so it will not obstruct him in his work to be a servant of the Creator, it is to the contrary. That is, he constantly makes sure that he gives it what it demands of him, and he gives to it because he thinks that by so doing, it will stop disturbing him. But then we see the exact opposite—this receiver actually grows stronger by his satisfying its needs, meaning it becomes even more evil.

And now he sees how right our sages were when they said (*Beresheet Rabbah* 25:8), "Do not do good to a bad one," meaning do not do good to a bad person. It is the same for us, who learn everything in one person. The meaning will be that it is forbidden to do good to the will to receive, which is the evil inclination, since out of any good that a person does to it, it later has more strength to harm him. And this is called "returning a favor with evil." They are like two drops in a pond; that is, to the extent that he serves it, just so is its power to harm him.

However, one should always remember what is the evil that the receiver causes him. This is why one must always remember the purpose of creation—to do good to His creations—and believe that the Creator can impart endless delight and pleasure. It is written about it (Malachi 3:10), "'And test Me now in this,' says the Lord of hosts, 'if I will not open for you the windows of heaven and pour out for you a blessing until it overflows.'"

The reason why a person does not feel the delight and pleasure that the Creator wishes to give is because of the disparity of form between the Creator, who is the giver, and the receiver. This causes shame upon reception of the delight and pleasure. To avoid the bread of shame, there was a correction called *Tzimtzum* [restriction]—to not receive unless it is in order to bestow contentment upon one's Maker. This is called "equivalence of form," as our sages said, "As He is merciful, so you are merciful."

This means that as the Creator is the giver and there is no reception in Him whatsoever—since from whom would He receive?—man, too, should strive to reach that degree of not wanting to work for himself, but to keep all his thoughts and desires on pleasing his Maker. And then he receives suitable *Kelim* [vessels] for reception of the upper abundance, which is the general name for the delight and pleasure that the Creator wished to give to the creatures.

In general, the abundance divides into five discernments, called *NRNHY*. Sometimes they are called *NRN*. Also, the upper abundance can simply be called *Neshama* [soul], and the receiver of the *Neshama* is called *Guf* [body], but those are not fixed names, but depend on the context.

Thus, who is the obstructor to receiving the above-mentioned delight and pleasure? It is only the will to receive. It obstructs and does not let us out of its authority, called "reception in order to receive." It is on this discernment that the *Tzimtzum* took place—to correct the vessels of reception so they will be in order to bestow, at which time he will be similar to the giver.

And there is equivalence of form here, called *Dvekut* [adhesion]. At that time, through *Dvekut* with the Creator, a person is considered alive, since he is attached to the Life of Lives. And through the receiver in him, he is separated from the Life of Lives. This is why our sages said, "The wicked—in their lives, are called 'dead.'"

Thus, it is clear who is obstructing us from being given life: it is only the receiver in us, and we should determine that through the above-mentioned calculation. It turns out that it is the cause of all the troubles and afflictions we suffer. Clearly, the moniker, "evil inclination," suits it, since it causes all our troubles.

Let us imagine a sick person who wants to live. There is only one cure that can save his life, by which he will be rewarded with life; otherwise, he will have to die. And there is one person who is stopping him from having this medicine. Clearly, this person is called "an evil man." It is the same for us. When one learns that only through the desire to bestow is it possible to be rewarded with spiritual life, that there is where the real delight and pleasure are found, and that this will to receive detains us from receiving, how will we look at it? Of course we should see it as the angel of death. Meaning, it is causing us not to be granted life!

When a person comes to realize this—that our receiver is the evil in us—and wishes to be "Israel," meaning he does not want to commit idolatry, which is the evil inclination in man's body, and wishes to repent for having committed idolatry all that time, and wishes to be a servant of the Creator, in that state, when he wishes to exit the domination of the evil inclination, what should he do?

To that, there is the answer that our sages said (*Kidushin* 30b), "So says the Creator to Israel, 'My sons, I have created the evil inclination, and I have created for it the spice of Torah. If you engage in Torah, you will not be given into its hand, as it is written, 'If you do well.' And if you do not engage in Torah, you will be given into its hand, as it is written, 'Sin crouches at the door.''" In other words, only engagement in Torah has the power to come out of the domination of the evil inclination and enter *Kedusha*.

It therefore follows that one who engages in Torah—when speaking of the work—the purpose of the study must be clear to a person, meaning the reason that causes him to engage in Torah. This is so because there are two opposites in the Torah, as our sages said (*Yoma* 72b), "Rabbi Yehoshua Ben Levi said, 'Why is it written, 'And this is the law that Moses put'? If he is rewarded, it becomes a potion of life to him. If he is not rewarded, it becomes a potion of death to him.' For this reason, when a person engages in Torah, he should see that the Torah does not bring him into death."

However, it is difficult to understand how there can be such a distance between being rewarded and not being rewarded, to the point that they say that if he is not rewarded by engagement in Torah, it becomes a potion of death to him. Would it not be enough that he were not rewarded? Why is he even worse than one who did not engage in Torah at all? That is, one who did not engage in Torah does not have the potion of death, and one who engaged in Torah obtained death in return for his work. Can such a thing be?

This question is presented in the "Introduction to The Study of the Ten Sefirot" (p 20, Item 39): "However, their words require explanation to understand how and through what does the Holy Torah become a potion of death for him. Not only are his work and exertion in vain, and he receives no benefit from his labor and strain, but the Torah and the work themselves become a potion of death for him. This is indeed perplexing."

In the "Introduction to The Study of the Ten Sefirot" (Item 101), "Since the Creator hides Himself in the Torah, since the matter of the torments and pains that one experiences during the concealment of the face are not similar between one who possesses few sins and has done little Torah and *Mitzvot* and one who has engaged in Torah and good deeds extensively. The first is quite qualified to judge his Maker favorably, to think that the suffering came to him because of his sins and scarceness of Torah. For the other, however, it is much harder to judge his Maker favorably."

It is similar with us. When he places the goal before his eyes, meaning that the upper one wishes to delight His creatures, but to avoid the shame, we must have vessels of bestowal. And since we are born with the will to receive, which is considered a strange God, whom we serve even above reason and it enslaves us and we cannot come out of its power, we believe in our sages who said, "The Creator said, 'I have created the evil inclination; I have created the spice of Torah.'"

This is the reason that makes one engage in Torah, and then the Torah brings him life. In other words, through the Torah he comes out of the domination of the evil inclination and becomes a servant of the Creator, meaning that his intention is only to bring contentment to his Maker. And he will be rewarded with *Dvekut* with the Creator, meaning that at that time, he will adhere to the Life of Lives. Indeed, only in that state, when a person studies with this goal, is the Torah regarded for him as a potion of life, since through the Torah he will be rewarded with life.

The Meaning of the Strict Prohibition to Teach Idol Worshippers the Torah

And yet, if he does not engage in Torah for this purpose, through the Torah that he is studying, the will to receive will grow stronger and acquire more strength to keep him under its control. This is because the receiver lets him understand that he is not like other people because, thank God, he is a man who has acquired good deeds and Torah, and certainly, the Creator should not treat him as He treats ordinary people. Rather, the Creator should recognize him for who he is.

And if he works in concealment, he is certain to have complaints against the Creator, since if he suffers from something, he tells the Creator, "Is this the reward for the Torah?" Thus, he always has grievances against the Creator, which is called "doubting the *Shechina* [Divinity]," referring to the Creator. By that, they are separated from the Life of Lives.

This means that where they should have longed to be annulled before the Creator and to have all that they do be only to serve the Creator, those who work for the receiver wish for the Creator to serve them: All that their receiver needs, the Creator should satisfy. It follows that they are working opposite from those who want to be rewarded with life by their engagement in Torah.

Therefore, we can understand what we asked about why Rabbi Ami says, "Torah is not to be given to idolaters." If this is in the work, meaning in the person himself, and he is in a state of idolater, the reason that it is forbidden to learn is that it is pointless. This is so because in the work we learn that we should study Torah in order to come out of the domination of the evil inclination. But if he does not want to break free from the enslavement of the evil inclination, why does he need the Torah? It follows that if he were to be given Torah, it would be pointless. It is a waste of effort for the one who will teach him.

However, Rabbi Yohanan adds to Rabbi Ami and says, "Not only is it pointless, but if an idol-worshipper engages in Torah, it will harm him." He is risking his soul because for idol-worshippers, meaning those who study Torah without the goal of exiting the domination of the evil inclination, but wish to stay under it and serve it willingly, this is called "idolatry."

It is written about it, "A strange God in man's body." Thus, he is taking for himself the potion of death. This is why Rabbi Yohanan said, "An idol-worshipper who engages in Torah must die." It means that he is risking his soul because the Torah will be a potion of death for him. However, what Rabbi Meir would say is, "Where is it from that an idol-worshipper who engages in Torah must die? Rather, he is like the high priest, as it was said, 'If a man does them, he shall live by them.'"

And we asked about it, A) Why is he saying that he is like the high priest? Isn't an ordinary priest a high degree? This is so far from the words of Rabbi Yohanan, who thinks that he must die. So what is the reason for this exaggeration that he is as the high priest? B) The interpreters ask, the evidence that Rabbi Meir brings, where it says, "The man," Rabbi Shimon says that "the man" actually means Israel and not idolaters.

We should interpret what Rabbi Meir says, "An idol worshipper who engages in Torah," as referring to what we explained above. Rabbi Meir's intention is that a person has come to realize that he is an idol-worshipper, that he sees that from the day he was born until now he has been serving idols, a foreign God, meaning the evil inclination, which is inside a man's body. He sees how he is enslaved and is under its control and has no strength to defy its word. And although he often understands with his mind and reason that it is not worthwhile to serve it, but to the contrary, the evil inclination should serve the *Kedusha* [holiness], he still subdues his reason and serves it as if he realized that it was worthwhile to serve it.

When a person comes to realize it, when he sees that there is no power in the world that can help him, and he sees that he is lost and will be cut off from life forever, to deliver himself from death—being "The wicked in their lives they are called 'dead'"—in that state he comes to believe the words of our sages. They said, "This is what the Creator said to Israel: 'My sons, I have created the evil inclination;

The Meaning of the Strict Prohibition to Teach Idol Worshippers the Torah

and I have created for it the spice of Torah. If you engage in Torah, you will not be given into its hand.'"

It is about *this* kind of idol-worshipper that Rabbi Meir said that he was like the high priest. And he brings as evidence that it is written, "If a man does them, he shall live by them." He interprets that if one engages in Torah in order to "live by them," if the reason for his engagement in Torah is that he wishes to be rewarded with life and not to be wicked—an idolater, which is a foreign God in a man's body—but his sole aim is to be rewarded with life, this verse, "If a man does them, he shall live by them," is about him.

This is so because if he engages in Torah, he will be as the high priest. And not just a priest, but he will be a priest, meaning obtain the quality of *Hesed* [mercy], which is called "a priest," meaning he will be rewarded with vessels of bestowal, and he will also be rewarded with *Gadlut* [greatness/adulthood]. This is why he says that he is like the high priest.

Accordingly, we should ask why Rabbi Meir says, "Even an idolater." As we explained, it is to the contrary, since such an idol worshipper is worthy of being as the high priest. We can explain and say that the word "even" means that even if a person comes to such lowliness that he sees that he is truly an idolater, that he sees that thus far he gained nothing in his life, but only served his evil inclination. In other words, all his thoughts and desires have been only in favor of the receiver. He hasn't even touched the path of truth, meaning had the ability to believe in the Creator above reason, but only according to what the reason of the receiver allowed him to see—that specifically by working for it, it will give it energy to engage in Torah and *Mitzvot*. To such a person, Rabbi Meir comes and says, "Do not regret this lowliness. Instead, you should believe that even when you have come to such a low, the Creator can still help you out of the exile of being under its control all this time." So the reason is to the contrary: The meaning of what he says is, "Even if the world agrees."

However, in truth, only now is there a need for the Torah. Only now you have the real *Kelim* [vessels], a real need for the Creator to help you, since you have come to the point of truth, as our sages said, "Man's inclination overcomes him every day. Were it not for the Creator, he would not prevail over it." Now he sees the truth, that he really needs the help of the Creator.

Now we can understand the above-mentioned words of *The Zohar*, where he says that on the face of it, we should make three discernments in the work: 1) idol-worshippers, 2) Jacob, 3) Israel. The difference between them is that idol-worshippers are forbidden to study even the literal Torah. And we learn this from what is written, "He has not done so with any nation." In general, it is permitted to teach him the literal, specifically in the revealed matters. It concludes that from the verse, "He declares His words unto Jacob," which is an inferior degree. When he is at a superior degree, it is permitted to teach him the secrets of Torah. It concludes this from the verse, "His statutes and His ordinances unto Israel."

It is written in *The Zohar*, *Yitro* (Item 265): "'Thus shall you say to the house of Jacob,' to that place which befits their degree. 'And tell the children of Israel,' since Jacob and Israel are two degrees. Jacob is the degree of *VAK*, and Israel is the degree of *GAR*. However, Israel is called 'the wholeness of everything,' which means showing *Hochma* [wisdom] and speaking in the spirit of *Hochma*."

And it is written in *The Zohar*, *Yitro* (Item 260): "'Thus shall you say to the house of Jacob' is to the females, 'And tell the children of Israel' is to the males." Also in *The Zohar*, *Yitro* (Item 261): "'Thus shall you say to the house of Jacob' meaning with a saying, from the side of *Din* [judgment]. 'And tell the children of Israel' is as they said, 'And he shall tell them his covenant.' Telling is *Rachamim* [mercy] for the children of Israel, meaning the males, who come from the side of *Rachamim*. This is why it states 'telling' about them."

We should understand the distinctions in the words of *The Zohar*, which says in the portion *Aharei*, that Jacob and Israel are two degrees: 1) Jacob is below, with whom one studies the literal;

The Meaning of the Strict Prohibition to Teach Idol Worshippers the Torah

2) Israel is the degree above, with whom one studies the secrets of Torah.

It is written in *The Zohar, Yitro* (Item 260): "Jacob is females; Israel is males." It says (Item 261), "Jacob is from the side of *Din*. This is why it writes, 'saying,' and Israel is *Rachamim*, for telling is *Rachamim*." It says (Item 265), "Jacob is considered *VAK*, and Israel is considered *GAR*. This is why it is written, 'And tell the children of Israel,' meaning to show *Hochma* and to speak in the spirit of *Hochma*, since telling implies *Hochma*."

First, we will explain what *The Zohar* interprets about the discernment of Jacob. It says, 1) *VAK*, 2) females, 3) *Din*, 4) a revealed degree, the lower degree, the literal.

The order of the work that a person should begin in order to achieve the goal is to know his state in the work of the Creator and what is the goal that he must reach. In other words, what is the wholeness that a person must achieve?

The first state is for a person to know that he is an idol-worshipper, called "idolater." This is the evil inclination that exists in man's body. It is called "a strange God" or "a foreign God." This is to clarify his state, where he truly is—that he is truly in a state of idol-worshipping.

However, one should make great efforts to see the truth because it is impossible to reach the truth unless through Torah and work, as our sages said, "From *Lo Lishma* [not for Her sake], one comes to *Lishma* [for Her sake]." In a state of *Lo Lishma*, when a person exerts in Torah and work, it is human nature to look at people in his surroundings. And he sees that there are no other people like him, dedicating so many hours to the work of the Creator.

In that state, he feels superior to others, which causes him to forget the goal, meaning that the main thing is to achieve *Lishma*. This is because people on the outside caused him to feel wholeness, and that wholeness is why he cannot feel that he is devoid of the main goal—reaching *Lishma*.

It is especially so if he is respected for being a servant of the Creator. Indeed, all the people who honor him instill their views so that he will believe what they think about him, that he is a highly virtuous man without any faults. Thus, how is it possible that a person will say about himself that he is in a state of idol-worshipping, that he is still uncircumcised? It follows that his *Dvekut* to the masses, meaning their *Dvekut* to his Torah and work brought him wholeness. In the work, this is called "a grip to the external ones."

And what is he losing by their having a grip? The answer is that the grip is the reason why he cannot see his real state, that he is still in a state of idol-worshipping, and should seek advice to exit the domination of the evil.

The second state of a person is when he circumcises himself. "Circumcision" means that he cuts off the foreskin. The foreskin is the three impure *Klipot* [shells/peels], called "Stormy Wind," "Great Cloud," and "Blazing Fire," and the will to receive comes from there.

However, it is not within one's power to cut off this foreskin. Baal HaSulam said about this that the Creator should help in order for a person to be able to cut off the foreskin. It is written about it, "And made a covenant with him." The meaning of "With him" is that the Creator helped him. However, the person must begin.

Yet, if we say that he cannot circumcise himself by himself, then why should a person start, if we say that he cannot finish? It seems as though his work is in vain. However, it is known that there is no light without a *Kli* [vessel], and a *Kli* is called "a deficiency," since where there is no deficiency, there is no filling.

Thus, a person having to start refers to the deficiency. It does not mean that a person should start with the filling. Rather, when we say, "start," it is about giving the need and the lack. Afterward, the Creator comes and gives the filling for the lack. This is called "And made a covenant with him," that the Creator helps him.

This is also regarded as the right line, which is the meaning of "Father gives the white," as explained in *The Study of the Ten Sefirot*.

This means that when the upper light shines—meaning *Ohr Hochma* [light of *Hochma*], called *Aba* [father]—it is possible to see the truth, that the foreskin—will to receive—is a bad thing. Only then does one realize that he should throw away the self-love. This is the help that a person receives from the Creator: he comes to the recognition of evil.

In other words, before a person comes to the resolution that it is not worthwhile to use the receiver, one cannot use the vessels of bestowal, since one contradicts the other. For this reason, a person must circumcise himself, and then he can take upon himself the desire to bestow.

It follows that removing the foreskin, called "circumcision," comes by help from above. In other words, it is precisely when the upper light shines that one sees his baseness, that he cannot receive anything because of the disparity of form. In the worlds, this is called "Father gives the white."

And after he comes to the recognition of evil comes a second correction: he begins to work in order to bestow. But this, too, requires help from above. This is called "His mother gives the red." In *The Study of the Ten Sefirot*, he interprets that this relates to the desire to bestow. It follows that both the power to annul the will to receive and the power that can perform acts of bestowal are given by the upper one. In other words, the help comes from above.

This brings up the question, "What does the lower one give?" Since it is said that the lower one must start. With what does he start, so that afterwards the Creator will give him the necessary assistance?

As it was said, all that the lower one can give to the Creator is the lack, for the Creator to have a place to fill. In other words, one who wishes to be a servant of the Creator and not an idol-worshipper must come to feel his lowliness. To the extent that he feels this, a pain gradually forms within him for being so immersed in self-love, actually like a beast, and that he has no connection with the discernment of a human.

Yet, sometimes a person comes to a state where he can see his lowliness and not care that he is immersed in self-love, and he does not really feel that he is in such lowliness, to the point of needing the Creator to deliver him from it.

In that state, a person should tell himself, "I am not inspired that I am like a beast, doing only beastly things, and my only concern in that state is that I ask of the Creator to let me feel more delight in corporeal pleasures, and I feel no desires otherwise." In that state, a person should tell himself that now he is in a state of unconsciousness. And if he cannot pray for the Creator to help him, there is only one solution: to bond with people whom he believes do feel the flaw, that they are in lowliness and who ask the Creator to deliver them from trouble to relief and from darkness to light, although they have not been delivered yet—by the Creator bringing them closer.

Afterward, he should say, "Of course they still have not completed their *Kli* of deficiency, called 'the need to be delivered from this exile.' However, they have probably traversed the majority of the way to feeling the real need." Thus, through them, he can receive their sensation, too, meaning that he will feel pain at being in lowliness, too. However, it is impossible to receive the influence of the society if he is not attached to the society, meaning *if he does not appreciate them.* To the extent that he does, he can receive from them the influence without any work, simply by adhering to the society.

It follows that in the second state, when he is circumcised and has gone through the two discernments—1) removal of the evil, which is the annulment of the vessels of reception, 2) obtaining the vessels of bestowal—it is considered that now he receives the degree of *VAK*. This is considered half a degree, since a complete degree means that he can use the vessels of reception in order to bestow, as well.

And since he only obtained the vessels of bestowal, to be in order to bestow, after he was circumcised, it is merely regarded as the degree of *VAK*. This is called "the degree of Jacob." It is also called "female," as in, "His strength is as weak as a female," which means that he cannot overcome and aim them in order to bestow, but only with the vessels of bestowal.

And this degree, too, is called *Din*. It means that there is still *Midat haDin* [quality of judgment] over the vessels of reception, that it is forbidden to use them because he cannot aim in order to bestow. It is also called "a revealed degree," to know that there is another degree, which is hidden from him. It is also called "a low degree," to know that there is a high degree. We need to know this so as to know that there is more work to be done, meaning to still reach a higher degree.

This degree is also called "the literal," since now that he has circumcised himself, he has become "a simple Jew." That is, before he was circumcised he was an idol-worshipper. Now he is simply discerned as "Jewish."

Also, now he is called "Jacob," as it is written, "Thus shall you say to the house of Jacob," meaning "saying," which is a soft speech, since the degree of Jacob is regarded as working only with vessels of bestowal, which are pure *Kelim*. This is why there is "saying" there, which is soft speech.

This is not so with the discernment of "Israel." *The Zohar* interprets Israel as being 1) the degree of GAR, wholeness of everything, 2) males, 3) *Rachamim*, 4) a high and hidden degree, the secrets of the Torah.

We shall explain them one at a time.

1) The degree of GAR. Since each degree comprises ten *Sefirot*, which divide into *Rosh* and *Guf* [head and body, respectively], the *Rosh* is called GAR, meaning *Keter-Hochma-Bina*, and the *Guf* is called ZAT. They are two halves of the degree. This is why VAK is considered the low degree and GAR is considered the high degree. It is known that when speaking of the degree of VAK, it is called "half a degree." This is a sign that the GAR is absent. For this reason, when saying, "the degree of GAR," it means that there is a complete degree here, since the rule is that when two degrees are together, the

higher one is mentioned and includes the lower one. This is why *The Zohar* calls the perfection of everything, "Israel."

2) The degree of males. Each degree contains two kinds of *Kelim*: *Zach* [pure/fine]—which are vessels of bestowal, and *Av* [thick], which are vessels of reception. It is possible to use them only if the intention to bestow is placed on them. And since in order to bestow is against nature, it requires great effort with much strength against nature. And when one can overcome only the fine *Kelim*, this is called "a female," implying that his power is as weak as a female's. But when he can overcome the vessels of reception, too, he is called "a man," "male," "strong." And since Israel is considered GAR, the perfection of everything, using the vessels of reception, too, Israel is considered "males."

3) The degree of *Rachamim*. Since there was a *Tzimtzum* [restriction] and *Din* [judgment] over the vessels of reception, and it is forbidden to use them unless one can do it in order to bestow, when one cannot aim to bestow with vessels of reception, there is *Din* over them and it is forbidden to use them. This is why a female is called *Din*.

But a male means that one can overcome in order to bestow in vessels of reception, too, and the *Din* is removed from them. He is using the vessels in order to bestow, and this is called *Rachamim* [mercy]. It is considered that the previous *Din* has been mitigated by the quality of *Rachamim*, that now he is receiving on the degree of in order to bestow. This is why a male is called *Rachamim*.

This means that males are called *Rachamim* and not *Din*, as written in *The Zohar* (Item 261): "Thus shall you say to the house of Jacob," meaning "saying" is from the side of *Din*, and "Tell the children of Israel" means that "telling" is from the side of *Rachamim*.

RASHI interprets the verse, "Thus shall you say to the house of Jacob": "The name *Mekhilta* [an interpretation on the book *Exodus*] are the women, tell them with soft speech, and 'Tell the children of Israel,' the males, the words are as hard as tendons."

The Meaning of the Strict Prohibition to Teach Idol Worshippers the Torah

We should interpret the words, "To the women with soft speech." It was mentioned above that females are those who do not have much strength to overcome, but only over the fine *Kelim*. This is called "soft," meaning it is soft and not so difficult to overcome the vessels of bestowal ["difficult" is the same word as "hard" in Hebrew].

But the vessels of reception are very hard to overcome. Hence, the males—those who are in a state of males, who have the power to overcome—were given work in things that are as hard as tendons, referring to the vessels of reception. But why does *The Zohar* write that males are *Rachamim*? Rather, it says, "As hard as tendons," and hard means *Din*, not *Rachamim*. Hence, on the one hand, it says that males means as hard as tendons, and on the other hand it says that they are *Rachamim*.

We should interpret that males have the power to overcome the vessels of reception, too, which are hard to overcome. And when overcoming the vessels of reception, called *Midat haDin* [quality of judgment] that is on them, there is *Rachamim* on that place, and not *Din*. But with females, who have no power to overcome the vessels of reception, there is *Midat haDin* on them and they are forbidden to use.

4) A high and hidden degree, considered "the secrets of the Torah." "Hidden" means that even if a person has already circumcised himself and has been rewarded with the literal, meaning with being a simple Jew, that is, he has come to a state where he is not committing idolatry but serves the Creator, the light of *Hochma*—revealed over the vessels of reception—is still hidden from him.

But one who has been rewarded with the highest discernment, who is a male and has the power to overcome the vessels of reception, too, the light of *Hochma*, called "the secrets of Torah," appears on those *Kelim*. This is why *The Zohar* says (Item 265), "And tell the children of Israel," meaning to show *Hochma* and to speak in the spirit of *Hochma*, since "telling" implies *Hochma*, as it is written, "And he shall tell them his covenant."

It follows that saying that it is forbidden to teach Torah to idol worshippers should be interpreted in the work as, "It is impossible to teach idol-worshippers Torah." As Baal HaSulam said, when speaking in matters of the work, where it writes, "forbidden," it means "cannot." But after he is circumcised, there are two degrees—upper and lower—meaning literal and hidden.

What Is Preparation for Reception of the Torah?

Article No. 18, Tav-Shin-Mem-Zayin, 1986-87

The writing says, "And the Lord came down on Mount Sinai, to the top of the mountain." Concerning the people, the writing says, "And they stood at the foot of the mountain."

We should understand what "came down" means for the Creator, which means a descent, lessening. After all, this was at the time of the giving of the Torah, so why should this be regarded as a descent for the Creator, as this was a time of joy?

Our sages said about "and they stood," that it teaches that "He forced the mountain on them like a vault" and said, "If you accept the Torah, very well. But if you do not, there will it be your burial" (*Shabbat* 88). He asked there in the *Tosfot*, "Forced the mountain on them like a vault," although they had already preceded doing to hearing. There are many answers to this question, but we should also understand the meaning of forcing on them the mountain like a vault in the work.

To understand the above, we must remember the known rule that there is no light without a *Kli* [vessel]. That is, there cannot be filling without a lack. It is impossible to enjoy something without yearning for it, and yearning for something is called "preparation," meaning a need. The need for something determines the yearning, and the level of the pleasure corresponds to the level of the yearning.

It therefore follows that prior to the giving of the Torah, there had to be a preparation for the reception of the Torah. Otherwise, there could not be joy of the Torah. That is, they had to prepare the need to receive the Torah, and the need yields the above-mentioned yearning. According to the level of the yearning, so is the measure by which we can enjoy the Torah. However, we should know what indeed is the need for the reception of the Torah.

Our sages said (*Baba Batra* 16), "The Creator created the evil inclination, He has created for it a spice." RASHI interpreted "Created for it the Torah as a spice," which cancels thoughts of transgressions, as was said (*Kidushin* 30), "If you encounter this villain, pull him into the seminary." And there, in *Kidushin*, they said, "Thus the Creator said to Israel: 'I have created the evil inclination, and I have created for it the spice of Torah. If you engage in Torah, you will not be given into its hands,' as was said, 'and if you do well.' 'But if you do not engage in Torah, you will be given into its hands,' as it was said, 'Sin crouches at the door.'"

Accordingly, we see that the Torah is a correction to come out of the governance of the evil inclination. This means that one who feels he has the evil inclination, who feels that the evil inclination, with all the counsels it gives to a person about how to be happy and enjoy life, aims to harm him. That is, it obstructs him from achieving the real good, called "*Dvekut* [adhesion] with the Creator." This is why a person says about it that this inclination is bad and not good.

However, it is very difficult for a person to say about it. That is, the evil inclination makes him understand that it is in his interest to see to his enjoyment in life, to feel pleasure from the things he does, meaning that all his actions will be only for his own sake. It makes him understand that a person should know the rule that all the counsels it gives him are only with one thing in mind: his own benefit. And even though sometimes it says that he should do something for another, it is with good reason that it tells him to work in favor of another. It is calculated in advance that this act will later yield benefit for himself. Therefore, how can a person say about it that it is an evil inclination, when it tells him to believe that it has no other aim but his own good, and not the good of anyone else?

For this reason, a person has a lot of work to come to feel that his will to receive is bad, to the extent that a person will know with absolute certainty that he has no greater enemy in the world than the receiver in him, as King Solomon would call it, "enemy." It is as it is written, "If your enemy is hungry, feed him bread." It is very difficult for a person to determine once and for all that he is bad and wants only to fail him from walking on the good path, which is the very opposite of the way of the receiver, since the path of truth is only to bestow, while the receiver wants only to receive. It follows that here is where one must choose if he is to be called "good" or "bad."

Our sages said about it (*Nida*), "Rabbi Hanina Bar Papa says, 'That angel appointed over pregnancy is called Laila [Hebrew: night]. It takes a drop and places it before the Creator and says to Him: 'Master of the world, what shall become of this drop? Will it be a mighty one or a weakling, a wise one or a fool, rich or poor?' But 'wicked or righteous' it did not say. Rather, this was given to man's choice.'"

We should interpret that choice means to determine, decide, and name the receiver in a person, or that it is truly a good inclination because it tends to man's benefit and is not distracted for even a minute into caring for others whatsoever. For this reason, it is worthwhile to listen to it, since it cares only for his own benefit, meaning that he will be happy. Therefore, it should be trusted and not veer off from it to the right or to the left, but carry out all its commandments and not deviate from it one bit.

There is also the opposite view, that it is indeed bad because by listening to it and engaging in self-love, we become remote from the Creator due to disparity of form. Then the quality of judgment is on a person, which was done by the correction of *Tzimtzum* [restriction] that was done on the light of doing good to His creations. For this reason, the name of the Creator, The Good Who Does Good, cannot be revealed where there is self-love. And for this reason, a person must decide once and for all that self-love is the real bad and harm-doer for a person.

However, the question is, from where can one receive the strength to make a choice to say about the receiver that it is so bad as to say that from this day forward he will not listen to it?

The truth is that this, too, requires help from the Creator to show him the truth, that the receiver for himself is man's real wicked one and enemy. When a person comes to feel this, he is immune from sinning. Then, all the concealments and punishments are removed from him because when he already knows that this is the angel of death, he will certainly run away from death. This is the time when the delight and pleasure that is in the purpose of creation can be revealed. At that time a person comes to attain the Creator, who is called The Good Who Does Good.

Accordingly, we should interpret what is written (Genesis 8:21), "And the Lord said in His heart, 'I will curse no more the earth because of man, for the inclination of a man's heart is evil from his youth.'" Nachmanides interpreted "in His heart" as not revealing the matter to the prophet at that time. And Even Ezra adds and says, "Afterward, He revealed His secret to Noah."

It is difficult to understand that verse, for did the Creator see only now that "the inclination of a man's heart is evil from his youth" and before this, He did not know?

In the work, we should interpret that the Creator now disclosed, after all the work that a person has put into awakening to achieve the truth, meaning to really know why he was born and what goal he should achieve, so now the Creator disclosed to him that the inclination of a man's heart, which is the receiver, is evil from his youth. That is, it cannot be said that now he sees that the inclination has become bad. Rather, it is evil from his youth. However, until now he could not determine that it was really evil; therefore, the person was in states of ascent and descent. In other words, at times he would listen to the inclination and say that from now on I will know that this is my enemy and everything it advises me to do is to my detriment.

But afterwards, the esteem of the inclination rises again and once again he listens to it and works for it wholeheartedly, and so on and so forth. He feels that he is as "a dog returning to its vomit." That is, he has already determined that it was unfit for him to listen to it because all the nourishments that the inclination gives him are but food fit for beasts and not for man. But all of a sudden, he returns to animal food and forgets all the decisions and views he had before.

Afterward, when he regrets, he sees that he has no other way but for the Creator to make him see that the inclination that is called "evil" really is evil. Then, once the Creator has given him this knowledge, he does not go astray again but asks the Creator to give him the strength to overcome it each and every time the inclination wants to fail him, so he will have the strength to overcome it.

It therefore follows that the Creator should give him both the *Kli* [vessel] and the light, meaning both the awareness that the inclination is evil and there is a need to emerge from under its reign, and the correction for this is the Torah, as it is written, "I have created the evil inclination, I have created the Torah as a spice." Accordingly, the Creator gave him both the need for the Torah, as well as the Torah. This is regarded as the Creator giving him the light, as well as the *Kli*.

According to the above, we should interpret the above verse, "And the Lord said in His heart." The interpreters interpreted that not revealing the matter to the prophet is regarded as "in His heart." Afterward, He revealed His secret. What is the secret? That the inclination of a man's heart is evil from his youth.

Thus, the order is that first one must see by himself and choose and determine that the name of the inclination in his heart is "evil." Afterward, he sees that he is unable to determine resolutely that he will not go back on his word and say that the inclination is a good thing and it is worthwhile to listen to it, and so on and so forth. At that time, it is regarded that the Creator says "in His heart," that the inclination of a man's heart is evil from his youth, but to one who engages in choice, the Creator still did not reveal that secret that the inclination is called "evil" because it is evil. This is done in order to give man room for choice and to determine that it is evil.

But afterwards, when a person sees that he cannot say that it is utterly evil, but regrets every time, then comes the state where he cries out to the Creator, "Help me!" This is the meaning of what Even Ezra says, "Afterward, He revealed His secret to Noah." It means that Noah is called "serving the Creator." That is, when the Creator reveals to a person that the inclination is evil from his youth, which is nothing new that the evil inclination is evil, "but I did not tell you. Now that I am telling you this secret, that Man's inclination is evil, you can be certain that you will no longer listen to it, since I myself revealed this to you. Therefore, I will no longer curse," since there will not be any need for more punishments, since everything will be okay, as it is said, "And I will strike no more all the living, as I had done."

This means that before the Creator disclosed that the inclination of a man's heart is evil, there had to be ascents and descents. That is, in the beginning of the work you had vitality, but in order to walk on the right path, you had to strike all the living, meaning I took from you the vitality you had in the work, and you descended from there to a state of lowliness because you have evil, which is the evil inclination. Then there can be, "I have created the evil inclination, I have created the Torah as a spice." But before he has this evil inclination, he feels the necessity for the Torah. For this reason, only after the Creator revealed the secret that the inclination of a man's heart is evil can there be the giving of the Torah, since there is no light without *Kelim* [vessels], and only where there is a need it is possible to give him what he needs.

However, the Creator revealing to him that the inclination of a man's heart is evil is also called "light," meaning filling, and there is no filling without a lack. For this reason, a person cannot be rewarded with the Creator revealing the bad to him before he has a need for it, since there is a rule that it is not man's way to act needlessly, and it is even more so with the Creator, who does not do anything needlessly.

Accordingly, from where can one receive the need for the Creator to reveal to him the above-mentioned secret? For this reason, one needs to begin the work and know that his receiver is his evil, and he must escape from its ruling, and everything he does in Torah and in prayer, or when he engages in *Mitzvot* [commandments/good deeds], it is to try to make all these actions bring him the recognition of evil. When he feels that he is bad and wants to perform acts of bestowal, he begins to receive vitality. When he falls from his degree, he loses the vitality.

It is the Creator Himself who makes him fall from His degree, since he still does not see the real evil in him. But through the descents he has each time, he asks the Creator to reveal to him once and for all that the will to receive is evil and not to be taken after it.

It follows that the descents he has, come to him from the Creator, as it is written, "And I will strike no more all the living," to receive from Him the vitality in the Torah and work and to remain without any vitality of *Kedusha* [sanctity/holiness] because man has already been completed with the need for the Creator to help him recognize the evil permanently, so as not to yearn once more to listen to the voice of the evil. It is so because man has come to the need for the Creator to help him, since now he sees that it is impossible that he will ever be fond of the evil inclination and want to listen to it, and will go astray again endlessly. This is the reason why he needs the Creator now, to help him know that the inclination within him is bad, and is the reason why he cannot achieve the delight and pleasure that the Creator has created for the creatures.

This is why a person has many descents, for by this a desire forms within him to yearn for the Creator to help him feel that the inclination of a man's heart is evil.

Now we can understand what we asked: What is the preparation for the reception of the Torah? The answer is—the evil inclination. When a person knows that he has evil in him, which is after the Creator has informed him this, a new need is born in a man: how to defeat it. Yet, this can be only through Torah, as our sages said, "I have created the evil inclination, I have created the Torah as a spice." This is the preparation for the reception of the Torah. That is, the need for the Torah is called "the preparation for the reception of the Torah."

By this we will understand what we asked about the meaning of the words, "And the Lord came down on Mount Sinai, to the top of the mountain." What is "the top of the mountain," and how can a descent be said about the Creator? It is known that in spirituality, the name is according to the action, as it is written about Manoah with the angel who said, "Why do you ask for my name?" Rather, it is according to the action.

For example, an angel who heals will be called Angel Refael [the Creator's healing], and so forth. Likewise, when the Creator sends healing to a person, the Creator is called "Healer of the sick." According to the above, the Creator revealing to man that the inclination of a man's heart is evil is regarded as the Creator revealing to a person in what state of descent the man was born, as it was written, "evil from his youth," meaning from the day he was born. Then, the Creator is named after the action, showing to the man his lowly state, and this is called "And the Lord came down on Mount Sinai."

We find two wordings here: 1) Regarding the Creator, it is written, "And the Lord came down on Mount Sinai, to the top of the mountain." 2) Regarding the people, it is written, "And they stood at the foot of the mountain."

We must understand what is a "mountain." The word *Har* [mountain] comes from the word *Hirhurim* [thoughts], which is man's intellect. Anything that is in the intellect is regarded as "in potential." Afterward, it can expand into actual fact. Accordingly, we can interpret "And the Lord came down on Mount Sinai, to the top of the mountain," as the thought and intellect of man, meaning that the Creator informed all the people that the inclination of a man's heart is evil from his youth. After the Creator informed them in potential, meaning at the top of the mountain, that which was in potential expanded in actual fact.

For this reason, the people came to actually feel and everyone now sensed the need for the Torah, as it is written, "I have created the evil inclination; I have created the spice of Torah." Now they said that through actually feeling that they were forced to accept the Torah, meaning without choice, since they saw that if they received the Torah they would have delight and pleasure, and if not, there it would be their burial. In other words, if we remain in our current state, our lives will not be lives but they will be our burial place.

Accordingly, we should interpret "And the Lord came down to the top of the mountain" to mean that once the Creator informed them on the mountain, in the intellect, that the evil is man's heart, and once this has been set in their minds, in their thoughts and intellect, it immediately operated, as it is written, "And they stood at the foot of the mountain." In other words, the descent that was on the mountain operated on them and they stood at the foot of the mountain, meaning the above descents controlled them.

It follows that "forced the mountain on them like a vault" means the descent and the information they received on the mountain, meaning with the thought about them that now they will have to receive the Torah because this mountain, meaning this descent, causes them the need to receive the Torah, so they can overcome the evil in their hearts.

The meaning of "forced ... on them" is that the reason that now they must receive the Torah and they have no other choice is the mountain, meaning the information they received in the thought and intellect that they are in a state of descent because they have evil in the hearts. This is like a vault, meaning that it is coercive and they have no choice. This is regarded as the mountain controlling them at the bottom.

Accordingly, we should ask what does it mean that through the miracle on Purim, our sages said, "kept and received"?

It is that thus far coercively, henceforth willingly (*Shabbat* 88). It said, "Raba said, 'Nevertheless, the generation received it in the days of Ahasuerus,' as it is written, 'The Jews kept and received.'" RASHI interpreted that it was for the love of the miracle that was done for them.

We should explain this as it is written in the "Introduction to the Study of the Ten Sefirot" (p 41): "There is conditional love, where because of the pleasure he feels in Torah and *Mitzvot*, he keeps them. But there is a higher degree called 'unconditional love,' that because of the miracle, they took upon themselves to observe Torah and *Mitzvot* without anything."

What Are Revealed and Concealed in the Work of the Creator?

Article No. 19, Tav-Shin-Mem-Zayin, 1986-87

The writing says (Micah 6:8), "He has told you, O man, what is good, and what does the Lord require of you but to do justice, love mercy, and to walk humbly with your God?" Here in this verse we see two things revealed before us: 1) "To do justice," where we see that He does justice. 2) "Love mercy," where we see that He loves mercy. How do we know this? We see that He does mercy. He must certainly love it or He would not do mercy. And one thing that was said here is concealed, as it is written, "and to walk humbly with the Lord your God."

We need to understand the meaning of walking humbly. In the literal, it is interpreted that the two above-mentioned things—doing justice and loving mercy—should be in concealment, so no one will see his good deeds. But what does this mean in the work?

It is known that there are the acts of *Mitzvot* [commandments/good deeds] and the intention of the *Mitzvot*. In the actions, everyone is equal; there is no difference between a great righteous and an ordinary person, since it was said about the practicing *Mitzvot*, "Do not add and do not subtract." We do not say that the righteous has two mezuzahs [text from the Torah placed on the right hand doorpost], one on the right side of the door and on the left side. Rather, the difference between great and small is only in the intention.

In the intention we should also make two discernments: 1) to aim that now he is performing the *Mitzvot* of the Creator, 2) aim for the reason that makes him observe the *Mitzvot* of the Creator.

However, in this regard we should make several discernments: 1) He is observing the *Mitzvot* of the Creator for by this, people around him will respect him and so forth. It follows that what compels him to keep the Creator's *Mitzvot* is people and not the Creator. That is, if there were no people around him, he would not observe the *Mitzvot* of the Creator.

And in this discernment, too, we should discern whether he is doing this out of coercion. That is, a person who desecrates the Shabbat [Sabbath] might work for a religious person. The rule is that if he can force him not to desecrate the Shabbat, the rule is that he must force him. For example, if he does not observe the Shabbat, he will fire him from the job. If he has no place else to work, he will certainly promise him that he will not desecrate the Shabbat.

It turns out that he is observing the *Mitzvot* of his boss, meaning he follows the commandments of the giver of the work, and he has no connection with the Creator. However, in terms of the law, we see that this, too, is regarded as observing *Mitzvot*. Otherwise, why would he need to force him to observe *Mitzvot*?

It turns out that this servant is only working out of coercion. It is as we said (Article No. 29, *Tav-Shin-Mem-Vav*) that Maimonides said (*Hilchot De'ot*, Chapter 6), "In matters of above, if he did not revert in concealment, he is shamed in public. He is despised and cursed until he repents." It follows that he is observing the Mitzvot because the public is forcing him.

Concerning the reason that people are compelling him, we should discern whether he enjoys performing that Mitzva or not. When he performs the Mitzvot because he is respected and so forth, he enjoys observing the Mitzvot. But if he is observing Torah and Mitzvot because of coercion, he always yearns to come out of that exile so he will not suffer from the Torah and Mitzvot, which is to him as "will pass on his own will, and will not be killed" by the people compelling him to observe the Torah and Mitzvot.

It therefore follows that one who observes because of respect from people can observe the Torah and Mitzvot gladly. But one who observes coercively, cannot be in happiness. Rather, he sits and waits for an opportunity to escape from this exile, since he is not observing the Mitzvot of the Creator because he wants to observe what the Creator said, but he must observe because people on the outside are chasing him, and he cannot suffer greater torments than the torments of observing Mitzvot. For this reason, this manner is worse than the first.

It follows that there are two discernments in aiming to observe Torah and Mitzvot: 1) out of fear and coercion, 2) out of love, when he is happy when he observes Torah and Mitzvot.

There is also another discernment in the reason that makes him observe Torah and Mitzvot. It is called "walking humbly." This refers to the actions—so everything he does, no one sees or hears of his good deeds, and he does everything in concealment. In terms of the intention, it is certainly hidden from the eye of every living thing.

But in the intention, there are two discernments to make: 1) He is observing Torah and Mitzvot and there is nothing here that is because of people, since no one knows about his work. Rather, the reward that the Creator pays for listening to Him is the reason compelling him to observe Torah and Mitzvot.

This manner is regarded as believing in the Creator and believing in reward and punishment. Thus, the reward and punishment is the reason compelling him to engage in Torah and *Mitzvot*. We can call this manner "working *Lishma* [for Her sake]," meaning for the Creator and not for people to respect him.

This is certainly clean work, which is entirely for the Creator: 1) With respect to actions, he does not want anyone to see his good deeds so they will reward him for it. 2) With respect to intention, he does not require people to pay him anything for this work in Torah and *Mitzvot*. Rather, he wants the Creator to pay his reward for his work.

However, this manner of walking humbly is still incomplete, although it is more important than the two prior manners, which is when people compel him: 1) the first is because of fear and coercion, 2) the second is because of love.

Here, however, the reason is only that the Creator compels him. Yet, since he wants reward in return for his work, by this he becomes separated from the Creator due to disparity of form. For this reason, his work is still incomplete.

Complete work means that he works in concealment, his intention is that only the Creator compels him to engage in Torah and *Mitzvot*, and other people have no grip on his work. At the same time, he is working not in order to receive reward, but only for the Creator. This is regarded as wanting to adhere to the Creator, as in, "As He is merciful, so you are merciful."

This means that all his work is in order to bestow, and he derives great satisfaction from the privilege of serving the King. From this he derives pleasure and joy, and he has no other need to be given anything. Rather, when he observes Torah and *Mitzvot* in utter simplicity and cannot aim any intentions, he settles for this as though he can serve the King with an important service.

It is like a person working for the king as a cleaner compared to one who is the king's minister and advises the king wherever the king needs his help. There is certainly a great difference from the king's cleaning man, both in salary and in the respect of the king's minister.

The lesson is that there is certainly a difference between one who is serving the king when he has been rewarded with "The secrets of Torah are revealed to him and he entertains himself with the King," and one who is a commoner, observing Torah and *Mitzvot* without any understanding of the intellect of the Torah. Rather, he is happy that he has been privileged with observing the King's *Mitzvot*, which He has given to him. He enjoys this more than any worldly pleasure, since the pleasures of this world seem to him as though they are serving the body, which is flesh and blood. But when he engages in utter simplicity, which is the simplest work, like a cleaner in the King's house, but says, "At the end of the day, whom do I want to please? The King." He does not want to serve himself, called "will to receive for his own sake," but his intention is that the Creator will enjoy his work.

It follows that a person should receive pleasure, since without pleasure a person cannot work. Because of the nature that the Creator has created, according to the thought of creation, which is His desire to do good to His creations, a desire and yearning to receive pleasure are imprinted in us.

However, there are great differences regarding the things from which we can receive pleasure. That is, pleasure is called "light," and there is no light without a *Kli* [vessel]. It follows that the pleasure that one wants to receive is placed in some *Kli*. This means that there are pleasures clothed in corporeal pleasures, such as lust. Yet, in lust, too, there are several discernments to make. It is likewise with respect, and one can also derive pleasure from learning knowledge. Every person can derive pleasure from the *Kelim* [vessels], which are generally called "lust," "respect," and "knowledge."

However, there is a fourth degree, which is serving the Creator. Baal HaSulam said in the "Introduction to The Book of Zohar" that there are four degrees called SVAS (still, vegetative, animate, and speaking): 1) "Still" is called "lust," 2) "Vegetative" is called "honor," 3) "Animate" is called "knowledge," and 4) "Speaking" is called "serving the Creator."

It follows that each one must receive pleasure, except there is a difference from which clothing a person can derive delight and pleasure. In this we should distinguish one from the other. For this reason, it turns out that the beginning of man's work on the path of truth is to achieve the degree of "walk humbly with your God."

That is, his work is in concealment, where no one has any contact with his Torah and *Mitzvot* because he is concealed from people. However, there is another thing that should be here: "Walk humbly with your God." "With" means in *Dvekut* [adhesion]. His work should be in *Dvekut* with your God and not in separation. This is so because specifically when he works not in order to receive reward, but entirely to bestow, he has equivalence of form, called "*Dvekut* with the Creator." But if his intention is to receive reward from the Creator for his work, then he is deemed a receiver, and the Creator is the giver. It follows that there is no *Dvekut* with the Creator here, but to the contrary, there is separation, for he is in oppositeness of form from the Creator.

By this we will understand what we asked, "What is the meaning of 'Walk humbly with your God'?" The literal meaning is that here is the beginning of the work called *Lishma*. It is as Rabbi Meir said, "He who learns Torah *Lishma* [for Her sake], henceforth, he is rewarded with many things and the secrets of Torah are revealed to him, and he becomes like a springing stream."

It therefore follows that we should distinguish between the work of the general public and the work of the individual.

The work of the general public refers to the whole of Israel, who learn Torah as a practice. In other words, in actual fact. There are seventy nations in the world, and there are good people with good qualities, and there are the opposite: wicked. In other words, in the world in general, there are many people. There, the order of the work is that the act is what matters. It is impossible that they will mind the intention, to make it *Lishma*. Instead, they are told, "From *Lo Lishma* [not for Her sake], we come to *Lishma*."

Also, their work does not need to be in concealment. Instead, the order is that each one tells his friend how much good deeds he has and how much time he dedicates to Torah and work. This is so on purpose, and there are two benefits from it: 1) It benefits the teller, since when he sees that someone is envious of him, it motivates him to work. That is, he has the power to work for others because he thinks that his friend will respect him for his work. It follows that this gives him fuel for work.

The reason is that anyone who makes any effort must have reward in return for it. The reward can be in money or in respect. That is, sometimes, the act that he does makes people respect him. This is already regarded as reward, like money. That is, some people work for respect, and respect pertains precisely to where there are people who see his actions.

However, there is a difference between money and respect from the perspective of the giver. Where one works for money, he does not care who gives the money. The giver can be a common person, but if he pays a higher price than a respectable person, in monetary payment, it is not the giver's personality that determines if the work is worthwhile, but the sum of money determines the place of the work.

This is not so with one who works for respect. Here, the giver is precisely the one who determines. If the giver is a distinguished person, it is not so difficult to work for respect. However, this depends on the level to which the person is regarded by the public as an important personality.

It therefore follows that it is difficult to serve the Creator not in order to receive reward, and a person expects some return. It is not enough for a person to serve the King because he lacks the faith in the greatness of the Creator, since otherwise, it is natural that the small one annuls before the great one, when a person is accepted by the public as a great personality.

For this reason, when a person can no longer feel the greatness of the Creator, he must work in *Lo Lishma*. This is why a person engages in Torah and *Mitzvot* in order for people to respect him. However, this is so only where he is in an environment that respects servants of the Creator. When one is among secular people, he certainly works in concealment so as not to receive contempt from them instead of respect.

However, once a person has crossed the stage of the general public, if a person awakens and wants to come out of the general public, meaning be to enslaved to the public, meaning that according to what the general public determines as the work of the Creator, this is what he can observe.

But what is not accepted by the public, and he feels that the work of the general public is not the final stage, but he has an inner drive that there is the issue of work that pertains specifically to individuals, where each individual contains the collective, then the matter of *Lishma* begins to be revealed to him. It is as Maimonides says (end of *Hilchot Teshuva*), "Until they gain more knowledge and acquire much wisdom, they are shown that secret bit by bit. They are accustomed to this matter calmly until they attain Him and know Him, and serve Him with love."

It follows from all the above that there is the wholeness of the action and the wholeness of the intention. Once a person keeps the wholeness of the action, which pertains to the general public, then begins the work on the wholeness of the intention. This is when one must try to make the cause compelling him to observe Torah and *Mitzvot* be the Creator, since he wants to bestow upon the Creator because he believes in the greatness and importance of the Creator.

For this reason, he regards it as a great merit if he succeeds in serving the King. This work is called "concealed work." Here, the work is primarily on the intention, which is not revealed to anyone. That is, not a single person in the world can know the reason that compels his friend to work in Torah and *Mitzvot*.

But in the work of the general public, called *Lo Lishma*, this is the revealed work, which is the practical part. This means that their wholeness is in the action. However, they were not given work on the intention, to make the intention whole, as well, meaning *Lishma*. Instead, they are taught to engage in Torah and *Mitzvot Lo Lishma*, as Maimonides says.

It is written in *The Zohar* (*Nasso*, Item 50): "'The concealed things belong to the Lord our God' are fear and love, which are in the mind and in the heart. These are the *Yod-Hey*. 'And the revealed things belong to us and to our children,' meaning the Torah and the *Mitzva* [singular of *Mitzvot*], which are in the externality of the *Guf* [body] and the *Rosh* [head]. This is the *Vav-Hey*. The meaning of the matter is that no one knows if a person fears the Creator or loves Him, since it is something that is revealed only between him and his Maker."

But a person who engages in Torah and engages in practical *Mitzvot*, this is revealed to everyone, since here the Creator has made it that he should engage in Torah openly, and eyes to look at it and ears to hear it. The Creator has also made man hands, legs, and a body with which to perform *Mitzvot*.

It is known that the name *HaVaYaH* comprises five worlds, called *AK* and *ABYA*. The tip of the *Yod* consists of *AK*. They contain five *Partzufim* called *Galgalta*, *AB*, *SAG*, *MA*, and *BON*. These comprise five *Sefirot*: *Keter*, *Hochma*, *Bina*, *ZA*, and *Malchut*. This means that each and every *Behina* [discernment] is included in one letter in the name *HaVaYaH*.

The Zohar says about the verse, "This is My name forever, and this is My remembrance to all generations," "My name" with *Yod-Hey* [in Hebrew] is 365 in *Gematria*, which implies to the 365 negatives [commandments not to perform certain actions]. "My remembrance" with *Vav-Hey* [in Hebrew] is 248 in *Gematria*, implying the positive *Mitzvot* [commandments to perform certain actions].

Baal HaSulam explained why the negatives are implied in *Yod-Hey*, which imply *Hochma* and *Bina*, and why the positive *Mitzvot*, which are certainly things with which to serve the Creator, are at a lower degree and are implied only in the *Vav-Hey*. He said that in the world of *Tikkun* [correction], it is in order to prevent another breaking of the vessels, since the reason for the breaking was that there were great lights in small vessels.

Hence, a correction was made that only small lights would shine, called "lights of VAK." And because it is forbidden to extend lights of GAR, and GAR is called *Yod-Hey*, which are *Hochma* and *Bina*, it is nonetheless necessary to extend lights of VAK. For this reason, the lights of VAK are implied in the name *Vav-Hey*. Therefore, the positive *Mitzvot* are in *Vav-Hey*, which is VAK, but the lights of GAR, which are forbidden to extend, are called "negative *Mitzvot*," meaning that it is forbidden to extend.

Accordingly, we can explain the meaning of *HaVaYaH* that includes fear and love, which are *Yod-Hey*, and Torah and *Mitzva*, which are *Vav-Hey*. We will explain them one at a time.

1) Fear means that one should be afraid lest he will bring little contentment to his Maker, as it is written in the "Introduction of The Book of Zohar" (Item 203): "Both the first fear and the second fear are not for his own benefit, but only for fear that he will lessen bringing contentment to his Maker."

Fear is the first *Mitzva* because it is impossible to truly believe in whole faith that he will not come into heresy before he has been rewarded with fear. It is as it is written in the "Introduction of The Book of Zohar" (Item 138): "It is a law that the creature cannot receive disclosed evil from the Creator, for it is a flaw in the glory of the Creator for the creature to perceive Him as an evildoer. Hence, when one feels bad, denial of the Creator's guidance lies upon him to the same extent, and the superior Operator is concealed from him."

Yet, when a person does all his works in order to bestow, at that time the *Kelim* are fit to receive the delight and pleasure, and then there is faith upon him because in that state, he attains the Creator as the good who does good. It is as it is written in the *Sulam* [Ladder commentary]: "Thus, it is no wonder that we are still unworthy of receiving His complete benefit. For this reason,

His guidance of good and evil has been prescribed for us." It follows that this is the root of faith by which we can be rewarded with permanent faith.

2) Love. Since through fear he is rewarded with delight and pleasure, at that time love appears. In love, too, we should discern between conditional love and unconditional love, as it is written in the "Introduction to The Study of the Ten Sefirot."

3) Torah. This extends from fear, since precisely through fear we can obtain the desire to bestow, as our sages said, "The light in it reforms him." For this reason, specifically through Torah we can come to fear and trepidation lest he will not be able to bring contentment to his Maker.

This is why the Torah is over the disclosure of fear. That is, if he is truly learning Torah on the path of truth and not for the sake of knowledge, and his intention in the Torah is to achieve fear. For this reason, the order of the work is from below upward. This is why the Torah, which is *Vav* of *HaVaYaH*, comes first, since through it he later achieves fear.

However, one who learns Torah with a different aim, not in order to achieve fear of heaven, this is not regarded as Torah, but as knowledge. It is as our sages said (*Midrash Rabbah, Eicha Rabatti* 2:17), "Should a man tell you, 'There is wisdom in the nations,' believe, 'There is Torah in the nations,' do not believe," since Torah belongs to those who learn in order to achieve fear of heaven.

4) *Mitzva*. This is *Hey* of *HaVaYaH*, and extends from love, which is the first *Hey* of *HaVaYaH*. Because of this, performing the *Mitzvot* should be with love and joy of observing the King's commandments. Here, too, we learn from below upward, meaning by a person exerting to observe the King's *Mitzvot* with love, by an awakening from below that causes an awakening of above, where the Creator reveals His love for Israel, as it is written, "You loved us and wanted us."

It follows that through Torah, fear appears, and through *Mitzva*, love appears. This means that a person should begin the order of the work from below upward: 1) first *Mitzva*, which is the last *Hey* of *HaVaYaH*, 2) then Torah, which is *Vav* of *HaVaYaH*, 3) then love, which is the first *Hey* of *HaVaYaH*, 4) and then fear, which is the *Yod* of *HaVaYaH*.

But in the order of bestowal that comes from above, fear appears first, then love, then a person attains love, and then he attains Torah, and then *Mitzva*.

However, the matter of the inclusion of the souls in the name *HaVaYaH* is specifically in the last *Hey*. It is as the holy ARI says, that the soul of *Adam HaRishon* is from the internality of *BYA*, and *BYA* emerged from *Malchut* of *Atzilut*, called "last *Hey* of the whole of *Atzilut*." For this reason, *Malchut* is called the "Assembly of Israel," as it includes within it all the souls.

And for this reason, man's work belongs to *Malchut*. That is, by observing Torah and *Mitzvot*, they cause the unification of the Creator and His *Shechina* [Divinity], since *Malchut* is called "a vessel of reception for the upper abundance," and the Creator is called "the Giver." This is why there is no unification here, called "equivalence of form." But when we engage here below in acts of bestowal, each one causes equivalence of form in the root of his soul, and this is called "unification," like the Creator, who is the Giver.

It is as it is written in *The Zohar* (*Nasso*, Item 29): "The letter *Hey* is a confirmation of things." The meaning of the matter is "Take with you things and return to the Creator. Certainly, when a person sins, he causes the *Hey* to move farther from the *Vav*, since *Ben Yod-Hey*, which is *Vav*, comprises *Yod-Hey-Vav*, and departed from the letter *Hey*. This is why the Temple was ruined and Israel were removed from there and were exiled among the nations. And this is why anyone who repents causes the *Hey* to return to the letter *Vav*, and redemption depends upon this.

What Is Man's Private Possession?

Article No. 20, Tav-Shin-Mem-Zayin, 1986-87

The *Zohar* (Korah, Item 4) interprets the verse, "And Korah took." It asks, "What is 'took'"? And it replies, he "took a bad advice for himself. Anyone who chases what is not his, it escapes him. Moreover, he loses even what he has. Korah chased what was not his; he lost what was his and did not win the other one."

We should understand in terms of the work, what is the thing that we can say that it belongs to a person, that we can say that it is his, and what is the thing of which we want to say that it is not his. *The Zohar* says about Korah that he chased what was not his and lost what was his, as well. What do these words tell us in the work, so that a person will know how to keep himself from Korah's punishment?

It is known that the primary innovation in creation is the will to receive, as it is written (*The Study of the Ten Sefirot*, Part 1, *Histaklut Pnimit*), "His desire is to do good to His creations, which is the connection between the Creator and the created beings. He has created a deficiency, meaning a desire and craving to yearn to receive delight and pleasure. Otherwise, it is impossible to enjoy anything."

It is known that it is forbidden to speak of that which preceded creation. Instead, all that we speak of is by way of "By Your actions, we know You." This means that we speak of that which exists in the creatures. Yet, why did the Creator make such a reality? He could have done it differently! Of this, we are forbidden to speak.

We see the nature that is in creation, that it is impossible to enjoy anything unless there is craving for it. Moreover, the craving for something determines the amount of pleasure that we can derive from the thing we crave.

For this reason, we attribute this *Kli* [vessel], called "will to receive delight and pleasure," to the *Kli* that the Creator has made. We have no permission or ability to revoke this *Kli*, or to spoil that will to receive. Once that *Kli* has come out and received the abundance that the Creator wanted to give her, the *Kli* felt that the root is the giver and the *Kli* is the receiver, that there is no equivalence of form here. For this reason, the *Kli* desired to be a giver like her root. She placed a *Tzimtzum* [restriction] on the quality of reception in a manner that the *Kli* is a receiver and the Emanator is the giver. Instead, she said that she will not receive anything but only to the extent that she can receive in order to bestow.

We attribute that *Kli*, who receives only if it is in order to bestow, to the creature, since this is an opposite action from what the Creator has created. The Creator created the lower one to receive, as this is the purpose of creation, called "His desire to do good to His creations," so the creatures will enjoy. But the lower one took the opposite action: It wants the Creator to enjoy. This is its gauge; it does not consider itself, its own pleasure, and in every act it calculates whether it should do this or not.

In other words, if it brings contentment to the Creator, it will do it. But if it does not see that it will bring contentment to the Creator, it avoids taking this action. This means that all the calculations it does prior to any operation are according to the ability to delight the Creator.

The abundance that spreads over this *Kli*, called "in order to bestow," is called "the light of line." It means that the light illuminates according to a line and a measure that the receiver can aim to bestow, which is equivalence of form. It does not regard its own pleasure because it wants *Dvekut* [adhesion]. Hence, it turns out that all the many worlds and *Partzufim* and *Sefirot* were made because of the receivers.

This means that while the light was illuminating in the *Kli* of the Creator, called "desire to receive in order to receive," called *Malchut*, that *Kli* had the ability to receive the delight and pleasure that was in the thought of creation because certainly, to the extent of delight and pleasure that He wants to give, He has created the size of the *Kli*. Therefore, the *Kli* received all the light and there was only one, simple light there, as it is written in the book *Tree of Life*, that "Prior to the *Tzimtzum*, the upper, simple light filled the whole of reality."

In other words, *Malchut*, called "will to receive," received all the abundance that He wanted to give, since that *Kli* came from the Emanator. For this reason, He certainly made the *Kli* whole, so she could receive what He wanted to give. But afterwards, *Malchut* said that she did not want to receive with the *Kli* of the Creator, but that she had her own *Kli*, which she has made. But since the lower one, who is the created being, cannot make a *Kli* like the Creator, instantaneously, but rather, the lower one is limited in what it should do, hence, that *Kli* was made slowly-slowly, according to the ability to aim in order to bestow.

Many degrees emerge from this, meaning that the light shines according to the ability of the *Kelim* [vessels] of the lower ones. He interprets likewise (*The Study of the Ten Sefirot*, Part 1) what the *Tree of Life* says, that the light expanded slowly-slowly. He asks, "How can it be said, 'slowly-slowly,' in spirituality, since there is no time there, and 'slowly-slowly' implies time?" He explains there in *Ohr Pnimi* [Baal HaSulam's interpretation to the text of the ARI] that slowly-slowly means that the light does not expand at once, but by degrees, to the extent that the lower ones can receive in order to bestow. This is regarded as "slowly-slowly."

It therefore follows that we have two *Kelim*: 1) The *Kli* that we attribute to the Creator. This is the *Kli* called "will to receive in order to receive." That *Kli* emerged in whole because from the perspective of the Creator, she has wholeness. 2) The *Kli* we attribute to the creature, namely the desire to bestow. That *Kli* is established slowly-slowly because the lower ones cannot make that *Kli* at once.

We should know that all of our work is based on a single point, meaning that the Torah and *Mitzvot* [commandments/good deeds] that we are commanded to observe are in order to obtain the *Kli* that we should make. We can make that *Kli* only through Torah and *Mitzvot*, as Rabbi Hananiah Ben Akashia says, "The Creator wanted to refine Israel, therefore He gave them plentiful Torah and *Mitzvot*, as was said, 'The Lord desired for His righteousness; He will increase the Torah and glorify.'" It is also written in the essay "Preface to the Wisdom of Kabbalah," And it is known that refinement comes from the word *Hizdakchut* [becoming refined]. It is as our sages said, that the *Mitzvot* were given only so as to cleanse Israel."

It follows that we only need to make the *Kli*, called "vessel of bestowal." We lack nothing else. It is as it is written, "And I will bless you in all that you do." That is, "doing" refers to the *Kli*. If we make the *Kli*, the Creator will fill it with blessing, meaning abundance, called "His desire to do good to His creations."

The vessel of bestowal is prepared for us in both mind and heart, since the Creator has given us a *Kli* to receive. For this reason, we have a yearning to understand everything with our intellect, since that desire has given us the yearning to gain knowledge. This causes us to want to understand the Torah and *Mitzvot*. However, at the same time, we have a yearning to understand Providence, meaning that man contemplates how the Creator behaves with him in a manner of guidance of good and doing good.

Here we need to believe above reason. Since a desire to understand and learn was installed in the body, it is clear that a desire to understand the ways of the Creator has awakened in him. However, that desire to understand and to learn was said about the

Torah, not about Providence. In other words, with this desire, with this force, we must understand everything only with regard to the Torah, and not with regard to Providence.

Baal HaSulam once explained what we say in the blessing, "Who has formed the man and created in him holes-holes, hollows-hollows. It is revealed and known before Your throne that should one of them open, or one of them become blocked, it will be impossible to exist and stand before You." He said that the difference between "holes" and "hollows" is that a hole should be blocked, but a hollow should remain hollow.

Interpretation: There are "law" and "justice." "Law" means that we should accept the matter as a law above reason. This is faith, and acceptance of faith should be above reason. It follows that lack of knowledge, understanding, and the intellect of something keeps it as a hollow, without knowledge. Each time, one must be careful not to fill up this hollow.

In the blessing, "who has created," we say, "[should] one of them become blocked, it will be impossible to exist." However, a hollow, meaning a place of lack of knowledge, must not be filled. Rather, we should always go above reason. This is called "mind," in order to bestow.

This is not so with justice, which is the Torah. Here, specifically, is the place where one should try to do what he can in order to understand the Torah. The Torah is called "the names of the Creator," and it is upon us to understand and attain. And here, in the Torah, the lack that is called "hole" should be blocked, meaning there should be no lack, and the more the better.

For this reason, we say, "should one of them be opened ... it will be impossible to exist." That is, "should one of them be opened" means that the hole will be opened, that there will be a hole and a lack in understanding the Torah. In such a state, a person has no existence or establishment, and instead, he should immediately see to filling that lack with the light of Torah, since the light of Torah reforms him. This is the *Kli* that is suitable to receive the upper abundance. Afterward, the light that is clothed in the Torah comes to him, called "613 deposits," as it is written in the "Introduction of The Book of Zohar."

However, normally, it is to the contrary. That is, the burden of the kingdom of heaven, which we should accept above reason, specifically here everyone wants to understand the Creator's Providence over people within reason. But with regard to the Torah, here they agree to go above reason and do not place sufficient attention to understanding.

It is written in *The Zohar* (*Hukat*, Item 2): "This is the statute of the Torah." It is also written, "This is the Torah," and it is not written, "statute." "This is the Torah" is to show that everything is in one unification, to include the assembly of Israel, which is *Malchut*, with the Creator, who is ZA, so that all will be one, without separation. "This" is general and particular together, meaning male and female together, since *Vav* is male, meaning ZA, which is the general. "This" is *Nukva* [female], meaning *Malchut*, who is particular. But "this" without an addition of *Vav* [in Hebrew] is the statute of the Torah. Of course, she is *Malchut*, called "statute," and she comes from ZA, who is called "Torah." She is only the judgment of the Torah, the decree of the Torah, which is *Malchut*.

We should understand the meaning of ZA being called "Torah" and "general," and "male" and *Vav*, while *Malchut* is called "the judgment of the Torah," "the decree of the Torah," "particular," *Nukva*, and the "assembly of Israel."

According to the above, we can interpret that the Creator is called ZA, as the ARI says, that the guidance of the world is in the form of ZA and *Malchut*, where ZA is called "general," meaning that everything extends from him. However, the one who receives from him, always takes only parts. That is, each time a part of the general appears in the parts. From that perspective, *Malchut* is called the "assembly of Israel," assembling within her parts of Israel, who is called ZA. This is with regard to *Malchut* being the receiver of abundance from ZA.

However, there is another interpretation. *Malchut* is called the "assembly of Israel" because she contains all the souls. From that perspective, we should interpret that *Malchut* takes abundance from ZA and bestows upon the souls of Israel. However, we should discern between the bestowal of ZA, called "Torah," and the bestowal of *Malchut*, called "the judgment of Torah" or "the decree of Torah," which is called "statute."

It is known that *Malchut* is called "faith," meaning that the kingdom of heaven should be accepted as a law above reason, for such is the decree of Torah, to accept the faith above reason. This is the meaning of her being regarded as "mind." Also, in the "heart," there should also be above reason and not consider what the body explains to us about what we should do and what we should not. Instead, everything must be above reason.

But the Torah is regarded as "general," meaning that everything extends from it. It means that doing good to His creations, which is the delight and pleasure, is included in His bestowal, and the strength to take upon himself the above reason is also included in the giver. That is, ZA, who is called "the Creator," must give that force so that the lower one will have the strength to overcome its reason and go above reason.

This force is called "light," and any light comes from the upper one. Only the *Kli* pertains to the lower one. A *Kli* means a lack, and a lack pertains to the lower ones. That is, if the lower one feels that he is lacking that force, meaning that he wants to go above reason but he cannot, this is called "a *Kli*." It was said about this, "There is no light without a *Kli*," as it is known that "There is no filling without a lack."

In that respect, we can call ZA by the name "general," since he includes everything. That is, he gives both the faith above reason and the Torah, called the "names of the Creator." We already said that the "names of the Creator" refers to the delight and pleasure revealed through the Torah, as the general name of the Creator is The Good Who Does Good. It is explained in the Torah how within each and every letter in the Torah, a special light is revealed. This discernment is called "the Torah, and Israel, and the Creator are one."

Accordingly, we understand that when he refers to ZA by the name "Torah," it is with respect to the names of the Creator. This is called "written Torah," where there is nothing to add or to subtract, since there is no attainment whatsoever in the giver, called "the Creator."

For this reason, there is nothing to add or to subtract, but rather everything that there is in the giver is revealed in the receiver. That is, what exists in the giver manifests in the receiver.

Yet, not everything that is in the giver is revealed in the receiver. Instead, each time, another detail is revealed in the receiver. For this reason, *Malchut*, which is the receiving *Kli*, is called "particular," and ZA is called "general." For this reason, *Malchut* is called "oral Torah," where "oral" means disclosure, for it discloses what is in the written Torah, called ZA.

However, *Malchut* is called the "judgment of Torah," which means that each discernment of the Torah that appears in *Malchut* is according to the judgment concerning what is permitted to be revealed. In other words, since *Malchut* is called the "receiver," and there was a judgment over the vessels of reception that it is forbidden to receive except to the extent that it is possible to aim to bestow, for this reason there are ups and downs in *Malchut*.

She is called "statute" because with regard to faith, she is a law without knowledge. If we ask ourselves, why should faith be a law? the answer is that such was His decree, that we should serve Him above reason, and this is why it is a law.

From that perspective, *Malchut* is called the "decree of the Torah," meaning that the Torah decreed that such would be the order of the work on work above reason. It is as RASHI says about the verse, "This is the statute of the Torah": "Since Satan and the nations of the world cause Israel to say, 'What is this *Mitzva* [commandment] and what is its purpose?' This is why it is written about it, 'statute,' 'It is a decree before Me,' and you have no permission to doubt it."

This is why we should not ask why the Creator wants us to serve Him above reason in regard to this, as well. That is, on this question, too, comes the answer that it is above reason, since common sense dictates that if our work is within reason, meaning that the body understood the ways of the Creator's guidance with the creatures, there would be no room for heretics and secular people to turn away from *Kedusha*. Rather, everyone would be servants of the Creator. It was said about this (Isaiah 55): "'For My thoughts are not your thoughts, and your ways are not My ways,' says the Lord."

This is why *The Zohar* writes "and this" with a *Vav* [in Hebrew]. It is to show that everything is in one unification, and to include the assembly of Israel, who is *Malchut*, in the Creator, who is ZA. We should interpret that unification is equivalence of form. For this reason, when the lower ones engage in Torah and *Mitzvot* with the aim to bestow, by this they cause, each in the root of his soul, which is *Malchut*, that it will be in order to bestow like ZA, who is called "male," meaning a giver.

This means that including the assembly of Israel, which is *Malchut*, in the Creator, who is ZA, by this appears all that there is in the general, which is ZA, the giver, in the *Malchut*, who is the receiving *Nukva*. Through the unification, each time, a new detail emerges in *Malchut*. This is why *Malchut* is called "particular."

According to the above, we should understand what we asked, What is private property, of which we can say that it belongs to the individual alone? According to what we explained, a person has in his world only the *Kelim* that he has made, called "vessels of bestowal." This is all that belongs to a person. But what enters the *Kelim* of reception does not pertain to man because that *Kli*, the Creator has made it.

For this reason, anything that enters these vessels does not belong to man as well, and all that a person has is what he placed in vessels of bestowal. For this reason, when *Korah* wanted to receive in *Kelim* that were not his, meaning in vessels of reception, he lost his *Kelim*, as well, which he had from the desire to bestow.

What Are Dirty Hands in the Work of the Creator?

Article No. 21, Tav-Shin-Mem-Zayin, 1986-87

The *Zohar* says in Balak (Item 43) about the verse, "When they come to the tent of meeting, they shall wash in water and will not die": We learn from this verse that "One who is not concerned with this and appears before the King with dirty hands must die. What is the reason? It is because man's hands are at the top of the world, where he (The *Hassid* Rabbi Shmaiah) said that every filth and every dirt goes up to the *Sitra Achra* because the *Sitra Achra* feeds on that filth and dirt. This is why the *Hassid*, Rabbi Shmaiah, said that one who blesses with dirty hands must die."

We should understand why this prohibition is so grave that one who blesses the Creator, who does something good, if his hands are dirty he must die. Can this be? That is, if he did not bless the Creator, he would not have to die. But if he blesses the Creator but his hands are unclean then he deserves death for it. And we should also understand why he says that man's hands are at the top of the world. What does this imply to us in the work of the Creator?

What Are Dirty Hands in the Work of the Creator?

It is known that our purpose in the work of the Creator is to achieve *Dvekut* [adhesion] with the Creator, which is equivalence of form, as our sages said, "As He is merciful, so you are merciful." This is all that we must do.

In other words, the reward for all the labor that we do in Torah and *Mitzvot* [commandments] should be that we will be rewarded with vessels of bestowal, which are *Kelim* [vessels] of *Dvekut*. Beyond that, the Creator gives everything.

It is known that from the perspective of the Creator, the purpose of creation is to do good to His creations, meaning for the creatures to receive delight and pleasure. However, in order for the delight and pleasure to be complete when the lower ones receive, and so as not to have shame in them, to establish this there was a judgment that it is forbidden to receive any pleasure in order to receive, but rather in order to bestow.

And since by nature, man is born with a will to receive in order to receive, and it is known that it is hard to go against nature, this causes us work and labor when we want to begin to walk on the path of bestowal and to avoid receiving anything in vessels of reception, but rather in vessels of bestowal, called "receiving in order to bestow."

It therefore follows that for the *Kelim* to be ready to receive the upper abundance, they must be in equivalence of form with the light. If they are not, there is a judgment because of the *Tzimtzum* [restriction] that was placed, whereby that *Kli* [vessel] must remain in an empty space. For this reason, all of our labor is to provide for ourselves clean *Kelim*, called *Ohr Hozer* [Reflected Light]. This means that as the Creator wants to bestow upon the creatures, the creatures want to bestow upon the Creator.

In other words, there is the *Ohr Yashar* [Direct Light], meaning that the abundance that comes from the Creator to the lower ones is called *Yashar* [straight/direct], meaning that the intention of creation to do good to His creations was about this. This is called *Ohr Yashar*. However, when *Malchut* of *Ein Sof* [infinity] received the

Ohr Yashar, she desired *Dvekut*, called "equivalence of form." For this reason, *Malchut* does not receive more *Ohr Yashar* than she has *Ohr Hozer*. In other words, the measuring she does on how much abundance to receive by looking at how much she can aim to bestow upon the Creator, which is called "light that returns to the Creator."

It is known that the main reward we hope to receive in return for the work in Torah and *Mitzvot* is only to receive that *Ohr Hozer*, as it is said in the preface to the book *Panim Meirot uMasbirot* (Item 3): "Know that the *Masach* [screen] in the *Kli* of *Malchut* is the root of the darkness by the force of detaining that exists in the *Masach* on the upper light, not to expand in *Behina Dalet*. This is also the root of the labor in order to receive reward because labor is an act that is not desirable, as the worker is content only when he rests. However, because the landlord pays his salary, he revokes his will before the will of the landlord. You should know that there is not a thing or a conduct in this world that is not rooted in the upper worlds, from which branches spread into the lower worlds. It follows that the power of detaining in the *Masach* is equal to the level of the labor, and the salary that the landlord gives to the worker is rooted in the *Ohr Hozer* that emerges through a *Zivug de Hakaa* whereby through the *Masach*, a root for the *Ohr Hozer* is made, and all the benefit in this comes to her because of the above-mentioned detainment."

We therefore see that one must make an effort in order to receive reward. What is the reward we hope for? The reward is that we will obtain vessels of bestowal. That is, through the labor, which is the root of the *Masach*, when we detain ourselves from receiving into our will to receive, meaning for our own sake, what do we want in return for this detainment? We want the Creator to give us a desire—that we will want to please the Creator.

This means that we give our desire to the Creator and we do not want to use it. In return for this, He will give us His desire. That is, as the Creator's desire is to bestow upon the creatures, He will give us the desire to bestow contentment upon Him, and this will be our reward. In other words, we want Him to change the *Kelim* we have by nature, called "receiving in order to receive." What we have we relinquish, and receive in return the vessels of bestowal.

This is as our sages said (*Avot*, Chapter 2, 4), "Revoke your will before His will so that He will revoke the will of others before your will." This means that a person should revoke his will to receive, which is the *Masach* we spoke of earlier, being the root of the labor and what detains the will to receive before the will to bestow, for the will to bestow is called "the will of the Creator," and it revokes the desire for self-benefit before the Creator's benefit.

However, man has no power to go against nature. Our sages said about this, "He who comes to purify is aided," so he may revoke the will of others. In other words, all the desires that awaken in the body and resist his having the ability to engage in the desire to bestow—the Creator does this. In other words, the Creator gives him the ability to revoke. It was said, "so that He will revoke the will of others before your will": You want to engage in the desire to bestow but you cannot; your reward will be that you will receive assistance from the Creator.

This means that in order for the Creator to revoke the will of others, meaning the will to receive, which is the will of others, and not of *Kedusha* [sanctity], a person must first begin this work, and then the Creator gives him the assistance required for it. This is so for the known reason that there is no light without a *Kli* [vessel]." That is, nothing comes from above unless there is a desire below, since the desire is called the need for it.

This is the meaning of what our sages said, "Revoke your will," meaning the will to receive, "before His will," meaning before the will of the Creator, for the will of the Creator is to bestow. Then, when you begin, according to the labor you will give in order to revoke the will to receive, to that extent, the need to ask the Creator to help you will form, and then you receive a complete desire and need for His help.

Saying "Revoke your will" means that a person should begin to revoke the will to receive "before His will," meaning before the desire to bestow, which is the Creator's will. "So that He will revoke the will of others before your will" means that once you have a desire and need for the desire to bestow, but you cannot revoke the will to receive, the assistance comes from above, meaning it "revokes the will of others," which are not of *Kedusha*, pertaining to the will to receive. "Before your will" means that now your will is to be in *Kedusha*, for the work to be in order to bestow. Now a person receives this strength, meaning comes out of the governance of the will of others, meaning the *Sitra Achra* [other side], which is only to receive and not to bestow, and now he uses the vessels of bestowal.

According to the above, we can interpret what we asked about what *The Zohar* said, "Man's hands are at the top of the world." What does this imply in the work? It is known that hands imply man's vessels of reception. This comes from the verse, "For the hand attains." It is as was said (*Ketubot* 83a), "My hand is removed from her," meaning that he removes himself from ownership over the field.

"[The hands] are at the top of the world" means that the existence of the world depends on the hands, which are man's vessels of reception. In other words, the purpose of creation, which is to do good to His creations, should be received in man's hands. In other words, if the hands, which are man's vessels of reception, are fine, meaning clean, and have equivalence of form with the Creator, meaning that they are in order to bestow, under such conditions, the upper abundance expands to the lower ones. However, if the hands, namely the vessels of reception, are not clean, it is necessary to stop the upper abundance from coming to the lower ones, since the vessels of reception do not belong to *Kedusha*, but only to the *Klipot* [shells/peels].

It is known that all the lower branches follow the upper roots. For this reason, in corporeality, too, when a person wants to place something in some *Kli*, he cleans the *Kli* and washes it with water. If the *Kli* is too dirty, he uses a detergent to clean the *Kli*. Otherwise, he will spoil the food or drink or clothes that he will place in the *Kli*.

If he places expensive clothes, he even cleans the suitcase, all in order to avoid spoiling the things or the food. If he does not follow the correct order and places objects or food in dirty *Kelim* [vessels], everything goes to the outer ones. This means that a person takes everything in his hands and gives them to the outer ones, meaning throws out the food and the objects and does not keep them in the house.

It is likewise in the ways of the work: If a person's hands are unclean and can spoil the abundance to the point that he takes the abundance and transfers it to the outer ones, meaning if his *Kelim* are dirty with the will to receive for himself, which is in oppositeness of form from *Kedusha*, the abundance goes to the *Klipot*. It is so because he places the abundance that had to be in *Kelim* of *Kedusha*—which are vessels of bestowal—into the *Klipot*, by which the *Klipot* grow much stronger.

Now we will understand why it says, "Every filth and every dirt goes up to the *Sitra Achra* because the *Sitra Achra* feeds on that filth and dirt." As we explained, dirt and filth are vessels of reception for one's own benefit. When his intention is not the benefit of the Creator, this is really the *Sitra Achra*, meaning the "other side," which does not belong to *Kedusha*. *Kedusha* is called "bestowal," as was said, "You will be holy, for I am holy," which means that as the Creator gives, likewise, the creatures should engage only in giving.

It therefore turns out that if a person works in order to receive and not in order to bestow, he is providing for the *Sitra Achra*, for they are only about reception and not about bestowal. This is the meaning of the verse, "Every filth and every dirt goes up to the *Sitra Achra*," who are sustained only by the vessels of reception.

This is as he says in *The Study of the Ten Sefirot* (Part 11, *Ohr Pnimi*): "Even on weekdays, the *Melachim* [kings] and the *Klipot* take their nourishments from *Atzilut*, as a thin light. This is done by the iniquities of the lower ones, who always cause lights of *Hassadim* to retire from illumination of *Hochma* and descend to the *Klipot* for their nourishment, and even more than is necessary for them."

It is also written there, "Yet, the whole grip of the *Sitra Achra*, which can be on the day of Shabbat, for when a person moves from the private domain to the public domain, he causes lights of *Hassadim* to spread from *Atzilut* to the place of *BYA*, and they must spread without illumination of *Hochma*. Because of this, they die, and as a result, there is the matter of 'He who desecrates her shall be put to death.' Because they cause the exit of the lights from the domain of *Atzilut* and retire from illumination of *Hochma*, their punishment is to die. This is the meaning of 'He who desecrates her shall be put to death.'"

Accordingly, we see that through the iniquities, they cause spreading of *Kedusha* to the *Klipot*, and all the sins come only from the will to receive. By this they cause death in the lights of *Hassadim*. For this reason, the punishment in terms of the work is death, as he says, "He who desecrates her shall be put to death." This is why it was said, "one who blesses with dirty hands," whose vessels of reception are unclean so as to work in order to bestow, but are dirty with the will to receive, "must die," since he caused death in the light of *Hassadim*.

Hence, when a person blesses the Creator, meaning when he wants to extend blessings, but his hands are dirty with the will to receive in order to receive, and the abundance he wishes to draw will all go to the *Klipot*, which are called "dead," at that time a person is in a state of "The wicked in their lives are called 'dead.'" In other words, although he wants to extend life, which is called "in their lives," he is still in the state of "wicked." That is, he does not want to work for the sake of the Creator but for his own sake, and this is separation from the *Kedusha*. Also, the wicked are called "dead" because they cause the abundance go to the *Klipot*, as he says about the verse, "He who desecrates her shall be put to death."

Therefore, when a person wants to walk on the path of truth, to observe Torah and *Mitzvot* in order to bestow, what should he do? The advice for this is to first of all aim before every action, which reward he expects for the actions he is about to do. At that time he needs to tell himself, "Since I want to serve the Creator, and since

I cannot, since the will to receive within me will not let me, hence, through the actions I am about to do, the Creator will give me the real desire to bring contentment to the Creator, and I believe in our sages, who said, 'The Creator wanted to refine Israel, therefore He gave them plentiful Torah and *Mitzvot*.'"

What Is the Gift that a Person Asks of the Creator?

Article No. 22, Tav-Shin-Mem-Zayin, 1986-87

It is written in *The Zohar* (Pinhas, Item 180): "It is written, 'My God, save Your servant.' 'Delight the soul of Your servant.' 'Give Your strength to Your servant.' Three times did David become a servant in this praise, corresponding to the three times that the authors of the Mishnah established that man should be a servant in the prayer. In the first blessings, he should be as a servant who praises his teacher. In the middle ones, he is as a servant who asks for a gift from his teacher. In the last blessings, he is as a servant who thanks his teacher for the gift he has received from him, and he walks away."

We should understand why they compared man's prayer to a servant receiving a gift from his teacher, and not to charity or other things. What does this teach us in the work?

It is known that from the Creator, two things come to us directly: 1) the light, 2) the *Kli* [vessel] to receive the light.

1) We learned that the purpose of creation is His will to do good to His creations. It follows that the Creator wanted to do good to the creatures even without an awakening from the lower ones, for there were still no creatures in the world from whom to receive awakening. This is regarded as the light coming from the Creator without any involvement of the lower one.

2) The Creator created—existence from absence—a *Kli* called "desire and yearning to receive delight and pleasure." This means that what we see is as in "By Your actions we know You," meaning that we speak only of what we see that exists in the nature of creation. We see that it is impossible to enjoy anything, whatever it is, unless there is a yearning for it. For this reason, we learned that from the perspective of the light that created this *Kli*, called "will to receive," it underwent four *Behinot* [discernments], meaning four stages until the will to receive acquired the complete form of yearning. After the light created the *Kli*, this *Kli* received the delight and pleasure that He wished to give.

These two above-mentioned things, the light and the *Kli*, pertain to the Creator. We learn that in this respect, there was complete perfection and there is nothing to add to this.

However, afterwards, something new was born, which we attribute to the creature and not to the Creator. In other words, we attribute the matter of giving to the Creator, who is the giver, for His desire is to do good to His creations, which is to give abundance to the creatures and receive nothing from them. Yet, afterward, something new was made, as it is written in *The Study of the Ten Sefirot* (Part 1), that the first receiver, called *Malchut de Ein Sof*, craved a decoration called "decoration at the point of desire": to have equivalence of form called *Dvekut* [adhesion]. For this reason, the *Tzimtzum* [restriction] was made, meaning that she diminished her will to receive on the *Kli* called "will to receive," hence the light departed.

Malchut invented a new *Kli*, called "will to bestow," meaning not to receive delight and pleasure according to the level of the yearning for the light, but according to the level of her desire to bestow. This means that *Malchut* calculated how many percent of the abundance she could receive with the aim to bestow. On the part she would receive in order to receive, if she were to receive, she would not receive.

It follows that we attribute this *Kli*, which the lower one gives, to the lower one, since the *Kelim* [vessels] of the upper one, which the upper has made in order for the lower one to be able to enjoy the light, is only the will to receive. That *Kli* will never be revoked because what the Creator has created must always exist.

However, the lower one can add to the *Kli* of the Creator, as it is written, "Which God has created to do." This means that God has created the *Kli* called "desire to receive pleasure," and man must add to it a correction called "the intention to bestow," as was said above, that *Malchut de Ein Sof* decorated herself at the point of the desire. This means that her decoration was in that she placed on the will to receive the aim to bestow.

There, in *Malchut de Ein Sof*, was only the root. From her, it extended to the lower ones that it is forbidden to receive, following the rule, "A desire in the upper one becomes a binding law in the lower one." It extended from this discernment until the *Sitra Achra* [other side] was born—the opposite of *Kedusha* [holiness/sanctity]. In *Kedusha*, there is only the desire to bestow, which is *Dvekut*. But those who want to receive in order to receive become removed and separated from the Life of Lives. For this reason, they said in *The Zohar*, "The wicked in their lives are called 'dead,'" and said the verse, "The grace of the nations is a sin," about the wicked, "All the good that they do, they do for themselves."

It therefore follows that Creator gives two things directly to the creature: 1) the delight and pleasure, 2) the desire to yearn for pleasures.

However, unpleasantness, called "shame," extends indirectly from the Creator. That is, the Creator wants the lower one to receive delight and not suffering, but indirectly, meaning that the upper one, the Giver, does not want the lower one to feel shame upon reception of the delight.

This is why the correction of the *Tzimtzum* was made. Because of the *Tzimtzum*, the abundance does not come to the *Kelim* [vessels] that the Creator has made, unless the creature has placed a correction of the intention to bestow on the *Kli*. If a person does not have this *Kli*, he remains in the dark without light, and the name The Good Who Does Good is hidden from him because he does not have the right *Kelim* for reception of the abundance, which is called "equivalence of form."

It follows that the whole novelty that was made after the *Tzimtzum* is that only the aim to bestow is missing, but the two discernments that extended prior to the *Tzimtzum* did not change. In other words, in the first *Behina* [discernment], which is His desire to do good, there was no change, and after the *Tzimtzum* He still wants to impart delight and pleasure. In the second *Behina*, which is the will to receive, there was also no change. It is as we learn that there are no changes in spirituality, but only additions. It follows that after the *Tzimtzum*, it is impossible to receive any upper abundance unless we add to the will to receive the aim to bestow. This is all of our work in Torah and *Mitzvot* [commandments]: to be rewarded with vessels of bestowal.

Our sages said about this (*Kidushin* 30), "I have created the evil inclination; I have created the spice of Torah." It is known that the will to receive is called "evil inclination" because it causes remoteness from the Creator, since it is in disparity of form from the Creator. The Creator aims to bestow, whereas the evil inclination wants only to receive. For this reason, all the delight and pleasure in the thought of creation is hidden from it.

However, how can we obtain these *Kelim*, since this is against our nature?

The answer is that this is why we were given the Torah and *Mitzvot*. Through them, we can obtain these *Kelim*. Yet, why are not everyone awarded with vessels of bestowal through Torah and *Mitzvot*? The reason is that there is no light without a *Kli*.

It follows that if a person does not know for certain that all we need are only these *Kelim*, he still does not have real *Kelim*. In other words, he does not have a need for these *Kelim*. It follows that the light is in Torah and *Mitzvot*, which can assist a person to attain in these *Kelim*, but he does not have a real need to be given these *Kelim*.

If we look a little deeper in, and thoroughly examine those who observe Torah and *Mitzvot*, whether they want to be given vessels of bestowal and to give in return the will to receive, the vast majority of the workers will say that they pass on this. Instead, they want to observe Torah and *Mitzvot* in order to receive. It follows that they have no need for vessels of bestowal. For this reason, how can they say that the Torah and *Mitzvot* they labor in should give them a reward for which they have no need? On the contrary, they are afraid lest they will lose the vessel of reception called "self-love."

This is as Maimonides says (end of *Hilchot Teshuva*), "Our sages said, 'One should always engage in Torah, even if *Lo Lishma* [not for Her sake], since from *Lo Lishma* he will come to *Lishma* [for Her sake]. Therefore, when teaching little ones, women, and uneducated people, they are taught to work only out of fear and in order to receive reward. Until they gain knowledge and acquire much wisdom, they are taught that secret little-by-little and are accustomed to the matter calmly until they attain Him and serve Him with love.'"

It therefore follows that one should yearn to obtain vessels of bestowal. Although he sees that the will to receive disagrees with it, meaning that it does not let him pray that the Creator will give him these *Kelim*, for that, too, one must pray to the Creator to give him a desire to understand the necessity that there is in these *Kelim*. He asks the Creator to have the strength to overcome the desire of the body, which wants to remain specifically in vessels of reception. Moreover, when he sees that a desire can emerge from this thing—that the person will later want to come to vessels of bestowal—he promptly feels this and begins to instantaneously resist.

However, a person does not come easily into seeing that he cannot work in order to bestow. Instead, a person thinks that now he still does not have the desire to bestow, but whenever he wants to work in order to bestow, the choice is in his hands, meaning he will be able to work in order to bestow. The awareness that he thinks he has calms him down so as not to be impressed by the fact that he is not engaging in work of bestowal, since whenever he chooses, he will be able to. For this reason, he is not worried about this.

However, the truth is that this is not within man's power, as it is against human nature. Our sages said about this: "Man's inclination overcomes him every day. If the Creator does not help him, he will not overcome it." However, in order to receive help, a person must see and exert to have a need for His help. This is why it was said, "He who comes to purify," then the Creator helps him.

We asked, Why does man have to begin the work and only then the Creator helps him? Why does the Creator not give him this strength right away, meaning that even if a person does not ask for help, the Creator will help him as soon as he begins the work of the Creator? According to the rule that there is no light without a *Kli*, a person must begin. When a person sees that he cannot, he has a need for the Creator's help. Therefore, specifically when one has begun the work and sees he is unable, in that state he receives a *Kli* for the Creator to impart him this force, called "desire to bestow."

However, normally, when a person begins the work of bestowal and sees that it is difficult for him, and sees that in his view, he has already asked the Creator many times to help him but received no help at all, a person escapes the campaign and says that this work is not for him. Indeed, precisely in this place, when he has resolved that this is difficult for him alone and only the Creator can help, a person must trust the Creator that He will help him.

However, this still does not complete the *Kli*, meaning the need for His help. Each time he asks for help, although he still does not feel His help, we must believe above reason that the Creator does help, but that we still do not need to see in order to reveal the real need for this.

According to the above, we should interpret that the verse, "For the ways of the Lord are straight. The righteous walk in it and the wicked fail in them." This means that precisely at this point, when a person comes to a resolution that it is not within man's power to obtain vessels of bestowal because he sees that not a single organ in his body agrees to this, now he has arrived at the point of truth. Now he should make an honest prayer for the Creator to help him. Certainly, he will receive the help from the Creator, who sits and waits for man to give him the *Kli*, meaning the need for it. It is precisely here that a person escapes from that state, and precisely here is where the help can come to him. Yet, he escapes the campaign and for this reason he is called "a criminal."

Yet, the righteous does not despair because specifically now he is rewarded with vessels of bestowal. It follows that in the same place where "the righteous walk," meaning receive an ascent in degree, in that very same place "the wicked fail." Precisely in this place where they should receive help, they fail and escape the campaign.

It follows from all the above that man should ask for the Creator's giving, meaning that the Creator will give him as a gift the vessels of reception, just as He has given him the *Kli* called "will to receive." In other words, on one hand, we say that the Creator has given the *Kli* and the light, meaning both the desire and the yearning to receive the pleasure, as well as the pleasure. Only the addition to the *Kli*, which is the will to bestow, we attribute to the creatures, as it is written, "Which God has created to do." "Which has created" refers to the will to receive, called "created," which is something made existence from absence, called "creation." On this, man should place the aim to bestow, meaning that this really does belong to the creatures and not to the Creator.

However, the truth is that the Creator should give even this *Kli*, called "addition." When we say that this pertains to the creatures, it means that man should ask the Creator to give him this *Kli* called "intention to bestow." That is, only the lack, his lack of desire to bestow, is what the lower one should exert to have.

But regarding the will to receive, it cannot be said that there is an awakening of the lower ones for this because if the desire to receive still does not exist in the world, who would ask to be given a desire to want to receive pleasure? It is impossible to say that before a person is born, he wants something. This is why we say that the will to receive belongs entirely to the Creator.

But afterwards, once the will to receive pleasures has been born, comes the time when a person feels that this will to receive, without additions, but as it came from nature, is bad because he cannot receive real pleasures with this desire, but only as a "thin light," which the Creator has given to the *Klipot* [shells/peels] so they would not be canceled. When a person comes to this awareness, he receives a need to have the ability to aim to bestow. Before he has the need for this, he cannot be given the *Kli*, as was said that "there is no light without a *Kli*," and a *Kli* is called "need" and "lack." That lack is not apparent as such unless he suffers torments and pains from needing this thing and not having it.

A regular lack is when a person sees that he does not have something and understands that he needs it. However, if he knows that he can live without it, it still cannot be said about him that he has a real lack. A real lack means that he knows that without the thing he lacks, he cannot go on living. This is called a "real need."

It is likewise in the work: Many times a person knows, understands, and feels that he is lacking the desire to bestow. He asks the Creator to give him the ability to overcome the body called "will to receive," and he knows that he has already asked the Creator several times but the Creator did not want to listen to him. Seeing that he still did not receive this strength from the Creator puts him off and he does not have the strength to ask the Creator once again to give him what he wants, since he sees that the Creator is not listening to him. Hence, he can no longer pray to the Creator.

But in truth, we should say that a person still does not have the real need for the Creator's help. The need that the person has, where he sees that he is unable to aim to bestow, is still not regarded as a real need. Rather, a real need means that he sees that if he does not have what he needs, he cannot exist in the world. This is regarded as a real need.

For this reason, when a person realizes that unless he obtains the desire to bestow he will be separated from *Kedusha*, and he has no hope of ever achieving spirituality, called "*Dvekut* with the Creator," but he will be constantly immersed in self-love and have no chance of entering *Kedusha*, and he will remain in the *Klipot*, and this pains him and he says, "In that case, I am better off dead than alive," this is called "a real need." Then, when a person prays that the Creator will grant him the vessels of bestowal, this is called a "real need," and it is only this that we can attribute to the lower ones, meaning the lack, that he is lacking vessels of bestowal. This is called a *Kli*, meaning a need.

The filling for this, meaning the desire to bestow, belongs to the Creator. In other words, as the Creator has given the first *Kli*, which is the will to receive, He also gives the *Kli* called "desire to bestow." The only difference between the first *Kli* called "will to receive," and the *Kli* called "desire to bestow," is that the first *Kli* was without an awakening of the lower one, since before he was born, who would ask? But afterwards, when the will to receive was born, he began to feel what that will to receive is causing him. To the extent of the understanding of the need for vessels of bestowal, so does a person awaken to feel the need, and it is only the need for vessels of bestowal that we attribute to the creatures.

Accordingly, we can interpret what we say and ask, "Grant me the treasure of a free gift." This is perplexing, since we need to serve the Creator not in order to receive reward, much less ask for a free gift. So, why does it say (in the prayer, *May It Please*, before saying Psalms) "Grant me the treasure of a free gift?"

What Is the Gift that a Person Asks of the Creator?

The meaning is "Give us a free gift, grant me." That is, give us the gift of the vessel of bestowal, just as You have given us the *Kli* of the will to receive. We are asking You, since we feel the need for the vessel of bestowal. And what are the vessels of bestowal? To be able to work for free, without any reward, but rather that our work will be only in order to bestow. That is, in the first *Kli*, called "will to receive," a person can only work for a reward, and this *Kli* is called "a new *Kli*," a new creation that did not exist before He has created it.

Now, give us a *Kli*, meaning a desire from Your treasure. And what is it? The desire to bestow. This was also before He has created the will to receive, for the desire to bestow is the reason for the desire to receive. The desire to bestow is called "existence from existence," and the will to receive is called "existence from absence, since it is known that there is no will to receive in the Creator because from whom would He receive? For this reason, we ask for "the treasure of a free gift," meaning from Your treasure. Since You have a desire to bestow, You give that desire for free. Give it to us, so we, too, can work for free, without receiving reward.

By this we will understand what we asked, How can we ask the Creator to give us a free gift? The meaning is that we are asking the Creator to give us the ability to serve Him for free. In other words, the vessel of reception that a person receives is called "a free gift."

Thus, what is the gift that one should ask the Creator to give him? We asked, How can one ask for presents, since it is known that you can ask for charity, but a gift? Who asks for gifts? Normally, we give gifts to those we love.

The answer is that since a person wants to love the Creator, and since the will to receive is the obstructor, a person asks for this gift called vessels of bestowal, where through this gift that he will receive from the Creator, a person will be rewarded with the love of the Creator and not with self-love. This is why it is called a "gift," and this is what a person should ask.

This is the meaning of what we asked, What gift should one ask of the Creator, which is permitted to ask, and on which our work in

Torah and *Mitzvot* stand, where by observing them we will receive a need for this request and understand that "they are our lives and the length of our days"? That need is that we are lacking *Dvekut* with the Creator, called "equivalence of form," by which we can adhere to the Life of Lives. And if we are not rewarded with *Dvekut* and remain in self-love, we will be separated from the Life of Lives, which is the meaning of "the wicked in their lives are called 'dead,'" due to the separation between them.

Concerning the request for the gift, the main point is the need for the matter. Through Torah and *Mitzvot* we receive a need, and through the need there is room to ask for this gift, regarded as Him giving us the *Kli* called "desire to bestow upon the Creator."

It is written about it (*Hagigah* 7): "As I am for free, you are for free." In other words, a person should exert to work in order to bestow and not want to receive any reward. Although the Gemara interprets this differently, this, too, is implied there, as it is called *Dvekut*.

According to the above, we can interpret what we say in the blessing for the food, that even on Shabbat [Sabbath], when it is forbidden to speak of mundane matters, we ask the Creator, "Do not make us need the gift of flesh and blood." Such a prayer is suitable on weekdays, when we ask for provision, but not on Shabbat.

We should interpret that the request on Shabbat not to "need the gift of flesh and blood" refers to the *Kelim* of flesh and blood, which flesh and blood use, namely vessels of reception. They ask the Creator to help them not need to use their *Kelim*, but the *Kelim* of the Creator, which are vessels of bestowal, and on these *Kelim* we ask of the Creator, for they are *Kelim* of a free gift.

Peace After a Dispute Is More Important than Having No Disputes At All

Article No. 23, Tav-Shin-Mem-Zayin, 1986-87

Concerning peace, Rabbi Shimon Ben Halafta said in *Masechot Okatzin*: "The Creator did not find a *Kli* [vessel/receptacle] that holds a blessing for Israel but peace, as it was said, 'The Lord will give strength to His people; the Lord will bless His people with peace.'" The verse says (Isaiah 57), "'Peace, peace, to the far and to the near,' says the Lord, and I will heal him."

We should understand his words when he says, "The Creator did not find a *Kli* that holds a blessing for Israel but peace." He says "blessing" and he says "peace." This means that the blessing is the main thing and the peace merely holds the blessing. We should also understand why he says, "a *Kli* that holds a blessing for Israel." This implies that for the nations of the world, peace is not a good thing. Can it be said that there is a place where having peace is not good?

We should also understand the meaning of "Peace, peace, to the far and to the near." It means that the Creator gives peace to those who are far. Certainly, He gives peace to those who are near to the Creator, but what does it mean when He says, "to the far and to the near"?

In order to understand this in the work, we must understand the matter of the purpose of creation and correction of creation, which we have discussed many times before. The purpose of creation is for man to be awarded delight and pleasure, since this is why He has created the creatures. It follows that as long as a person has not been awarded this, that person is regarded as one who has not achieved wholeness because he is far from the goal. Thus, a person must exert to be rewarded with the goal, meaning with the delight and pleasure for which he was created.

However, before a person engages in Torah and *Mitzvot* [commandments] in order to thereby achieve the goal, he must engage in the correction of creation, meaning to know how to receive the delight and pleasure so he will be able to enjoy it. If he does not know the order of corrections, he will spoil the abundance. For this reason, before a person engages in the purpose of creation, he must exert to learn the order of corrections—to know what he should correct so as not to spoil the gift that the Creator will give him.

It is known that all the corrections pertain to *Malchut*, as it is written, "To correct the world with the kingdom [*Malchut*] of *Shadai*, and all the flesh shall be calling Your name." What does it mean that *Malchut* must be corrected? Since His will was to do good to His creations, He has created existence from absence a lack called "desire to receive delight and pleasure." This *Malchut* spreads with her will to receive over several *Behinot* [discernments].

There is a rule in spirituality that disparity of form divides the degree into two. For this reason, once this *Malchut* craved a decoration at the point of desire and wanted equivalence of form with the Creator, as in, "As He is merciful, so you are merciful," because of this, she wanted to be a giver, just as the Creator is the giver.

After this correction, called *Tzimtzum* [restriction], there was a judgment that it is forbidden to receive unless when it is possible to aim to bestow. That judgment became the root from which *Klipot* [shells/peels] extended, which are the opposite of *Kedusha* [holiness/sanctity]. *Kedusha* is called "bestowal," as it is written, "You will be holy," meaning "You will retire," as in, they will retire from receiving in order to receive. Instead, the intention should be only to bestow upon the Creator like the Creator bestows upon the creatures.

It is written, "for I am holy." That is, as the Creator gives, Israel, too, should give to the Creator. The opposite of this, meaning the opposite of bestowal, is considered the opposite of *Kedusha*, and this is *Tuma'a* [impurity], or *Sitra Achra* [other side] or *Klipa* [singular of *Klipot*]. For this reason, the will to receive later became *Klipot*, which want to receive in order to receive.

It is written in the "Introduction to The Book of Zohar" (Item 10):

"Indeed, first we must understand the meaning of the existence of the *Tuma'a* and the *Klipot*. Know that this great will to receive, which we determined was the very essence of the souls by creation—for which they are fit to receive the entire filling in the thought of creation—does not remain in that form within the souls. If it remained in them, they would have to remain eternally separated from Him.

"In order to mend that separation, which lies on the *Kli* of the souls, He has created all the worlds and separated them into two systems. These are the four worlds ABYA of *Kedusha*, and opposite them the four worlds ABYA of *Tuma'a*. He imprinted the desire to bestow in the system of ABYA of *Kedusha*, removed the will to receive for themselves from them, and placed it in the system of the worlds ABYA of *Tuma'a*.

"Now we can see what corrections we must perform—correct the vessels of reception so as to have the aim to bestow. It is as he says there (in Item 10): "And the worlds cascaded onto the reality of this corporeal world, to a place where there is a body and a soul and a time of corruption and a time of correction. For the body, which is the will to receive for himself, extends from its root in the thought of creation, traversing the system of the worlds of *Tuma'a*, as it is written, 'a wild ass's colt is born a man' (Job 11:12).

"He remains under that authority for the first thirteen years, and this is the time of corruption. By engaging in *Mitzvot* from thirteen years of age onward, in order to bestow contentment upon his Maker, he begins to purify the will to receive for himself imprinted in him, and slowly turns it to in order to bestow. And so he accumulates degrees of *Kedusha* from the thought of creation in *Ein Sof* [Infinity] until they aid a person in turning the will to receive for himself in him to be entirely in the form of reception in order to bestow contentment upon his Maker, and not at all for his own benefit."

Now we can see that all our work in Torah and *Mitzvot* is to correct the *Malchut*, which is called "receiving for oneself" after her root in *Ohr Yashar* [Direct Light] in the world of *Ein Sof*. From this stems the order of the work.

Also, there is an order of work for beginners, and there is an order of work for advanced. It is as Maimonides writes, "When teaching little ones, women, and uneducated people, they are taught to work in order to receive reward. Until they gain knowledge and acquire much wisdom," then they are taught *Lishma* [for Her sake], meaning not in order to receive reward.

From this we see that there is an order of work for the general public, and there is an order of work for individuals, and that order of work is not for the general public. This is according to the rule we spoke of, that there is one line, which is the work of the general public. In one line, it is explained that there is above and below, meaning of higher importance and of lower importance. A person must always walk on one line, meaning that he has but one intention when he engages in Torah and *Mitzvot*—to observe the Torah and *Mitzvot* that the Creator has commanded us through Moses, in return for which we will be rewarded in this world and in the next.

On this path, which is regarded as one line, we discern that he is gaining all the time because every act he does is whole from the perspective of the act and there is nothing to add to it, as it is written, "Do not add and do not subtract." It follows that this person cannot not gain. However, at times he gains a lot, when he works many hours in Torah and *Mitzvot*, and when he works less, he gains less.

It follows that one line means that he is walking on the path of the Creator in one way. But one who does not engage in Torah and *Mitzvot* has no line at all. That is, he has no way in the work. Instead, when he is walking on the path of the Creator and observes Torah and *Mitzvot*, this is regarded as walking by one line. It is called so since he is working only in action: That which he must observe, he observes with all its details.

But those who want to work as individuals, who want to be rewarded with a personal "the Lord your God," must work on the intention, on the reason that compels them to observe Torah and *Mitzvot*, meaning why they are observing Torah and *Mitzvot*, since there is no act without a reason. Therefore, a person must sort out the real reason why he has taken upon himself to work "as an ox to the burden and as a donkey to the load" and engage in Torah and *Mitzvot*.

However, when he looks at the reason that causes him to engage in Torah and *Mitzvot*, this criticism on the actions is regarded for him as a left line, and the acts he performs are now emerging from one line and are given a new name: right line. In other words, when there are not more than one line, it cannot be said that I have a right line, since there is only one line. But when he has another line, it can be said that one is called "right," and the other is called "left."

However, we must understand why we call the work in practice "right line" and the work on the intention "left line." The rule is that something that does not require correction is called "right," and something that does require correction is called "left." It is as our sages said (*Minchot* 37), "The Gemara asks, 'Placing on the left, from where is it (how do we know that placing a hand *Tefillin* is on the left hand and not on the right hand)?' Rav Ashi said, 'From your hand is written with a blunt *Hey*, and RASHI interpreted that writing with a blunt *Hey* means female, meaning in the left, as was said, 'she is as powerless as a female.'" For this reason, wherever we learn about a weak side, a weak way, or a weak place we call it "left." In other words, anything that requires correction, which is in itself weak, is called "left."

It therefore follows that with respect to actions, there is nothing to add there. For example, we do not say, "Today I put *Tefillin* on the left hand and tomorrow I will put *Tefillin* on the right hand, too," or "Today I placed a *Mezuzah* [box with text from the Torah attached to door posts] on the right hand side of the door, and tomorrow I will try to place a *Mezuzah* on the left hand side of the door, as well."

Rather, as it is known, concerning practical *Mitzvot*, it is said, "Do not add and do not subtract." For this reason, those who only observe the actions and whose only intention is for the action to be proper, and who do not regard the intention, meaning what reward they want for their work, since they are working and observing Torah and *Mitzvot*, there must be some reason that compels them to observe. And since there are many reasons, such as fear of punishment or because of love, or in order to receive pleasures in this world and in the next world, they do not get into the scrutiny of the reasons, namely the real reason. The real reason is that the Creator wants them to put in work in order to obtain that which the Creator wants.

What is the reason that it can be said that the Creator wants us to work for? First, we need to understand what can we say that the Creator lacks, whereby our work He will receive pleasure from our giving Him what He needs.

To this there is one answer: If we look at the purpose of creation, we will know what He needs. The purpose of creation is to do good to His creations, meaning that He has created creatures in order to give them abundance, and the *Kelim* [vessels] in which they can receive delight and pleasure is the desire to receive pleasures, as it is known that we cannot enjoy something for which we have no yearning.

For this reason, in every creature there is a yearning for pleasures. However, in order not to have shame, a correction should be added to the will to receive: to make it in order to bestow. Since that correction is not to receive, we attribute that correction to the creatures, meaning that the creatures do not want to receive before they have the intention to bestow.

To the Creator, however, we attribute everything He gives. Since the Creator wants that when the creatures receive the pleasures, it will be without the flaw of shame, we say that the upper one accepted and agreed to the *Tzimtzum* that the lower one has made—not to impart abundance to the lower ones unless according to the correction that *Malchut de Ein Sof* has made.

It follows that we attribute the correction primarily to the lower one, but in what the upper one seemingly agreed to the view of the lower one. For this reason, it is impossible to receive any spirituality if there are any limitations and restrictions that the lower one has made. Rather, the upper one bestows according to what the lower one can receive in order to bestow. For this reason, after the cascading of the worlds, when man was created after the *Klipot* manifested in the world, for this reason, a person wants to receive in *Kelim* of self-reception, and he has no connection to the correction that *Malchut* of *Kedusha* had done.

Therefore, the upper one cannot bestow abundance below before the lower ones take upon themselves to use only vessels of bestowal, as was said above, that the upper one agreed to the *Tzimtzum* performed by *Malchut de Ein Sof*, who is called "the root of all the receivers" who later emerged.

For this reason, the upper one awaits the vessels of bestowal that the lower one will give to the Creator so as to have the ability to impart it with the complete delight and pleasure, meaning that there will be no shame upon the reception of the abundance.

However, how can a person receive vessels of bestowal when it is against his nature? He was born with a desire to receive for himself because he was extended after the system of *Klipot* emerged. For this reason, in order for a person to have vessels of bestowal so the Creator could impart abundance, He has given us Torah and *Mitzvot*. It is as our sages said, "The Creator wanted to refine Israel, therefore He gave them plentiful Torah and *Mitzvot*, as was said, 'The Lord desired for His righteousness; He will increase the Torah and glorify.'"

It therefore follows that the real reason that compels a person to observe Torah and *Mitzvot* is that through the Torah and *Mitzvot* he will award himself an exit from his *Aviut* [thickness], which is self-reception, and will receive vessels of bestowal. These are the *Kelim* that the Creator awaits because specifically in vessels of bestowal, a person can receive delight and pleasure from the *Kedusha*.

For this reason, a person who wants to walk on the path of truth, must, before every act in Torah and in prayer and in good deeds, see that he has a real reason for which to engage in Torah and *Mitzvot*. That is, the Torah and *Mitzvot* should give him the purpose for which he is working and doing what he can to obtain it.

However, as there is work in observing *Mitzvot*, whether or not to do good deeds, meaning that there is choice there, we should know that the work of choice is harder on the intention, since the intention is man's work, as in, "You are called 'man,' and not the nations of the world." We interpreted that a "man" is one who bestows, which is MA in *Gematria*, called "male," meaning a giver. But a beast is called "female," and a beast is BON in *Gematria*, which is a receiver.

It follows that when he is in the action and does not consider the intention, he is observing Torah and *Mitzvot* for beastly reasons. That is, the reward he expects to receive for his work is reception, called a beast and not a man, as *The Zohar* says about the verse, "The grace of the nations is a sin; all the good that they do, they do for themselves."

This means that in terms of the work, this work is regarded as receiving reward into what is regarded as man's "nations of the world." Although it is also difficult to engage in Torah and *Mitzvot* in action, it is regarded as *Lo Lishma* [not for Her sake], which is for his own sake. However, we should know that this is the first degree, that we must begin from here, and that there is no other way, as Maimonides said.

This is already regarded as "man" and not a "beast." When we say that they are as "the nations of the world," it is nonetheless the "nations of the world" in man, the beast in the man. Conversely, those who have no connection even to the action are called "a nation that is similar to an ass."

For this reason, we should know that the degree of *Lo Lishma* is a very important degree, and we haven't the intellect to appreciate the importance of Torah and *Mitzvot Lo Lishma*. Baal HaSulam said that "as much as one may appreciate the work *Lishma*, which is important work, he should know that *Lo Lishma* is more important than the importance that a person attributes to *Lishma*, since one cannot properly assess the importance of observing Torah and *Mitzvot* even *Lo Lishma*, although observing Torah and *Mitzvot* should be *Lishma*.

It therefore follows that although the real reason for observing Torah and *Mitzvot* should be to be rewarded with vessels of bestowal, that it is specifically in those *Kelim* that the Creator has the ability to give the upper abundance, since the Creator wants the creatures to feel only pleasure and no shame upon the reception of the abundance, for this reason, He awaits our work in Torah and *Mitzvot* with the intention to thereby be rewarded with vessels of bestowal.

However, the beginning of the work is specifically in action. At that time, we need not think and scrutinize quite which reward we hope to receive from the Creator in return for our work. Instead, he observes

Torah and *Mitzvot* only because he is following the Creator's orders. This is called "satisfactory work for the general public." That is, they should not think at all about the intention, but all their thoughts will be about observing Torah and *Mitzvot* in action.

Certainly, there is the matter of choice here, and the war of the evil inclination that it is impossible to observe Torah and *Mitzvot* even in *Lo Lishma*. Indeed, his reward is great indeed, as Baal HaSulam said, that the *Lo Lishma* is very important in the eyes of the Creator, since keeping Torah and *Mitzvot* even in action requires great efforts and a person must relinquish corporeal things in order to be able to observe what the Creator has commanded. Still, true work begins when a person wants to scrutinize the intention of *Lishma*, meaning that he wants to work in order not to receive reward.

In the work on intention, which is the real reason for observing Torah and *Mitzvot*, here begins the real division between good and bad. When a person wants to work for the Creator, since the Creator is called The Good Who Does Good, who is the giver, the body, called "evil," comes and obstructs him. The will to receive for oneself is called "bad" because the quality of judgment is on it because there was a judgment and restriction that it should remain in the dark and is unfit to receive any light.

Since man is born by nature with the desire to receive and must work against nature, here lies the real dispute. It is so much so that one cannot defeat and subdue his will to receive and be able to work for the Creator and not for his own sake.

Here we can say that they are called "two things that deny one another." The will to receive is the complete opposite of the will to bestow, and then comes the third party and decides between them, meaning until the Creator comes and makes peace between them. In other words, the Creator gives him a gift: the desire to bestow. Then, opposite the giving of the Creator, the evil surrenders, bringing the above receiver under man's good.

In other words, we learn that there are two forces in the body, two kinds of desire. But the desire to bestow begins to work in a person only when he wishes to begin the work on the intention. But in the work of the general public, it is still not apparent that there are a desire and a need in the body to aim to bestow, and to say about it that the will to receive resists since there is still no one to resist.

Rather, specifically when a person begins to work in order to bestow and contemplates whether he wants to work in order to bestow, it is up to him, meaning depends only on his will. But when he begins to work he sees that he is not the landlord who can do whatever he wants, but that he has another view with him, meaning the will to receive objects.

In that state, we feel the hardest work. This is even harder than the work of choice that a person needs to place on the act of *Mitzvot*, since he wants to do truly clean work for the sake of the Creator, as was said, that he wants to do the work of *Kedusha*, which is in order to bestow.

At that time begins the real dispute between good and bad. In terms of action, it was still not clear to the body that it wanted to walk on the path of not receiving anything for itself, but that everything will be for the Creator. It thought that everything would be for the receiver.

Since they are two forces within man, and the will to receive comes to a person as soon as he is born, as it is written in *The Zohar* (*Vayeshev*, Items 3-4), "an old and foolish king. A king is the evil inclination, who is called a 'king' and a 'ruler' in the world of men. He is old and foolish, since he is with man from the day one is born into the world. For this reason, he is an old and foolish king."

It is also written there (Item 8): "For this reason, the evil inclination immediately connects itself to man from the day he is born, so he will believe him. Later, when the good inclination comes, man will not be able to believe it and its words will seem burdensome to him."

It is also written there (Item 9): "Because the evil inclination comes first and makes its arguments before him, later, when the good inclination comes, it will be bad for man to be with it, and he will not be able to raise his head, as though he has been burdened with all the burdens in the world."

We therefore see that there are two forces within man, but the bad force is stronger because it comes with its arguments that one must tend to one's own benefit. Hence, its governance is stronger since it comes before the good inclination. This is called "In a quarrel, the first one is right," as it is written there (Item 10), "For this reason, any judge who accepts the words of a litigator before his colleague arrives is like one who takes upon himself another god to believe in."

It is also written there (Item 11): "But a righteous who fears his Master, how much evil does he suffer in this world so as to not believe or partake with the evil inclination? But the Creator saves him from all of them, as it is written, 'Many are the ills of the righteous, but the Lord delivers him from them all.' Thus, one who suffers many ills is righteous because the Creator wants him. This is so because the ills he suffers remove him from the evil inclination. For this reason, the Creator wants that person and delivers him from them all."

According to the worlds of *The Zohar*, when does the Creator save a person? Only when he suffers many evils. Afterward, the Creator comes and saves him. This is perplexing. Why should a person suffer many troubles and then the Creator helps him? Why should the Creator mind if He saves the righteous before he suffers many evils?

The answer is that it is known that there is no light without a *Kli*, and a *Kli* is called a "need." If a person is given something he does not need, he will not keep it and will lose it. Therefore, when a person begins to work on the intention to bestow, which is against nature, the body resists this because it is the opposite of its quality.

At that time the dispute is between the two beings. Since the receiver comes to the person first, and "In a quarrel, the first one is right," therefore, its governance is very strong. To the extent of the effort that a person makes in order to defeat his self-receiver, but he is unable to do so, he therefore feels very bad. Each time he overcomes and thinks that he is winning and the receiver has surrendered because he can see the losses—that the receiver is causing him troubles by not letting him aim for the Creator, and now he sees the truth, all of a sudden he falls into its net once more.

He does not even feel when he departed from the *Kedusha* into a state of lowliness. But after some time he realizes that he is in the domain of the receiver for himself with all its lowliness. Finally, a person is bewildered, how such a thing can be.

That is, it is known that everything deteriorates gradually. But here he sees that while he felt that now he was at the top of the world, suddenly he sees that he is at the bottom of the pit, and there were no stops in between. He realizes that he has fallen not in the middle of the fall, but when he is already lying on the ground. Only then he regains consciousness and he sees that he is on the ground. Also, there is no fixed interval between the fall and the realization that he has fallen.

We should understand why this is so, for it seems that such is the order of the work. The thing is that through the ascents and descents, a great need for the salvation of the Creator forms in him. This is the meaning of the verse, "Many are the afflictions of the righteous." That is, one who wishes to be righteous, and it is known that righteous is the quality of *Yesod*, and *Yesod* means a "giver," that is, one who wishes to work in order to bestow is regarded as "wanting to be righteous." He suffers many afflictions, meaning many descents, and each descent causes him pain and sorrow for being under the control of the receiver.

According to the many evils that he feels, a need forms in him, called a *Kli*, for the Creator to help and save him, since he sees that there is no way out of that governance and only the Creator can help him. It follows that through the suffering he suffers, these evils give him the need called a *Kli* for the Creator to give him the filling for this lack.

But before he suffers from his inability to work in order to bestow, if the Creator gives him some illumination that reforms him, he will not appreciate it because he has no need for it. Although he asked to be given the desire to bestow, he immediately regrets it because the need for it has not been carved within his heart.

This is the answer to why the Creator does not help him as soon as he prays, and especially when he has prayed to the Creator several times and the Creator did not hear his prayer, a person becomes angry with the Creator. Sometimes thoughts come to a person that he has grievances and says, "If I were to ask the Creator to help me for my own sake, I could understand that I am still not worthy of the Creator hearing me. But when I ask the Creator because I want Him to help because I want to work for His sake, for the sake of the Creator, why does He not want to help me?" For this reason, a person escapes the work.

Now we will explain the question that we asked. It stands to reason that where there is no dispute, that place is more important than a place where there is a dispute, although afterwards, someone gets involved in the matter and makes peace between them. We must say that it would certainly be better if there was no dispute, and they would not have to make peace.

In the order of the work, we see otherwise: Our sages said (*Berachot* 5), "One should always anger the good inclination over the evil inclination, as it was said, 'Be angry but do not sin.'" RASHI interprets "anger the good inclination" to mean that he should make war with the evil inclination.

This means that although there is peace there and the evil inclination does not obstruct his engagement in Torah and *Mitzvot*, still, one should make war with it. We should also ask, If it does not disturb him from engaging in Torah and *Mitzvot*, why is it called "evil inclination"? And moreover, we need to anger it. Why do we need to anger it if the evil inclination does not harm him?

In the work we should interpret simply that he is accustomed by upbringing to engage in Torah and *Mitzvot* in all its details, and he has nothing to add to the actions. But according to the order of the correction of creation, a person should correct the receiver for himself to work in order to bestow. For this reason, when a person begins to think about the intention, meaning when he begins to organize for himself, prior to making the Mitzvot, for which reason he is going to perform the Mitzvot, and he comes to the true intention, meaning that the Torah and Mitzvot were given in order to cleanse people, so that from this day onward he hopes that by the merit of Torah and Mitzvot, he will not give to his receiver anything, for this he should anger it.

He tells the body to work and observe Torah and Mitzvot, and that its reward for its work will be that he will not give it anything, unlike how it was thus far, when all his thoughts were only about how to please his receiver. Now he says to the receiver: "I ask you to engage in Torah and Mitzvot with a new aim, meaning that I will not give you anything."

Would this not anger? The evil inclination is right. Whoever heard of such a thing? It is insolence to tell a person, "I want you to work for me, and I will give the reward for your work to another. Moreover, I will give the reward that you deserve for the work to a person who hates you."

Our sages said about this: "One should always anger the good inclination over the evil inclination." It is as it is written in *The Zohar* that the Creator hates the bodies (*Vayeshev*, Item 28). But still, a person angering the evil inclination does not make sense. After all, it did not do him any harm so why anger it?

King Solomon called the evil inclination "enemy," as it is written, "If your enemy is hungry, feed him bread." We should understand what this comes to teach us. Normally, when someone has a bad neighbor whom he hates, it is normal for an enemy and a bad person to do harm to the neighbors. But sometimes a person meets someone and asks him, "Where do you live?" He tells him, "In the house of so and so, and we are only two neighbors." He asks, "How are you getting along with your neighbor? since I heard that he is a very bad man." He replies, "I don't know about this because he's never done me any harm." So he tells him, "How can this be?" and he asks some more: "How do you behave with him?" So he tells him, "Each day before I leave the house I ask him what he needs. Even what he does not tell me, I understand that he needs it. Likewise, with other things, before he asks me, I immediately do his wish." So he replies to him: "Now I understand that he is really a bad man, but he has no reason to harm you because he is afraid that he might lose the services you give him. Try not to serve him and you will see his evil, that in truth, he hates you but he doesn't want to lose the service you are giving him."

The lesson is that when everything we do, whether in Torah and *Mitzvot* or in corporeal matters, is for the sake of the receiver, it does not reveal its evil. Only when we tell it, "Thus far I have been working for you; henceforth, I want to work in order to bestow upon the Creator, and I also want you to work for the *Kedusha* and not for the *Tuma'a*." When it hears these words, it immediately becomes angry.

Now we will understand why our sages said to anger it. It does not mean that we must anger it if it causes us no trouble or harm. However, we need to advance in man's work, which is the intention, to aim to bestow upon the Creator. If a person wants to know if he really wants to work henceforth only for the Creator, the sign is if the evil inclination becomes angry. This is the indication that the person wants to walk on the path of construction of *Kedusha*. This is why the evil inclination becomes angry.

In other words, the anger is a result of a person wanting to work for the Creator. But if a person says that he wants to work for the Creator only as lip-service, this does not anger the evil inclination because why should it care if a person speaks and does not even know what he is saying? In other words, the person does not even know the meaning of "for the sake of the Creator."

It therefore turns out that the meaning of what RASHI said, to anger, means to make war with it. We should understand why RASHI adds by interpreting that he should make war with it. The answer is that "angering" means making war with it. In other words, he should not serve it but rebel against it and tell it, "Thus far I have been serving you with all my might. Now I will no longer give you anything. On the contrary, I want to enslave you, so you will work for the Creator."

By this he will see that the evil inclination becomes angry with the good inclination. If you make war and do not see that the evil inclination is angry with you, it is a sign that you do not even know what "for the sake of the Creator" means. Rather, you only heard that it is written in the books that we should do everything for the sake of the Creator. You say that you want this, too, but in truth, you have no idea what this is about.

It follows that the bad is actually within us, but we do not see it. Only through the dispute does it appear. Hence, if a person is at peace with it, he is hopeless because he will never be able to achieve the purpose of creation, since he will not have vessels of bestowal, but only vessels of reception, and these *Kelim* cannot receive the upper abundance because of the oppositeness of form.

A person does not know the power of the evil—that he should escape it—before he feels what the evil causes him. For this reason, specifically through the wars it makes with it, it has constant ascents and descents, and according to the sensation of pain from the descents, this makes him hate the evil.

This is the meaning of "You who love the Lord, hate evil. He keeps the souls of His followers, delivers them from the hands of the wicked." One who wishes to love the Creator, meaning that his only aim in life is to have but one desire—to be able to bring contentment to the Creator—must first hate the evil. It is impossible to work for the Creator unless one is not working for his own benefit. And since the receiver, called "evil inclination," disrupts him from working for the sake of the Creator, this causes man to hate his evil, called "self-benefit."

For this reason, specifically when a person tries to work for the sake of the Creator and sees that this is the obstructor, it causes him each time a measure of hatred for his evil, for one who does something bad to another once is not as one who harms him each and every day. It follows that the hatred is measured by the amount of bad that he suffers from it. This is why it was said, "Man's inclination overcomes him every day and seeks to put him to death. If the Creator did not help him, he would not be able to overcome it, as it was said, 'The Lord will not leave him in its hand'" (*Kidushin* 30).

According to the above, we can understand why it is necessary for man's inclination to grow each day and then the Creator will help him, and why the Creator does not help him once and for all. Why do I need this work, each day the same thing? The person understands that each day he needs to advance, since the order is that in whenever a person wants to acquire something, each day he advances, at times less and at times more. But here a person sees the complete opposite: Not only is he not advancing, but he sees that he is constantly regressing.

However, the truth is that as Baal HaSulam said, each and every day, a person who wants to walk on the path of truth advances closer to the truth each day. That is, each day a person sees more of the truth—that the will to receive for oneself is bad. That is, by the receiver causing him troubles by removing him from working to benefit the Creator, each day when a person suffers new troubles and afflictions in that the Creator does not let him work for the sake of the Creator, it follows that the afflictions a person receives from the evil inclination cause a person to hate the evil inclination.

This is the meaning of what is written, "You who love the Lord, hate evil." That is, those who love the Creator must first come to hate the evil. This comes to him by the evil afflicting him. This is the reason why he hates it. At that time a person falls into great fear that he will remain under the control of self-love and will never be freed from it.

This is when the promise that the Creator will help him comes, as it is written, "The Lord will not leave him in its hand," of the bad. But if a person has not come to fear that he might stay in the hands of the wicked forever, since he sees that he is not afraid that he will remain in the hand of the receiver because it still does not pain him, causing him to feel troubles and afflictions over being unable to do anything for the Creator, it means that he still does not have the need. Thus, how can the Creator help him? If something is not necessary, a person does not value it. Therefore, if the Creator helps him, he will promptly lose it, since the help of the Creator is as it is written in *The Zohar*, which writes about what our sages said, "He who comes to purify is aided. He asks, 'With what?' and he replies, 'With a holy soul.'"

When he obtains this but he has no need, it is impossible to value the upper abundance. He will lose it and the *Klipot* will take it away from him because he will not understand the importance of *Kedusha*—that it must be kept from the outer ones, from those outside of *Kedusha*.

However, a question arises here: When can one feel the bad, meaning that the will to receive is called "bad"? During the descent, when a person falls into the corporeal world, he does not even think about the work because he is completely immersed in the lusts of this world. In that state he is a slave to the receiving master and loves him wholeheartedly. Thus, how can he feel that the receiver is called "bad"? If he could feel that receiving for himself is called "bad," he would not serve it wholeheartedly, so when is the time of evil, meaning when is the time when one feels that receiving for himself is called "bad"?

Baal HaSulam said that the sin among those who are working, who want to walk on the path of truth, is actually during the ascent. This is the time when one can make scrutinies concerning the work of the Creator. During the descent, there is no one to speak of because then he is not a man but a beast, since his only concerns are beastly concerns. For this reason, during the ascent, if a person does not guarantee that his work is in the right order, he is thrown out and he falls into the netherworld, since he did not conduct himself during the ascent the way he should have and did not pay attention to this.

For this reason, during the ascent, a person must calculate what he has lost during the descent and what he must obtain and raise up the rungs of *Kedusha*, and why he is not ascending now to a state of greater wholeness than where he is now. He should also see if indeed he is currently at the highest level and there is no higher degree than the situation he is in now. He should also calculate the value and importance that he feels when he senses that he is in a state of ascent, and what he should do henceforth: If he has been rewarded with the secrets of Torah, does he even hope to be rewarded with it? and so forth. He can think about all this only during the ascent.

It therefore follows that only during the ascent, when he calculates what he gains and what he loses by being enslaved to the will to receive, that he cannot gain and only loses, that calculation that he does can make him feel how his inclination is harming him.

In each and every ascent, he must calculate what he lost from the descent. By this he sees that the inclination is causing him many harms. In order to set in his heart the need for the help of the Creator, many troubles come to him and he suffers from it, as in the words of *The Zohar*, which explained about the verse, "Many are the afflictions of the righteous," that the righteous suffers many troubles from the inclination.

According to what we explained, we should interpret the verse, "Many are the afflictions of the righteous." That is, after the righteous has suffered many afflictions, since "righteous" is named after the future, meaning one who wants to be righteous, who wants to work for the Creator, he suffers many afflictions until many afflictions are accumulated. This is why it is written, "from all of them," meaning that when he has many afflictions, the Creator will save him, since then he has a real need for the Creator's help and he will know how to appreciate the Creator's salvation, since there is no light without a *Kli*.

Peace After a Dispute Is More Important than Having No Disputes At All

Now we will explain the question that we asked, Why does it say, "The Creator did not find a *Kli* [vessel/receptacle] that holds a blessing for Israel but peace"? It seems as though peace is specifically for Israel, whereas for the nations of the world, peace is not good. Can this be? For whom is peace not good? That is, it implies that for the wicked, dispute is better than peace; how can such a thing be?

According to what we explained above, "wicked" means the bad in a person's body. These wicked need to undergo correction, as we learned that the will to receive must be corrected so as to serve the *Kedusha*. This is the meaning of "And you shall love the Lord your God with all your heart, with both your inclinations." But how can the inclination undergo such a correction? This can happen specifically through the dispute with the good inclination, as was said above, that the good inclination should anger it, meaning make war with it.

Through these wars, the evil in him appears. That is, he feels the troubles that the evil inclination causes him, and then a person determines that the receiver for himself is called the "evil inclination." If the receiver for himself does not cause him harm, a person works for it wholeheartedly and all his concerns and thoughts are only for the sake of the receiver.

This receiver, which does many things against *Kedusha*, is named in plural form, meaning "wicked." For these wicked ones, peace is not good, but rather dispute, for through the dispute they will be corrected, as it is written (Isaiah 57), "'There is no peace,' says my God, 'for the wicked.'"

Now we can interpret the meaning of sins becoming to him as merits and how such a thing can make sense. That is, if the evil inclination causes him constant descents that compel him to descend once more into the netherworld, where he becomes completely separated from *Kedusha*, can such matters and actions ever be merits?

According to the above, through many evils that the righteous suffers from the wicked, where the inclination keeps harming him, this gives him a need for the Creator's help, or he is doomed. "From all of them" means when many evils accumulate, it comes to a point where a person makes a heartfelt prayer, and then the Creator helps him.

It is as it is written (Psalms 85), "I will hear what the Lord God will speak, for He will speak peace unto His people and unto His followers, and let them not turn back to folly." Thus, who caused it that "the Lord God will speak, for He will speak peace unto His people ... and let them not turn back to folly," meaning that he will not sin again? It was specifically these evils and troubles that the wicked in him caused his sins, and he has already come to the lowest possible lowliness, as it is written, "Many are the afflictions of the righteous."

It is also written in *The Zohar* that when the righteous suffers many afflictions, the afflictions he suffers remove him from the evil inclination. For this reason, the Creator desires that person and saves him from all of them. In other words, by suffering afflictions he realizes that the inclination, namely the receiver for himself, is evil.

It follows that the suffering he receives from the inclination removes him so as not to want to work for it, and then he has a need to cry out to the Creator to help him out of its control. Thus, why does the Creator desire specifically that person? It is because that person has a need and a *Kli* that the Creator will help him, as it is said, "There is no light without a *Kli*."

It follows that specifically the sins that the evil inclination has given to that person caused him the *Kli*. The Creator can impart the peace into that *Kli*, and this is called "sins becoming as merits to him," since all the peace he had been rewarded with hearing from the Creator was thanks to these sins. This is why they became merits.

Now we can understand what we asked about what our sages said, "The Creator did not find a *Kli* that holds a blessing for Israel but peace." We asked, What is the blessing and what is peace? We should understand according to the rule that there is no light without a *Kli*, that nothing in reality exists without a reason. If there is no reason for it, the matter must be canceled. This is why our sages said that the *Kli* that holds a blessing is only the peace. Otherwise, the blessing must depart. In other words, the blessing is the light and peace is the *Kli*, as it is written, "A *Kli* that holds a blessing for Israel."

However, we should understand what is the merit in peace by which the blessing can be specifically through peace, and otherwise it must depart. It is known that the light is called "blessing." When a person is rewarded with His light, he no longer lacks anything. Instead, he is in utter wholeness because it is impossible to say that that person is whole if he is lacking something.

This is as it is written, "The Lord blessed Abraham with everything." What is "with everything"? We should say that "everything" means that he did not lack anything. Otherwise it is not regarded as a blessing if there is some lack. For this light to stay in a person and not depart from him, it needs a *Kli* where it can be without becoming spoiled. Otherwise, if we see that, for example, a drink stays in a *Kli*, it must become spoiled, so we take the drink out of the *Kli*.

The lesson is that in spirituality, since the light is the giver, in order for the abundance to be in the *Kli*, the *Kli*, too, needs to have an aim to bestow. Otherwise, the light will become spoiled.

This means that since the outer ones, meaning *Klipot*, want to enjoy the light, it is regarded as the wine being spoiled. Thus, that wine is no longer fit for human consumption, as in, "You are called 'man,' and the nations of the world are not." For this reason, before the *Kli* spoils the wine, the wine is taken out.

Likewise, before the *Kli* blemishes the abundance, the abundance is taken out and the light departs. It is as our sages said, "A person does not transgress unless a spirit of folly has entered him (*Sotah* 3). People ask about this: Therefore, why does the spirit of wisdom depart from a person? If it did not depart, the person would not sin.

Baal HaSulam explained that it is known that "The eye sees and the heart covets." This means that when a person sees something, seeing it causes him to covet. A person cannot do anything about seeing, since this is not up to him. Also, it does not necessarily require seeing with the eyes to bring one to covet, but even by imagining. That is, a thought might come to him, and that thought will cause him to covet.

Therefore, if a person does not want to covet, for coveting is already a sin, he should repent on the seeing, and then he will not covet. Otherwise, he will have to covet, and coveting is already a sin.

For this reason, a correction was made that in order for a person not to blemish the *Kedusha*, if he does not repent immediately after seeing, the light of *Hochma* departs from him, and a spirit of folly enters in its stead. Then, the flaw is not so grave. This is why the spirit of *Hochma* [wisdom] departs from him, where our sages have told us what correction is done from above on man's behalf—that the spirit of wisdom departs from him.

Now we can understand why we need a *Kli* that can hold the blessing that he is given from above, and so it will not need to be taken away from him again. It is that the spirit of wisdom is taken away from him so he will not blemish the *Kedusha*. Likewise, if a person has been rewarded with a blessing from above to receive abundance from above, if the person is improper, meaning that the *Kli* in which the abundance is clothed is inappropriate and can spoil the abundance, like the wine, then there is correction from above that the blessing is taken back.

Rabbi Shimon Ben Halafta comes and says about this: "The Creator did not find a *Kli* that holds a blessing for Israel but peace." He advises us how the blessing can continue and never stop, namely peace. Yet, what is "peace"? We should interpret it according to the verse, "I will hear what the Lord God will speak, for He will speak peace unto His people ... and let them not turn back to folly."

We explained above that there should be a dispute within man, as it is written, "One should always anger the good inclination over the evil inclination." RASHI interprets that he should make war with it. Specifically through the war, the evil in him will appear. Each time evil appears, it is regarded as the appearance of a wicked. Through many appearances, it is revealed that there are many wicked within man, as in the words of *The Zohar*, "Many are the ills of the righteous, but the Lord delivers him from them all."

When these wicked appear in a person, they create the need called "a *Kli* for the Creator's help," as it is written, "He who comes to purify is aided. With what?" *The Zohar* says, "with a holy soul." In other words, he is rewarded with the upper light, called a "soul," and this reforms him.

Now we will understand the meaning of peace, of which it is written, "for He will speak peace unto His people ... and let them not turn back to folly." When the Creator helps him by giving him a soul as assistance to defeat the evil, this is called "peace." In other words, it is when the evil surrenders under the good and now serves the *Kedusha*, as it was said, "And you will love the Lord your God with all your heart, with both your inclinations." That is, the evil inclination, too, has become a lover of the Creator, meaning that now it can work in order to bestow contentment upon the Creator.

This peace, which was made in man so he will not turn back to folly, this *Kli* keeps the light from stopping. When we said that the *Kli* can blemish the abundance, this can be if the will to receive for himself awakens in the *Kli*. At that time the abundance can be extended to the *Klipot*. For this reason, the abundance must depart. But when the Creator tells him, "Peace, so he will not turn back to folly," this is the *Kli* that holds the blessing.

By this we will understand what we asked, "If the Creator says, 'Peace to those who are far,' He certainly says, 'Peace to those who are near.'" Thus, what does it mean to us when it says, "Peace to those who are near"? When does the Creator say, "Peace" [in Hebrew: also "hello" or "goodbye"]? It is when there is someone who is far, when the evil is revealed through the dispute, and it is apparent that the receiver for himself removes him from the Creator. This is called "far."

Certainly, this matter applies specifically if someone wants to be close to the Creator. He makes war with Him, and he is called "near." Specifically through both of them, meaning when one can make peace with the far and with the near together, then the Creator says, "Peace" [or "hello"]. This is why it is written, "Peace, peace, to the far and to the near."

What Is Unfounded Hatred in the Work?

Article No. 24, Tav-Shin-Mem-Zayin, 1986-87

Our sages said (*Yoma* 9b), "The Second Temple, when they engaged in Torah and *Mitzvot* [commandments] and charity, why was it ruined? Because there was unfounded hatred in it." We should understand what is the gravity of unfounded hatred, to the point that our sages said that even though there were Torah and *Mitzvot* there, and charity there, since there was unfounded hatred, it is powerless to protect from the ruin of the Temple. We should also understand why there was a need to destroy the Temple if there were all three things there. That is, if there is unfounded hatred there, is there no more room to keep the Temple standing and it must be ruined?

Therefore, we must understand the connection between unfounded hatred and the Temple. Also, we must understand what it means that it is for unfounded hatred, whereas if there were hatred there that was not unfounded, the prohibition would not have been so grave and the Temple could have remained.

It is written in the Torah (Leviticus 19:17): "You shall not hate your brother in your heart." There it means as RASHBAM interprets "If he does you harm." If he does you harm, it is still forbidden to hate him, much less for nothing. But this is only one manner of prohibition. If that prohibition were over nothing, the Temple would not have the right to exist and it would have to be ruined. That is, had there been hatred there, but the hatred was not unfounded, the Temple would not have been ruined. The whole reason for the ruin of the Temple was only because the hatred was for nothing. Therefore, we should understand the connection between unfounded hatred and the Temple.

In the prayer "May It Please," which we say before saying Psalms, it is written, "The merit of King David will protect, so You will be patient until we return unto You with complete repentance before You, and grant me the treasure of a free gift."

We should understand the connection between asking for complete repentance, meaning that we lack nothing and we ask for nothing at all, and immediately after, we ask, "Grant me the treasure of a free gift," implying we want something more besides complete repentance. This also implies that we actually do want a reward for our work, but because we are full of iniquities and crimes, we ask that You will atone for our sins and we want to repent. This is why we do not deserve a reward. This is why we are not asking for reward, and why we are asking You, "Grant me the treasure of a free gift."

We should understand this. After all, we should work for the sake of the Creator and not to receive reward, yet we ask Him to grant us. We cannot say, "Reward us," since we do not deserve it because we are sinners. Therefore, we want a free gift. Accordingly, how is it permitted to ask that He will give us for free? After all, we need nothing for ourselves, but only for the sake of the Creator. Thus, why are we asking Him to give us "the treasure of a free gift"? Is receiving for ourselves from there permitted?

However, we learned that the essence of our work is that since the Creator created a *Kli* [vessel] to receive the delight and pleasure called "will to receive for oneself," meaning that without yearning, we cannot enjoy anything because this is our nature, for this reason, the original *Kli* that can enjoy is called "desire to receive pleasure."

However, afterwards there was a correction called "equivalence of form," which is not to use the will to receive for oneself but to the extent that one can aim to bestow. In other words, the Creator created the world called "desire to receive pleasure," and that desire is regarded as having been created "existence from absence," since the desire to bestow that exists in Him created a new thing.

In order not to have shame, we need to invent for ourselves the desire to bestow that He has had before He created us with the will to receive. But since the desire to bestow is against our nature, we ask Him that as He has given us the will to receive, now He will give the desire to bestow that He has, and for which He has created in us the will to receive, for we haven't the power to go against nature, but the Creator, who has given us this nature, can give a second nature. That is, only He can make us use the vessels of bestowal.

By this we should interpret that when we are asking the Creator, "Grant me the treasure of a free gift," it means that the will of the Creator, who has created the world, was a free gift, since to whom was He indebted? Also, we ask Him to grant us of this treasure called a "free gift," meaning that we, too, will have this power to do the holy work for free, called "not in order to receive reward."

By this we will understand what we asked about the connection between asking and saying, "Be patient with us until we return to You with complete repentance before You," and then we ask Him to give us the treasure of a free gift. He begins with repentance, which is all that we lack, and we promptly say, "Grant us." Repentance means that we want to return to the root, as it is written about it, "Repentance means, 'The *Hey* returns to the *Vav*.'" This means that the *Hey*, called *Malchut*, which is reception, will return to the *Vav*, called the "bestower."

This means that by wanting to do everything in order to bestow, we cause the root of the soul of each and every one, which is *Malchut*, to be completely in order to bestow. It therefore follows that the repentance we ask is that we want to work only in order to bestow, and we immediately say, "Give!" meaning that we are asking, "Grant me the treasure of a free gift."

According to what we explained above, the meaning of a "treasure of a free gift" is an explanation about repentance, meaning which repentance we are seeking. This is what we promptly explain. That is, we want You to give us the desire to bestow, called "the treasure of a free gift." That is, that desire, with which You have created the world, called "His desire to do good to His creations," with nothing in return, but only for free, as it is known that the creation of the world was "by donation." Give us this desire.

It follows that asking to be given "the treasure of a free gift" explains which repentance we want, as it is written in *The Zohar*, "repentance means that the *Hey* returns to the *Vav*." Now we can understand what we asked about what our sages said, that the Second Temple was ruined although there were Torah and *Mitzvot* and charity there. Still, since there was unfounded hatred there, it could not exist, and Torah and *Mitzvot* and charity did not have the power to save the Temple from ruin.

We explained that a "free gift" means that we need *Kelim* in which the *Kedusha* [holiness/sanctity] can be. Otherwise, the *Kedusha* must depart because there is no equivalence of form between the light and the *Kli*. *Kedusha* means to bestow. If the *Kli* works in order to receive, the light must depart. For this reason, we ask, "Grant me the treasure of a free gift."

Since there was unfounded hatred in the Second Temple, meaning that they hated the "free," meaning to work for free, without any reward, but rather not in order to receive reward, hence, even though they engaged in Torah and *Mitzvot* and in charity, because they did not have the aim to bestow, there was no room for the *Kedusha* to settle there due to the oppositeness of form between them. This is why the Temple had to be ruined.

The order of the work is that we need Torah and *Mitzvot* and charity so they will bring us to work for free. That is, they are only means to achieve the goal, which is to achieve *Dvekut* [adhesion] with the Creator, which is equivalence of form, as it is written, "And to cleave unto Him," and our sages said, "As He is merciful, so you are merciful."

The 613 *Mitzvot* in that state are the means by which to achieve *Dvekut*, and *The Zohar* calls them "613 counsels." This is as it is written ("Introduction of The Book of Zohar," "Mirrors of the Sulam," Item 1), "*The Zohar* calls the *Mitzvot* in the Torah by the name *Pekudin* [deposits]. However, they are also called '613 *Eitin* [counsels].' The difference between them is that in everything there is *Panim* [anterior] and *Achor* [posterior]. The preparation for something is called *Achor*, and its attainment is called *Panim*. When observing Torah and *Mitzvot* as "doers of His word," before we are rewarded with hearing, the *Mitzvot* are called '613 counsels' and they are regarded as *Achor*. When rewarded with hearing the voice of His word, the 613 *Mitzvot* become *Pekudin*, from the word 'deposit,' since there are 613 *Mitzvot* and in each *Mitzva*, the light of a special degree is deposited."

In the above-said, it is explained to us that the order of the work during the preparation is that we should observe Torah and *Mitzvot*. This is an advice by which we can achieve *Dvekut*, called "equivalence of form." Only afterward, when they have *Kelim* that can receive the upper light, the 613 *Mitzvot* become deposits and they are rewarded with all the lights intended for each and every *Mitzva*, according to its essence.

Since there was unfounded hatred there, when they hated the work for free, without reward, meaning that they had no need to work not in order to receive reward, but rather the Torah and *Mitzvot* and charity were all in order to receive reward, hence this work is called "If he is not rewarded, it turns for him into the potion of death." For this reason, the observing of Torah and *Mitzvot* and charity during the Second Temple could not prevent the ruin of the Temple, for in order to maintain the *Kedusha* there is a need for vessels of bestowal. Since they did not have them, the Temple was ruined.

It therefore follows that man is born out of the *Kli* that the Creator has given him, called "will to receive for himself," and all his work and profits belong to the receiver, and no one has a claim over what man has acquired. In other words, both the man and the possessions belong to the receiver for himself.

It is as he says ("Introduction to The Book of Zohar," Item 11), "For the body, which is the will to receive for himself, extends from its root in the thought of creation, passes through the system of the worlds of *Tuma'a*, and remains enslaved to that system for the first thirteen years."

It therefore follows that indeed, everything belongs to the receiver. Thus, how is he told after thirteen years, "Know that although until now everything belonged to you, but henceforth, you and all the property you see should be handed over to the authority of the Creator, and there is nothing for you. In other words, until now you were a gentile, and now everything that the gentiles have is taken away and transferred to the authority of Israel."

But what is "the authority of Israel"? It is the authority of the Creator, called *Yashar-El* [straight to the Creator]. This means that everything that Israel has enters the singular authority. It follows that everything that was in the authority of the receiver, each and every detail, which together are called the "nations of the world," is now required, since everything that belonged to them, now they are told that the receiver for himself must relinquish everything he has and transfer it to the authority of Israel.

And what is "the authority of Israel"? As said above, the Creator is the authority of Israel, for they have no authority of their own, but rather they all want to annul before the Creator.

Now we can interpret the words of RASHI in his interpretation on the word *Beresheet* [in the beginning]: "Rabbi Isaac said, 'The Torah should have begun with, 'This month is to you...' which is the first *Mitzva* that Israel were commanded. What is the reason that he began with *Beresheet*? It is because 'He has made known to His people the power of His works, to give them the inheritance of the nations.' Thus, if the idolaters should tell them, 'You are robbers, for you have conquered seven nations,' they would reply, 'The whole of the Earth belongs to the Creator. He has created it and He has given it that whom He saw fit. Upon His will, He gave it to them, and upon His will, He has taken it from them and has given it to us.'"

We should understand what this teaches us in the work. As we explained, we can understand this simply. The Creator created the world with the aim to do good to His creations, which is that the receiver for himself will enjoy. In order to have *Dvekut* with the Creator, called "equivalence of form," a correction was made not to work for the receiver for himself but for the sake of the Creator, which is called "in order to bestow."

It is known that in order to bestow is called "Israel," and in order to receive is called the "nations of the world." Since there are seven qualities of *Kedusha*, which are HGT NHYM, there are also seven bad qualities in the *Klipot*, which are called "seven nations." Everything must be taken away from their authority and transferred to Israel, meaning that the owners of the seven qualities will be Israel and not the nations of the world, which are the seven nations corresponding to seven *Klipot*.

As he says (there in the introduction), "Until the age of thirteen, man is in the authority of the *Klipot*. Afterward, he must come out of the *Klipot*, and this is the time called 'idol-worshipping,' and enter the *Kedusha*, called 'Israel.'" At that time, the *Klipot* come with the argument, "But the Creator has created us, meaning the will to receive for ourselves, and has placed you under our control, so why after thirteen years you want to exit our control? Moreover, you want to govern us!" This is the grievance of the body against a person when he wants to exit being an idolater, called "self-reception," and become Israel, which is to do everything in order to bestow upon the Creator.

It is written, "You are robbers, for you have conquered seven nations." They reply, "The whole of the Earth belongs to the

Creator," meaning that He is the owner of the world. That is, the Creator, who has created the world in order to do good to His creations, first created the receiver for himself to receive from Him the delight and pleasure. Later, in order for the creatures not to feel any flaw in receiving the delight and pleasure, a judgment was passed and the light departed from the receiver for himself. Instead, the light was given to the receiver in order to bestow, and the receiver for himself remained in the dark, without light.

Later, upon the creation of the souls and in the world of *Tikkun* [correction], two systems extended from this: ABYA of *Kedusha* [sanctity/holiness] and ABYA of *Tuma'a* [impurity], and man comes out and is born. For thirteen years, he is under the authority of ABYA of *Tuma'a*. Afterward, through the power of Torah and *Mitzvot*, he exits their control and takes everything along with him to the side of *Kedusha*.

This is the meaning of the nations' complaint, "You are robbers, for you have conquered seven nations." It means that the nations of the world in a person complain to him: "Why are you making a fuss? You can see that the Creator has created the will to receive for itself, and He must want the will to receive to enjoy the world. Why do you want to do the opposite, meaning take all the pleasure from self-reception and give it all to 'Israel,' called 'in order to bestow'? In other words, you want to be a thief, and you are saying that the Creator agrees to this. Is this possible?"

To this comes the answer that it is as it is written, "Stolen water is sweet" (Proverbs 9). Through the stealing, they will be mitigated [sweetened], when everything is taken away from the receiver for himself, called "idol-worshipper," which are the seven nations. "Sweet" means that specifically through Israel, who take parts from the *Klipot* and raise them to *Kedusha*, this will be their correction. Only by stealing, when they think that what they have is taken away from them—they will receive correction.

This is so because in their *Kelim*, meaning in idol-worshipping, which are the seven nations, they want to receive. And they do receive, but it is only a tiny light compared to what the Creator wants to give. It is written about it, "To do good to His creations, is generously, not with a very thin light." This was given to them only so they would persist until they truly receive all the light that was intended in the thought of creation. At the end of all the corrections, says *The Zohar*, "The angel of death will become a holy angel." It also says, "SAM is destined to become a holy angel."

It follows that specifically by stealing, when the nations of the world say, "You are robbers," they receive mitigation, when each time a part of them is transferred to the *Kedusha*. By this they receive correction. This is the meaning of the words, "Stolen water is sweet."

What does this verse tell us in the work? We should know that to the extent that we can take possessions away from the *Sitra Achra* [other side] and the *Klipot*, which are reception, to that extent we mitigate the bad and it receives complete correction. When all the discernments that have fallen into the *Klipot* enter the *Kedusha*, then will be the end of correction and everything will be completed.

What Is Heaviness of the Head in the Work?

Article No. 25, Tav-Shin-Mem-Zayin, 1986-87

Our sages said (*Berachot* 30b), "One does not pray unless with heaviness of the head."

RASHI interprets that heaviness of the head means subduing. Our sages also said there, "One does not pray out of sadness, and not out of lightheadedness." RASHI interprets that lightheadedness means the opposite of heaviness of the head.

We should understand that when he says, "only out of heaviness of the head," it means that if he does not have heaviness of the head he should not pray. But afterwards it is written, "One does not pray, and not out of lightheadedness." This means that if there is no lightheadedness then one can pray, and there is no need [to wait] for heaviness of the head.

Rather, this implies that if he does not have lightheadedness then he has heaviness of the head. And also to the contrary, if he does not have heaviness of the head then he is already lightheaded. That is, there is nothing in the middle between heaviness of the head and lightheadedness. Because of it, there is no contradiction between the phrases. However, we should understand how it is possible that there is nothing between heaviness of the head and lightheadedness.

And mainly, we should understand what is the prayer, of which they said, "One does not pray unless," according to the conditions that our sages said. In other words, what is a prayer? There must be these conditions there; otherwise, it is impossible to pray.

Our sages said (*Taanit* 2), "To love the Lord your God and to serve Him with all your heart." Which is work that is in the heart? It is prayer.

We should understand why a prayer is called "work in the heart," more than the rest of the *Mitzvot* [commandments] in the Torah. Is the study of Torah not as great a work as prayer?

We should also ask why is it that specifically prayer is called "work in the heart." We cannot say that only a prayer belongs to the heart and not the Torah, since the Torah belongs to the heart, as well. It is as Rabbi Eben Ezra says (presented in the introduction to the book *Panim Masbirot*), "Know that the Torah was given only to men of heart."

Thus, we should understand 1) why a "prayer" is regarded as work more than the rest of the *Mitzvot*, 2) why specifically a prayer is called "the work in the heart," and not "the work in the mind." Concerning prayer, which is work in the heart, our sages told us, "One does not pray unless out of heaviness of the head." This means that precisely through this his prayer will be in order. Thus, we should understand what is "heaviness of the head."

To understand the above, we first need to reiterate what is known concerning the purpose of creation. Although it is clear, we should reiterate in order to remember the goal, which is a guarantee that they will not miss the goal. Concerning the purpose of creation, we should speak of only two topics: a) the Creator, who is the Giver, b) the creatures—the receivers of the abundance.

The purpose of creation, which is "His desire to do good to His creations," has created creatures to receive what He wishes to give them, meaning to receive the delight He wishes to impart upon them. This is the meaning of doing good, since it cannot be said that one is receiving something good without enjoyment. In other words, if he does not enjoy it, why is it regarded as good?

Yet, we see that a person enjoys only what he craves. For this reason, He has created in the creatures a desire to crave to receive pleasures. This is called "will to receive for one's own sake." In the upper worlds, the will to receive for one's own sake is called *Malchut*, and also *Aviut* [thickness], once the will to receive for oneself has been disqualified and it is forbidden to use this *Kli* [vessel] without corrections.

However, a correction was placed here on the will to receive, not to use it as it emerged upon its creation, meaning in the first root when it was born, due to the disparity of form between it and the Creator, since the Creator is the giver and the creatures will be receiving.

In order to have equivalence of form, meaning that the receiver, too, will be regarded as a giver, or else there will not be equivalence of form, causing the creatures to feel unpleasantness upon reception of the delight and pleasure, called "shame." In order to spare the creatures this shame, a correction was made called "receiving in order to bestow." This means that although he is receiving with his *Kli*, called "craving," meaning that it is impossible to enjoy the benefit unless he craves to receive it, but the correction is that he should place an intention over the act. That is, he must see that although the desire to receive it is in full power, if he cannot aim to bestow contentment upon his Maker, he relinquishes the pleasure despite his yearning.

The reason he relinquishes it should be only because he wants *Dvekut* [adhesion] with the Creator, called "equivalence of form," as our sages said, "As He is merciful, you are merciful." From that correction extends to us a *Tzimtzum* [restriction] and concealment.

That is, before the lower ones have this aim and can relinquish even the greatest pleasures if they cannot aim to bestow upon the Creator, there is darkness in the world.

In other words, the Creator is hidden from the creatures; they do not feel Him. Yet, we must believe above reason that He has connection with the creatures and He has created them in order to impart upon them delight and pleasure. This is not so with what appears to our eyes. Before we can aim to bestow, we are placed under the governance of the darkness and nothing spiritual illuminates. At that time the purpose of creation, to do good to His creations, is not disclosed because at that time they see only suffering and pain in the world, and do not see the guidance of The Good Who Does Good. Yet, we must believe that the purpose of creation, to do good to His creations, is the absolute truth, and the reason we do not see this is because of a correction for us, which is called "*Tzimtzum* and concealment of the face."

This is as he says (in "Preface to the Wisdom of Kabbalah," Item 10), "Thus, you find that this soul, which is the light of life that is dressed in the body, extends existence from absence. As it traverses the four worlds ABYA, it becomes increasingly removed from the light of His face until it comes into its designated *Kli*, called *Guf* [body]. And even if the light in it has so diminished that its origin becomes undetectable..."

This causes us to have work on faith because it is no longer apparent in our soul that it comes from the Creator. Instead, we need special work to believe in the Creator, that He is the one leading all the creatures. It therefore follows that all the heaviness we feel in the work of bestowal is not because it is hard for us to work without reward because of our nature, called "will to receive." Rather, there is a completely different matter here, since according to the rule that Baal HaSulam said, there is a trait in our nature that every lower one wants to annul before the upper one, who is the most important to him. A common person derives pleasure from serving an important person, as our sages said (*Kidushin* 7), "With an important person, she gives, and he says, 'You are hereby sanctified,'" for his reception, which is in order to delight the one who gives him, is regarded as complete bestowal and giving to her.

The reason for this is that by nature, a person enjoys giving and bestowing upon an important person. This brings up the question, Why is it difficult for us to observe Torah and *Mitzvot* in order to bestow? The answer is that because of the correction of the bread of shame, a correction was made called "*Tzimtzum*, concealment, and darkness," whereby as long as the creatures are under the control of the receiver for himself, they are so removed from their root that their origin becomes undetectable.

Instead, we were given the work above reason, where although we do not see or feel any spiritual matter, we must do everything above reason. This causes us the heaviness in the work of bestowal. It therefore follows that when we want to walk on the path of truth in the work, we must ask the Creator to give us the power of faith.

It is written (in the prayer of Rabbi Elimelech, "A Prayer before a Prayer"), "Set Your faith in our hearts forever, ceaselessly." This means that the Creator will give us the power of faith so we will feel that we are serving the King of Kings, and our body will certainly annul "as a candle before a torch."

However, since we are born with an inherent mind and reason, which is our leader, our guide, who tells us what is good and what is bad for us, for this reason, anything that we do not understand with our reason, it tells us it is not good for us.

Therefore, when we are given the work of faith above reason, our reason comes and makes us think that we should not walk on this path. Instead, it argues, "Did the Creator give us a mind for no reason? He certainly created everything for our sake," meaning so we will enjoy it. And it brings as evidence the verse, "One should praise according to one's intellect."

All of a sudden, the person comes to the body and says, "It's true that until now you have been my guide, and I never did anything against reason, meaning I followed your command. But henceforth, know that anything you tell me to do, I will not listen to you, but only according to what I heard from books and authors. I take upon me the burden of the kingdom of heaven above reason, and I want to serve the Creator as befits a great king. From now on, I do not want to be concerned with it at all, but that my thoughts will be only for Your sake, the Creator."

It therefore follows that in order to be able to get to the truth, all that a person lacks is faith above reason. The body resists this with all its might, and from this extends our lack of progress in the work of the Creator. This is called "heaviness of the head," for "head" means man's reason. If a person follows what the reason tells him, it is called "lightheadedness," meaning it is something that is easy for the reason to tolerate, for one to do things that the reason dictates to him.

But if a person wants to go above reason, this is called "heaviness of the head," meaning it is difficult for the reason, called "head," to tolerate when a person wants to go against reason, and regards it as a burden and a load. This is called "heaviness of the head."

By this we should interpret what is written, "One does not pray unless with heaviness of the head." In other words, our sages advise us how one should pray. They tell us, "only with heaviness of the head." This means that one should see what he needs before he prays, and on this lack he prays that the Creator will satisfy his lack.

Therefore, one should first check oneself to see if he can take upon himself to walk in faith above reason, called "heaviness of the head," and only then will pray that the Creator will establish the faith in his heart, for if there is faith above reason, then he has everything, as was said, that the small one annuls before the great one.

This is the meaning of what RASHI interpreted, that heaviness of the head means subduing. What is subduing? It is when a person subdues before the great one and heeds the view of the great one. This means that if a little child tells something to a grownup, and the grownup sees that what the child is saying makes sense, the grownup will certainly listen to him. Yet, this does not mean that the grown one subdued before the little one.

Rather, what is subduing? If a person seeks the advice of the great one about what he should do, and the great one tells him, "Do this and that," and the person sees that it makes no sense at all, and if he asked someone if he should listen to what the great one said, he would certainly tell him that it makes no sense and he must not listen to him, yet if that person subdues himself, meaning subjugates his reason and the reason of the public, which are against the reason of the great one, and listens to him, this is called "subduing," when he listens to the great one above reason.

This is very difficult to do, and it is called "The matter is heavy to do." It is also called "I am of heavy mouth and heavy tongue," said about Moses. Mosses is called "the faithful shepherd," since Moses is called "faith," and with faith there is no mouth or tongue, for mouth and tongue mean that he explains the matters with mind and reason, while Moses is faith above reason.

From this we can understand what RASHI interprets about lightheadedness being the opposite of heaviness of the head, and why he does not interpret directly but says that it is the opposite of heaviness of the head. It is so because he wants to interpret to us more clearly what is heaviness of the head, that it is about faith above reason. This is why he tells us that lightheadedness is the opposite of faith above reason.

In other words, he explains to us that there is nothing in between them, but either faith above reason, called "heaviness of the head," or within reason, called "lightheadedness," since something that is clothed in mind and reason is easy for the head to agree for a person to do these actions, which are built on a foundation that the outer intellect understands.

But if a person is told to do things that contradict the mind and reason, it is heaviness of the head. That is, it is a heavy burden for the intellect to tolerate. Therefore, when one is told to take upon himself the burden of the kingdom of heaven "as an ox to the burden and as a donkey to the load," he objects.

What Is Heaviness of the Head in the Work?

According to the above, we can understand why the Mishnah says, "One does not pray unless with heaviness of the head." It means that if he has no heaviness of the head, he must not pray. The Gemara says, "One does not pray out of lightheadedness."

We were wondering, for here it means that if he has no lightheadedness, even though he has no heaviness of the head, he can already pray. This means that there is no in between here. And according to the above, there really is no in between. Rather, either he has faith above reason, called "heaviness of the head," or faith within reason, called "lightheadedness," since it is easy for the mind to understand and agree if the intellect mandates that he should do these actions.

But in between, there is nothing. Therefore, one who wants to pray to the Creator certainly has faith, or he would not come to pray. However, a) either he prays on a basis of faith within reason, called "lightheadedness," as RASHI interpreted, that he has no subduing, b) or he prays with heaviness of the head, when he has subduing. That is, he subdues his reason and does not look at it, as though it is worthless, and his entire basis is built on faith above reason.

Now we can understand the question we asked, Why is prayer called "work"? Moreover, it is called "work in the heart"! It is known that "work" means that a person needs to do something that the body does not enjoy doing. This is called "work." For this reason, a person cannot work without reward. But if a person enjoys the work, it is not regarded as exertion.

This means that the same act that a person does, to one who does not enjoy doing it, it is regarded as "labor," and to another, who enjoys what he is doing, it is not regarded as labor or work. Hence, naturally, he does not need to receive any reward in return for it. Because a person cannot do anything without pleasure, when he does something he does not enjoy, why does he do it?

The answer is that he is expecting to benefit from the work he is doing now at a later time, meaning that he will receive reward for the work and will enjoy. It follows that when one does something without pleasure, from where does he derive strength to work? We must say that he is looking at the reward, and this gives him fuel for the work.

For example, assume that the ADMOR of Lubavitch lands at the airport and he has a suitcase. He gives it to the porter, whose job is to take the suitcase to the taxi. Afterward, he will demand his payment for his work. This is so because he does not recognize the importance of the rabbi. Yet, if the rabbi were to give the suitcase to one of his followers, and the rabbi would want to pay him for his work, the follower will not want to receive, since he already received pleasure while working, for he considers it a fortune to serve the rabbi.

It is as we explained, a prayer should be with heaviness of the head, meaning when a person feels that he does not have faith above reason, meaning that the reason does not mandate him to work in order to bestow, yet the person understands the primary goal should be to be rewarded with *Dvekut* [adhesion] with the Creator. Since the reason objects to this, he must go against reason, and this is very hard work.

Since he is asking the Creator to give him something to which all of his organs object, it follows that each and every prayer he makes to the Creator has its special work. This is why a prayer is called "work in the heart," meaning that he wants to go against the intellect and the mind, which tell him the complete opposite.

This is why it is not called "the work of the brain," since the work of the brain means that a person exerts to understand something with his mind and reason. But here he does not want to understand with his reason that we should serve the Creator in a state of knowing. Rather, he wants to serve the Creator specifically with faith above reason. This is why a prayer is called "work in the heart."

Accordingly, we should interpret "One does not pray," for a prayer is a lack. When a person lacks something and cannot obtain his wish by himself, he asks others to help him. Therefore, when one comes to pray to the Creator to help him, he first needs to see what he really needs, meaning that if he were given what he asks, he will be a complete person who lacks nothing.

This pertains specifically to faith, for when a person is rewarded with permanent faith above reason, he is rewarded with everything. This is why they said, "One does not pray unless with a lack of heaviness of the head," meaning for the Creator to give him the light of faith.

What Is a Light Commandment?

Article No. 26, Tav-Shin-Mem-Zayin, 1986-87

It is written, "And it shall come to pass that because you listen, the Lord your God will keep with you the covenant which He has sworn to your forefathers, and He will love you and bless you." RASHI interprets, "And it shall come to pass that because you listen" to mean that if the *Mitzvot* [commandments] are light [easy/unimportant], which a person tramples with his heels, "you will listen." "[God] will keep" means He will keep with you His promise, thus far his words.

We should understand why it is written that if the *Mitzvot* are light, which a person tramples with his heels, you will hear, meaning that the Creator can give what He has promised to the forefathers. But if they do not observe the light *Mitzvot*, will the Creator not be able to give what He has promised us?

We cannot say that it means that even light *Mitzvot* should be observed. It should have said simply that if one *Mitzva* [commandment] of the 613 *Mitzvot* is missing, you will not receive what He has promised to the forefathers. However, the words "light *Mitzvot*" imply that because they are light *Mitzvot*, the Creator cannot give the delight and pleasure.

What Is a Light Commandment?

Therefore, we should understand why specifically the light *Mitzvot* are the reason, as though they prevent the giving of delight and pleasure to the creatures.

Our sages said (*Avot*, Chapter 2), "Be careful with a light *Mitzva* as with a grave one, for you do not know the reward for the *Mitzvot*." We should also understand what is a "light *Mitzva*" and what is a "grave *Mitzva*," as well as the reason for which we should be careful with a light *Mitzva* as with a grave one. It is implied here that we should be careful with a light *Mitzva* as with a grave one only because we do not know the reward for the *Mitzvot*. But if we did know the reward for the *Mitzvot*, would it be permitted to make distinctions in the caution? Can we say this?

In order to understand the above, we should first know the meaning of the 613 *Mitzvot* that we were given to observe, and for whose sake they were given. Our sages said (*Avot*, Chapter 1), "Rabbi Hananiah Ben Akashia says, 'The Creator wanted to cleanse Israel, therefore He gave them plentiful Torah and *Mitzvot*.'"

In the essay "Preface to the Wisdom of Kabbalah" (Item 1), he explains that cleansing Israel comes from the words "merit" and "purification." This means that through the Torah and *Mitzvot* we can achieve *Hizdakchut* [cleansing/purification]. He explains there what we need to cleanse. He says that since we are born by nature with a desire to receive for our own sake, which separates us from the Creator because in spirituality, disparity of form causes remoteness and separation, and having equivalence of form, which is called "the power of bestowal," is against our nature, it is therefore difficult to work in order to bestow. For this reason, He has given us Torah and *Mitzvot*, by which we will be able to receive the power to overcome and will be able to work in order to bestow.

Accordingly, we should interpret "The Creator wanted to cleanse Israel" to mean that through the cleansing they will be fit to receive the delight and pleasure that He wished to give us, but we did not have the suitable *Kelim* [vessels] for the abundance. It follows that the Torah and *Mitzvot* were given to us as qualification by which we will purify ourselves and will be able to receive the delight and pleasure.

It follows that observing Torah and *Mitzvot* is for our sake. That is, by this we will be able to receive the delight and pleasure. Hence, when can a person receive the delight and pleasure? Specifically when he can work without reward. That is, specifically when he is not concerned with his own benefit and everything he does is only for the sake of the Creator, then he is fit to receive the good, since he already has equivalence of form. Then, it is considered that he has *Kelim* in which the abundance can be without being spoiled. This is regarded as *Kelim* that are cleansed from self-love, and are corrected with the desire to bestow. For this reason, they have equivalence with the abundance, which comes only because His desire is to bestow, and in such *Kelim* the abundance can be.

Apparently, it means that one who wants to receive delight and pleasure, enjoy the world, and lead a happy life should obtain vessels of bestowal in order to later receive delight and pleasure. Accordingly, we should say that he bestows so as to later receive. This is similar to bestowing in order to receive, which is called *Lo Lishma* [not for Her sake].

The answer is that indeed, a person should crave to adhere to the Creator, meaning to come to feel in his organs that any pleasure he wants to receive will be on the path of truth. The truth is that a person should come to a state where he can say wholeheartedly, "Blessed is our God, who has created us for His glory."

This means that a person thanks the Creator for creating him for the glory of the Creator, meaning to increase the glory of the Creator in the world, meaning that everyone will see His greatness in the world.

It is written about it (*Midrash Rabbah, Beresheet*), "When the Creator wanted to create the man, the angels said to Him: 'What is man that You should remember him, and the son of man that You should care for him? Why do You need this trouble?' What is this like? Like a king who had a tower filled abundantly, but no guests.

What pleasure has the king with the abundance? Promptly, they said to Him: 'Do that which pleases You.'"

We need to understand what the argument between the Creator and the angels teaches us, as though the Creator had to have their consent to man's creation. We should interpret that the argument with the angels comes to teach us about the purpose of man's creation, meaning for which purpose man was created. The Creator said to them, "What is your question, Who is man, that You should remember him?"

That is, the angels asked Him, What could man receive from Your creating the world for the purpose of delighting His creations, and by this imprinted in him the desire to receive delight and pleasure? He will be in disparity of form from You, without any *Dvekut* [adhesion] or connection with You, so how will he be able to receive the delight and pleasure? To this comes the Creator's reply that man should work in order to bestow and not in order to receive, as you think.

However, they will say, "But the King has created the tower filled abundantly, and what pleasure has He if He has no guests?" Over this allegory, man will receive the delight and pleasure, meaning that man relinquishes his own benefit and does not want to receive anything. Rather, he wants to bestow in order to bestow. But since the King derives no pleasure from creating a tower filled abundantly, for this reason they want to receive the delight and pleasure.

By this we will understand what we asked, that it seems to mean that man works in order to obtain vessels of bestowal in order to be able to receive the delight and pleasure. It seems that it is as though he is bestowing in order to receive, which is called *Lo Lishma*.

The answer is that after a person has achieved the degree of *Lishma* [for Her sake], meaning that he has no need to receive the delight and pleasure for himself because he has been rewarded with *Lishma*, then comes the allegory about the Creator's reply to the angels, that it is like a king who has a tower filled abundantly but no guests, so what pleasure has the king from having made the tower filled abundantly?

With this intention, a person comes to receive the delight and pleasure. This is called "receiving the delight and pleasure in order to bestow." In order for the Creator to enjoy, having made the tower filled abundantly, and so He may have guests, the person tries to be among the guests receiving the delight and pleasure, since this will please the Creator.

This is called that we must say, "Blessed is our God, who has created us for His glory." That is, the fact that we receive from Him delight and pleasure is with the intention that we will be able to tell the glory of the Creator to everyone by their receiving of the purpose of creation, which is His desire to do good to His creations. This is called "the revelation of His Godliness to His creations," and this is why he wants to receive the delight and pleasure.

It therefore follows that the lower one has no intention to receive reward for his work. Instead, all he asks of the Creator is to help Him so he can bring contentment to the Creator. In other words, since the whole body objects to this view that he should do nothing for his own benefit, but only that which pleases the Creator, he insists on this and asks the Creator to help him defeat his own body, so he will have the power to overcome self-love.

According to the above, we should interpret what our sages said, "Be careful with a light *Mitzva* as with a grave one, for you do not know the reward for the *Mitzvot*." We said that this implies that we are looking at the reward because they said that you do not know their reward, and therefore should be careful with a light *Mitzva* as with a grave one. But then, they said, "Be as slaves serving the great one not in order to receive reward." Thus, what does it mean that you do not know the reward for the *Mitzvot*?

We should interpret that the purpose of the creatures is to achieve *Dvekut* with the Creator, meaning to do everything in order to bring contentment to the Creator. This is why they said that you do not know, meaning that you do not want to know the reward for

What Is a Light Commandment?

the *Mitzvot* because you are working without reward. Hence, what is the difference between a light *Mitzva* and a grave one? In any case, you do not want to work for a reward, but for free.

However, how can one know if he is truly working in order to bestow? For this, our sages gave us a place where we can discern: If we can be careful with a light *Mitzva* as with a grave one, and tell ourselves that we are working without reward and all our works are in order to bestow upon the Creator, then we are careful even with the slight thing as though it were a great thing.

Say, for example, that a person knows for certain that when he speaks inside the synagogue it is not an offense, for he would certainly not transgress in public, where everyone can see that he is committing so many offenses in one hour. But in truth, speaking inside the synagogue during service is an offense, but a person does not regard it as such. This is regarded as a person trampling with his heels because he does not feel that this is such a great offense that he should be careful with it.

Yet, if a person calculates and says, "I do not care if this is a great or small offense," that is, if I were working for a reward, then I would distinguish between a light *Mitzva* and a grave one. But I am working without reward, but only in order to serve the King, so why should I mind whether I am observing a light *Mitzva* or a grave one? On the contrary, I want to be careful with a light *Mitzva* as with a grave one in order to know about myself that I am working only for the Creator. By this, I can know if I am considering the reward or the service of the King. If a person can exert the same efforts with a light *Mitzva* as on a grave one, he can be certain that his actions are just fine.

But if he sees that he cannot exert the same efforts on light *Mitzvot* as he exerts on grave *Mitzvot*, it is a sign that his intention is only the reward, and not the actions that he wants to please the Creator. Rather, it is all for his own benefit.

The allegory I have given, about the person who speaks during service at the synagogue, does not mean that this is a light or a grave *Mitzva*. I only used this as an example because it is common to slight this custom. But what is a light *Mitzva* or a grave one is a personal matter, and each one determines for himself what is grave and what is light.

According to the above we can understand what we asked, that it implies that the Creator cannot give what He promised to the forefathers, as it is written, "The Lord your God will keep with you the covenant which He has sworn to your forefathers, and He will love you and bless you," for they will not be observing the light *Mitzvot*, which a person tramples with his heels.

The answer is that in order to be able to receive the delight and pleasure that He promised to the forefathers, this light must have suitable *Kelim* [vessels] for this, meaning vessels of bestowal. Therefore, if we have the vessels of bestowal, He will be able to give us the delight and pleasure. But if the creatures have only *Kelim* for reception for themselves, there is no place where the light of the Creator can be because of the disparity of form.

This is the meaning of what is written, "And it shall come to pass that because you listen." That is, the light *Mitzvot*, which a person tramples with his heels, you will hear as though they were the gravest of the grave. But this can be only when a person does not consider the reward, and therefore does not mind whether it is a light *Mitzva* or a grave one, since he is serving the teacher not in order to receive reward, but only to bestow. Therefore, he does not mind what he is doing for the King, as long as he is giving contentment to the King. It follows that specifically with light *Mitzvot* it is apparent that a person is working for the sake of the Creator.

Accordingly, the meaning of the condition of the heel is not that specifically if you listen to the *Mitzvot* that a person tramples with his heels, He will give the delight and pleasure. Rather, the meaning is that the Creator has given us a sign concerning observance of Torah and *Mitzvot*, that we said that it is that by the merit of Torah and *Mitzvot* we will be able to obtain the vessels of bestowal, with which we will be able to receive the abundance. The text comes to teach us that if we observe the light *Mitzvot*, which a person tramples with his heels, it is a sign that we are walking on a path toward obtaining the vessels of bestowal.

It is not so with one who chooses between the *Mitzvot*. What is he choosing? Where he can get more; this is what he chooses. This indicates that his intention by observing Torah and *Mitzvot* is not to be rewarded with vessels of bestowal. Rather, he engages in Torah and *Mitzvot Lo Lishma*, but for the sake of receiving reward. This is why he examines each and every *Mitzva*, where is there a greater reward.

For example, we see that our sages said, "Circumcision is great, for it is equal to all the *Mitzvot* in the Torah" (*Nedarim* 32), "Good deeds are greater than charity" (*Sukkah* 49), and there are many other examples from our sages.

It follows that when a person says, "I want to do this in order to please the Creator," and he has no consideration of the reward, here is a place where the Creator can give all the blessings, since here is a place that is called "vessels of bestowal." This is regarded as what is written, "Every place where I mention My name, I will come to you and bless you."

The question is, it should have said, "Where you mention." However, it means that if the Creator can say that this place is His, since a person has given this place to the Creator and has cancelled his own authority, this is why the Creator can "mention," meaning say that the person is saying, "This place is the Creator's."

What Are "Blessing" and "Curse" in the Work?

Article No. 27, Tav-Shin-Mem-Zayin, 1986-87

It is written, "Behold, I am setting before you today a blessing and a curse. The blessing, that you hear the commandments of the Lord your God, which I am commanding you today, and the curse, if you do not hear the commandments."

Here, we need to understand the following: 1) Why does he begin with singular form [in Hebrew], "Behold," and then speaks in plural form [in Hebrew], "before you"? 2) Why is it written, "today"? 3) "A blessing and a curse." It is written, "The bad and the good do not come from the mouth of the upper one" (Lamentations 3). Hence, why is it written, "I am setting before you today a blessing and a curse"? 4) We see that in the corporeal world there is a place where the blessing is present, and a place where the blessing is absent, but there is also no curse there, and there is a place where the curse is present. It follows that there is a middle between a blessing and a curse. But here it says, "I am setting before you today a blessing and a curse," meaning that there is nothing between them but either a blessing or a curse.

What Are "Blessing" and "Curse" in the Work?

The interpreters of the Torah ask these questions. To understand all the above, we must reiterate what we have said thus far. We should examine what it is we have to know in order to know what we must do while we are in this world.

It is known that we should be cognizant of two purposes: 1) the purpose of the Creator, which we learn is to bestow upon His creations, 2) the purpose of the creatures, which is to do good to the Creator.

We should know that the purpose of the Creator is just fine. We must believe that He leads the world in benevolence, but our purpose—to do good to the Creator—is far away from us. Since our goal is the complete opposite of the Creator's goal, and since the purpose of the Creator must be fulfilled, namely that the creatures will receive delight and pleasure as the Creator wants it, His installing in us a desire and yearning to receive pleasure is fixed and cannot be revoked. This means that a person cannot exist in the world if he cannot enjoy life. It makes no difference what he enjoys, but without pleasure, it is impossible to live.

Therefore, when we begin to work on our goal, which is to do good to the Creator, and not use our will to receive, which is what the Creator gave us by nature, we have no strength to go against nature. For this reason, when we begin to work in bestowal, we think that we can revoke nature, but in the end we realize that we cannot.

He has no other counsel but prayer. It is as our sages said, "He who comes to purify is aided." Only through help from above can he achieve the goal of the created beings to equalize in form with the Creator. That is, as the Creator wants to do good to His creations, the creatures should want to bestow upon the Creator, which is called "doing good to the Creator."

The order of the work should be that we must believe above reason in the importance and greatness of the Creator. When we feel the greatness of the King, by nature, we annul before the King. We do not need to exert on this, since we see that by nature, the Creator has given the small one the power to annul before the greater one, since when the smaller one serves the greater one, it feels pleasure in this. It follows that the pleasure it feels while serving the great one does not contradict the nature of the creature, called "will to receive pleasure," since it receives pleasure while working for the great one.

It is known from the allegory that a famous ADMOR [distinguished rabbi] comes and many people greet him at the airport. He gives his suitcase to someone to take it to the taxi. If the rabbi were to give the suitcase to a porter, who does not recognize the greatness of the rabbi, the rabbi would have to pay the porter. Sometimes the porter would even argue over the wages and would want more money than the rabbi gave him. However, if the rabbi were to give his suitcase to one of his followers and would want to pay him, he would not accept it, since there is a rule that one cannot do anything unless he feels pleasure in it. While doing it, work without pleasure is called "labor." That is, the person would not do this if he did not know he would be paid for the effort.

It turns out that if he is serving the great one, and it is inherent in nature that there is pleasure when serving the great one, it follows that he does not need a reward because this is his reward. That is, he is receiving reward, called "pleasure," while serving. It follows that all we need in order to be able to work in order to bestow is the recognition of His greatness, and then the body will naturally annul before Him.

However, since there was a concealment on His light for the purpose of correction, so that the will to receive will work in order to bestow, for this purpose we were given the work of faith, to believe in the greatness of the Creator and depict His greatness every time so we will be able to work in order to bestow and receive nothing in return.

It follows that the person asks the Creator to remove the concealment from himself. This brings up the question, How can one pray to the Creator to remove the concealment from himself,

What Are "Blessing" and "Curse" in the Work?

since it was given for our benefit, so that the shame would be corrected? Thus, how can we pray that the concealment will be taken away from us?

The answer is that the concealment was placed because man is born with a desire to receive for his own sake, and there is no greater pleasure than being in the King's palace. Yet, when receiving pleasure, it will be for our own sake, and this is called "disparity of form."

For this reason, there was a concealment, meaning that before a person is rewarded with vessels of bestowal, so he can receive in order to bestow, a person feels only *Tzimtzum* [restriction] and concealment of the face. For this reason, although man has not been rewarded with vessels of bestowal, and all his work is currently in order to be able to bestow in order to bestow, and he does not want to receive anything for his own sake, he cannot do so because the body is enslaved to self-love.

For this reason, he asks the Creator to remove the concealment from himself, not in order to enable him to enjoy His light. On the contrary, he wants the Creator to remove from him the concealment of the face so he will be able to bestow upon the Creator. It follows that the intention that he wants the Creator to give him is the ability only to bestow.

His intention is not that the Creator will open his eyes and give him the revelation of the face in order to derive pleasure for his own benefit. This is called "disparity of form." Rather, he wants the opposite from the Creator—to have equivalence of form, meaning to have the power to bestow upon the Creator, called "equivalence of form."

Once a person has been rewarded with vessels of bestowal. and can act in order to bestow upon the Creator, comes the work with vessels of reception. That is, he says to the Creator, "Now I want to receive delight because Your will is to do good to His creations. For this reason, I want to do Your will, which You want to give to us."

It is as we interpreted *Midrash Rabbah, Beresheet,* concerning the Creator's reply to the angels who complained about the creation of man. He said, "What is this like? It is like a king who has a tower filled abundantly but no guests." For this reason, a person wants to receive the delight and pleasure from the Creator, so as to delight the King, as said above (Article No. 26, *Tav-Shin-Mem-Zayin*).

By this we can explain the third question, about the verse, "I am setting before you today a blessing and a curse." It is written, "The bad and the good do not come from the mouth of the upper one." But according to what we learned, the purpose of creation is to do good to His creations. Thus, there is no good and bad in this purpose; it is all good! Hence, from where do those two discernments of good and bad come?

This extends from the point of *Tzimtzum*, which is the root of the judgment. *Malchut de Ein Sof,* which received the light in the vessel of reception, desired equivalence of form, as there is in the light. For this reason, she performed the *Tzimtzum*, not wanting to receive any longer with this *Kli* [vessel]. It follows that *Malchut* has made all the boundaries between light and darkness, and this is why we attribute the *Tzimtzum* to the lower one.

It is written (in the commentary *Panim Masbirot*) that "No force from the Emanator is revealed as a boundary. This light that comes to them is called *Ohr Pnimi* [Inner Light], yet it is a restricted illumination because of the point itself."

In other words, the boundary on receiving only in order to bestow is the point itself, which is regarded as *Malchut,* called "a vessel to receive for herself." She made the good, meaning to receive in order to bestow, as well as the bad, not to receive in order to receive. And because that which is a will in the upper one becomes a binding law in the lower one, for this reason, one who wants to receive in order to receive has a sensation of bad and separation from the Life of Lives.

It follows that the reason for the good and bad was made by the lower one. That is, the lower one made a reality of good and gad. It is as was said above, that by *Malchut* desiring equivalence of form, from here extends good and bad in the world. This means that if the lower ones follow the path of the *Tzimtzum* and want only to work in order to bestow, they will have delight and pleasure. But if they do not follow this line, examining everything so it is precisely in order to bestow, they will have darkness and not light.

It follows that from the upper one, meaning the abundance that emerged from the upper one, it was all good. There was no place for bad there, as it is written (beginning of the book *Tree of Life*), "Before the *Tzimtzum*, there was He is one and His name One." That is, there was still no issue of distance between the light, called "He," and the *Kli*, called "His name." Only after the *Tzimtzum* did the will to receive become different in form.

By this we will also understand the fourth question, where it is written "blessing and curse," which means that there is no middle between them. In corporeality, we see that there is a place where there is a blessing, or a place where there is a curse. But there is also a place where there are neither blessing nor curse. For the most part, a person who trades or goes to live in some city does not insist that it will be specifically a place of blessing, since normally, if it is not a place of curse, that place is regarded as a place where he can live. Here, however, the verse, "I set before you a blessing and a curse" implies that there is nothing in between.

The answer is that the good who does good, who is called "Life," if we give vessels of bestowal, it is possible to adhere to the "Life of Lives." It follows that only in this way can one be rewarded with the delight and pleasure called "blessing." But if a person has only vessels of reception, he must be separated from the Life of Lives and he has no *Kelim* in which to receive the delight and pleasure. It follows that he is in the dark and has no light or spiritual life, and no curse is worse than this.

But in the corporeal world, we see that there is a middle between blessing and curse, since the order of the work is that when a person wants to commence in the work of the Creator, to work for the sake of the Creator, he must begin with an in between. That is, he wants to exit the curse and enter the blessing.

But since by nature, he is in a state of "curse," meaning that there was a *Tzimtzum* and concealment on the will to receive with which man was born, so the light of life will not shine there, he wants to come out of there. For this reason, there must be something in between, called *Lo Lishma* [not for Her sake]. This means that the things he does are acts of bestowal—both between man and God, and between man and man. However, he still does not have the intention to bestow.

Since from *Lo Lishma* we come to *Lishma* [for Her sake], this is called "middle," between a curse and a blessing. Since all that is missing in order to be rewarded with the blessing is the aim to bestow, and since this world is called the "world of action," meaning the "place of work," hence, according to the order of the work there is a middle.

But from the perspective of the goal, there are no two things but only one thing. This means that either he is rewarded with the goal, called "blessing," or he is not rewarded with the goal. It follows that he remains inside the curse, which is death, as it is written, "The wicked, in their lives, are called 'dead.'" Therefore, there is no middle here, but either a curse or a blessing in that he is rewarded with *Dvekut* [adhesion] with the Creator.

According to the above we can understand the first question we asked, Why does it begin with singular form, "behold," and then says "before you," in plural form? It is because there is a matter of a giver here, who is the Creator, and a receiver, who are the people of Israel, and it is known that from the perspective of the Creator there are no degrees, as it is written, "I the Lord do not change," but all the changes are only in the receivers.

Therefore, when speaking from the perspective of the giver, He says, "I am placing before you one thing," since from the perspective of the giver, the light of doing good to His creations is called by the name, "one simple light," He therefore speaks to the entire collective and says, "I am placing one thing before you." But when speaking from the perspective of the receiver, there are many degrees in the receivers, as our sages said, "As their faces differ, their views differ" (*Berachot* 58).

For this reason, when speaking to the receivers, He said, "Behold," in singular form, since each individual has his unique vision. This is the reason for the singular form, "Behold," which means that each one should see for himself and should not rely on the vision of one's friend. It is as the ARI wrote, that one cannot correct that which one's friend corrects, but each one has his own correction.

Therefore, the word "Behold" refers to the receivers, who each receive a unique vision. And when speaking from the perspective of the giver, He gives the same thing to everyone. This is why the words, "I am setting before you," speak to the entire collective.

Now we will understand what we asked, What does it imply to us when it says, "Which I am setting before you today"? It means that this matter of blessing and curse applies each and every day, that each and every day there are special corrections, as the ARI says (the writings of the ARI, book, *Gate of Intentions*, in the beginning of "Intentions for Shabbat"), "Moreover, in the weekdays themselves there is a big difference between the prayer on one day from the prayer on the next day. There is not one prayer, since the day when the world was created to the end of the world, that will be similar to another in any way." This is why he says the word "today," as it applies to each and every day.

What Is Do Not Add and Do Not Take Away in the Work?

Article No. 28, Tav-Shin-Mem-Zayin, 1986-87

It is written (Deuteronomy 4:2), "You shall not add to the word which I am commanding you, nor take away from it, to keep the commandments of the Lord your God which I command you."

The interpreters ask, we can understand that the Torah should say, "Do not add," that you should not even think of adding, since it can be said that it is good to add because this will increase the glory of heaven. Yet, for what purpose do the words "and do not take away from it" come, saying that should not lessen? It is simple: If the Creator has given us Torah and *Mitzvot* [commandments], we must certainly observe them and not breach the *Mitzvot* of the Creator.

In the literal, there are many answers. But what does this teach us in the work? Also, we should understand why indeed we are forbidden to add. It makes sense that it is good to add to the *Mitzvot*, especially since in the work, the order is that a person adds each time.

What Is Do Not Add and Do Not Take Away in the Work?

It is known that there is a matter of one line in the order of the work, and there are two lines, called "right" and "left," and there is a middle line, as is explained in previous articles. We will reiterate it here as needed.

We should also know that there is a rule, meaning one rule, which applies to everyone, to the whole of Israel, and there are also individuals in Israel. That is, there are people who cannot be like the general public, meaning behave in regard to Torah and Mitzvot like the general public. Instead, they understand and feel that the work of the general public and its aspirations—what the general public aspires to achieve through the work in Torah and Mitzvot—do not satisfy them. Instead, they have other aspirations and goals than the general public.

Still concerning observing Torah and Mitzvot, it is said, "You will have one law [Torah]" (Numbers 15:29), there is no difference between a complete righteous and an ordinary person. However, this is so with regard to actions, meaning that they should aim to keep the commandments of the Creator as He has commanded us through Moses, and this is called "the intention of the work of Mitzvot," and in this, everyone is equal.

But regarding the intention, meaning what one intends while observing the Torah and Mitzvot, meaning what he wants in return for his work, when he relinquishes other things and dedicates his time and all his energy to observe Torah and Mitzvot, in this there are already discernments, which in general are called Lo Lishma [not for Her sake], or that his intention is Lishma [for Her sake]. For the individual, there are many discernments in Lo Lishma and many discernments in Lishma.

Concerning Lo Lishma, the rule is that everyone begins in Lo Lishma. Afterward, there are individuals who emerge from Lo Lishma and come to the degree of Lishma. At that time they should be discerned by way of lines. That is, all those who, as long as they agree with Lo Lishma, there is a matter of correction in them. This is considered that they cannot see the true path of the work. Instead, they must feel that they are walking on the path of truth. Otherwise, they will not be able to keep observing Torah and *Mitzvot*, since naturally, a person needs to benefit from his work. If *Lo Lishma* is not the truth, but what is truth, it is that *Lo Lishma* is very important. But since they will not think of *Lo Lishma*, there is a correction that they think that they are working *Lishma*, so they will value their actions, for how can one benefit from a lie?

Baal HaSulam said that we should believe that to the extent that a person imagines that *Lishma* is very important, he should believe that *Lo Lishma* is even more important than he appreciates the *Lishma*, and that the importance of *Lishma* is beyond man's ability to grasp.

In the work of the general public, there is only one line, meaning the action. This is one way. That is, he should know that with each and every act he does he is advancing, and many pennies make a great amount. It is as the allegory we said about it, that a person receives a rent from a factory that he has rented to someone. Each year he receives a certain sum, so he is certain that with each passing year, his fortune is growing.

It is likewise in the work of the general public. For example, if a person reaches the age of twenty, he has seven years of wealth of Torah and *Mitzvot*. If he has reached the age of forty, he knows that he has the wealth of twenty-seven years, and so on. It follows that he has nothing to worry about because his reward is secured. And so it is, since a reward is received for *Lo Lishma*, as well. But this is called "one line" or "one way," and there are no contradictions here in the path of the work on which he is going.

However, when a person wants to break away from the path of the general public and enter the work of *Lishma*, we should discern two lines: 1) "right," which is called "wholeness," where there are no lacks. This can be in one of two ways. The first way that there is on the right is that he reflects and says, "Everything is in private Providence and man has no choice for himself." If that is the case, he calculates and sees how many people there are in the world to whom the Creator did not give a thought and desire to observe the commandments of the Creator, while he did receive from the Creator a thought and desire to have some grip on Torah and Mitzvot. Although he sees that there are people who have been rewarded with higher degrees in quantity and quality, when he looks back he sees that there are people who have no grip on spirituality. Instead, their entire lives are about what they can find in corporeal lusts. They do not feel more than any animal, nor think of any purpose, that the world was created for some purpose. Instead, they settle for being able to satisfy the same wishes they had had as children. If they can satisfy those wishes, they consider themselves happy.

Yet, he sees that the Creator has given him mind and reason not to live like an animal, but to know that he is human, that being human means being at a higher level than animals, meaning having contact with the Creator—the ability to keep the commandments of the Creator. He believes that he is speaking to the Creator both in the blessing for the prayer and in the blessing for pleasure. He prays to Him for this little bit of grip that he has on spirituality, he walks about happy, and feels joy in life. He feels that he is not like other people, whose goal in life is only that of children, without any spiritual notion. This is called "right," since he feels himself as a complete person who lacks nothing.

The second manner that is found on the right is as Baal HaSulam said, that one should believe above reason as though he has been rewarded with complete faith, that thus he should depict to himself, as though he already feels in his organs that the Creator leads the whole world as good and doing good, meaning that the whole world receives from him only benefits, and he is one of them. How elated he should feel at that time, when he is going above reason, as though he has a world filled abundantly, and he has only to thank and praise the Creator for awarding him with achieving the delight and pleasure. This, too, is called "right."

This right line gives to a person that only here he has a place where he can thank the Creator for benefitting him, and only in this way he is regarded as whole and blessed because he lacks nothing.

At that time he can be adhered to the Creator, since "the blessed clings to the blessed."

From this a person can receive vitality because a person cannot live on negativity. It follows that through the right line he receives vitality in the work of the Creator because only from wholeness can one receive joy, and life without joy is not considered life.

There is another merit to the right line: By thanking the Creator for bringing him closer, although a person has only a small grip on spirituality, if he is grateful for a small thing, it causes the goal of serving the Creator to receive greater importance in his eyes each time. And since the *Shechina* [Divinity] is in exile, or as it is written, "the *Shechina* is in the dust," meaning that spiritual work is unimportant, only corporeal things matter and a person appreciates them, and man is influenced by the public, hence, corporeality is more important than spirituality for him, as well. By walking on the right line, meaning by thanking the Creator for every single grip he has on spirituality, it increases his importance of spirituality.

Baal HaSulam said that by seeing above how a person appreciates everything that is spiritual, and the evidence of this is that he is thankful for everything, it causes some illumination from above to be given to him, since it is apparent that he will know how to keep it. It is as our sages said, "Who is a fool? He who loses what he is given." The rule is that anything that is not so important is not kept from being lost. For this reason, an illumination from above is not given if a person does not know how to keep it. When they see that that person appreciates every little thing in *Kedusha* [holiness/sanctity], he will certainly keep what he is given. It follows that the person's exertion to praise and thank the Creator for giving him the mind and reason to draw a little nearer to *Kedusha* causes him to be given some illumination from above.

However, one should also walk on the left line. Right and left are regarded as "two lines that deny one another." The left is called "something that requires correction." The left line entails criticism, when a person should see his true state in spirituality, if he is truly on the path of a desire to bestow or is deceiving himself, or is he altogether oblivious.

It is known that the most important is to achieve *Dvekut* with the Creator, which means thinking only about things that yield equivalence of form, and not the contrary. That is, he criticizes the order of his work, if he has already advanced in his work toward achieving the goal, or to the contrary, meaning that he is regressing and should think what he must do in order for his actions to be complete. In other words, he must see his powers in the work, whether he has the power to overcome, and if not, what should he do.

At that time he sees that only the Creator can save him from his state, so he can emerge from self-love and work only for the sake of the Creator. This means that he sees that only the Creator Himself can help him, as it is written, "I the Lord your God, who brought you out from the land of Egypt, from the house of slavery." This means that the people of Israel were enslaved to the discernment of Egypt, which is the will to receive for oneself, and they were slaves to the Egyptians and had no possessions in *Kedusha* because the Egyptians, meaning self-love, took everything.

This is called "The wicked, in their lives, are called 'dead,'" for "the poor is as important as the dead" because the *Sitra Achra* [other side] took all their possessions. Nothing went into the domain of *Kedusha* until the King of all Kings appeared to them and redeemed them. This matter is always valid, meaning that whenever a person is in exile and prays to the Creator to deliver him from exile, the Creator delivers him.

This is the meaning of "He who comes to purify is aided." However, alone, a person cannot come out of exile and enslavement to self-love. It follows that the left line is a place where he should pray to the Creator to deliver him from exile. Otherwise, without a left line, he can never know that he is in self-love because while in the right line, it is impossible to see any flaws, so there is nothing to correct.

Now we can understand the order that we have in the prayer, of chants, singing, and praising, and the meaning of prayer and request. Our sages said (*Berachot* 32), "One should always praise the Creator and then pray."

The question is, If a person wants to ask something from the Creator, he should first establish the praise of the Creator: why he should do this. We can understand that when we ask a favor from flesh and blood, it can be said that first he needs to show him that he regards him as important. It is as though he is bribing him, giving him pleasure, and afterwards asks him to do him a favor, as though the giver will return a favor to the receiver like the receiver did a favor to the giver by giving him the contentment of praising him. But with regard to the Creator, can such a thing be said?

As we explained concerning the need for the two lines, right and left, we should understand that when a person wants to come into the holy work, he must first know what it is about, meaning whom he wants to serve. That is, first he must appreciate the greatness and importance of the King whom he wishes to accept him as a slave, to be as "slaves serving the great one not in order to receive reward." Who is it who gives him the desire to serve the King without any reward? Only the greatness and importance of the King gives him the fuel to want to work without any reward.

Therefore, the order is that he begins to walk on the right line, and then all his work is to imagine the importance of the King and thank Him for giving him the desire and thought to take part in spirituality. It could be anything, even if he is given a small thing, to have a little bit of a grip on spirituality, he regards it as great and important, as said in the clarification of the right line. It is the same with the second interpretation of the right line, as it is written in the name of Baal HaSulam, that "right" means "turn to the right."

This means that he must believe above reason and imagine that he has already been rewarded with faith in the Creator that is felt in his organs, and he sees and feels that the Creator leads the entire world as the good who does good. Although when he looks within reason he sees the opposite, he should still work above reason and it should appear to him as though he can already feel in his organs that so it really is, that the Creator leads the world as the good who does good.

Here he acquires the importance of the goal, and from here he derives life, meaning joy at being near to the Creator. Then a person can say that the Creator is good and does good, and feel that he has the strength to tell the Creator, "You have chosen us from among all nations, You have loved us and wanted us," since he has a reason to thank the Creator. And to the extent that he feels the importance of spirituality, so he establishes the praise of the Creator.

Once man has come to feel the importance of spirituality, which is called "One should always establish the praise of the Creator," then is the time when he must shift to the left line. He must criticize how he truly feels within reason the importance of the King, if he is truly willing to work only for the sake of the Creator.

When he sees within reason that he is bare and destitute, that state when he sees the importance of spirituality, but only above reason, that calculation can create in him deficiency and pain for being in utter lowliness. Then he can make a heartfelt prayer for what he lacks.

But if he does not have the right line even though he has prayed to the Creator to help him, it is as though he is asking the King to do him a favor and save him and have mercy on him. Since the King is merciful, he is asking Him for money to buy himself some bread. But a person does not know that he is in prison among those who have been sentenced to death, and now he has a chance to ask the King to save his life, meaning pardon him, and the King will pardon him and give him a chance to live a life of happiness, and he asks the Creator to have mercy on him and give him bread, and he settles for this, it is because he has been incarcerated for so long that he has forgotten everything, that there is a world where he can lead a happy life.

This is the benefit from first establishing the praise of the Creator and then praying. The reason is that once he knows the importance of spirituality, that it is "for they are our lives and the length of our days," hence, when he prays, he knows what he needs and for what he must ask the Creator's mercy on him and to give him life. It is so because while he was on the right line, he felt that corporeal life is as "the wicked, in their lives, are called 'dead.'"

By this we will understand what we asked, Why should one establish the praise of the Creator and then pray? This is appropriate for a flesh and blood, whom we must first appease and praise, which makes the giver compassionate and giving, as the pleading person told him, that the giver has good qualities. But why do we need to establish the praise of the Creator before we pray?

According to the above, this is simple. It is in order for him to know what he is missing, for then he will know for what to ask the Creator's help. This is similar to the allegory I once said, that a person was very ill, and a party of physicians came to examine him and diagnose his illness. The patient showed the doctors a tiny sore on his finger and told them he was in pain, but they did not want to look at it. He asked them, "Why aren't you looking at what I'm telling you, and no one wants to look at it?" They replied to him, "You are in mortal danger, between life and death, and you want us to look at something so trivial?"

It is likewise with us. When a person has no idea what he is missing and he asks for something small like that sore, when in truth he is in the domain of *Tuma'a* [impurity], as in, "The wicked, in their lives, are called 'dead,'" how can they regard him from above when he is in the domain of the dead? He needs to ask to be given life, as it is written, "Mention us to life." But although we say, "Mention us to life," which life do we expect? This is the question!

However, once a person has begun to walk on the right line, he begins to know what he is missing. That is, afterward, when he shifts to the left line, he has an example from the right. Yet, this, too, is not acquired at once, but is constant work, as it is written in the prayer for every day, that we must first establish the praise of the Creator and then pray.

Yet, the two lines must be balanced, meaning that one will not be greater than the other. Instead, he must always walk as in the corporeal allegory, on two legs—the right leg and the left leg. It cannot be said that he should walk on one leg more than on the other, and walking on only one leg is altogether impossible. Therefore, those who want to walk on the path of truth and achieve *Dvekut* with the Creator, must walk on both the right and the left, but not walk on one leg more than on the other.

Now we should interpret what we asked, What is the meaning of "Do not add and do not take away from it"? We asked, How does it pertain to the work that we should not add in the work? And on the other hand, it is perplexing: "Do not add" can be said when the Torah tells us, "Do not add." But why the commandment, "Do not take away"? How can we think that it is permissible to take away from the 613 *Mitzvot*, but the Torah should tell us that we are forbidden to take away?

According to the order of the work, we should interpret this in regard to the two lines. It means that it is forbidden to add on the right path. Instead, a person who wants to walk on the path of truth must dedicate a certain amount of time to the right path, and then he must walk on the left line. It is in this regard that the commandment not to add comes—on one way more than on the other, nor take away from the lines. That is, one should not say, "Today I want to walk on the right line," or to the contrary, "Today I want to walk on the left line." It is about this that the commandment, "Do not add and do not take away," comes. Rather, as our sages said, "One should always establish the praise of the Creator and then pray."

The right path is called "wholeness." At that time a person can be very grateful to the Creator. Afterward, he must shift to the left line. On the left path is the time to see his real state, as it seems to him within reason. Then, he has room to pray, since prayer pertains precisely to a place of lack, and the greater the lack, the more heartfelt is the prayer.

This is the meaning of what is written, "From the depth I called You, O Lord." Therefore, the two lines must be equal "until the third writing comes and decides between them." Then, after the work in two lines, he is rewarded with *Dvekut* with the Creator. This is called the "third writing." That is, the two lines pertain to man's work, but the middle line pertains to the Creator. This means that by walking in two lines, from those two, a place is made where the Creator can place His blessing. This is called "until the third writing comes and decides between them."

Now we can interpret what *The Zohar* says (*Pinhas*, Item 321), "'Their leg is a straight leg.' The authors of the Mishnah said that one who prays should correct one's legs in one's prayer, as the ministering angels, so that his legs will be straight."

We should understand why if the legs are not straight, his prayer cannot be accepted. It means that his legs imply something, that for this reason, when he prays, he feels deficient and comes to the Creator to satisfy his lack, his legs must be straight.

According to the above, we can understand the meaning of his "legs." The "right leg" is the right line or the right path. This is the place to praise and thank the Creator. The left leg refers to the left line and the left path, and the prayer cannot be accepted before both lines are straight and not that one is bigger than the other.

What Is "According to the Sorrow, So Is the Reward"?

Article No. 29, Tav-Shin-Mem-Zayin, 1986-87

Our sages wrote (*Avot*, Chapter 5), "Ben Ha Ha says, 'According to the sorrow, so is the reward.'" We should understand this condition. What can we understand from "The work is according to the reward"?

It is written (in the song, "All who Sanctify"), "His reward is plentiful, according to his work." Therefore, we should understand what is "According to the sorrow, so is the reward." Instead, it should have said, "According to his work, so is his reward," so what is "According to the sorrow is the reward"?

This is similar to what we find in *The Zohar* (*Ki Tetze*, Item 54): "Likewise will be the redemption. If they are rewarded, they will come out with mercy, as it is written, 'Before her pain came, she gave birth to a male,' and they came out with mercy. If He does not precede mercy, they will come out with pain. It is better to precede sorrow and judgment in order to extend mercy. For this reason, the authors of the Mishnah established, 'According to the sorrow, so is the reward.'"

The words of *The Zohar* require clarification: 1) Why does it require preceding sorrow and judgment in order to extend mercy, as it is written, "It is better to precede sorrow and judgment in order to extend the mercy"? 2) They said, "According to the sorrow, so is the reward," meaning "according to the sorrow, so is the reward." But our sages said (*Avot*, Chapter 1), "He would say, 'Be not as slaves serving the great one in order to receive reward.'" Thus, why is it permitted to work for a reward, since they said, "According to the sorrow, so is the reward"? Are we not forbidden to work for a reward?

To understand this, we first need to know what they call "sorrow," "labor," and "judgment." Which reward are they referring to in "According to the sorrow, so is the reward"? It is known that there is no light without a *Kli* [vessel]. That is, we cannot fill a lack where there is none. Rather, where there is a lack, it can be said that it requires filling. For this reason, the Creator created a lack called "desire and yearning for pleasure."

This is called *Malchut de Ein Sof*, which is called "creation." It is known that this is called "creator of darkness," in order to give her light and pleasure. We learned that it is called *Ein Sof* because this discernment, called "will to receive" in order to satisfy the lack in the yearning for pleasure, did not put a stop. That is, she did not say, "I do not want to use this *Kli*." Instead, she received the delight and pleasure.

Afterward, this *Kli*, which took the abundance, said, "I do not want to be a receiver. Rather, I want to be like the Creator, meaning a giver, too." But how can this be? That is, if we are speaking of spirituality, and she is craving *Dvekut* [adhesion] with the Creator, how can she say, "I don't want to receive," which contradicts the intention of the Creator, since His will is to do good to His creations? How could *Malchut* say, "I don't want the intention of the Creator to be carried out"? since the Creator's will cannot come true unless the lower one receives what He wants to give. If the lower one does not receive, the Creator's intention will never come true.

The answer is that *Malchut* said, "I do want to receive; I don't want to go against the will of the Creator, who wants to give, as it is written, 'His desire to do good to His creations.' However, I don't want to receive in order to calm my yearning. Although I feel a great deficiency and I want to satisfy my desire with upper abundance, yet, I do not want to receive for this reason. Instead, with this intention He will receive, meaning because of the will to receive in me. I want to relinquish this, meaning to leave a vacant space without abundance, and because the Emanator wants the lower one to receive delight and pleasure, for this reason I will receive. In other words, I will receive because the Creator wants to give, for His pleasure is that He gives. For this reason I will receive." This is called "receiving with the intention to bestow," since by this I am bestowing upon the Creator, whose will, which is called "His desire to do good," is carried out.

In the words of Kabbalah, this is regarded as placing a *Masach* [screen] on the upper abundance and not receiving it until she calculates this abundance to see what percentage she can receive in order to bestow. This she receives. If she receives the rest, it will be in order to receive, and this will remain vacant, without abundance.

According to the rule, "A desire in the upper one becomes a mandatory law in the lower one," it follows that *Malchut* saying, "I don't want to receive in order to receive," which is called *Tzimtzum* [restriction], caused a prohibition on receiving in order to receive from her and below. If we do want to receive, we become separated from the Creator, since He is the bestower, and the receiver is in oppositeness of form, and "disparity of form causes separation in spirituality." From here, the place for the *Klipot* [shells/peels] was made, who are separated from "The Life of Lives," and are called "dead."

Afterward, two systems emerged from this: *Kedusha* [sanctity/holiness] and *Klipa* [singular of *Klipot*]. It is written about it ("Introduction to The Book of Zohar," Item 10), "And in order to mend that separation, which lays on the *Kli* of the souls, He created all the worlds and separated them into two systems, which are the four worlds ABYA of Kedusha, and opposite them the four worlds ABYA of Tuma'a. He imprinted the desire to bestow in the system of ABYA of Kedusha, removed from them the will to receive for themselves, and placed it in the system of the worlds ABYA of Tuma'a. The worlds cascaded onto the reality of this corporeal world, to a place where there is a body and a soul and a time of corruption and correction. For the body, which is the will to receive for oneself, extends from its root in the thought of creation through the system of the worlds of Tuma'a, and remains enslaved thirteen years, and this is the time of corruption. By engaging in Mitzvot from thirteen years onward, he begins to purify the will to receive for himself, imprinted in him, and slowly turns it into working in order to bestow. By this he extends a holy soul from its root in the thought of creation. It passes through the system of the worlds of Kedusha and dresses in the body. This is the time of correction."

The above order, where he says that for thirteen years a man is under the control of the Klipot, is when one satisfies all his needs completely. There is no one who does not walk on this path of the time of corruption, since this way is natural. That is, everything he does, does not blemish the will to receive for himself.

But after thirteen years, when a person begins to work in Torah and Mitzvot with the aim to emerge from the governance of Tuma'a, and wants to work to the contrary, meaning that by the force of Torah and Mitzvot that he observes, he will have the strength to revoke the will to receive, which extends from the system of Tuma'a, the work becomes heavy, since it is against nature. [And I, Michael Laitman, heard from my teacher, the RABASH, that Baal HaSulam mentioned the number thirteen in order to obscure the matter.]

Man is born inside the will to receive for himself. Suddenly, he comes to the body and says, "Listen, until now you worked in thought, speech, and action for your own sake. From now on, I want you to work only for the sake of the Creator, meaning that everything you do will be with the intention to bestow contentment upon your Maker."

What Is "According to the Sorrow, So Is the Reward"?

When the body hears these words, it resists with all its might, both in mind and in heart. According to one's prevailing, to that extent he reveals its resistance through all kinds of arguments, such as the arguments of the spies, who spoke about the land of Israel, as *The Zohar* interprets (*Shlach*, Item 59). It writes, "And they went up the Negev." It means that people ascend in her in *Negev* [desert/dryness], meaning with an idle heart, as though one is working for nothing, with dryness, and thinks that there is no reward in it. He sees that the wealth of the world is lost for her, and thinks that everything is lost.

It is also written there (Item 63), "'And they returned from touring the land.' That is, they returned to the bad side and reverted from the path of truth saying, 'What will we get out of it? To this day, we have not seen good in the world. We have toiled in Torah but the house is empty. We sat among the lowliest in the nation, and who will be rewarded with that world? Who will come into it? It would have been better had we not toiled so. That upper world is good, but who can be rewarded with it?'"

According to the above, we see that the complaint of the spies came only after the exertion, when they already began to work in order to bestow, as it is written in *The Zohar*, that they said, "To this day, we have not seen good in the world. We have toiled in Torah." They also said, "It would have been better had we not toiled so." That is, they had made great efforts to come to work in order to bestow, which is called "the land of Israel," for *Eretz* [land] is called *Ratzon* [desire], and *Ysrael* [Israel] is called *Yashar-El* [straight to the Creator], meaning that they want everything to be straight to God, directly to the Creator, and not to the *Klipot*, whose control is in the will to receive for oneself.

Yet, the spies said, "That world is good, but who can be rewarded with it?" We see that the bad in a person interferes with entering the path of truth, which is to work only in order to bestow. It does not appear at once, but rather everything goes by way of "one opposite the other": To the extent of overcoming in order to bestow, the "in order to receive" increases.

For this reason, a person thinks that he is regressing and not progressing. But in truth, he is progressing, and he can see this by the fact that the more he exerts to work in bestowal, the more attraction he receives toward the will to receive.

That is, before he exerted to walk on the path of bestowal, he did not have such an attraction for self-love. But once he has commenced in the work of bestowal, he sees that where the desire to bestow should have been stronger in him and the will to receive weaker, he is asking, "What have I gained from my work for "in order to bestow"? The will to receive has strengthened, meaning ascended in degree and became more important, while the desire to bestow grew weaker. In other words, it is at a lower degree in him after he has begun this work of acquiring vessels of bestowal.

It follows that only when he begins to work in bestowal comes the argument of the spies. Before he began to work in bestowal and his work was like the general public, he knew that he was learning Torah and engaging in *Mitzvot*, and he had no sorrow while engaging in his work in Torah and *Mitzvot*. But once he has begun the work of bestowal, he feels sorrow and suffering even during the work.

Indeed, concerning the argument of the spies that comes into his mind at that time, he sees that they are right in everything they say. This causes him to doubt the beginning. That is, he is angry with the one who admitted him into this work of bestowal. He lived in a world that was all good and felt that he was "happy in this world and happy in the next world." But now he is hearing the argument of the spies coming from his body: "We labored in vain, and who will be rewarded with the upper world?"

It follows that he feels destitute because now he sees the truth—that the evil controls him and he has no permission to disobey it and go against the will and view of the will to receive for himself. He actually feels that he is completely separated from *Kedusha* and is in the group of the dead, as in, "The wicked, in their lives, are called 'dead,'" since they are separated from The Life of Lives. Now he can actually feel this.

Conversely, before he began the work of bestowal, he would tell himself that he belongs to the group of servants of the Creator, and all the energy he put into the work brought him pain and sorrow when he saw that there are people who are not walking on the path of the Creator. But concerning himself, he was more or less certain that he was already considered a "servant of the Creator."

But now he sees what has happened to him because of the advice to walk in the above-mentioned way: only sorrow and pain for not having this world. That is, in this world, he sees that he is not fine with the Creator, meaning he feels that he would like to work for the sake of the Creator and does not find satisfaction in his own benefit. Although he cannot exit self-gratification, he also cannot find satisfaction in it.

Now, in the next world, how can he hope and tell himself that he will be rewarded in the next world, so now he sees the truth—that he has no intention to work for the sake of the Creator, to be able to say, "I deserve reward for working for the Creator."

Accordingly, we see that precisely when a person begins to walk on the path of bestowal, he comes to a state of pain and sorrow, and feels the labor that exists in serving the Creator. That is, the labor begins to work when one wants to work for the sake of the Creator. Only then do the arguments of the spies come to him. It is very difficult to overcome them, and many people escape the campaign and surrender to the argument of the spies.

But those who do not want to move, but rather say, "We have nowhere to go," suffer from not being able to always overcome them. They are in a state of ascending and descending, and every time they overcome, they see that they are farther from the goal that they want to be rewarded with *Dvekut* with the Creator, which is equivalence of form.

The measure of sorrow that they must tolerate is because in truth, a person cannot emerge from the control of self-reception by himself, as it is the nature in which the Creator created man, which only the Creator Himself can change. In other words, as He has given the created beings the desire to receive, He can later give them the desire to bestow.

However, according to the rule, "There is no light without a *Kli*, no filling without a lack," first one needs to obtain a deficiency. That is, he must feel that he is deficient of this *Kli* called "desire to bestow." And concerning feeling, it is impossible to feel any lack if one does not know what he is losing by not having the *Kli*, called "desire to bestow." For this reason, man must introspect on what causes him not to have the desire to bestow.

To the extent of the loss, he feels sorrow and suffering. When he has the real lack, meaning when he can pray to the Creator from the bottom of the heart for not having the strength to be able to work for the sake of the Creator, then, when he has the *Kli*, meaning the real lack, this is the time when his prayer is answered and he receives assistance from above. It is as our sages said, "He who comes to purify is aided."

By this we will understand what we asked, "What is the meaning of 'According to the sorrow, so is the reward'?" It means that according to his lack, meaning to the extent that he feels sorrow at not being able to emerge from the control of the bad, and bad means that he feels that it is something bad, meaning he sees what bad that the vessels of reception cause him, then he feels actual sorrow. This gives him the need that the Creator will help him, and he receives the reward, meaning the reward for the sorrow he had had. This is the meaning of the words, "According to the sorrow," to the full extent of the sorrow, meaning the understanding of the lack, is the reward. Then comes the time when the reward comes, for "there is no light without a *Kli*."

Now we can understand what we asked according to what our sages said, "Be not as slaves serving the great one in order to receive reward." In other words, it is forbidden to work in order to receive reward because receiving the reward separates us from the Creator, who is the giver, while man wants to receive.

What Is "According to the Sorrow, So Is the Reward"?

The answer is that the reward he is asking for his labor is to be able to overcome the vessels of reception and be able to work in order to bestow. Such a reward will bring him *Dvekut* with The Life of Lives. That is, the reward he expects is to be given the strength to work without reward that comes to the vessels of reception, by which he becomes separated. Rather, the reward comes to the vessels of bestowal, by which he becomes close to the Creator.

By this we will also understand what we asked about what we sing in the songs of Shabbat [Sabbath], "His reward is plentiful, according to his work." We should understand the following: 1) Is it permitted to work for a reward? If so why does he say, "His reward is plentiful"? 2) "His reward is plentiful, according to his work." What is the novelty? In everything, if he works more he receives more reward. So, what is "his reward is plentiful"? I would understand it if he said, "His reward is plentiful although he did not make such great efforts, yet he received a great reward."

According to the above, we should interpret that "work" does not pertain to corporeal work, where one is rewarded according to the output that a person produces. The output is positive, relating to what the worker did, and to the extent of the output so is his reward.

But here, "according to his work" means according to his labor and exertion without seeing anything positive in the work. On the contrary, each time, he sees more negativity in his work. That is, each time he sees that he does not want to work for the sake of the Creator. Thus, how can he ask for a reward, so as to say, "His reward is plentiful, according to his work," although he sees no progress? On the contrary, he is regressing every time, yet he does not escape the campaign or grow idle in the work. Instead, he works as though he is advancing. It follows that "according to his work" means to the extent that he overcomes each time, and according to the sorrow and exertion that he puts into this work, it causes him to be able to obtain a real *Kli* and need for the Creator's help.

It follows that unlike corporeality, where we are rewarded according to the output, meaning that one looks at the work he did. Here, it is the opposite.

Also, why is it permitted to receive reward here? It is because the reward he is asking is not a reward that will separate him from adhering to Him. Rather, he hopes that all of the reward he hopes to be given is the ability to bestow upon the Creator, and through this reward he will adhere to Him.

This is the meaning of what is written, "It is good to precede sorrow and judgment in order to extend mercy." We asked, why the need for sorrow and judgment if we want mercy? The reason is that the sorrow is the *Kli* and the need, for there is no light without a *Kli*. And what is the "light"? It is mercy, as our sages said, "As He is merciful, so you are merciful." This is what he should be given.

What Is a War Over Authority in the Work - 1

Article No. 30, Tav-Shin-Mem-Zayin, 1986-87

RASHI interprets the verse, "When you go to war against your enemies," that the verse speaks of a War Over Authority. Afterward, it is written, "And the Lord your God delivers them into your hands and you take them away captive. And you see among the captives a beautiful woman, and you desire her and take her as a wife for yourself, and she shall shave her head and do her nails."

We should understand what all this comes to teach us in the work. Since the Torah is eternity, we should understand the following: 1) What is a War Over Authority? 2) What it means when he says, "And the Lord God delivers them into your hands." Clearly, every Jew believes that any war can be won only with the help of the Creator. 3) What does a beautiful woman mean in the work? 4) What is the meaning of the corrections, what does it imply to us in the work that "she shall shave her head and do her nails"?

To understand all the above in the work, we first need to know what is work. That is, what discernment is called "work" when walking in the path of the Creator, and which reward we expect to receive in return for the work. It is known that no one can work without reward, for because our root is in a state of rest, we can exert only in return for a reward, which is pleasure that we obtain following the exertion.

Since we cannot live without pleasure, which is also because our root is the source of the pleasure, it follows that this is what makes us need pleasure. But there is another reason for our inability to live without pleasure: Since the Creator created the creatures because of His desire to do good to His creations, He has imprinted in the creatures a desire and craving to receive delight and pleasure.

For this reason, since labor is not in our root, if we want to do something that is not in our root, it is difficult for us to do it. And yet, we do the work because it is impossible to live without pleasure, so we relinquish the rest and make an effort in order to thereby obtain delight and pleasure.

It follows that labor is something in which there is no delight and pleasure. Therefore, since there is no pleasure in it, why do we do it? The answer is that thanks to the work, we will receive reward in return for it, and the reward is called "delight and pleasure." We see that this is what is done in corporeality. But in spirituality, what is the work that we do not enjoy, which is called "work"? And, what is the reward in spirituality, from which we can derive delight and pleasure?

It is known that there are two discernments in the lights:

1. A light that is called "the purpose of creation." This is the delight and pleasure that a person should receive, which the Creator wanted to give to the creatures, and for which He has created in the creatures a desire and craving to receive pleasure. However, in order to bring to light the perfection of His deeds, He has made a *Tzimtzum* [restriction] and concealment, by which the matter of the "bread of shame" (shame) upon the reception of the pleasure will be corrected, as it comes because of the disparity of form between the giver and the receiver.

2. The light of the correction of creation. In other words, the correction is for the lower one to receive the lights in order to bestow, by which there will be equivalence of form, called "*Dvekut* [adhesion] with the Creator." At that time the shame will be cancelled.

It follows that this light, called "light of *Hassadim*" [mercies], is named so after his will to do *Hesed* [mercy] with the Creator, meaning to bestow upon the Creator. Conversely, the light of the purpose of creation is called "light of *Hochma* [wisdom]" or the "light of life." This is the light that the Creator wants to do good to His creations.

It therefore follows that since there was a judgment that it is forbidden to use the *Kli* [vessel] called "desire to receive for oneself," although the Creator created this desire in the creatures, still, indirectly, shame is poured upon the receiver. To correct this, a person must cancel this *Kli*, which comes to him by nature. This is called "work" because it is against nature, for nature is that we should receive delight and not relinquish it. When a person does not receive delight, it is labor, since it is against nature. So why does he do this work? It is because he wants *Dvekut*, called "equivalence of form."

However, in this work, when he relinquishes the delight and does not receive it, he still does not become equal. That is, by not wanting to receive any delight, it is not regarded as achieving the degree of equivalence of form because as the Creator bestows, if man, too, wishes to achieve the degree of equivalence of form, he should be a giver, too, meaning come to want to bestow upon others, just as the Creator bestows.

We should also say that by engaging in love of others, in bestowal, he still does not achieve equivalence of form if he derives no pleasure from performing acts of bestowal and not receiving any reward in return. This is so because the Creator enjoys giving to the creatures, for His desire is to do good to His creations, as our sages said (*The Zohar*, *VaYera*, Item 399), "Rabbi

Yehuda said, 'There has never been such joy to the Creator as the day when the world was created.'"

Therefore, if a person engages in bestowal but derives no pleasure, he certainly has no joy. Joy is only a result of a person's enjoying something; this brings him joy. Therefore, if a person attempts to engage in bestowal but derives no pleasure from engaging in bestowal, then he is still lacking equivalence of form because when the Creator bestows He derives pleasure, whereas man does not derive pleasure. It therefore follows that when one wants to be rewarded with *Dvekut*, he needs to meet three conditions: 1) not to use the will to receive for his own sake, 2) engage in acts of bestowal, 3) enjoy while bestowing.

However, we should understand how one can enjoy giving everything to the Creator in a manner of coercion. It can be said that although the body does not agree to work only for the Creator, meaning that before he does anything, he will calculate if the Creator will enjoy the act he is going to perform, since this is against nature, and although we can understand that he is doing this compulsively, he is forcing and tormenting himself in order to do things that please the Creator.

Yet, there is no pleasure in what is done compulsively. For example, if a person goes to the hospital to undergo surgery, he is certainly doing this against his will, although he goes to the hospital by himself and no one is forcing him, and he also pays a lot of money to the surgeon. However, this, too, is regarded as coercion because he is not enjoying this. However, by having himself operated on, despite the suffering and the fear of danger, he knows that by this he can save his life. Yet, he would certainly be more pleased if he were healthy and did not need the operation.

It follows that although he is performing an act from which he is not pleased, by knowing that he will save his life, this awareness pleases him and he has the operation. Thus, we should note here that he is performing the act, and although he does not enjoy the act itself, but to the contrary, he suffers from it, yet because he is considering the reward of saving his life, he has the strength to do things he does not like.

It is likewise in corporeality. A person works and toils although he does not like the work, since he would prefer to rest. Still, when he considers the reward, he has the strength to work willingly, and this is not regarded as compulsory work, since he is not saying, "I relinquish this work and want to be paid for nothing." Instead, because of the shame, he agrees to work on the condition that he will be paid. Conversely, a patient who admits himself into a hospital in order to be operated on would certainly be happier if he did not have to do this.

By this we see that we should discern three manners in man's work in corporeality:

1. Work that a person does in order to receive reward, at which time he likes the work. In other words, he is not saying, "I would give up the work and I want only the pay," since a person is ashamed to eat the bread of shame.

2. A person works in order to receive reward, though he does not like the work. In other words, he would be happier if he did not have to do the work, as in the allegory of the man who admitted himself to the hospital to have himself operated on. Although he does this work voluntarily and no one is forcing him, he does it because of the reward or the punishment. That is, he can either save his life, or avoid death, whereas if he avoids doing this, he will be punished with death.

3. He works for the sake of others. That is, he wants no reward at all, but only the benefit of others. It is as though he is going to work somewhere and gives his salary to charity. This brings up the question, From where does he take fuel for such a work? meaning to work without any reward. The simple reason is that there is the matter of honor. He is in an environment that respects those who work for the sake of others, and this gives him the strength to work.

In the essay "The Peace," it says about it, "But when all the work of bestowal upon others is based solely on the benefit of society, it is a rickety foundation, for who and what would obligate the individual to toil for society?"

Not every person is fit to work for the sake of the society in order to receive respect. This is already a second degree to lust, and it is known that there are four discernments in man's degrees, called "still, vegetative, animate, and speaking."

It is said in the "Preface to The Book of Zohar" (Item 20): "Thus, in the first category—the necessary measure for one's sustenance—and in the second category—the physical desires that exceed one's measure for sustenance—one is nourished by things that are lower than the person: the still, vegetative, and animate. However, in the third category, the human desires such as power and respect, one receives and is nurtured by his own species, his equals. In the fourth category, knowledge, one receives and is nurtured by a higher category than one's own—from the actual wisdom and intellect, which are spiritual."

Thus, a person cannot work without any reward. Even for respect, not every person is able to work, but they are already regarded as a higher degree than mere ordinary people. Yet, sometimes a person can work for others because of jealousy. That is, although he relinquishes honor, meaning he cannot work and toil although by not working for the sake of others he will not gain respect. But because of jealousy, when he sees that those who work for respect, when he sees that they are respected and no one is looking at him, these torments—that another has respect—pain him. Because of these pains it is possible that he, too, will work for the sake of others.

However, when beginning to work in spirituality, meaning to observe Torah and *Mitzvot*, many things are complicated. The main reason is that in spirituality there is the matter of faith. That is, a person must believe in reward and punishment. And where one must believe, the body disagrees, since the will to receive for himself enjoys when it understands and sees the profitability in the matter. But when he is told that he should believe, the work in heaviness begins. This follows the rule, "Doubt does not precede certainty."

That is, he sees the labor, that he will certainly have to relinquish rest, but he is doubtful of the reward.

Therefore, then the *Lo Lishma* [not for Her sake] is also difficult to do because first he must take upon himself faith above reason and believe in reward and punishment. Once he has taken upon himself faith in the kingdom of heaven in general, comes the time to think about details. That is, he should discern between partial faith and complete faith, as he says in the "Introduction to The Study of the Ten Sefirot" (Item 14), "It is like a person who trusts his friend and lends him money. He may trust him with a pound, and ... he may trust him with all his possessions without a hint of fear. This last faith is considered 'whole faith,' and the previous forms are considered "incomplete faith." Rather it is partial faith, whether more or less."

In this there is a difference between spiritual work and corporeal work, since the reward is based on faith. Since the basis of Judaism is faith, we therefore have many discernments: 1) He has partial faith, and in addition, he adds a little bit of knowledge, meaning that the reward is in knowledge. This can happen while he is working *Lo Lishma*, but in order to receive money or respect. He does not need to believe in the money or the respect. Rather, he sees if he can receive money or respect, or avoid disgraces. That is, when he actually suffers disgraces, it causes him to work and toil. Or, when he is given honors and money, it is in actual fact. This is why there is no issue of faith in this.

It follows that in *Lo Lishma*, too, there are two discernments to make: 1) He does not like the work he does, as with the allegory of the person who is going to have himself operated on. In other words, one who works because of coercion does not like his work. He would be happier if he did not have to work. But this applies only to those who work and observe Torah and *Mitzvot* [commandments] because of punishment. That is, if his boss is religious and he tells him that if he does not observe Torah and *Mitzvot* he will fire him and he will remain without provision, then his need to observe

Torah and *Mitzvot* is for fear of punishment. Hence, he awaits the day when he can be freed from observing Torah and *Mitzvot*.

It is likewise with one who observes because of disgrace. That is, assume he is used to learning the daily page [of Gemara] each night. And because of the commandment to learn Torah, how he is in a state where his faith is weak and he has no desire to come to the lesson on the daily page. However, because he is ashamed of the friends, who might despise and not respect him, he comes to study Torah. It follows that he does not like this work and would be happier if this reason, for which he must toil, did not exist.

2) The *Lo Lishma* that he learns in order to receive reward or respect or money and so forth—this work does please him. That is, he does not say, "I wish I did not have to work." He cannot say this because a person does not want to lose gains.

However, there is a discernment called *Lishma* [for Her sake], meaning that he works because of faith and not because people are forcing him to work. Rather, the faith in the Creator is the reason why he observes Torah and *Mitzvot*. This is called "working for the Creator," and not for people. This is a very important degree. Sometimes he wants to be certain that he has no thought of working because of people, so he does everything in concealment and no one in the world knows the measure of his work or how much effort he exerts in serving the Creator; only the Creator knows.

However, this degree, too, which is entirely for the Creator, is still not regarded as "work in completeness," since the completeness of the work is to achieve *Dvekut* with the Creator, called "equivalence of form," as our sages said, "As He is merciful, you are merciful." That is, a person must work not in order to receive reward. Instead, he wants to completely annul his authority and wants there to be only one authority in the world, a singular authority, that only the authority of the Creator will be in the world, and wants his own authority annulled.

It therefore follows that the war of the inclination that a person has is done in several manners:

What Is a War Over Authority in the Work - 1

1. A War of *Mitzva* [commandment]—when he is at war with the evil inclination over controlling the evil inclination so it does not disrupt his observing of the *Mitzvot*. Or, the war is about having the power to overcome the evil inclination so he does not transgress. This is called "a war of *Mitzva*," where his entire war concerns the observance of Torah and *Mitzvot*.

2. A War of Authority—when a person wages war with the evil inclination over the authority. That is, the evil inclination argues that there are two authorities: a) that of the Creator, b) that of man. His argument is that this was the purpose of creation, namely for the creatures to receive delight and pleasure from the Creator. It follows that the authority of the creatures should remain, so why do you want to revoke the authority of the creatures? The man, on the other hand, says the opposite.

In this work of the war of authority, a man is powerless to conquer the authority of the body and transfer it to the authority of the Creator. It was said about this, "He who comes to purify is aided." Since annulling the authority contradicts nature, for as the body argues, the Creator created the world in order to do good to His creations, hence, it is imprinted within man to receive everything into his own authority.

It is written, "When you go to war against your enemies and the Lord your God delivers them into your hands." We asked, what does the verse come to tell us? since it is known that all the wars where the people of Israel come to conquer is only with the help of the Creator. According to the above, the verse comes to teach us that we should know that we cannot win the War Over Authority. We should know that knowing this saves us from despair, since once a person has made efforts to conquer this authority so as to enter the *Kedusha* [sanctity/holiness], he sees that on the contrary, in his eyes, he has become worse than when he began the War Over Authority. In other words, while he was engaged in a War of *Mitzva*, he saw that he was advancing in the work, for each day he saw that he was conquering commandments and good deeds. But with the War Over Authority, he thinks he has regressed.

The verse tells us about this that specifically now that you have recognized that you are unable to win this war, do not escape the campaign. Rather, now is the time when a person can pray from the bottom of the heart because he sees that by himself, he cannot do a thing.

It follows that through the work that he has done thus far, he has gained the need for the salvation of the Creator. And since now he has a *Kli* [vessel], called a "need," now is the time when the light can come and really clothe within that *Kli*, as it is written, "and the Lord your God delivers them into your hands," for only the Creator can give you the conquest in the War Over Authority.

It follows that this knowledge is so important that it is difficult for a person to believe this, and he falls into despair. But if a person believes it—that specifically now is the time when the Creator will help him—he will certainly not escape the campaign and will now walk on the path of truth and will be rewarded with conquering this authority and taking the authority away from the *Klipot* [shells/peels] and admitting it into the *Kedusha*.

According to the above, we should interpret what our sages said (Sanhedrin 97), "Three come absentmindedly: the Messiah, finding, and a scorpion." "Absentmindedly" means that in his eyes, he keeps falling into despair and has already stopped thinking about it. That is, many times he thought that this work of taking the authority away from the *Klipot* and giving it to the *Kedusha*, namely the War Over Authority, was not for him, for he saw that he was unfit for it.

The reason for this is very simple. He has already made great efforts, and in his view, he has regressed and not progressed. Each time he overcame above reason, yet nothing helps him. This is why it was said that one should know he must not regard what he sees, but say that the "Messiah," which will redeem him from the exile of sitting among the nations, this authority of being enslaved to the seventy nations, the Messiah will redeem and take everything away from the authority of the *Klipot*, which are called "seventy nations of the world." These correspond to the seven qualities of

Kedusha, called *HGT NHYM*, and since each *Sefira* consists of ten, they are seventy.

Opposite them there are seven *Klipot*, and each consists of ten, hence they are seventy nations. The "Israel" is under their control and the Messiah will deliver us. Also, everything that exists in the general public, we learn within the individual. Thus, each and every individual must be rewarded with personal redemption.

According to the above, we should interpret what they said there: "Son of David does not come until all pennies are emptied from the pockets." We should understand what "all the pennies are emptied from the pockets" means in the work. Money is something by which we buy good things that we need. Money is a substitute for labor. That is, a person works and labors, and in return receives money with which he buys for himself things that he needs.

Accordingly, when a person has done all that he could, and all the labor he thinks that he can do, he has already done, and he has no more labor to add, this is called "Ben David does not come," meaning that redemption—when He redeems the authority from the *Klipot* and lets it into the authority of the *Kedusha*—will not happen before a person has made every effort he could make and he cannot make any more efforts. This is regarded that he has not a penny, meaning he has nothing more with which to buy *Kedusha*.

Then comes the time when he is pitied from above and is admitted into the *Kedusha*, called Ben David, referring to redemption. At that time, the verse "and the Lord your God delivers them into your hands" comes true, meaning that at that time comes help from above. The words, "and you take them away captive" mean that a person has conquered the authority of the body, which was under the control of the *Sitra Achra* [other side], and man is the ruler.

Now we will explain the third question we asked, What is a beautiful woman in the work? It is written, "And you see among the captives a beautiful woman, and you desire her and take her as a wife for yourself." It is written (*Avot*, Chapter 6), "Rabbi Meir says, 'Anyone who engages in Torah *Lishma* is rewarded with many things, and the secrets of the Torah are revealed to him." It is known that the Torah is called a "woman," as it is written (*Kidushin* 30b), "To teach him a craft. From where is this? Hezekiah said, 'Behold a life with a woman you love, if she is a real woman. As he must marry him a wife, so he must teach him a craft. If it is Torah, as he must teach him Torah, so he must teach him a craft.'" Thus, they interpret that a woman is the Torah.

The souls come from *Malchut*, who is regarded as Rachel, which is the revealed world. This means that *Hochma* is revealed in her and she is called "beautiful," as it is written (Genesis 29:17), "And Rachel was of good looks and good appearance."

Baal HaSulam said that where it is written, "beautiful," it refers to *Hochma*, for *Hochma* [wisdom] is called "beauty," as it is written, "of beautiful eyes," for eyes are called *Hochma*, as it is written, "the eyes of the congregation," who are the sages of the congregation. This means that Torah is called a "woman of good appearance," and the souls that extend from *Malchut* in the form of the revealed world are also called a "woman of good appearance."

By this we can interpret "And you see among the captives a beautiful woman" to mean "once the Creator has given you" this authority that was in the hands of the *Klipot*. Then, when you engage in the Torah, it will all be *Lishma*, and you will naturally be rewarded with the secrets of Torah. That is, the Torah is the soul of Israel, as it is written in *The Zohar*, "The Torah, the Creator, and Israel are one." And you see among the captives the soul of the Torah, and you desire her, meaning that then begins the work of the *Masachim* [screens].

That is, this is when a person begins to work with the will to receive spirituality, for it is known that each degree that is higher than its predecessor requires that the work begins anew, to receive it in order to bestow. Thus, although he has already been rewarded with learning *Lishma*, when he receives a higher degree than he had had, new corrections are required in order to receive it not out of craving, called "will to receive." Instead, he must perform corrections, which are called *Masachim* in Kabbalah. It is as we learn that there are five *Behinot* [discernments] in the *Masach* [screen], as it is written in the "Preface to the Wisdom of Kabbalah" (Item 17), "And these corrections, said the Torah, and shaved her head and did her nails."

Now we will explain the fourth question we asked, What is "and shaved her head and did her nails in the work"? It is known that "hair" is called "judgments," as it is written in *The Zohar* (*Nasso*, Item 78), "Rabbi Yehuda said, 'A woman's hair that is disclosed causes another hair to be disclosed, meaning the forces of the *Sitra Achra*, which grip to the hair and blemish her. For this reason, even the walls of her house should not see one hair of the woman's hair, much less outside. Go and see how many flaws the woman's hair causes—causes above and causes below.'"

But why does the hair blemish above and below? We should understand the meaning of hair in spirituality. We learned that "In the beginning, He created the world with the quality of judgment. He saw that the world could not exist, He associated with it the quality of mercy." It is known that "judgment" means vessels of reception, for on them was the judgment that they must not be used unless one can place on them the intention to bestow. Yet, it is very difficult to go from one end to the other, meaning from the will to receive for himself, and do everything in order to bestow. For this reason, "He associated with it the quality of mercy," which is *Bina*, bestowal. By this, through the power of Torah and *Mitzvot*, it will be possible to turn her into aiming to bestow.

It is written in the "Preface to the Wisdom of Kabbalah" (Item 58), "He saw that the world could not exist." That is, in this way, it will be impossible for man, who must be created from this *Behina Dalet* [Fourth Phase], to be able to adjust his works to bestowal and by him the world will exist in the desired quality of correction. Hence, He first took the quality of mercy and associated it with the quality of judgment. Through this association, sparks of bestowal were included in *Behina Dalet*, which is the quality of judgment, making it possible for man's body, which emerges from *Behina*

Dalet, to do good deeds in order to bestow contentment upon his Maker. By this, the world will achieve the desirable correction from the creation of the world.

According to the above, we can understand the meaning of the hair. Hair is vessels of reception, which come from the quality of judgment and belong to the worlds before the correction, where they were still not regarded as hair. However, there, those *Kelim* received the lights, causing the breaking of the vessels. Hence, a correction was made not to use these *Kelim* any longer. For this reason, when the lights with these *Kelim* came to the world of correction, the lights departed, and these *Kelim* received the name *Se'arot* [hair], from the word *se'ara* [storm], since these *Kelim* lacked the lights they had had.

He says in *The Study of the Ten Sefirot* (Part 13, Reply No. 112): "They are called *Se'arot* from the verse, 'For He bruises me with a hair,' which means storm. They are called so because of the force of the judgments that is in them, since they come from *Malchut* of *Tzimtzum Aleph* [First Restriction]." In other words, *Malchut* of *Tzimtzum Aleph* is called the "quality of judgment" and is not used in the world of correction.

By this we should interpret what is written concerning the corrections of a beautiful woman, "And she shall shave her head," meaning not use the vessels of reception, called "the quality of judgment," when the light illuminated in *Gadlut* [adulthood/greatness], which is called "And she shall shave her head," meaning the *Se'arot*, which are the *Kelim* that come from the quality of judgment, but rather use the *Kelim* that are corrected with the quality of mercy, which is a smaller degree. For this reason, it will be easier for him to aim to bestow the secrets of the Torah called *Neshama* [soul].

But if he receives it as he is, he will receive the pleasure of the light of *Neshama* because "you desire her" and not because of a desire to bestow, for he will not have the strength to aim over the *Kelim* of the quality of judgment and receive the light in order to bestow. It is as our sages said, "The Creator saw that the world could not exist, He stood and associated with it the quality of mercy."

In this way we can interpret the second correction, where it says, "And did her nails." The Unkelus Translation interprets "did her nails" to mean that she makes her nails bigger. Yonatan Ben Uziel interprets "and did her nails" to mean that she made her nails bigger. In the work, this means that she will take her *Gadlut* [adulthood/greatness] from the nails and not from the flesh of the fingers.

To understand the meaning of the fingers, we need to know what is written in *The Zohar* (*Beresheet*, Item 129, essay, "Illuminations of Light; Illuminations of Fire"): "A man's fingers are the concealments in the degrees and are upper secrets. There are *Panim* [anterior] and *Achoraim* [posterior] in them." By this you will understand the words of our sages, who said (*Taanit* 31), "The Creator is destined to pardon the righteous. He sits among them in the Garden of Eden, and each one points with his finger, 'Behold, this is our God,' for the fingers are *Mochin de Hochma*, and *Mochin de Hochma* are seeing and the light of the eyes. For this reason, they said, 'points with his finger,' as the *Achoraim* of the fingers are in their externality, which implies the fingernails. For this reason, a person is permitted to look at the nails at the end of Shabbat [Sabbath] because then they illuminate from the same candle and illuminate from the same fire, to govern the weekdays. This is the meaning of the words, 'And you will see My back, but My face shall not be seen.' That is, a person should not look at the inside of the fingers while blessing at the end of Shabbat, 'creator of the illuminations of fire,' as they are regarded as internal *Panim*, of which it was said, 'and My face shall not be seen.'"

It therefore follows that in the work, nails imply that the light called "illuminations of fire" can be received as "seeing," called *Hochma*, but only as *Achoraim*, called "nails," which is *Katnut* [smallness/infancy], and not as *Panim*, which is *Gadlut*. The prohibition is that in a greater degree, in which there is greater light, the passion is greater because the pleasure is greater and harder to overcome.

It is written, "And you desired her." Hence, the *Neshama* that he obtains after the conquest of the authority of the body, called "self-love," and all he wants is to bestow contentment upon his Maker, still, there is a distinction of degrees in the reception of the abundance, to have the ability to do everything in order to bestow.

It is known that there are four degrees in general: 1) receiving in order to receive. This is regarded as how a person is born by nature. He cannot understand how it is possible to do something without benefit for himself. 2) Bestowing, but on condition that he receives reward. This is called *Lo Lishma*. 3) Bestowing in order to bestow, which is called *Lishma* [for Her sake]. 4) He can receive pleasure and his intention is to bestow.

It follows that after the conquest of the War Over Authority, it is considered the third degree, which is *Lishma*. It is as Rabbi Meir says, "He who learns Torah *Lishma* is rewarded with many things and the secrets of Torah are revealed to him." At that time he should achieve the fourth degree—to receive the pleasure of the light of *Neshama*, called "a beautiful woman and you desire her." The secrets of Torah clothe in vessels of reception, and *Lishma* is in vessels of bestowal, since that light dresses in the *Kelim* of the reception of the pleasure and not in vessels of bestowal, which are *Kelim* that give and do not receive. At that time begins the order of corrections by which he has the ability to receive in order to bestow.

This is the meaning of the words, "And you see among the captives," for "seeing" refers to the disclosure of the light of *Neshama*. It is to this that the words, "and she did her nails," imply, as the Targum interprets, she makes her nails bigger. This means that her *Gadlut* will be in the form of *Achoraim*, called *Katnut*, regarded as "nails," as in the words of *The Zohar*.

Now we can understand what our sages said (*Berachot* 63), "Words of Torah can be only in one who puts himself to death over it." The question is, If he puts himself to death over it, who is the one observing the Torah and *Mitzvot*? since it is written, "The dead are free." Our sages said, "When a person dies, he becomes free from the

Mitzvot" (Jerusalem Talmud, *Kilaim* 9:3). We should interpret "Puts himself to death over it" to mean he should revoke the authority. When he says that it is for himself, he should cancel this authority and transfer it to the authority of the Creator, meaning to say that there is no other authority in the world, but everything belongs to the Creator. This is called "annulment of the authority."

This is the time when the Torah exists in him. That is, everything that the Torah promises to a person if he keeps the Torah, all those things cannot be in a person until he has the ability to receive in order to bestow, and this can happen only when a person annuls his authority, called "self-love." At that time he becomes a servant of the Creator, meaning that he is what is regarded as "He who buys a servant buys his teacher." This means that the slave has no authority in which to place the delight and pleasure that the Torah has promised. Instead, everything, meaning all the delight and pleasure he receives, he puts into the authority of the Creator and the person has no other authority in the world. This is called "The Torah exists only in one who puts himself to death over it."

But "the view of landlords is opposite from the view of Torah," and everything he sees as worth receiving, he wants it all to be on his name, meaning in his authority, where he is the owner of all things. That is, he wants to take away from the authority of the Creator and place it in his own authority. By this we will understand the meaning of the War Over Authority.

What Is Making a Covenant in the Work?

Article No. 31, Tav-Shin-Mem-Zayin, 1986-87

It is written, "that you may enter into the covenant with the Lord your God, which the Lord your God is making with you today." RASHI interprets "that you may enter into the covenant" as "in passing." "Thus would the makers of a covenant do: a partition from here and a partition from here, and they pass in between." The writing also says there, "And not with you alone am I making this covenant, but with those who stand here with us today before the Lord our God and with those who are not with us here today."

We should understand the following: 1) What is the meaning of making a covenant in the work? That is, what does making a covenant give us, by which we will have correction in the work? 2) Why RASHI interpreted that makers of a covenant would make a partition from here? What does this mean to us in the work? 3) What does "those who stand here with us today ... and those who are not with us here today" mean to us in the work? What are the two times in the work?

What Is Making a Covenant in the Work?

Baal HaSulam said, "What is the merit of making a covenant"? It seems redundant, for why are they making a covenant between them? If they think that they should love one another, then because they love one another, what does making a covenant add to us? He said that sometimes, they might come to a state where each one sees that the other is not behaving properly with him, and he should therefore hate the other.

When he makes the covenant with him, the intention is that even if he sees that he is not treating him properly, he will go above reason and say, "Since I made a covenant with him, I will not break my covenant."

It follows that the covenant is not for the present but for the future. It might be that the love between them will cool off; therefore, they make a covenant so that the future will be as it is now in the present.

The work in Torah and *Mitzvot* [commandments] is primarily when beginning to walk on the path that leads to *Lishma* [for Her sake]. That is, when a person begins the work, he begins in *Lo Lishma* [not for Her sake], as our sages said, "One should always engage in Torah *Lo Lishma*, and from *Lo Lishma* we come to *Lishma*."

For this reason, the beginning of his work was with enthusiasm because he saw that by observing Torah and *Mitzvot* he would achieve happiness in life. Otherwise, he would not begin. Therefore, in the beginning of his work, when he is still working *Lo Lishma*, meaning that when he works, he constantly looks at the reward he will receive after his work, he has the strength to work.

As in corporeality, a person is used to working in a place where he knows he will be rewarded for his work. Otherwise, a person cannot work for free, if not for his own benefit. Only when he sees that self-benefit will come from this work does he have the strength to work enthusiastically and willingly, since he is looking at the reward and not at the work.

The work does not matter if a person understands that here he will receive from this employer twice as much as he would receive from working for the previous employer, before he came to the job where they pay twice as much. This means that according to the salary, so the work becomes easier and smaller.

Accordingly, we should interpret in the work that making a covenant means that when a person takes upon himself the work, even if in *Lo Lishma*, he must make a covenant with the Creator to serve Him whether he wants to or not.

Yet, we should understand on what the enthusiasm depends. It depends only on the reward. That is, when there is a big reward, the desire for the work does not stop. But when the reward is doubtful, the desire for the work vanishes and he shifts to rest. That is, at that time he feels more pleasantness in rest.

It is so much so that he says, "I relinquish the work, and anyone who wants can do this work because it is not for me." But making a covenant is when he begins to work even in *Lo Lishma*. And since now he wants the work, for who would force him to come into the work of the Creator, now he must make the covenant and say, "Even if there comes a time of descent," meaning that he will have no desire for the work, "I still take upon myself not to consider my desire but work as though I have a desire." This is called "making a covenant."

However, we should understand the reason that he comes to a state of descent. In corporeality, we see that when a person works in order to receive reward, are there ascents and descents there? So, why do we see that in the work of the Creator there are ascents and descents?

We should understand this matter in two ways:

1) Even in a state of *Lo Lishma*, when he works in order to receive reward, we can understand the reward only by way of faith, since "The reward for a *Mitzva* [commandment] is not in this world." This means that the reward for the *Mitzvot* is not given in this world, but he will receive the reward in the next world, as it is written, "To do them today and to receive the reward for them tomorrow," meaning in the next world.

What Is Making a Covenant in the Work?

Since the basis of the reward depends on the faith, as it is written (*Avot*, Chapter 2), "You can trust your landlord to pay for your work, and know that the reward for the righteous is given in the future." It is known that concerning faith, there are ascents and descents, since the whole matter of faith is to believe above reason.

This means that sometimes a person can go above reason, where faith contradicts the reason. For example, twenty percent of the faith are against reason, and he can overcome twenty percent. But sometimes he sees that there has been a change, since now he sees that faith contradicts by thirty percent, and to such an extent he is not immune and has the power to overcome and go with faith. Hence, at that time he must descend from his state, where faith illuminated for him.

This causes him descents and ascents, when it does not coincide with his power to overcome. This is not so with a corporeal reward. Faith does not apply to the reward; therefore, in corporeality, it cannot be said that he has a descent in corporeal work, since the reward is in this world and he does not need faith.

2) In a state of *Lishma*, he does not need anything in return for his work. The cause of the descents is also the reason that he bases his entire work on faith. But there is a difference: It is not about the reward but about the landlord. That is, to the extent that he believes in his landlord, that he is so important that it is worthwhile to serve Him, meaning that it is a great privilege to serve the King of Kings, who will pay for his work.

This means that the reward for the work coincides with the measure of faith in the greatness of the Creator. Since by the nature of creation, man derives great pleasure from serving an important person, as in the famous allegory that if an important rabbi comes and wants to let someone carry his suitcase to the taxi, a porter will certainly take money for it. But if the rabbi were to give it to a student, the student would certainly take no charge for the work, since the service he is giving to the rabbi is his reward and he would need nothing more.

Accordingly, "You can trust your landlord" means that to the extent of the faith, that he believes in the greatness of the Creator, to that extent is the measure of the reward, which is measured by the amount of faith he has in the greatness of the Creator.

It turns out that when he believes that the Creator is great indeed, his reward is great indeed. If his faith in the Creator is not so great, his reward will not be so great either. It therefore follows that whether he works *Lishma* or *Lo Lishma*, the whole basis is only faith.

But the difference is this: In *Lo Lishma*, the faith relates to the reward; in *Lishma*, the faith relates to whom we serve. In other words, the amount of pleasure depends on the greatness of the Creator, as our sages said (*Avot*, Chapter 2), "Rabbi Elazar says, 'Know before whom you toil, and who is the owner of your work, who will pay you the reward for your work.'"

As said above, we must believe in the greatness of the owner of the work, for upon this depends His paying the reward for the work. That is, the measure of the reward depends on the greatness of the owner of the work, who is the Creator. In other words, there is a difference in the pleasure between serving the greatest in the city, the greatest in the country, or the greatest in the world. Upon this depends the reward, meaning according to the greatness of the King.

Since the basis is faith, there are ascents and descents here because as long as one has not been awarded permanent faith, there must be ascents and descents. It follows that there could be a time when the love between them cools. For this reason, now, in the beginning of his work, he takes upon himself the burden of the kingdom of heaven, to make a covenant, so that whether or not the body agrees to be a servant of the Creator, he takes upon himself not to change a thing. Instead, he will say, "I spoke once and I will not change." Instead, I will go above reason as I have taken upon myself when making the covenant in the beginning of the work.

By this we will understand what RASHI interpreted, "that you may enter into the covenant" in passing. Thus would the makers of a covenant do: a partition from here and a partition from here, and they pass in between." Accordingly, we should interpret that through the making of the covenant they would imply that sometimes there will come a time when there is a partition from here, meaning a partition that separates this one, and a partition from here, meaning that the other one would also have a separating partition.

In other words, even if both of them have a partition that stops the love that was between them, still, now they are taking it upon themselves not to part from one another. Instead, they will remind themselves the covenant that they had made, and this will make it possible not to break the covenant. They will pass in between, meaning that they pass over the separation that was made between them, and it is all by the power of the covenant that they had made.

In this work, this means that a person must make a covenant with the Creator. As he began the work now, and now he certainly has love for the Creator, otherwise who would make him take upon himself the burden of the kingdom of heaven? So now he must make a covenant with the Creator forever. That is, even if there is a time when he feels that the love of the Creator has cooled in him, he will remember the covenant that he had made with the Creator.

But in the work, we must remember that in the matter of making a covenant between the Creator and a person, it might be that the love will cool only between man and the Creator. But how can it be said that the love will grow cold in the Creator? That is, since the covenant applies to both, it means that there could be a descent between the two of them concerning the making of the covenant, but how can we speak of changes or a descent in the Creator?

Baal HaSulam said that in both man and the Creator there is the matter of "As in water, face reflects face, so the heart of man reflects man." He interpreted about what is written (Exodus 33:13), "And now, if I have found favor in Your eyes, let me know Your way that I may know You, so that I may find favor in Your eyes." He asked,

How did Moses know, when he said, "If I have found favor in Your eyes"? He replied that it is because beforehand, it is written, "You have said, 'I have known you by name, and you have also found favor in My eyes.'" By this Moses knew that the Creator favored him, since Moses favored the Creator, following the rule, "As in water, face reflects face, so the heart of man reflects man" (Proverbs 27).

According to the above, we should interpret that when we say that the love cools within a person and he feels that he is in a state of descent, meaning that now he does not have such love for the Creator as he had in the beginning of his work, this causes him to feel that the Creator, too, does not love him and does not listen to his prayer, to what the person asks of the Creator. This causes the person an even greater descent because he begins to doubt what is written, "For You hear the prayer of every mouth." At that time, he thinks that the Creator has no connection with the creatures, which causes him great descents as his faith grows weaker every time.

It follows that although there are no changes in the Creator, a person feels this way because "As in water, face reflects face," he feels this way. This follows the rule that all the changes we learn in spirituality are according to the receivers.

Now we can understand what we asked, What does it mean in the work, "those who stand here with us today before the Lord"? The making of the covenant is whether he is standing today before the Creator, when he is at a time of ascent. However, he is taking it upon himself that even should a time of descent come, called "and those who are not with us here today" before the Lord our God, when he does not feel that he is standing before the Lord our God, he still takes upon himself, above reason, not to mind anything, but to remember the making of the covenant, and this will be unwavering.

Tav-Shin-Mem-Het
(1987 - 1988)

Why Life Is Divided into Two Discernments

Article No. 1, Tav-Shin-Mem-Het, 1987/88

Our sages said (*Berachot* 18), "For the living know that they will die. Those righteous, in their death, are called 'living.'" RASHI interprets, "Those righteous, how do they know they will die? They pay attention to the day of death, and avoid transgression." "And the dead know nothing. Those wicked, in their lives, are called 'dead.'" RASHI interprets, "The wicked know nothing," meaning "they pretend not to know and sin."

It therefore follows that there is life that is called "death." In other words, to the wicked, their lives are called "death." Also, there is death that is called "life," which is among the righteous.

That is, there are two discernments to life: 1) the life of the wicked, 2) the life of the righteous.

It is not written what the life of the righteous is called. Rather, what is written is that the death of the righteous is called "life." And we should certainly say that if the death of the righteous is called "life," then the life of the righteous is certainly a higher degree.

According to RASHI's interpretation, it seems that in their death, meaning when looking at when they are discerned as dead, therefore they do not sin. Yet, how does this pertain to life? Does one who does not sin already have life? Also, RASHI interprets that the wicked in their lives are called "dead." Why? It is because the wicked know nothing, meaning they pretend not to know. We should interpret that they do not know about the day of death.

This, too, we should understand. Does one who does not remember the day of death must sin? After all, our sages said (*Berachot* 5), "One should always vex the good inclination over the evil inclination. If he defeats it, good. If not, he should engage in Torah. If he defeats it, good. If not, he should read the *Shema* reading. And if not, he should mention to it the day of death." This means that even if he does not remember the day of death, he does not have to sin. Thus, what does it mean that RASHI interpreted that they pretend not to know about the day of death and therefore sin? Does this imply that one who does not want to sin must always remember the day of death?

In order to understand all the above, we should remember all that is ahead of us, meaning the purpose of creation, as well as the matter of the correction of creation, which is done later. We should also understand the rule that there is no light without a *Kli* [vessel]. It is known that the purpose of creation is to do good to His creations. It is also known that there is no light without a *Kli*. This means that there cannot be a filling without a lack. For this reason, the Creator created existence from absence a lack and craving to receive pleasures. This is called a "desire to receive delight."

On this *Kli*, called "will to receive," there was later a correction called *Tzimtzum* [restriction]. This means that since because of the reception of the abundance there was no equivalence between the giver and the receiver, and that *Kli* craved equivalence of form, called *Dvekut* [adhesion]. For this reason, she did not want to receive into her will to receive. Instead, on that discernment there was to be a *Tzimtzum* and she would receive only where she can aim to bestow.

This is the correction of creation, so the creatures would not feel unpleasantness when receiving pleasures from the Creator.

Now we understand that the purpose of creation is for the creatures to receive delight and pleasure, and the correction of creation is for the creatures not to feel unpleasantness upon reception of the pleasures. A *Kli* is called a "lack," and "light" is called the "filling." It follows that the *Kli* in which life is clothed is called "desire," and the life that is clothed in her is called "light."

From this we learn that we have two kinds of *Kelim* [vessels]: 1) a *Kli* without the correction of creation, called "receiving in order to receive," 2) a *Kli* with the correction of creation, called "receiving in order to bestow."

According to the above, life is called "light." It follows that we have life that is clothed in the *Kelim* of the will to receive, by which we receive disparity of form from the Creator, which causes us to part from the Life of Lives. For this reason, this life is called "death," due to the separation that occurs there.

There is also life that is called "light," which is clothed in *Kelim* on which there is the correction of creation, called "receiving in order to bestow." By this, although they are called "receivers," since the aim is to bestow, they remain in *Dvekut* even while receiving the pleasures. It follows that the light that he receives, meaning life, is called "life," since the light remains attached to the Life of Lives.

By this we can interpret what was said, "The wicked, in their lives, are called 'dead,'" since they receive all that they receive in vessels of reception, which causes separation. This is why it was said, "The wicked, in their lives, are called 'dead.'" Also, this clarifies why "The righteous, in their lives, are called 'living,'" since they receive the filling of the *Kli*, meaning the light and the pleasure, in vessels of bestowal, by which they adhere to the Life of Lives, although they become receivers.

However, according to this, how can we interpret what our sages said, "The righteous, in their death, are called 'living'"? The thing is that in the order of the work, we begin in *Lo Lishma* [not for Her sake], and from *Lo Lishma* we come to *Lishma* [for Her sake]. Thus, when a person begins the work, the intention is for his own sake, called "reward and punishment." Afterward, he is rewarded and is shown from above—by an awakening from above—that he should walk on the path of truth, which is to do everything for the sake of the Creator.

When he is shown from above what does it mean for the sake of the Creator and not for his own sake, the body escapes from this work and no longer wants to work, at that time a person thinks that he is in a state of descent.

That is, when he began to work he was in a state of ascent, meaning that he was finer and not so materialized. Hence, the body did not object to his work. But now the body has become materialized and therefore does not want to work. It says, "This work is not for me because I see that not only have I stopped progressing, I am even regressing. Therefore, it is a waste of my time and effort. Since I cannot acquire spiritual life, at least I will acquire corporeal life like the rest of the world, which does not think of spirituality, but only of corporeality.

"I will be like them and at least try to enjoy what I can in this world. Otherwise, I will be left empty handed in both ways." At that time, it says, "I will do what our sages said (*Yoma* 72), "Raba said to the Sages: 'I beseech you, do not inherit a double Hell!'" RASHI interprets "double Hell" as laboring and toiling in Torah in this world. "And you will not observe it and you will inherit Hell upon your death, and in your life, you did not enjoy in your world."

By this we should interpret that when a person comes to a state of descent, called "death," meaning when he feels the taste of death, if he follows the path of bestowal, meaning that everything he does will be only to thereby bring contentment to the Creator, and for himself he wants nothing, it is called "serving the Creator devotedly." To a person, this feels like death.

Indeed, this brings up the question we asked, It is known that "A *Mitzva* [good deed/commandment] induces a *Mitzva*." Thus, why does a person come from a state of feeling the taste of life while engaging in Torah and *Mitzvot* [plural of *Mitzva*] to a state where when he only begins to say that he is going to observe Torah and *Mitzvot* for the sake of the Creator, he feels in this a taste of death and not of life? Where is the rule that a *Mitzva* induces a *Mitzva*, as it is written (*Avot*, Chapter 4, 2), "Ben Azai says, 'Run to a light *Mitzva* and flee from transgression, for a *Mitzva* induces a *Mitzva* and a transgression induces a transgression, for the reward for a *Mitzva* is a *Mitzva*, and the reward for a transgression is transgression.'"

The thing is that when he begins in work *Lo Lishma* and dedicates himself to the work wholeheartedly, and takes upon himself everything seriously, he is therefore endowed from above with the knowledge that there is work in order to bestow and not for his own sake. The reason he is awarded to feel that knowledge in his organs was because a *Mitzva* induces a *Mitzva*, for not just anyone is rewarded with feeling what it is that all his work is for the sake of the Creator and not for his own sake. This pertains specifically to those who work with all their might in *Lo Lishma*. By this, they come to feel the *Lishma*, and to this, the body certainly does not agree.

However, now that he sees that in the work of bestowal, the body has nothing to receive, the person stands before a dilemma: He can say that now he is in a state of descent, called "transgression." At that time, he falls into despair and says that now he sees that the most important is to bestow, but he cannot work in order to bestow, therefore he must escape the campaign and return to at least enjoy the corporeal life. Or, he can say that when he began this work, all the actions were with the aim *Lo Lishma*. At that time the work was not against the will to receive, so the body did not object. But now that he has been rewarded with knowing about the existence of *Lishma*, called "working for the sake of the Creator," the body should certainly object because it is against nature. So, how can we work for the sake of the Creator? The answer is that it is inherent in nature that the small can serve the great without any reward, since it feels great pleasure in serving it.

This brings up the question, Why does the body not agree to work for the sake of the Creator? The answer is that the body does not believe in the greatness of the Creator, for where there is a need to believe, the body objects, since faith is something unimportant. This means that if His greatness is not revealed within reason, but we should believe, a person regards it as "lowly" and "inferior." The body cannot stand this work.

Therefore, we should ask why the Creator created the concealment and the *Tzimtzum* [restriction] so His greatness will not be revealed. Rather, if a person wants to feel the greatness of the Creator, he can achieve this only by faith. The answer is known. When a person is still not cleansed of vessels of reception, he will take everything, meaning all the revelations of the Creator, into *Kelim* of self-love. This will separate him from spirituality and will be as "knowing one's Master and aiming to rebel against Him."

If a person is righteous, as our sages said, that "righteous is he who justifies his maker," meaning says that his current feeling of a time of descent is certainly not because the Creator has rejected him from serving Him, but it is rather a great correction for him. That is, now he was given room to believe above reason in the greatness of the Creator, and was also given the need to ask the Creator to illuminate His greatness for him.

He does not want to feel the greatness of the Creator because of the pleasure in this revelation. His intention is not to delight his vessels of reception. On the contrary, since he wants to cancel all the self-love in him, and the body does not want to surrender, he is asking the Creator to illuminate for him, and remove the concealment from him so that the will to receive for himself will annul before the Creator.

By this we will understand what Ben Azai said, "Run to a light *Mitzva*." That is, a person stands before a dilemma: He can say that the descent, his falling from his previous degree when he had desire and craving for the work into a state where he feels a taste of unpleasantness in the work, without any vitality, but everything is done by coercion, this came to him from above. It is because they want him to walk on the path of truth, meaning with faith above reason, which is a light *Mitzva*, which a person slights because it is unimportant to a person when he must go above reason.

Or, he can say the opposite: It is not because "a *Mitzva* induces a *Mitzva*," but simply that he is a coarser person and with worse qualities than other people. Therefore, he commits transgression and is unworthy of the work of holiness. Instead, "a transgression induces a transgression." Since what I do now in Torah and *Mitzvot* is compulsory, and I have no love for the holy work, hence, I will commit another transgression and leave the path of coercion. When I am in good spirits, I will engage in Torah and *Mitzvot*. In the meantime, I will return to my corporeal life and at least enjoy this world, as in the words of Raba.

For this reason, when a person faces a dilemma, Ben Azai says, "Run to a light *Mitzva*," meaning run and choose a light *Mitzva*. This means that this state is regarded as a light *Mitzva*, and was given to you from above so that you would walk ahead on the path that leads to the truth. The reason is that "a *Mitzva* induces a *Mitzva*." Since you began in *Lo Lishma*, and your intention was to devote yourself wholeheartedly to Torah and *Mitzvot*, hence, "a *Mitzva* induces a *Mitzva*." For this reason, you were given from above the knowledge of the matter of *Lishma*, and you began to feel it. This is the time when a person has the need for the Creator to bring him closer, since then he sees what our sages said, "Man's inclination overcomes him every day. Were it not for the help of the Creator, he would not overcome it."

"...and escape from transgression." That is, run from saying that the state you are in now is a transgression. Instead, say that a *Mitzva* induces a *Mitzva* and this cannot be a transgression. If you do not say so, but rather say it is a transgression, then know that "a transgression induces a transgression." Hence, you will be forced to commit another transgression, meaning you will have to return to the corporeal life and leave the work you have begun because you will want to at least enjoy this world, as in the words of Raba, who said, "You will not inherit Hell upon your death, and in your life, you will not have enjoyed in your world."

According to the above, we can understand what we asked about RASHI's commentary, who said that it is written, "The living know that they will die; those righteous, in their death, are called 'living.'" "How do they know that they will die?" They pay attention to the day of death and avoid transgression, while the dead know nothing. Those wicked, in their lives, are called "dead." He says that they pretend not to know and sin.

According to RASHI, it seems that one who does not pay attention to the day of death is already a sinner. We asked, 1) about his interpretation that the righteous, in their death, are called "living," since by knowing they will die they do not sin. It follows that one who does not sin already has life. What is the connection between one who does not sin and life? 2) It seems from the words of RASHI that he says about the righteous that "the living know that they will die," that they pay attention to the day of death and avoid transgression. From his words, it seems they do not sin because they pay attention to the day of death, otherwise they, too, would sin. But our sages said that it is not necessarily the day of death that prevents sin (*Berachot* 5), as is said, "One should always vex the good inclination over the evil inclination. If he defeats it, good. And if not, he should engage in Torah. And if not, he should read the *Shema* reading. And if not, he should mention to it the day of death."

Therefore, we see that it is not necessarily the day of death that prevents a person from sinning. Accordingly, we should understand, and this is why we should be precise about what he said, "the day of death," meaning it is when a person comes into a state of descent, when he feels no taste in the Torah and in the prayer, and everything he does in Torah and *Mitzvot* is compulsory, and he has no vitality, which really feels like death.

The person asks himself, "What is the reason I have descended from my previous state? That is, before I began the work of bestowal, I was happy and confident that I would be a worker of the Creator. This always invoked me to exert, and I did not know any weakness or idleness. Rather, I was always alert to everything. But once I have begun to work on the path of bestowal, I have lost all the vitality in the work, and I do everything lazily. I feel the taste of death in this work. Our sages said that a *Mitzva* induces a *Mitzva*, but now I see the opposite."

Indeed, a person should pay attention to the state of death that he feels now. This is why he says, "The living know that they will die; they pay attention to the day of death and avoid transgression." The meaning of "pay attention to the day of death" is that according to the rule "a *Mitzva* induces a *Mitzva*," it should have been day now. That is, when he begins to work *Lishma*, he should have been more alive because now he is marching on the path of truth. So, why does he feel death now, which is darkness and not life, but is regarded as night?

However, one who is righteous justifies his maker and says, "Certainly, the descent that the Creator has now given me is to my benefit. That is, now the Creator has let me know what it means when a person is working not for himself, but only for the Creator. Of course the body resists this, as it is against its nature. Conversely, before he began the work of *Lishma* and was a servant to self-benefit, therefore the body did not resist it.

It follows that this is a sign that he was notified, so he would know that he is walking on the right path, since the body is resisting. Otherwise, the body would not resist. Therefore, now he has a need, called *Kli*, that the Creator will help him, as it is written, "He who comes to purify is aided." This is so because it takes the Creator's help to go against nature, for anything that is natural, a person can do. But that which is against nature, this is called "a miracle from above," meaning that only from above can he be given strength to be able to go against nature.

Thus, the meaning of "paying attention to understanding the day of death" is that this death that I feel is really a day and not a night. "The day of death" means that there is room for choice here, to say that it is "day," called "life," or say it is "death." This came to me once I have labored honestly and extensively to achieve the goal for which I was born. And since I began in *Lo Lishma*, and *Lo Lishma* is not opposite from nature, the body did not resist.

But now, I have been rewarded from above with walking on the path of Lishma. This is why the body resists and does not want to give energy to work, as it is against nature. This is why now I feel the taste of death. Therefore, if I say that now is "day" and not "death," I receive from that state confidence that I will succeed on the path on which I am now going.

I avoid saying that this state, where I feel death, is because I am in a state of transgression, called "a descent," and because of it I have nothing more to do in the work, since I see that I am declining, so it is a waste of my time. Instead, I say that this state is not a descent, but an ascent in degree; I have embarked on the path of truth.

The words, "avoid transgression" mean that they avoid saying that this state is a transgression, and naturally, a transgression induces a transgression, meaning it is better for me to leave the whole campaign. Instead, I say that I have ascended in degree because a Mitzva induces a Mitzva.

It follows that we can interpret "a Mitzva induces a Mitzva" in relation to the past and in relation to the future. That is, if he says that this state is a Mitzva, then a Mitzva induces a Mitzva, meaning that now he has faith and confidence that he will be rewarded with ascending in the degrees of holiness and will be rewarded with achieving the goal.

By this we will understand why we say, "Remember us to life, O King who desires life, and write us in the book of the living, for Your sake, the living God." We should understand the ending, when we say, "for Your sake, the living God." We can see that there are two kinds of life: 1) of the wicked, 2) of the righteous. The life of the wicked is in vessels of reception, called "separation from the Creator." The life of the righteous is in vessels of bestowal, which is Dvekut [adhesion] with the Creator. For this reason, when we say "Remember us to life," which life? "For Your sake," meaning to bestow. That is, we ask for life in vessels of bestowal.

What Is the Extent of *Teshuva* [Repentance]?

Article No. 2, Tav-Shin-Mem-Het, 1987/88

It is written (Hosea 14), "Return, O Israel, unto the Lord your God." This means that the extent of *Teshuva* [repentance] is "unto the Lord your God." However, we should understand the meaning of "unto the Lord your God," for it implies that up to this place we must repent, and when arriving at that place he no longer needs to repent because he has returned to the place from which he came. We should understand what it means that a person walks away from a place and is told he must return to the place from which he came, which is called *Teshuva* [*Teshuva* means "returning"]. Accordingly, What is the place from which he went and to which he must return?

It is known that Kabbalists wrote that man's soul is a part of God above, as it is written ("Introduction to The Book of Zohar," Item 2), "Inquiry No. 3: This deals with what Kabbalists have said, that man's soul is a part of God Above, in such a way that there is no difference between Him and the soul, but He is the 'whole' and the soul is a 'part.'"

It is also written ("Introduction to The Book of Zohar," Item 9), "And you find that in spirituality, the disparity of form acts like the ax that separates the corporeal things. From this we learn that since the will to receive His delight has been imprinted in the souls, that disparity of form that the souls acquired separates them from His essence. Through that disparity of form, the souls were separated from the Creator and became creatures." It is also written ("Introduction to The Book of Zohar," Item 11), "And the worlds cascaded onto the reality of this corporeal world, a place where there is a body and a soul, and a time of corruption and a time of correction." And it is also written ("Introduction to The Book of Zohar," Item 12), "And through Torah and *Mitzvot* [commandments/good deeds], they finally turn the form of the will to receive to be as the form of the will to bestow. Then they can receive all the good that is in the thought of creation. Along with it, they are rewarded with strong *Dvekut* [adhesion] with Him, because through the work in Torah and *Mitzvot* they have been rewarded with equivalence of form with their maker, which is deemed the end of correction."

It therefore follows that all we need to do in this world is correct and qualify ourselves to be able to receive the delight and pleasure that exist in the thought of creation. Thus, by being created with a will to receive, which is opposite from the Creator, it is considered that a person has departed from the place. From what place? From the root, since the soul is a part of God above. It has departed because of the disparity of form from the Creator and has descended into this world so as to be clothed in a body.

It was mentioned above that in this world there is a time of corruption and a time of correction. Through the remedy of Torah and *Mitzvot*, that which was corrupted will be corrected. Since the corruption is only that the will to receive removes a person from the Creator, once a person engages in Torah and *Mitzvot* in order to receive the quality of the aim to bestow, which is called "equivalence of form," it corrects the corruption.

By this we can understand the question, What is the place from which man emerged, as he is told that he should return to his place,

What Is the Extent of Teshuva [Repentance]?

which is called *Teshuva*? We should interpret that since the soul is a part of God above, and was removed from the Creator into being merely a part and not the whole, all this was because of the disparity of form. Therefore, when he corrects this through the power of Torah and *Mitzvot* with the intention that it will bring him the correction of the ability to do everything in order to bestow, he will naturally reconnect to the whole. This is called "*Dvekut* with the Creator," and this is the extent that one should know how much he must work until he achieves *Teshuva*.

To this comes the answer, "Return, O Israel, unto the Lord your God." "Your God" is said in singular form. That is, the will to receive that exists in man divides him into two authorities and he becomes removed from the Creator. When a person corrects himself and does everything in order to bestow, in this way he achieves *Dvekut*. It follows that the disparity of form divided man and removed him from his source. This is regarded as a person being removed from his place and that he has now returned to his place. This is called "your God," in singular form, where nothing separates the Creator from the creature.

This is called *Teshuva*, when a person returns to his place, as he was prior to creation, when the soul was included in the whole. Subsequently, through the will to receive, she divided from the whole, and now the singular authority has been created and this is called *Teshuva* [returning]. This is the meaning of "Return, O Israel." To what extent must he return? The prophet tells us, "unto the Lord," until He becomes "your God," the singular authority.

According to the above, we see that the writing wants to show us what is *Teshuva*. That is, the general public is taught to engage in Torah and *Mitzvot Lo Lishma* [not for Her sake]. There, in the general public, a person needs to repent for the act. That is, if a person takes care to observe Torah and *Mitzvot* with all its details and specifics, in this manner, a person must believe above reason that he has not done his duty in observing Torah and *Mitzvot*, and he always searches—perhaps he slandered or spoke idle words.

That is, if he wants to acquire wholeness, he is always busy looking into the work he does. But normally, a person does not see his own fault. Also, it is the same with humbleness, as our sages said, "be very, very humble." In this, too, he searches for faults by which he will be able to tell himself that he is worse than others, since a person must be humble, and lying is certainly forbidden. Therefore, he is always concerned and thinks about finding some flaw in himself, so he will be able to say that he is worse than others.

Certainly, it is very difficult for a person in this state to repent. All he can say after all his efforts is that he might have prayed improperly, or perhaps slandered and did not notice. That is, he finds in himself a place where he can repent for sins he might have committed.

Also, about humbleness, he says, "Perhaps I am worse than others." It turns out that his entire *Teshuva* is on a possible transgression. That is, he believes above reason that he probably still lacks wholeness. But, all this pertains to people who belong to the general public.

However, for people who belong in the individuals, whose aim is to be rewarded with *Dvekut* with the Creator, which is equivalence of form, meaning they want all their actions to be for the sake of the Creator, here begins a completely different order. Their gauge in Torah and *Mitzvot* is not necessarily the act. Rather, they want the intention to be for the Creator, too. That is, they do not settle for observing the Creator's commandments only in action. They observe Torah and *Mitzvot* because the Creator commanded us to observe the Torah and *Mitzvot*, and not because the environment commits them to observe the Torah and *Mitzvot*. That is, they observe not so the environment will respect or disrespect them, and this is what obliges them to observe Torah and *Mitzvot*.

Rather, they do everything in concealment "with the Lord your God." They do not demand from the environment respect and so forth, but rather want to observe the Torah and *Mitzvot* with the aim not to receive reward, but only for the sake of the Creator. They see that the body does not agree to this work. But since they want to achieve the truth, from above they are constantly shown the truth—according to the merit of their work—about how the will to receive is in oppositeness of form from the Creator. Yet, each time they overcome more forcefully in that they want to work only for the sake of the Creator.

That person does not see that he has any merit in spirituality. He sees that he is more materialized than the rest of the servants of the Creator who engage in Torah and *Mitzvot*. And the reason is, as said above, that it is because that person exerts more efforts to reach the truth. Then, he is shown from above the true state of the evil. At that time he sees that he is unable to help himself, and he has a need, called a *Kli* [vessel], that the Creator will help him emerge from the control of the evil within him.

It therefore follows that the words "Return, O Israel, unto the Lord your God" were said so that a person would not deceive himself and say, "I don't see any sins in myself," and may doubt that he has transgressions on which he needs to repent. This is why the verse says, "Return, O Israel."

And should you ask, What is the extent of the *Teshuva*, so that I may know for certain that I must repent? The verse says to us in this regard, "Return, O Israel, unto the Lord your God." That is, if he sees that he still has two authorities, meaning that he wants the Creator to give delight and pleasure to man's authority, called "will to receive for himself," then he knows for certain that he is removed from the Creator, that he has become a separate part from the whole, and he should do all that he can to return to his origin and root, meaning return to his place, which is called "the Lord your God."

This means that there is only one authority—the authority of the Creator—as was said, "On that day, the Lord will be one, and His name One," meaning one authority.

What It Means that the Name of the Creator is "Truth"

Article No. 3, Tav-Shin-Mem-Het, 1987/88

It is written in *The Zohar, Haazinu* (Item 210): "Happy is he who has been summoned to the King and knows how to call upon Him properly. If he calls and does not know Whom he calls, the Creator moves away from him, as it is written, 'The Lord is near to all who call upon Him.' To whom is He close? He reiterates, 'To all who call upon Him in truth.' But is there anyone who calls upon Him in falsehood? Rabbi Aba said, 'Yes, it is he who calls but does not know Whom he calls.' How do we know? Because it is written, 'to all who call upon Him in truth.' What is 'in truth'? It is with the seal of the King's ring, which is the completeness of everything."

It is very difficult to understand the answer of *The Zohar* to the question, Does anyone call Him in falsehood? To this comes the answer, "Rabbi Aba said, 'Yes, it is he who calls but does not Whom he calls.'" This is very perplexing. Why does one who does not know Whom he calls is regarded as lying? We could say that he is mistaken, but not lying! Also, the evidence he brings to the interpretation, "truth," saying that it is with the King's ring, which is the completeness of everything, what evidence is this, that we must know whom we are calling or it is called a "lie"?

To understand the above, which is necessary because according to the words of *The Zohar*, "One who prays but does not know to Whom he calls, the Creator moves away from him," can we understand this? But how can one know to whom he is calling? Certainly, every person calls upon the Creator. Otherwise, to whom does he pray? So, what does it mean "to whom he calls." What is even more difficult to understand is why he says, "and does not know to whom he calls." After all, we learned that one should believe and not know to whom he calls.

We need to establish the matter of the purpose of creation and correction of creation first, and then we will know what man must correct. It is known that the purpose of creation is for the lower ones to receive delight and pleasure, and for this reason He has created in them the will to receive pleasure, and otherwise they cannot exist in the world. This desire forces them to do everything they can in order to obtain pleasure, and by this they can exist in the world.

Yet, along with it, as it is written in the introductions, upon the reception of the pleasure, shame is born within this will to receive—that it receives in a dishonest manner. In order to correct this, there was the *Tzimtzum* [restriction] and concealment, where the spiritual pleasure is hidden from us and is revealed only to the extent that the will to receive for oneself departs, to that extent, the spiritual pleasure is revealed. If the will to receive is present in some place, the abundance promptly departs from there, and both cannot be in the same place.

Accordingly, we can understand the correction of creation, when corrections are made so that creation will achieve the goal for which it was created—meaning to receive complete delight and pleasure without any bread of shame. We learned what is the order of the work, meaning what a person must do so the shame will be removed from him when he receives pleasure from the Creator, since before a person obtains this *Kli* [vessel], which is to receive with the aim to bestow, at which time there is no shame, meaning that while receiving, he will not feel unpleasantness due to oppositeness of form.

This means that as long as the lower one has no will to receive, and that will to receive will not make any disparity of form in relation to the light and the abundance, the *Tzimtzum* and concealment are still on it. This means that the upper abundance does not reveal, and anything of *Kedusha* [sanctity/holiness] he looks at, he sees as dark and not as light.

However, this applies to people who truly want to draw near to *Kedusha*. This order applies to them because from above, they do not want them to waste time needlessly, since they are fit to achieve the holy work in purity, meaning in order to bestow. In these people, if they do not aim in order to bestow, they see darkness and not light.

Conversely, in people who belong to the general public there is the matter of the general light, which shines for them as surrounding. They are satisfied by this and do not feel their lacks that they must correct. This light illuminates in *Lo Lishma* [not for Her sake].

However, when a person wants to emerge from the general public and be a worker of the Creator, built on the basis of faith above reason, when he does not want to receive the gift of flesh and blood—as we explained that sometimes when one's faith is not enough to commit him to engage in Torah and *Mitzvot*—but since he is in an environment where all the friends engage in Torah and *Mitzvot*, he receives a gift from the friends. It is as though they give him part of their desire, and through the gifts of parts of desire he receives from the friends, it causes him to also engage in Torah and *Mitzvot*. It follows that the Torah and *Mitzvot* that he observes is built on the basis of the gift of flesh and blood and is not based on the Creator. In other words, the power of faith in the Creator that he has is not enough to compel him to engage in Torah and *Mitzvot*. Rather, the reason that causes him to observe Torah and *Mitzvot* is the gift of flesh and blood.

Now we can interpret what we say in the blessing for the food, "And do not make us need, the Lord our God, neither the gift of flesh and blood nor their lending, but only Your full and open hand, so we will never ever be ashamed or disgraced." When a person blesses the Creator and thanks Him for giving him food, during the blessing for the food a person should pay attention and think that thanks to the food he exists in the world, that if he did not have food he would suffer hunger, and now the Creator has provided him with food, and for this he thanks the Creator, for the good that a person feels that the Creator has given him.

From corporeal nourishments, a person must contemplate on spiritual nourishments, which spiritual nourishments he received from the Creator. A person has to know that without corporal food he cannot live in corporeality. It is likewise in spirituality, called "the life of a Jew." It has many names: Some call it a "life of Torah" or a "life of *Kedusha* [sanctity/holiness]," and some call spiritual life by the name "life that is connected to the Creator," meaning that he says that the Creator gives him everything.

Sometimes, the Creator wants a person to ask Him for something, and then He will give him what he wants. The reason is not that the Creator longs for the creatures to ask Him for a favor and then He will give them, as with flesh and blood. Rather, we should interpret what our sages said (*Yevamot* 64), "The Creator longs for the prayer of the righteous."

The reason is that there is no light without a *Kli*. Therefore, the Creator cannot give them when they have no need or desire. It follows that "longing for the prayer of the righteous" is longing for them to have a need and a *Kli* for the abundance, since the desire and need of the righteous is in order to bestow upon the Creator, and this *Kli* and need can hold the abundance and it will not go to the outer ones, as with the breaking of the vessels. Conversely, He does not long for the prayer of the wicked, since their *Kli* and need do not gain anything because He cannot impart abundance, as it will go to the *Klipot* [shells/peels], and all the gains of the Creator is in what He bestows.

Accordingly, we should say that the life that a person wants to have contact with the Creator, whether in prayer, when he asks Him to give him something, or when he thanks the Creator for what He has given him, in the end, at that time he is speaking to the Creator. The connection of speaking to the Creator brings him life, if he appreciates the fact that he is conversing with the Creator and he extends life because at that time he lacks nothing. That is, if a person can pay attention and picture to himself that if he could speak to a flesh and blood king, which everyone reveres, it is inherent in nature that a person can give everything he has in order to speak with the king. That person, if he can strengthen his faith that he is speaking to the King of Kings, who does not speak with just anyone, then as we said, we should make three discernments in this:

1. The person does not know that this country has a king.

2. Even if he knows there is a king, he does not know that the king has come to town.

3. Even if he knows the king has come to town, he does not know the importance of his king, who is revered the world over, and all the kings and ministers in the world yearn to speak to his king, while he was fortunate to receive permission to speak to the king, and what else does he need? That is, he does not need the Creator to give him what he asks, for simply the privilege of speaking to the king is enough and gives him life. The reason he is asking something from the king is not so that the king will give him what he wants, since the prayer itself is enough for him, as though he has already granted his wish.

Likewise, when he thanks the Creator for what He has given him, he does not mind the size of the gift, but the fact that now he has the opportunity to speak to the King and thank Him—this is all His importance. This means that he does not consider the giving that the Creator has given him, or what he wants Him to give him. Rather, his entire importance is that he believes that now he is speaking to the King.

In such a state, when a person has no value for what he has, when he does not regard what enters the vessels of reception but measures the importance of what enters the vessels of bestowal, this is called "spiritual life," since all his thoughts are about being rewarded with *Dvekut* with the Creator and not for his own benefit.

In these people, it is said that there is the matter of ascents and descents. At one time they feel the importance of *Dvekut* with the Creator, and sometimes there is the *Tzimtzum* and concealment and they feel the taste of death in the state they are in, without spiritual vitality.

Now we will explain what we asked about the name of the Creator being "truth," and for this reason, one who calls upon Him in falsehood, He moves away from him. Rabbi Aba interpreted that falsehood is one who does not know whom he calls. We asked, Why is one who does not know called a "liar"?

To understand the meaning of truth, we will bring here what is written (*The Study of the Ten Sefirot*, Part 13), where he explains the seventh correction of the thirteen corrections of *Dikna*: "Therefore, this *Tikkun* [correction] is called in relation to Him, 'and truth,' since by revealing these two holy apples below, the truth of His Providence over the lower ones is revealed. This is why the revelation of His Providence is called 'and truth,' for it is the truth of His will, and all the concealments present in the worlds come only to reveal this truth in His Providence, which is to do good to His creations."

It therefore follows that what is written, that the name of the Creator is "truth," means that the truth that the purpose of creation is to do good to His creations is apparent. This is why Rabbi Aba says that "'in truth' means with the seal of the King's ring, which is the completeness of everything." We should understand what it implies to us that truth is the completeness of everything.

As we learned, the completeness of creation is for the creatures to achieve the purpose of creation, which is that the Creator's will is for the creatures to receive delight and pleasure. The completeness of everything is that when they receive delight and pleasure from the Creator, they will not part from the *Dvekut*, called "equivalence of form." This can be specifically that when they receive delight and pleasure, their intention will be to bestow. This is called "the completeness of everything."

It therefore follows that when a person asks the Creator to satisfy his wish, he should know the name of the Creator when he calls upon Him. Otherwise, it is not regarded as truth but as falsehood and the Creator moves away from him.

We asked, Why is it considered a lie if he does not know His name, and why does the Creator move away from him? The answer is that when a person comes to pray to the Creator, he should believe that the name of the Creator is "truth." That is, the Creator wants the quality of truth to be evident, that the Creator wants to do good to His creations. If he calls upon the Creator but does not believe that the name of the Creator is "truth," that He wants the creatures to receive delight and pleasure, it follows that he does not believe in the purpose of creation, which is to do good to His creations. Thus, he is calling in falsehood. That is, he is asking someone to do him a favor while not believing that that man can do him any good.

Thus, when he calls upon Him to do good to him, he calls in falsehood because he does not believe that the Creator is good and does good. Because of this, the Creator moves away from he who calls upon Him in falsehood.

In corporeality, too, we see that if someone asks someone for a favor, and the other one knows that he does not believe that he can do him a favor but he is asking him for no reason, clearly, that person will move away from him and will not even want to hear what he will say to him.

Likewise, the Creator knows that the person speaks falsehood, that he is not calling Him by His name, which is "truth," that the Creator truly does good to His creations. Naturally, the Creator moves away from him.

It therefore follows that when a person comes to pray to the Creator to help him, if that person comes to pray to the Creator to bring him closer, to adhere to the Creator, the order is that prior to the prayer he should first examine to Whom he is praying, meaning to which name of the Creator he is praying.

That is, the Creator has many names. The names of the Creator are given after the operations that manifest from Him. It is as our sages said, that each angel is named after the operation.

For this reason, first and foremost, a person must believe that the name of the Creator is The Good Who Does Good, and that the purpose of creation was to do good to His creations, and that His name is "truth." At the end of correction, His real name will be revealed, that His intention in our suffering was not vengeance, as is done among corporeal people. Rather, it was all with one intention—to do good to His creations. That is, the suffering they suffered were corrections that qualified them to receive the delight and pleasure.

When a person has this faith and he asks the Creator to bring him closer, meaning to give him strength from above to achieve the degree of qualification where all his actions are in order to bestow, and this is what he asks of the Creator—that His glory will be revealed in the world, and not as it is now, when the *Shechina* [Divinity] is in the dust—and he prays that His glory will be revealed in the world, this is considered that he knows the name of the Creator and is not calling Him in falsehood, but in truth.

What Is the Prayer for Help and for Forgiveness in the Work?

Article No. 4, Tav-Shin-Mem-Het, 1987/88

Our sages said (*Kidushin* 30b), "Man's inclination overcomes him every day and seeks to put him to death. Were it not for the help of the Creator, he would not overcome it." This means that when the Creator helps him, he can overcome it. Hence, the question is, Why should a person ask the Creator for forgiveness for the sin, since our sages said that a person himself cannot overcome it unless with the help of the Creator? It follows that if a person sins, it is not his fault, for what could he do if the Creator did not help him?

To understand this, we first need to understand the root of sins. That is, what is the source and the reason that causes all the sins? Although the answer is simple and known to all, that the reason for all the sins is the evil inclination, we should know the source and the root of the evil inclination, which incites the creatures to sin. In other words, why does He want the creatures to sin in the world? We should also understand what is the good inclination, which wants specifically that the creatures will engage in Torah and *Mitzvot* [good deeds/commandments].

As we learned, the purpose of creation is to do good to His creations. For this reason, the Creator created creatures that want to receive delight and pleasure, meaning to have a desire and craving for pleasures, or they feel that they have no point in living. They must receive pleasure or they feel torments. That will to receive, imprinted in the creatures, is the root of all the evil inclination, which incites the creatures to sin.

However, we need to understand, if the Creator created this will to receive in the creatures, and it is the reason why the creatures are called "creatures," which is as it is written, that the creatures are called "existence from absence," which is something new that did not exist before He created it, then why is it the root of the evil inclination?

The answer to this is presented in *The Study of the Ten Sefirot*. Since every branch wants to resemble its root, had this will to receive remained in its form, which is in order to receive, that desire, which is opposite from the Creator, would feel unpleasantness upon reception of the pleasures. For this reason, there was a correction on this, called *Tzimtzum* [restriction]. This means that it will not receive the light in this *Kli* [vessel] called "receiving for oneself," but will receive the abundance specifically when it has the intention to bestow.

This means that all that a person wants to receive for himself became forbidden because any desire in the upper one becomes a binding law in the lower one, meaning that the lower makes a prohibition if he receives for himself, and not with the aim to bestow contentment upon his Maker.

It follows that all the sins extend from a person wanting to receive for his own sake. It is as it is written, "I have created the evil inclination; I have created the Torah as a spice." It follows that the Torah and *Mitzvot* that we were given to observe are with the aim to bring us to the intention to be able to aim our hearts to do everything in order to bestow. This is called *Kedusha* [holiness/sanctity]. From this extends that the *Klipa* [shell/peel] and the *Sitra Achra* [other side], which want to receive for their own sake, are in this, opposite from *Kedusha*.

For this reason, we call the will to receive for one's own sake by a new name, "evil inclination," since by wanting to satisfy its own wish and enjoy for itself, it prevents us from observing Torah and *Mitzvot*. By observing Torah and *Mitzvot*, even if *Lo Lishma* [not for Her sake], we come to *Lishma* [for Her sake]. Hence, even in *Lo Lishma*, the evil inclination prevents us from observing Torah and *Mitzvot*, since from *Lo Lishma* we come to *Lishma*. For this reason, for the mere doubt that "it may come," it already disrupts.

Lishma means that a person does everything for the sake of the Creator and not for his own sake. It follows that when a person engages in Torah and *Mitzvot*, the evil inclination loses so much that it disappears from the world. In other words, by observing Torah and *Mitzvot*, the person kills it. It is as our sages said (*Berachot* 61b), "Tania Rabbi Yosi from the Galilee says, 'The righteous, the good inclination judges them, as it was said, 'My heart is slain within me.'" RASHI interprets, "'My heart is slain within me' is the evil inclination. It is as though dead within me, meaning that he can force it."

Accordingly, everything that the evil inclination does, which obstructs him from engaging in Torah and *Mitzvot*, it does justly, since the person wants to put it to death through the Torah and *Mitzvot*. For this reason, the will to receive is called "evil," since it harms a person, for the evil inclination prevents a person from achieving *Dvekut* [adhesion] with the Creator, which is called "life," as it is written, "And you, who cling unto the Lord your God, are alive every single one of you this day."

When a person realizes that the will to receive for himself prevents him from reaching the world of the living and wants the person to remain in the world of darkness and death, is there anything worse in the world than obstructing him from reaching life? At that time a person names the will to receive for himself, "evil inclination." This means that when a person feels the troubles it causes him, he names it "evil." Before a person comes to feel that the will to receive for himself prevents him from reaching the delight and pleasure, the person does not refer to the will to receive for himself by the name "evil inclination."

From this we see that the will to receive for oneself is right when it prevents a person from observing Torah and *Mitzvot*, since the will to receive for oneself sees that the person wants to put it to death, as in the words of our sages about the verse, "My heart is slain within me," that in the righteous, who observe Torah and *Mitzvot*, the evil inclination becomes as though dead. It is as our sages said, "I have created the evil inclination; I have created the Torah as a spice."

It follows that this will to receive, which is imprinted in the creatures, is the root of all the sins. It does not let the creatures observe the commandments of the Creator because it sees that they want to remove it from the world. It is as is written in the essay "Preface to the Wisdom of Kabbalah" (Item 1): "Rabbi Hanania Ben Akashia says, 'The Creator wanted to cleanse Israel; hence, He gave them plentiful Torah and *Mitzvot*.'" It explains there that by observing Torah and *Mitzvot*, they are rewarded with cleansing from the will to receive for themselves. Hence, we understand very well why the will to receive is what prevents us from observing Torah and *Mitzvot*, and is the root and the cause for all the sins.

It therefore follows that those who want to work on the path of bestowal, the war against the evil inclination is more difficult for them, since these people really want to kill and put to death the will to receive for themselves. That is, they want to walk in the path of Torah, which is opposite from the view of landlords. The view of landlords is that they are not doing anything unless it is for their own good. Hence, when they engage in Torah and *Mitzvot*, their whole intention is to thereby gain reward for their own sake.

That is, they will stay in their will to receive. Before they began to engage in Torah and *Mitzvot*, they wanted reward in this world, while engaging only in corporeal matters, for one who works for the landlord wants the landlord to pay his salary. But now that they have begun to work and observe Torah and *Mitzvot* that the Creator has commanded us, they want the Creator to pay their reward. It follows that it is all by way of self-gain. But afterward, when they begin to observe Torah and *Mitzvot*, it is with the intention to receive reward for their will to receive—the next world.

Thus, the evil inclination, called "will to receive," did not resist them so much, since the will to receive objected to them only over doubt, meaning since from *Lo Lishma* we come to *Lishma*. That is, he began to engage in Torah and *Mitzvot* in order to reward himself, but by this he could later come to *Lishma*, meaning to work only for the sake of the Creator and not for his own sake.

Conversely, one who wants, from the beginning, to work not in order to receive reward, meaning he does not want to work for his own sake, the evil inclination certainly resists him every step of the way. The evil inclination wants to keep "He who comes to kill you, kill him first." Hence, their work is much harder than those who work in order to receive reward, since from the beginning, they say that they want to observe Torah and *Mitzvot* as a remedy by which to kill the evil inclination, as was said, "And my heart is slain within me."

Now we can understand the question we asked according to what our sages said, "Man's inclination overcomes him every day. Were it not for the help of the Creator, he would not overcome it." Thus, why is it man's fault if he did not receive the required help from the Creator? And accordingly, why should one ask forgiveness from the Creator? The answer is simple: It is because he did not ask for help. Our sages said, "He who comes to purify is aided." It follows that the help comes from the Creator after he asks for help.

Thus, man's sin is that he did not ask the Creator for help. Had he asked for help, he would certainly get help from the Creator. But if a person says that he asked for help and the Creator did not help him, to this comes the answer that a person should believe that the

What Is the Prayer for Help and for Forgiveness in the Work?

Creator hears the prayers, as it is written, "For You hear the prayer of every mouth." If he truly believed, his prayer would be complete, and the Creator hears a complete prayer when a person yearns with all his heart that the Creator will help him.

But if his prayer is not constantly on his lips, it means that he does not have the real faith that the Creator can help him and that the Creator hears everyone who asks Him, and that small and great are equal before Him, meaning that He answers everyone. It follows that the prayer is incomplete. This is why he should ask forgiveness for his sins, for not asking for the required help from the Creator.

And although there are other answers in the literal, in the work, when a person wants to walk on the path of bestowal and not by way of reception, the sin is mainly that a person did not ask the Creator to help him overcome the evil. For this, he asks forgiveness, and from here on he will ask for help.

What Is, "When Israel Are in Exile, the *Shechina* Is With Them," in the Work?

Article No. 5, Tav-Shin-Mem-Het, 1987/88

It is written in the *Megillah* (p 29): "Tania Rabbi Shimon Ben Yochai says, 'Come and see how fond is the Creator of Israel; wherever they exile, the *Shechina* [Divinity] is with them, as was said, 'And the Lord your God returned from your captivity.' It did not say, 'will return,' but rather 'returned,' showing that the Creator returns with them from the exiles.'"

We should understand in the work, 1) What it gives us in the work if the *Shechina*, too, is in exile. That is, what is the benefit from the *Shechina* being in exile, as it is written, "Israel are beloved by the Creator," in that the *Shechina*, too, is in exile. Thus, we should understand what this adds to us in the work. In other words, What is the correction that we find in the *Shechina*, too, being in exile?

2) What does it mean that our sages said, "It is the sorrow of the *Shechina* that she is in exile"? Our sages also said, "A person should be sorry for the sorrow of the *Shechina*." How can it be said that there is sorrow above, that we must ask the Creator to raise the *Shechina* from the dust, meaning that we should ask the Creator to pick her up from the dust?

3) What does it mean in the work to understand that the *Shechina* is in the dust, that she herself cannot rise up by herself, but needs the Creator to raise her?

4) In order for the Creator to raise her, we must pray for this. It is as though without our prayer, the Creator cannot raise her from the dust.

To understand all these we first need to understand which discernment we call the Creator, and which discernment we called *Shechina*. Baal HaSulam said a commentary about what is written in *The Zohar*: "He is the *Shochen* [dweller in male form] and she is the *Shechina* [where the dweller dwells]." We should know that the many discernments we make in upper worlds are only from the perspective of the receivers. But from the perspective of the Creator, it is written, "I the Lord do not change." Therefore, all the worlds are discerned by two discernments: 1) The Creator, who is the *Shochen*. He is called "light," "bestower," "giver," and "reviver."

2) The place where the Creator is revealed, meaning the place where we feel Him and attain Him according to the value of the *Kli* [vessel] that has equivalence of form. This correction emerged after the *Tzimtzum* [restriction]. Accordingly, he said that the place where the *Shochen* is revealed is called *Shechina*. Thus, they are not two things but are light and *Kli*. The light is called *Shochen*, and the *Kli* where the light is clothed is called *Shechina*.

According to his words, we should interpret the whole work we have ahead of us concerning the correction of creation, that it is only the correction of the *Kelim* [vessels], meaning how the upper abundance that He wants to impart upon His creatures, so the *Kelim* are suitable to receive the abundance and the abundance will not go to the outer ones. This is our only work, and nothing more.

It follows that the Shochen wants to be revealed, meaning that the delight and pleasure will be revealed to the creatures. To the emanator, we attribute only bestowing and giving, as this was the purpose of creation.

However, from the perspective of the lower ones, for the Kli where the delight and pleasure should be revealed, since she desired equivalence of form with the root, namely to be a giver like the root, she said that she does not want to receive in order to receive, and on this she placed a Tzimtzum.

Only when there is an ability to aim to bestow, the Kli will receive the delight and pleasure. This was done in the upper worlds, which are regarded as the roots of the souls, meaning that the souls, too, will receive the abundance only under such conditions that are called "in order to bestow." This causes a delay that the delight and pleasure cannot be revealed until the lower ones are fit to receive the abundance.

It therefore follows that if the lower ones do not give the place where the Shochen must be revealed, since they haven't the strength to place the aim on the gift that the Shochen will give so the reception will be in order to bestow, this is called "the sorrow of the Shechina." That is, it is that the Creator cannot impart the delight and pleasure as He wishes, for His desire is to do good to His creations.

It follows that the sorrow of the Shechina means that the Creator regrets being unable to reveal the delight and pleasure because the creatures cannot give the place that is suitable to receive, for if He gives them the delight and pleasure, it will all go to the Sitra Achra [other side]. Therefore, it follows that He cannot impart the delight as He wishes.

By this we will understand that a person should be sorry for the sorrow of the Shechina. We asked, Why does the Creator not raise her from the dust, but must instead ask the lower ones to aim that their actions—meaning what they do—will be only with the intention to "raise the Shechina from the dust"?

The answer is that all that the Creator gives is delight and pleasure, for His purpose of to do good to His creations. But to

What Is, "When Israel Are in Exile, the Shechina Is With Them"?

raise the *Shechina* from the dust, meaning for the Creator to be able to give the abundance without the abundance going to the *Sitra Achra*, this can be only when the lower ones do not want to receive for their own benefit, but only in order to bestow.

Yet, this pertains to man's work, and not to the Creator. What pertains to the Creator is giving, but not giving does not pertain to the Creator but to the creatures. In other words, the creatures do not want to receive for themselves unless it is in order to bestow. It is as our sages said, "Everything is in the hands of heaven except for the fear of heaven."

Baal HaSulam interpreted that the Creator gives everything. Everything means that every good that is given, the Creator gives it, and "fear of heaven," which is not to receive for oneself, is all that man must do. Therefore, it is upon man to correct himself so the Creator may give the delight and pleasure.

Thus, the question is, What is the benefit from man's work for the Creator? What does the Creator need that we should work for the sake of the Creator, which the Creator receives from man's work? We can say that it is only one thing: a place where He can impart the delight and pleasure that He wished to impart at the time of the creation of the world, namely to do good to His creations.

Therefore, when we say "the sorrow of the *Shechina*," we mean that the Creator cannot reveal to them the delight and pleasure. It turns out that there is seemingly sorrow for His inability to do good to the created beings. This is called "the sorrow of the *Shechina*," sorrow that He cannot bestow impart upon the *Kelim*, as we said that the *Kelim* are called *Shechina*, where the *Shochen* is present.

The reason we should aim all our actions toward the sorrow of the *Shechina* is that we should achieve equivalence of form, called "in order to bestow and not to receive for our own sake." The rule is that a person cannot work aimlessly. Therefore, a person must see before him what he wants from his effort, meaning what he wants to obtain in life, so he will know that if he obtains it, he will be the happiest man in the world.

Therefore, he is told that nothing is greater or more important than satisfying the Creator's wish and not the will to receive for himself. At that time a person should know what is missing in the King's palace, the lack that he can fill. That is, what can be said that causes the Creator sorrow, that He misses, and that if He is given it, He will be happy.

To this comes the answer that a person should be sorry for the sorrow of the *Shechina*, meaning that the Creator is seemingly sorry that He cannot impart delight and pleasure upon the creatures, as in the allegory in the *Midrash*, which says that it is similar to a king who has a tower filled abundantly but no guests.

To understand the allegory of the *Midrash*, we can use allegory about a person who held a wedding for his son, and invited food for five hundred guests, but for some reason, no one came and he could barely get a *Minyan* [ten people] for the *Huppah* [wedding ceremony]. What sorrow that person felt that he had food for five hundred people but they did not come.

It is on this reason that a person needs to work to be rewarded with bringing contentment to the Creator—by receiving from Him the delight and pleasure. A person who achieves this degree is the happiest person in the world.

But if a person observes Torah and *Mitzvot* [commandments] in order for the Creator to give abundance into his vessels of reception because he wants to delight himself, that person is far from the abundance, since the upper abundance can only come into vessels of bestowal. Hence, the reason he observes Torah and *Mitzvot* must be because by this he will be among those who want to please the Creator, as in the allegory.

Yet, since man is born with a *Kli* for self-reception, how can he change his nature and say that he is not concerned with himself in any way, and the only thing that pains him, and for which he is sorry, is the sorrow of the *Shechina*, meaning the sorrow that seemingly exists above because he is unable to satisfy His will.

That is, since He desires to do good but He cannot execute this benefit because the creatures haven't the suitable *Kelim* to receive it, and since by observing Torah and *Mitzvot* he will be able to make suitable *Kelim*, as our sages said, "I have created the evil inclination; I have created the Torah as a spice," this is why he works with all his might to observe Torah and *Mitzvot*, so that by observing Torah and *Mitzvot* he will emerge from self-love and will be rewarded with vessels of bestowal. Then, he will be able to bring contentment to the Maker, from whom he receives the delight and pleasure.

By this we will understand the second question, How can it be said that there is sorrow and lack above? The answer is that it is because He wants to give abundance to the created beings, yet the creatures cannot receive due to disparity of form. His inability to give to the place where the *Shochen* must be revealed, which is called *Shechina*, this is called "the sorrow of the *Shechina*," meaning sorrow that there cannot be a place where the *Shochen* can be, for *Shechina* is called the *Kli* where the light is revealed.

Accordingly, we can understand the third question we asked, What does it mean in the work that the *Shechina* is placed in the dust, and that the Creator needs that only the creatures can raise her from the dust, as though He Himself cannot?

We should interpret that since the place where the *Shochen* can be revealed is when there is a *Kli* with the intention to bestow, and among the creatures, who were born with the will to receive for themselves, the place for bestowal is called "the taste of dust," since it is against their nature, hence, each time they want to work with an intention to bestow, they feel in this the taste of dust, since bestowal goes against nature. Hence, the creatures must perform deeds and actions that can correct the place so it is fit to receive the delight and pleasure.

Therefore, when speaking of the correction of the *Kelim*, the lower one must correct itself to be able to receive. And according to the rule, each one must see that he is fine and that he can do what he should do. Hence, what the giver should do pertains to the giver, and what the receiver should do pertains to the receiver. That is, the receiver should try to have suitable *Kelim*, meaning that the *Klipot* will not take from him what he will receive. In other words, the receiver should try to be able to have the aim to bestow while receiving, or the upper light will not be able to reach those *Kelim* due to disparity of form. For this reason, the lower one must erect the quality of bestowal in order to receive the bestowal from above.

Now we can understand what we asked, What is the benefit in what our sages said, "When Israel are exiled, the *Shechina* is with them," in the work? Our sages said (*Tanhuma, Nitzavim* 1), "When torments come upon Israel, they surrender and pray. But the nations of the world kick them and do not mention the name of the Creator."

We should interpret this in the work. In the work, suffering is when a person comes into a state of descent, and suffers from having no flavor or vitality in Torah and *Mitzvot*, and the whole world grows dark on him, and he finds no peace of mind.

He begins to look into the past, meaning what is the reason that he has come to a state of lowliness and cannot find anything to which to attribute this descent. Moreover, it is hard for him to understand how come before he began the work of bestowal, he felt that he was in a world that was all good, and it was great work for him to observe what our sages said, "Be very, very humble."

But now he sees that he is the worst in the world. He sees that the whole world lives and enjoys engaging in Torah and *Mitzvot*, and when they pray, they feel that each word they utter leaves an impression above. And because they believe that it leaves an impression above, this leaves an impression below. That is, each one feels in his heart that today he did a great thing by praying or by learning Torah, and he continues similarly each and every day.

Yet, he sees himself as the worst in the world because the whole world has grown dark on him. That is, the sun that shines to the world does not shine for him and he does not see that he has a right to exist in the world.

At that time, a person faces a dilemma: He can say that he is regarded as Israel. He believes in the Creator, that everything is under His Providence. That is, the situation he is in now, the Creator who sent him this descent. His suffering at being in a state of lowliness comes from Him, meaning that certainly, the Creator wanted him to ascend in degree and not remain in a state where all his work is for his own sake, for by this he becomes separated from *Dvekut* [adhesion] with the Creator.

Instead, the Creator wants him to see his real state, how remote he is from working for the benefit of the Creator. For this reason, the Creator has taken from him the flavor he felt in *Lo Lishma* [not for Her sake], which leaves him lifeless. It follows that the Creator is tending to him and wants to admit him into *Kedusha*.

Therefore, now he must pray to the Creator to help him, since now he needs His help. Otherwise, he sees that he is completely lost. This is regarded as having obtained a *Kli* and a need for the Creator's help, since now he sees that he is truly separated from the Creator because he has no life, for one who adheres to the Creator has life, as it is written, "For with You is the source of life."

Now he can certainly pray from the bottom of the heart, for a real prayer is specifically from the bottom of the heart. Accordingly, he should be thankful to the Creator for letting him see his true state. Now he sees that he needs the Creator to give him the necessary assistance, as our sages said, "He who comes to purify is aided." And *The Zohar* asks, "With what is he aided?" and it replies, "With a holy soul."

Therefore, now the Creator has given him an opportunity to obtain a holy soul. He should be delighted about the state of descent and suffering that he feels in this state. For this reason, he should say that he is not in a state of descent, but on the contrary, he is in a state of ascent.

By this we can interpret what our sages said, "When torments come upon Israel, they surrender and pray." This means that when they come into a state of descent, they see their true state, that they are in lowliness. This is considered that they surrender, since they see their state—that they have parted from the Life of Lives, for one who has *Dvekut* with the Creator is alive. Otherwise, he feels only suffering. Therefore, it is clear to him that now is the time for prayer from the bottom of the heart. This is the meaning of the words, "They surrender and pray."

But it could be said to the contrary—that it is an argument that belongs to "the nations of the world" and not to "Israel." That is, he does not believe that the Creator has sent him this state—that he sees that he is in a state of descent and feels that now he has no taste in Torah and *Mitzvot*, but that he is in a state of suffering and generally has no meaning in life and he "ponders the beginning," meaning he regrets he put himself into the path of bestowal.

That is, he says that before he began the work of bestowal, he had joy from the work of engaging in Torah and prayer and observing the *Mitzvot*. At that time he knew that he did not have to make any calculations and his only concerns were about increasing the quantity, meaning to dedicate more time for prayer and Torah. As for the quality of the work, he had no need to pay attention and think about the goal for which he was doing the holy work. He relied on the general public because at the time, it did not occur to him that there was a need to think about the reason that compels him to engage in Torah and *Mitzvot*. For this reason, he always felt in complete wholeness.

But now that he has begun to ponder the reason for which he wants to observe Torah and *Mitzvot* and to engage for the sake of the Creator—in order to bestow and not in order to receive for himself—the work has become more difficult for him and it is more difficult for him to overcome his evil inclination.

He says that where he wants to walk on the path of truth, it makes sense that the evil inclination should yield and weaken. Yet, now it is the complete opposite: Everything in *Kedusha* that he wants to do in order to bestow, the evil inclination overpowers him and it is difficult for him to overcome. He asks, "Where is the justice?" From all the work of having to constantly overcome, he falls into a descent.

At that time he comes to the argument of the spies and says, "I'm fed up with this work," and he escapes the campaign. He argues that where he should have progressed, he is regressing. Therefore, he "ponders the beginning" and kicks this path of having to work on the intentions and the actions are not enough, but the intention is what counts, as it is written, "Better a little bit with intention than a lot without an intention." He says that this work is not for him.

Now we can interpret what our sages said, "But the nations of the world," when suffering come upon them, "kick them and do not mention the name of the Creator." This means that when suffering comes upon him, meaning when he suffers during the descent because he feels no flavor or vitality in Torah and work, and the suffering is so intense that the whole world grows dark because of them, and he finds no other solution but to escape the campaign, this is considered that they "kick them."

We should know that this escape comes for only one reason, as it is written, "But the nations of the world kick them and do not mention the name of the Creator." That is, in a state of descent, when he feels suffering, they "do not mention the name of the Creator," saying that the Creator has sent him this state of descent so as to know his situation in complete clarity, to what extent he can work for the sake of the Creator, and to feel that now he sees that without His help, it is impossible to emerge from the control of reception for oneself.

Now he does not need to believe the words of our sages, who said, "Man's inclination overcomes him every day, and if the Creator did not help him, he would not overcome it," for now he sees that he needs assistance from above. So, now is the time when he can pray from the bottom of the heart, for a real prayer is specifically from the bottom of the heart. That is, he prays with all his heart, for the heart understands that without assistance from above, he is lost.

In the book *A Sage's Fruit* (Vol. 1, p 301), Baal HaSulam interprets the matter of the prayer having to be from the bottom of the heart: "There is no happier situation in man's world than when he finds himself despaired with his own strength. That is, he has already labored and done all that he could possibly imagine he could do, but found no remedy. It is then that he is fit for a wholehearted prayer for His help because he knows for certain that his own work will not help him. As long as he feels some strength of his own, his prayer will not be whole because the evil inclination rushes first and tells him, 'First you must do what you can, and then you will be worthy of the Creator.'"

We should interpret what he says, that "the evil inclination rushes first and tells him, 'First you must do what you can, and then you will be worthy of the Creator.'" Ostensibly, it speaks like a righteous man. Why is this regarded as the evil inclination speaking to him? The answer is that the evil inclination tells him good things, but what it means by those good words is that he does not need to pray to the Creator, that he still has time to ask of the Creator. Therefore, when he has done everything he could, the evil inclination can no longer come to him arguing that he still has time to pray to the Creator, for then a person immediately replies to the evil inclination, "There is nothing more that I can do that I haven't done, and it did not help." Therefore, now is the best time to pray to the Creator.

However, when a person has done what he could and the evil inclination has no more words to say to a person that he still has time to pray, since there is still more to do, since he has already done everything he could, then the evil inclination has other, worse words, with more poison and the potion of death.

These are that they "do not mention the name of the Creator." In other words, he does not say that the Creator sent him the state of suffering he feels during the descent. Instead, what does he do during the descent? It is written, "But the nations of the world," during the descent, when they feel suffering, "kick them." That is, they leave the campaign and escape from the work of bestowal.

Now we can understand the question we asked, What is the meaning of "When Israel are in exile, the *Shechina* is with them"? As

What Is, "When Israel Are in Exile, the Shechina Is With Them"?

Rabbi Shimon Ben Yochai said, "Wherever they exile, the *Shechina* is with them." What is the benefit from this in the work, that he says about it, "How beloved are Israel by the Creator"?

We should interpret that when a person feels that he is in exile, meaning feels the taste of exile in the work and wants to escape from the exile, the meaning will be that a person must believe that wherever they are exiled, the *Shechina* is with them. That is, the *Shechina* let him feel the taste of exile. "With them" means that the *Shechina* is attached to them and they are not separated from the *Shechina*, that they should say that it is a descent. On the contrary, now the *Shechina* is giving him a push so he will climb the degrees of *Kedusha* [holiness/sanctity], and dresses herself in a garment of descent.

When a person knows and believes that this is so, it will encourage him so he does not escape the campaign or say that the work of bestowal is not for him because he always sees that he is in states of ascents and descents, and he sees no end to these states and falls into despair.

But if he walks in the path of faith and believes in the words of our sage, then he must say the opposite. If the order of the work of the rest of the people is proper, meaning that they feel themselves as whole and see that thank God, they are observing *Mitzvot*, pray, and learn Torah, and what else do they need, it means that they do not have from above special treatment every step of the way, or are told if their work is proper or not.

This is similar to people learning in a seminary. Assume there are a hundred people in the seminary, and some town needs a rabbi. The town's people send a request to the principal of the seminary to send them a rabbi. Then, the principal chooses a team that will test which of the students can be a rabbi there. From among the one hundred students in the seminary, the best ones are chosen. Assume that five students are selected and tested. The test contains questions that they must answer. However, they need not to answer all the questions. Rather, if they answer ninety percent, they are already considered worthy of being among the select elite of the people. But some answer less than ninety. Can it be said that those students in the seminary that are tested in Torah and wisdom are ordinary people, while the ninety-nine percent of the students in the seminary who are not tested, are they fine in Torah and wisdom, and because they are greater, they do not need to be tested?

Likewise, here in the order of the work, there is a rule. Let us say, for example, that ninety-nine percent of the workers of the Creator are not tested to see if they are fine. That is, they are not shown their situation, whether they are fine in their Torah and work. If they are not tested, certainly, everyone thinks that he is fine.

But let us say that those five percent who can achieve wholeness and be admitted into the King's palace, these people are tested. They are shown from above their true state in Torah and *Mitzvot* so they may know what to correct. The corrections are called "faith," "prayer," and "labor."

This is similar to what Baal HaSulam said about the verse, "And he said, 'I beseech You, please show me Your glory … And the Lord said, 'Behold, here is a place with Me.'" Our sage said, "'with Me' is an acronym [in Hebrew] for 'faith,' 'prayer,' and 'labor.' Through these corrections it is possible to achieve real wholeness."

Accordingly, we can see what is the real way in Torah and *Mitzvot*. The way is to achieve *Dvekut* with the Creator, called "equivalence of form," by which we are rewarded with life, as it is written, "For with You is the source of life." Also, ascents and descents are given to the capable ones, who are better capable of entering the King's palace.

Accordingly, we should interpret what we asked, what does knowing that the Creator, too, will return from exile, like Israel, add to us in the work, as our sages said about the verse, "And the Lord your God returned from your captivity"? They said, "It was not said 'will return' but rather 'returned,' meaning that the Creator returned with them from the exiles."

However, first we must understand how can we speak of "exile" in relation to the Creator. Exile means that He has departed from the place where He was and had to go to foreign places and be governed by other kings. Also, He has no choice but to do and obey every wish of every ruler under whom He is. Yet, we must believe what is written, that "The whole earth is full of His glory." Thus, how can we speak of exile in relation to the Creator?

We should also understand toward whom we say that the Creator is in exile. In relation to Himself, we cannot say because we do not know His thoughts, as it is written in *The Zohar*, "There is no thought or perception in Him whatsoever." Rather, all that we say in relation to the Creator is, as in, "By Your actions, we know You." Therefore, we must say that the Creator is in exile in relation to Israel. In other words, the people of Israel see that the Creator is in exile among the nations. Hence, we should understand how it is expressed that it seems to the people of Israel that He is in exile. Also, we should understand what is exile, and then we will be able to understand that one who is in exile feels the taste of exile.

We should also know that concerning exile, we find two discernments: 1) When the people of Israel were in the holy land and had a Temple. Nebuchadnezzar came, destroyed the Temple, and exiled Israel from the land, as it is written (Esther 2), "There was a Jewish man in the capital, Susa, whose name was Mordecai, who had been exiled from Jerusalem." It follows that exile means that they have been exiled from a place of happiness and tranquility to go and suffer and wander, and have no peace of mind. 2) We find that in the exile in Egypt, they were not exiled from a place of tranquility, but where they were, they began to feel that they were in exile. They saw that they were enslaved to Pharaoh king of Egypt, meaning that what the king of Egypt required of them, they had no free choice but had to obey his wish in everything he demanded of them.

Accordingly, what does it mean that the Creator was exiled from His place? After all, it is written, "The whole earth is full of His glory," so how can we say that the Creator has been exiled from His place unto another place? According to the second interpretation of exile, such as the exile in Egypt, when Pharaoh King of Egypt ruled over the children of Israel, they felt exile in this. But how can we speak of exile in relation to the Creator, for does anyone govern Him that we can say that the Creator is in exile?

Certainly, when we speak of exile in relation to the Creator, it is only from the perspective of the creatures. That is, it is according to the attainment of the creatures that there is the matter of exile and redemption. Sometimes they perceive the Creator as a great King dwelling in His palace with *Seraphim* and animals and wheels of holiness standing around Him, and sometimes they perceive Him as a King who has been exiled from His palace, captive under the rule of another king. This is regarded as the King being in exile.

Accordingly, we should interpret that the people of Israel went out of the land of Israel and the Temple was ruined. In the work, we should interpret that the people of Israel went out and did not feel the flavor of Torah and *Mitzvot*, and their heart, which was a place for feeling the *Kedusha*, called "The Temple," that place was ruined.

The other king, called "an old and foolish king," conquered their hearts and took all the *Kelim* of *Kedusha* out of there. This means that he took out all the thoughts of *Kedusha* that they had in their hearts and inserted instead, an idol in the palace of the Lord. That is, where previously there was *Kedusha*, he took out all the thoughts of *Kedusha*, where *Kedusha* means thoughts for the sake of the Creator. Yet, he conquered their hearts and installed in their hearts thoughts that are only about their own benefit. This is regarded as a foolish old king conquering the Temple and exiling Israel from within it. That is, the quality of Israel is no longer in their bodies.

This is as it is written (Psalms 79, "A Psalm for Asaf"), "God, the nations have come into Your inheritance; they have defiled the Temple of Your holiness, laid Jerusalem in ruins." That is, the quality of Israel departed from their hearts and in their stead came gentiles.

Accordingly, this means that the Creator has been exiled with them. That is, He departed from His palace because of Israel, meaning that this is how they feel, that He does not have the importance that they felt before they were exiled from the land of Israel.

What is the benefit of the Creator being in exile with them? We can understand this by what Baal HaSulam said about the words of our sages, "'A person does not sin unless a spirit of folly has entered him.' People ask about this, 'Why did a spirit of folly enter? So he would sin.'" He said that since there is a rule that "The eye sees and the heart covets," if a person sees something bad, whether in sight or in thought, he must come to covet it. Therefore, although he cannot prevent this with his eyes, because both thoughts and looking come without any preparation, hence, this is still not considered a sin, but from this we come into a sin that is called "coveting."

If a person immediately repents on the seeing, he will not come to covet and will not sin. But if a person does not immediately repent the seeing, he must come to the sin called "coveting."

A correction was made above, that in order for man not to blemish the glory of the King, He took out of him the spirit of wisdom and installed in him the spirit of folly. Thus, we see that even in the courthouse of below, a fool is not punished in the same manner as a sane person. It follows that here, when gentiles entered his heart and he does not feel the taste of life in Torah and *Mitzvot*, it is considered that for him, the Creator, too, is in exile. In that state, he does not have the faith in the Creator he had had before he suffered the descent. Hence, the blemish is not so great.

And there is another meaning to the Creator being in exile with them, when the people of Israel are in exile. When the nations govern them, the Creator is in exile, too. Therefore, we ask for the Creator to come out of exile, since we must be careful not to pray for self-love but only for the sake of the Creator. Hence, when he asks the Creator to take His people out from exile, he is asking for the sake of the creatures, and not for the sake of the Creator.

For this reason, when we believe that the Creator, too, is in exile, we ask for the sake of the Creator. That is, we pray for the glory of heaven. It is as is said in the litany: "Have mercy on us, O Lord, why should the nations say, 'Where is their God?' For Your sake, Be merciful with us and do not delay.'" It follows that by knowing that the Creator, too, suffers from the exile, this gives them a place to pray for the Creator and not for himself.

However, how can we say that He is in exile and that the gentiles seemingly control Him as they control Israel? The answer is that since the purpose of creation is to do good to His creations, and over the good that the creatures must receive, there was a correction that they will aim to bestow, hence, when Israel are in exile among the nations—when they are placed under the governance of self-love—they cannot receive the delight and pleasure clothed in Torah and *Mitzvot*.

For this reason, they cannot feel the taste of life that there is in *Kedusha*. And since the exile among the nations of the world is on them, anything they will receive will have the taste of the concealment of the face. But since the Creator desires the existence of the world, He must dress Himself in dresses that are not of *Kedusha*. That is, He bestows upon the world vitality in dresses of corporeality, meaning that He bestows upon the world pleasure and life only in corporeal things.

This means that the world can receive delight and pleasure only in dresses called "envy," "lust," and "honor." That is, He illuminates and sustains the world with dresses of *Klipot* [shells/peels], dresses that separate them from the Creator, since these pleasures come clothed in *Kelim* of self-love.

It follows that the Creator suffers from their being in exile, meaning that while they are placed under the governance of the nations of the world, the Creator must hide Himself from His sons so they would not know that He is the one giving them the taste of exile in Torah and *Mitzvot*, and that they find all the life in vessels of reception. That is, this correction of having pleasures in vessels of reception and being unable to feel the taste in Torah and *Mitzvot*, the Creator made the correction so they would not blemish the *Kedusha* and to prevent everything going to the *Klipot*. That is, they would not draw farther from *Kedusha* by feeling more flavor in self-reception, since wherever the pleasure is greater, they move farther into the vessels of reception, which separates them from *Kedusha*.

It therefore follows that by knowing that the Creator is in exile, that He must hide Himself as though He is in exile, by this a person can know that there are no *Klipot* in the world, but that a person should ask for everything only from the Creator, and there is no other force.

What Is the Difference between a Field and a Man of the Field, in the Work?

Article No. 6, Tav-Shin-Mem-Het, 1987/88

It is written in *The Zohar* (*Toldot*), "'And Isaac loved Esau because he had game in his mouth.' He wrote here, 'a skillful hunter, a man of the field,' and it is written there, 'He was a mighty hunter.' As there, it means that was hunting people's minds and misleading them into rebelling against the Creator, so here, 'a man of the field' means in order to rob people and to kill them. He is a man of the field because his inheritance is not in an inhabited place, but in a desolate place, in the desert, in the field. For this reason, he is called 'a man of the field.'"

Concerning Isaac, we also see that it is written "field," as it is written (Genesis 24:63), "And Isaac went out to wander in the field." Also, it is written about Jacob, "And he said, 'Behold, the scent of my son is as the scent of a field that the Lord has blessed.'"

We should understand the difference between the fields, where it was said about Esau, who is called "a man of the field," that *The Zohar* interprets "to rob people and to kill them," whereas concerning Isaac, it is written, "to wander in the field," which is a great thing, as our sages said that Isaac established the afternoon prayer because of the verse, "And Isaac went out to wander in the field." We should also understand why it is written about Jacob that Isaac said, "The scent of my son is as the scent of a field that the Lord has blessed." Therefore, we should understand the differences between "a man of the field," "to wander in the field," and "the scent of a field."

It is known that *Malchut* is called a "field." Since *Malchut* has many changes because of the *Tzimtzum* [restriction], *Malchut* has many names, one of which is a "field." When we speak of *Malchut*, the rule is that we speak of *Malchut* of *Ohr Yashar* [Direct Light], where she was using the will to receive for herself. In that respect, there are no changes in her but is as the Emanator created the will to receive in order to receive the delight and pleasure that He wished to impart upon the creatures. This is called *Malchut* with respect to the *Ohr Yashar* in her.

For this reason, this *Malchut* is called *Ein Sof* [infinity/no end], for *Malchut* did not put a stop on the upper light, meaning she did not say, "No more!" I do not want to receive with my self, called "receiving in order to receive." While she was receiving with her self, there were no changes, which is why it is called by the name, "Everything was one light."

However, afterward, *Malchut* desired equivalence of form, called "decoration," at the point of desire. That is, she did not want to receive in order to receive, but in order to bestow. In that respect, we can call *Malchut* by the name "field," meaning that the field must be plowed, and plowing means inverting that which is below and placing it above, and that which is above, we place below.

Likewise, here in *Malchut*, who is called a "field," for the will to receive, reception is important and is considered "of superior importance," while matters of bestowal are of inferior importance. In *Kedusha* [sanctity/holiness], there is the matter of plowing, that we must till the land, meaning turn the will to receive, which is on top, to be below, and the will to bestow to be on top. Specifically by this can we yield crops that are good to eat. Otherwise, there is no way we will be able to eat food of *Kedusha*, as it is written (Proverbs 14:4), "Much crop comes by the strength of the ox." That is, the force of the ox yields much crop.

The meaning of "ox" is as our sages said, that *Malchut* [kingdom] of heaven must be as an ox to the burden and as an ass to the load." Baal HaSulam said that "an ox to the burden" means that the burden of faith must be as one places the yoke on the ox so as to plow the field, without any consideration of its will, if it agrees with it. Instead, we place the yoke on it against its will. Likewise, man must take upon himself the burden of the kingdom of heaven, since an ox means knowing, as it is written, "The ox knows its master." For this reason, faith is regarded as a burden to one who needs knowledge.

It therefore follows that a field is *Malchut* with respect to self-reception, which requires plowing, which is the correction of the field to turn the vessel of reception, which is of high importance, and make it low importance, while the vessels of bestowal, which are of low importance, raise them so as to be of high importance.

It is known that the will to receive is in mind and heart, and both require correction. In the mind, the correction is faith above reason. In the heart, the correction is that every pleasure he receives will be in order to bestow. And more precisely, every act he does will be in order to bestow; otherwise, he will not make a single move.

Accordingly, we can interpret why it is written about Esau, "a man of the field," meaning that while he is in a state of "field," and must assume the burden of the kingdom of heaven as an ox to the burden, he thinks he is complete and does not need any corrections. This is called "for he had game in his mouth." This is as it is written in *The Zohar* (above), "And Esau said that he was in the field in order to pray, and he hunted and deceived Isaac with his mouth."

In the work, we should interpret that "he had game in his mouth" means that his mouth and heart were not the same. His mouth is externality, meaning that in actions, he was righteous, because there is nothing to add to actions, but in his heart, meaning the intention, he was not as the act. The act that is apparent to people implies that he wants to observe the commandments of the Creator in order to please Him by doing His will in observing the *Mitzvot* [commandments/good deeds]. But in his heart, he thinks only about his own benefit and not about the benefit of the Creator. Thus, his mouth and heart are not the same.

Therefore, in action, Esau appeared complete, like a completed person. This is the meaning of "Esau was a man of the field," meaning that he had no more work to do in the field, since the work of the field begins with plowing, which is about inverting the vessels of reception. This is not for him because it is enough for him to keep everything in externality, which is called "his mouth," meaning that his mouth and heart are not the same. This is why Esau is called "a man of the field," meaning that a field is receiving for oneself, and in this he is complete and has nothing more to add.

This is not so with Isaac and Jacob. To them, the work of the field was labor and prayer in the field, as it is written about Isaac, "And Isaac went out to wander in the field," which is prayer. It is as our sages said, that Isaac established the afternoon prayer, when he prayed to raise the *Shechina* [Divinity] from the dust, meaning that the vessel of bestowal, which should be in the kingdom of heaven in mind and heart, will be in order to bestow.

However, Esau, who was a man of the field, corrected nothing so as to work in order to bestow. Rather, with him, everything was only for his own sake. This is why *The Zohar* interpreted "'a man of the field,' to rob people and to kill them." *The Zohar* also interprets "a man of the field," since his inheritance is not in an inhabited place, but in a desolate place, in the desert, in the field. This is why he is called "a man of the field."

When one works only for oneself, that state is regarded as stealing the aspect of man that is in him, meaning the aspect of "You are called 'man,' and the nations of the world are not called 'man.'" That aspect is robbed from him when he works for his own benefit.

Even worse, because transgression induces transgression, he kills the man when he is for himself. This is the meaning of the words of *The Zohar*, "And to kill them." It says about it, "Because his inheritance is not in an inhabited place," where "an inhabited place" is where people dwell, as in "You are called 'men,'" "but in a desolate place," the place of the breaking of the vessels, for because the will to receive for himself was revealed there, the world became desolate.

However, it is written about Jacob, "And he said, 'Behold, the scent of my son is as the scent of a field that the Lord has blessed,'" since Jacob established the evening prayer, as it is written, "And he came to a place," meaning he established the evening prayer. It is also written about Jacob, "And behold, a well in the field, and three flocks of sheep lying there beside it." *The Zohar* interprets (*VaYetze*, Item 92), "'And he looked, and behold a well in the field.' He saw the well of above, which is the *Nukva*, one opposite the other, meaning that the well of below was directed opposite the well of above."

We should interpret that when Jacob established the well of below, his intention was his own well, which is the field, meaning that he established it to be as above. That is, as above, *Malchut* of *Kedusha* is a *Masach* [screen], meaning that on the will to receive for himself, there is a *Masach* that raises *Ohr Hozer* [Reflected Light], meaning that everything she wants to receive is because she wants to bestow. Likewise, he established himself so that all his actions would be in order to bestow.

Hence, when Jacob came to Isaac, since Jacob is the middle line, where all the wholeness appears, this is why it is written that Isaac said, "And he said, 'Behold, the scent of my son is as the scent of a field that the Lord has blessed.'" That is, when the kingdom of heaven, called a "field," received the correction of the middle line, it is called "a field that the Lord has blessed," meaning that here appear the delight and pleasure that the Creator has prepared for the creatures. This is the difference between "a man of the field," "wander in the field," and "as the scent of a field."

What Is the Importance of the Groom, that His Iniquities Are Forgiven?

Article No. 7, Tav-Shin-Mem-Het, 1987/88

Our sages said, "Three are forgiven their iniquities: A gentile who converted, one who becomes great, and one who marries a woman. From this we learn that this is why she is called Mahalat, since his iniquities *Nimhalu* [have been forgiven]. Conversely, in the portion *VaYishlach*, she is called Bosmat, daughter of Ishmael" (presented in RASHI, *VaYishlach*).

This verse requires explanation. Our sages tell us that forgiving the iniquities of the groom on his wedding day comes from Esau, who took the daughter of Ishmael, whose name was Bosmat, daughter of Ishmael. Since it is written in the portion *Toldot*, "Esau went to Ishmael, and took Mahalat the daughter of Ishmael," it is an evidence that on his wedding day, the groom is forgiven his iniquities.

What Is the Importance of the Groom, that His Iniquities Are Forgiven?

It follows that we learn this entire basis from wicked Esau, who took the daughter of wicked Ishmael. This is difficult to understand. After all, what is a wicked one? It is one who says that there are no sins in the world and he can do what his heart desires because a wicked one believes in nothing. Thus, the wicked one says that he never sins. Therefore, why does he need his iniquities forgiven? Is a person given that which he does not want? After all, there is no light without a *Kli* [vessel], no filling without a lack.

It is even more difficult to understand what is the real reason that he deserves absolution. What is his privilege? Is it because he took a wife that he deserves his iniquities forgiven? It makes sense that one who does a great deed, which we cannot appreciate the importance of the matter, then we understand that he deserves a great reward for this, to the point of absolving his iniquities. But what great thing did he do by taking a wife?

Also, we see that saying a litany is a great thing. There is the matter of thirteen qualities there, as well as kneeling. But if there is a groom in the synagogue, we do not say the litany. We should understand the importance of taking a wife, that all seven days of the "seven blessings," it has the power to cancel a prayer, which is so important, because he took a woman, who is now called "a bride."

There are many explanations in the literal, but we should interpret this in the work. What does it come to teach us? The wicked Esau is when a person has realized that the bad thing in the world, which prevents all created beings from achieving the delight and pleasure for which the world was created—which is the meaning of bad—has become in him as Esau, from the word *Assiya* [doing]. His evil has been completed with clear knowledge that it is the will to receive for himself. At that time comes the order of "turn away from evil," meaning that before a person knows that the will to receive is called "bad," it is impossible to turn away from it and not listen to it.

Afterward begins the matter of "and do good." "Do good" means assuming the burden of the kingdom of heaven. However, a person cannot be rewarded with the quality of "a woman who fears God."

Rather, a person must receive this from above, as it is written, "He who comes to purify is aided." The Zohar says that he is given a soul, and this is the assistance that the person receives.

It follows that this soul was born by the Creator hearing him when he came to purify. This soul is called a "daughter," which was born out of the Creator hearing his prayer once a person has come to the recognition of evil, called Esau.

This is the meaning of what is written, "And Esau went and took Mahalat the daughter of Ishmael." "Went" means to a higher degree, once he has come to the recognition of evil, called Esau, to *Yishma-El* [Ishmael, meaning "the Lord will hear"]. That is, at that time he engaged in the form of "do good," praying to the Creator to hear his prayer and give him a soul, as it is said in *The Zohar*. This is the meaning of "He took Mahalat," meaning he took the absolution of iniquities by which he was rewarded with a daughter from which the Creator heard his prayer. This is called "the daughter of *Yishma-El*."

This follows a certain procession: 1) Exertion to see the truth, as much as he understands that the will to receive for himself is harming him. At that time he can determine once and for all not to use it, and this is called Esau. 2) Afterward, he is rewarded with taking a woman by forgiving the iniquities. At that time it is possible to be rewarded with it.

We can understand the meaning of a woman, which is the soul he is given from above, according to what is explained in the "Introduction to The Study of the Ten Sefirot" (Items 53-55): "Then the Creator helps him and one attains open Providence, meaning the revelation of the face. Then, he is rewarded with complete repentance, meaning he cleaves to the Creator once more with his heart, soul, and might, as though naturally drawn by the attainment of the open Providence. Naturally, one who is imparted this open Providence is certain that he will not sin again, as one is certain that he will not cut in his own flesh and cause himself terrible suffering. In addition, one is certain that he will not neglect a *Mitzva* [commandment/good deed] without performing it the

What Is the Importance of the Groom, that His Iniquities Are Forgiven?

instant it comes to his hand, as much as one is certain that he will not neglect any worldly pleasure or a great profit that comes into his hand." This repentance is regarded as his iniquities being forgiven.

According to the rule that all the *Mitzvot* [commandments/good deeds] extend from branch and root—meaning that each *Mitzva* in corporeality has its root in spirituality—we can say that what extends from this is that in corporeality, too, when a man takes a woman, his iniquities are forgiven, which implies to spirituality.

Now we can interpret what our sages said, "How to dance before the bride?" and did not say, "How to dance before the groom?" Conversely, concerning the wedding meal, they said, "One who enjoys a groom's meal and does not delight him (*Berachot*, p 6) transgresses in five voices: the voice of merriment and the voice of gladness, the voice of the groom and the voice of the bride, the voice of those who say, 'Thank!'" They did not say that we must delight the bride, and they did not say that there is a bride's meal, but only a groom's meal.

We find that on Jacob's wedding, Laban made the meal, as it is written, "And Laban assembled all the men of the place and made a feast," meaning that the meal came from the side of the bride, that the bride's father made the meal and not Jacob, who was the groom.

According to what Baal HaSulam explained—that "groom" means Torah, and "bride" means faith—we should interpret what we asked. Until a person acquires permanent faith, he has ascents and descents, since a person is born with a vessel of reception, and that vessel wants to engage in things that the mind says are worthwhile to engage in, meaning they will benefit the will to receive for himself. Otherwise, he cannot work.

Also, since faith is above reason, meaning that the reason cannot stand them, there is a matter of ups and downs here. This is called a "dance," since we see that when dancing, we lift our legs and bring them back down repeatedly. This implies that since *Raglaim* [legs] comes from the word *Meraglim* [spying], meaning that when one should take upon himself the burden of the kingdom of heaven and serve Him only *Lishma* [for Her sake], the person's intellect immediately comes and makes him see that he should not be rash, but first see if it is worthwhile to serve the Creator not in order to receive reward.

Therefore, when lifting the legs, meaning when we go above our reason and intellect, it is regarded as lifting our legs above the earth. However, a person cannot always overcome and go above reason, and this is considered placing one's feet on the ground once more. This is the meaning of what he says, "How to dance before the bride?" (*Ketubot* 16b). "Before the bride" means during the ascent, called *Panim* [face/anterior]. What should he say about the bride? What is the merit that he has found in faith, meaning what did he see in it that we should say that this is why he took upon himself the burden of faith?

Beit Shammai [House of Shammai] say, "A bride, the way she is," meaning that according to how he feels her importance, so he takes upon himself the faith. That is, he does not need to find any merit in her. Even if he feels no importance about her, he takes upon himself what we were told to believe, and this is all of our merit—if we can take upon ourselves this work, which we believe is the Creator's will, and we need not look for any merits, but simply believe and take upon ourselves by coercion, "as an ox to the burden and as a donkey to the load."

Beit Hillel [House of Hillel] say, "A bride, fair and pious." We should interpret that this means that a person should say about what he sees, "They have eyes and do not see." And considering what he hears, he should say, "They have ears and do not hear." That is, seeing is not necessarily with the eyes, but there is seeing in the mind. That is, the mind shows him depictions that contradict faith, and he often hears what the mind makes him see—that work for the sake of the Creator is not for him. He should overcome all this and say, "They have eyes and do not see." That is, what the mind tells him and makes him see is not the truth. This is called "They have eyes and do not see" the truth; "they have ears and do not hear" the truth. Therefore, their thoughts, meaning what the will to receive for himself tells him, is not the truth. Rather, he should tell himself that indeed, she is a fair and pious bride, except he is unfit to see the truth right now.

Yet, the truth is that all the delight and pleasure that the will to receive can receive in his *Kelim* [vessels] is but a slim light compared to the light that dresses in the vessels of bestowal. This is called "a fair bride." Yet, a person cannot always overcome his mind and reason. This is why there is the matter of dances in faith, of which our sages said, "How to dance before the bride." That is, what can we say to the *Panim* [face/anterior] of the bride, since *Panim* pertains to "a man's wisdom illuminates his face." Thus, he should say what is the praise that there is in the bride, called "faith." This is the difference between Beit Shammai and Beit Hillel, whether to say, "a bride, the way she is" or "a bride, fair and pious."

This is not so with the groom. The Creator is called "Torah," and Torah is considered a gift. There, there is no dancing because when a person receives a gift, it cannot be said that he has a descent, meaning that he does not want to receive gifts. Only where there is labor and a person must overcome against the reason, it can be said that at times he can overcome and at times he cannot. Conversely, when receiving gifts, how can it be said that he has no need for gifts? This is why they did not say, "How to dance before the groom?" but "How to dance before the bride?"

Conversely, considering a meal, it is written, "One who enjoys a groom's meal," and it is not written, "One who enjoys a bride's meal." The reason is that a groom is regarded as the Torah, and the Torah is a gift, as our sages said, "From Matanah [gift] to Nahaliel" (*Iruvin* 54), where it writes, "Why is it written, 'And from the desert to Matanah, and from Matanah to Nahaliel, and from Nahaliel to Bamot, and from Bamot to the valley'? He said to him, 'If a man makes himself like this desert, which everyone treads, the Torah was given to him as a gift. And since it was given to him as a gift, he inherits God, as was said, 'From Matanah to Nahaliel [rivers of God].'"

It is known that the Creator has many names, according to what He reveals to the lower ones. That is, it depends on the extent to which He bestows upon the lower ones. That is, according to the merit of the lower ones, He bestows abundance upon them. And since there are many discernments in the receivers, as it is written, "As their faces are not similar to one another, their views are not similar to one another," and as we learn in the work, that a person himself also undergoes changing states, therefore, the abundance of the Creator changes into many discernments, but the Creator has no name, since "there is no thought or perception in Him whatsoever." Rather, it is as it is written, "By Your actions we know You." That is, according to the abundance He bestows, so we name Him.

For this reason, with regard to the Torah, the Creator is called "groom." When He bestows faith, He is called "bride." With respect to the purpose of creation, which is His will to do good to His creations, for the whole world to enjoy, meaning enjoy in the way that is called "His desire to do good," meaning that He sustains the *Klipot* [shells/peels], as well, or they would not be able to exist in the world. This is as *The Zohar* says, that they have but a slim light. But in Torah and *Mitzvot*, the light is clothed there by way of "The whole Torah is the names of the Creator," whose general name is The Good Who Does Good.

According to the above, the Creator is called "groom" because He is the Giver and bestows upon the lower ones. The creatures' enjoyment from the joy He gives them, and as was said that what the whole world enjoys comes from Him, all the pleasures are called "meal." It follows that the whole world is enjoying the King's meal.

However, there is a difference from the perspective of the lower ones. There are lower ones who believe that this is a meal that comes from the King. And there are secular people, who do not believe that the meal comes from the Creator, who is called "the King." With regard to his being the Giver, He is called "a groom." This is as our sages said, "One who enjoys a groom's meal and does not delight him transgresses in five voices." That is, although they believe that the meal is a groom's meal and thank him for their pleasure, there is still a higher level, meaning that by enjoying, they should delight the King.

According to the above, that the Creator is called "groom," how can we speak of delighting the Creator? It is known that joy comes as a result of something. When a person obtains something new that he yearned for and received, it engenders joy in a person. But what can we say that the Creator is missing that if He receives it He will be happy?

The Zohar says (VaYera, Item 399), "There was no joy before the Creator since the day the world was created like the joy He is destined to have with the righteous in the future." We should also understand this verse. How can it be said that the Creator receives delight. As we learn, the purpose of creation is to do good to His creations. It follows that when the lower ones receive the delight and pleasure that He has prepared for them, He derives pleasure from this, as it is known from the allegory about the king who has a tower filled with abundance but no guests.

Therefore, we attribute the meal to the Creator as a groom, that He is regarded as the Torah, a gift, Nahaliel [rivers of God]. When the creatures receive the delight and pleasure, called "meal," they must receive everything in order to bestow and not because of self-reception. This is the meaning of what our sages said, "One who enjoys a groom's meal and does not delight him," but receives for his own sake, "transgresses in five voices." The five voices imply the completeness of the degree that must be revealed to the creatures. That is, His will to do good to His creations is revealed in five discernments, called "five parts of the soul," which are *Nefesh, Ruach, Neshama, Haya,* and *Yechida*.

This is why our sages said, "One who enjoys a groom's meal and does not delight him," meaning his intention in enjoying the meal is not to please the Creator, in that the purpose of creation is achieved in its complete correction, but rather his own benefit, then he causes five voices, meaning the *NRNHY* that should be revealed, to move away from him, since there was a *Tzimtzum* [restriction] on the vessels of reception for himself. Thus, the light does not extend to that place, and that place requires correction in order to bestow. Yet, he does not regard it, and therefore causes the abundance not to reach the lower ones.

It therefore follows that our sages warn us that we must prepare ourselves with much work and labor to 1) Believe that any pleasure we receive in the world is regarded as the King's meal. However, we must believe this. And because of it, our sages have set up a specific blessing for each and every pleasure: a blessing for the prayer, a blessing for the Torah, and also for corporeal pleasures. 2) We must try to receive any pleasure that we receive from the King's meal in order to bestow, and not for our own sake.

Conversely, when the Creator bestows upon the lower ones as a "bride," which is faith, it is still not regarded as a meal, but rather there are ups and down there. This is why there are dances there.

What Does It Mean that One Who Prays Should Explain His Words Properly?

Article No. 8, Tav-Shin-Mem-Het, 1987/88

The Zohar (VaYishlach [And Jacob Sent], Item 70) brings evidence that one who prays should explain his words properly through what is written about Jacob, who said, "Deliver me, I pray Thee." It writes, "'Deliver me, I pray Thee, from the hand of my brother, from the hand of Esau, for I fear him, that he might come and strike me and the mothers with the children.' This implies that one who prays his prayer should explain his words properly. He said, 'Deliver me, I pray Thee.' It seems as though it should have sufficed, since he does not need more than deliverance. Yet, he said to the Creator, 'Should You say that You have already delivered me from Laban?' This is why he explained, 'from the hand of my brother.' And if you say that other kin are called brothers, too, as Laban said to Jacob, 'Because you are my brother, should you serve me for nothing?' he therefore explained, 'from the hand of Esau.' What is the reason? It is because we must explain the matter properly. If you say, 'Why do I need deliverance?' It is because I fear that he might come and strike me. All of this is to explain the matter above, and not obscure it."

It is very difficult to understand this. When a person prays to the Creator, who knows the thoughts of man, should we interpret our words properly, or He might not know what the person needs? Rather, we should interpret this with respect to man. That is, the person himself should know what he needs and scrutinize every single lack separately. A person should not say in general, that he is not okay and he would like the Creator to help him. The reason is that there is a rule: "There is no light without a *Kli* [vessel], no filling without a lack." Hence, it is upon man to arrange for himself all the things he needs. That is, deliverance from Laban is not like deliverance from Esau, and so forth.

We can understand this the way Baal HaSulam said about what is written concerning Laban, who said to Jacob, "Laban replied to Jacob, 'The daughters are my daughters, and the children are my children, and the flocks are my flocks, and all that you see is mine.'" Concerning Esau, when he spoke to Jacob, it is written that Esau said the opposite: "And he said, 'What is this company of yours that I have met?' And he said, 'To find favor in the eyes of my lord.' And Esau said, 'I have plenty, my brother; let what is yours be yours.' And Jacob said, 'then take my present from my hand.'"

He said that sometimes the evil inclination dresses as Laban, who is righteous, and walks with a white garment. Sometimes it dresses as Esau, saying that man has already done everything completely, and there is nothing more to add, installing in him a spirit of pride. The order is that before the work, it tells him: "You should not get into the work *Lishma* [for Her sake], as this is difficult and no work for you. Rather, you, everything you do is for me, and you cannot aim anything for the sake of the Creator." With these arguments, the evil inclination can prevent a person from engaging in Torah and *Mitzvot* [commandments/good deeds] in truth. This is before the work, and this is the meaning of what Laban said, "The daughters are my daughters."

What Does It Mean that One Who Prays Should Explain His Words Properly?

After the work, Jacob comes and tells him, "Now I see that you are right, meaning that all my thoughts were only for you," meaning *Lo Lishma* [not for Her sake]. "Thus, now I must ask the Creator to give me repentance so I will have the strength to work for the sake of the Creator." The evil inclination comes and dresses as Esau, from the word *Assiya* [doing/action], that "You really did everything for the sake of the Creator and you are a great righteous, and you are not like your friends." Then Jacob told him, "then take my present from my hand," meaning he said, "I have plenty," meaning that all the work I did so far has been for you. But Esau told him, "Let what is yours be yours," meaning you did not work for me.

Accordingly, we should explain why we need to interpret "When he prays, he should explain his words properly." It means that the person himself should scrutinize the order of his work so he will clearly know what to pray for, since sometimes a person prays for the opposite of what he needs. The prayer is the disclosure of a lack within a person, for a lack is called a *Kli* [vessel], and there is no light without a *Kli*. Hence, a person should pray so as to have a *Kli* that the Creator will fill. If there is no *Kli*, it is impossible to speak of the Creator filling the lack.

This is similar to what we pray in the Beginning of the Month Prayer: "May the Lord grant our heart's wishes favorably." "Wishes" are *Kelim* [plural of *Kli*]. When there are *Kelim*, the Creator can fill the *Kelim*. We should understand what we are saying in this prayer of the blessing of the month, "May the Lord grant our heart's wishes favorably." What does it imply that we add the word "favorably"? Would one ask for the unfavorable?

We can understand this by what *The Zohar* says, "One who prays should explain his words properly," as it is written, "Deliver me from the hand of my brother." Laban is also called "my brother," as it is written that Laban said to Jacob, "Because you are my brother." This is why he clarified, "from the hand of Esau."

According to what Baal HaSulam explained, at times the evil inclination is called Laban, and at times it is called Esau. The difference between these names relates to before the fact and after the fact. Before the fact, it is called Laban. After the fact, it is called Esau.

By this we should interpret that when a person prays for the Creator to help him since he wants to do some good deed but feels that he does not have the power to overcome, he must not pray that the Creator will deliver him from Esau, meaning to think about how he does everything not for the sake of the Creator and that his work is worthless. He should ask the Creator to deliver him from Esau's words, who says, "Your work is indeed worthy and highly regarded above, and your intention is not to work for me," meaning for the evil inclination, which is now regarded as Esau.

Instead, he wants the Creator to help him feel that he is doing everything not for the sake of the Creator, and will see the truth—that his work is worthless. It follows that if he really feels that his work is worthless, what will he gain by receiving such help from the Creator? He will certainly not succeed in doing anything good, since a person cannot work for a lost cause. Rather, one must see some benefit from the work.

This is the meaning of what *The Zohar* says, that "he should explain his words properly." It is because a person must know what he is missing so he can observe Torah and *Mitzvot*. For this reason, his prayer should be "Deliver me, I pray Thee, from the hand of Laban," meaning from what Laban would make him see, that "All that you see is mine." Laban claims that all he did was for his own sake, for the sake of the evil inclination, and his work is worthless.

At that time he prays that the Creator will give him the feeling, and that he will see that the Creator enjoys everything he does, and every little thing in spirituality is a very important matter, and we cannot appreciate its importance. Then he will have the strength to work because now he is working for a purpose, meaning that with his work, he will do a great thing for the entire world. It is as our sages said (*Kidushin*, p 40), "Rabbi Elazar, son of Rabbi Shimon, says, 'Since the world is judged by its majority, and the individual is judged by its majority, if he performs one *Mitzva* [commandment/good deed], happy is he, for he has sentenced himself and the entire world to the side of merit.'"

When he has this feeling, he certainly gets energy for the work. But if he asks, "Deliver me from the hand of Esau," it will be to his detriment. Since there is no light without a *Kli*, when a person prays, he should "explain his words properly." What is "properly"? It means that his prayer should be suitable for reception because it is to his benefit.

However, after the fact, one should shift to the left line. That is, he should examine and see if the work was really in utter completeness, and check if he has more to correct so that through the Torah and *Mitzvot* he is doing, he will achieve *Dvekut* [adhesion] with the Creator. At that time, the evil inclination dresses as Esau and tells him: "You have no flaw that anyone can point to, since everything you do is only for the Creator." This is called Esau, from the word *Assiya* [action/doing]. That is, your work is called "complete work," and there is nothing to add to it. At that time comes the prayer, "Deliver me from the hand of my brother, Esau, since I want to have the strength to examine and see what I really should correct."

If, after the fact, he asks, "Deliver me from the argument of Laban," who said that everything he did was not for the sake of the Creator, but for his own sake, which is the authority of the evil inclination, then he is controlled by Esau, meaning he is doing everything for the sake of the Creator. In that case, he would always remain with his flaws because Esau claims that he has nothing to correct and he is doing everything for the sake of the Creator. He would never be able to see the truth.

This is why *The Zohar* says that he should explain his words properly. That is, one should obtain the right *Kli* where the right help may enter, since "There is no light without a *Kli*." With this we will understand what we asked, "What does it mean that we say that the Creator should grant our heart's wishes favorably?" Would a person ask the Creator for something bad? Rather, it is that each prayer should be in its place.

What Does It Mean that the Righteous Suffers Afflictions?

Article No. 9, Tav-Shin-Mem-Het, 1987/88

The *Zohar* (*VaYeshev*, Item 11) interprets the verse, "Many are the afflictions of the righteous": "'Many are the afflictions of the righteous, and the Lord will deliver him from them all.' It is not written, 'Many are the afflictions to the righteous,' but rather 'Many are the afflictions of the righteous,' indicating that one who suffers many afflictions is righteous because the Creator wants him. And because of it, the Creator wants that person and delivers him from them all."

We should understand these words: 1) Why should the righteous suffer afflictions? 2) If afterward, "the Lord delivers him," then what is the point in afflicting the righteous if the Creator must then save him? It seems like pointless work.

It is known that the order of the work for those who want to walk on the path of truth, called *Lishma* [for Her sake], meaning in order to bestow and not for themselves, is that they want to be righteous and not wicked, called "receiving in order to receive" in the work. That is, even the acts of bestowal that they do with their intention to receive are considered wicked in the words of *The Zohar*, as it says about the verse, "'And the mercy of the nations is a sin,' for all the good that they do, they do for themselves." This means that all the good that they do, their intention is their own benefit, and this is their sin.

Conversely, those who want to serve the Creator must work only for the sake of the Creator and not for their own sake. Therefore, the nature of the creatures is only for their own sake, as it is known that the desire to do good to His creations created a lack for this purpose, meaning for the creatures to yearn to receive pleasures, for without yearning, a person cannot enjoy anything. Moreover, the extent of the pleasure depends on the measure of the yearning.

For this reason, when a person is told he must relinquish his own benefit and work for the sake of the Creator, for only by this can he achieve *Dvekut* [adhesion] with the Creator, and this is man's purpose and is considered repentance, since the quality of reception separates a person from the Creator due to disparity of form because the Creator is the giver and the creatures receive from Him what He gives them, for this reason when a person comes to a degree where all he wants is to bestow, this is called "equivalence of form." This is regarded as the creature returning to its root, meaning unites with the Creator. At that time he reaches the degree of "righteous," since he is no longer working for his own sake, but for the sake of the Creator.

Therefore, when a person does not want to work for the sake of the body, the body resists his work and does not let him do anything that is in order to bestow. When a person forgets the intention to bestow and begins to work in order to receive, he can once again continue the work. Yet according to the rule, from *Lo Lishma* [not for Her sake] we come to *Lishma* [for Her sake], an awakening from above comes to him that we must work in order to bestow. Then, he immediately encounters resistance from the body, which does not let him continue with the work of bestowal and he begins to feel the troubles that the body inflicts on him.

He repeatedly overcomes his body to some extent but then descends from his work once more and feels the bad in him. It follows that one who wants to be righteous constantly feels the afflictions that the body causes him. That is, each time he wants to do something to bestow, the wicked one comes and asks, "What is this work for you?" But when a person works for himself there is no place for the wicked to ask "What is this work for you?" because he is working for the sake of the wicked, called "will to receive for himself." It follows that the wicked's question comes specifically when he wants to work for the sake of the Creator.

Now we understand why specifically the righteous suffer many afflictions. It is because man's inclination overcomes him every day. That is, when the evil inclination sees that a person has some light, called "day," that he is on the right path, it immediately overcomes him and wants to fail him with its complaints, telling him, "What will you get from wanting to work to bestow?" And that same order happens each and every day.

This is as our sages said (*Kidushin* 40), "One should always see himself as if he is half guilty, half innocent. If he performs one *Mitzva* [commandment/good deed], happy is he, for he has sentenced himself to the side of merit." Yet, if "One should always see himself as half guilty, half innocent. If he performs one *Mitzva*, happy is he, for he has sentenced himself to the side of merit," then how can he say again, "half," since he was already sentenced to the side of merit, so why do they say "always"?

As was said, "Man's inclination overcomes him every day." The minute the evil inclination sees that now it is "day" for him, it immediately overcomes him. It follows that according to the measure of good that he did, the evil promptly overcomes him, and then he is once more "half guilty, half innocent."

This is the meaning of "overcomes him every day." That is, each day there is new overcoming. We should interpret that "man's inclination overcomes him every day" means that the bad in him is increasing, as in, "a growing stream of adding evil." For this reason, it is "One opposite the other." As soon as a person overcomes and does a good deed, the evil inclination overcomes him.

It follows that the righteous suffers many afflictions. That is, each day, the bad in him grows and according to his good deeds, so the evil becomes revealed in him. It is as our sages said, "Anyone who is greater than his friend, his inclination is greater than him."

We should understand what the words "than him" imply to us. According to what we explained, "than him," meaning the fact that his inclination has grown, comes as a result of man's growing, since he tried to be a man and not a beast. From this, the inclination grew, as well, as it is written, "One should always be half guilty, half innocent," so as to be able to defeat the evil.

It is impossible to defeat the evil at once. Hence, the evil appears to a person slowly. Each time a person does something good, there is a place to reveal some more evil. This repeats itself until a person corrects all the evil within him. It follows that this is why the righteous suffers many afflictions.

We could ask, Why does all the evil not appear in a person at once? The answer is that a person would not be able to overcome all the evil within him. Only when the bad in him is not more than the good and the two are equal, a person can overcome through the power of Torah and *Mitzvot* [commandments/good deeds]. For this reason, the bad emerges in a person gradually, meaning to the extent that he has obtained the good, some bad is revealed to him from above, until over time, all the bad in a person will be corrected.

This extends from the order of scrutinies, as it is written, that it is permitted to sort only the 288 sparks, which are the upper nine that exist in each path of the 32 paths, but *Malchut* in each path is forbidden to scrutinize. This is called the "stony heart," as in, "And I will remove the stony heart from your flesh," since it is impossible to correct this evil during the six thousand years. After the six thousand years, when the 288 sparks have been sorted, all the evil will be sorted, as it is written in *The Zohar*, "The angel of death will become a holy angel," and this is called "Death will be swallowed up forever."

In this manner, when a person corrects the evil in him, meaning the vessels of reception, so they work in order to bestow, it is impossible to correct it at once. Rather, the vessel of reception in him, which is the source of evil that separates us from the Creator, divides into many parts. This is a correction from above. By dividing into many parts, each time we correct a part into *Kedusha* [holiness/sanctity], another part immediately comes—a bigger piece than what we needed to correct before. Because a person becomes accustomed to the work, he is given a bigger piece of the evil in him to correct each time.

It is like a person practicing weight-lifting. Each day he is given a heavier weight to lift. Likewise, in the work, each day we are given a bigger piece of evil to raise. This causes us to see as if we are not advancing in the work, but are regressing. That is, each day we see that the work is growing harder to overcome. But the reason is that each day we are given a bigger piece to correct.

"The Lord will deliver him from them all." We asked, If the Lord should deliver us from the bad, why does He give us the bad, to suffer for no reason? That is, if man could overcome by himself, we could understand that it is given to man to correct. But if the Creator saves him, then what is the point of giving him many afflictions?

We already asked, Why can't a person overcome by himself and only the Creator must save? And if we are given the choice to overcome, why are we not given the strength to be able to overcome? According to what Baal HaSulam said, this is so deliberately, so that a person will ask the Creator for help, and the help He gives is that He gives him a higher soul, in order for a person to need to receive a higher degree.

Since man must attain the *NRNHY* of his soul, and without a need, meaning without a *Kli* [vessel], it is impossible to receive filling, it was deliberately made so that man should begin the work. When he sees that he cannot overcome, he must not despair but rather pray to the Creator, as *The Zohar* says, "He who comes to purify is aided. And with what? With a holy soul."

What Does It Mean that the Righteous Suffers Afflictions?

Accordingly, there are two things here: 1) A person must begin to work in bestowal so as to have a need for the Creator to help him, since if he could overcome by himself, he would not need the Creator's help. This is considered that he does not have a *Kli* [vessel], and there is no light without a *Kli*. 2) Man was not given the ability to overcome by himself. It follows that this is why he must begin but cannot finish.

By this we understand what we asked, Why the righteous deserve to suffer many afflictions? It is because the suffering that the righteous suffer from the afflictions obstructs him from achieving *Dvekut* with the Creator, and this causes him to have a *Kli*. And the reason why there are so many afflictions until he cannot overcome them, but the Creator "delivers him from them all" and a person cannot defeat them by himself, is on purpose, since the Creator cannot give a person a higher degree if he has no need for it. For this reason, the Creator gives him the parts of his soul as deliverance, as it is written, "And the Lord delivers him from them all."

For this reason, two things are required: 1) The righteous must have many afflictions, which are the *Kli*. 2) Then, He gives him the parts of the soul as deliverance.

However, normally, when people ask, they begin to ask the Creator to help them out of the evil and give them a soul over a piece that has already been recognized as evil. But why does the Creator want a person to reveal a certain measure of evil and then the Creator will help him?

This is how it seems to man. However, we should make two discernments here: 1) Indeed, the Creator helps a person by revealing to him the bad in him, so he will know the truth. 2) This is revealed only to those who are capable of walking on the path of bestowal. This is why they are shown the evil, so they will have the ability to correct it. But to people who have no connection to the work of bestowal, the evil is revealed only in general.

This is similar to what we do in this world. When a person suffers from an incurable disease, he is not told what is his illness.

Instead, he is told that he has other illnesses, but the truth, that he has a terminal illness, is not shared with him. The reason for this is simple: What will happen if he is told of the bad in him if he cannot correct it? For this reason, in spirituality, a person is shown the evil very slowly, to the extent of his ability to work.

Accordingly, if a person does not have the revelation of evil to an extent that he has a *Kli* and a need that is fit to contain a soul, it is impossible to place a soul in half a *Kli*. It is like an embryo in its mother's womb, as our sages said, "There are three partners in a person: The Creator, his father, and his mother. The father gives the white; the mother gives the red, and the Creator gives the soul."

Clearly, everyone knows that if the father and the mother do their part, a half fetus might still be born. That is, if they do their part, the embryo might be born without a head, but only a body, or vice versa, it might be born with a head but no body. Do we want to ask the Creator to do His part, meaning to give a soul to half an embryo and this is how it will be born? Of course, no one is so foolish.

It is likewise in the work of the Creator. When a person begins the work, he first begins with the white. His father and mother are called the "parents." They are the reason that a person will be born. The father is called "male," meaning "wholeness," and this is called "white," where there are no lacks. That is, he is content with his lot and thanks the Creator for any contact he may have with the work of the Creator, for rewarding him and giving him a thought and desire to have some contact with the work of the Creator. It is as our sages said, "Walks but does not do, the reward for walking is in his hand."

Afterward, he shifts to the left line, called "the mother's red." The mother is regarded as a female, a lack, criticizing his good deeds to see if they have the aim to bestow. At that time he sees the truth, that he is far from it. This gives him the need to pray that the Creator will bring him closer so he will be rewarded with *Dvekut* with the Creator. Then, a person expects, since he already has two lines and he already feels that he has a need and a *Kli*, so what else does he need? Only that the Creator will do His part, meaning give the soul.

However, if the father's white and the mother's red are still not worthy, since they have not been completed, and for example, they might produce only half a baby, the Creator certainly cannot do His part, which is to give the soul. For this reason, the Creator waits for the right and left lines to be completed, so it will be possible to create a complete thing. Then, the Creator gives the soul.

For this reason, a person cannot say that the Creator does not want to help. On the contrary, the Creator assembles each and every action until there is a complete measure, sufficient for the soul to shine in.

It is written about it in the book *A Sage's Fruit* (Vol. 1, p 196): "It is written, 'Take no rest, and give Him no rest until He establishes, and He makes Jerusalem a praise in the earth.' So we rush our pleas above, knock by knock, tirelessly, ceaselessly, and do not weaken at all when He does not answer us. We believe He hears our prayer but waits for us, for a time when we have the *Kelim* [vessels] to receive the faithful bounty, and then we will receive a reply for each and every prayer at once, since 'the hand of the Lord will not be short.'"

It follows that one should not say that he is praying every day but he is not receiving help from the Creator. Instead, he should believe that the Creator takes each prayer a person prays and adds it to the rest of the prayers that the person has prayed so far, and waits until the measure is full so it is fit to receive the soul from the Creator.

Also, we should make two discernments concerning the prayer in request for the Creator to help and give strength from above to overcome the evil: 1) A person asks the Creator to be able to admit the vessels of bestowal into *Kedusha*, meaning to have the ability to use them with the intention to bestow. 2) He asks that the Creator will give him the power to overcome the vessels of reception, too.

This is considered that he can aim with the vessels of reception in order to bestow.

By this we should interpret what our sages said (presented in RASHI, VaYeshev), "We should also explain about it, 'and [Jacob] sat,' Jacob wanted to sit in peace; Joseph's anger jumped on him. The righteous wish to sit in peace. The Creator said, 'It is not enough for the righteous that they have what is set up for them in the next world; they also wish to sit in peace in this world."

It is seemingly difficult to understand what they said, "The Creator said, 'It is not enough for the righteous that they have what is set up for them in the next world; they also wish to sit in peace in this world.'" There is an explicit *Mishnah* (*Avot*, Chapter 6:4): "Such is the way of Torah: Toil in the Torah. If you do so, happy are you in this world and happy are you in the next world." This means that there should be peace in this world, too.

We should interpret this in the work. It is known that *Bina* is called the "next world," meaning a vessel of bestowal, since everything consists of two discernments: 1) what she receives, 2) what she gives. These are called "the quality of *Malchut*" and "the quality of *Bina*," which are giving and receiving.

When a person begins the order of the work, he begins to sort out the best first. We begin to sort out and elicit the *Kelim* that are placed inside the vessels of reception, meaning that all the vessels—both of reception and of bestowal—fell during the breaking of the vessels into the *Klipot* [shells/peels], which are receivers, and in the terminology of Kabbalah, they are called *Kelim de Panim* [anterior vessels/vessels of the face] and *Kelim de Achoraim* [posterior vessels/vessels of the back].

For this reason, once the righteous have corrected for themselves the vessels of bestowal so as to have the intention to bestow, which is called "learning Torah *Lishma* [for Her sake]," this is regarded as "set up for them for the next world." The righteous do not settle for this, but want to "sit in peace in this world," namely that the vessels of reception, too, which are *Kelim de Achoraim*, called "*Kelim* of

Malchut," for *Malchut* is called "this world," will also enter *Kedusha*, meaning that they will work in order to bestow.

This is the meaning of what he says, "Jacob wanted to sit in peace; Joseph's anger jumped on him." Joseph is called *NHY*, which are *Kelim de Achoraim*, the place of disclosure of *Hochma*, which are vessels of reception, regarded as "this world." That is, the anger is that he still did not correct them so they will enter *Kedusha*. This is why he says, "It is not enough for the righteous," etc.

What Are the Four Qualities of Those Who Go to the Seminary, in the Work?

Article No. 10, Tav-Shin-Mem-Het, 1987/88

Our sages said (*Avot*, Chapter 5:17), "There are four qualities among those who go to the seminary: He who goes but does not do has the reward of going in his hand. He who does but does not go has the reward of doing in his hand. He who goes and does is a *Hassid*. He who neither goes nor does is wicked."

We should understand the following: 1) Why does he not say about one who goes and does that he has the reward of going and doing, but merely calls him a *Hassid*? 2) He says, "Four qualities among those who go to the seminary, and counts one who neither goes nor does as one of the qualities of those who go to the seminary. But he is not doing anything, so why does he count him as one of the qualities?

What Are the Four Qualities of Those Who Go to the Seminary, in the Work?

First we need to understand the reward for going and the reward for doing. It is known that it is forbidden to work for a reward, as our sages said, "Serve the Rav [great one] not to receive reward." However, we should understand what is written (Avot 2:1), "Calculate the loss of a Mitzva [commandment/good deed] opposite its reward." Thus, we do need to work for a reward, as it is written, "If you learned much Torah, you are given a great reward, and you can trust your landlord to pay for your work."

We see that the whole world works for a reward. However, reward does not necessarily mean money, which is a return for the effort. Rather, anything that a person receives in return for his work, something he needs and which will make him happy, counts as a reward. For this reason, we see that a person might work and toil for money, but one might also pay money for respect. Sometimes, a person gives money and respect in order to get his life. In other words, a reward is that which a person needs, as it is written, "Man will give all that he has for his life."

Thus, what is the reward we can receive in return for observing Torah and Mitzvot [plural of Mitzva]? It is Dvekut [adhesion] with the Creator, as it is written, "What does the Lord your God ask of you? To cling unto Him." It is written in the essay "A Speech for the Completion of The Zohar": "It is known that the desired purpose of the work in Torah and Mitzvot is to cleave unto the Creator, as it is written, 'and to cleave unto Him.'"

Dvekut means repentance. Since man was created with an inherent desire to receive for himself, which is called "separation" due to disparity of form, meaning that because of it, a person becomes far from Him, in order to achieve equivalence of form, called Dvekut, he must make great efforts in order to struggle with his nature, which is a desire to receive for himself and not to bestow. Also, the measure of bestowal that a person much achieve is "with all your heart, and with all your soul, and with all your might." He must not leave any existence for himself, to the extent that a person cannot achieve equivalence of form by himself.

Instead, what one must do is only to be as "he who comes to purify." In other words, a person should prepare a *Kli* [vessel] and a need for the Creator to help him. It is known that there is no light without a *Kli*. It follows that the measure of the labor is that a person must install within him a lack, that he is deficient of equivalence of form, called "repentance." He yearns to repent, but he is unable to achieve it by himself.

Thus, for what does he pray and labor in order to be rewarded for his labor? Only for yearning for repentance, since through the exertion he puts in order to achieve repentance, it gradually installs in him a lack and need by which a person sees that he needs the help of the Creator. At that time, "He who comes to purify is aided" comes true. *The Zohar* asks, "With what is he aided?" It answers, "With a holy soul." At that time he is rewarded with a soul, as in, "Man's soul will teach him."

By this we will understand what we asked, "Is it permitted to work and toil in order for the Creator to reward us, since they said, 'Be as slaves serving the Rav [great one] in order not to be rewarded.'" However, we should understand why it is forbidden to receive reward. It is so because a person must work in order to achieve equivalence of form. If one asks for reward for his work, then he is under the authority of self-reception. This is the opposite of equivalence of form, and why it is forbidden to work for a reward.

But one who works and toils and prays for the Creator to reward his labor, what reward is he aiming for? The reward he wants is for the Creator to give him the strength to make all his thoughts and actions be only about bestowal upon the Creator, and not for his own sake. Thus, this reward he is asking brings him to equivalence of form, which is called "repentance," when he returns to *Dvekut* with the Creator, from whom he parted.

This is similar to what he says in the book *A Sage's Fruit* (Part 1, p 116): "It is known that the soul is a part of God above. Before it comes in a body, it is as adhered as a branch to the root." It is also written there that "the purpose of the soul when it comes in the body is to be rewarded, while clothed in the body, with returning to its root and to clinging unto Him."

We therefore see that a person should try to be rewarded for his work, and the reward is repentance. That is, we do not say that a person should aim while working in Torah and *Mitzvot*, that the work will be without an intention to be rewarded. On the contrary, a person must always have a clear goal before him, as it written in *The Zohar*, "Man's prayer should be sufficiently explicit and clear." In other words, a person must know what he needs, and he should try to obtain it through labor and prayer.

However, it is known that the prayer must come from the bottom of the heart. In other words, a person must clearly know that alone, he cannot achieve repentance, which is to adhere to the Creator in equivalence of form. This awareness comes to a person only when he has done everything he could do. Then it can be said that now he knows for certain that it is out of his hands, and only the Creator can help him.

Now we will explain what we asked concerning what our sages said about the four qualities among those who go to the seminary: 1) "He who goes but does not do has the reward of going in his hand." In the work, this means that he is going on the way to achieve *Dvekut* with the Creator, called "the way of bestowal." However, he sees that he is not doing anything with the aim to bestow.

He "has the reward of going in his hand," meaning that the fact that he wants to walk on the path of truth is already considered a reward. In other words, he should thank the Creator for rewarding him with a desire to walk on the path of truth, while others, who engage in Torah and *Mitzvot*, do not have this desire. They settle for simply working, without considering their intention while engaging in Torah and *Mitzvot*, as is the general public.

2) "He who does but does not go has the reward of doing in his hand." This means that he engages in Torah and *Mitzvot* in everything he can observe, in every detail and intricacy. However,

he is not walking on the path that leads directly to *Dvekut* with the Creator. Instead, he settles for what he does without the intention. He "has the reward of doing in his hand." Although he is not going, his reward is that he should be pleased because the Creator has given him a desire and yearning to observe Torah and *Mitzvot*. He does not see any merit in himself compared to other people, to whom the Creator did not give this desire and yearning, while he did receive from the Creator this desire. He believes that everything happens through private Providence.

For this reason, he gives many thanks to the Creator for being able to have a part in Torah and *Mitzvot*, while the rest of the people were not privileged with this. This is considered that he "has the reward of doing in his hand," that he thanks the Creator. This degree applies to both the general public and to individuals. That is, those who are advancing on the individual path also have times when they do not want to be among those who are "going," so they should be happy with "doing."

3) "He who goes and does is a *Hassid*." We asked, Why in the first two discernments, it is written that he has a reward in his hand, while here in the third discernments, it does not say that he has a reward in his hand, but rather that he is a *Hassid*?

We should interpret we must know that whether he "goes but does not do" or "does but does not go," a person still has his own authority. That is, he has still not been rewarded with annulling his self-authority and inclusion in the Creator, which is called "repentance." Our sages said, "The Torah exists only in he who puts himself to death over it." We interpreted that he has annulled his self-authority and then he has only the singular authority, which is the authority of the Creator, while he himself does not even appear in reality.

Therefore, in a state of "going and doing," it cannot be said that he has a reward in his hand, since he has no hand. That is, he has no self-authority of which we can say that there is he who can receive. This is why they said *Hassid*, meaning he is in a state where he says,

What Are the Four Qualities of Those Who Go to the Seminary, in the Work?

"Mine is Yours, and Yours is Yours." There can be reward between two authorities, similar to an employee working for an employer. The employer pays him for his work.

But if a son works for his father and the son is supported by his father, meaning he is still living in his father's house and has no independence, then the son does not receive a salary from his father. However, when the son begins to think that he wants to be independent and not be dependent on his father, his father begins to pay him a salary for his work.

The same applies here in the work, when a person is rewarded with "going and doing" everything for the sake of the Creator. At that time, he has no self-authority, but rather he annuls himself before the Creator. This is called "*Dvekut* and equivalence of form," and it is called "repentance." At that time, it cannot be said that he has a reward in his hand because he has no hand to buy, meaning his own authority. This is why they did not say, "reward in his hand," but said that he is regarded as a *Hassid*.

Now we will explain what we asked when he says, "four qualities among those who go to the seminary," and one of them is "he who neither goes nor does." If he does not do anything, why is it regarded among the four qualities of those who go to the seminary?

It is known that when a person wants to work on the path to achieve *Dvekut* with the Creator, which is equivalence of form, the body objects to everything. He might come to a state where he feels that he has come to the worst lowliness, meaning he sees that he is "not going," meaning he is not advancing in bestowal, and he is "not doing" either, meaning he is unable to do good deeds, and anything he does requires tremendous efforts.

That is, now he sees that he is worse than when he began to work on the path of bestowal. Previously, he was very happy when he was doing good deeds, and especially during prayer. But now he has come to such lowliness that it is very difficult for him to pray. That is, all the things he would do with joy before he began to work on bestowal, now he sees them as lowly.

Now he feels the meaning of "*Shechina* [Divinity] in the dust," meaning that all the sacred things have the form of dust, namely they taste like dust. Every little thing he does is unbearably hard because it has lost its value. Thus, now he sees that he has regressed, meaning he is neither going nor doing. It is about this that our sages said that he is wicked.

However, the question is, Why has he come to this state after all the efforts he has made because he wanted to walk on the path of truth? According to what Baal HaSulam said, the time of answering the prayer, for man to receive permission to enter the King's palace so that He will bring him closer to Him and he will be rewarded with *Dvekut* with the Creator, is specifically when a person sees that, he is lost and powerless to do anything. At that time a person gives a real prayer, since he sees that he is simply wicked. That is, he has no grip on *Kedusha* [holiness/sanctity].

For this reason, when a person comes into a descent, he should not be startled and escape the campaign. On the contrary, this is the time to make a heartfelt prayer.

In this regard, we should interpret what our sages said (*Hulin* 7b), "Israel are holy. Some want and do not have." RASHI interprets that some want to please others with what he has but is unable to, and from him, I do not want to enjoy. "Some have and do not want." RASHI interprets that he has the ability but does not want to delight others. "So said Rabbi Pinhas to Rabbi."

The question is, Why is the one who has but does not want to give to others regarded as holy? The *Tosfot* explains, "He who has but does not want, even so they are called 'holy,' for he invites his friend to eat at his place because of shame."

We should interpret "Israel are holy" in the work. There is he who wants to work in order to bestow but does not have. When he considers his actions, he sees that he is immersed in self-love and cannot do anything in order to bestow. He is called "holy" because he is walking on the path of truth. Although he sees that he is regressing, he still clings to the path of truth. In the end, he will touch the truth, meaning that he is truly in *Dvekut* with the Creator. Because the most important are the *Kelim* [vessels], called "desire," and since he wants to achieve *Dvekut*, he will be rewarded.

It is as Baal HaSulam said about what is written, "Will give wisdom to the wise." He asked, "It should have said, 'Will give wisdom to the fools.' However, 'wise' is he who desires wisdom. Then he has a *Kli* [vessel] in which to bestow. But fools have no desire for wisdom whatsoever, as it is written, 'the fool has no desire for understanding.'"

It follows that one who wants to walk on the path of *Kedusha* is called holy. "Holy" means as it is written, "You will be holy," which means that they retire from self-reception. For this reason, he is holy. This is the meaning of the words, "Israel are holy; there is he who wants but does not have." And there are also those who have but do not want. This means that he has *Mitzvot* and good deeds, but he does not want to walk on the path that leads to "in order to bestow." Instead, he settles for *Lo Lishma* [not for Her sake]. He, too, is called "holy," since the act is fine and he has nothing to add in actions.

What Are the Two Discernments before Lishma?

Article No. 11, Tav-Shin-Mem-Het, 1987/88

The *Zohar*, Exodus, asks about the verse, "These are the names of the sons of Israel who are coming to Egypt with Jacob; they came each one with his household." Why does it begin with Israel and end with Jacob? It explains there in relation to the upper degrees. We should understand the meaning of the two degrees during the period of preparation, too, before a person is rewarded with *Lishma* [for Her sake]: "Israel" implies wholeness, since Israel is *Li-Rosh* [a *Rosh* (head) unto me], and Jacob is a smaller degree.

The order is that a person begins the work of the Creator in *Lo Lishma* [not for Her sake]. At that time the work he does is in practice, meaning without the intention, which should be to bestow. Therefore, in the practice, a person sees that he is making good progress, and each day his possessions of Torah and *Mitzvot* [commandments/good deeds] increase. A person feels that he is in a state of ascent, since he sees that he is rising in degree, meaning he sees that he is accumulating more each time.

In that state he receives vitality in his work from the Surrounding Light, which shines for everyone, meaning the light that shines for the whole of Israel, as it is explained (in *The Study of the Ten Sefirot*, Part 1) that the Surrounding Light shines even for the vessels of reception. Conversely, the Inner Light shines specifically to the vessels of bestowal, since the first restriction, which was over *Behina Dalet* [Phase 4], not to receive light within it, caused the light to depart from the *Kli* [vessel], for the light was shining in the interior.

Concerning the Surrounding Light, it is explained in *Panim Masbirot* that "The fourth is the Surrounding Light itself, since now *Ein Sof* [infinity/no end] illuminates bestowal from its place in remoteness from the place. That is, since the point of desire of *Behina Dalet* has been diminished and contained no will to receive, she lost her vessel of reception and could not receive within her the light of *Ein Sof* as before, and the middle point became removed from the light. For this reason, we call this "Removal of place to *Ein Sof*."

This means that the light of *Ein Sof* shines as surrounding even in places where the *Kli* is still unfit to receive in order to bestow. Rather, this is called "restricted illumination." Conversely, the Inner Light shines abundant bestowal, as explained there.

For this reason, in the state of *Lo Lishma*, a person feels that he is regarded as Israel. But when a person wants to begin the work of bestowal, meaning to have *Kelim* to receive Inner Light, when he wants to emerge from self-love, then he comes into the exile in Egypt. That is, then a person sees how he is remote from *Dvekut* [adhesion] with the Creator in equivalence of form. Instead, whether in mind or in heart, the *Klipa* [shell/peel] of Egypt governs.

In that state, he sees that he is far from being Israel. Instead, he is in a state of Jacob, a state of *Katnut* [smallness/infancy] from the words *Akev* [heel] and *Sof* [end]. In other words, he is in utter lowliness, seeing that each day, he is farther from the Creator and has no grip on *Kedusha* [holiness/sanctity].

This is called the "exile in Egypt." This is the meaning of Pharaoh coming to a person and asking, "Who is the Lord that I should obey His voice?" That is, each time, thoughts of Pharaoh come and ask him this question, and a person has but one counsel, to cry out to the Creator to help him out of these thoughts, which are a concealment that hides the faith in the Creator. This is also called *Metzar-Mi* [narrow/distress-who], when *Mitzraim* [Egypt] ask, "Who is the Lord that I should obey His voice?" This is *Metzar-Yam* [narrow-sea].

In that state, he is always in doubt. This is the meaning of the words, "who are coming to Egypt," meaning *Metzar-Koh* [narrow/distress-Creator]. "With Jacob" means that they have come to the degree of *Akev* [heel], the *Sof* [end] and conclusion of *Kedusha* [holiness/sanctity], which they felt in the *Koh* [Creator] when they had to take upon them the kingdom of heaven. They regretted not being able to do so because of the questions of Pharaoh, King of Egypt, who governed them with the "who" and "what" questions, which are regarded as "mind" and "heart," meaning "Who is the Lord that I should obey His voice," and "What is this work for you?"

This is the meaning of the words, "From the narrow place, I called on *Koh* [the Lord]." The prayer is because they suffer troubles from the Egyptians, as it is written, "And they cried out to the Lord in their distress; He will save them from their afflictions." It is known that *Tzar* [narrow/distressing] means narrow in *Hassadim* [mercies]. That is, they could not engage in bestowal. In other words, when they wanted to take upon themselves the kingdom of heaven—called *Koh*—in order to bestow, they felt narrowness [also troubles], that they could not do anything in *Hesed* [mercy].

The difference between bestowing and working in order to receive is great. When we want to use the vessels of reception, we can derive delight and pleasure from the fact that sparks of light, called "vessels of reception," were placed in the *Klipot* [shells/peels] from the beginning, so that the world would exist. For this reason, when a person wants to use the vessels of reception, he has a place from which the pleasures called "slim light" extend and shine in the world so it may exist.

But when a person does not want to use the vessels of reception, but he has not obtained vessels of bestowal, he is in an uncomfortable state. He still does not have the place from which to draw delight and pleasure. Hence, when he wants to work in bestowal and receive delight and pleasure in vessels of bestowal, since he still does not have vessels of bestowal, when he feels the exile he cries out, "From the narrow place, I have called on *Koh* [the Lord]; answer me in the wide expanse, *Koh*." "Wide" means expansive in *Hassadim*, when the Creator helps him with the quality of *Hassadim*, meaning gives him vessels of bestowal.

This is regarded as emerging from the exile in Egypt and entering redemption, in that now he can work in order to bestow because he already feels the importance of the greatness of the Creator, since he has vessels of bestowal, called "equivalence of form." This is so because when the Creator gives him the expansion of the vessels of bestowal, the *Tzimtzum* [restriction] and concealment are removed from him, which he had through the power of the control of the *Klipa* of Egypt with their questions and dominations. Now, however, he receives the kingdom of heaven not as something "narrow," as before, but "expansively." This is the meaning of "Answer me in the wide expanse, *Koh*." At that time it is regarded that he has been rewarded with work *Lishma*.

It follows that we should make two discernments in the work even before we achieve *Lishma*. The first is Israel, when he feels that he has wholeness, as in *Li-Rosh* [a head unto me]. This applies to the work of the general public, at which time he receives the general surrounding, which shines from afar. That is, even when a person is still remote from the Creator, meaning he is still immersed in his will to receive for himself, even in this *Lo Lishma* there are pleasures that are mixed together with his work. These are pleasures he receives from other people who respect and honor him, etc., which he receives from people because they know that he is working for the Creator. Here he receives the pleasure of "slim light," which is given to corporeal pleasures, which are generally called "envy," "lust," and "honor." Because of it, they feel themselves as whole, as Israel.

The second discernment is when he begins to enter the work of *Lishma*. At that time he begins to go down to the exile in Egypt, and the body begins to betray the person and does not let him do this work by asking all kinds of questions that cannot be answered within reason, while above reason, a person cannot always overcome it. At that time he begins to feel ascents and descents because each time, he is shown from above what is the work of bestowal and not for his own sake. Although every person understands this, when it comes from above, when he is given the understanding, he comes to feel it. This is when the work with "mortar and bricks" begins, when they feel the hardships of the enslavement of the exile.

According to the above, we should interpret "And the king of Egypt died." This pertains to the work for their own sake, called the "*Klipa* of the King of Egypt." They have stopped working for him, meaning they felt that working for themselves, called "the control of the king of Egypt," is regarded as death. Instead, they took upon themselves to work for the sake of the Creator, but then they had no power to work because the king of Egypt governed them.

It follows that they do not work for their own sake, yet cannot work for the sake of the Creator. This is the meaning of the verse, "And the children of Israel sighed from the work, and they cried out, and their cry rose up to God from the work." That is, what is the meaning of "and they cried out"? It is that "their cry rose up" pertained to "God from the work." That is, the fact that they wanted their work to be for the sake of God and not for their own sake, but could not do the work, this was their cry.

It is known that there is no light without a *Kli*. In other words, it is impossible to give something to someone by force, as it is known that there is no coercion in spirituality. Therefore, when a person is afflicted and suffers pain and suffering from not being able to emerge from self-love and work only for the sake of the Creator, he cries out to the Creator to help and give him what he wants. That is, if the Creator gives him this: the ability to revoke his own authority and annul before the authority of the Creator, for he wants only the singular authority to be in the world, namely the authority of the Creator; this is his only salvation. This is considered that he has a *Kli* and a need for the Creator's help.

This is the meaning of the words, "And God heard their groaning." That is, once they had a *Kli*, which is a desire and need to have the ability to work for the sake of the Creator, then comes the time when "God heard their groaning," meaning that then the redemption began—delivering them from under the afflictions of Egypt.

However, it is known that we must walk on two lines, meaning on the right line, too. This means that a person must thank the Creator for letting him see what he was lacking. In other words, the fact that his suffering is from being remote from the love of the Creator, that these are his troubles and pains, whereas other people, the Creator does not give them this suffering, but their troubles and suffering are from being unable to satisfy their corporeal needs, which pertain to self-love, meaning that they are as beasts and have no idea of anything other than self-reception. For this they were in gladness and gratitude to the Creator.

However, this is hard work, since the left line cancels the right line. Hence, there is always new work to rebuild it. This is the meaning of the words, "And they made their lives bitter with hard work with mortar and with bricks." Their work was with *Homer* [mortar], meaning on the left line, when they saw the gravity of their situation, how remote they were from the love of the Creator. Afterward, the work on the right line is to be in gladness because the Creator showed them the truth about the state that they are in. This is called *Levenim* [bricks].

What Are Torah and Work in the Way of the Creator?

Article No. 12, Tav-Shin-Mem-Het, 1987/88

Our sages said (*Avot*, Chapter 2, 2), "Raban Gamliel, son of Rabbi Yehuda Hanasi, says, 'It is good to learn Torah with work, for exertion in both, mitigates iniquities, and any Torah with which there is no work is ultimately canceled and induces iniquity.'" This verse is very perplexing to understand literally. Can it be that one who learns Torah without working alongside, the Torah stops being Torah? Moreover, Torah with which there is no labor induces iniquity!

The previous verse is also difficult to understand. Why is it that specifically exertion in both mitigates iniquity? After all, our sages said (*Kidushin* 30), "I have created the evil inclination, I have created for it the Torah as a spice." They did not say that in order to revoke the evil inclination, the Torah also requires labor in order to revoke the evil inclination.

We should interpret this in the work. It is known that the evil and iniquity is primarily the nature in which man was created, whose origin is the dust, as it is written after the sin of the Tree of Knowledge (Genesis 3:19), "For you are dust, and to dust you shall return."

Dust is *Malchut* (as it is written in *The Study of the Ten Sefirot*, Part 16, Item 43, *Ohr Pnimi*); it is the will to receive for one's own sake. On this desire was a *Tzimtzum* [restriction] and concealment, which means that this place became a space vacant from light. That *Tzimtzum* was in order not to have the bread of shame. Rather, to the extent of equivalence of form, the concealment is removed and upper light comes instead of it.

For this reason, Maimonides says that when beginning to teach women and children and uneducated people, they are accustomed to learn *Lo Lishma* [not for Her sake]. When they gain knowledge and acquire much wisdom, they are taught that secret, meaning *Lishma* [for Her sake]. This is so because *Lishma* contradicts our nature, as we were born with a desire to receive for ourselves. For this reason, the only way to begin with Torah and *Mitzvot* [commandments] is in *Lo Lishma*. However, through *Lo Lishma* we come to *Lishma*, as it is written, "By engaging in it, the light in it reforms them" (*Midrash Rabbah, Pticha de Eicha*).

It therefore follows that the whole work that we must do is to invert our will to receive so as to aim to bestow. But this work is very difficult, and it is also called "work." That is, normally, the smaller one annuls before the greater one, and there is great pleasure in the smaller one serving the greater one. Accordingly, each one should have had a desire to serve the Creator in order to bring contentment to the Creator. Yet, this work is hard to keep, as well, and this is called "It is good to learn Torah with work."

This is so because of the *Tzimtzum* and the concealment that was on the will to receive. For this reason, the light does not shine in this place, but there are rather darkness and concealment here in the vessels of reception for oneself. Hence, it is upon the person to take upon himself everything in faith above reason. Yet, this, too, is difficult because our will to receive is not used to doing things against reason. In order to be able to emerge from the control of the will to receive for himself, our sages said, "The Creator said, 'I have created the evil inclination; I have created the Torah as a spice,'" meaning that "the light in it reforms him."

Concerning "the light in it reforms him," it is written in the book *A Sage's Fruit* (Vol. 2, p 159): "The majority of the words of the Torah are for study. This reconciles why the Torah speaks at length on parts that do not concern the practical part but only the study, meaning preceding the act of Creation," etc., "and, needless to say, legends and commentaries. Yet, since they are where the light is stored, his body will be cleansed, the evil inclination subdued, and he will come to faith in the Torah and in reward and punishment. ...Clearly, when one ponders and contemplates words of Torah that pertain to the revelation of the Creator to our fathers, they bring the examiner more light than when examining practical matters. Although they are more important with respect to the actions, with respect to the light, the revelation of the Creator to our fathers is more important. ...Since the whole of the wisdom of Kabbalah speaks of the revelation of the Creator, naturally, there is no better teaching for its task. This is what the Kabbalists aimed for—to arrange it so it is suitable to engage in."

It follows that we engage in the Torah in order to subdue the evil inclination, meaning to achieve *Dvekut* [adhesion] with the Creator, so that all our actions will be only in order to bestow. That is, by ourselves, we will never be able to go against nature, since the mind and heart that we must acquire require assistance, and the assistance is through the Torah. It is as our sages said, "I have created the evil inclination; I have created the Torah as a spice. By engaging in it, the light in it reforms them."

However, this was said—that it is beneficial to elicit the light from the Torah—if he aims while engaging in the Torah, to learn in order to receive the reward of the Torah, called "light." At that time, the learning of Torah is good for him. But when he is distracted from the purpose of studying Torah, the Torah does not help complete the work of making the vessels of bestowal and not using the vessels of reception for one's own sake. Otherwise, his Torah vanishes from him. That is, the force of Torah and that should have subdued the evil inclination is cancelled. This is the meaning of the words, "Any Torah with which there is no work," meaning when he does not aim for the Torah to do the work of turning the vessels of reception to work in order to bestow, "is finally cancelled," meaning that that force is cancelled.

However, we should understand why the Torah induces iniquity. Is it not enough that the Torah is cancelled, but it also induces iniquity? Can this be? The question is presented in the "Introduction to The Study of the Ten Sefirot" (Item 39): "We need clarification so as to understand how and through what the Torah becomes a potion of death to him. Not only is he toiling in vain ... but the Torah and the work itself become to him a potion of death."

There (in "The Study of the Ten Sefirot," Item 101), he says, "It is written that the Creator hides Himself in the Torah. Regarding the torments and pains one experiences during the concealment of the face, one who possesses few transgressions and has done little Torah and *Mitzvot* is not as one who has extensively engaged in Torah and good deeds. This is because the first is quite qualified to sentence his Maker to the side of merit. ...For the other, however, it is very difficult to sentence his Maker to the side of merit because in his view, he does not deserve such harsh punishments."

Accordingly, we can understand why he says, "Any Torah with which there is no work is finally cancelled and induces iniquity." It is so because on one hand, he sees that he engages in Torah and *Mitzvot*, so why does the Creator not treat him as he thinks he deserves? Therefore, there are two things here: 1) It is finally cancelled. 2) It causes iniquity.

For this reason, prior to the study, a person should examine with which purpose does he want to observe the *Mitzva* [commandment] of learning Torah? That is, does he engage in Torah because of the Torah itself, in order to know how to observe the rules of doing the *Mitzvot*, or is the learning of Torah itself his whole intention, and knowing the rules of doing the *Mitzvot* is a completely different matter for him? meaning he is learning Torah for two reasons.

However, even while learning Torah for the sake of learning Torah, he should still distinguish with which intention he is learning. Is it to observe the commandments of the Creator, as it is written, "And you shall reflect on Him day and night," or is he learning in order to receive the light of Torah because he needs the light of Torah in order to cancel the evil within him, as our sages said, "I have created the evil inclination; I have created the Torah as a spice"? It turns out that he is learning in order to obtain the spice, as our sages said, "The light in it reforms him."

Certainly, prior to learning Torah, a person should examine the reason for which he is learning Torah, for any act needs to have some purpose that causes him to do the act. It is as our sages said, "A prayer without an aim is as a body without a soul." For this reason, before he comes to learn Torah he must prepare the intention.

This is what he says there, in the "Introduction to the Study of Ten Sefirot" (Item 17): "Hence, prior to the study, the student must pledge to strengthen himself in faith in the Creator and in His guidance in reward and punishment ... In this way, he will be rewarded with benefitting from the light in it, that his faith, too, will strengthen and grow through the remedy in this light. Thus, even one who knows about himself that he has not been rewarded with faith, still has hope through the practice of Torah. For if one sets one's heart and mind to attain faith in the Creator through it, there is no greater *Mitzva* than that. ...Moreover, there is no other counsel but this."

It therefore follows that a person must make a great effort before he comes to learn so that his learning will bear fruit and good results, meaning so the learning will bring him the light of Torah, by which it will be possible to reform him. Then, through the Torah, he becomes a wise disciple.

What is a "wise disciple"? Baal HaSulam said that it is a student who learns from the wise. That is, the Creator is called "wise," and a person who learns from Him is called a "disciple of the wise." What should one learn from the Creator? He said that a person should learn only one thing from the Creator. It is known that the Creator wishes only to bestow. Likewise, man should learn from Him to be a giver. This is called a "wise disciple."

According to the above, we should interpret what our sages said (*Nedarim* 81), "Why are no wise disciples emerging from among them? Rabina says, 'It is because they do not bless in the Torah first.'" We should understand these words in the work, meaning that it all applies to one body. Hence, we should interpret the question, "Why are no wise disciples emerging from among them?"

It is known that "father" and "son" are called "cause" and "consequence." That is, the first state causes the second state. Accordingly, when a person learns Torah, this is called a "wise disciple." Also, we learned that "the light in it reforms him." What does "reforming" mean? It is as our sages said, that the Creator said, "I have created the evil inclination; I have created the Torah as a spice, which cancels the evil inclination." When the evil is cancelled, and evil is the will to receive for himself, he becomes a wise disciple, according to the interpretation of Baal HaSulam.

For this reason, the answer to the question, "Why are no wise disciples," which is the first state, "emerging from among them?" That is, the second state does not emerge from them, which is that he should become a disciple of the wise, to be rewarded with all his actions being only in order to bestow.

But there is a rule, "The light in it reforms him," and we do not see that the wise disciple has the ability to elicit sons who are wise disciples. To this comes the answer that they did not bless in the Torah first.

Yet, this answer is also difficult to understand. We see that anyone who comes to study, first says the blessing of the Torah before the learning. Thus, how can they interpret that the reason they are not begetting sons who are wise disciples is that they did not bless in the Torah first?

We should interpret the words, "they did not bless in the Torah first." Since we see that one who is going to make a substantial purchase, where through the merchandise that he will buy he will make great profits, his friends bless him with luck in this activity. That is, that he will make a lot of money.

It is likewise here in the work. When a person comes to learn Torah, there should be a purpose before his eyes, namely the reason he is going to study. Clearly, it is in order to benefit from the study of Torah, for without a benefit it is impossible to work. Hence, he must know that the purpose, meaning the benefit he needs to acquire from the Torah is "the light in it," which "reforms him."

In the work, where we speak of one body, he should bless himself with success in his learning and with obtaining much light from the Torah that he is now going to learn. Otherwise, if he does not bless prior to learning Torah, he does not remember the goal he must elicit from the learning, which is called "sons." The sons are the result of the study, as was said, that the Torah is the reason, the father, and the light he elicits from the Torah is the son.

Accordingly, prior to learning, each and every one must contemplate the purpose of the study, meaning why he exerts in the Torah. Certainly, one should not exert without reward, and certainly, when a person learns Torah, he believes in "You can trust your landlord to pay for your work" (*Avot*, Chapter 2, 21). But to which reward is he aiming? He should pay attention to keep the reward always before him, meaning to have confidence and faith that the Creator will pay his reward.

The reward he hopes to receive should give him energy to work. That is, the reward is the fuel on which his work is based. Clearly, the greater the reward, the more energy there is to work. But if the reward is not so important, that reward cannot give him the strength to work devotedly, meaning to make him see that the Torah is so important, as it is written, "For they are our lives and the length of our days." Certainly, if a person feels this way, that it is truly the

Torah of life, each person, according to his feeling, would give his whole life to obtain life.

However, feeling the vitality in the Torah requires great preparation to prepare his body to be able to feel the life in the Torah. This is why our sages said we must begin in *Lo Lishma*, and through the light of Torah he obtains while still in *Lo Lishma*, it will bring him to *Lishma*, since the light in it reforms him. Then, he will be able to learn *Lishma*, meaning for the sake of the Torah, which is called "Torah [law] of life," as he has already attained the life in the Torah, for the light in the Torah will have given such qualification to a person as to be able to feel the life that is in the Torah.

In the "Introduction to the Study of Ten Sefirot" (Item 38), he asks, "Why is complete engagement in Torah and *Mitzvot* regarded as Torah *Lishma*? We should understand this title, Torah *Lishma*, why the complete and desirable work is titled *Lishma*. According to the literal meaning, one who engages in Torah and *Mitzvot* must aim his heart to bring contentment to his maker and not for his own sake. This should have been named and defined as Torah *Lishmo* [for His sake] and Torah *Lo Lishmo* [not for His sake], meaning for the Creator. After all, the text proves that Torah *Lishmo*, meaning to bring contentment to one's maker, is still not enough. Instead, we also need the engagement to be *Lishma* [for Her sake], meaning for the sake of the Torah, for it is known that the name of the Torah is 'Torah [law] of life,' as was said, 'For they are life to those who find them' (Proverbs 4:22). As was said, 'It is not a vain thing for you, for it is your life' (Deuteronomy 32:47). Therefore, the meaning of Torah *Lishma* is that engagement in Torah and *Mitzvot* brings him life and longevity, for at that time the Torah is as its name."

According to the above, it implies that once a person has reached the degree of bestowing contentment upon his maker, as this is regarded as engaging in Torah and *Mitzvot* for His sake, then begins a second degree, when he engages in Torah and *Mitzvot* for Her sake, meaning for the sake of the Torah, as the name of the Torah is "Torah of life."

In order for a person to achieve a degree of doing everything for the Creator, called Torah *Lishmo* [for His sake], it requires the light of Torah, for this light reforms him. That is, he will be able to emerge from self-love and do everything for His sake. Only this light can help him, as our sages said, "I have created the evil inclination; I have created the Torah as a spice." That is, once he has been rewarded with the light of Torah, he can be rewarded with the Torah itself, called "Torah of life."

Accordingly, we should interpret what our sages said, "Should one tell you, 'There is wisdom in the gentiles,' believe. 'There is Torah in the gentiles, do not believe'" (*Eicha Rabbah* 2, 17). When a person learns Torah, he should discern two things in it: 1) the wisdom and the intellect in it, called the "clothing of the Torah," 2) who is wearing the clothing of the Torah.

We must believe in the words of *The Zohar* that the whole Torah is the names of the Creator, meaning that the Creator is clothed in the clothing of the Torah. Hence, we should discern two things in the Torah: 1) the clothing, 2) the one who wears it.

It is as it is written in the book *A Sages Fruit* (Vol. 1, p 118): "However, the Creator is the light of *Ein Sof*, clothed in the light of Torah that is found in the above 620 *Mitzvot*. ...This is the meaning of their words, 'The whole Torah is the names of the Creator.' It means that the Creator is the whole, and the 620 names are parts and items."

It follows that one who has faith in the Creator can believe that the giver of the Torah is clothed in the Torah. Conversely, a gentile, who has no faith in the Creator, how can he learn Torah, since he does not believe in the giver of the Torah? He can learn only from the clothing of the Torah, but not from the one who wears it, since he has no faith. The outer clothing is called "wisdom" and not "Torah," since Torah is specifically when he is connected to the giver of the Torah.

By this we understand what our sages said, "Should one tell you, 'There is wisdom in the gentiles,' believe." It is so because they can learn the clothing with the one who wears it, which is only called "wisdom," without any connection to the giver of the Torah. But "Should one tell you, 'There is Torah in the gentiles,' do not believe," since they have no connection to the giver of the Torah.

Since the essence of our work is to achieve *Dvekut* [adhesion] with the Creator, as it is written, "to cling unto Him," it follows that the Torah is the means to adhere to Him. That is, while learning Torah, we should aim to be rewarded with connecting to the one who wears it. This is done through the clothing, which is the Torah, in which the Creator is clothed.

In the above-mentioned verse, "There is wisdom in the gentiles, believe, there is Torah in the gentiles, do not believe," when we interpret this in the work, we should know that "gentiles" and "Israelis" are in the same body. That is, before a person is rewarded with faith, he is still regarded as a "gentile." Only after he is rewarded with faith, he is called "Israel."

However, if a person wants to achieve complete faith, although he has still not been rewarded with complete faith, he is already regarded as Israel. It is as Baal HaSulam said about "Let wisdom be given to the wise." He asked, Should it not have said, "Let wisdom be given to the fools"? He said that a person who seeks wisdom is already called "wise" because any person is judged by his goal, meaning by what he expects to achieve, after this a person is called. Accordingly, we should interpret that all those who want to achieve complete faith are already called "Israelis."

For this reason, if in the beginning of his study, when a person comes to study, there is no desire to thereby achieve complete faith, which he can achieve through the light in the Torah by wanting to adhere to the one who wears it, who is clothed in the Torah and gives the light of Torah and none other, it follows that he is learning Torah, which is the clothing of the Creator. Through it, he wants to achieve complete faith, adhere to the one who wears it, who is the giver of the Torah.

Here there is unification of three discernments: 1) the Torah, which is the clothing of the Creator, 2) the Creator, who is clothed in the Torah, and 3) Israel, the person who is learning Torah with the above intention.

This is called "unification," called "the Torah and the Creator and Israel are one." Although *The Zohar* speaks to those who have already been rewarded with "the names of the Creator," which is called that they have been rewarded with a "hand *Tefillin*," called "faith," and a "head *Tefillin*," called "Torah," yet, those who walk on the path of achieving Torah and faith also receive a surrounding from this unification.

Now we can understand what is written, "There is wisdom in the gentiles, believe." That is, if a person does not aim to be rewarded with faith in the Creator through the study of Torah, then he has no connection to the Torah, since Torah means the clothing and the one who wears it together, namely the Torah together with the giver of the Torah.

Although he still does not feel the giver of the Torah, still, the purpose of the study is to come to feel the giver of the Torah. If a person does not place the goal of reaching the giver of the Torah in front of him, he is regarded as a gentile, meaning one who has no need for faith. That is, he should have the need to seek advice to achieve faith. This is why he is still considered a gentile and not "Israel." Hence, regarding wisdom, believe that he has it, meaning only the clothing without the need for the one who wears it. This is the meaning of the words, "there is Torah in the gentiles, do not believe," since he has no connection to the Torah.

However, believing or not believing also does not refer to two bodies. Rather, believing or not believing refers to the person himself. The person himself must pay attention to whether or not he has Torah. Since a person exerts and makes efforts, the intention is certainly to be rewarded with the Torah. The person thinks that even without the aim to achieve complete faith he can be rewarded with the Torah. Our sages said about this that one should know that it is impossible to be rewarded with the Torah without complete faith.

For this reason, prior to the study, a person must pay attention and introspect with which aim he is making his effort in learning Torah. That is, what does he want to achieve by learning Torah? Certainly, when a person makes an effort, it is because he lacks something. Through his effort, he will be given what he thinks he needs and his lack will be satisfied in return for the toil. A person should believe what is written, "I labored and found."

For this reason, sometimes a person understands that what he lacks is the knowledge of Torah. Hence, all his thoughts are toward being rewarded with the knowledge of Torah. This is the clothing of the Creator, and he feels that all he needs is the outer clothing of the Torah. This is called "wisdom."

But Torah means that he needs the one who wears, who is clothed in the Torah. That is, he still lacks complete faith in the Creator and he feels that there is evil in his heart, and he wants to be rewarded with the mind and heart that will be all for the sake of the Creator.

Since our sages said, "The Creator said, 'I have created the evil inclination; I have created the Torah as a spice because the light in it reforms it,'" it follows that he needs the Torah as a means, where through the Torah he will be rewarded with complete faith in the Creator. Afterward, through the Torah he will be rewarded with the Torah that is called "Torah of life," since he will be rewarded with the one who wears together with the clothing.

That is, he will be rewarded with the clothing called "Torah," together with the one who wears it, called "the Creator." It is as *The Zohar* says, "The Torah and the Creator and Israel are one."

This is the meaning of what is written (*Midrash Rabbah, Truma*, Chapter 33), "'And let them take for Me a contribution.' You have merchandise that he who sells it is sold with it. The Creator said to Israel, 'I have sold to you My Torah [law]. It is as though I have been sold with it,' as was said, 'And let them take for Me a contribution.'"

According to the above, we should interpret the words of the Midrash where it says, "It is as though I have been sold with it." The Torah is regarded as "The Torah and Israel and the Creator are one," since the Torah is the clothing of the Creator, and through the Torah, man must be rewarded with the one who wears it, which is called "adhering to the Creator," it follows that we must be rewarded with two things: the Torah and the Creator. This is the meaning of what is written, "It is as though I have been sold with it."

For this reason, there is completeness of three things here: 1) Israel, 2) the Creator, and 3) the Torah. It is as it is written in the book *A Sage's Fruit* (Vol. 1): "What can a person do in order to come to feel the need for the Torah, in which the Creator is clothed? It is our sages said, that the Creator said to Israel, 'I have sold you My Torah. It is as though I have been sold with it.' This is the meaning of having a merchandise that one who sells it is sold with it."

This means that the Creator wants that when a person takes the Torah, he will seemingly take the Creator with him. Yet, a person does not feel he needs this. Primarily, a person takes after the majority. And since when beginning to teach women, children, and the general public, Maimonides says we should begin in *Lo Lishma*, and normally, everyone takes after the beginning, meaning that the reason they were given for why we need the Torah are reasons of *Lo Lishma*, and not because "I have created the evil inclination; I have created the Torah as a spice." Naturally, the majority of the world does not even understand that there is a reward called "*Dvekut* with the Creator."

For this reason, the view of the majority controls a person—that he does not need to study Torah so that by this he will be able to achieve the real intention. That is, that through the Torah he will be able to aim in order to bestow and not for his own benefit, that it will bring him *Dvekut*, to adhere to the Creator. For this, meaning in order to correct the creatures so they achieve *Dvekut*, the multiplicity of worlds, *Partzufim*, and souls were made.

It is all in order to correct creation, called "will to receive." Through the reception, creation has moved away from the Creator, and by these corrections that were made, it will be possible to correct everything so it works in order to bestow. When all the vessels of reception work in order to bestow, this will be the end of correction.

This is called "the perfection of His deeds," as the holy ARI said (*The Study of the Ten Sefirot*, Part 1), "When it came up in His simple will to create the worlds and emanate the emanations, to bring to light the perfection of His deeds, His names and appellations, which was the reason for the creation of the worlds, *Ein Sof* restricted Himself and there was room where the emanations could be." There (*The Study of the Ten Sefirot*, Part 1), he interprets in *Ohr Pnimi* as follows: "It follows that the very reason for the *Tzimtzum* [restriction] was only the craving for the new form of reception in order to bestow, which is destined to be revealed by the creation of the worlds."

Accordingly, we see that the creation of the worlds and souls was primarily with one intention—to correct everything so that it works in order to bestow, which is called *Dvekut*, equivalence of form. The Creator said about the Torah, "I have created the evil inclination; I have created the Torah as a spice." That is, once man receives the Torah as a spice, the evil inclination will be corrected to work in order to bestow, as it is written in *The Zohar*, "The angel of death is destined to be a holy angel."

A person cannot see all this because he takes after the majority, called "the whole of Israel." It was said that the beginning of the education everyone receives is in *Lo Lishma*, meaning that the engagement in Torah and *Mitzvot* is in order to receive reward in *Kelim* [vessels] of self-benefit, and the *Lishma* is forbidden to reveal to a person upon the admission of a person into the observance of Torah and *Mitzvot*, as mentioned in the words of Maimonides.

This causes a person to understand with his intellect that he needs to learn Torah only in order to know the rules, how to observe the *Mitzvot*, as our sages said, "An uneducated person is not a *Hassid*." Although they also learn Torah that does not pertain to practical *Mitzvot*, learning that part of the Torah is because of the commandment to learn Torah, as it is written, "And you shall reflect on it day and night." That is, he learns because it is a *Mitzva*, just like the rest of the *Mitzvot*.

However, concerning what our sages said, "You have a merchandise that one who sells it is sold with it," when the Creator said to Israel, "I have sold you My Torah, it is as though I have been sold with it." To this, one has no connection, for what will it give him if he believes that the Creator is clothed in the Torah? Should one who takes the Torah know that the Creator is clothed in the Torah, and he should be rewarded *Dvekut* with the Creator, who is clothed in it?

All of his work is with the intention *Lo Lishma*, and all he hopes for is to observe Torah and *Mitzvot* with the intention for self-benefit. Naturally, he has no connection to the one who is clothed in the Torah, but rather settles for just one thing: To the extent that he has faith in reward and punishment, to that extent depends his work in observing Torah and *Mitzvot*, since he looks at nothing but the reward. But the essence of the Torah and *Mitzvot* that he performs does not interest him.

Conversely, if a person wants to work and observe Torah and *Mitzvot* without any reward, only because he wants to serve the King, then he needs to know the greatness of the King, for the measure of his work depends on the extent of his faith in the greatness of the King, for only the greatness and importance of the King gives him fuel for work.

It is as it is written in *The Zohar* about the verse, "Her husband is known at the gates." It means that each according to what he assumes in his heart. By this, he tells us that to the extent that a person assumes in his heart the greatness and importance of the Creator, to that extent he dedicates himself to serving the King.

For this reason, people of this kind, who want to work only in order to bestow, and the whole reason that compels them to engage in Torah and *Mitzvot* is the importance and greatness of the Creator, as it is written in *The Zohar* that "The essence of fear is to work because He is great and ruling," when these people believe that the Creator is clothed in the Torah, and believe what the Creator said to Israel, "I sold you My Torah; it is as though I have been sold with it," when they learn Torah they want to elicit the light of the Torah that reforms him. This is the meaning of what our sages said, "He who comes to purify," through the Torah, "is aided," since the Creator is clothed in the Torah.

Accordingly, we should interpret what we say ("Everlasting Love," prior to reading the *Shema*), "Enlighten us in Your Torah." It seems as though the words "Enlighten us," should be said of a place of darkness and concealment, but in regard to the Torah, it should have said, "Let us understand Your Torah," so what is "Enlighten"?

According to the above, we should interpret that since we should discern within the Torah, the clothing of Torah, in which the Creator is clothed, and this is concealed from us because we see only the clothing, and not the one who wears it, we therefore ask the Creator to enlighten us so we may be rewarded with seeing and feeling the Creator, who is clothed in the Torah. This is the meaning of "Enlighten us," that we may see that You are clothed in Your Torah.

We should also understand what is said in *The Zohar* about the verse, "They who seek Me will find Me." They asked about this, "Where do you find the Creator?" They said that you find Him only in the Torah. Also, they said about the verse, "Indeed, You are a God who hides," that the Creator hides Himself in the holy Torah.

It is written in the "Introduction to The Study of the Ten Sefirot" (Item 41) concerning what our sages said, "You have merchandise that he who sells it is sold with it." This means that the Creator is clothed in the Torah, except a person must seek and find Him since He hid Himself in the Torah as long as the learners of Torah are unworthy of it. But through the labor and prayer, they find Him.

It was said about this, "I labored and found." The question is, What is the connection between laboring and finding in the Torah? Through the labor, we find the Creator, how He is clothed in the

Torah. This means that one should not say, "I learned much Torah but I do not find the Creator, how He is clothed in the Torah." Instead, we should seek Him and not despair, but believe what is written, "They who seek Me will find Me," since the concealment is a correction that a person will not attain Him before he has vessels of bestowal, which is called "equivalence of form" and "*Dvekut* with the Creator."

Accordingly, we should interpret what our sages said (*Nedarim* 81), "Be careful with the sons of the poor, for from them Torah will emerge," as was said, "Water will flow from his bucket," for from them Torah will emerge. It seems to mean that Torah will emerge specifically from the sons of the poor, but from the sons of the rich it will not. Can we say this?

In the work, we should interpret that "poor" is as our sages said (*Nedarim* 41), "One is poor only in knowledge." For this reason, when a person learns Torah and wants to achieve the Torah, meaning to a state of "Enlighten us in Your Torah," meaning to adhere to the Creator, who is clothed in the Torah, for "Your Torah" refers to the Creator, who is clothed in it. Yet, he sees that as much as he has exerted and worked to find the Creator in the Torah, he cannot find Him. Although it is written, "They who seek Me will find Me," he sees that he is poor in knowledge. Yet, he wants to keep what is written, "Know the God of your father and serve Him," and what is written, "A soul without knowledge is not good," but he is far from it, for each time he sees that it is utterly impossible to find Him in the Torah. This is called "poor in knowledge."

At that time a person understands that finding the Creator in the Torah was not said for him, since he thinks that he has already looked for Him in the Torah but has found nothing, and he wants to escape the campaign.

This is why our sages came and said, "Be careful with the sons of the poor, for from them the Torah will emerge." The reason is according to the rule, "There is no filling without a lack, no *Gadlut* [greatness/adulthood] without *Katnut* [smallness/infancy]." This means that if we want to give something to a person but the giver is afraid that if he is given immediately, as soon as the receiver asks of him, the receiver will not be able to appreciate the giving and will probably lose it, or other people might take that thing from him.

Since the giver knows the importance of the matter, he does not want the receiver to spoil it. For this reason, he does not give him what he asks immediately. Instead, he wants the receiver to ask him many times. Thus, through the demand, a need for the matter is formed in the receiver. Otherwise, he would have had to stop asking.

When he does not stop asking him, this can be only if each time he must understand the necessity of the matter. That is, if he wants to ask of him again—that the giver will give him—a person must contemplate whether he really needs that thing, for only then does he have the strength to ask again, once he has already asked but received no answer to his question.

This is so because a person cannot ask of someone who takes no interest in his requests. However, since the thing that he is asking is necessary, and his whole life depends on it, the necessity of the matter does not let him rest and he goes even above reason to ask time and time again. He has nowhere else to go because he understands that this is his life and without it, he says his life is pointless, since he has come to feel that it is not worth living for other things.

It follows that he has no choice since he has no satisfaction in his life. That is, since there is a rule that a person cannot live without provision, since the Creator created the creatures with the intention that they will enjoy, which is called "His desire to do good to His creations," and the three things that can give a person provision—to sustain the body so it is satisfied, and which are called "envy," "lust," and "honor"— do not satisfy him, for this reason a person must seek spirituality. If he is a Jew, he believes that through *Dvekut* with the Creator and His law he can obtain provision, to provide for the body and be able to say wholeheartedly, "Blessed is He who said, 'Let there be the world,'" since he enjoys it if he is rewarded with *Dvekut* with the Creator, as it is written, "And you, who cling unto the Lord your God, are alive everyone of you today," for then he will be rewarded with real life.

This gives him the strength not to despair from asking the Creator to bring him closer and open his eyes in the Torah. It is written in the "Introduction to The Study of the Ten Sefirot" (Item 83), "The first degree of the revelation of the face comes to a person only through His salvation, when he is rewarded with opening of the eyes in the holy Torah with wonderful attainment, and he becomes like a never ending stream."

However, this depends on the extent to which he believes that the Creator hears a prayer and can justify Providence and say what he thinks, that he did not receive what he asked for not because the Creator did not pay attention to his prayers, but he believes that the Creator stands and waits for his prayers and collects them, as in, "Penny by penny join into a great amount."

In other words, since it is known that if you give something important to a person who does not know its value, and there are people who do know its importance, that thing will move to those people either by theft or by losing it, for the person will not know how to keep it, and there are people who know its value and they will steal or find it and not return it to the owner.

It is known that opposite *Kedusha* [sanctity/holiness] there is the *Sitra Achra* [other side], who do know the value of spirituality. For this reason, there must be keeping so it does not come into their authority. This is why the Creator does not give him what he wants, but stands and waits. By prevailing each time with faith above reason to ask the Creator to help him and open his eyes in the Torah, and he believes in faith in the sages, who said that working on faith is the best way to be rewarded with the importance of the goal, which is *Dvekut* with the Creator. When the Creator knows that he already knows how to keep the King's present, the Creator will certainly help him and grant his prayer, which is his request that the Creator will open his eyes and he will be rewarded with opening the eyes in the Torah, and He will certainly give him.

This is the meaning of the words, "Be careful with the sons of the poor." That is, do not underestimate the situation where he feels that he is poor in knowledge because he has not been rewarded with opening the eyes in the Torah and he has not been rewarded with "The light in it reforms him," since "from them, Torah will emerge." That is, he should believe that by feeling that he is poor in knowledge, and each time he must overcome, he must believe that these descents come to him from the Creator, and by this he will receive the vessels and the need to appreciate the gift of the Creator from the outer ones, meaning that not everything will fall into the vessels of reception, which are *Kelim* [vessels] that belong to the *Klipot* [shells/peels]. By overcoming with faith that the Creator hears a prayer, and each and every prayer that he asks of the Creator, the Creator adds it to the great amount until a person knows the value of the matter.

This is the meaning of what is written in the book *A Sage's Fruit* (Vol. 1, p 88): "For this reason, this *Klipa* [singular of *Klipot*] is called Pharaoh, with the letters [in Hebrew] *Peh Ra* [evil mouth]. In the exile in Egypt, that *Peh Ra* had control and they returned to their bad ways. For this reason, even though they were rewarded with some illumination from the upper nine, it could not be swallowed in the *Guf* [body] because the *Peh Ra*, which is the opposite of the *Peh* [mouth] of *Kedusha*, namely the back of the neck, stopped the abundance that came down from the *Rosh* [head] and sucked all the abundance that began to come down for Israel."

It therefore follows that we should make several discernments in the Torah: 1) one who learns Torah in order to know the rules, to know how to observe the *Mitzvot* of the Torah, 2) one who learns Torah in order to observe the *Mitzva* of learning Torah, as it is written (Joshua 1), "This book of Torah shall not move from your mouth, and you shall contemplate it day and night." RASHI interprets "contemplate it" as "looking in it," every thought in the Torah is in the heart, as he said, "The contemplation of my heart is before You." 3) He learns Torah in order to be rewarded with the light of the Torah, as it is written, "I have created the evil inclination; I have created the Torah as a spice because the light in it reforms him." By this he will be rewarded with faith, and to adhere to the Creator, and then he will become "Israel" for he believes in the Creator in complete faith. 4) Once he has been rewarded with faith, he is rewarded with the "Torah, as in the names of the Creator." In *The Zohar*, this is called "The Torah and Israel and the Creator are one." At that time he is rewarded with the purpose of creation, which is to do good to His creations, when the creatures receive what the Creator wants to give to the creatures.

And concerning what RASHI interpreted about the verse, "You shall contemplate it day and night," he says "look in it. Every thought in the Torah is in the heart." We should understand what he means by saying that the thought is in the heart, since when we learn Torah, it is in the mind and not in the heart, so why does he tell us, "Every thought in the Torah is in the heart"?

We should interpret that this does not pertain specifically to the Torah that relates to rules he learns in order to know how to observe the *Mitzvot*. Instead, he wishes to say that the Torah also includes the last two discernments just mentioned: 1) that he learns in order to receive the light of Torah, 2) that he is then rewarded with the Torah, called "the names of the Creator."

Those two belong specifically to the heart, as Rabbi Abraham ibn Ezra says (in the "Introduction to the book Panim Masbirot," Item 10), "Know that all the *Mitzvot* that are written in the Torah or the accepted ones, which the forefathers have established, although the majority of them are in deed or utterance, they are all in order to correct the heart. This is because the Lord wants all the hearts, and He understands the inclination of every thought. It is written, 'To those whose hearts are straight,' and conversely, 'a heart filled with thoughts of transgression.' Know that the Torah was given only to men of heart."

We should interpret the words of RASHI, as Rabbi Abraham ibn Ezra says. Accordingly, we should note about the above four discernments, that the last two pertain to the work of the individual, while the first two pertain to the general public. It is as Maimonides says, "When teaching children, women, and uneducated people, they are taught to work only out of fear and in order to receive reward. Until they gain knowledge and acquire much wisdom, they are taught that secret little by little, and are accustomed to it calmly until they attain Him and serve Him with love."

We see from the words of Maimonides that the beginning of the work of the general public is in *Lo Lishma* and in order to receive reward. Therefore, they must learn Torah in order to know the rules how to observe the *Mitzvot*. This is the first discernment. Also, his learning of Torah is in order to know with the intellect what is written there, that he will be rewarded through the *Mitzva* of learning Torah. This is the second discernment. Those two do not belong to the work of the heart, as said in the words of Rabbi Abraham ibn Ezra.

But the last two discernments already pertain to the heart because they pertain to *Lishma*. When one wants to walk on the path of *Lishma*, he is shown, as Maimonides says, that "What we told you before, that you should learn *Lo Lishma* but in order to receive reward, was because by nature, a person cannot work for the sake of the Creator, but only for his own sake. Therefore, now we are telling you that you must know that the real work is *Lishma*. But how do you achieve this? The advice is "From *Lo Lishma* we come to *Lishma* because the light in it reforms him."

The question is, What is the evil we should correct so as to be good? We are told that it is our inability to do anything for the sake of the Creator. Only the light of Torah will correct the heart, for the heart is called "desire," and by nature, it is a desire only to receive. But how can a person go against nature?

This is why the Creator said, "I have created the evil inclination; I have created the Torah as a spice." It follows that he is not learning

Torah for the intellect, to understand, but he is learning in order to understand so as to achieve *Dvekut* with the Creator, who is clothed in the Torah, and this pertains to the heart. Through the light he will receive, it reforms him, meaning that the will to receive for his own sake can receive strength from above that enables it to work for the sake of the Creator.

It follows that when he wants to begin the work of *Lishma*, which pertains to the work of the individual, he is shown that learning *Lo Lishma* is not the end of the road, as he first thought, in the beginning of his learning. Rather, the learning *Lo Lishma* should aim to bring him into learning *Lishma*. For this reason, once he has learned about the intention to achieve the aim to bestow by receiving the light of the Torah, he comes to the fourth discernment in the study of Torah, called "Torah of life."

It is written (*Avot*, Chapter 6), "Rabbi Meir says, 'Anyone who engages in Torah *Lishma* is rewarded with many things and the secrets of Torah are revealed to him.'" This means that then he is rewarded with the "Torah, which is the names of the Creator." This is what *The Zohar* calls, "The Torah, and Israel, and the Creator are one."

Accordingly, we should make two discernments in the Torah, which pertain to the heart: 1) The light of Torah pertains to establishing faith in the heart. This is the meaning of "The light in it reforms him." 2) Torah that pertains to the heart, as it is written (Exodus 28:2), "And you shall speak to all the wise-hearted whom I have filled with the spirit of wisdom." In the words of *The Zohar*, this is called, "One who does not know the ways of the upper one and the commandments of the upper one, how will he serve Him?"

It is written about it in the book *A Sage's Fruit* (Vol. 1, p 119), "Hence, you'd best grip unto the goal of yearning for the commandment of the upper one, for one who does not know the ways of the upper one and the commandments of the upper one," which are the secrets of Torah, "how will he serve Him?"

Thus, the meaning of "Torah and work" is that he learns Torah in order for the Torah to bring him the light of Torah. By this, he will be able to invert the vessels of reception to work in order to bestow, and with these *Kelim* he will be rewarded with *Dvekut* with the Creator, called "learning Torah *Lishma*."

By this we can interpret what our sages said (*Kidushin* 40), "A good thought, the Creator adds it to an act." When a person learns Torah in order to come to actions, meaning an act of making the vessels of bestowal, since a person cannot do this by himself due to the evil in his heart, when the Creator sees that a person has a great yearning for this act, the Creator gives him the light of Torah, which reforms him. This is the meaning of "the Creator adds it to an act." That is, now He does the act. By giving him the light of Torah, an act results.

Accordingly, we see that in truth, from man came nothing more than a good thought. That is, he thought that vessels of bestowal were a good thing. But in truth, who did the work for man to be rewarded with these *Kelim*? Only the Creator—by giving him the light of Torah, which is the one who wears, who is clothed in the Torah.

This is why it is written, "A good thought that a person has, the Creator makes it so there will be an act here, too." It is as our sages said, "He who comes to purify is aided." It turns out that on the part of man, there is nothing more than coming to purify, which is called a "good thought." Afterward, the Creator gives him the assistance, adding it to an act.

In light of the above, we should interpret what is written, "And you will speak to all the wise-hearted, whom I have filled with the spirit of wisdom." We asked, What is the connection to the wise-hearted, since wisdom pertains to the mind? The thing is that we should make two discernments in the Torah, which pertain to the *Lishma*: 1) *Kli*, 2) light.

The *Kli* that is fit to receive the light must be in equivalence with the light, for on this was the *Tzimtzum* and the concealment. We learned that *Malchut de Ein Sof*, which is the root of the creatures, desired *Dvekut*, called "equivalence of form," and all the corrections are only about performing this correction, to correct the vessels of reception so they work in order to bestow.

Therefore, a person who is born with the will to receive and wants to correct it into working in order to bestow, since this is against nature, he has only one counsel: Only the light of Torah can invert him into working in order to bestow, as it is written, "I have created the evil inclination; I have created the Torah as a spice," and the light in it reforms the heart. It is said that "evil" is receiving for one's self, and "good" is when his heart is only about bestowal and not about reception.

For this reason, those who engage in Torah not necessarily in order to know the rules and customs how to observe the *Mitzvot*, but have another, exalted role, that they are learning Torah in order to correct the heart, these are called "wise-hearted," since everything is named after its action. For this reason, the Torah they learn with this intention is called "wise-hearted" and not "wise-minded," since they need the Torah in order to correct the heart.

In this way we should interpret what is written, "Whom I have filled with the spirit of wisdom." Once they have *Kelim* that are suitable for the light, where as the light that comes from above is to bestow, so the *Kli* should aim to bestow, since they already have this *Kli*, which they have obtained through the light of Torah, they are called "wise-hearted," since they learned Torah in order to correct the heart. That is, they have suitable *Kelim*; therefore, they should receive the Torah, which is called "Torah of life."

This is the meaning of the words, "whom I have filled with the spirit of wisdom," pertaining to the light. That is, the light, too, goes to the heart because once they have acquired new *Kelim*, called "vessels of bestowal," and they want to bestow contentment upon the Creator, they see that only one thing is missing in the King's house. Since our sages said (*Midrash Rabbah, Beresheet*), "The Creator said to the angels when He came to create *Adam HaRishon* and the angels slandered him, What is this like? Like a king who has a tower filled abundantly but no guests. What pleasure has he from his work?"

Therefore, when a person wishes only to bring contentment to the Creator, his heart, which wants to enjoy giving something to the King, to please Him, finds only one thing that the King can enjoy—that they will receive from Him the delight and pleasure that He wishes to give to the creatures. Since there is a tower filled abundantly, and he wishes to be the Creator's guest, he should come into the tower and receive from Him delight, as this is the King's pleasure. It follows that the light of Torah that a person wants to receive as "Torah of life" is for man's heart, so he will have something with which to delight the King.

This is the meaning of the words, "And you will speak to all the wise-hearted, whom I have filled with the spirit of wisdom." That is, the spirit of wisdom filled him. Whom? The wise-hearted. This pertains to the light, for the light comes to the wise-hearted. The heart is called "desire," and it wants to receive the Torah of life in order to thereby delight the Creator, as in the allegory about the king who has a tower filled abundantly but no guests.

According to the above, we should interpret what our sages said (*Berachot* 58a), "He would say, 'A good guest, what does he say? What trouble has the host gone through for me, and all his trouble were only for me.'"

It is known that it is possible to be a guest only where there is a host. Therefore, when a person believes in the Creator, that He is the landlord of the world, and a person feels that he is a guest, yet wants to adhere to Him, as our sags said about the verse, "And to cling unto Him," which means "cling unto His attributes: as He is merciful, so you are merciful," this is called a "good guest."

The meaning of "good" is as is written (Psalms 85), "My heart overflows with a good thing; I say, my work is for the King." It means that all of his actions will be only for the King, meaning for the Creator. This is called "a good thing." When all his actions are in order to bestow, then he is regarded as "wise-hearted," and comes to a state of "Torah of life," which is the names of the Creator, where the delight and pleasure that He wished to give to the creatures is found.

At that time, he says, "Everything that the host did, he did only for me," and not at all for himself, as in the allegory about the king who has a tower filled abundantly but no guests. Now we can interpret the "secrets of Torah," meaning which secret the Torah reveals.

We should interpret this in two discernments: 1) The Torah reveals something new to a person, which he did not know before. This is so because man is born with a nature of wanting to receive. When told to work with a desire to bestow, it is to him unimportant and despicable. The body wants to run away from such desires, since it can only lose if it uses the vessels of bestowal.

However, when a person learns Torah with the aim to be rewarded with the light of Torah because this light reforms him, this light of Torah reveals something new to him, which he did not know before. That is, now he knows the complete opposite of what he thought before. Before he was rewarded with the light of Torah, he knew that what is important to man is primarily the vessels of reception, for with the vessels of reception he can receive the joys of life in this world. Conversely, with acts of bestowal he can only do good to others, that they, too, will enjoy the world through his help.

However, this is only for the purpose of *Mitzva*, because he feels sorry for others who cannot provide for themselves, and he is helping them. Certainly, he expects those people whom he benefits not to be ungrateful and respect him.

But now, by being rewarded with the light of Torah, which reforms him, something new has been revealed to him: By using the vessels of reception, he loses life and delight and pleasure for himself. If he uses the vessels of bestowal for the sake of others, he will receive *true* delight and pleasure for himself. Only through vessels of bestowal does he gain for himself delight and pleasure, whereas with vessels of reception he loses delight and pleasure. This secret has now been revealed to him through the light of the Torah.

By this we can interpret what our sages said (*Pesachim* 50a), "I saw an opposite world, the upper ones below, and the lower ones above." We should interpret that something new has been revealed to him: What is regarded as "upper ones" in the world of falsehood, meaning vessels of reception, which is an important thing called "upper ones," in the world of truth, meaning when one is rewarded with the light of Torah, regarded as being "rewarded with the truth," then we see the lower ones above.

In the world of falsehood, the vessels of bestowal are regarded as having inferior importance and are degraded. Sometimes, when a person must work with them, he tastes in them the taste of lowliness, since he does not see what the will to receive for himself gains from them. But there, in the world of truth, they are of superior importance because only through them it is possible to acquire any delight and pleasure. Therefore, it turns out that the lower ones are of superior importance.

This is the meaning of the words, "upper ones below." The vessels of reception are appreciated in the world of falsehood, for we use only the vessels of reception for ourselves because we think that through them we can enjoy. But in the world of truth, when one is rewarded with the light of Torah, we see something new that has been revealed—the vessels of reception only cause us losses in life. They interfere with our attainment of the delight and pleasure. It turns out that the upper ones are of inferior importance. This is the secret for which the Torah is called the "secrets of Torah," as it reveals the truth to man.

2) The Torah reveals that the name "secrets of Torah" is given for before he attains the vessels bestowal through the light of Torah, he attains only the clothing of Torah, where the Creator is clothed in the clothing. Now, the one who wears, who is clothed in the Torah, also becomes revealed to a person. This Torah is called "Torah of life," which is the names of the Creator. This is called "the Torah and Israel and the Creator are one."

By this we will understand what we asked, What are Torah and work, in the work? The answer is that he learns Torah in order to be able to do the work, which is called "which God has created to do." That is, the creatures must do the work of turning the will to receive into a desire to bestow, by which they will have *Dvekut*, which is equivalence of form, and they will also be able to receive the delight and pleasure, which is the purpose of creation.

What Is "the People's Shepherd Is the Whole People" in the Work?

Article No. 13, Tav-Shin-Mem-Het, 1987/88

It is written in *The Zohar* (*Beshalach*, Item 68): "'And Moses said to the people, 'Do not fear; stand by and see the salvation of the Lord.'' Rabbi Shimon said, 'Happy are Israel that a shepherd such as Moses walks among them. It is written, 'And He remembered the days of old, Moses is His people.' 'And He remembered the days of old' is the Creator. 'Moses is His people,' since Moses was tantamount to the whole of Israel. We learn from this that the people's shepherd is really the whole people. If he is rewarded, the whole of the people are righteous; and if he is not rewarded, the whole of the people are not rewarded and are punished because of him.'"

We should understand this in the work, where we learn everything in one body, meaning that both Moses and Israel are in the same body. We should also understand why if he is not rewarded, meaning the people's shepherd, they are punished because of him. We learned that if the shepherd is righteous, the people are also righteous. But why should the people be punished because of him? What did they do that they are to blame for the fault of the shepherd?

It known that *The Zohar* calls Moses "the loyal shepherd." Baal HaSulam interpreted that he was nourishing the people of Israel with faith. He said that man does not lack any power in order to be able to observe Torah and *Mitzvot* [commandments/good deeds] in full, but only faith. To the extent that he has faith, to that extent he can exert in the work.

He says in the "Introduction to The Study of the Ten Sefirot" (Item 14): "I once interpreted the saying of our sages, 'He whose Torah is his trade.' The measure of his faith is apparent in his practice of Torah because the letters of the word *Umanuto* [his trade] are the same [in Hebrew] as the letters of the word *Emunato* [his faith]. It is like a person who trusts his friend and lends him money. He may trust him with a pound, and if he asks for two pounds he will refuse to lend him. He may also trust him with all his property without a hint of fear. This last faith is considered 'whole faith,' and the previous forms are considered 'incomplete faith.' Rather it is partial faith." Thus, we see that man lacks no power but only faith, and this is what gives man the power to work.

By this we can interpret what Rabbi Shimon said, "Happy are Israel that a shepherd such as Moses walks among them." It means that the people of Israel have within them faith, which is called "Moses, the faithful shepherd." Then, since they have faith, they have the strength to engage in Torah and *Mitzvot*. In other words, within every person there is faith in the Creator, which is called "Moses, the faithful shepherd." At that time the whole people are righteous, meaning that all of man's organs, namely his thoughts and desires, which are called "organs," and this is called "a people."

This is the meaning of what is written, "'And He remembered the days of old' is the Creator. 'Moses is His people,' since Moses was tantamount to the whole of Israel." We learn from this that "the people's shepherd is really the whole people," for the faith in man is the whole of man. That is, if he has the quality of Moses, which is called "faith," then the whole people are righteous. This is why he says, "If he is rewarded, the whole people are righteous," for "rewarded" means that his shepherd is faith, called Moses.

He says, "If he is not rewarded, the whole people are not rewarded and are punished because of him." It is known that if there is a righteous, he protects the generation, and if there is no righteous, we can say that there is no one to save the generation. Yet, why are they punished because of him if he is not rewarded? Why is it the generation's fault?

According to the rule that Baal HaSulam said, all the heaviness in the work of the Creator is only the lack of faith, since when a person is rewarded with complete faith, he yearns to annul before the Creator as a candle before a torch. Naturally, all his organs, meaning his thoughts and desires, follow what faith obliges him to do, they do it. This is why he says that if he is rewarded, all the organs are righteous, since thoughts and desires of the righteous extend from faith in the Creator.

Accordingly, it is obvious that if the people's shepherd is not rewarded, meaning that his faith, which should be cleansed, meaning complete faith, yet he has only partial faith, as it is written ("Introduction to the Study of the Ten Sefirot," Item 14), "the whole people are not rewarded." This means that all his organs do things that are suitable for those without complete faith. "They are punished because of him," meaning that it is not their fault that they have thoughts and desires unfit for one who has faith.

That is, if their shepherd had complete faith, the organs would listen to him and would have thoughts and desires of a righteous. This is why they suffer because of him, since he does not have complete faith. This is why such thoughts are born out of this shepherd.

Therefore, when a person wants to walk on the path of truth, he cannot say that he has worse qualities than others, and less intellect than others. That is, he cannot exempt himself from the work because he has a weak character or no talent. Instead, the only difficulty in the matter is the lack of faith. For this reason, a person should do all his work and all his actions in order to acquire faith in the Creator, for only this gives everything.

For this reason, when a person learns Torah or engages in *Mitzvot*, or when he prays, he should focus his thoughts on wanting reward for all his good deeds—that the Creator will give him complete faith. This is as it is written in the prayer of Rabbi Elimelech ("A Prayer before a Prayer"): "And do fix Your Faith in our hearts forever and ever, and let Your Faith be tied to our hearts as a stake that will not fall." This is the meaning of "The people's shepherd is really the whole people."

In order to achieve complete faith, they said, "He who comes to purify is aided." The reason is that since faith requires assistance from the Creator, and there is a rule, "There is no light without a *Kli* [vessel]," it means that it is impossible to fill up a place where there is no lack, which is called a need, namely a *Kli*, as he said, "there is no light without a *Kli*."

In order to come to feel the need for faith, a person must first imagine what benefits he can derive through faith, and what he loses when he has only partial faith. First, he must depict to himself the purpose of creation, meaning for what purpose the Creator created creation. Then, he must believe in the sages, who said that the purpose of creation is to do good to His creations.

When a person begins to examine creation with his eyes, meaning which form of good and doing good he sees that the creatures are receiving from Him, the opposite view appears to man. He sees that the whole world suffers torments, and it is hard to find one person who can say that he feels and sees how His guidance is in the form of good and doing good.

In that state, when he sees a dark world, and he wants to believe above reason that the Creator behaves with the world in Private Providence as good and doing good, he remains standing on this point, and all kinds of foreign thoughts come into his mind. Then, he must overcome above reason, that Providence is good and does good. At that time he receives a need for the Creator to give him the power of faith that he will have the strength to go above reason and justify Providence.

Then he can understand the meaning of "*Shechina* [Divinity] in the dust," since then he sees that where he should do something for the Creator and not for his own sake, the body promptly asks, "What is this work for you?" and does not want to give him strength to work. This is called "*Shechina* in the dust," meaning that what he wants to do for the sake of the *Shechina* tastes to him like dust and he is powerless to overcome his thoughts and desires.

At that time a person realizes that all he lacks in order to have strength to work is that the Creator will give him the power of faith, as said above (in the prayer of Rabbi Elimelech), that we must pray, "And do fix Your Faith in our hearts forever and ever." In that state, he comes to the realization that "If the Creator does not help him, he cannot overcome it."

Now we can interpret what our sages said (*Berachot* 6b), "Any person in whom there is fear of heaven, his words are heard," as it was said, "In the end, all is heard, fear God." This is difficult to understand literally. After all, there were many prophets and righteous and great people, so why were their words not heard, but Israel remained in their state and would not listen to those who admonish? In the literal, there are probably many explanations to this.

However, in the work, where we learn the whole Torah in one body, we should interpret this verse. One who wants his body, meaning all the organs, which are the thoughts, desires, and actions, to be purely sacred, the advice for this, for the body to obey all his demands, is to obtain complete faith, which is called "fear of heaven."

There are many degrees in faith, as it is said in *The Zohar* ("Introduction of The Book of Zohar," Item 191), "Fear, which is the most important, is when one fears one's Master because He is great and ruling, the essence and the root of all the worlds, and everything is considered nothing compared to Him." Interpreting the words teaches us that there are three manners in fear of the Creator, only one of which is regarded as real fear: 1) He fears the

Creator and observes His commandments so his sons may live, and he will be kept from bodily punishment or a punishment to his wealth. This is a fear of punishments in this world. 2) He fears punishments of Hell, as well.

Those two are not real fear, for he does not keep the fear because of the commandment of the Creator, but because of his own benefit. It follows that his own benefit is the root, and fear is a derived branch of his own benefit.

3) Fear, which is the most important, means that he fears the Creator because He is great and rules over everything. He is great because He is the root from which all the worlds expand.

It follows that the most important point about fear or heaven is to believe in the greatness of the Creator, for the greatness and importance of the Creator is the reason that commits him to observe Torah and *Mitzvot*, and not for his own sake. It is as he says there, "And he will place his heart and desires in that place called 'fear.' He will cling to fear of the Creator willingly and eagerly, as is befitting and proper with the King's commandment."

When a person is rewarded with such faith, meaning that he feels in his heart the greatness of the Creator, the body and all the organs, meaning the desires, thoughts, and actions, annul before the King as a candle before a torch.

The Need for Love of Friends

Article No. 14, Tav-Shin-Mem-Het, 1987/88

There are many merits to it:

1) It brings one out of self-love and to love of others. It is as Rabbi Akiva said, "Love your friend as yourself is the great rule of the Torah," since by this he can come to love the Creator.

However, we should know that loving others or working for the sake of others is *not* the purpose of creation, as the secular understand it. The world was not created for one to do good to another. Rather, the world was created for each one to receive pleasure for himself. Saying that we must work for the sake of others is only the *correction* of creation, not the *purpose* of creation. The correction is that in order to prevent the matter of shame, there was a correction of bestowal, which is the only way for the creatures to receive the complete delight and pleasure for themselves without the flaw of shame.

In that regard, we should interpret what *The Zohar* says about the verse, "'The mercy of the nations is a sin;' all the good that they do, they do for themselves."

We can interpret "all the good," meaning the acts of mercy that they do, as referring to their intention, which is called "for them," meaning for themselves. This means that it is according to their own understanding and not as we were told to observe, according to "love your friend as yourself," as a commandment of the Creator, who created the world with the aim to do good to His creations. The *Mitzvot* [commandments] we were given are only to *cleanse people*, by which they will achieve *Dvekut* [adhesion] with the Creator. This will help them receive delight and pleasure, and they will remain in *Dvekut* with the Creator.

2) When the friends unite into a single unit, they receive strength to appreciate the purpose of their work—to achieve *Lishma* [for Her sake]. Also, the rule by which they were brought up is, as Maimonides said, "Women, children, and uneducated people are taught to work out of fear and to receive reward. Until they gain knowledge and acquire much wisdom, they are taught that secret bit by bit."

And since we must wait "until they acquire much wisdom" to tell them that they need to work in *Lishma*, and a great number among the masses naturally remains in *Lo Lishma* [not for Her sake], and since the minority naturally annuls before the majority, when the friends wish to walk on the path that leads to *Lishma*, to avoid annulment before the collective, the friends unite and each one is dedicated to the others. Their aim is *to achieve love of the Creator, which is the purpose, through the love of others*, as it is written, "And you shall love the Lord your God with all your heart and with all your soul."

It follows that by becoming one collective, although it is a small collective, they are already regarded as a collective, and this collective is not enslaved to the majority of the collective. Thus, they can work on love of friends with the aim to achieve the love of the Creator.

Although the commandment to love your friend as yourself applies to the whole of Israel, the whole of Israel are not walking on the path of coming from love of others to love of the Creator. Also, there is a rule that when people unite they absorb each other's views, and the matter of *Lishma*—the essential aim of Torah and

Mitzvot—has not yet been fixed in a man's heart, meaning that the main intention is that through observing Torah and *Mitzvot* they can achieve *Lishma*. Hence, by bonding with others, the views of the others weaken his view of *Lishma*. For this reason, it is better to serve and to bond with the kind of people who understand that "love your friend as yourself" is only *a means to achieve the love of the Creator*, and not because of self-love, but his whole aim will be to benefit the Creator. Hence, one should be careful in bonding and know with whom one bonds.

This is the benefit of love of friends in a special group, where *everyone has a single goal—to achieve love of the Creator*. But when bonding with regular people, although they engage in Torah and *Mitzvot*, they are not on the path of achieving the aim to bestow upon the Creator, since they were brought up in order to receive, called *Lo Lishma*. Hence, if they unite with them, they will adopt their views and will say that it is not worthwhile to walk on the path of *Lishma* because *Lishma* is more difficult than *Lo Lishma*, since *Lishma* is against nature. For this reason, one should be careful not to bond with people who have not acquired much wisdom and have not come to know that the essence of the work of the Creator is for the sake of the Creator and for their own sake.

But the matter of "love your friend as yourself" applies to the whole of Israel. Yet, we were given the keeping of knowing in advance with whom to bond. The reason is that before a person is rewarded with exiting self-love, he always feels that it is hard. This is because the body resists it, and if he is in an environment of a group of people who are united under one view, that considers the goal and not the work, then his goal will not weaken in him.

But if he is not always together with his friends, it is very difficult for one to hang on to the goal of bestowal. He needs heaven's mercy not to weaken in his mind, which previously realized that it was better to work and to walk on the path of the work of bestowal.

Yet, all of a sudden he gets thoughts that it is better to follow the crowd, that one should not be an exception, although while he was united with the friends he thought differently. It is as we said above: While he is not bonded with the collective of the small group, he immediately surrenders to the collective of the masses and absorbs their views that it is enough to observe Torah and *Mitzvot* in all its details and precisions, and to aim that we are observing the King's commandment, who commanded us through Moses and through the sages following him. We are content with this, since we will receive reward for this, and we believe in our sages who told us, "You can trust your landlord to pay you for your work," and why should we think about anything more than that? As they say, "If we observe this, we are content."

It is as Rabbi Hananiah Ben Akashiah says, "The Creator wished to cleanse Israel, therefore, He gave them plentiful Torah and *Mitzvot*." This means that all the Torah and *Mitzvot* we were given are so we may have a great reward.

Thus, now the person has become smarter than while he was united in the society, when he understood that one simply needs to work for the Creator and not for his own benefit, and should emerge from self-love and be rewarded with *Dvekut* with the Creator. And although he saw that it was difficult to emerge from self-love, he realized that this was a true path, meaning that a person should come to work *Lishma*.

But while he is separated from that society, he immediately falls into the majority view, which is the majority of the world. In other words, the majority of Israel has not yet come to what Maimonides said, "Until they gain much wisdom, they are taught that secret," which is the necessity to work *Lishma*.

And when that person enters the society, whose way is that it is necessary to achieve *Lishma*, the question arises, "How did this person end up in such a place?" We must believe that it came from above.

Accordingly, we should understand why, afterwards, he drifts away from the society. We should say, as Baal HaSulam said, that when a person begins to walk on the path of *Lishma*—and certainly this aim comes to a person who is given an awakening to the path of truth—and afterwards, for some reason, he becomes negligent in this work and relapses to the path of the collective, he asked, "Why is he not given another awakening from above?"

He gave an allegory about this. It is similar to a person who is swimming in the river. Halfway across the river, he grows weak, and a person swimming next to him gives him a push so he will start swimming by himself. The person who is trying to save him gives a few pushes, but if he sees that he is not participating, he leaves him and moves away. Only when he sees that when he pushes him, he begins to swim by himself does he keep pushing him each time until he's out of danger. But if he is not participating, he leaves him.

It is the same in the work. A person receives an awakening from above so he will come to a place where people work knowingly in order to come to bestow contentment upon the Creator. And a person is given several awakenings, but if he does not make an effort to achieve this, he finds excuses for himself and must escape the campaign. Thus, a person remains righteous; that is, by leaving this society, he is always right. And by justifying himself, he truly feels that he is righteous.

Therefore, *one must cling to the society*. And since they are united, they are regarded as a collective, too. However, theirs is a big collective, while his society is a small collective. And a collective does not annul before a collective.

3) There is a special power in the adhesion of friends. Since views and thoughts pass from one to the other through the adhesion between them, each is mingled with the power of the other, and by that each person in the group has the power of the entire society. For this reason, *although each person is an individual, he has the power of the entire group*.

What Is "There Is No Blessing in an Empty Place" in the Work?

Article No. 15, Tav-Shin-Mem-Het, 1987-88

It is written in *The Zohar* (*Truma*, Item 525): "This table stands in the Temple to have food on it, and to extract food from it. Hence, it should not be empty even for a moment. The other table, that of the *Sitra Achra* [other side], is a table of emptiness, since there is no blessing above in a place of deficit and lack. This is the table before the Creator. The table on which a man blesses before the Creator should also not be empty because there is no blessing in an empty place."

We should understand why there cannot be a blessing in an empty place, and what this means in the holy work, that a person who wants to receive a blessing from the Creator must try to have something, for only in this manner can the Creator give him a blessing.

Our sages said, "The cursed does not cling to the blessed." For this reason, Abraham did not want to take the daughter of Eliezer,

What Is "There Is No Blessing in an Empty Place" in the Work?

Abraham's slave. Therefore, when a person prays to the Creator to give him what he asks of Him, and when a person prays an honest prayer, from the bottom of the heart, the person certainly feels deficient. He feels that he is more deficient than the entire world. Otherwise, if there are other people who are as deficient as he, this is no longer regarded as a prayer from the bottom of the heart, after the rule, "a shared trouble—half a comfort."

Hence, his lack is no longer complete because it is only half a lack, since half of what he lacked is complemented by the others. For this reason, he has only half a *Kli* [vessel] to receive the filling, the part that the others cannot give him since they do not have it. Hence, he has no more than half a need to receive filling.

For this reason, the prayer that a person asks the Creator to grant him his wish should be from the bottom of the heart. This means that since the heart is called "desire," if the desire does not come from the bottom of the heart, since he does not have the real need to receive the filling, his prayer is therefore not accepted.

For this reason, a person must see himself as the worst in the world, and the matter of "a shared trouble—half a comfort" will not pertain to him because he is worse than everyone, as it is known that satisfaction in life concerns specifically a time when he lacks what others have. He may be earning more than others, and even have more important things than his environment, yet, he may still be dissatisfied with it.

Women feel this more. If they lack something, even if they have much more than their friends, they feel deficient. A woman might say, "I'd rather die," and take no comfort in having more things than her friends. If the lack touches her heart, she says she feels more miserable than the entire world.

The reason is that when a person feels a real lack, it does not comfort him that others also do not have it. The suffering of not satisfying the desire determines, and can even bring a person to commit suicide. Only this is regarded as a real deficiency.

Here, in the work, if he sees that there is someone who is similar to him with regard to the desire for spirituality, he can become satisfied by way of "a shared trouble—half a comfort." For this reason, he might fall into despair because he accepts the situation because then he says that it is impossible to obtain this thing that he understands he lacks, for after several attempts when he began the work but failed, he promptly decides that it is difficult and not for him. And the reason why he decides promptly is that the desire for that thing has weakened in him because he received a filling for half the lack in the form of "a shared trouble—half a comfort."

This is similar to a person who loses something and is searching for it. There is a rule concerning how much time he must dedicate to searching for the object: It depends on the value of the object. If the object is very valuable, he will dedicate a lot of time to look for it. If it is less so, he will dedicate less time.

It is likewise here in the work. If it is very important to him to work in order to bestow, he does not give up immediately, but persists and searches for ways to come to this. This is not so if he sees that there are other people who do not engage in Torah and *Mitzvot* [commandments] with the intention to achieve *Lishma* [for Her sake], but settle for observing the Torah and *Mitzvot* as Maimonides says, that the secret of having to work *Lishma* is not to be revealed to everyone, and they feel that by observing the Torah and *Mitzvot* as they were brought up, they are happy with it and do not search for other ways, and this is what pleases them.

This is the reason that even if they receive some awakening that they must search for the real intention in Torah and *Mitzvot*, that desire is not so important to them. Hence, they searched several times for the way to walk in the path of bestowal, and since they do not find it easily and have no real lack, they begin to walk in the path of *Lishma*, and then leave it and follow the masses.

However, we should understand the words of Maimonides when he says, "Until they gain knowledge and acquire much wisdom, they are taught that secret bit by bit." We should understand what it means when he says that they are taught that secret. What secret are they revealed when they are told that they must work *Lishma*? Who does not know that we must serve the Creator as it is written, "And you shall love the Lord your God with all your heart, and with all your soul, and with all your might"?

We say this four times a day: in the readings, *Shema de Korbanot*, *Shema de Yotzer Ohr*, *Shema de Arvit*, and *Shema al Hamita* [four times the *Shema* text is read during the day]. Even children say the *Shema* reading. Thus, everyone knows that we must work for the sake of the Creator, so what is the secret that is revealed to them, which there was no need to reveal to them before "they gain knowledge and acquire much wisdom"?

We should also understand the measure of "gain knowledge." How do you measure their knowledge so as to know that now it is possible to reveal to them the secret of *Lishma*, which was not so before? And also, what does it mean, "and gain much wisdom"? We should understand what is "wisdom" and what is "much wisdom."

We should interpret that wisdom and knowledge are what they received from the teachers in the beginning of the study, when they were taught in *Lo Lishma* [not for Her sake]. That is, by believing in the Creator and in the sages, they will be rewarded, and if they do not, they will be punished. It follows that they understand that by observing the Torah and *Mitzvot* and loving the Creator "with all your heart," He will reward us, and the reward will be that we will receive reward for observing everything He has commanded us. In other words, in order not to feel shame upon receiving the pleasure, He has given us commandments to follow, and He pays us for the effort. In this way, they will not receive something for free, but rather a payment for the effort of working for Him. In this way, there will be no matter of shame.

Now we can understand what are "knowledge" and "wisdom." It is what they received in the beginning of their learning, when they could not understand more than the reward accepted in *Kelim* [vessels] of self-love. That is, they still did not have the wisdom and knowledge to understand that it is worthwhile to do something in that which is not for one's own benefit, since they did not see what the will to receive for oneself would gain from this. However, they did understand that it is worthwhile to observe Torah and *Mitzvot* because they would have wisdom. They believed that they would receive reward, which is the wisdom and knowledge that they have gained—that it is worthwhile to observe Torah and *Mitzvot* for self-benefit.

It therefore follows that "much wisdom" means that they can understand by receiving the knowledge to understand something new. This is called "until they gain knowledge and acquire much wisdom." In other words, now they see that it is worthwhile to work for the Creator and not for themselves. But prior to this, they did not have the wisdom or knowledge to understand that it was possible not to work for self-benefit.

It follows that the prohibition on revealing the secret of *Lishma* at the beginning of the learning does not mean that it is forbidden, but that it is impossible, since they would not be able to understand this. Therefore, they must be given a reason for which it is worthwhile to work.

Hence, when "they gain knowledge and acquire much wisdom," they can hear the secret that they were forbidden to hear before. That is, even if they had been told that the real work is the work of bestowal, it would have remained a secret to them because they would not be able to understand it whatsoever.

Rather, after they "gain knowledge, they are taught that secret bit by bit." "Bit by bit" means that they begin to understand that it is worthwhile to work for the sake of the Creator and not for one's own sake. For this reason, we should interpret "until they gain knowledge" as pertaining to the view of Torah, which is the opposite of the view of landlords. The view of landlords is to work so that all the profits will be in his own domain. That is, he wants to be the landlord of all the work he does, meaning do everything for his own benefit.

Its opposite is the view of Torah, as our sages said, "The Torah exists only in one who puts himself to death over it." We interpreted that this means that he must put his self to death, meaning the will to receive for himself, and cling to Him, which our sages interpreted as "Cling onto His attributes; as He is merciful, so you are merciful."

In other words, a person must achieve a level of annulment of the desire for self-love, and his only aim is to love the Creator. That is, everything he does should be only with the aim to bestow.

This is the meaning of what is written, "until they gain knowledge and acquire much wisdom," when they can already hear the secret of the work of bestowal, and because they can understand that this work is real work because they want to work for the Creator and not for themselves.

Now we will explain what we asked, How do we know that they already have much wisdom, as he said, "Until they gain knowledge and acquire much wisdom"? As Baal HaSulam said, this knowledge and wisdom come to them from above, as awakening from above.

Yet, how do we know this? The answer is that since these people received an awakening from above, they cannot live in peace, but search from place to place for who will be able to guide them toward achieving the work of bestowal. By searching for a way to go forward, and having no satisfaction in their regular work, it is a sign that he has received knowledge and awakening from above. That person, when he is told that there is the matter of having to work for the sake of the Creator, will be able to understand this secret, since he already has the discernment, "until they gain knowledge." Hence, since he has the knowledge to understand, it is no longer a secret, for a secret is as long as we do not know, contrary to when we do know.

However, Maimonides says, "And they are taught that secret bit by bit." We should interpret that we cannot understand at once that the essence of the work is to engage in order to bestow. Rather, there are ups and downs in this understanding because this work is against nature. For this reason, once a person understands that we must work *Lishma*, the body overcomes him and argues that we must work for our own sake and not for the sake of the Creator. This is the meaning of "bit by bit." That is, this awareness, that he should know once and for all, does not come at once, but one at a time.

In order to be rewarded with working in order to bestow, a person cannot achieve this by himself. Rather, this requires help from the Creator. Our sages said about this, "He who comes to purify is aided." This means that one who wishes to purify himself from vessels of reception and work in bestowal, receives assistance from the Creator. However, one who seeks help from the Creator, his prayer should be from the bottom of the heart. That is, the lack he feels, that he cannot do something for the sake of the Creator, but only for his own sake, this is the desire of the entire heart, and he has no need whatsoever for the Creator to help him, except for this, since he feels that if he cannot work for the sake of the Creator but only for himself, he does not consider this "life."

By such a feeling, he feels that he is the worst and lowliest man in the world. Although he sees that there are people in the world who are respected for having much Torah and many good deeds, although he does not see that they are working *Lishma*, yet, they feel no deficiency in themselves. Hence, he can say to the Creator that He must help him achieve *Lishma* because he is the worst in the world.

The reason he needs to feel that his state is worse and he suffers more than the entire world, is that otherwise he will not have a complete *Kli* for the Creator to fill. This is called "the bottom of the heart." Since the Creator is complete, when He gives to a man inside his *Kli*, that *Kli* should also be complete, meaning a complete desire without any mixture with another desire.

Therefore, when a person sees that there are others who do not engage *Lishma*, yet do not feel that they are in such a bad state, and "a troubled shared—half a comfort," they complement half his lack with their filling. Then, he does not need the Creator to help on only half a lack. It follows that he has only half a *Kli*, but the Creator gives His filling only in a complete *Kli*, meaning on a complete lack.

For this reason, when he sees that there are people who have less life than he does, and he sees that they can live although they do not have such a need for the work of bestowal, and in any case he is not worse than they are, for this reason, his lack is filled by the others. But if he sees that he is worse than they, in that he cannot deceive himself and say that he is doing something for the sake of the Creator, it follows that only then he is unable to receive assistance from others. Hence, he feels that he has a real lack, meaning that he is suffering more than everyone from not being able to work in order to bestow.

According to the above, we should interpret what our sages said (*Avot*, Chapter 1), "Be not as slaves serving the great one in order to receive reward." We should interpret that when you come to pray to the Creator to grant your wishes, your desire should not be to receive reward, meaning half a filling, that you pray that He will satisfy only half your lack, since half of the lack has already been filled by the others, as in "A trouble shared—half a comfort," since he does not feel that his state is the worst in the world.

But when he sees that his state is worse than the entire world, he does not receive any filling from the public. Naturally, when he prays that the Creator will grant his wish, he has a complete *Kli* with a lack. This is not so when he receives a reward from others, for *Pras* [reward] comes from the verse, "*Paras* [cut in half] at dawn and *Paras* at twilight."

Now we can interpret what we asked if there is no blessing on an empty place, this is because the cursed does not cling to the blessed. For this reason, he cannot receive filling for his prayer, since the blessing cannot come into a place of curse, as in the words of *The Zohar*.

According to what we explained, the prayer is not regarded as a real prayer unless he feels that he is the worst person in the world, and that there is no one else in the world who suffers like he does from the evil within him. It follows that he is called "cursed," and how can he receive filling for his lack, since "the blessed does not cling to the cursed."

The answer is that "cursed" is regarded as the opposite of *Kedusha* [holiness/sanctity]. *Kedusha* is blessing and life, and in a lack, there is nothing that can have some life in it, since the poor has nothing from which to receive vitality, as our sages said, "The poor is regarded as dead." For this reason, they said in *The Zohar* that a table on which a person blesses before the Creator must also not be empty, since there is no blessing in an empty place.

However, when a person reflects on whether he is truly as he feels, that the fact that he cannot do anything for the sake of the Creator is truly a state of evil and lowliness, that there could not be worse than him. If so, the question is, What is the merit that he has, in that he was rewarded with seeing the truth, while others were not rewarded, but rather think they are complete?

Although they, too, feel that they still do not have real wholeness, they still feel that they are standing above the general public, since they have Torah and work, except they need to add a little more in quantity. But in quality, although they understand that there is more to add, it is not so bad; there are worse people. They believe that there is always more to add, but they can do without the addition to what they have.

Thus, why does that person feel that he really has nothing? Who revealed to him this secret that we must work *Lishma* and that he is still far from it? For this reason, he suffers and feels that he is poor, that he has nothing, and many times he thinks he would be better off dead.

He sees that he is no better than others, but what is the reason that he was rewarded with seeing the truth? He says that knowing this must have come to him from above, and not from his own powers. Hence, now he sees that the Creator is more considerate with him than with others. It follows that on this, that He has revealed to him from above the truth, which is what Maimonides says, that this secret is not revealed until they gain knowledge and acquire much wisdom, now a person sees that from above, the secret of having to work *Lishma* has been revealed to him.

Now he prays that the Creator will bring him closer and will give him the assistance, as our sages said, "He who comes to purify is aided." That is, he already has something and he is no longer regarded as having an empty table, for the fact that he came to purify, meaning knowing that he feels the need for the work *Lishma*, is itself regarded as a blessing, meaning that a person has been rewarded with knowing the truth.

About this, about knowing this, a person should thank the Creator. This is called "a blessing." On this there can be a blessing from above, for it is not an empty thing—that the person has been rewarded with knowing that we must walk on the path of bestowal. This means that the fact that he wants to walk on the path of bestowal, he does not feel this as luxury, as an addition to the work. Rather, he feels this as the core. That is, the essence of man's work is that we were given Torah and *Mitzvot* to cleanse Israel with them. He does not see any progress in this cleansing. On the contrary, each time, he sees how far he is from the work of bestowal, and sees that now he is more immersed in self-love.

It therefore follows that now he has in his prayer a life that he has received from above, and for which he must thank the Creator. This is regarded that he already has a blessing, and the upper blessing has something on which to be. This is no longer regarded as an empty thing. It can be said about this, "Serve the Lord with gladness."

This raises the question, How can one be glad when he should pray from the bottom of the heart? which means that he has nothing, so how can he be glad? The answer is that he believes that his praying to the Creator will bring him closer to working for the sake of the Creator, and that this is the essence of man's work, and he received this from above. This awareness can make it possible to be in gladness that he has been rewarded with understanding the truth of what he lacks and for what to pray.

Now we see that man should receive life from the present, from what he has now. This is regarded as the table on which a person blesses before the Creator is not empty, as said in *The Zohar*. That is, he has something from which to receive life, as it is written, life and blessing. And what he asks is that he wants to receive and enjoy the future. That is, a person receives vitality from what he can be glad about now, and this is regarded as living from the present.

That is, when can we say that he has nourishment from the present? If he knows how to appreciate the fact that the Creator has given him the knowledge of the truth. At that time he sees that the Creator is indeed considerate with him and watches over him to see that he walks in the path of truth. If he can believe this then he has nourishment, he nourishes himself from the fact that he has life. And a person can see his measure of faith according to the gratitude he gives to the Creator for this. This means that if he cannot thank the Creator for the lack that the Creator has shown him, it is for lack of faith that the Creator watches over him with Private Providence.

You could ask, If he can be glad and believe that the Creator guides him in Private Providence, why should he pray to the Creator? Moreover, if he thanks the Creator for the lack, how can he then pray from the bottom of the heart and say that he is suffering from being far from the Creator? One contradicts the other. If he has joy in the present and receives vitality from this, what should he ask about the future, that the Creator will grant his wishes?

The answer is that we say that the fact that a person is happy stems from the fact that he has come to know the truth that on the path of bestowal, which is the essence of our work, he has not even begun. Therefore, it pains him that he is remote. And if he does not suffer from his remoteness from the Creator and he is still immersed in self-love, what kind of truth is this, that we can thank the Creator for revealing the truth to us—that we are at the bottom of the pit, the place of *Klipot* [shells/peels] and the *Sitra Achra* [other side]. By knowing this, the Creator saves him from death.

If he agrees to remain separated from the Creator and derives satisfaction from this, then he is still in a state of "secret," for *Lo Lishma* is called "the potion of death," since he wants to remain in that state. It follows that even the gratitude he gives to the Creator is not the truth, since he still does not know the secret that the wicked in their lives are called "dead" because they are separated from the Life of Lives and want to remain in *Lo Lishma*.

Rather, precisely to the extent that he asks about the future, that the Creator will deliver him from the governance of self-love, that now the Creator has told him the secret that the essence of the work is *Lishma*, and he suffers from this and wants the Creator to help him as soon as possible, then it can be said that he is happy that the Creator has revealed to him the truth. Hence, we should understand these two opposites in one subject: One is in the present, that he has achieved the recognition of evil, and from this state he must escape, and the satisfaction of the deficiency is in the future.

It follows that the blessing in the beginning is because he has come to know the truth, and from this he must derive joy in the present. This is called "serve the Lord with gladness." Afterward, there is a blessing, meaning in the future, that he will receive the filling, that the Creator will give him the assistance, as our sages said, "He who comes to purify is aided." This is what it means that when a person comes to pray, he should not be in a state of cursed, but be in a state of blessed.

Accordingly, we should interpret what our sages said, "One should always establish the praise of the Creator and then pray" (*Berachot* 32). That is, before the prayer, he should see that he is not an empty *Kli*, but that he has blessing from receiving from the Creator the awareness of the truth—that we must work for the sake of the Creator and not for our own sake. He thanks the Creator for letting him know for what to pray.

It is written, "establish the praise of the Creator." Which praise should he say? The answer is that it is for the Creator revealing to him the truth he did not have, and that he will not deceive himself that he is fine, like the general public thinks. Instead, the Creator has revealed to him that he is missing an essential thing, and if he prays for it, meaning if he knows the great need to know what he really lacks, as he understands now, then he has a *Kli* that the Creator can fill, since now he is giving a prayer from the bottom of the heart. This is called "a complete *Kli*."

A person needs to know that in fact, he does not need anything but the ability to be able to do everything for the sake of the Creator, since only then he will be able to receive the delight and pleasure, since the Creator created the world only for this purpose—to do good to His creations.

According to the above, we can interpret the words of *The Zohar* where it says, "The other table, that of the *Sitra Achra*, is a table of emptiness." As we explained concerning the table of *Kedusha*, which *The Zohar* calls "The table on which a man blesses before the Creator should not be empty because there is no blessing in an empty place," this is so because the cursed does not cling to the blessed. The table is a place on which we receive the blessing of the Creator. Hence, *Kedusha* means that he believes that the Creator has given him the knowledge what to ask.

This is a great blessing when we know the reason for the illness. This is not so with the *Sitra Achra*. That is, when a person asks the Creator to grant his wishes and send him a blessing, but does not believe that the Creator has given him room to pray, this is the *Sitra Achra*, which is unlike *Kedusha*.

What Is the Foundation on which *Kedusha* [Holiness] Is Built?

Article No. 16, Tav-Shin-Mem-Het, 1987-88

With a corporeal building, we see that anyone who wants to build a building must first dig the foundations, and on the foundation he builds the building. In digging the foundation, we see that we should discern between having to build a one-story building—meaning only the ground floor—or a multi-story building. Thus, the digging of the foundation into the ground should be according to the height of the building. The foundation is not dug at once. Rather, each day the foundation is built so that it will be deeper, and then one can build a tall building.

The same order applies in spirituality. When a person wishes to build a one-story building, he does not need to dig very deep. He only digs a little, and he can build his building in observing *Torah* and *Mitzvot* [commandments/good deeds]. And what is digging in spirituality? It is a deficiency, when a deficiency is dug in the heart, since the heart is called "desire," a heart is called *Malchut*, and a heart is called "earth" or "ground."

As in corporeality, you dig a deficiency in the ground. In other words, before we go and build a building, we must first dig in the ground, that is, take out whatever there is in the digging site. Once the place where we want to build is empty, we begin to build. If the place is filled with earth, we must not build on it because the building will fall.

Likewise, in spirituality we must dig in the ground, meaning in the heart, and take out the dust in the heart from there, and then the heart remains empty, without any filling. Then begins the time of building. It follows that when the heart is filled with corporeal things, it is impossible to build any building on that ground because the whole building will tumble, since nothing can exist if there is no need for it.

Rather, only where there is a need, and he feels the lack from not having what he craves, when he obtains it, that thing is entitled to exist, because he needs it. And then he knows—the measure of importance is according to the measure of the need, and he knows how to watch over the building so his enemies will not ruin it.

Here begins the matter of digging the foundations, meaning the depth of the digging in the ground depends on the height of the building that a person intends to build. Sometimes a person says that he is content with a ground-level building. In other words, he wishes to observe Torah and *Mitzvot* by which to be rewarded with a building that is at ground level, meaning not far from the ground.

This means that he wishes to remain in earthliness, which is regarded as vessels of reception, meaning the reward in which he wishes to dwell. As when building a building to live in, the reward is considered the building where he lives. Thus, it is known that a person wants to live only by reward, and reward means that he is receiving delight and pleasure in return for his work, and this is the person's life—that a man wants to live only for delight and pleasure.

The order of the work in Torah and *Mitzvot* begins with *Lo Lishma* [not for Her sake], as it is written in *The Zohar*, "Some observe Torah and *Mitzvot* in order to be rewarded in this world, and some work in Torah and *Mitzvot* to have the next world." However, his reward is only what he will receive in vessels of self-reception, regarded as earthliness. This manner is called "people of the earth," meaning that they do not move from the earth, which is called the "will to receive."

It is as Maimonides said (*Hilchot Teshuva* (*Penance Laws*), Chapter 10), "When teaching little ones, women, and people of the earth [uneducated people], they are taught only to work out of fear and to receive reward."

Conversely, according to what Baal HaSulam said, being a wise disciple means that he is learning the qualities of the Wise, and the Creator is called "Wise." Therefore, one who walks on the path of bestowal is regarded as learning from the wise. Hence, he is called "a wise disciple."

It follows that those who engage in Torah and *Mitzvot* to be rewarded with a building called "reward of this world or reward of the next world for one's own benefit" are defined as "people of the earth." This is considered that he wishes to build only the ground floor. Thus, he does not need to dig a deep foundation, meaning dig each day to make the digging deep. Instead, he digs once and the digging is enough for him.

In other words, when he understands that he has a need and desire to observe Torah and *Mitzvot* so as to be rewarded, when he understands this deficiency, this reason, he can already work in order to obtain the building of the reward. This is so because as long as a person does not wish to exit self-love, the body does not object to Torah and *Mitzvot*. Therefore, he does not need to dig each day, meaning he does not need to search for a need and desire to engage in Torah and *Mitzvot* because the body does not resist his need, for it understands that it is worthwhile for it to work for its own benefit.

This is considered that his digging does not need to be so deep. Rather, the need to understand that it is good to engage in Torah and *Mitzvot* is enough to motivate him for the work. It follows that the digging he did once always remains with him and he can continue the work. Thus, his digging does not need to be deep.

However, if he wishes to build a multi-story building, meaning to be rewarded with a *Neshama* [soul] that consists of NRNHY, he can be rewarded specifically if his intention is in order to bestow, that all his thoughts and desires are only for the Creator's sake and not for his own sake. In this way, when he wishes to create a foundation, to build such a building, the digging of the foundation—meaning the need for it—is not made in a single time.

This is so because after a person works with himself and lets his body understand that it is worthwhile to work to bestow, this digging does not come easily to him. During the digging he hits rocks, which are difficult to make holes in. It is hard to make even a small hole in a rock.

In other words, when he wishes to understand—when he has a big desire, when he sees that he cannot do anything in order to bestow and wishes to ask the Creator to give him what he wants, meaning to give him the light of Torah that reforms him—in the middle of the digging he finds a big rock.

In other words, a thought arises in him that he wishes to understand why he needs to work for the Creator and not for himself. After all, it is known that "Your life and the life of your friends—your life comes first." And he has nothing to answer to that perception. Thus, he pauses in the digging because that rock is too hard to be able to make a hole in it.

For this reason, he needs a valuable instrument by which it is possible to break the stone. This instrument is called "faith above reason," and only this instrument can break the stone, which is called "external reason," meaning that this reason is outside of *Kedusha* [holiness] because it only serves the *Kedusha* as a shell that precedes the fruit.

What Is the Foundation on which Kedusha [Holiness] Is Built?

Thus, since only with faith above reason is it possible to break the stone, there is the matter of ascents and descents here, since one cannot always go above reason. It follows that all his digging and finding of some deficiency to ask the Creator to give him strength to go by the path of bestowal has been sealed again by the rock.

As a result, he must dig once more, repeatedly. Each time he begins to dig out the earth, in the middle of the digging he finds a rock again. Once again he begins to ask questions within reason. And again, he overcomes and uses the faith above reason. Once more, he obtains a place of lack and begins to pray to the Creator to bring him closer to His work, meaning to do the work of the Creator for the sake of the Creator, and not for his own sake.

Since his whole construction is built on above reason, the digging is sealed again, meaning that his need disappears again and he has nothing to ask; that is, he has no need for the Creator to bring him closer. Thus, he must start digging again, meaning to work in order to find a deficiency, so he will have a basis upon which to ask the Creator to build his building.

In this digging, we find that when we dig in the ground, we find dust and rocks. Dust is called "heart," meaning the will to receive for oneself. This is still not so terrible because with great efforts, one can take out the dust from the earth. But when he finds rocks in the middle of the digging, when the reason begins to ask questions, then he needs heaven's mercy to receive strength to overcome above reason.

Therefore, there is great work on the foundation because the digging is not finished in a day. Rather, immediately after the digging come the rocks and fall in his mind, meaning he receives foreign thoughts. That is, after he has overcome above reason, for a time, he cannot maintain it but suffers another decline and must begin anew. However, one must believe that no work is lost. Rather, everything remains but there is a correction during the work, not to see what he has already done.

Therefore, it is considered that each day when a person digs the foundation, he digs into the depth of the ground and does not go back to working on what he has already worked yesterday. But the progress is in deepening, and the measure of the depth of the digging is until he receives a genuine need for the Creator's help, to help him have the desire to work in order to bestow.

"Penny by penny accumulates into a great amount." Finally, from all the digging, he arrives at such a depth that it is possible to build on it a building that is worthy of being rewarded with NRNHY of the *Neshama*, with which one should be rewarded.

We understand the construction of *Kedusha* [holiness] in two ways: 1) *Kli* [vessel], 2) Light.

A *Kli* means that the Creator gives a desire and craving to bestow upon the Creator.

"Light" means that once he has a desire to bestow, which is called *Dvekut* [adhesion], he receives a degree of *Neshama*, until he is rewarded with NRNHY. It is written in the "Introduction to the Study of Ten Sefirot" (Item 133), "So it is in the work of the complete righteous, that the choice that applies during the concealment of the face is certainly not applied once the door for attainment of open Providence has been opened. Instead, they begin with the primary part of His work—in disclosure of the face. At that time, one begins to march on the many degrees, as it is written, 'The righteous go from strength to strength.' These works qualify them for the will of the Creator, that His thought in creation would be realized in them: to delight His creations."

Now we see that there is a degree of being rewarded with *Dvekut* with the Creator, meaning obtaining the degree of wanting to bestow. Afterward, there is the order of being rewarded with the light, which is called NRNHY, which are degrees in the disclosure of the light.

According to the aforesaid, we can interpret what is written (Genesis 26:15), "And all the wells which his father's servants had dug in the days of Abraham his father, the Philistines sealed. ...

And Isaac sat and dug the wells of water which had been dug in the days of his father Abraham, and the Philistines sealed them. And Isaac's servants dug ... And the herdsmen of Gerar quarreled with the herdsmen of Isaac, saying, 'The water is ours!'... And they dug another well, and quarreled over it too ... and [he] dug another well, and they did not quarrel over it; and he named it Rehovot, for 'At last the Lord has made room for us, and we will be fruitful in the land.' And he went up from there to Beersheba."

The digging that they dug was to find a lack and a need for the salvation of the Creator; they were for the *Kli*, meaning to ask the Creator to give them the need to bestow. And they see that they cannot because the body resists it by nature, for it is born with a desire only to receive.

However, in this, too, we should make two discernments: 1) When he prays for the Creator to give him the strength to overcome the will to receive and work in order to bestow, and he wishes for the Creator to give him this power. 2) Sometimes, one cannot ask the Creator to give him the desire to bestow because the body resists the prayer, as well. The body is afraid that perhaps the Creator might help him and he will lose the desire to receive. It follows that he must pray that the Creator will give him the strength to overcome the body and that he will have the strength to pray to the Creator for help in overcoming the will to receive and working in order to bestow.

It follows that he is praying, and what is his request? It is to be able to pray. This is called "a prayer for a prayer." It is called that the Creator must help him with the *Kli*, meaning to understand that what he needs is the power of bestowal. It turns out that the Creator helps him and gives him a desire to want to understand that all that one needs is the desire to bestow in mind and heart.

Afterward, when he has the need and he wishes to work in order to bestow, but cannot, the Creator gives him the light, meaning light that comes for the correction of the *Kli*, to be able to work in order to bestow. And that light is called *Kli*, as it is known that the light is named after the act.

Since the light gives him the desire, called *Kli*, it is considered that the Creator gave him the vessel of bestowal. This is called "the foundation," and on such a foundation it is possible to build a multi-story building. In other words, once he has obtained the foundation, which is the vessel of bestowal, he begins to be rewarded with a full level of *NRNHY* in his soul.

However, concerning the Philistines sealing the wells that his father's servants dug in the days of Abraham, we should interpret it in the work. Abraham is the quality of *Hesed* [mercy/grace]. Abraham's servants are those who follow the path of the quality *Hesed*, meaning those who wish to go by the path of bestowal, called *Hesed*. They dug this deficiency for themselves, meaning the need for vessels of bestowal. But the more they dug to find deficiencies, their deficiencies were sealed, and they always had to work anew, to dig again, repeatedly.

Now we can interpret the dispute between the herdsmen of Gerar and the herdsmen of Isaac, as it is written, "And Isaac's servants dug ... and the herdsmen of Gerar quarreled with the herdsmen of Isaac... So he named the well Oshek, because they *Hitashku* [contended] with him. And they dug another well, and they quarreled over it, too, and he named it Sitnah [Hebrew: enmity]. And [he] dug another well, and they did not quarrel over it; and he named it Rehovot ... And he went up from there to Beersheba."

We must understand the meaning of "Herdsmen of" in spirituality, and the difference between "the herdsmen of Gerar" and "the herdsmen of Isaac" in the work, as well as why there was a quarrel over the digging of the first two wells and none over the digging of the third well, as it is written, "And they did not quarrel over it."

It is known that one cannot live without provision. "Provision" is considered that which sustains one in life and of which he says, "This is worth living for." Certainly, there are many degrees of man's provision. Some are content with little, meaning that if a person has the food that animals settle for, he says, "This is enough for me and such provision is worth living for." Compared to the provision of others, he is regarded as settling for little.

And some say that they settle for such nourishments that are enough to provide for little children. This is an addition to animals, since they have interests: they play hide-and-seek, with toys and so on. They settle for this and say, "What we enjoy does not have to be real. Even if it is a lie, we can still find our provision there." On the contrary, it is the real things that we find completely meaningless.

As an allegory, I said many times that we see that there are little girls whose parents bought them rag dolls to play with. Sometimes, the mother is in the kitchen preparing a meal, with a year-old baby in the house, and the baby is crying. The mother says to her little girl, "Go play with the baby. By that, the baby will enjoy and I will enjoy because I will be able to prepare the meal."

But we see that in reality, the girl will not go. If we were to ask the girl, "Why don't you want to play with the baby? You're only playing with your doll, kissing it, but why won't you play with a real baby instead of a baby made of rags? Moreover, you can see that your mother is doing the opposite. She never kisses your doll, but the real baby." The girl would probably answer, "My mother does not want to enjoy life; this is why she cannot play with a doll. But I still want to enjoy life, so I can't play with a real baby."

Similarly, in the work, one cannot enjoy the truth in the work. Rather, man is impressed specifically with lies and takes pleasure and liveliness from this. If he is told, "It is unbecoming for you to enjoy work with unreal things," he says, "I still want to enjoy the world; this is why I settle for little in my engagement in Torah and *Mitzvot*."

For the most part, each person in the general public that observes the holy work and observes Torah and *Mitzvot* chooses his own measure of time he must dedicate to Torah and *Mitzvot*. Each one measures for himself what he understands as sufficient for him in both quantity and quality, and says that he settles for little. He does not have to be among the wealthy, who have great possessions. Instead, each understands his measure in Torah and Mitzvot with good reason.

It is as *The Zohar* says about the verse, "Her husband is known at the gates," each according to what he measures in his heart. This means that according to the greatness of the Creator that he measures in his heart, he knows how much time he must dedicate to Torah and Mitzvot and how much he must exert if it is hard for him to observe the Torah and Mitzvot.

However, there are a chosen few who do not settle for the provisions of the general public. According to the ARI, the dissatisfaction that they feel is a matter of the root of the soul. They need to advance more than the general public, and they begin to understand that the main work should be to sustain themselves on man's food, not on the food of beasts or the food given to little ones. As Maimonides puts it, "When teaching the little ones, they are taught to work for a reward, and they are not told of the matter of *Lishma* [for Her sake]."

However, here begins the main exertion, when he wishes to go by the path of bestowal upon the Creator and not for his own benefit, and to this, the body resists. Then he begins to think thoughts that wish to make him see that "You don't need to be an exception. As others settle for the provision of reward for labor in this world and in the next world, this should be enough for you, too. Why are you making a fuss about wanting to work specifically in a manner of bestowal? Can't you see that this is difficult? If it weren't, others would work in bestowal, too." With these arguments, these thoughts seal the diggings, meaning the deficiencies and the need to obtain the desire to bestow.

Now we can interpret what are "The herdsmen of Gerar," "The herdsmen of Isaac," and what is the dispute between them. "Herdsman" means provider. "The herdsmen of Gerar" means that their provision is in following the crowd. In other words, thoughts come to them that they do not need to work like the work of the few, who wish to reach the truth, called *Lishma*, meaning in order to bestow. Instead, they settle for being workers who observe Torah and *Mitzvot* to receive reward in this world and in the next world. This means that here, too, in observing Torah and *Mitzvot*, he can follow a path of settling for little.

"The herdsmen of Isaac" means what sustains Isaac. This is considered sustaining the quality of Isaac, the quality of bestowal. As long as he can bestow upon the Creator, this is his provision, and from this he makes a living.

That was the quarrel between the herdsmen of Gerar, who were telling him that any digging to find deficiency and need to engage only in the path of bestowal is not worth digging and searching for such deficiencies. They seal the need by saying, "We must follow the masses and not be exceptions."

The herdsmen of Isaac dug and looked for a need and deficiency to find pain and suffering from not being able to do things with the aim to bestow. This means that they understood that the most important thing was to work in bestowal, and they did not feel pain and suffering from this deficiency. Thus, they dug and sought advice concerning how to feel suffering, and the herdsmen of Gerar came and blocked the deficiencies that they had found. In other words, they promoted the understanding that it is not so terrible; we can follow the masses who say, "We are content with little."

This caused suffering to Isaac's herdsmen, since they had made great efforts to find that their deficiencies could not work in bestowal and to be pained by it. And they were already able to pray from the bottom of the heart, and they already had a place of blessing, meaning to give thanks to the Creator for showing them a place of lack, which is the most important in the work of the Creator. In other words, if they cannot aim the actions to benefit the Creator, they are not considered servants of the Creator, but their own servants. And the herdsmen of Gerar suddenly came and pulled them to follow the provision of the masses. By this they sealed all the well of Isaac's herdsmen, and this is the issue with the quarrel that they had between them over the digging of the wells.

Now we will explain what we asked: Why did the herdsmen of Gerar quarrel over the first two wells and did not quarrel over the third well? It is known that the order of the work is in three lines—right and left, which are opposite to one another, and then comes the middle line and peace is made.

It is also known, as we said, that the masses belong to a single line. Therefore, there is no one to oppose him, to make contradictory arguments, since he has only one line. This is why the matter of ascents and descents hardly applies to them. But with the right line, the left line stands opposite it. Therefore, in the right line there are already ascents and descents.

It is known that the right line is a line of truth. A single line, however, is not so true. Also, it is known that anything that is far from the truth is easier to observe. This is why the way of the masses, who are taught to go by a single line, means that they have not come to know and understand that there is more than actions. Rather, when they observe the 613 *Mitzvot*, they aim that the Creator commanded us to observe them, by which we will receive reward, and this is a complete righteous.

The only distinction among the workers is in quantity, in the amount of time each one gives for his engagement in Torah and *Mitzvot*. Therefore, since he is not so close to the truth, to being in *Lo Lishma* [not for Her sake], there aren't that many ascents and descents in those states, called "provision of the masses," since if he only believes in reward and punishment, to the extent of his faith, the body agrees to work and to exert in observing Torah and *Mitzvot*, for the reward he expects to receive in his vessels of reception are not in contrast with the body, called "will to receive for himself." Thus, they can work with great diligence.

There is another reason why there aren't so many descents in them: They find success in the work. In other words, they see that each day they advance in Torah and *Mitzvot*. It is human nature that

What Is the Foundation on which Kedusha [Holiness] Is Built?

when we see that we succeed in some work, there is motivation to work. All this is considered one line.

This is not so when a person begins to work in order to bestow, meaning when the reward he expects to receive in return for his work is to obtain *Dvekut* [adhesion] with the Creator, when his intention in observing Torah and *Mitzvot* is to have only the desire to bestow upon the Creator and not for himself. And as much as he exerts to be rewarded with vessels of bestowal, he does not move an inch. On the contrary, he sees that he is not succeeding in the work. Thus, from where will he receive livelihood so he can continue with the work?

The correction is to know the truth: that he is still immersed in self-love and he is still remote from the Creator. But then he must tell himself, "Although I still do not see any progress in the work, I have the great privilege of being able to do something in Torah and *Mitzvot*."

Then he must believe above reason that although he still does not feel His greatness, doing little things in Torah and *Mitzvot*—even if by coercion—makes him happy that he has some grip in Torah and *Mitzvot*. And for that he is grateful to the Creator. This is considered that the gratitude he gives to the Creator is given in truth.

In other words, he knows the truth—that he is remote from the Creator—yet he is happy that he has the strength to do something in Torah and *Mitzvot*, although he is not doing it wholeheartedly. But what is important to him is that he is serving the Creator, even though he still does not feel the greatness of the Creator. Nevertheless, he is thankful to the Creator for allowing him to do anything for Him.

And this is true. He is not deceiving himself into thinking that he is regarded as a servant of the Creator because he knows the truth, that everything he does is completely by coercion and not willingly.

But those who walk on a single line, who thank the Creator for rewarding them with engaging in Torah and *Mitzvot*, there are two drawbacks there: 1) One considers himself a worker of the Creator, and this is not the truth, since he is working for himself. 2) The Creator is not the one who is important in his eyes, meaning that it is worthwhile to work for the Creator. Rather, all the importance of the work is in how much reward he will receive for his labor. In other words, he is looking at the reward—whether he will receive a weighty salary—and not whether the giver of the salary is important.

But those who go by the right line consider the giver of the work, how important He is to them. Their desire is always that the giver of the work will be important to them, and this is their reward. This is considered that they always long to see the greatness of the Creator.

It follows that they are not after the reward they will receive for their work. Rather, when they observe His commandments, they always look to see that the commander, the Giver of the commandments, will be more important in their eyes each time, and this is their reward in their exertion in Torah and *Mitzvot*. For this reason, they say that even a small grip in Torah and *Mitzvot* is a great thing, and they are delighted and receive livelihood.

Now we can explain the quarrel over the first digging, since the matter of the three diggings comprises the whole work. In other words, there are many diggings that belong to the right line, many diggings that belong to the left line, and many diggings that belong to the middle line. The reason for it is that not all the diggings can be done at one time. Rather, in each line there is much to dig until the lines are acquired in full.

Concerning the first well that they dug, it is written, "And he named the well Oshek, because they *Hitashku* [contended] with him." We should explain Oshek. It means that with the first well, which implies the right line, they engaged in Torah and *Mitzvot* in these diggings.

This is so because the right line is called "wholeness," since the left line is called "deficiency." Right is called "wholeness," meaning that in the right, they had the strength to engage in Torah and *Mitzvot* with joy for the above-mentioned reason: Whatever grip they have in Torah and *Mitzvot*, they believe that it comes to them from above, that the Creator gave them the desire and craving to be able to engage a little in Torah and *Mitzvot*. This is why the herdsmen of Isaac argued, "Whatever grip we have, it is important to us and we thank the Creator for it."

Conversely, the herdsmen of Gerar were following what the masses say: "We observe Torah and *Mitzvot* by our own strength, and for this reason, we demand of the Creator to pay for our labor in Torah and *Mitzvot*." By this they seal the well that the servants of Isaac had dug, who said, "We can receive vitality from here because even a small thing is important to us, meaning that the Creator gave us the desire and craving to do anything in the work of the Creator. But we see that there are people who do not have the desire and craving to do anything in the work, since the Creator did not give them this desire."

This is why the servants of Isaac received life from this well. The herdsmen of Gerar came and sealed that well so they would not be able to receive life from there. They would tell them, "Your insistence on this inferior work is worthless. You will not receive any reward for it because it is completely unimportant, since the majority of people regard it as inferior."

This is why in the first well, which they called *Oshek* [contending], they said, "It is not contention that it is worthwhile rejoicing with this petite work, about which you are making a fuss. After all, there is nothing to look at, as you yourselves are saying that it is only a very small work. And your focus on the Giver—this, we do not understand."

Afterward, the herdsmen of Isaac's servants shifted to working on the left line, criticizing their situation, that they are still immersed in self-love. They see that they are unable to work for the Creator by themselves; hence, they dig in the bottom of their hearts to find deficiencies and pain. In other words, they seek advice how to feel suffering over being remote from the path of bestowal. And certainly, when they have suffering, they will receive help from the Creator, as during the exodus from Egypt, as it is written, "And the children of Israel sighed from the work ... and God heard their groaning."

Thus, by digging into the bottom of their hearts, they found a well, meaning a place where they could pray. "And they quarreled over it, too, and he named it Sitnah [enmity]." This means that the herdsmen of Gerar became their slanderers, not letting them pray that the Creator would fulfill their wish, meaning that the Creator would grant them the strength to overcome the vessels of reception so they could work for the sake of the Creator and not for themselves.

It follows that through their quarrel, they sealed the diggings they had dug in the left line so they would have a need for the Creator to grant their wishes favorably. "Good" means in order to bestow, as it is written, "My heart overflows with a good thing. I say, 'My deeds are for the King.'" The meaning of "My deeds are for the King" is that everything he does will be for the King, that his intention is to bestow upon the King.

And the herdsmen of Gerar were their slanderers so they would not be able to pray because they were following the majority saying, "The act is what counts, and the intention of doing it *Lishma* is not our business. Rather, it is for people who are pure at heart and gifted from birth. And the work in bestowal is not for us." Thus, they sealed off the need for prayer. This is why they called the second well, *Sitnah*, from the word *Satan* [which also means "slandering"].

And in that line, too, they did not make the second well in a single time. Rather, they dug many times in each line. However, all of them, meaning all the diggings, fall under the name of the three wells.

But afterwards, once they completed the process of work in two lines, they were rewarded with the middle line. It is as we said in previous essays, that the right line is called "his father," the left line is "his mother," and the middle line is called "the Creator," as it is written, "Three partake in man—his father, his mother, and the Creator."

"His father gives the white." This means that there is no deficiency there. Rather, everything is white, meaning that he is content with his lot, with the little grip on spirituality that he has.

"His mother gives the red." This means that he is not in a good situation, but is rather filled with deficiencies, and then he has room for prayer.

Afterward, "The Creator gives the soul." When the Creator helps him, giving him the soul, Satan no longer has room, meaning he has nothing to slander. This is the meaning of the words, "And [he] dug another well, and they did not quarrel over it; and he called its name Rehovot, for 'At last the Lord has made room for us...' And he went up from there to Beersheba."

We asked, "What is the reason that the herdsmen of Gerar did not quarrel over the third well?" Where there is a deficiency in *Kedusha* [holiness], there is room for the *Sitra Achra*. Hence, when a person goes on the right line, when he knows that he is immersed in self-love and all of his actions are not for the Creator, but he wants to be a worker of the Creator and in the meantime he is serving himself, and despite all the baseness that he is in, he wants to thank the Creator for giving him some contact with the work of the Creator, even if it is *Lo Lishma*.

And he believes above reason that the Creator gave him the thought and desire to engage a little in the work. Since he believes as much as he can in the greatness and importance of the Creator, above reason, although he was not rewarded with feeling the importance within reason, he still has the privilege of doing simple things. He is thankful and praises the Creator, and he is delighted and wishes to thank the Creator like those people who are in one line, meaning those who feel that the work they are doing is truly in wholeness and all they need to add is in quantity.

In quality, however, they feel that they are so complete that they need to work on humbleness, as our sages said, "Be very, very humble." They exert much work in this, in finding some lowliness in themselves, and it is all because they know only one line. This is the work of the masses.

But one who wishes to go by the right line, who knows that there is a left line, too, which weakens the right line, must make great efforts to believe above reason that even a little work in spirituality—even if incomplete, as they themselves feel—is important. Also, he must thank the Creator and be happy, and feel that now he has a life worth living for.

This means that by believing above reason that there is no end to the greatness of the Creator, and it is very important for him that he can serve the King, this is called "right line." This is a lot of work, and one should feel that the work in the right line is important. He should strive to have the same extent of vitality as when he was working in a single line, or at least no less than when he was working in a single line, before he came to work in the right line.

Yet, here in the right line, there is much work in it, and it does not come as easy as while working in a single line. This is because there he knew that the deeds he was doing were great and important, so it was easier for him to work. But in the right line, he sees for himself that his deeds are worthless in and of themselves, since he is not working wholeheartedly. Thus, he cannot say that he is doing great things and that the Creator will certainly grant him much reward in return for his work.

However, in a single line, there is no resistance on the part of the body, so he can work easily, without obstructions. But in the right line, he has a lot of work because he says that he wants to work for the Creator and not for the body, so the body naturally resists and he must constantly struggle with the body. Thus, he must always work with it and defeat it.

And there is another issue. If he wishes to continually walk on the right line and have strength to work, he must constantly exalt the Creator and make great efforts seeking advice how to obtain the greatness and importance of the Creator. If he appreciates the actions, meaning that he says, "My actions are very important above," it will certainly be a lie because they are not *Lishma*, since self-love—instead of love of the Creator—is involved in everything he does.

However, in a single line they do appreciate the deeds because in a single line they speak only of actions and not of the intention—whether his intention is in order to bestow or not. There, the order of the work is to not be meticulous about the actions. But when beginning to work on the aim to bestow, which is called "right line," it cannot be said that the actions are fine, that he is happy with the work he does.

However, if he extols the Creator as much as he can, above reason, he will never overemphasize his faith in the greatness of the Creator, since we must certainly say that the Creator is greater than man can exalt Him. Hence, saying that the Creator is important turns out to be the truth, and thus he is going on the path of truth.

And then a person can say, as in corporeality: "We see that concerning an important person, even if one can do a small service for him, it makes him happy and gives him high spirits." This means that it is not the act that is the most important, meaning the service that he gives, but whom he serves. Thus, when a person walks on the right line, it is a line of truth.

However, since the right line is a line of truth, there is great resistance on the part of the *Sitra Achra*, who does not permit walking on the path of truth, which leads to the correction of the world. This is because the building of the *Klipot* [shells] comes from the world of shattering and corruption. This is why all the things in the world that belong to destruction and corruption have strength to do their deeds. We see it clearly with little children, who can work on breaking and corrupting, but cannot work on things that bring about correction, such as in the allegory of the little girl.

This is so because of the shattering that occurred in the upper worlds. Hence, the corporeal branches follow the same routes. This is why there is energy to work on corruption and shattering, but for correction, it is hard to work on things that bring about the correction of the world in the corporeal branches because the correction above has not been completed.

This is why it is very difficult to walk on the right line. In other words, one must see how people exert on the path of one line, while they should have at least as much energy and high spirits while walking in the right line.

When a person wishes to appreciate the right line, the herdsmen of Gerar come and quarrel. They make him understand that "This is the wrong way. How do you want to thank the Creator for such a small work? You're thanking the Creator for something worthless. Conversely, those who walk on a single line know that what they do is important, and they can thank the Creator for it. But for trifling things? After all, you yourself are saying that your actions are worthless, since they are not from the heart, since you are saying that you are not working for the Creator. Thus, your gratitude is like flattery, and how do you derive joy and high spirits from a lie?"

The herdsmen of Gerar *Gorerim* [drag] him to the view of the majority, who can thank the Creator only for important things. And this is true, "While you are walking in a lie."

This *Klipa* [shell] is a big *Klipa*, which does not allow a person to be happy and receive vitality from the truth. Instead, it wishes to bring man into sadness and depression. Sometimes it brings him to a point where his life becomes meaningless, and then the only thing that can give a person joy is sleep, since while he is asleep he enjoys not being in a state of despair and pointlessness in life.

This is similar to a person who must undergo surgery at a hospital. There is a special physician who is called "anesthesiologist." This is the doctor that one wishes to see so he can give him a tip on how he can sleep for at least three months. This *Klipa* completely ruins the *Kedusha* because it is impossible for one to be able to say that the Creator is called The Good Who Does Good. A person defines that state as a descent, but there remains the question, "Where is he descending?"

The answer is that he is descending to the netherworld. If a person becomes stronger in that state, he says (in a Hanukkah song), "Lord, you have lifted my soul from the netherworld." Therefore, it is one's duty, when the herdsmen of Gerar come to a person and wish to drag him into the domain of the majority, meaning how they regard a person who is doing something small when they know that it is small and they are unappreciative of such an act.

"So how do you do two opposite things? On one hand, you admit that when doing such an act while being aware of doing it, it is an act full of faults," since during the action there are many foreign thoughts, each according to his degree.

For example, they make a blessing and thank the Creator saying, "...who sanctified us with His commandments." But during the blessing, they know that they are not feeling anything during the performance of the commandment, and they express much gratitude for this. Thus, he says that the blessing and the gratitude he gives are not because he is doing something important.

And afterward, you say that one should receive vitality and be happy because he was rewarded with performing a *Mitzva* [good deed/commandment], even if it is unimportant, and to thank the Creator for rewarding you, and say, "Who has chosen us." Moreover, you say, "An everlasting love, Your people, the house of Israel, the love of Torah and *Mitzvot*."

This brings up the question, "If you cannot see anything in the *Mitzva* that you are observing, why are you saying that the Creator gave us good things because He loves us? What is the point of this *Mitzva*, which you say that He gave you for love? We, the majority, say that He gave us Torah and *Mitzvot* because He loves us. It is as Rabbi Hanania Son of Akashia said, 'The Creator wished to reward Israel; thus, He gave them plentiful Torah and *Mitzvot*.'

"Thus, since He wished to reward us with having the next world and this world, with receiving great reward without feeling shame—for it is known that when one eats the bread of shame, he is ashamed— He therefore gave us plentiful Torah and *Mitzvot*, by which we would be able to receive a great reward. Yet, we know that with a small and incomplete deed, this would be the bread of shame."

Therefore, when a person walks on the right line and wishes to receive vitality and high spirits from doing something small, he thanks the Creator for rewarding him with doing something for the Creator and he believes above reason that the King is a great King, called "The Great, Mighty, and Terrible God."

It is said that something is important in one's eyes according to the importance of the King, even if he is only permitted a small service to the King, even one that is not important and with many faults, as long as he has some contact with the King. This is so because he is not seeking reward.

The order is that if one brings something to someone and wants a reward, then the order is that the thing is checked to see whether the reward that is demanded for the object is worth it or not. But those who walk on the right line have no wish for any reward. Instead, what they do for the King is their entire reward. Hence, they believe above reason that they are doing some service for the King, and this gives them vitality, joy, and high spirits that they were rewarded with doing some service for the King.

Since it is true both that they say that the Creator is very important, and we do not have the power to appreciate His greatness, and also vice versa, that from the perspective of the act, there cannot be a smaller and more important act than the one they are doing. It follows that it is true on both sides, and everything is built on the basis of faith above reason. Baal HaSulam said, "Everything that is built on above reason enters *Kedusha* and is considered internality, and within reason is considered externality."

Therefore, since the right is built on the basis of truth, the herdsmen of Gerar immediately awaken and wish to drag a person to the view of the majority. Then this *Klipa* begins to attack a person and makes him understand the view of the majority—that what they say is true. At that time, a person begins to believe this *Klipa*, when she wishes to kill him and extract all the vitality of *Kedusha* from him and throw him to the netherworld. This *Klipa* dresses in a clothing of hypocrisy and says that all she is telling you now is only so you will not fool yourself on a path of falsehood.

Hence, all that one can do then is stand guard while the thoughts of the herdsmen of Gerar come to his mind like jagged arrows dipped in poison, which kill a person instantaneously, leaving him without the spirit of life of *Kedusha*.

This *Klipa* comes to a person and sends him her views and ideas, and they do not come so he will not be a worker of the Creator. On the contrary, they make one understand that "Since now you clearly know what is the work of truth, that the intention must be for the Creator, and you know for yourself that you cannot aim for the Creator, thus your prayer is certainly worthless, as is the Torah that you are learning. You are wasting your efforts in vain. Therefore, it is better for you to work on the intent you must make. Thus, it is better, instead of praying or studying and doing trifle things, all *Lishma*."

And since he is in her domain, he certainly has no strength to do anything in *Lishma*, and by this she kills him. "It is better for you to think about the purpose of the work and engage in thought and not in action. This is why it is better that you engage in the work of intentions, that you must do everything *Lishma*."

And since he is under her authority, he certainly has no strength to do anything *Lishma*. By this she kills him. "Thus, when you pray, you do not need to overcome yourself if you wish to speak to someone during the prayer, since your prayer and your Torah are meaningless. Thus, when you are not studying, if you have someone to speak to, or if you have someone to speak to during the prayer, it is a waste trying to refrain from speaking, since you are not losing anything anyway, since both your prayer and your Torah are worthless.

"This is so because in the prayer, you see that you have no connection to the words you are uttering. And in the Torah, what are you losing by stopping in the middle of the study? You yourself are saying that the important thing is to aim for the Creator. Thus, what are you gaining if you know a few pages of Gemara or other words of Torah?

"And likewise in actions: Why do you need to be so meticulous about actions? I am not telling you that you should eat forbidden things; rather, I am speaking of the meticulousness of customs, that you want to follow this path. After all, you know that the most important is to aim for the Creator. Thus, leave these actions and do what you understand that you must do. And meticulous observance of customs is not for you. Rather, those deeds are for simple folk, who do not think and do not know what real work is. Therefore, it is best for you to think about the thought, how to bestow upon the Creator."

And when a person obeys this *Klipa*, called "the herdsmen of Gerar," how they speak only in favor of the work of truth, a person believes what they say and begins to neglect the schedule of the prayer and the Torah studies, and begins to listen to the voice of this *Klipa*. And since now a person has no vitality, since he has no action by which he can receive vitality of *Kedusha*, when he begins to contemplate doing something for the Creator, the body laughs at him and shows him only dark depictions in the work for the Creator.

Thus, a person remains without vitality and no longer has the strength to say above reason that the Creator is good and does good. He falls under the dominion of heresy, and has no strength to contemplate spirituality. Then he comes to a state where the world darkens on him. This is the meaning of what is written, that the herdsmen of Gerar quarreled with the herdsmen of Isaac. In other words, they furnished Isaac's servants with their views until they dragged them into their own authority, and killed them, and took all of their vitality.

In other words, they would suck out what little faith they had, and they remained bare and empty. This is called "the *Klipa* of the right," which does not let them follow the path of truth, meaning to say that although their actions are incomplete, they believe above reason that the Creator is so important that even doing the smallest service for the King is considered a great thing.

Since that small act is true, and their belief above reason that the Creator is a great and important King is also true, it follows that then they are adhered to the quality of truth. They can rejoice in doing their Master's will even a bit, since truth is a great thing in and of itself.

This is why we must beware of this *Klipa* when beginning to walk on the right line. Only when a person is strong in overcoming the *Klipa* of the right does the work on the left line begin. This means that the person himself evokes his criticism on himself, and not the *Klipa*.

Hence, while a person does not have vitality and can take the right line, he must not walk on the right line. Rather, once he is full of life and joy from the work of the right, the time comes for him to engage in the left line, meaning to see the lowliness of his state and why he has not been rewarded with the Creator admitting him into the King's palace.

Baal HaSulam said about what is written (Psalms 57), "Awake, my glory ... I will awaken the dawn." Our sages said, "I awaken the dawn, and the dawn does not awaken me." He said, "The literal meaning is that King David said that he does not accept the *Shahar* [dawn]—from the word *Shahor* [black], and darkness, which comes to him—and he awakens from the blackness. Rather, 'I awaken the dawn,' meaning when he feels that he is fine, he himself awakens the blackness."

We should interpret his words that a person does not accept criticism that his actions are not fine and that everything he does is worthless while the *Klipa* comes to him and dresses in a cover of righteousness, and ostensibly wishes for a person not to deceive himself in the work, but to work for the Creator.

But when such thoughts come and he does not evoke them, he should know that they are not coming from the side of *Kedusha*. Rather, the *Klipa* of Gerar sees that a person receives vitality from small things, that he settles for little and says that he believes above reason that there is no limit to the importance of the Creator, and he says that it is considered a great privilege that he was rewarded with the Creator giving him even a small desire and thought of serving Him, and he sees that there are many people in the world who do not have this privilege. Therefore, he is grateful and praises, and is very thankful to the King. And he is delighted and receives high spirits from that state.

At that time, the above-mentioned *Klipa* comes and wishes to kill him, to take out all the air of *Kedusha* that there is in him. She does not allow him to praise the Creator, but throws him into the netherworld and takes whatever faith he had. Then the person is considered dead because he has no life of *Kedusha*.

And who was the cause of this? Only the *Klipa*, which comes to a person in false appearance and speaks only in favor of *Kedusha*. This is called "The dawn does not awaken me," meaning that he did not wish to receive darkness and blackness from the *Klipot*.

Rather, "I awaken the dawn" will mean "Whenever I want, I awaken the dawn." In other words, I myself awaken the darkness and the blackness within me—that I am still immersed in self-love and I still do not have love for the Creator. I am still without the glory of the Torah and I still do not have the importance of the Torah to know that it is worthwhile to do everything to obtain the light of Torah, as well as how to appreciate the importance of observing the *Mitzvot* that the Creator commanded for us.

When I need to perform some *Mitzva* and intend that it will be in order to bestow, the resistance in the body promptly awakens in full force. And he has a great struggle to do anything and he sees the ascents and descents each time. And then he has room for prayer. This is so because a person awakens himself at the right time, meaning when he feels that he will be able to pray instantaneously, and not that the black will bring him sadness and depression, that he will not have the ability to pray for the blackness.

What Is the Foundation on which Kedusha [Holiness] Is Built?

One can see for himself whether it comes to him from the side of *Klipa* or not. The sign for this is that something that comes from *Kedusha* is always in the form of "increasing holiness and not decreasing." In other words, one always asks the Creator to elevate him to a higher degree than the one he is on. But when the blackness comes from the side of *Klipa*, a person cannot ask the Creator to raise him above his state.

"Rather, they bring down," meaning bring him down to the netherworld, and he loses the small portion of faith that he had and he remains seemingly dead, without the spirit of life. Then his only vitality is if he can sleep, meaning escape and forget his state of depression.

According to the above, we should interpret the words of *The Zohar* when it says, "It is forbidden to raise the hands without prayer and litany." We should understand what this means that our sages prohibited the lifting of hands in vain, and only if one can pray and make a request is there no prohibition, since there is prohibition only in emptiness.

According to the above, we should interpret that "hands" comes from the words, "If a hand ... obtains." This means that when a person raises his hands to see what he has obtained in the work of the Creator, if he has Torah and fear of heaven and good deeds, if he believes in complete faith that the Creator is benevolent, if he is ready and has the strength to overcome, then if he sees that he has none of the things he thought he would obtain through his labor in Torah and *Mitzvot*, he will not despair. On the contrary, he will have the strength to pray for the Creator to help him.

And he will have the strength to tell himself, "My seeing that I have nothing good in my hands is because the Creator has now allowed me to see the truth, that I truly am an empty vessel, and there are neither Torah nor fear of heaven or good deeds in me. Rather, everything I do is only for my own benefit, and now I have a *Kli* [vessel] and a real need, from the bottom of the heart, for the

Creator to grant my wish, since the help that I need Him to give me is necessity and not an accessory.

"Thus far, I thought that I needed the Creator's help for redundancies, not for necessities, because I knew that I am not like other people, who have no hold on spirituality whatsoever, but now I see within reason that my situation is worse than that of the rest of the people because I feel that I have nothing. Therefore, I am suffering and in pain because of my situation. But for the masses, it is not so bad because they do not feel what I feel. Therefore, I cannot derive satisfaction from the fact that they, too, have nothing, as this is what I think, and this is what my reason makes me understand—that this is the state of the others."

That is, perhaps they have good states, since one does not know what is in one's friend's heart. But a person determines his friend's state according to what he sees with his eyes, and from this he deduces how to behave. For example, if his friend is a hidden righteous, he thinks about him that he is not so orthodox.

What can one learn from this hidden righteous? Only frivolity. Therefore, when a person looks at the majority, it does not matter what is the real degree of the majority. What is important is what a person thinks about the majority. Therefore, at that time a person sees that his state is worse than that of the others; hence, he says that the Creator should help him because he is suffering more than the majority.

It follows that if he can assume that when he raises his hands to see what he has in his hands, and he will be able to pray, then he will know that his calculation came from the side of *Kedusha*. And then he is permitted to shift from the right line to the left line. Otherwise, if he does not know in his heart that he has the strength to pray, he must not shift to the left line, since then he will face the *Klipa* called "the herdsmen of Gerar."

It is written in *The Zohar* (*Vayikra*, Item 401): "Rabbi Yehuda started and said, 'Or make his sin known to him.' He asks, 'Make his sin known to him,' on whose behalf? Who made it known?' It should have said, 'Or knew his sin.' What is 'Make his sin known to him?' He replies that the Creator commanded the assembly of Israel to make the sin that he sinned known to man."

It is written in *The Zohar* (*Vayikra*, Item 404): "Here, too, the Creator said, 'Make his sin known to him, which he has sinned.' One who rises at night to engage in Torah, the Torah makes his sin known to him. And not by a way of judgment, but as a mother who tells her son with soft words, and he repents before his Master."

We must understand why, specifically, when the Creator alerts him that he has sinned, it is considered that now he is aware of the sin, but if his friend sees that he has sinned and his friend sees that he still did not repent and alerts him to his sin, it is not considered knowing. Also, what is the reason that if specifically the Creator alerts him that he has sinned, he knows that he has sinned and this is the time to repent, but if the Creator does not alert him, it is not yet time for him to repent for the sin?

We should also understand what *The Zohar* says, that one who rises at night to engage in Torah, the Torah alerts him, and one who studies all day, the Torah does not make it known to him that he has sinned. But when he studies at night, even when he does not study during the day, the Torah does make it known to him. Thus, we should understand the advantage of studying at night over the day. We should also understand what is written, that the Torah makes his sin known to him "Not by a way of judgment, but as a mother who tells her son with soft words." What is the difference between judgment and soft words?

RASHI interprets the verse, "Or make his sin known to him." "When he sinned, he thought it was permitted. Afterward, he was informed it was forbidden." We should understand this in the work. What is this sin? It is known that all the work that was given to the lower ones is in the form of "Which God has created to do."

It is known that creation is named after His creating existence from absence, which is called "will to receive," and "craving to receive pleasure." Because of the equivalence of form, called *Dvekut* [adhesion], another *Kli* [vessel] must be made, so we can receive the light of the pleasure. In other words, we must add the aim to bestow over it, or else it is forbidden to receive the abundance.

Even if we want, it is still not given. However, if we wish only to receive in order to receive, this is already called "a sin" in the work. This is so because through this desire, a person becomes more remote from the Creator, and it becomes more difficult for a person to be able to repent, which is called "returning to the root," meaning the giver.

A person must return to his source, since the disparity of form made him remote from the root, which is about bestowal. Therefore, when a person acts but does not intend for it to be in order to bestow, but instead, his intention is only to receive for himself, he is farther away, and this is his sin.

But in the order of the work, when we begin to work, we begin in *Lo Lishma*. This is why at that time we understand differently, meaning that what appears to a person in the order of the work are only two things: 1) to do, which is the 248 positive *Mitzvot* [commandments to perform certain actions]; 2) not to do, which is the 365 negative *Mitzvot* [commandments to avoid certain actions].

In other words, there is a transgression and there is a *Mitzva* [good deed]. Then, when a person believes in the Creator and in His law, a person knows very well what is a sin and what is not. Should he forget or err in some action because he did not know it was forbidden, if his friend sees, his friend can alert him that he has sinned. Thus, he himself did not know, but his friend, who saw, can tell him, and then a person repents for the sin he had committed.

But when speaking of the work on the path of truth, which is with the intention to bestow, which is only an intention, this is hidden from one's friend, since one cannot know what is in one's friend's heart. For this reason, his friend cannot alert him that he has sinned by not intending for it to be in order to bestow.

Now we can interpret what we asked, that this implies that it is specifically the Creator who can alert him that he has sinned, and his friend cannot tell him that he has sinned, since his friend cannot see his friend's intention. Thus, only the Creator knows which intention he had while engaging in Torah and *Mitzvot*.

However, there truly is a profound matter here, in the explanation of *The Zohar* that the Creator alerts him that he has sinned. And since when one sees in the Torah that what one needs to observe are positive and negative *Mitzvot* and he will already know what is a sin and what is not, this is so in the beginning of his studies. It is as Maimonides says, "When teaching women and little ones, they are taught in order to receive reward." Only afterward, "When they gain much knowledge, are they told" that they must study *Lishma*, meaning in order to bestow.

It follows that one cannot understand that if he does not have the intention to bestow, it is considered a sin in the work on the path of truth, since the majority are still in *Lo Lishma*, and he wishes to walk in *Lishma*. For example, if he does not have the aim to bestow, it is considered a sin, but a person cannot feel this for himself. It is similar to a person performing an act that is prohibited in the Torah, such as desecrating the Sabbath or eating forbidden food, etc., meaning he will have the same feeling while performing some *Mitzva* without intending to bestow, as when committing a grave transgression.

This brings up the question, "Who can alert the person that if he does not perform in order to bestow it is considered a sin and he should repent for it, meaning ask of the Creator that he will not sin again?" In other words, here we must understand, a) that if there is no intent to bestow, it is a sin, and b) that he should have the desire to repent so as to not sin again, as our sages said, "Repentance is remorse for the past and acceptance for the future."

This matter of a person feeling that it is a sin—that he will feel that this is a general sin, that it is all the evil that exists in man—this is something that only the Creator can make us understand. The Torah and *Mitzvot* that were given to us are to correct that evil, which is called "will to receive for oneself," and it is not within one's power to understand that this is all the evil that separates the creatures from the Creator.

And this is what *The Zohar* says about the verse, "Or, make his sin known to him, which he has sinned." In other words, "make his sin known to him, which he has sinned" means that the Creator makes it known to him what the sin that he has sinned, since for the person himself, it is difficult to accept it and say that if he works for his own benefit, in the work on the path of truth, it is considered a sin.

Only when the Creator gives him this awareness can he feel that it is a sin. For example, when one person kills another person, of course he feels that he has committed a grave sin, such as if a person has a chauffeur, and that chauffeur hit someone with the car and killed him, and this was at night and no one knows about it. It is not necessarily the chauffeur who feels that he has killed a man, but even the employer, who was travelling with him, feels that sin, as well.

In spirituality, when the Creator alerts him that he has sinned and he is killing the quality of man each day, only the Creator can give such a feeling in spirituality. But the person himself cannot know or understand it.

Now we can understand what RASHI explains about the verse, "Or make the sin known to him." These are his words: "When he sinned, he thought it was permitted. Afterward, he learned it was forbidden."

To understand his words in the work, we should interpret "When he sinned" as "While he engaged in Torah and *Mitzvot* in order to receive." He still did not know it was forbidden. Rather, if he kept Torah and *Mitzvot* only in action, he felt it was permitted. Only afterward did it become known to him that there was a prohibition here, that his aim was in order to receive reward. But who informed him that it was forbidden, that using the vessels of reception is prohibited? *The Zohar* interprets that it is the Creator who alerted him, for without the help of the Creator it is impossible to feel it.

It therefore follows that in the work, the primary evil and sin is the will to receive, which is the only cause that stops us from receiving the good that the Creator wants to give to the creatures, and why we cannot be rewarded with *Dvekut* with the Creator. As we learn, the light of *Neshama* divides into five discernments, called NRNHY, which clothe only in one's vessels of bestowal.

Thus, for a person to have the sensation of evil and darkness, that it all comes from this harm-doer called "the will to receive for himself," only the Creator can alert him that it is a sin. This is so because a person is accustomed to using the will to receive even when he begins with the work of the Creator.

It is as our sages said, "One should always study *Lo Lishma*." Thus, he already has permission from our sages to study, since by that he will come to *Lishma*. Thus, since there is permission from our sages that we must study *Lo Lishma*, it is difficult for a person to say that it is a sin, since they said that it is permitted to study *Lo Lishma*. Thus, there is no reason to believe that this is indeed the biggest sin because this is all that obstructs the achieving of *Dvekut* with the Creator.

With the above said, we can interpret what we asked about the words of *The Zohar*, which writes that for one who rises at night to engage in Torah, the Torah alerts his sin to him. We asked why specifically those who study at night, and should it be particularly the Torah which alerts his sin to him.

The answer is that specifically through the Torah one can come to feel that receiving for himself is called "a sin," meaning that the will to receive for himself is called "a sin." But uneducated people cannot know, as Maimonides says that the matter of *Lishma* is not revealed to women, little ones, or uneducated people. And the meaning of "not revealed" is because they cannot understand. Rather, specifically through the Torah, for that the Torah can bring such a feeling to a person that will make him see that reception for himself is considered a sin.

But why is it specifically Torah that is studied at night that has the strength to alert his sin to him? In other words, what is the advantage of the night over the day, which implies that specifically at night, as it was written that for one who rises at night to engage in Torah, the Torah makes his sin known to him? To understand this, we must first understand the meaning of "day" and "night" in the work.

"Night" is, as our sages said (*Pesachim* 2b) about the verse, "The murderer arises at dawn ... and at night he is as a thief." "Does that mean that light is day? The meaning there is this: If the matter is as clear as light to you that he comes to take life, he is a murderer. But if you are in doubt, like the night, you must regard him as a thief." Thus, we see that our sages use "day" and "night" for "certain" and for "in doubt."

We can interpret that "day" in the work means that when a person engages in Torah and *Mitzvot*, he can be certain that he will receive reward for his labor. Then he is content and has no room for prayer for the Creator to help him, since what is he lacking? It is, however, possible that one will say, "I should do more," but he probably has excuses of not having enough time for some reason or because of health issues. However, on the whole he is fine because he believes that he will be rewarded. He believes in reward and punishment in this world and in the next world, and this is called "studying Torah at daytime."

"Studying Torah at nighttime" means that he in doubt, since doubt is called "night." This occurs when a person wishes to walk on the path of truth, meaning with the aim to bestow. That is, he wishes to work in Torah and *Mitzvot* on a different quality level than the way he worked on the path of the majority, with the intention to receive reward in this world and in the next world. Instead, he wishes to engage in Torah and *Mitzvot* not in order to receive reward. But the body resists this path. Hence, alien thoughts always come to him, bringing him constant doubts in his work.

And what are the doubts? Sometimes he thinks that he should walk on the path of bestowal, and then the body begins to resist. Then, thoughts come to him that perhaps the majority is right, meaning that he does not have to work in a manner of bestowal because it is hard to fight against the body. Therefore, it is better to follow the majority view, since the majority are certainly more fine-looking and have a more important place in the world. And they chose to walk on the path of aiming that only the actions are for the Creator, and not the aim to bestow. This means that they observe Torah and Mitzvot because the Creator commanded us to observe His commandments and keep His law, and not for money or for honor, meaning that by engaging in Torah and Mitzvot he will be respected or will be called "Rabbi." Rather, they observe Torah and Mitzvot for the Creator because He commanded us, and in return, we will receive reward. This must be the best way.

And since this does not contradict self-love, it is not so difficult to walk on this path. But on the path of bestowal one always has doubts because this way is unaccepted by the majority and the body is naturally inclined toward the view of the *Klipot*, which are only about reception. This is why he has constant work fighting these thoughts.

And even when a person overcomes the body and makes him understand, "But you see that by nature, one wishes to serve the great one without reward, but only in pure bestowal." Then the body stands against him and makes a true argument: "In corporeality, you see that you are 'great,' and you see that everyone respects you. Thus, you can be influenced by the majority, by the majority appreciating him as great. Therefore, there it is worthwhile to work in bestowal. But here, you are in concealment because the greatness and importance of the Creator is not revealed, and you just want to believe that this is so, that the Creator is important and worth serving without any reward."

Thus, at that time a person becomes weak against the body and has no answer, since at that time, there is only one thing to say—that he is going above reason. It follows that he cannot prevail over the body's argument with his mind, and then it is heaven's mercy that he needs in order not to escape the campaign.

This is called "night," when a person is in doubt because of the complaint with the body. And then this Torah reveals his sin to him, meaning that his sin is primordial and deeply rooted, since then he sees that he is lacking faith in the Creator. In other words, he cannot believe that the Creator is great and ruling and worth serving and giving to, and that He will have contentment from him.

In other words, there is no contentment for a person in serving a great king. As *The Zohar* says ("Introduction of The Book of Zohar," Item 195), "Fear is the most important, meaning that he will fear the Creator because He is great and rules over everything, since He is the root from which all the worlds expand, and His greatness appears in His deeds."

Without Torah, one cannot feel what he is lacking because there is a rule that absence must precede presence, and it is impossible to feel absence, meaning that he is lacking something, unless he feels that there is something good in the world that is good, and that he does not have it. Then you can talk about absence. In other words, when there is someone who feels the absence, you can say that he should try to satiate what is missing.

Who created the first absence? The Creator did, in the world of *Ein Sof* [infinity]. We learn that He is one and His name is One. The first absence is the *Tzimtzum* [restriction], when the light departed and left a lack. The light of the line should fill up the deficit made by the Creator, who is the presence, and He created a new thing—He created absence.

Thus, when one studies Torah, through the Torah he comes to feel that there is a Creator and a leader, because by studying Torah he receives the light of Torah that reforms him. Then he begins to feel through the Torah that there is the giver of the Torah, and then he begins to understand that it is a great privilege to serve Him.

And when he begins to converse with the body concerning this, the small feeling that he begins to feel—that it is worthwhile to serve the Creator—is met with the resistance of the body, which vehemently opposes the sensation of receiving from above in the form of "The light in it." In other words, it is not at once that one receives the light of Torah sufficiently to reform the body. Rather, it comes bit by bit. This is why there are ups and downs, and for each ascent that he receives and begins to understand that he must walk on the path of bestowal, the nature of the body immediately resists.

However, this is so deliberately, from the Creator. The reason for this is that "There is no light without a *Kli* [vessel]." What comes from above is called "awakening from above." In other words, the need and the satisfaction come as one. At that time, he doesn't have a reason for an awakening of the desire that it is worthwhile to serve the Creator. This is why, when the feeling that comes from above departs, gradually a need builds in his heart to work in bestowal, and this is when he begins to ask the Creator to give him the strength for it. Then this state is called "light and *Kli*."

There is another reason why one needs awakening from below: When the upper one gives without preparation on the part of the lower one, the receiver cannot feel it as important. According to the rule that anything that a person wishes to enjoy depends on the importance of the matter, before the upper one lets him feel something, it cannot be said that he wants something.

Rather, after one experiences some awakening to the work of the Creator, one must believe that the fact that a person has awakened to the need to engage in the work of the Creator is because the Creator sent him these thoughts without any messengers. In other words, when no one tells him that he should engage in the work, a person certainly says that it came to him from above.

However, even if some person comes and makes him understand, and explains to him that it is worthwhile to begin with servitude of the Creator and he is awakened by it, he still should not say that so-and-so showed him the merit of the work of the Creator. Rather, that person, too, was a messenger of the Creator to awaken him. Thus, sometimes one must say that the Creator gave him the desire without messengers, and sometimes he should say that this desire came from the Creator through an emissary.

And since that desire came to him without any preparation of his own, he cannot appreciate the importance of the matter. Thus, a person is not so impressed and cannot enjoy that thing because he does not know its value. It is like a person who sends a gift to his friend, but his friend does not know how to appreciate it.

Let us say, for instance, that the receiver of the gift thought that it was worth about 100 dollars, but the giver of the gift paid 10,000 dollars for it. The giver knows that the receiver appreciates the value of the gift only according to his own understanding. Thus, we understand that the giver of the gift seeks advice and tactics to make the receiver of the gift understand the value of the gift, so he can enjoy the gift as much as the giver wants him to.

This is the cause for ascents and descents in the work, which are called "day" and "night." When we study Torah during the "night," in that overcoming one sees how remote he is from the Creator by not being able to exit self-love, and the Torah brings him the sense of importance. When he is in an ascent, he must say that the Creator is bringing him closer, meaning that the Creator is not hiding Himself from him, and this is why he feels that it is worthwhile to have *Dvekut* with the Creator.

It is as we learned in *The Study of the Ten Sefirot*, where he gives an explanation about the four phases of Direct Light and says, "What is the difference between *Hochma* of Direct Light and *Malchut* of Direct Light? If there is the same light in the *Sefirot Hochma* and *Malchut*, then why is one called *Hochma* and the other is called *Malchut*?"

The answer is that in the *Sefira* of *Hochma* there was still no preparation on the part of the lower one, since the lower one still did not exist, meaning sensed itself as lower, in need of something and having to receive from the upper one, so he would complement its deficiency. Therefore, the lower one takes no pleasure in receiving the abundance from the upper one, as there is a desire in the upper one for the lower one to enjoy Him.

The desire of the upper one is to do good to His creations, meaning for the lower one to enjoy. But because of the lack of preparation on the part of the lower one—since when the lower one was born it was born along with the abundance—there was no time for it to equip itself with a deficiency, meaning to crave the abundance.

But *Malchut* comes after the abundance has departed from the *Sefirot* above her. Thus, she already had the preparation, meaning the need for the light that illuminated in the *Sefira* of *Hochma*. Thus, only *Malchut* can receive pleasure from the abundance that the giver wishes for the lower one to enjoy.

With all the above, we discern two things concerning the gift of the giver: 1) One should know what to want, meaning what he needs. 2) He must want to have that deficiency filled, meaning make all the preparations to be able to receive the gift.

Thus, how can one begin to feel a need for the work of the Creator when he does not know of the work of the Creator whatsoever, meaning that there is such a thing at all? In other words, if he does not know about it, how can a desire for it awaken in him?

The answer is that as we learned about the *Sefira* of *Hochma* that the Creator, who is called "desire to do good," created the light and the *Kli* together, the sensation of the spiritual comes to a person from above. He receives the light and the desire for the light simultaneously. Either the awakening comes to him directly from the Creator, or the awakening for the work comes to him through a messenger that the Creator sent in order to make a person understand, and influences the person that it is worthwhile being a worker of the Creator. However, everything comes to him through the awakening, without any preparation on the part of the lower one. And as was mentioned here, it is impossible for the lower one to have real pleasure from the work of the Creator, due to lack of preparation.

Rather, we said about the *Sefira* of *Malchut* that she craves the abundance that was in the *Sefira* of *Hochma*, when there is preparation on the part of the lower one, she receives the pleasure that the giver wishes to give. Similarly, here in the work of man, a descent comes to him from the awakening he had, and he begins to want what he had before. Then the lower one can prepare to receive the abundance.

Yet, the desire and craving for real *Dvekut*—to really be able to receive, and to regard it as important as the Creator wishes—does not occur at once. This is why there are many ups and downs. However, without the first awakening on the part of the upper one, it would never be possible for the lower one to want something that he did not know what it was.

Now we will explain what we asked about the meaning of the Torah making his sin known to him, and not by a way of judgment, but as a mother who informs her son with soft words. Also, what are judgment and "soft words?"

As we explained concerning that quarrel between the herdsmen of Gerar and the herdsmen of Isaac, something that provides is called "herdsmen." The herdsmen of Isaac were saying, "We can receive sustenance only from the truth, and not from falsehood." Hence, when they wished to work on the right line, they would say, "We are content with little, although in truth, the deeds we do are worthless because they are not done with the real intention.

"Still, if we consider to whom we wish to bestow—to a great and ruling King—any work is enough for us and we consider it a great privilege because we are serving such a great and important King. Hence, as much as we are allowed to serve the King, we thank and praise Him even if it is a small service."

This is called "The herdsmen of Isaac," who wish to serve the Creator with Isaac's dedication but the body does not agree to it. But when they know that they should serve like Isaac, they are content with it and bless the Creator for it.

And when the *Klipa* of the herdsmen of Gerar sees that they are happy with the Creator, they immediately begin to quarrel with the herdsmen of Isaac saying, "Why are you happy with the Creator? You yourselves are saying that the service you are doing is not as it should be when serving a King. The way is to do everything in full."

"Therefore," they ask, "Why this joy? We, who follow the majority, have something to rejoice about, since we say that we settle for doing the actions that the Creator commanded us. And in return, we believe that we will receive reward for observing Torah and *Mitzvot*, and we are happy. But you, who say that the important thing is *Lishma*, and you can see for yourselves that you cannot work in order to bestow, you see that you are not doing anything. See for yourselves how much effort you have already made, yet you did not advance one bit. Why are you working for nothing? You are unworthy of approaching the Creator because you are too immersed in self-love, so you are wasting your time for nothing."

Thus, what did this *Klipa* do? She extended the quality of judgment over that person and killed him. This is considered that the *Klipa* informs the sin with the quality of judgment, and then there is nothing he can do but fall into despair and escape the campaign. She takes from him whatever faith he had, and he remains without spiritual life. But he is also unable to receive corporeal satisfaction, as he did before he began the work. Thus, he remains melancholic and sad, and all because this *Klipa* came to him in a disguise of righteousness and care only for his well-being.

This is the meaning of what is written, that the *Klipa* makes his sin known to him in a manner of judgment. But for one who rises to engage in Torah at night, the Torah makes his sin known to him as a mother who informs her son with soft words, and he repents before his Master.

We should understand the meaning of "soft words." The end of the essay comes and interprets "He repents before his Master." In other words, she informs him of the sin not because she wishes to remove him from the work of the Creator like the *Klipa* of Gerar, who informs him of the sin with the quality of judgment–that it is impossible to repent and to work in order to bestow, and thus she pushes him away.

Rather, she informs him as a "mother to her son," making him understand with soft words that he should not think that he cannot repent and work in order to bestow. "In soft words" means that it is not as hard as you think, since the Creator wishes to help a person when he feels that it is hard for him.

However, we must understand that the Creator Himself made it difficult, as it is written, "Come unto Pharaoh, for I have hardened his heart ... that I might show these My signs." In other words, the Torah makes one to understand that the fact that he is feeling that it is hard to walk on the path of bestowal is not because he is incompetent, but because "I have hardened his heart." Why? "That I might show these My signs."

Baal HaSulam interpreted that it is in order to have a need for the letters of the Torah, the Creator made the hardening of the heart so that by that, one will be needy of the Torah. Otherwise, he would have no need for the Torah. But since a person wishes to go on the path of bestowal and the Torah alerts him that the will to receive for himself is the sin, that this is the actual evil inclination, and one who wishes to walk on the path of bestowal, it is written (Psalms 1), "Happy is the man who has not walked in the counsel of the wicked, nor stood in the way of sinners."

We should interpret "Who has not walked in the counsel of the wicked," meaning the herdsmen of Gerar—who want him to follow them—that they make him understand that it is not worthwhile to follow the path of bestowal. Instead, they wish to hear the herdsmen of Isaac, who say, "One who walks on the path of receiving reward, it is called 'a sin.'" And when they understand that this is a sin, they immediately cry for the Creator to bring them out of that state and wish to keep what is written, "Nor stood in the way of sinners."

In other words, they do not wish to remain in the state of sinners, and ask for the Creator's help, that He will give them the light of Torah because "The light in it reforms him," and he, too, wants to serve the King and be a true worker of the Creator.

The Zohar says that one should know the ways of Torah because "One who does not know the commandment of the upper one, how will he serve Him?" It follows that by being unable to emerge from his will to receive for himself, and by feeling that he needs the Creator's help, the need for assistance of the Creator is born within him.

His help is through Torah, in which there are two things: 1) "The light in it reforms him," meaning he receives vessels of bestowal. 2) When he has vessels of bestowal and he wishes to bestow upon the Creator but does not know what the Creator needs for him to give Him. In *The Zohar*, this is called "One who does not know the commandment of the upper one, how will he serve Him?"

And here we should discern between a) the *Klipa* alerting him that he is a sinner, in the quality of judgment, whose aim is to remove a person from the work, and b) the Torah, which alerts a person that he has sinned "As a mother who informs her son with soft words, and he repents before his Master."

The Torah alerts that he can correct this sin through the Torah in the two above-mentioned manners: 1) through the light in it, which reforms him; 2) by being rewarded with flavors of the Torah and flavors of the *Mitzvot*, for "One who does not know the commandment of the upper one, how will he serve Him?"

This is why *The Zohar* concludes, "And he repents before his Master." But when the *Klipa* alerts him of his sin, he is incapable of repenting. Instead, he falls into despair and complete departure from the work of the Creator.

It follows that when a person walks on the right line, he must not hear the thoughts of the *Klipa* of the herdsmen of Gerar, as our sages said that David said, "The dawn does not awaken me." But afterward, one must shift to the left line, which is called "I awaken the dawn."

This means that he awakens the dawn. That is, a person has a special preparation of wishing to awaken the blackness. This means that he summons it, and not the thoughts of blackness, when the *Klipa* alerts him that he is in the wrong. It follows that he summons the left and examines how to correct his deeds—to see the measure of his remoteness from equivalence of form, and the measure of pain and suffering—he feels all that when he sees the lowliness of his state. He sees that sometimes he does not care that he is remote from *Dvekut* with the Creator. This is the time to ask the Creator to deliver him from the exile he is in.

Here, too, we should discern two things: 1) He does not feel that he is in exile. In other words, he has no wish to escape self-love. Rather, he is in a state that *The Zohar* calls *Hav, Hav* ["give-give," but also the sound of a dog bark], like a dog, referring to the words, "The leech has two daughters, who bark like dogs, *Hav, Hav*." It interprets, "*Hav* [give] us the wealth of this world, and *Hav* us the wealth of the next world."

This means that they wish to observe Torah and *Mitzvot*, but in order to receive everything in the will to receive for themselves. This is considered that he does not feel any exile, so as to want to be redeemed from the exile.

He feels all this when he enters the left line. But when he walks on the right line, he must not scrutinize if his work is complete or not. Instead, he is thankful to the Creator for whatever grip he has.

This state is called "concealment within concealment," as it is written (Deuteronomy 31:18), "And I will surely hide My face in that day." We should interpret that when he is in concealment, he does not feel that he is in exile. What is the exile? It is as it is written, "It is for our sins that we have been exiled from our land and were sent far from our land."

It was written, "It is for our sins." Sin concerns using the will to receive for oneself. This is what caused us the remoteness from "Our land." It is known that "desire" and "land" are called *Malchut* [kingdom], meaning the kingdom of heaven. The kingdom of heaven means that a person takes it upon himself to enslave himself to heaven, meaning to the Creator, who is called "heaven," as it is written, "Lift up your eyes on high, and see: who created these?"

This is the meaning of "We have been exiled from our land," meaning from our land, called "the kingdom of heaven," to serve and to toil for the glory of heaven; we have been exiled from this will. But into which desire did we enter? The desire of "the nations of the world," called "receiving in order to receive."

What Is the Foundation on which Kedusha [Holiness] Is Built?

It is written, "[We] were sent far from our land." *Adamah* [land] comes from the words *Adameh la Elyon* [I will be like the Most High], which is equivalence of form. And since we engaged with our own will to receive, we have become far from our land, from being in equivalence of form with the upper one. And when a person does not feel the exile, that he is under concealment, the exile, which is called "concealment," is hidden from him. Thus, he is in a state of concealment within concealment.

However, concealment within concealment also means a certain measure of disclosure. Indeed, there is concealment within concealment, but we should ask, "Where did this awareness that he is in concealment come from?" We should say that this awareness, too, came from the Creator, either directly or through a messenger.

In that regard, we should interpret the verse, "Maker of light and creator of darkness." This darkness refers to a person's feeling that he is inside a concealment, that he does not feel that the Creator is hidden from him, and he has no desire to search where He is, so that from this place he will surrender before Him and will have the great reward of serving Him.

He also does not feel the concealment in the sense that the Torah is the clothing of the Creator, or regrets it. Instead, he is in a completely different world, meaning the fact that there is a Creator and the Creator wishes to give delight and pleasure to the creatures do not interest him at all. This feeling, called "concealment within concealment," is called "darkness," and the Creator created and gave him this darkness.

But we see that a person usually does not see the negative in himself. He always knows that he is fine, whether he is religious or nonreligious. It is as it is written, "A bribe blinds they who see." And since a person is close to himself, he can never see the truth. Thus, a person who sees that he is not alright should say that he was alerted this from above.

2) He is in a single concealment. In other words, he feels that he is under concealment. This means that it pains him that he is

far from the Creator, meaning that the Creator is hidden from him and that he does not feel the Creator to the extent that he will wish to annul before Him. Yet, it pains him that he is remote. Then, he has no other way but for the Creator to help him, to make him able to approach the Creator, called "*Dvekut* and equivalence of form."

All this scrutiny that he does, which is called "left line," should be at a certain time. That is, particularly after he has walked on the right line that day and praised the Creator extensively for giving him even a small service, and he rejoiced in that. As said above, this is the path of truth.

Afterward, he can shift to the left line for a short while, but not for long. That is, while he engages in Torah and prayer, he should be careful not to go out to the left line, but to be specifically in the right, for this is called "The blessed adheres to the blessed."

This is the time when he can be rewarded with a higher degree, as it is written, "Divinity is present only out of joy." But when he is in the left line, which is a time of criticism, that time is the place to see only faults. But the work of the left should give him the need to pray. Prayer relates specifically to a place where there is a deficiency, and a place of deficiency is called "cursed." But then, "The cursed does not adhere to the blessed." For this reason, it is impossible to rise to a higher degree. On the contrary, the right line is the place for ascension, for then he is in a state of wholeness.

The Main Difference between a Beastly Soul and a Godly Soul

Article No. 17, Tav-Shin-Mem-Het, 1987/88

It is written in *The Zohar* (*Tazria*, Item 1): "Rabbi Elazar started, 'On my bed night after night I sought Him whom my soul loves.' He asks, 'He says, 'On my bed.' It should have said, 'In my bed.' However, the assembly of Israel spoke before the Creator and asked Him about the exile, since she is seated among the rest of the nations with her children and lies in the dust. And because she is lying in another land, an impure one, she said, 'On my bed I ask, for I am lying in exile,' and exile is called 'nights.' Hence, 'I sought him whom my soul loves,' to deliver me from it.'"

We should understand why he says that "On my bed at night" refers to the exile. Exile can be understood in three ways: 1) She is "seated among the rest of the nations with her children." This is plural form, "among the nations." 2) She "lies in the dust." 3) "Because she is lying in another land, an impure one," which is singular form.

Also, we should understand what is "the assembly of Israel with her children" in the work, and that they lie in exile and she is lying in the dust, in the work.

It is known that the assembly of Israel is called *Malchut*, who is the root of all the souls, for *Malchut* contains within her all the souls. Generally, we learn that all the corrections in the world are named after *Malchut* because *Malchut* is the general *Kli* [vessel] that receives all the lights imparted upon all the worlds.

Baal HaSulam said a rule that we must know: 1) In general, all the lights that exist in the worlds are regarded as the light of *Ein Sof*. 2) The general receiver that we discern in the worlds and in the *Sefirot* is *Malchut*. 3) All the multiplicities are only from the perspective of the receivers. 4) Each and every discernment we make is to the extent that *Malchut* is impressed by the lights she receives.

That is, according to the power of the *Masach* [screen] that *Malchut* raises *Ohr Hozer* [Reflected Light], she feels the light bestowed upon her. Since there are many discernments in the *Masachim* [plural of *Masach*], as we learned, there are also many discernments in the light.

To understand the need for a *Masach* and *Ohr Hozer*, which causes many discernments, we must remember what is said in *The Study of the Ten Sefirot*, Part 1, where he says that we begin to speak of the connection between the Creator and the creatures, and that connection is called "His desire to do good to His creations." For this reason, He created existence from absence, and this "existence" is called "will to receive for oneself." This is something new, which did not exist before that desire was created. Hence, this desire, called *Malchut*, received that light as one discernment, without distinguishing degrees, since the Creator, who created the will to receive delight and pleasure, was precisely a desire to receive to the extent that the Creator wants to give.

For this reason, it is written in the beginning of the book *Tree of Life*, that prior to the *Tzimtzum* [restriction], the upper light had filled the whole of reality, and there was no beginning or end, until after *Malchut* of *Ein Sof* received the light. And since the power of the upper one, which is the desire to bestow, is included in the light, once *Malchut* received the light, she wanted equivalence of form, like the light she had received. For this reason, she restricted herself from receiving in order to receive and will not receive any more abundance than the extent to which she can aim to bestow.

Since we attribute this *Kli* to the receiver, and it is against the nature of *Malchut*, who was created with a will to receive, and now she needs to do something against her nature, making such a *Kli* does not happen at once. That is, *Malchut* cannot receive all the light she had prior to the *Tzimtzum* and take it in order to bestow.

This is why we discern many discernments in *Malchut*, which is the general vessel of reception, to the extent of the ability of the *Masachim* that she is able to do. That is, from the perspective of the Creator, His intention was to bestow endlessly, meaning according to the measure of the will to receive. But from the perspective of the lower one, which wants to receive only in order to bestow, we get all the multiplicities called "corrections of *Malchut*."

Generally, we speak of *Malchut de Atzilut*, who was the only one to beget the souls. Through the cascading of the worlds, *Malchut de Atzilut* emerged, and the souls she begot correct her. That is, the souls that come from her, each one corrects at the root of his soul in *Malchut*, to be a corrected part in the will to receive in her in order to bestow. And to that extent, *Malchut* bestows upon the lower ones.

That is, to the extent of equivalence of form that the lower one causes above in *Malchut*, to that extent it is bestowed upon the lower one, who caused the correction in her, so she can receive from her upper one because there is already equivalence of form between the receiver and the Giver. This is called "the unification of the Creator and His *Shechina* [Divinity]." That is, unification is called "equivalence of form." When the receiver is corrected with the aim to bestow, this aim makes the receiver be regarded as giver because everything follows the intention.

As said above, the purpose of creation is to do good to His creations, meaning for the souls to receive delight and pleasure. For this reason, since equivalence of form mandates that there will be work in the lower ones, to obtain that intention to bestow, and since the creatures were created with the nature to work in order to receive, which is against the *Kedusha* [holiness/sanctity] because all the light of pleasure that comes from the Creator is because He desires to bestow and the lower one who receives it is the opposite of this, hence, the question is, From where will the creatures take life, so they can exist, before the creatures obtain the vessels of bestowal so they will have equivalence of form, since any life and pleasure come from the Creator, and disparity of form separates them from the Creator? Thus, who would give them vitality and pleasure, since without this it is impossible to exist because of the law of the purpose, which is "to do good," and if the creatures have no delight and pleasure, they cannot exist in the world.

Rather, the *Kedusha* sustains the *Klipot* [shells/peels] so they will not be cancelled. For this reason, even before a person is rewarded with vessels of bestowal, in order to be able to receive the light of *Kedusha*, he is nourished by the *Klipot*, from what the *Kedusha* sustains *Klipot* with, so they will not be cancelled. This is as it is written in the "Introduction to The Book of Zohar" (Items 10-11): "In order to mend that separation, which lies on the *Kli* of the souls, He created all the worlds and separated them into two systems, as in the verse: 'God has made them one opposite the other.' These are the four worlds ABYA of *Kedusha*, and opposite them the four worlds ABYA of *Tuma'a* [impurity]. He imprinted the desire to bestow in the system of ABYA of *Kedusha*, removed the will to receive for themselves from them, and placed it in the system of the worlds ABYA of *Tuma'a*. Because of this, they have become separated from the Creator and from all the worlds of *Kedusha*. The worlds cascaded onto the reality of this corporeal world where there is a body and a soul and a time of corruption and a time of correction. For the body, which is the will to receive for oneself, extends from its root in the thought of creation, through the system of the worlds of *Tuma'a*."

Accordingly, we see that the *Klipot* are necessary to us since the *Guf* [body] extends from them and receives vitality from them. Only afterward, by the power of Torah and *Mitzvot* [commandments/ good deeds], when he engages in order to bestow contentment upon his Maker, he (the body) begins to purify the will to receive for himself imprinted in it, and gradually inverts it into working in order to bestow. By this, it extends a soul of *Kedusha* from its root in the thought of creation, and it passes through the system of the worlds of *Kedusha* and dresses in the body, as it is written there (in Item 11).

For this reason, the *Kedusha* must give vitality to the *Klipa* [shell/ peel] so they can exist. It is as it is written in the book *Tree of Life* (*Panim Masbirot*, Branch 39): "It is necessary to have some tiny sparks of *Kedusha*—which are the 11 marks of the incense—within those *Klipot* [shells/peels]." This is the meaning of what is written, that nothing can exist without sparks of *Kedusha*.

For this reason, we discern two souls in man: 1) a beastly soul, 2) a soul of *Kedusha*.

The beastly soul is that which sustains the body and maintains its existence, since it is impossible to live without pleasure. Pleasure is light that comes from above, and "there is no light without a *Kli*." For this reason, the pleasure must dress within some *Kli*, and it cannot be said that a person wants pleasure without any clothing, but only the pleasure. Rather, there must be (pleasure) clothed in some *Kli*. Generally, the dresses where the light of pleasure is clothed are called "envy," "lust," and "honor."

By and large, there are three dressings, but in each clothing there are many discernments. For example, in "lust," we should discern eating, drinking, and so forth. Likewise, there are many discernments in eating, as well as in drinking.

In other words, in each clothing, we feel a different pleasure, which is different in taste. Thus, the taste of eating bread is unlike the taste of eating cake, etc. Although the light of pleasure is one, the dresses in which the light of pleasure clothes make the differences.

All of this is called "the beastly soul." This means that there is "beast," and there is "man," as our sages said, "You are called 'man,' and the nations of the world are not called 'man.'" We should understand that "beast" means that one has no relation to the work of the Creator. For this reason, "the beastly soul," which sustains the body, has no need for faith in the Creator. Even those who have no faith can receive the light of pleasure that sustains the body, which is called a "beast," although we should believe that there is nothing that does not extend from the Creator, meaning that the *Kedusha* sustains the *Klipot*. Yet, the body being called "a beast" means that it does not feel that the light of pleasure comes from the Creator. We must believe that the Creator did this on purpose—that they would not know that He has given them life—because it is for man's correction. Otherwise, man would have been regarded as "knowing his Master and aiming to rebel against him."

Conversely, the "Godly soul" is that to the extent of the faith he has, the Godly soul spreads within him, meaning the feeling that he has a Godly soul that sustains him spreads within him to the extent of the faith that he has. The extent of the faith can be in a person according to the measure of his work in order to bestow, as explained in the *Sulam* [commentary on *The Zohar*] ("Introduction of The Book of Zohar"), where he says that a person cannot obtain faith before he has vessels of bestowal.

We should believe, as we see, that the beastly soul that sustains the body, according to the measure of clothing in the dresses, so we feel the flavor, where the beastly soul is clothed in the dresses. Although the beastly soul is one, through the dresses it wears, we see that each clothing yields a different taste. Certainly, we should say that the one who wears, who is clothed in the dresses, changes according to his dresses.

Likewise, we should believe that a Godly soul also clothes in its dresses, called Torah and *Mitzvot*. Although we say that there are no changes in the light, the dresses engender different flavors, so we cannot feel the taste of light that is dressed in Torah and *Mitzvot* as similar to one another.

Since a different light is dressed in each *Mitzva* [commandment/good deed], which is the meaning of the 613 *Mitzvot* that *The Zohar* calls "613 deposits," meaning that in each *Mitzva*, a different light is deposited, meaning a different flavor, since the changes come due to the dresses.

This is similar to what is written in the *Sulam* (*Mar'ot HaSulam*, Part 1), that when we are rewarded with "hearing the voice of His word," the 613 *Mitzvot* become *Pekudin*, from the work *Pikadon* [deposit], since there are 613 *Mitzvot*, and in each *Mitzva*, the light of a unique degree is deposited, corresponding to a specific organ in the 613 organs and tendons of the soul and the body. It follows that by making the *Mitzva*, he extends to its corresponding organ in his soul and body, the degree of light that pertains to that organ and tendon. This is regarded as the *Panim* [face/anterior] of the *Mitzvot*."

Although the light is one, since there are no changes in the light, but "there is no light without a *Kli*," meaning without dresses. It follows that the dresses change the flavors in the light. Many discernments extend from this, both in corporeal pleasures and in spiritual pleasures.

However, we must know that the primary discernments we make in spirituality are the *Masachim*. To the extent that we can aim to bestow, which in spirituality is judged by the *Ohr Hozer* [Reflected Light] he has, so he dresses the upper abundance. In the order of our work, it is called "to the extent that a person can aim to bestow," to that extent the light appears to him.

Now we will return to explaining what we asked about the assembly of Israel lying in the dust. *The Zohar* calls the exile by the name "nights," and by the name "seated among the nations," and by the name, "the other, impure land," and by the name "dust." According to the above, the issue of the souls having to correct the *Malchut* from where they were born, is that since by nature, the

Creator created *Malchut* with a desire and yearning to receive delight and pleasure, since this was the purpose of creation, but because of the correction of creation, in order not to have shame, she should be corrected into working in order to bestow. This correction is for the souls to do.

That is, we learn that "His desire to do good to His creations" refers to the souls, that they will receive delight and pleasure, and all that we learn about the upper worlds is only a preparation where by the restrictions and cleansing and various changes that we learn in the upper worlds are but preparations for the souls to emerge in the way that the Creator wanted them to emerge—ready to receive delight and pleasure. For this reason, when we say that *Malchut* engendered the souls, it means that the souls should receive the abundance from her under the conditions by which the abundance can stay in their possession, meaning that they will receive in order to bestow. This means that it is as though the souls say to *Malchut*, "Give us delight and pleasure into our *Kelim*, which we awaken ourselves, so everything we do will be only in order to bestow."

Now we can understand that the words "*Malchut* is in exile with her children" are because this concerns the desire to bestow, which are the *Kelim* with which we can receive the delight and pleasure and that it will not depart (the abundance). Otherwise, if the will to receive for oneself comes in the middle, the abundance must depart since the *Kelim* of the desire to bestow are called "man," as our sages said, "You are called 'men,' and the nations of the world are not called 'men,'" where "man" means bestowing and "beast" means receiving, and "man" means male and "female" means receiving.

It is known that each person in the world is considered a small world in and of itself, as it is written in *The Zohar*. That is, each person consists of seventy nations, which means that "God has made them one opposite the other." There are seven qualities of *Kedusha*, called HGT NHYM, and each consists of ten *Sefirot*. Hence, the seven qualities of *Kedusha* are sometimes called "seventy faces." Opposite them are seventy nations of *Tuma'a* [impurity], and everything is included within man.

The Main Difference between a Beastly Soul and a Godly Soul

This means that the "man" in him, regarded as "the point in the heart," is in the dark, under the rule of the seventy nations in him, which enslave the Israel in him so he will not be able to engage in bestowal, which is "man," but rather the beastly soul governs. It follows that the quality of "Israel" is in exile among "the rest of the nations," meaning that self-reception, called "the nations of the world," controls "Israel."

This is regarded as the *Shechina* seated among the rest of the nations with her children, as in, "When Israel are in exile, the *Shechina* is with them." It follows, that she is in exile with her children. Generally, *Malchut* is called *Shechina*, and her children are every quality of Israel within each and every one. "Being in exile" means those who feel that they cannot emerge from the control of the nations of the world. The measure of suffering in the exiled is judged by the measure of wanting to come out from the exile, from the governance of the rest of the nations.

However, sometimes, a person comes to a state, as it is written, "And they mingled with the nations and learned from their actions." That is, they do not feel any difference between them and the nations. That is, he does not say that he wants to do otherwise except the nations are ruling over him. Rather, he himself wants to behave like all the nations. That person is not in exile. That is, he has no *Kelim* for exile, since one whose *Kelim* are in exile means that he wants to work in order to bestow but the body resists him. Then it can be said that the seventy nations in his body control the Israel in him.

At that time he can say that the vessels of bestowal are under the control of the body, and when he cries out to the Creator to deliver him from exile, he knows what he wants with clarity. It is as it is written in *The Zohar*, that a person should see while he is praying, that he knows how to pray clearly.

We asked, Does the Creator not know what is in man's heart? So, why does *The Zohar* say that one must speak to the Creator clearly? The answer is that it must be clear to man what he is asking of the Creator, for the reason that there is no light without a *Kli*, and therefore no redemption without an exile.

By this we should interpret that exile means the *Shechina* with the souls are in exile. In order for *Malchut* to receive delight and pleasure for the souls, they must be in equivalence of form, which is the desire to bestow. Yet, that desire is placed under the rule of the *Klipot*, called "land of the nations" or "the impure land." When a person wants to work in order to bestow, he feels a taste of dust in the work of bestowal. Only when he engages in order to receive for himself does he feel the taste of food.

This is similar to how we interpreted the words, "And you will eat dust all the days of your life," as our sages said, "A serpent, its only food is dust." We should interpret that as long as one did not correct the sin of the primordial serpent, anything he eats, meaning all the flavors that a person feels in Torah and *Mitzvot* taste like dust. However, once a person has been rewarded with correcting the sin of self-reception, called "the primordial serpent," he begins to feel the flavor of Torah and *Mitzvot*, as it is written, "nicer than gold and sweeter than honey."

This is the meaning of the words, "The *Shechina* is lying in the dust." This means that each one who wants to work in order to bestow, meaning to take upon himself the burden of the kingdom of heaven, feels the taste of dust, due to the sin of the primordial serpent, as Baal HaSulam said about what our sages said, "The serpent came over Eve and cast filth in her."

He said that the meaning is that the serpent cast in *Malchut Zu-Ma* [this-what], meaning he blemished the kingdom of heaven. One who wants to take upon himself the kingdom of heaven, the serpent comes and asks that person "this" "what," meaning "What will you get out of wanting to work for the sake of the kingdom of heaven?" That serpent is the evil inclination. That is, we must believe above reason that through the kingdom of heaven, we will receive the delight and pleasure, which is the purpose of creation, and the only reason we cannot receive this good thing is because of that serpent, called "will to receive for oneself."

This is the meaning of what is written, that we understand the exile in three ways: 1) She is "seated among the rest of the nations."

The Main Difference between a Beastly Soul and a Godly Soul

He means that the point in the heart of each and every one is sitting in exile among the seventy nations that exists in each of them. 2) She is "lying in the dust," meaning they feel the taste of dust. 3) Generally, she is "lying in another, impure land," which is called "the primordial serpent," where she should have been dressed in a place of desire to bestow, called "the land of Israel." That is, instead of all his actions being *Yashar-El* [straight to the Creator], she is in another land, an impure land. Naturally, she cannot bestow upon the creatures the delight and pleasure because of the disparity of form between the creatures and the Creator.

This is the meaning of the words, "On my bed," which *The Zohar* interprets as referring to the exile. It refers to those who suffer from the exile and want to escape from the will to receive for themselves, but the nations of the world control them and they cannot emerge from their control. About those she says, "I seek that which my soul loves, to bring me out of it," meaning that the Creator will give the strength to come out of exile, since there is already an "awakening from below," called *Kli* and "desire." At that time it is possible for the light to spread, where the light of redemption removes the control of the nations of the world.

Now we can understand the difference between a beastly soul and a Godly soul. That is, in truth, both come from the Creator, since there is no life in the world but that which the Creator gives. But the difference is that the Creator gives the beastly soul to man, and a person does not need to know that the sustaining soul comes from the Creator. Instead, he thinks it comes through nature's messengers. This is considered that "over the nations of the world, He has given governance to ministers." That is, they do not need to believe that it comes from the Creator. Conversely, He alone governs the people of Israel, meaning that the quality of Israel in man believes that it comes from the Creator, and there is no other force in the world, but rather He alone does and will do all the deeds.

When Is One Considered "a Worker of the Creator" in the Work?

Article No. 18, Tav-Shin-Mem-Het, 1987/88

The Zohar (*Tazria*, Item 10) asks about the verse, "When a woman inseminates and delivers a male child: "Rabbi Aha said, "And delivers a male child.' Since she inseminates, does she also deliver? After all, this requires pregnancy. This verse should have said, 'If a woman is impregnated, she delivers a male child.' What is, 'If she inseminates, she delivers'? Rabbi Yosi said, 'Since the day of insemination and conception to the day of delivery, a woman has not a word in her mouth except her offspring, whether it will be a male. This is why it is written, 'If a woman inseminates and delivers a male child.'""

We should understand what it means that the woman says, "Since the day of insemination and conception to the day of delivery, a woman has not a word in her mouth except her offspring, whether it will be a male," and that this is why the verse says, "If a woman inseminates." What does knowing this give us?

Certainly, there are answers in the literal. But we will explain in the work, what is the importance of a woman being worried whether her child will be a male as soon as she inseminates. First, we need to know what is insemination in the work. In corporeality, we see that when we sow a seed in the soil, the seed rots in the ground, and then yields crop that sustains people. That is, the sowing brings us food. If a person did not sow a seed, he will certainly not reap, as it is written, "They who sow in tears shall reap in song."

What is sowing in the work of the Creator? We should interpret that there are two forces in man: 1) the force of bestowal, which is what man wants to bestow upon others, 2) the force of reception, meaning wanting to receive from others and enjoy for oneself. Whichever force he wants to annul, this is called "sowing." He places this force in the ground, such as when placing seeds in the ground so they will rot. Then they are annulled in the earth and later yield crop for food and for nourishment and life to the world.

Likewise, in the work, when a person wants to annul the will to receive for himself, it is regarded as placing it in the ground, as wanting to annul it "as the dust of the earth," and that a desire to bestow will grow out of it. A "woman" is called "desire to receive for oneself." When wanting to revoke and uproot it from the world, the desire to bestow emerges from it, which yields nourishment and life and peace to the world, since through the *Kli* [vessel] of the desire to bestow, called "equivalence of form," we receive the delight and pleasure that the Creator wants to bestow upon the creatures. It is as it is written, "When a woman inseminates and delivers a male child." That is, by burying the vessels of reception, the desire to bestow emerges from it, which is regarded as a male.

However, the male is not born as soon as one sows. Rather, there are nine months of pregnancy. In the work, they are called "ascents and descents." Sometimes a pouring rain comes down and takes all the seeds out of the soil. In the work, this is called the arrival of "evil water," which are *Mi* [who] and *Ma* [what], and *Mi* and *Ma* together are called *Mayim* [water], which takes all the seeds outside.

That is, after he has thrown the will to receive for himself into the ground several times, the thoughts of "who" and "what," where "who" is the argument of Pharaoh, who said, "Who is the Lord that I should obey His voice?" and "what" is the argument of the wicked, who asks, "What is this work for you?" These thoughts take the seeds that were already placed in the earth, in utter lowliness and degradation back up from the ground, and once again, we want to use these *Kelim* [vessels], which are vessels of reception. And once again, we cannot hope to have something with which to furnish ourselves with the abundance that should furnish the spiritual, but we haven't the *Kelim* to receive the abundance, for there is no light without a *Kli*.

However, afterward, another awakening from above comes to a person and he begins once more to inseminate the "woman" in him, called "will to receive for himself." Once again, he buries it in the ground, and once again comes a bad wind or a flood of rain, and so on and so forth. This causes many ascents and descents, and this is regarded as what is written, "They who sow in tears." They are regarded as crying because it appears to them that they are always on the degree at which they began to come into the work of the Creator.

It follows that when they are about to inseminate once more, they sow in tears because they see that each time they begin from the same place and they never move even one step forward. On the contrary, they see that they are going backward. Hence, all their sowings are in tears.

We have already spoken about why the Creator made it so there would be many ascents and descents, meaning who gains from it. The answer is that it is in man's benefit, since there is no light without a *Kli*, meaning no filling without a lack. And since the Creator wants man to need help from above, since through the help, the Creator bestows upon him illumination from above, it is considered that each time, he receives additional *Kedusha*. Thus, at the end of his work, after he has come to a greater lack each time, a person receives a holy soul from above. By this, he is rewarded with being permanently in *Kedusha*, as *The Zohar* says, "He who comes to purify is aided." With what? *The Zohar* says, "with a holy soul," and all this came to him through ascents and descents.

By this we will understand why specifically "They who sow in tears, reap in song." It is because they sow in tears, meaning that each time, he sees that he must begin to sow anew, as though until now he has done nothing. He sees that time is moving forward and that he is going backward, causing him sorrow and pain. By this, he constantly becomes more needy of the Creator's help.

This means that each time, he sees himself, how inherently incapable he is to exit self-love, except through a miracle from above. From all this suffering, a true need and *Kli* is created in him, meaning that now he sees what is written (Psalms 127), "Unless the Lord builds a house, they who built it worked in vain." Only the Creator can help.

It follows that specifically through "They who sow in tears," a person can obtain the need for the Creator's salvation, for then "reap in song" comes true. Sowing means making the *Kli*, and reaping means the reception of the light. That is, the light comes into the *Kli*. This means that when the deficiency is filled, this is called "reaping."

Accordingly, we should interpret what *The Zohar* says, "Since the day of insemination and conception to the day of delivery, a woman has not a word in her mouth except her offspring, whether it will be a male." We asked, What does this come to teach us in the work? When a person begins the holy work, to make it pure, which means that he is working for the sake of the Creator and not for his own sake, that person is called "a woman inseminates first."

This means that the beginning of his work is that he wants to bury in the ground the quality of *Nukva* [female], called "a woman."

He sows that desire in the ground the way one sows seeds in the ground. By this, food grows to furnish the created beings. Likewise, when sowing the will to receive for oneself in the ground, so it will rot, meaning so that the use of the will to receive will be cancelled if it is without an intention to bestow, and to use it only on condition that he can use it in order to bestow, then "she delivers a male child." That is, he is rewarded with the quality of "male," meaning that he has the power to work for the sake of the Creator and not for his own sake.

However, it does not grow at once, as soon as we plant the seed in the soil. Rather, in corporeality, sometimes there are torrential rains that flood the whole area, and all the seeds come out even before they decayed in the soil. It is likewise in the work: A person wants to grow the quality of male as soon as he plants the seed in the ground, meaning that he will be rewarded with the desire to bestow right away.

But since the order is that it is impossible to go against nature at once, since man is born with a desire to receive for himself, hence, there is always the matter of overcoming, meaning that each time, a person begins to overcome the state of descent. That is, once the winds of the world came and took the seeds out of the ground, and the "winds of the world" are thoughts that are foreign to the spirit of *Kedusha*, called "desire to bestow," a person has to overcome and sow once more the will to receive for himself in the ground.

And each time, he tells himself, "Now I will certainly have a male child." That is, *Adama* [ground/soil/earth] comes from the words *Adame la Elyon* [I will be like the Most High], meaning equivalence of form, which is the quality of male. The female, which is the will to receive, will be annulled in the "I will be like the Most High." We should interpret what *The Zohar* says, "Since the day of insemination and conception to the day of delivery, a woman has not a word in her mouth except her offspring, whether it will be a male." That is, each time a person overcomes, he must be certain that now he will be rewarded with the quality of male.

It follows that in each and every sowing, the intention is only to be a male. Otherwise, if his intention is not to be a male, it is not regarded as sowing anything. This is the meaning of what is written (Ecclesiastes 11:4), "He who guards the wind will not sow." Sporno interprets this as follows: "'He who guards the wind will not sow.' Even though sometimes the seed is lost in the stormy wind, which disperses it, still, we should not avoid sowing because we are worried about it."

We should interpret his words in the work. A person sees that he has many descents, and many times he has overcome and sowed, and did not regard the wind, meaning the alien thoughts, called "winds of the world," dispersing them. And as he says, he should not look at the stormy wind, since she is the hardest *Klipa* [shell/peel], opposite the world of *Assiya*, as the ARI says, whose desire is to spread all the seeds that place the will to receive in the ground, since it is against her will. Therefore, the writing says that we must not look at this wind, which wants to disperse the seeds, but overcome and not avoid sowing, and we must believe in the Creator, that "the salvation of the Lord is as the blink of an eye."

Baal HaSulam interpreted that "He who guards the wind will not sow" means that one should not say, "I cannot do anything and I am waiting for the Creator to send me the spirit from above, and then I will have the strength to work. In the meantime, I sit and wait." The writing says about this, "guards the wind," from the verse, "And his father kept the matter," meaning that one who sits and waits will never sow. Rather, a person must make "an awakening from below," and by this comes "an awakening from above." It is as our sages said, "He who comes to purify is aided." However, the person must begin.

Now we can interpret what is written (Malachi 2), "If you do not listen, and if you do not take it to heart to give honor to My name, I will send the curse upon you. I will rebuke your semen and I will spread feces on your faces." The Even Ezra interprets this as follows: "I will rebuke the semen so it will not grow, since My table is empty." The *Metzudat David* interprets this as "I admonish you.

Because of you, I will rebuke the semen so it does not grow. 'And I will spread feces on your faces,' I will spread manure on your faces." He reiterates and interprets, "Manure from beasts that you sacrifice to Me, which is the most loathsome thing in the beast, I will spread it in order to degrade you, the same way you degrade My name."

We should interpret this that in the work, it is when we sow a seed in the ground so it will decay and annul in the ground, which is regarded as "I will be like the Most High," so that a male will grow out of this sowing. But in the middle of the sowing, a person regrets giving "honor to My name," to do everything to glorify His name. Rather, as soon as one sows, a person receives from the "winds of the world," and they ask the person, "What about your own glory?"

That is, what will the person receive for himself from this work of sowing in the ground that will yield a desire to bestow? It follows that by a person degrading the glory of heaven before his own glory, saying that it is not worthwhile to annul his own glory before the glory of heaven, for this reason, the Creator says, "I will send the curse upon you," the curse that the seed will not grow so that you will not be able to receive through this vessels of bestowal because as soon as you receive the thoughts from the "winds of the world," you immediately say that they are right and it is not worthwhile to work for the glory of heaven.

This is the meaning of what the Even Ezra says, "I will rebuke the semen so it will not grow because My table is empty." This means that they engage in Torah and *Mitzvot* [commandments/good deeds], but their intention is not for the sake of the Creator. It follows that the table of the Creator is empty, and everything that you do in Torah and *Mitzvot* is all for man's table, for one's own sake. Thus, you have no need or a *Kli* for me to give you the quality of "male," called "desire to bestow," since there is no light without a *Kli*.

However, the question is, If a person does not want to dedicate one hundred percent of his strength to work for the Creator, and only a small part of him understands that it is worthwhile to work for the Creator, and in that small part, the Creator places a curse that no vessels of bestowal, called "male," will grow out of it, how can one ever be rewarded with vessels of bestowal?

We should interpret this according to the rule that everything that the Creator does is for the purpose of correction. That is, the curse not to grow seeds is also for the benefit of the creatures. This should be interpreted as we interpreted the verse, "He brings down to the netherworld and He lifts up." That is, by seeing that each time he sows, the wind comes and disperses the seeds, a person understands that he must pray to the Creator to give him the strength to stand against the winds.

That is, the Creator should let him feel the importance of obtaining a life of service to the King of the world, since each time he overcomes and sows, the wind promptly disperses it and takes it out of the ground. By this he feels, while engaging in Torah and work, the taste of manure while he is thinking about the aim to bestow.

As the *Metzudat David* interprets, "I will spread manure on your faces," I will spread it to degrade you the way you degrade My name. That is, when you do not pay attention while engaging in Torah and *Mitzvot*, and you do not think that they should be for My name, and do not feel the flaw that you are doing, I will make you feel the taste of manure, so you will not have the strength to do anything even in *Lo Lishma* [not for Her sake], since you will feel the taste of manure even when you engage in *Lo Lishma*. This will cause you to need vessels of bestowal, since you will have no vitality in *Lo Lishma*.

It follows that this curse is when you begin to sow your vessels of reception in the ground so that the will to receive for oneself will be cancelled in the ground. But you do not pay attention to regard the matter of bestowal as much as you need, and you make these sowings without any awareness that it is a key matter, and our lives, for otherwise it is impossible to achieve wholeness. Instead, you do this not so seriously. This is why it says, "I will send," meaning that the Creator Himself has sent these thoughts and disperses the sowings so that you will walk on the path of truth, so they will understand the need for vessels of bestowal.

Now we can understand that a person must believe that all his descents, if they occur while he wants to walk on the path of truth, he must believe that they all come from the Creator. That is, all his descents are for his best; otherwise, he will remain in his current state and will never be able to reach the truth, since he will settle for what he has and will think that this is wholeness. For this reason, when a person comes to purify, specifically then he has descents, so he will not remain in his *Katnut* [smallness/infancy], according to his understanding.

Accordingly, we should interpret what is written in *The Zohar* about the verse, "For the portion of the Lord is His people." The Creator handed the seventy nations to ministers who rule over them, and took to Himself the people of Israel, to rule over them. That is, the Creator is the ruler of Israel, which is not so with the rest of the nations, whom He has given to the rule of ministers.

But what does it mean that he seemingly does not rule over the nations of the world? Is it because it is difficult for the Creator to rule over them because of their inferiority? That is, is it beneath Him to rule over them, so He needed someone to help Him rule over them? But we should believe that "He alone does and will do all the deeds."

In the work, we should interpret that this applies to a single person. When a person is under the rule of the seventy nations, which is generally regarded as "will to receive for himself," because of the restriction that took place, he becomes separated from the Creator. That is, he does not have the faith that the Creator alone "does and will do all the deeds." It follows that a person who receives vitality from the world through things that the Creator has prepared for the creatures while they are still not ready to receive their vitality from *Kedusha*, these people say that the Creator "has left His work" because it is "beneath Him" to tend to them.

When Is One Considered "a Worker of the Creator" in the Work?

This is as it is written in the "Introduction to The Book of Zohar" (Item 4): "I know that there are those who cast over their shoulders the burden of Torah and *Mitzvot*, saying the Creator has created the whole of reality, then left it alone, that because of the worthlessness of the creatures it is not fitting for the exalted Creator to watch over their mean little ways."

It follows that before a person believes that everything comes from the Creator, he says that the whole world was given to the leadership of seventy ministers, which are seventy qualities in nature, or "the rest of the winds," but they do not believe that the Creator oversees it. This is regarded as saying that He has given over the management of the world to seventy ministers. Conversely, one who is "Israel" and believes in the Creator, says that only the Creator is the leader of the world, that "He alone does and will do all the deeds."

Now we can understand what we asked, When is one considered "a worker of the Creator"? Is it specifically when he can work for the sake of the Creator, or is it even in the beginning of his work? According to what Baal HaSulam explained about the verse, "will give wisdom to the wise," the question is that it should have said, "will give wisdom to the fools," since the wise already have wisdom. He explained that "wise" means one who desires wisdom, whereas one who is not wise has no desire for wisdom, as it is written, "The fool has no desire for intelligence."

In the work, we should interpret that "a worker of the Creator" is one who wants to work for the sake of the Creator. Although he is not succeeding, since this requires a real prayer that the Creator will help him, if he began to walk on the right line, meaning that he already has a "left" that resists the right line, then the order of the path of the Creator begins. For this reason, he is already regarded as "a worker of the Creator," since his goal is to come to a state where all his works are for the sake of the Creator.

And although there are many descents and ascents along the way, everything follows the plan, meaning that the descents, too, a part of the work, since by this we acquire the need for the salvation of the Creator. Through the descents, a person comes to the decision that it is impossible to do anything by himself, but that only the Creator can help. This attainment, a person achieves specifically through the descents.

This is as it is written in the book *A Sage's Fruit* (Part 1, p 301): "There is no happier situation in man's world than when he finds himself despaired with his own strength. That is, he has already labored and done all that he could possibly imagine he could do, but found no remedy. It is then that he is fit for a wholehearted prayer for His help because he knows for certain that his own work will not help him. As long as he feels some strength of his own, his prayer will not be whole. It was said about it, 'The Lord is high and the low will see.' Once a person has labored in all kinds of works and has become disillusioned, he comes into real lowliness, knowing that he is the lowest of all people, and there is nothing good about his body. At that time his prayer is whole, since at that time the whole of Israel came to a state of despair from the work. It is as one who pumps out in a punctured bucket. He pumps all day but does not have a drop of water to quench his thirst. So were the children of Israel in Egypt: Whatever they built was promptly swallowed in its place in the ground. Similarly, one who has not been rewarded with His love, all that he has done in his work on purifying the soul the day before is as though completely burned the next day. And each and every day he must start anew as though he hasn't done a thing in his entire life. It follows from the above that anything, small or great, is only obtained by prayer."

Thus, the descents are also regarded as correction, for through them a person can come to be a true "worker of the Creator," when all his works are only in order to bestow. For this reason, as soon as one begins on the path that reaches the work in order to bestow, although there are many failures along the way that are hard for one to overcome, he is already regarded as "a worker of the Creator," since he wants to work for the Creator and not work for himself, meaning that all his thoughts will be only about satisfying the will to receive for himself with the wealth of this world and the wealth of the next world, as it is written in *The Zohar* that they howl as dogs, "Give us the wealth of this world and give us the wealth of the next world."

For this reason, a person must always overcome and believe that only the Creator can help.

What Are Silver, Gold, Israel, Rest of Nations, in the Work?

Article No. 19, Tav-Shin-Mem-Het, 1987/88

It is written in *The Zohar* (Yitro [Jethro], Item 40): "'And Jethro heard.' He started and said, 'Therefore, I will give thanks to You among the nations, O Lord, and I will sing to Your name.' King David said this when he saw that the glory of the Creator was not rising in exaltedness and was not glorified in the world, but only among the rest of the nations. And if you say, 'But is the Creator not glorified in the world only thanks to Israel?' So it is indeed, since Israel are the foundation of the candle to shine. But when the rest of the nations come and thank Him in subjugation to the glory of the Creator, the foundation of the candle is supplemented and strengthens over all His works in one connection, and the Creator alone rules above and below."

We should understand why he says, "So it is indeed, since Creator is glorified in the world only thanks to Israel because Israel are the foundation of the candle to shine. But when the rest of the nations come and thank Him, the foundation of the candle is supplemented." Yet, how is the foundation of the candle supplemented if the nations come and thank the Creator? It appears from this that the people of Israel take strength and assistance from the nations by their thanksgiving, as though the faith that the people of Israel believe in the Creator is so deficient that they must receive assistance from the nations about the greatness of the Creator, as it is written, that the nations add to the foundation of the candle.

This is very difficult to understand. Is it permitted to receive assistance for faith from the nations of the world? After all, the foundation of faith should be based on above reason, so how can a person receive strength that they will have power to go above reason? We learn about this that it is through the Torah, whose light reforms him.

Also, we should pray to the Creator to give us the power of faith in Him, as it is written in the prayer of Rabbi Elimelech ("A Prayer before a Prayer"), "May it please You, that You will set Your Faith in our hearts as a stake that will not fall." It follows that faith must be received from the upper one. Yet, here it implies that if the nations come and thank the Creator, the basis of the faith, called "the foundation of the candle," is supplemented.

In order to explain the above-said, we must remember what Israel and the rest of the nations mean in the work, according to the rule that they all pertain to one person. Israel is called "bestowal," whose actions are only to bestow. This is called "man's good inclination." The rest of the nations are man's vessels of reception, called "man's evil inclination."

It is as we explained about what our sages said, "'Love the Lord your God with all your heart,' with both your inclinations: the good inclination and the evil inclination." We interpreted that this refers to the vessels of bestowal, which are the good inclination, and the evil inclination, which are the vessels of reception. Likewise, we should interpret here what *The Zohar* says, "So it is indeed, since Israel are the foundation of the candle to shine." This means that the foundation upon which man's work is built is in the good inclination, called "vessels of bestowal," called "Israel."

However, this is considered half a degree. This degree is regarded as having superior importance because they are fine *Kelim* [vessels]. This is not considered that the Creator controls all of man's actions, since Israel is called "acts of bestowal," meaning that he can aim with acts of bestowal to bestow upon the Creator. This is why it is considered that the Creator controls him only with vessels of bestowal.

However, the *Sitra Achra* [other side] and the *Klipot* [shells/peels] control the vessels of reception. That is, he cannot aim that they will work for the Creator. These *Kelim* are called "the rest of the nations," "below," since the vessels of reception are of inferior importance.

According to the above, we can interpret what is written, that when the rest of the nations come and thank Him, by subjugation to the glory of the Creator, the foundation of the candle is supplemented. We asked, How can it be said that the people of Israel take strength from the rest of the nations, as it is written, "the foundation of the candle is supplemented"? We should interpret that it means that it is when man's vessels of reception come and admit that we must do everything in order to bestow. This is the meaning of the words, "and thank Him, by subjugation to the glory of the Creator."

It turns out that previously, only Israel could bestow upon the Creator, for Israel recognized the glory of the Creator and that they should enslave themselves to the Creator. But when the rest of the nations come and thank Him and subjugate themselves to the glory of the Creator, meaning that it is worthwhile to work for the sake of the Creator even with vessels of reception, they have the strength to overcome and work in order to bestow. Then, the foundation of the candle is supplemented, for the candle is called "the kingdom of heaven."

That is, the primary foundation is Israel, since the beginning of the work is in vessels of bestowal, called "Israel." Afterward, the foundation of the candle is supplemented, meaning that the vessels of reception, called "the rest of the nations," also enter the authority of *Kedusha* [sanctity/holiness], called "candle" and "kingdom," when the kingdom of heaven controls the rest of the nations.

This is the meaning of the words, "the foundation of the candle is supplemented and strengthens over all His works." This means that acts of reception also enter the *Kedusha*. "In one connection," as we learn from the *Kelim* of *Galgalta Eynaim*, which are vessels of bestowal, that they connect with the *Kelim* of the *AHP*, which are vessels of reception, and become one degree. This is called *Gadlut* [greatness/adulthood].

This is the meaning of what is written, "and the Creator alone rules," referring to the vessels, and not as it was previously, when He controlled only Israel. This is the meaning of the words, "the Creator rules above and below." That is, "He controls" means that both the vessels of bestowal, regarded as higher in importance, and the vessels of reception, regarded as lower in importance, have entered His authority. The Creator governs everything.

We should interpret that at that time a person receives real wholeness, since he already has the vessels for receiving—both *Hassadim*, called *Katnut* [smallness/infancy], and *Hochma*, called *Gadlut*, since now he has *Kelim* that are fit for receiving.

This is the meaning of the words "and the Creator alone rules above and below." This is why David said about this, "I will thank You in the nations, O Lord, and to Your name I shall sing." When the Creator's governance spreads over the nations, too, which are the vessels of reception that have entered the authority of the Creator, there is wholeness in everything.

However, in order to achieve wholeness, so that the rest of the nations in a person will also enter *Kedusha*, there is a process called *Tikkun Kavim* [lines] in *Katnut*, and *Tikkun Kavim* in *Gadlut*, and *Tikkun Kavim* in *VAK*. These are three manners bearing the same name, but there is a difference between them.

The Book of Zohar says (Jethro, Item 499), "'You shall not make with Me gods of silver, or gods of gold.' Rabbi Yosi said, 'What is the reason?' It is because it is written, 'Mine is the silver and Mine is the gold.' Although Mine is the silver and Mine is the gold, you shall not make with Me, meaning Me."

We should understand what it means in the work when the Creator says, "Mine is the silver and Mine is the gold," therefore, "You shall not make Me." We should also understand why He says, "Although Mine is the silver and Mine is the gold," still, "You shall not make Me." What is the "although" that he says?

The order of the work is in two manners: 1) A person craves *Dvekut* [adhesion] with the Creator. This is called *Kisufin* [longing/yearning], and is considered "right line," as it is written, "My soul yearns and also longs for the courtyards of the Lord; my heart and flesh shall sing unto the living God" (Psalms 84). This means that when a person walks on the right line, "my heart and flesh shall sing."

That is, as soon as he remembers the Creator, even if he has been occupied with other things the whole day long, both corporeal matters and spiritual matters, but did not remember about the love of the Creator, as soon as he remembers about the love of the Creator, although the body does not want to love the Creator, still, he longs for these moments when thoughts of love of the Creator come to him, and rejoices that he has remembered that there is a Creator of the world who watches over each and every one.

Hence, on one hand, now he sees how the body objects to these longings. That is, the body does not enjoy a person wanting to adhere to Him. Yet, "My heart and flesh shall sing to the living God." That is, he thanks the Creator for these longings, for having a grip on the Creator. That is, he regards his wanting to adhere to the Creator while the body resists him as a great privilege, too, for now he sees that in him, it is a state of "this and this judge them."

But before he remembered the matter of love of the Creator, he was completely removed from the love of the Creator. He has completely forgotten that there is such a matter called "love of the Creator," and his head was occupied with other matters. Primarily, when he is walking on the right line, he should believe that remembering about the love of the Creator is no coincidence. Rather, it is the Creator turning to him, and placing it in his mind now that there is a Creator and he should connect with Him.

That is, that thought did not come to him of his own, but the Creator turned to him and reminded him about the whole matter of work of the Creator. However, this is only for a short while. That is, this thought does not linger in his mind for long, since as long as a person has not been qualified for it, this thought is short-lived.

It is as it is written, "Behold, these wicked are short-lived and full of anger." Baal HaSulam interpreted that when the wicked obtain some "day," called "light from above," since they are still wicked, meaning they have not emerged from self-reception, the light departs from them. This is called "short-lived." For this reason, they are full of anger. They are angry at why the light has departed from them, for they long for the light.

Yet, when a person is righteous and justifies Providence, he says, "The Creator's taking the awakening away from me is for my own good," and he praises and thanks Him for having the privilege of the little awakening that the Creator has sent him. He rejoices over it. That state of thanking the Creator is called "right" because he yearns for the Creator and does not mind how long he tastes of the manner of "day," and he thanks and praises Him all day for letting him adhere to Him even for one moment. This is called "gods of silver," whose work is in the right, called silver, or the quality of mercy, where he desires only mercy.

2) The left line is called "gods of gold." Baal HaSulam interpreted that *Zahav* [gold] means *Ze Hav* [give this], which is the opposite of the right line, when he wants nothing, but rather yearns for the Creator and wants to annul before Him, while the person himself wants nothing and is happy with whatever he has as though he was given great possessions.

But in the left line, he says, "This I want, and this I do not want." He calculates the profitability. It is as though he points with his finger and says what he wants, specifically through the criticism that he gives. It is as it is written (Job 37:22), "From the north comes gold." *Tzafon* [north] refers to *Matzpunei Halev* [concealed contemplations of the heart], which are views and scrutinies of his actions, meaning what he wants in return for exerting in this world, what reward he hopes for. Corrections pertain specifically to the left line.

In other words, when a person begins to scrutinize the details in the work, meaning examining for whom he works and what for, he begins to feel the real labor that exists in serving the Creator. The person already thinks that he knows what is good for him and what is bad for him, and thinks that this is what is upon him—that his work will be in the way of the left line. This is called "gods of gold." Although the Creator gave him these thoughts, called "left line," still, the Creator said, "You shall not make with Me gods of silver and gods of gold."

By this we should interpret the words of Rabbi Yosi, who asked, What is the reason? It is because it is written, "Mine is the silver and Mine is the gold." Although Mine are the silver and gold, you will not make with Me, meaning Me. We should interpret that although I have given you the right line, called "gods of silver," and I have given you the left line, too, and I sent you all the thoughts that you are feeling, still, do not make Me, meaning that the real work is specifically in the middle line. This means that what the Creator said, "Mine is the silver and Mine is the gold," means that "Mine," meaning although I have given you, this is not the end, but you must walk on the middle line, as this line consists of both.

Yet, from where do we take the strength to be able to walk in all those ways? It was said about this, "I have created the evil inclination; I have created the Torah as a spice," as we interpreted, that everything is found in the Torah. That is, when we learn Torah, we should demand reward from the study of Torah, which we understand in two general ways: 1) Our reward will be as in "The light in it reforms him," meaning that he will be rewarded with vessels of bestowal, for without help from above, it is impossible to emerge from self-love. 2) To be rewarded with the Torah, as it is written in *The Book of Zohar*, "He who does not know the commandments of the upper one, how will he serve Him?"

This is the reward that one should ask through his exertion in the Torah. Clearly, the study of Kabbalah is better capable of eliciting the light of Torah. It is as it is written in the book *A Sage's Fruit* (Vol. 2, p 160): "Since the whole of the wisdom of Kabbalah speaks of the revelation of the Creator, naturally, there is none more successful teaching for its task."

In other words, when a person learns Torah with the aim to receive the light of Torah, we should understand that since the wisdom of Kabbalah speaks also of the topic of Godliness, whereas in the rest of the parts of the Torah, the Torah is clothed in corporeal subjects, it is therefore more difficult to elicit from there the light of Torah, for it is difficult to focus on the one who is clothed in the Torah, namely the Creator, although "The whole Torah is the names of the Creator."

In the introduction to the book *Utterances of Joseph* by the ADMOR of Spinka, he writes there in the name of the ADMOR from the Rabbi of Tsanz, who interprets the verse (Proverbs 25), "The glory of God is to conceal a matter, and the glory of kings is to examine a matter."

The question is, What is the difference between the glory of God and the glory of kings? That is, both certainly refer to spirituality, so, what is the difference between these two degrees?

He interpreted that if a person wishes to learn the wisdom of Kabbalah, to know how many worlds and *Sefirot* there are, meaning the glory of God, to know the measure of His glory, conceal the matter. However, if he wants to learn the wisdom, to know how to crown the Creator and serve Him with intention, and to sanctify his 248 organs and make them a chariot for *Kedusha* [holiness/sanctity], which is the glory of kings—how to crown and serve Him—examine the matter. We see that the study of the wisdom of Kabbalah is a special remedy that gives a person the power to sanctify himself and be a chariot to the Creator.

Our sages wrote (*Avot de Rabbi Natan*, Chapter 29,7), "Rabbi Yitzhak Ben Pinhas says, 'Anyone who has learning in his hand but no practice, does not taste the taste of wisdom. Anyone who has practice in his hand but no learning, does not taste the taste of the fear of sin.'" He interprets there, "does not taste the taste of the fear of sin": The sayings and the interpretations are filled with admonition, ethics, and allegories that bring to man the fear of sin. Moreover, the wise disciples, who engage in rules of times, their hearts are haughty and they believe that they are wise, and God forbid that they should come to pride, the evil inclination chases them because the engagement (of the evil inclination) is more with wise disciples, as it is written (*Sukkah* 52), "Anyone who is greater than his friend, his inclination is greater than him."

We should understand why the rules cannot yield fear of sin, and why interpretations are preferable to rules, since it is known that the whole Torah is the names of the Creator. We should also understand why rules are called "wisdom," meaning what does it imply to us that the rules are called "wisdom."

An interpretation is called *Drush*. The writing says (Jeremiah 30:17), "For they have called you Zion, no one demands her." RADAK interprets that the nations of the world called you and said that Zion is a city that no one demands to return to Israel. Our sages said, "Zion, no one demands her, meaning that it needs to be required."

It is known that *Malchut* is called Zion. "Demand" means "demanding and asking." That is, a person demands only what he needs, and then he asks to satisfy his need. When beginning to engage in Torah and *Mitzvot* [commandments], we begin in *Lo Lishma* [not for Her sake], as our sages said, "One should always engage in Torah and *Mitzvot Lo Lishma*, and from *Lo Lishma* we come to *Lishma* [for Her sake]." Therefore, when a person accustoms himself to work *Lo Lishma*, he does not feel a lack in his inability to work *Lishma*. Because he does not feel a deficiency in his situation, he has no need to correct it. This causes him that when the desire to bestow awakens in him—when we must work for the sake of the Creator and not for our own sake—he feels the taste of dust in this work. This is what *The Zohar* refers to when it says that man should exert in Torah and *Mitzvot* in order to raise the *Shechina* [Divinity] from the dust.

In other words, in the work, when a person must work for the sake of the *Shechina*, he tastes the taste of dust because he is accustomed to working only for his own sake. By engaging in Torah, the Torah reforms him, and then he feels the taste of life in his work, since through the aim to bestow he receives *Dvekut* with the Life of Lives.

However, a person should certainly ask the Creator to raise the kingdom of heaven, meaning to make it important. Because the lower ones are unfit to receive the abundance from her, which *Malchut* [kingdom] must bestow upon the lower ones, for *Malchut* is called "the assembly of Israel," the collection of all the souls, she must hide herself so as not to show what she has to give to the lower ones.

This is so for Israel's benefit. Otherwise, if she reveals her greatness, everyone will receive from her in order to receive. For this reason, she must hide herself, and all that is revealed of her is the taste of dust.

But even the taste of dust that we receive from her is also to man's benefit. That is, a person must know that this will make him research the reason for the taste of dust he finds in her when assuming the burden of the kingdom of heaven in order to bestow.

The Torah promised us that if we follow the path of the Creator, meaning that all our actions will be with the intention to bestow, we will feel the taste of life, as it is written, "Taste and see that the Lord is good." Thus, why do we feel the taste of dust? By this we see if we are truly marching on the path of truth, or not. The fact that we feel the taste of dust testifies to our work. We must know that this is so because we still do not have vessels of bestowal.

For this reason, the *Shechina* must be in the dust, and we must ask of the Creator to raise her from the dust by giving us a spirit of purity and removing self-love from our hearts. By this we will be rewarded with seeing the beauty of the *Kedusha* and will be able to understand what is written, that a person should pray to the Creator for the exile of the *Shechina* and the sorrow of the *Shechina*.

We should understand why the *Shechina* is in sorrow and the Creator does not raise her from the dust. Instead, we must ask the Creator to raise her, and without our prayer He will not raise her, as it is written (in the Blessing for the Food), "The Merciful One will establish for us the fallen tabernacle of David." That is, He needs us to ask. But what is the reason?

According to the above, we will understand that the concealment, when *Malchut* is in the dust and in the dark, is so that the lower ones can work in order to bestow. It follows that the sorrow of the *Shechina* is that she must hide the delight and pleasure that she wants to impart upon the souls but cannot because it will be to their detriment, for through the abundance she imparts upon them while they are in vessels of self-reception, they will be farther from *Kedusha*, as the abundance will go to the *Klipot*. It follows that in the upper one, sorrow means that he cannot bestow upon the lower ones. This is called "the sorrow of the *Shechina*."

For this reason, we pray to the Creator to give us the strength to overcome the vessels of reception for ourselves, and then we will be able to work only in order to bestow. At that time the *Shechina* will be able to show the glory and grandeur in her by having the ability to receive what she wants to impart. There is a rule: "The cow wants to feed more than the calf wants to eat." Thus, everything depends on the receivers.

It turns out that when a person engages in Torah and *Mitzvot* without aiming to receive in return for his work the light that reforms him, but rather learns rules without paying attention to the interpretation, meaning to the discernment, "Zion, no one demands her," when he has no demand and request to raise the

Shechina from the dust, it is as the RADAK says, "For Zion is a city that none demand to return to Israel." We should interpret the words of the RADAK, as it is written (in the *Selichot* ["asking for forgiveness," prayers said in the period leading up to the High Holidays]), "I shall remember God and I will wail when I see every city standing firm, yet the city of God is lowered to the bottom of the underworld."

This means that the city of God is called "Zion." Those who engage in Torah and *Mitzvot*, there is no one to see and demand that the city of Zion be returned to Israel, meaning that the kingdom of heaven, called *Shechina*, will return to the whole of Israel, and to the individual Israel that exists in each and every one.

By this we should interpret what our sages said, "Anyone who has practice in his hand but no learning, does not taste the taste of the fear of sin." This is because the fear of sin means that he is afraid that he might not be able to aim in order to bestow, but in order to receive for himself, as it is written in the *Sulam* ("Introduction to The Book of Zohar").

We should know that a person cannot have fear of not being able to work in order to bestow. Rather, a person has a demand for Zion, meaning that he works in order to "raise the *Shechina* from the dust" and wants the city of God not to be lowered to the bottom of the underworld. This can be specifically by wanting to work in order to bestow, or else *Malchut* must hide her importance so the abundance will not go to the *Klipot*.

It follows that precisely he fears sin, since for him, a sin means one who is not working in order to bestow. He regards reception as sin because this is the only obstructor, making the *Shechina* unable to be in revealed face, but rather in concealed face. This is called "the sorrow of the *Shechina*," that she is unable to give to the created beings the delight and pleasure she has in store for them.

It follows that if a person sympathizes with the sorrow of the *Shechina*, it means that he has reflected on what he causes by being immersed in self-love. That is, to the extent that a person wants to enjoy pleasures that pertain to, and can be accepted by the vessels of reception, that vitality is called "vitality of the *Klipot*," meaning the vitality that *The Zohar* calls "a thin light," which was given to the *Klipot* to sustain them.

They impart this vitality to all those who are still unable to receive the light of *Kedusha*, which is imparted specifically on vessels of bestowal. This means that we must believe that there is no vitality in the world except from the Creator. That is, even the vitality that is received in the vessels of reception is regarded as received by the *Klipot*. This means that the *Klipot* are the givers and not the Creator Himself, for it is impossible to be in permanent faith prior to attaining the vessels of bestowal, as explained ("Introduction of The Book of Zohar").

It follows that the vitality that they receive is through the *Klipot*, which is considered that He has given dominion over the nations of the world to ministers and not He Himself governs them. It is as we interpreted, that in the work this means that people who have only partial faith are regarded as "nations of the world," who say that ministers of above—whether ministers or nature or of other spirits—influence life in the world, and they cannot say that only the Creator governs.

It follows that they are given to the *Klipot*, meaning that they say so, but this is regarded as the sorrow of the *Shechina* in that she must hide herself from the creatures. This is similar to an allegory of a mother who must hide herself from her child. She hands over the child to some institution for retarded children, where the treatment is nothing like the mother's treatment of the child, and the child does not even know he has a mother. As a result, the child suffers and the mother suffers from not being able to raise her child and give him everything he needs, as with a mother and son. This is called "the sorrow of the *Shechina*" that she suffers.

For this reason, He has given us the work in Torah and *Mitzvot* to engage in them with the aim to raise the *Shechina* from the dust, so she will not suffer the sorrow of not being able to tend to her child, for it is for the benefit of the child not to know he has a mother who longs for him.

In other words, through engagement in Torah and Mitzvot with the aim because of the sorrow of the Shechina, it will mean that since the reason why the Shechina cannot be revealed to them is the disparity of form of the will to receive, and since the light of Torah reforms a person, we want to be reformed, meaning to be rewarded with vessels of bestowal through the Torah and Mitzvot, by which we are granted fear.

Through fear, we are rewarded with faith. At that time we are rewarded with knowing who governs Israel, that only He alone governs. This means that the Creator knows that He is the governor, but the lower ones do not feel it before they are rewarded with faith, as it is written in the "Introduction of The Book of Zohar" (Item 138), "It follows that although He alone does and will do all the deeds, it still remains hidden from those who feel good and bad."

It therefore follows that one should ask the Creator to give him vessels of bestowal so there will not be sorrow for the Shechina because she must be concealed from man. As was said, this is for man's benefit. However, it is for man's benefit only so that he will not go deeper into the authority of the Sitra Achra [other side], but from this, a person does not achieve the purpose, for the purpose of creation is for the creatures to receive delight and pleasure. Hence, as long as the creatures are unfit to receive the delight and pleasure, it is regarded as the sorrow of the Shechina, since she cannot impart upon them what the creatures should receive from her.

Now we can interpret why our sages said, "Anyone who has practice but no learning, does not taste the taste of the fear of sin." The interpretation of "learning" is as it is written, "Zion, no one demands her," meaning there is no one who demands and asks the Creator to bring the city of Zion back to the people of Israel. At that time he begins to understand the reason for her fall, as it is written, "She has fallen, she will not rise again, the virgin of Israel," which comes to us because we are in self-love.

By knowing the reason, we begin to understand what is the sin, so we may know what to correct. At that time we come to feel that the whole sin is that we are immersed in self-love. Hence, only by this can we come to the fear of sin, meaning to know what is the sin, for which we suffer because we cannot receive the delight and pleasure.

According to the above, we should interpret what is written, "Anyone who has learning in his hand but no practice, does not taste the taste of wisdom." It is known that there is no light without a *Kli* [vessel]. Generally, a light is regarded as the Creator's desire to give to the created beings. This is called "His desire to do good to His creations." This name includes the light called *Hochma* [wisdom]. But there is a second light, called "the light of the correction of creation." This is called "light of *Hassadim* [mercies]." This means that the Creator should give to the creatures two lights.

According to the known rule, that we do not speak of the world of *Ein Sof* [infinity] but begin to speak after *Tzimtzum Aleph* [first restriction], meaning once a judgment has been passed that it is forbidden to use the vessels of reception and we must build new *Kelim* that will be fit for reception of the abundance and there will not be separation. It is known that this is called "vessels of bestowal," which are *Kelim* that come from the correction of creation.

That is, once we already have creation, which is vessels of reception, which is the substance of all the creatures, namely the will to receive for oneself, on this *Kli* we can draw two lights: 1) The light of the correction of creation, which can be drawn through the light in the Torah, as our sages said, "The light in it reforms him." By this we obtain the *Kli* called "desire to bestow." This is regarded as having fear, meaning he already contemplates everything, whether to do it or not. If he sees that he cannot aim to bestow, he is careful not to touch it.

A person cannot make this *Kli*, as it is against the nature of creation, which was that the creatures would receive delight and pleasure. And what the creatures cannot receive for themselves comes later from *Tzimtzum Aleph*. However, this pertains to the creatures after *Malchut de Ein Sof* yearned for equivalence of form. We learned that then, the *Masach* [screen] was made. Through that *Masach*, by the power of rejection when it does not want to receive, a new *Kli* was born, called *Ohr Hozer* [Reflected Light].

That *Ohr Hozer* is born out of two forces: 1) the *Masach*, which is called "the detaining force," which does not want to be a receiver for itself; 2) the light, which wants to give, for the lower one to receive the abundance.

Out of those two, this *Ohr Hozer* is born. We should understand that the lower one receives great pleasure in wanting to bestow upon the upper one. At that time the lower one comes to feel what the lower one has to give to the upper one, that the upper will enjoy, because what does the upper one lack which the lower one can give to Him? At that time he comes to realize that all the pleasure of the upper one is in the lower one assisting Him to complete the purpose of the upper one. That is, the lower one gives the upper one the opportunity for the upper one to satisfy His desire. And since the desire of the upper one is to do good to His creations, for the lower ones to receive delight and pleasure, the lower one comes to receive from the upper one delight and pleasure, for this is His will, as it is written at length in *The Study of the Ten Sefirot* (Part 4, *Histaklut Pnimit*).

It therefore follows that once he has received new *Kelim* from the upper one, namely vessels of bestowal, which come to him through the learning, now is the time to receive the light into the new *Kelim* he has obtained.

2) This is the second discernment, to draw abundance from the upper one. This is called *Hochma* [wisdom], which is the purpose of creation, for the creatures to receive delight and pleasure. This light is called "light of wisdom," and it is regarded as learning rules, as it was written, "Anyone who has learning in his hand but no practice, does not taste the taste of wisdom."

We should understand the connection between *Halachot* [rules/practices] and wisdom. It is known that *Malchut* is called *Halacha* [rule/practice], from the word *Kalah* [bride]. Also, the *Kli* to receive the light of wisdom is *Malchut*, and the vessels of bestowal are called *Bina*. It is known that the light of *Bina* is called "the light of the correction of creation," which is light of *Hassadim*. Accordingly, "Anyone who has learning," meaning that he has been rewarded with vessels of bestowal, "has the fear of sin," meaning his fear is that he may not have the power to bestow, meaning that he has already obtained vessels of bestowal, called *Bina*.

At that time he should try to have *Halachot* [practices], meaning to exert in obtaining the *Kalah* [bride], which is *Malchut*, who is regarded as the vessel of reception for light of *Hochma*. It is as it is written in the *Sulam* [Ladder Commentary] ("Introduction of The Book of Zohar," Item 203): "Fear is a *Mitzva* [commandment] that contains all the *Mitzvot* in the Torah, as it is the gate of the faith in Him. And according to the awakening of one's fear, the faith in the Creator is in him. ...However, both the first fear and the second fear are not for his own benefit, but only for fear that he will decline in bringing contentment to his Maker."

Thus, we see that first we must be rewarded with fear, and then we are rewarded with the light of faith, since complete faith is when the light of *Hassadim* shines in illumination of *Hochma*. This is called *Halacha* [practice], as it is written, "Anyone who has practice, tastes the taste of wisdom," and the interpretation is—the taste of the fear of sin.

However, what can one do if even when he feels that he already has fear, meaning that he wants to bestow upon the Creator, and thinks that he will ascend degree by degree to the highest level, but he soon gets thoughts that show him he should look at the past, meaning that he has already had times when he thought he had been rewarded with something, and he was certain that from that day forward he would have no descents and he would not suffer from being unable to overcome his evil anymore, but as he finds taste in the work now, so it will continue.

But what happened afterwards? He fell from his degree back into a state of suffering that he does not have this world, meaning a life with satisfaction. Instead, he has neither satisfaction nor the next world, meaning the desire to do the holy work. Therefore, now that he is a little higher than the previous states and wants to engage in the holy work gladly, what can he do if his thoughts disrupt him with just thoughts?

In his opinion, there is nothing to reply to them. For this reason, he cannot do anything, as though now he is in a state of descent. Thus, what use is it that he has now been given help from above and believes that the Creator is calling him and wants to bring him closer? But the arguments of the thoughts tell him, "See for yourself, this happens to you every time. Each time you think you are above, you fall deep down. So what makes you certain that this time will not be the same?"

Yet, we should follow the path of our sages, who instructed us (*Sotah* 48b), "Anyone who has bread in his basket and says, 'What shall I eat tomorrow?' is among those of little faith." It is as Rabbi Elazar in *Metzudat David* (Zachariah 4), "'Who has despised the day of smallness [*Katnut*]?' Who caused the righteous to despise their future table? The smallness that was in them—that they did not believe in the Creator." We should understand what he says, "Who caused the righteous to despise their future table? that they did not believe in the Creator. This is their smallness. Yet, if they did not believe in the Creator, why are they considered righteous?"

We should interpret the writing that calls them "righteous" while they have no faith. It means that after a person receives an awakening from above, he comes to feel that the most important is to work in order to bestow, and it is not worth working for himself. Thus, now he feels that he is righteous and should thank the Creator for bringing him closer to Him and removing from him the concealment.

For this reason, now he wants to annul before Him. Now he understands and feels that reception for oneself is called "bad," and one who uses it is called a "sinner." It follows that at that time he is called "righteous," as it is written, "Anyone who has bread in his basket and says, 'What shall I eat tomorrow?' is among those of little faith."

This means that now he has faith and he believes that the most important is to adhere to the Creator, and it is not worth it to think of himself for even a moment. Therefore, he should be delighted that he has been rewarded with nearing the Creator. Yet, right away, thoughts come to him that the faith he has now is small, meaning that he will not be able to continue tomorrow. Instead, he thinks that soon this faith will leave him and he will fall once more into the control of the wicked, who care only for their own benefit. It follows that this is the question that he asks, "What shall I eat tomorrow?"

There is a rule that "tomorrow" does not mean the next day. Rather, "tomorrow" means "after some time." In other words, the "present" is called "today" and the future is called "tomorrow." That is, the moment he stands in now is called "present" and "today," and the next moment is called "tomorrow." This causes him not to be able to praise the Creator for having brought him closer.

These thoughts, "What shall I eat tomorrow," remove him from the Creator because he does not believe that this state will remain forever. It follows that although now he is at the degree of righteous, because he does not believe that it will stay permanently, he is regarded among those of little faith. That is, he has faith, but his faith will be with him briefly and then his faith will depart. This is called "of little faith."

Now we can interpret the words of Rabbi Elazar, "Why it is written, 'Who has despised the day of smallness [*Katnut*]?' Who caused the righteous to despise their future table?" The words, "Who caused the righteous" refer to those people who are in a state of ascent and yearn only to adhere to the Creator. At that time there are righteous who despise their future table. That is, that table, which is set for a meal, they despise them in the future, meaning that they say, "After the present," meaning after the state he is in now, when this table is fine, "afterward," meaning in the time that will come later, "it will be despised." That is, afterward, the table will be under the control of the *Sitra Achra*, meaning that it will fall once more into the control of the will to receive for oneself.

This is the meaning of the verse, "Who despises the day of smallness." The smallness that was in them is that they did not believe that the Creator can give a permanent state of nearing. It follows that a person must not awaken any lack in the gift of the Creator and say that now it is clear to him that the Creator cannot give something permanently, and bring evidence from the past, that he has had good states several times, which then departed from him, so there is no proof that the current state will be forever. Here comes the matter of faith, that one must believe above reason and not regard what reason dictates, but believe with faith in the sages that the way they determined is how we should go, and not look at the reason, for we must believe that going with faith is a wondrous *Segula* [virtue/remedy].

What Is the Reward in the Work of Bestowal?

Article No. 20, Tav-Shin-Mem-Het, 1987/88

Our sages said (*Avot*, Chapter 2:21), "If you learned much Torah, you are given a great reward, and you can trust your landlord to pay you for your work." We therefore see that we must work for the reward. Moreover, there is a special commandment that we must believe that the Creator will pay our reward. But there, in Chapter 1, they said the complete opposite: "He would say, 'Be not as slaves serving the rav [great one] in order to receive reward. Rather, be as slaves serving the rav not in order to receive reward.'" We should understand how these two statements are valid.

It is known that every branch wants to resemble its root. Since our root, which is the Creator, is in a state of complete rest, the creatures cannot make a single movement unless it improves man's state of rest. Otherwise, a person chooses rest, as it is written in *The Study of the Ten Sefirot* (Part 1, *Histaklut Pnimit*, Item 19): "It is known that the nature of every branch is equal to its root. Therefore, every conduct in the root is desired and loved and coveted by the branch, as well, and any matter that is not in the root, the branch, too, distances itself from them. ...For example, we love rest and vehemently hate movement, to the point that we do not make a single movement if not to find rest."

In other words, we do not make a single movement unless we know that this movement will improve our rest. That is, this improved rest that we receive is called "reward." This means that if movement causes us to enjoy rest more, we can move. Otherwise, we stay motionless.

Concerning the reward, there is a clear statement in the Torah: "If you follow My laws and keep My commandments and do them, I will give your rains in their time and the land will yield its crop." Thus, why did our sages say that we should work without reward, called "not in order to receive reward"? This is the complete opposite of what is written in the Torah. Also, one of the tenets is to believe in reward and punishment. So, how did our sages say that a person should work not in order to receive reward?

We should understand why our sages said, "Be as slaves serving the rav not in order to receive reward." This seems to contradict the purpose of creation, since the purpose of creation is to do good to His creations, and this is why the Creator created the creatures with vessels of reception, meaning to have a desire and yearning to receive delight and pleasure.

Thus, why must we relinquish the yearning for delight and pleasure and try only to bestow upon the Creator and not satisfy the yearning for pleasures, as He Himself created us in such a nature? Also, how can they afterward tell us, "No, although He created us with a nature for reception of pleasures, still, it is currently forbidden to use these *Kelim* [vessels], called "will to receive for ourselves."

The answer is that since every branch wants to resemble its root, as said above, and since the Creator is the giver, where a person needs to receive for himself there is the issues of shame. In order to correct the shame, there was a correction called "receiving in order to bestow." It therefore follows that saying that it is forbidden to receive for oneself is not because it is forbidden to enjoy. Rather, it is a correction: When a person receives pleasure, because during the reception of pleasure he is in disparity of form from the giver, he feels unpleasantness during the reception of the pleasure.

However, if he receives the pleasure because he wants to delight the upper one, by this he receives equivalence of form. At that time, he has two things upon reception of the pleasure: 1) He does not become far from the Creator upon receiving the pleasure. 2) He does not feel any deficiency upon receiving the pleasure.

It follows that the prohibition to receive for himself is for the sake of the created beings, and not because the Creator needs to be bestowed upon or loved. Everything is only for the sake of the created beings, who receive the pleasure from Him, and to have completeness in the pleasure.

With respect to the correction of the world, two systems were made: 1) ABYA de [of] Kedusha [holiness/sanctity], where there is only the order of reception in order to bestow, 2) ABYA de Tuma'a [impurity], where there is reception in order to receive.

Hence, before a person corrects his actions to be in order to bestow, he is fed by what he drew from ABYA de Tuma'a. Now we can understand what we asked, that we should believe in reward and punishment, yet we are told to work not in order to receive reward, meaning to work for no reward at all. The answer is that the Creator wants to give, as this was His purpose—to do good to His creations. However, there was a correction: "in order to bring to light the perfection of His deeds," that we will work not in order to receive reward. Only on this correction, not to receive reward, we must make great efforts and do much work, as it is against our nature. Only through the Segula [power/merit] of Torah and Mitzvot [commandments/good deeds] can we be rewarded with these Kelim, called "vessels of bestowal."

Our reward is that we should believe in reward and punishment. That is, if we observe the Torah and Mitzvot we will be rewarded with vessels of bestowal. If we do not observe the Torah and Mitzvot, we will remain in vessels of reception, which cannot do anything in

Kedusha. Hence, how will it be possible to receive the delight and pleasure that the Creator wants to give them?

Therefore, as soon as we begin to walk on the path of bestowal, the body begins to resist, and we must believe in our sages who said, "He who comes to purify is aided," and in what our sages also said, that the Creator said, "I have created the evil inclination; I have created the Torah as a spice," since through the Torah, "the light in it reforms him." We should believe that the Creator will give us this reward in return for our work in Torah and *Mitzvot*. Thus, there will be no contradiction between what they say, that we must believe in reward and punishment, and what they say on the other hand, that we must be as "slaves serving the rav not in order to receive reward."

The answer is that since we should work not in order to receive reward, and it is against our nature and we cannot correct ourselves in this correction, this is why they said, "Man's inclination overcomes him every day. Were it not for the help of the Creator, he would not overcome it." Thus, only the Creator can help him by giving him vessels of bestowal. This is the reward for which man should pray that He will give him, since by himself, he cannot obtain vessels of bestowal.

Moreover, one must believe that the Creator will give us this power because many times a person toils and labors to obtain vessels of bestowal, but from the perspective of the correction, which man cannot understand, sometimes a person begins this work of bestowal but sees otherwise—that he is regressing. That is, now that he has begun the work of bestowal, he has become more materialistic, meaning the will to receive for himself is working within him more vigorously.

It follows that he sees that the will to receive in him is working more vigorously each time, until a person despairs and says that he sees that there is no chance that he will ever be rewarded with the desire to bestow. At that point, he says, "I have worked for nothing. That is, I thought that through my labor in Torah and *Mitzvot* I would be rewarded and it would be as a gift for me to receive that which I have hoped for all the time—to be rewarded with bringing contentment to the Creator and emerging from self-love. But now I see that this is not for me, as I am more materialistic than the rest of the people. In the beginning of my work, I thought that I was not so immersed in self-love, so I thought that this work of achieving the aim to bestow would take as long as any profession we learn. It is not easy to learn a profession, and requires much learning until one acquires the profession he is learning, regardless of the craft—carpentry or a locksmith's work, or even medicine and so forth. They all require time. Some professions require three years to learn, or five years, but there is patience to wait until the time is up. There, a person can work because he sees that each day he is progressing, so he understands that there will come a time, at the end of the three or five years, when he receives his diploma and can get a job in his profession."

But in the work of bestowal, he sees that each day he is regressing. A year or two may pass and he sees that he has not moved one bit. At that time, he despairs and says that he will never be able to get a diploma that he is working in order to bestow. Naturally, he will not be able to receive the Torah, for only faithful people are admitted there, who will not spoil the Torah that they are given. Since he sees that he cannot get a diploma that he is working *Lishma* [for Her sake], he will never be rewarded with the secrets of Torah, as our sages said, "He who learns Torah *Lishma* is shown the secrets of Torah."

For this reason, he wants to escape the campaign. Our sages said about this state that a person must brace himself and believe that "You can trust your landlord to pay you for your work." That is, if a person exerts in Torah and *Mitzvot* in order to receive reward, to be given the power of bestowal, he should not pay attention to his stalled progress. He must believe that if a person makes an effort to be rewarded with vessels of bestowal, the Creator will certainly give him. It follows that this is the reward that we ask for our work: to be able to work without reward, but because "He is great and ruling."

Accordingly, we should interpret what is written (in the prayer, "May it please," before Psalms): "Grant me the treasure of a free gift." That is, we pray and say psalms with the intention that we are not only asking for a reward, but we also want You to give us from the treasure of a free gift. We should understand, since it is known that one must do everything not in order to receive reward.

However, we should interpret that we want You to give us abundance from the treasure of a free gift because if we receive abundance from there, we will be able to work for nothing, not in order to receive reward. Similarly, when someone needs healing, we ask the Creator to send healing from the treasure of healings. Or, if someone needs strength, he asks to be sent strength from the treasure of strengths.

Therefore, one who wants to receive strength from above so he can work for free, without any reward, asks the Creator to give him strength "from the treasure of a free gift," meaning to be given strength, which to him is a great gift, meaning to be able to do things for free. He regards this as a gift, as it is written, "As I am for nothing, so you are for nothing."

Now we can interpret what is written (Psalms 121), "I will lift up my eyes to the mountains; from where shall my help come? My help is from the Lord, Maker of heaven and earth." We should understand David's question, "From where shall my help come?" and afterward his finding that "My help is from the Lord." But every believing Jew says that a person has no other place to receive help but the Creator, so what is the novelty?

We should interpret in the above that it comes to tell us that in order to receive delight and pleasure, we lack nothing but vessels of bestowal, for then we will have equivalence of form with the Creator, as in, "As He is merciful, so you are merciful." Then we will be fit to receive the delight and pleasure.

For this reason, we should interpret according to the known rule that all of creation, which we define by the name "creation," is only the will to receive for oneself that was created existence from absence. That is, concerning the Creator, we should say that He is the giver and the bestower. But reception is a new thing that the Creator created from nothing. That is, "nothing" means that there is no reception there. This is why it is written, "from absence," meaning that what exists in the Creator is that He only bestows. If a person can come to that state, called "nothing," then "my help shall come." At that time, a person is ready to receive the delight and pleasure.

This is the meaning of the words, "My help is from the Lord, Maker of heaven and earth." Here he interprets the meaning of "nothing," meaning the opposite of reception, but rather bestowal. This is the meaning of the words, "Maker of heaven and earth." It means that He has made heaven and earth, meaning that He bestowed and engendered heaven and earth. When a person achieves the state of "absence," called "the power of bestowal," he will be fit to receive delight and pleasure, since nothing is missing from the perspective of the Creator, except for *Kelim*—for the lower one to be able to receive.

This is the meaning of the words, "From where shall my help come?" It is written that one should not think that anything big is missing in order to receive this delight and pleasure that the Creator wants to give to the created beings. That is, when a person exerts to complete the purpose for which he was created, yet sees that he has still not risen higher than the level at which he was when he was nine years old, and he understands the work of the Creator as he understood when he was nine, when he examines the reason, he says, "I must have been born untalented and I am powerless to overcome. If I were more talented, I would be more noble and I would achieve wholeness."

It follows that he thinks that he is missing many things. But in truth, man lacks nothing but equivalence of form, called "vessels of bestowal," as it is written, "As He is merciful, so you are merciful," for bestowal is regarded as "absence."

This is what he wants to tells us when he says, "From where shall my help come?" that all we lack is this, and not any talent or nobility. Rather, "My help is from the Lord," for the Creator made heaven and earth in order to bestow upon people. This is what I need the Creator to help me attain, as this is the *Kli* [vessel]. After a person has this *Kli*, called "vessel of bestowal," the light will come by itself, for such was the purpose of creation—to do good to His creations.

What Does It Mean that the Torah Was Given Out of the Darkness in the Work?

Article No. 21, Tav-Shin-Mem-Het, 1987/88

It is written in the Midrash (*VaYikra*, Chapter 6): "Our sages say, 'The nations of the world did not receive the Torah, since it was given out of the darkness. He says about them, 'for the darkness will cover the Earth' (Isaiah 60:2). But Israel received the Torah, since it was given out of the darkness, as it is written (Deuteronomy 5), 'As you hear the voice out of the darkness.' He says about them (Isaiah 60): 'The Lord will shine upon you and His glory will be seen upon you.'"

We should understand why the Torah was given out of the darkness, and why the nations of the world did not want to receive it out of the darkness. It is as though the Creator deliberately gave the Torah out of the darkness so the nations of the world would not

What Does It Mean that the Torah Was Given Out of the Darkness?

receive it. And we should also understand why Israel did receive the Torah out of the darkness.

First, we need to know what is darkness in the work. The thing is that because the purpose of creation was "to do good to His creations," when a person is satisfied with his life, it is considered that the world shines for that person, meaning he enjoys the world. But if he does not find satisfaction in life, he says, "The world has grown dark on me."

It is known that in the work, we call the vessels of bestowal "Israel," and we call the vessels of reception, "the nations of the world." Hence, when a person wants to draw near to the Creator, meaning use the vessels of bestowal, but he cannot because the body disagrees with it, since his body extends from vessels of reception, at that time a person feels that the world has grown dark on him, for he understands that if he cannot obtain vessels of bestowal, he will never be rewarded with the upper light, which is the light of "doing good to His creations."

It follows that the darkness he feels from not being able to obtain vessels of bestowal by himself gives him the need that someone will help him obtain those *Kelim* [vessels]. According to the rule, "There is no light without a *Kli* [vessel], no filling without a lack," it follows that now he has received a need for the light of Torah. It is as our sages said, "I have created the evil inclination; I have created the Torah as a spice."

Thus, the Torah is given specifically to the deficient, and that deficiency is called "darkness." This is the meaning of the words, "The Torah was given out of the darkness." That is, one who feels darkness in his life because he has no vessels of bestowal is fit to receive the Torah, so that through the Torah, the light in it will reform him and he will obtain the vessels of bestowal. Through them, he will be fit to receive the delight and pleasure, for those two are included in the Torah: 1) The *Kli*—that he wants to bestow. 2) Then he receives the delight and pleasure into the vessels of bestowal.

Conversely, the nations of the world did not receive the Torah, since it was given out of the darkness. In the work, "the nations of the world" means that the body comprises seventy nations that want the Torah not because they feel darkness when they have no vessels of bestowal. Rather, their only desire is the vessels of reception and they have no desire to emerge from that control. They want the Torah in order to add more light to themselves, meaning more pleasure than they receive from corporeal matters. That is, they also want the next world, as it is written in *The Zohar*, "They howl as dogs *Hav, Hav* [give, give], give us the wealth of this world, and give us the wealth of the next world." That is, the wealth of this world is not enough for them, but they also want the wealth of the next world.

It follows that the Torah was given specifically to those who feel that their will to receive controls them. They cry out from the darkness that they need the Torah in order to deliver them from the darkness that is the control of the vessels of reception, on which there was a *Tzimtzum* [restriction] and concealment so that no light will shine in that place. But that place is the cause for the need to receive the Torah.

For this reason, since the Torah came because of the darkness, the Torah did two things: 1) "The light in it reforms him." Then, the *Tzimtzum* and concealment depart from his vessels of reception because where he had vessels of reception, he has now been rewarded with vessels of bestowal. This is the meaning of the words, "And the Lord will shine upon you." That is, as the Creator wants to bestow, so man will be rewarded with a desire to bestow. 2) After he has been rewarded with vessels of bestowal, meaning he was granted the ability to work *Lishma* [for Her sake], which is called "learning Torah *Lishma*," then he is shown the secrets of the Torah, as Rabbi Meir says (in the Mishnah, *Avot*). This is the meaning of the words, "And His glory will be seen upon you," meaning the glory of the Creator, which is the revelation of Godliness. It "will be seen upon you," for then one is rewarded with "The Torah, and Israel, and the Creator are one."

What Does It Mean that the Torah Was Given Out of the Darkness?

However, the nations of the world, which do not need the Torah in order to emerge from the darkness, which are vessels of reception, but rather need the Torah in order to add the wealth of the next world to the wealth of this world, as was said, "Give, give," these people, who are in a state of "nations of the world," say that they do not need the Torah in order to deliver them from the darkness, since for them, they regard the vessels of reception for themselves as "light." Rather, they want the light of Torah to come into the receiver.

The verse says about them, "for the darkness will cover the Earth." That is, they will not be rewarded with the light of Torah because "the light of Torah was given out of the darkness." In other words, one who feels that he is in the dark is regarded as "Israel," who need the Torah in order to illuminate their darkness. They are rewarded with "The Lord will shine upon you," and "His glory will be seen upon you."

Now we can understand what our sages said (*Avot*, Chapter 1:17), "It is not the learning that matters, but the work." Also, in *Kidushin* (p 40), they said, "They were asked this question: 'Much learning or much work?' Rabbi Tarfon replied, 'Much work.' Rabbi Akiva replied, 'Much learning.' They all replied and said, 'Much learning, since the learning leads to work.'" We should understand their words in the work, since the literal provides many interpretations to this.

In the work, meaning when we want to come to work in order to bestow and not receive for ourselves, of course we must observe the 613 *Mitzvot* [commandments/good deeds] in actual fact. One who learns Torah but does not want to observe the 613 *Mitzvot de facto*, is learning knowledge, the way one learns external teachings. It is as our sages said (*Eicha Rabbah* 2:17), "Should one tell you, 'There is knowledge in the nations,' believe. 'There is Torah in the nations,' do not believe." This means that a person can learn Torah, but if he is a gentile, who does not observe the *Mitzvot*, which makes him a gentile, then the Torah he is learning is called "knowledge" and not "Torah."

For this reason, one who wants to work in order to bestow must begin to work in action, and then begin with the intention, meaning to place on it the aim to bestow. However, how can we achieve the aim to bestow, since it is known that a person can work under coercion, though "his heart is not with him." That is, a person might be compelled to work against his will. He can overcome his desire and do something against his will. Yet, changing the heart, meaning the desire and yearning, this a person cannot do.

Thus, since man was created with a nature of receiving only for himself, how can he aim to bestow? as this is against his nature! How can one work against his nature and desire, which is only to receive? Can he force himself to aim his heart with the intention to bestow?

Moreover, we must know that the Torah was given in order to cleanse Israel. That is, all the actions He has given us to do are only in order to obtain this aim to bestow. Thus, how can we do the above, since there cannot be coercion of the heart and the desire?

Baal HaSulam interpreted "which God has created to do." "Which God created" means that it is about this that man must "do," on what He has created. We should interpret "Which God has created" to mean that creation is called "existence from absence," referring to the will to receive. "To do" pertains to the creatures, who must place on it the aim to bestow. This means that all that the creatures must do is only to be able to aim to bestow. This is called "Which God has created to do." This doing belongs to the creatures.

Accordingly, we should interpret that the above words, "Much learning or work," do not concern work that the lower ones must do, for clearly, without work there is nothing, since first we must observe the 613 *Mitzvot* in action. Rather, we should interpret about the Torah itself that the Torah is called *Talmud* [learning]. Thus, the question, "Much learning or much work?" means that the Torah speaks from two angles: 1) From the perspective of the rules, meaning in which way we should observe the *Mitzvot*. There is the issue of the measure of the *Mitzvot*. Take *Tzitzit* [undergarment with four fringed corners], for example. We must learn the rules of the *Halacha* [Jewish law] concerning the required size of the *Talit* [prayer shawl] and the *Tzitzit*, and likewise regarding the rest of the *Mitzvot*. This is called the "revealed" part of the Torah, since these *Mitzvot* are visible and you cannot say that a person makes mistakes there, since that which is visible, if a person pays attention, he can observe these *Mitzvot* properly. This is why it is called "revealed." 2) The part of the Torah that does not speak of rules and laws that we keep in actions, but which speak of tales and legends of our sages and have no connection to the 613 *Mitzvot*. The question is, What part of the Torah is greater, meaning more important to a person, and to which he should pay more attention?

"Learning" refers to the part of the Torah that is only learning, without work, since we are not speaking of the practical part, how to observe. This is called "learning," meaning Torah without work.

Rabbi Tarfon says that work is greater. That is, the part of the Torah that speaks of performing the *Mitzvot*, which is the main thing to know—the rules that apply to the *Mitzvot*. Rabbi Akiva said that learning is great, and everyone answered and said as did Rabbi Akiva, "Much learning." What is the reason? For learning leads to work.

We should interpret what they said, that "Learning leads to work." It means that while it is true that the beginning of the work is in the revealed part of the Torah, which speaks of the observance of the *Mitzvot*, this is only the beginning, since the Torah and *Mitzvot* were given primarily in order to cleanse people. This means, as it is written (in the essay, "Preface to the Wisdom of Kabbalah"), that "cleansing" means emerging from the control of the will to receive for oneself and working only in order to bestow. This is called "which God has created to do." This work, which is done on creation, called "receiving for oneself"—to place the aim to bestow on it, this work is the main thing that the lower ones should do in order to be able to receive the delight and pleasure that the Creator wants to give them.

In order to achieve a state of "work," which means that a person should work only for the sake of the Creator and not for his own sake, a person can still overcome the revealed part in the 613 *Mitzvot* by forcing himself to observe the 613 *Mitzvot*. However, on the concealed part, which is the aim, is something that is given to the heart, and here a person cannot force himself. That is, if the heart does not want to work and love others, man is helpless.

In that state, when a person wants to work for the sake of the Creator and the body disagrees, a person realizes that he cannot work for the sake of the Creator by himself. It follows that now the person has learned something new, which he did not know before he began the work of bestowal: He is a complete wicked, since he does not want to work for the sake of the Creator. Before he began the work of bestowal, he also knew that he was still not working for the sake of the Creator, but at that time he thought that he is not doing everything for the sake of the Creator only because of negligence and idleness, but he would succeed in doing everything for the sake of the Creator the moment he would choose.

For this reason, he was not concerned that he is not doing so now. He could say it was for lack of time, but he is certain that it is within his power to do everything for the sake of the Creator. There is a rule that everything that a person can do does not concern him because he can always do this. He attributes not having it only to the view of others.

But now that he has begun the work of bestowal and has made great efforts, yet sees that he is not progressing, and worse yet, after all the labor he has fallen into despair, now he sees that the evil in him is so great that he decides that the work of bestowal was not meant for him. This recognition is called "wicked." That is, now he knows beyond any doubt that his body is unyielding and cannot be changed into working for the sake of the Creator. He can convince it to do only revealed things, in action, and to do good deeds. Yet, his heart is not with him. Therefore, only now can he determine that he has an evil inclination that is truly evil against the Creator, that he does not want to work for the Creator, but only for himself.

When a person comes to that state, when he sees that he has evil inclination, he must believe what our sages said, "I have created the evil inclination; I have created the Torah as a spice," since "the light in it reforms him." That is, his being enslaved to the evil inclination, when he was compelled to work for his own sake and not for the sake of the Creator, now, through the light of the Torah, he is reformed and can work for the sake of the Creator. This is called "good deeds," meaning only to bestow upon the Creator and not for his own sake.

Accordingly, we see that it is impossible to bestow without the light of the Torah. It follows that the part of the Torah that a person learns, which does not speak of rules and laws, this is called "work," as it is written, "much work," meaning the part of the Torah that discusses the doing of the *Mitzvot*.

And this is the meaning of "much learning," meaning the part of the Torah that speaks of tales and legends and interpretations of our sages, etc., the part of the Torah that does not pertain to the doing of the *Mitzvot*. This is called "learning." They all said immediately, "Much learning," "since learning leads to work." Here the meaning of "work" refers to the intention on the work, which is regarded as the revealed. He will be able to aim the heart to work for the sake of the Creator, and this is called "work," as it is written, "which God has created to do." Doing refers to the heart, so that man will have the strength to work, so the heart will want to work for the sake of the Creator.

What Are Merits and Iniquities of a Righteous in the Work?

Article No. 22, Tav-Shin-Mem-Het, 1987/88

It is written in *The Zohar* (*BaHar*, Item 67), "A complete righteous—all his merits are above, and his iniquities below. A complete wicked—his iniquities are above and his merits below. That is, a complete righteous—all his merits are kept for him above, for the next world, and he does not receive anything from them in this world. His iniquities, namely the punishments for his iniquities, are below in this world. A complete wicked—his iniquities are above, meaning he is avenged in hell after his passing from this world. And the merits he had done are below, meaning he is given his reward in this world. Intermediate—both judge him, meaning that both his reward and his punishment are below in this world."

We need to understand the meaning of "complete righteous," "complete wicked," and "intermediate" in the work, as well as what are "this world" and "the next world" in man's work, and the meaning of "above" and "below."

It is known that the purpose of creation is to do good to His creations, meaning that the created beings will receive delight and pleasure. For this reason, we see that the whole world, without exception, strives only to receive delight and pleasure, since this was the purpose of creation. However, in order to have equivalence of form, there was a correction that everything we do must be with the aim to bestow contentment upon the Creator and not for our own sake.

How can one do something not for his own sake when this is against nature? The answer is that when a person believes in the greatness of the Creator, to that extent a person can do things in order for the Creator to enjoy his work. In nature, when the small serves the great, he derives pleasure from it and does not need any reward. Just the privilege of serving him gives him vitality and makes him feel like the happiest person in the world.

Therefore, when a person achieves this degree where his only aim is to bestow upon the Creator, he is called "righteous." That is, when he can bestow upon the Creator, this is his only hope in life, and he does not need to be given anything else in life. If he sees that he is not permitted to serve the King, he says that he must have committed some iniquity for which he is punished with ejection from the King's palace into a place of litter, a place of waste.

That is, he is thrown into the pleasures he derived from self-gratification, of which he said that this was suitable for the "animate," not for the speaking, which is the human level, as our sages said, "You are called 'man,' and not the nations of the world." But now he is in a state where (he) can enjoy only that which pertains to self-benefit. At that time he says that he must have been punished for some iniquity, that he was not careful and was therefore punished. This is the degree of "complete righteous."

Conversely, the pleasures of the complete wicked are only those that can be received in vessels of reception, which is only for self-benefit. If he sees that no self-benefit would arise from this work, but rather everything will go toward bestowal without any reward, he cannot derive pleasure from this. Then he says that he must have committed some iniquity, which is why he cannot receive anything in the vessels of reception, and he looks and examines why he cannot make the vessels of reception enjoy.

It follows that when he thinks that the will to receive will not receive anything, he is very worried. He says about the state he is currently in that it is truly hell, that he is being punished above for his iniquities, and this is why the will to receive for himself (cannot) enjoy anything, meaning that now he has nothing to live on.

"Intermediate—both judge him." Once he agrees with the righteous, and once he says that the complete wicked is correct.

By this we can interpret what *The Zohar* says, "A complete righteous—all his merits are kept for him above." He regards merits as "above, in the next world," meaning that he can do things that belong above, namely in order to bestow above, to the Creator, who is of superior importance. He regards this as "the next world," and the next world is called "reward."

He does not receive from them anything in this world. This world is called "receiving." That which a person receives in the vessels of reception is called "this world," regarded as *Malchut*, whereas the next world is called *Bina*, which is a vessel of bestowal. For this reason, *Bina* is called "above," "the next world," and *Malchut* is called "this world." Hence, the righteous does not want to receive for himself anything in the vessels of reception, but rather only in order to bestow.

He says, "A complete wicked—his sins are above." This means that he sees, when he engages in Torah and *Mitzvot* [commandments/good deeds], regarded as "above" in importance, that he is wicked, meaning that he does not want to work in order to bestow upon the Creator, but to bestow pleasure upon himself, and this is why he engages in matters of above. That is, things he should bestow upward, when he sees that below, meaning the will to receive, will not gain from this work, the wicked says about this state, "Why am I unable to give something to the will to receive for myself? It must be because of iniquities; this is why the will to receive cannot enjoy."

He says, "He is avenged in hell after his passing from this world." "His passing from this world" means that he says that now that he no longer has vitality from this world, called "vessels of reception," which are now devoid of life, this is called "passing from this world." This is the meaning of "He is avenged in hell." Now that he feels that he has nothing from which to derive pleasure for the will to receive, he says it is a punishment and he is being punished in hell. This is why he has no life.

This is the meaning of "a complete wicked above." To the extent that he must engage in bestowal upward and receive below, it is regarded as a punishment. This is considered that now he feels that he has passed away, since he no longer has any life.

"And the merits he had done are below, meaning he is given his reward in this world." "This world" is that which the will to receive enjoys. He says about it, "The fact that I can receive delight and pleasure in the vessels of reception must mean that I have merits, and this is why I am given pleasure." This is the meaning of "his merits are below," meaning in the vessels of reception, regarded as being of inferior importance.

Accordingly, the meaning of "complete righteous" is that his intention is only to bestow contentment upon his Maker. A "complete wicked" means that he wants only to receive, and not to bestow at all. Yet, both apply to the same person, meaning when he works in Torah and *Mitzvot* and wants to begin the work of *Lishma* [for Her sake]. At that time, through work and overcoming, he comes to know that he is a complete wicked and does not want to annul his own authority, and not to think of himself, of how he can delight himself, and make all his concerns about bestowal. At that time he sees that this is difficult.

That person can see the truth—that he is far from the truth of working only for the sake of the Creator. At that time he decides that he is truly wicked because then he sees what his body wants, and he sees that he cannot be a worker of the Creator, but rather a worker of himself.

Conversely, those who do not begin the work of bestowal can never see that they are completely wicked. Instead, they sometimes see that they have not reached the degree of righteousness, but to see that they are completely wicked, there is no such thing, as it is impossible to see the truth before one begins the work of bestowal.

This world is called "vessels of reception," and the next world, "vessels of bestowal." Likewise, "below" means into the vessels of reception, and "above" means vessels of bestowal, namely that the lower one wants to bestow to above.

"Intermediate—both judge him," meaning not at once, but at two separate times. That is, once he thinks that he has already achieved the degree of "righteous," and once he sees that he is a "complete wicked." It follows that a righteous says, "All my merits are kept for me above, and my iniquities are below in this world." This means that while his pleasures are in vessels of reception, he considers it a punishment.

By this we can interpret the words of *The Zohar* (*Truma*, Item 522): "One's table must be clean, so the body will not approach eating its food unless when it, itself is clean. For this reason, one must first clear himself out, since that food, which he has prepared for himself, the Creator wants it, so he will not approach that table of feces vomit from the *Sitra Achra*. Once a person has eaten and been delighted, he must give a part to the *Klipot* [shells/peels]. And what is it? This is the last water, the filth of the hands that must be given to that side, which needs it. Because man is obliged to give him that part, there is no need to bless at all."

We should understand what is "cleanness" in the work, where he says, "For this reason, one must first clear himself out, before he eats the food of the pure table." We should also understand what he says, "Once a person has eaten and been delighted, he must give a part to the *Klipot* [shells/peels]. And what is it? This is the last water, the filth of the hands... Because man is obliged to give him that part." We should understand why before the meal he says not to give anything to the *Klipot*, and after the meal he says we should give some to the *Klipot*, and that it is even mandatory to give, but there is no need to bless.

It is known that the purpose of creation is to do good to His creations. But in order not to have shame in it, there was a correction that we must aim all the pleasures we receive to be in order to bestow and not for our own sake. The *Klipot* are called "wanting to receive for one's own sake." When all the vessels of reception are corrected to work in order to bestow, this will be called "the end of correction." That is, there will be nothing to correct into working in order to bestow because all the vessels of reception will have entered the authority of *Kedusha* [holiness/sanctity], called "in order to bestow upon the Creator and not for one's own sake."

Hence, in order for a person to be able to aim—while receiving the pleasure—in order to bestow, regarded as sitting at one's table, a person should say, "This is the table before the Lord." A "table" is the place from which a person derives pleasures. A "table" means the place of one's sustenance. It is called "table," as our sages said, "reliant on his father's table, reliant on others' table [dependent on others]." Also, during the blessing for the food, we say, "The Merciful One, He will send us much blessing in this house, and on this table on which we have eaten."

We should understand what are "this house" and "this table." A "table" is the place where one receives one's sustenance. This is why we say, "The Merciful One, He will send us much blessing," meaning that the provision we receive from the Creator will not be with envy, which is receiving for himself. That is, he asks of the Creator that the sustenance with which he is providing the body will not go into the vessels of reception of the body, which are called "envy," as our sages said, "He is envious of what others have."

Rather, it should be as "much blessing," which are vessels of bestowal, which is called "expansion," which is *Hassadim* [mercies], when he wants to do only *Hesed* [mercy]. From this should be his provision for himself, and (his provision) will not be with envy, called "receiving and not bestowing," since from those who receive for themselves, there cannot be sustenance to the world. That is, if the whole world worked in bestowal, the world would be sustained even in corporeality, as he writes in the book *Matan Torah* [*The Giving of the Torah*]. This is the meaning of what he says, "On this table."

Concerning the words "much blessing in this house," a house means *Hochma*, as it is written, "As the glory of a man to dwell (dwells) at home," and as it is written, "A house shall be built with wisdom [*Hochma*]." This is the meaning of what is written in *The Zohar*, "Three things broaden man's mind: a handsome woman, a handsome home, and handsome *Kelim* [vessels/tools]. A handsome woman is his soul; handsome *Kelim* are his organs, and the home is his heart." That is, the home is regarded as man's heart, and man's heart should be a Temple, as it is written, "And let them make Me a Temple and I will dwell within them."

This means that one should work on two things: 1) The correction of creation, which is *Hesed*, is called "much blessing." Expansion is called *Hesed*, the opposite of envy. This is called "the table of the Lord," and it is attained through the Torah, as our sages said, "The light in it reforms him." 2) Afterward comes the work of the purpose of creation, called "light of *Hochma* [wisdom]" or "light of life." This light is called "the wisdom of the Torah," regarded as "the Torah and the Creator are one," In general, this Torah is called "the names of the Creator."

This comes after a person has received *Kelim* of *Hesed*, which are vessels of bestowal with respect to the equivalence of form. This is as our sages said, "Rabbi Meir says, 'He who learns Torah *Lishma* [for Her sake],'" meaning he has vessels of bestowal, meaning only to bring contentment to his Maker, "'the secrets of Torah and shown to him,'" which is the names of the Creator.

Now we can interpret the meaning of cleanness in the work of the Creator. He says, "For this reason, one must first clear himself out before he eats food on the pure table." This means that it is impossible to place important things in dirty vessels, since everything will be spoiled by the dirt. So it is in the work of the Creator: Precisely when one works for the Creator and not for himself, meaning when he wants to bestow upon the Creator, the abundance can enter these *Kelim* because there is equivalence between the light and the *Kli* [vessel].

Conversely, if the *Kli* is mixed with reception for oneself, which is regarded as "dirty" compared to the light, which is all about bestowal, accordingly, before a person comes to receive sustenance from the Creator, which are delight and pleasure, he must clean himself up from self-reception. At that time, the abundance, which is the pleasure, does not go to the *Klipot*, regarded as reception for oneself. Rather, the abundance will go to *Kedusha* because he can aim to benefit the Creator while receiving the pleasure. This is called "eating the food on the pure table."

After the meal, it is to the contrary. He must give a part to the *Sitra Achra* [other side]. This means that he says that there is still dirt here, which belongs to the *Sitra Achra*, and I must still correct myself.

What Beginning in *Lo Lishma* Means in the Work

Article No. 23, Tav-Shin-Mem-Het, 1987/88

It is written in *Pesachim* (p 50), "Rabbi Yehuda said, 'Rav said, 'One should always engage in Torah and *Mitzvot* [commandments/good deeds], even if *Lo Lishma* [not for Her sake], since from *Lo Lishma* he comes to *Lishma* [for Her sake].'"

Maimonides said (*Hilchot Teshuva*, Chapter 10:5), "Sages said, 'One should always engage in Torah, even if *Lo Lishma*, since from *Lo Lishma* he comes to *Lishma*.' Therefore, when teaching little ones, women, and uneducated people, they are taught only to work out of fear and in order to receive reward. When they increase knowledge and gain much wisdom, they will be told that secret bit by bit and are accustomed to this matter with ease until they attain Him and know Him and serve Him with love."

And in *Pesachim* (p 50), it is written there in the *Tosfot*, "In Chapter Two of *Berachot* it is said, 'Anyone who engages in Torah *Lo Lishma* is better off not being born.' And Rabbi Yehuda says, 'There it is about one who is studying in order to brag and to annoy.'" And in *Berachot*, the *Tosfot* explains, "We should ask, for here it is about one who is studying only to annoy his friends, and there it is about one who is studying so as to be respected."

With the above said, we can see that in general, we should make two discernments in the work of the Creator: 1) *Lishma*, 2) *Lo Lishma*. We should know what exactly is *Lishma* and what exactly is *Lo Lishma*.

In *Lo Lishma*, we see that we have five discernments to make:

1) As Maimonides said, he engages in Torah and *Mitzvot* because the Creator commanded us, and he wishes to keep the commandments of the Creator, and this is why he engages in Torah and *Mitzvot*. But we should note what is the reason that commits him to observe the commandments of the Creator. Maimonides says that we should tell him, "Because of reward and punishment." In other words, if he observes the commandments of the Creator, the Creator will reward him: He will have a long life, wealth, and the next world. And if he does not observe he will be punished for not wanting to observe the commandments of the Creator.

However, we should make two discernments in reward and punishment: 1) As Maimonides says. 2) There is reward and punishment from pleasures in the Torah and *Mitzvot*. These matters, too, cannot be disclosed to beginners in the work or to little ones or women.

2) The second discernment in *Lo Lishma*, as the *Tosfot* says, is that he is studying Torah in order to be respected. This is worse than the first manner that Maimonides mentions, since here he does not demand of the Creator to pay his reward and this is why he works. Rather, he wants people to respect him—whether with wealth or with honors—and this is the reason that commits him to engage in Torah and *Mitzvot*. We could say that it appears as though he is observing Torah and *Mitzvot* because people compel him, for otherwise the people will not reward him, and not because the Creator commanded to observe Torah and *Mitzvot*. However, that, too, falls under the *Lo Lishma* that brings to *Lishma*.

The third discernment is as the *Tosfot* says, "One who studies Torah in order to annoy his friends." This is worse than the previous forms of *Lo Lishma*. It is said about it, "Anyone who engages in Torah *Lo Lishma* is better off not being born."

Let us explain what is *Lishma*, and the five discernments in *Lo Lishma*, and let us begin from the bottom up.

The *Lo Lishma* in order to annoy is the worst. It is so much so, that our sages said that one who walks on this path "is better off not being born." We should understand why "in order to annoy" is worse than one who studies "in order to be respected." After all, he is studying for the creatures and not for the Creator, similar to "in order to annoy," which is for the creatures.

We should explain the difference between them. It is known that we were given the commandment, "love thy friend as thyself." Rabbi Akiva said about it that it is a great rule in the Torah. It is presented in the essay *Matan Torah* ["The Giving of the Torah"], that this is the transition to emerge from self-love to love of others, which is love of friends, and to the love of the Creator. This means that it is impossible to work *Lishma* before one exits self-love.

This is why we should make two distinctions concerning love of others: 1) when he has love of others, 2) when he hasn't love of others. But there is a third discernment, which is hatred of others. In other words, he does things in order to hurt the other. This is called, "One who takes honor in one's friend's disgrace." In other words, he enjoys his friend being disgraced and tormented, and derives his pleasure from it. That person is regarded as engaging in hatred of people.

With this we can distinguish between one who is studying in order to be respected and one who studies in order to annoy. The purpose is to reach *Lishma*, and we were given the advice by which to achieve *Lishma*—through love of others. Hence, although one who studies in order to be respected is not engaging in love of others, he is still not acting toward hatred of people, since those who respect him enjoy him, and therefore respect him. Hence, he still has a chance to achieve *Lishma*, simply because of the doing—that he engages in Torah and *Mitzvot*, since the Torah and *Mitzvot* themselves bring him a spirit of purity so he will be able to rise in the degrees and reach the love of others and the love of the Creator.

This is why they said about it, "From *Lo Lishma* he will come to *Lishma*." But one who is studying in order to annoy, which is an act that brings him to hatred of others, yet still wishes to be honored with his friend's disgrace, will certainly never achieve love of the Creator, since his actions prevent the exit from self-love. Thus, how will he exit self-love and come to love of the Creator?

And yet, there is one more discernment to make in *Lo Lishma*: by way of coercion, as written in Article No. 19, 1986/87. For example, if a person works for an orthodox person and receives a good salary from him, and the employer tells him, "I want you to observe Torah and *Mitzvot*. Otherwise, I will not want you to work for me."

He comes home and tells his wife that the employer wants to fire him. His wife says, "What does it mean, observing Torah and *Mitzvot* because you have an orthodox employer? We don't believe in it. Are we going to sell our conscience for money?" But when he says to his wife, "I've been to several other places and it's very hard to find a job these days, so if we don't accept the employer's condition, we will starve."

"Therefore," says the husband, "We shouldn't sacrifice ourselves for our conscience, but we know the truth, that we do not believe in Torah and *Mitzvot*. Instead, we will observe Torah and *Mitzvot* not because the Creator commanded us to observe Torah and *Mitzvot*, but because the owner of the factory instructed us, and this is why we observe Torah and *Mitzvot*. We don't have to believe in the employer. So what if we observe Torah and *Mitzvot*? The act does not blemish our conscience or suddenly makes us believers. We remain nonbelievers in the Creator even when we do those deeds."

On the face of it, what is the importance of such Torah and *Mitzvot*, when he explicitly says that he remains in his views like the rest of the secular? What is the value of such deeds in our mind?

However, from the perspective of the *Halachah* [religious law], we must force him even if he says that he does not want to. It means that by that, he still observes the commandments of the Creator, but it is called *Lo Lishma*. It is as Maimonides wrote (*Hilchot De'ot*, Chapter 6), "But in matters of holiness, if he does not repent in secret, he is shamed in public, and he is disgraced and cursed until he reforms."

This means that even this manner is called *Lo Lishma*, since from that *Lo Lishma*, one also comes to *Lishma*, more than one who studies in order to annoy—of whom our sages said, "He is better off not being born." And here we should interpret that by observing Torah and *Mitzvot Lo Lishma*, he isn't doing something against the love of others. Rather, this does give pleasure to others. That is, the orthodox, who see that now he has become observant of Torah and *Mitzvot*, do not look at the reason, but at the act. Thus, they enjoy it. But one who studies in order to annoy acts contrary to what one should do.

By that, we explained the difference between one who studies in order to annoy, which is the worst, and one who works by coercion, who is forced to work by others, which is *Lo Lishma*, and stands above the one who is studying in order to annoy. And although it is difficult to say so, he is observing Torah and *Mitzvot* voluntarily, and not by coercion, but his will is to annoy, which is only a thought and not an act. But why is one who is observing Torah and *Mitzvot* by coercion, who is pressured by the public, better than one who is studying in order to annoy, if he acts not of his own free will?

Perhaps we should say that nevertheless, through the deed that he is doing, albeit coercively, the act itself has the power to bring him a good will and thought, as our sages said about the verse, "Will offer him at his will before the Lord." And they said (*Arachin* 20a), "Will offer him" implies that he is forced, and you can say it is against his will. The Talmud says it is of his own will. How is he forced? Until he says, "I want." For this reason, we can say that he is more important than one who is studying in order to annoy.

However, we should ask, "At the end of the day, he is performing the act in full, but thinks that by that he will receive honors from showing that he knows and the other does not. Why is it so difficult to achieve the goal called *Lishma* with *Lo Lishma* that is in order to annoy, to the point that they said that he would be better off not being born?"

We could say that one who is studying in order to annoy must be completely immersed in the Torah and probably considers himself a complete man in the Torah. If so, he will never think about the matter of *Lishma* because he sees that he delves in the Torah more than his friends, who are not putting in that much time or quality. And he observes himself, that he is making greater efforts in Torah than the friends by delving in, to know the right meaning that should be understood in the Torah, and he is not studying superficially like the others, but straining his brain. Thus, how can he think of himself as lacking? He can never come to the recognition of evil, to know that he should achieve *Lishma*. For this reason, he is doomed. This is why they said about him, "He is better off not being born."

And the most important in the *Lo Lishma* is that it brings to *Lishma*. It is as Maimonides said, "To receive reward and not be punished." The *Lo Lishma* that the *Tosfot* speaks of, which is to be respected, does things so people will see him and appreciate him. Thus, it seems as though he is observing the commandments of people, that he is working for them, and that people will pay his reward.

But one who works with the intention of reward and punishment is working for the Creator, except he wants the Creator to pay his reward for his labor in Torah and *Mitzvot*. He does not want people to pay his reward because he isn't working for people to pay his reward. Rather, he is working and observing Torah and *Mitzvot* because the Creator has given us Torah and *Mitzvot* to observe. And by that, we will receive reward for our labor in Torah and *Mitzvot*.

Hence, this is certainly a higher degree than the one the *Tosfot* speaks of, the *Lo Lishma* in order to be respected. This is because there he is working for people to respect him, but in reward and punishment, he is working for the Creator, which is called *Lishma*, meaning for the Creator, except he wants reward for his work, and this is why it is still not considered "actual *Lishma*."

However, we should note another discernment that is called *Lo Lishma*, as Maimonides said, though the reward and punishment are of a different form. Normally, we understand reward and punishment as being clothed in corporeal dresses, such as eating, drinking, etc. *The Zohar* says that our ability to enjoy corporeal desires is only a slim light from what had fallen from the world of shattering, the breaking of holy sparks into the *Klipot* [shells], and this is all the pleasure that is in them. And the whole world chases these pleasures. When it is written that the majority of the light is clothed in Torah and *Mitzvot*, this is the kind of reward and punishment that he wants.

And we should always pay attention, while speaking to someone about observing Torah and *Mitzvot*, we should first think which reason is suitable for that person. Everyone has his own thing that interests him, a reason for which he sees that it is worthwhile to observe Torah and *Mitzvot*, since by that he will receive something that is worth a great effort and toil. And he will be willing to give anything to obtain what he sees as worthwhile for him.

For this reason, we should always say to a person that which is important for him to an extent that it is worth his giving everything that he is asked for. Otherwise, without providing a reason that will make him see the profitability, he will not hear what is being said to him. Man settles for what he has and it is hard to change habits, unless he gains from it something that is important enough to give him the energy to change his ways and to start working differently than what he is accustomed to.

Hence, there are five discernments in *Lo Lishma* before us: 1) by coercion, 2) one who studies in order to annoy, 3) one who studies in order to be respected, as mentioned in the words of the *Tosfot*, 4) for reward and punishment, as in the words of Maimonides, 5) reward and punishment from non-corporeal things, which is something that everyone understands. But he wants reward and punishment of spiritual pleasures, as written in the "Introduction to The Book of Zohar" (Item 30), "And the final degree in this division (in *Lo Lishma*) is that he falls passionately in love with the Creator, as one falls passionately for a corporeal love, until the object of passion remains before one's eyes all day and all night, as the poet says, 'When I remember Him, He does not let me sleep.'"

But with the fifth discernment in *Lo Lishma*, we cannot tell a person to begin in this *Lo Lishma*, since not every person can understand it, meaning believe that there is pleasure in the light that is clothed in Torah and *Mitzvot*, more than one can enjoy the pleasure that is clothed in corporeal pleasures. That is, if the light of the pleasure that is clothed in Torah and *Mitzvot* would be immediately apparent, it would be called "open Providence." In that state, it would be impossible for a person to be able to work *Lishma* because the pleasure he would feel in Torah and *Mitzvot* would force him to do everything, and not because the Creator commanded to observe.

It is as he says in the "Introduction to The Study of the Ten Sefirot" (Item 43), "If, for example, the Creator were to establish open Providence with His creations in that, for instance, anyone who eats a forbidden thing would immediately choke, and anyone who performed a commandment would discover wonderful pleasures in it, similar to the finest delights in this corporeal world. Then, what fool would even think of tasting a forbidden thing, knowing that he would immediately lose his life because of it? ...Also, what fool would leave any commandment without performing it as quickly as possible, as one who cannot retire from or linger with a great corporeal pleasure that comes into his hand, without receiving it as quickly as he can?"

It follows that then there would be no possibility for choice, since the great pleasures that are clothed in Torah and *Mitzvot* are great lights. This is why this pleasure is concealed. Conversely, in corporeality, the pleasure in each act is revealed, which makes us crave any place where we see that there is some pleasure. And the body does not tell whether it is forbidden or permitted. Because of it, there is the matter of choice and the matter of reward and punishment.

It follows that while speaking to someone about taking on the burden of Torah and *Mitzvot*, one should thoughtfully consider which type of *Lo Lishma* to tell him, since, as said above, each one should be given the *Lo Lishma* that suits his character, so he will see that this *Lo Lishma* is worth taking upon himself the Torah and *Mitzvot*. For example, the first discernment [by coercion] is suitable for everyone. In other words, if one can force another, in coercion, it makes no difference whether the other understands or does not understand. In any case, it is called "coercion," meaning that one can do it even if he understands one hundred percent that he is right, but he has no choice. This is called "coercion." But with the other forms of *Lo Lishma*, each one has a different character, and it's important to say what is acceptable.

We can understand the three other forms of *Lo Lishma*—1) in order to annoy, 2) in order to be respected, and 3) to receive corporeal reward and punishment. However, each person has a different nature, so one should pay close attention to know which type of *Lo Lishma* he should tell him, meaning which *Lo Lishma* that person can see as worth toiling for.

But with the fifth type of *Lo Lishma*, craving the love of the Creator because he feels pleasure in Torah and *Mitzvot*, this we cannot understand because it depends on the feeling. And before a person begins to taste, there is no point speaking to him. This is why it is called "the final form of *Lo Lishma*," meaning that afterwards one enters the degree of *Lishma*.

However, we should understand that if a person reaches the degree where he craves Torah and *Mitzvot* in the measure that was said above, "When I remember Him, He does not let me sleep," why is this still considered *Lo Lishma*? Indeed, it is because the pleasure in Torah and *Mitzvot* is what compels him to observe

What Beginning in Lo Lishma Means in the Work

the Torah and *Mitzvot*. *Lishma* means that the greatness of the Creator, because He is great and ruling, causes him to observe Torah and *Mitzvot*. Thus, it is not the pleasure that is the reason that compels him, but the Creator is the reason that makes him observe Torah and *Mitzvot*.

Lishma is described in the "Introduction to The Book of Zohar" (Item 32), "The work in Torah and *Mitzvot Lishma*, in order to bestow and not to receive reward, and he becomes worthy of receiving the five parts of the soul called NRNHY."

However, according to the rule that man is a small world, comprised of seventy nations, he is comprised of Israel, too. Thus, we said that there are five discernments in *Lo Lishma*, that there are people who belong to a special type of *Lo Lishma*, but we should also say that all these types of *Lo Lishma* exist within one person, but come one at a time. Sometimes, the *Lo Lishma* "in order to annoy" acts in a person. Sometimes, he is working with the *Lo Lishma* in order to be respected, and sometimes he is using the *Lo Lishma* by coercion, as Maimonides said, "He is shamed in public, disgraced, and cursed until he reforms."

In other words, when a person comes to pray in the synagogue or comes to study Torah so that the friends will not despise him, since everyone will despise him in their hearts although no one will tell him, "Why are you not coming to the Torah lessons at the synagogue?" But he will know for certain that everyone is looking at him as inferior. Thus, the disgrace that he will feel makes him come to the synagogue. It follows that the cause of *Lo Lishma* that forces him is the coercion, as Maimonides says.

It is easier to use this *Lo Lishma* as an effective *Lo Lishma*, since *Lo Lishma* that is connected to suffering—the disgrace—gives more energy to overcome the obstructions that he has. Therefore, at times when a person is in the lowest decline, the *Lo Lishma* of shame can still act in him. It is considered coercion because of the shame, meaning the shame—which is the suffering—forces him to do things even though the body disagrees.

And sometimes a person strengthens himself with the *Lo Lishma* of reward and punishment, as Maimonides said. And sometimes he has reward and punishment from finding meaning in the work, while if he does not observe the Torah and *Mitzvot* he lacks the meaning, and this is the end of the *Lo Lishma*.

Reward and punishment of pleasure in the work: When he engages in Torah and *Mitzvot*, he feels pleasure. And if he does not observe Torah and *Mitzvot*, he suffers. It is like a person who feels the taste of a meal and this is the reason that he goes to the meal, since he wants the pleasure of the food. It follows that the pleasure of the food is the cause for going to the meal.

The Concealed Things Belong to the Lord, and the Revealed Things Belong to Us

Article No. 24, Tav-Shin-Mem-Het, 1987/88

It is written (Deuteronomy 29:28), "The concealed things belong to Lord our God, and the revealed things belong to us and to our children forever, to do all the words of this Torah [law]." We should understand what knowing this gives us. Would anyone consider that man can know the concealed? And if we can know the concealed, why did the Creator hide it from us? And we should also understand what are the concealed things. What does this imply that we must not look into, but it rather belongs to the Lord our God?

It is written about the verse, "When you raise the candles," RASHI interprets that "'When you raise' means that the flame goes up, meaning we must light up until the flame rises by itself." We should understand what it implies to us that we must "light up until the flame rises by itself." Certainly, if the candle does not burn properly, but burns only as long as the person is lighting it, we certainly have to wait until it burns by itself. Thus, what novelty is it to say, "until the flame rises by itself"?

Concerning the making of the menorah, it is written, "This was the making of the menorah [lamp], a hammered work of gold." RASHI interprets "hammered": "It was one talent [piece] of gold. He would strike with a hammer and cut with scissors to spread its pieces properly. It was not made by separate pieces connected. Likewise, He made the menorah." RASHI interprets, "It was done by itself by the Creator."

We should understand this: If the menorah was made by itself, why did they have to strike with a hammer and cut with scissors? Certainly, if the Creator makes the menorah, it should have been enough to take a talent of gold and it would be made by itself. Why was there a need to strike?

It is known that human nature is to want only to receive for one's own benefit. A person cannot do anything unless he sees that it will yield some benefit for himself. It is written about it in *The Zohar*: "The leech has two daughters: *Hav, Hav*" (Proverbs 30:15). *The Zohar* interprets, "The leech has two daughters that howl as dogs: *Hav, Hav* [Hebrew: give, give]. Gives us the wealth of this world, and give us the wealth of the next world." In other words, everything a person sees, from which he can derive some pleasure, he yells about it, *Hav, Hav*, which means "Give, give, I accept this with my heart and soul."

We were given the commandment to love the Creator, as it is written, "And you shall love the Lord your God with all your heart, and with all your soul, and with all your might." But how can this be observed if this is against our nature? Our sages said about the verse, "And dawned on them from Seir," that "He opened to children of Esau so they would receive the Torah, but they did not want it. 'He appeared from Mount Pharan,' He walked there and opened to the children of Ishmael to accept it." Yet, they did not want it, meaning they all asked, "What is written in it?" Esau did not want it because it is written, "You shall not commit murder," and it is written about

The Concealed Things Belong to the Lord; the Revealed Things Belong to Us

Esau, "You shall live by your sword." It is likewise with the children of Ishmael: What does it write? "Do not commit adultery." They did not want it. But when he came to the people of Israel, they said, "We will do and we will hear."

We should understand, does the evil inclination in the people of Israel agree to relinquish the bad qualities? If so, what does it mean that they said, "We will do and we will hear"? We should interpret that when the people of Israel saw that their evil objected to the Torah, meaning that they did not want to observe the commandments of the Torah, they said, "We will do it against its will," meaning by coercion, although our evil disagrees.

However, we should understand the merit of one who gives something to another by force. Can we say that he has given to him out of love? Since he does not love him, so this is not the reason for giving. Love is acquired by giving to each other good things. Then, it is natural that the receiver of the gift comes to love the giver. Yet, the giving does not make the giver love the receiver by the giving, so what is the reason that Israel said, "We will do against its will," although the evil disagrees? And also, how will this fulfill, "And you shall love the Lord your God"?

Our sages said that when Israel said, "We will do and we will hear," the Creator said, "Who revealed to My children this secret, the tool that the ministering angels use," as it was said, "Mighty in strength, doers of His word, and then hearing the voice of His word." This means that "doing" is regarded as "mighty in strength," meaning overcoming, though the body, which has the nature of self-reception, disagrees. Later, by doing through overcoming, although the evil inclination does not want, we are later rewarded with "hearing the voice of His word." The meaning of "I hear" is "I think," as our sages said, "I did not hear means I do not think" (*Iruvin* 102).

Accordingly, the literal meaning is that by saying "we will do," in overcoming by coercion, we will then be rewarded with "we will hear." That is, the matter will be reasonable and acceptable. This means that when we find it reasonable and acceptable, we will certainly be able to do everything with love and joy, and then everything will be voluntary and not compulsory.

According to the above said, we can interpret the words, "Who revealed to My children this secret," where we must understand what is the secret in saying, "We will do and we will hear," of which asks, "Who disclosed this secret?" However, we must understand what is a "secret" in the work. A "secret" means that it is not revealed, but we must believe that it is here. That is, there is a matter here that we want and need to know, and if we have no need to know it, we do not consider it a "secret."

This is similar to someone seeing two people whispering to one another. Clearly, they do not want him to hear. But if they are not speaking about him, he does not want to know what they are saying. In that case, what they are saying is not considered a secret that he wants to know. Even if he were told, he would still not want to hear, since every person has his own business that interest him. But if he thought that they were speaking of him, he would want to know what they are saying, for it is a secret that they do not want him to know.

The same orders that applies in corporeality, also applies in the work. For example, when a person learns Torah. When a person is learning rules, it can be said that the Torah does not speak in secret, things he does not know. On the contrary, the Torah tells him the rules by which to observe the *Mitzvot* [commandments/good deeds]. However, when he learns the stories in the Torah, or even the legends of our sages, if he believes that the Torah speaks of him but does not know the connection between the Torah he is learning and himself, and he wants to know what is written there, this is considered that now he is learning a secret.

That is, two things are required in order for something to be considered a secret: 1) He must believe that they are speaking of him. 2) He must want to know what the Torah says about him, meaning what the Torah speaks of that pertains to him. Only in this way is it regarded as a secret in the work.

Now we can understand what the Creator said, "Who revealed to My children this secret"? It means "Who revealed to My children the secret" of believing that by working in coercion, they will be rewarded with "Hearing Me," and that which was previously compulsory will then become voluntary.

It follows that "doing" is called "faith." That is, by believing that after the doing they would be rewarded with hearing, they were certain also during the coercion to do the things with joy and love, since they could be rewarded with hearing.

This is not so with the nations of the world. In the work, they are parts of man that do not pertain to the quality of "Israel." Rather, they want to do everything with the external mind, as it understands what they can achieve. That which the intellect deems worth doing, for this they are willing to work, but not for what concerns faith above reason.

In other words, they see with their reason that a person cannot revoke the will to receive by himself. Instead, we must believe that if the Creator gave us this work of working in order to bestow, He must have known that it was possible to do this, but we, with our tiny mind, do not understand how such a thing can be, that it is truly a miracle from heaven. But the Creator certainly knew that we can achieve this degree.

They do not know how there are such things; they cannot believe. This is called "the nations of the world." But "Israel" means that they can overcome and believe above reason. Hence, those who belong to the quality of Israel believe that bestowing is a secret to people, meaning that they do not know how to achieve the power of bestowal, but they do believe.

Conversely, the nations of the world in a person say that this is difficult and not for us. Hence, when we see that we are required to walk by way of faith above reason, they have no interest in this and escape the campaign saying that this is difficult for them.

This is why the "nations of the world" in man did not want to receive the Torah, for as we learn, receiving the Torah is regarded as

"Should a man die in the tent." Our sages said, "The Torah exists only in one who puts himself to death over it." This means that a person should revoke his self-benefit, and make all his concerns only for the benefit of the Creator. Because the body does not agree to cancel the self-benefit and to walk by way of coercion and believe that by "We will do," we will achieve "We will hear," this faith is unacceptable to the reason of the self-receiver. This is the whole difference between the nations of the world and Israel.

Now we can understand what we asked, What does it imply that they said we must "light up goes up until the flame rises by itself"? The thing is that lighting pertains to man, who must perform an act. To what extent must he perform the act? In coercion, it is "until the flame rises by itself."

"By itself" means without the work of the lower one. This is called "by coercion." However, he is rewarded with the Creator giving him hearing. Naturally, at that time a person does everything gladly, with love, and willingly, not as when he engaged in doing, which was compulsory and the body resisted when he wanted to bestow upon the Creator.

Now, however, it is by way of "And you will love the Lord your God with all your heart," with both your inclination. That is, the evil inclination loves the Creator, too, since he is annulled before the Creator as a candle before a torch. This is the meaning of a person having to "light up," to do things "until the flame rises by itself," and not by a person's own strength. Thus, "by itself" means by the power of the Creator.

Likewise, we should interpret what we asked about what our sages said about the making of the menorah: "This was the making of the menorah [lamp], a hammered work of gold. It was one talent [piece] of gold. He would strike with a hammer and cut with scissors to spread it properly. It was not made by separate talents connected." We asked, Since they said a literal commentary, "This is how He made the menorah: It was done by itself by the Creator." If the

Creator made the menorah, which is called "by itself," why did they have to strike with a hammer? Why must man do something, too?

However, a person should say, "We will do and we will hear." That is, a person should begin in coercion and believe that he will be rewarded with hearing. Since there is no light without a *Kli* [vessel], meaning that the Creator does not give a filling to a person unless he has a need for the Creator to fill it. Hence, the person must begin and see that it is difficult, then pray to the Creator to help him. At that time, a person sees that everything is done by itself, without man's help. Thus, what does the person do in the making of the menorah if the Creator does everything?

Answer: Man's work is required, for without it we would not have the knowledge that the Creator does everything. Rather, we would say that we can achieve wholeness by ourselves, as well, without the Creator's help, and "My power and the might of my hand have gotten me success." Conversely, after a person toils and labors and does all that he can do, yet did not move even one bit, he must say that the Creator has given him this strength—to be able to work in order to bestow—as a gift. This means that the Creator has given man permission to serve Him. This permission is called that He has given him pleasure when he bestows upon the Creator.

By this we will understand the words, "It was one talent [piece] of gold." The body is called "a talent of gold," as it is written in *The Zohar*, "The leech has two daughters that howl as dogs, *Hav, Hav* [Give, give]. Give us the wealth of this world and give us the wealth of the next world. That body, which is called "a talent of *Ze-Hav* [Hebrew: Give this. English: "gold"], was striking with a hammer."

Explanation: Any work that the body does coercively is regarded as striking with a hammer and cutting with scissors. That is, every coercion that a person does is as though he has cut off a part of *Ze-Hav* [Give this], meaning part of the will to receive for himself. This is the meaning of what is written, "To spread her organs properly," meaning to strip off from the organs the will to receive for oneself, and correct them to work in order to bestow. This is called "to spread her organs properly."

However, it was not so. That is, it was not done as one complete organ, one organ opposite one quality, in wholeness, and then another complete quality. Rather, one wholeness was made for all, which is in order to bestow, then all the organs were connected into one complete quality. However, it was not so, but on the contrary: Each organ that he wanted to correct, the bad appeared in its place, and not the good. Therefore, he had many organs that were spoiled until he came to a state where he saw that there was not a single organ in his receiver that was willing to work to bestow.

At that time, he saw that it was all a hammered work of *Ze-Hav* [gold]. That is, he saw that gold, meaning the receiver, is difficult to invert to working in order to bestow. At that time the *Kli* is completed, meaning the act on the part of the lower one. He sees that he cannot prevail over it, as it is written, "and the children of Israel sighed from the work, and their cry went up to God, from the work." Then the help from the Creator arrives, as it is written, "Likewise, He made the menorah," and RASHI interpreted that "It was done by itself by the Creator."

Thus, who made the menorah? The Creator Himself. But if so, what is Israel's work for?

The answer is, "In order to reveal the need, that only the Creator can change the nature He has created—that the creatures should have a desire to receive for themselves. Otherwise, a person thinks that he himself could turn the receiver into a giver."

However, we should also understand why the Creator should care if the creatures do not know the truth and think that they themselves can do this work of turning the vessels of reception into bestowal. Or, we can ask the question differently: Why did the Creator not give strength to man to be able to invert the vessels of reception into bestowal by himself?

Baal HaSulam said that the answer to this is that it is a correction. Otherwise, a person would remain in his lowly degree. That is, he would not need the light of Torah, but the Creator wanted to give them the Torah. Hence, by not being able to obtain vessels of bestowal by themselves, they will ask the Creator to help them. The help He will give them is specifically through the Torah, since "the light in it reforms him."

It follows that a man must receive the Torah, since the second phase after being reformed and receiving the vessels of bestowal—which is Phase 1—is that he receives the Torah as "the names of the Creator." This quality is called "His desire to do good to His creations," clothed in "the names of the Creator," and it is called "The Torah and Israel and the Creator are one."

Now we can interpret what is written, "The concealed things belong to Lord our God, and the revealed things belong to us and to our children forever, to do all the words of this Torah [law]." We asked, What does this come to teach us? The answer is that when a person begins the work of bestowal, he sees that he is not moving forward toward obtaining vessels of bestowal, but to the contrary. At that time, a person begins to see his bad state, how immersed he is in self-love, since according to the rule, the more a person wants his garment to be clean of any dirt, the more he sees the dirt.

There is a rule: "Anything which does not rest upon a man, he will do absentmindedly." It means that when a person does not pay attention to something, he does not see what is missing there. For this reason, when he begins to work in order to bestow and pays attention to the extent to which he is willing to work in order to bestow, he sees how far he is from bestowal and that he cannot do anything without reward.

Hence, what can a person do when he sees that he has no progress in the work of bestowal, but rather always sees that he cannot exit self-love? That is, in the beginning of the work, he thought that if he only decided to walk on the path of bestowal, he would promptly be able to. That is, he thought that he was his own landlord, for who would tell him what to do? You can say that on things he wants to do there can be interferences from people on the outside. But here, in work of bestowal, which is only the intention to bestow, meaning that he does not need to observe more than the 613 *Mitzvot* if he wants to aim to bestow. Thus, superficially, he is engaging like everyone else, like the general public, and he is not unusual so it can be said that the general public objects to his way, for who knows that which is in one's neighbor's heart? Thus, he thought that after a short time of work, he would begin the work of bestowal.

Yet, suddenly he sees that each day, the more he works and wants to acquire vessels of bestowal, the more he sees that they are far away from him, and he is utterly unable to ever exit self-love.

The verse tells us about this: "The concealed things belong to the Lord our God." That is, the aim to bestow, which is called "the concealed part," for one does not know one's neighbor's thoughts, this a person should know—that in truth, it is out of our hands. Rather, the hidden part, called "intention," belongs "to the Lord our God." He must give us this power and we are powerless to help Him. Yet, we can help Him by beginning to engage in this work of bestowal and seeing that we cannot exit the self-love in us. By this we help Him, by knowing that only He helps us. Had we not begun, we would have been unable to continue further. This is the correction—to know that He alone does everything.

It would be the opposite if we could exit self-love by ourselves. That is, we would think so, but we would be devoid of the awareness that "He alone does, is doing, and will do all the deeds." But when we see for ourselves that we cannot exit self-love, we do not need to believe that He has given us this power, for we evidently see it.

It follows that the text tells us not to be alarmed by the fact that we cannot prevail and exit self-love, which is called "the concealed part." This is in the hands of the Creator, as it is written, "The concealed things belong to the Lord our God, and the revealed things belong to us and to our children." That is, "revealed" means the part of the action, which we can do by coercion. This is why the verse tells us that the fact that we see that this is difficult for us is true. However, this, meaning the intention, was not given for us to do, but rather only the work. Yet, by seeing that we cannot do this by ourselves, this is called a "prayer," meaning a need for the Creator to give us this *Kli*.

Now we can interpret what our sages said (*Minchot* 29), "Making the menorah was difficult for Moses until the Creator showed him with His finger, as it is written, 'This is the work of the menorah.'" We should interpret this in the work: The "work of the menorah" means that the light of the Creator will shine. Yet, this requires vessels of bestowal. From where will they take the vessels of bestowal? This is difficult, as it is against nature. But the Creator showed him with His finger and said to him: "This is the work." That is, "You will do the work, and I will give the intention." This is considered that "You will do the revealed part, and I will give the concealed part." This is the meaning of the words, "Likewise, He made the menorah," meaning by itself.

What Is the Preparation on the Eve of Shabbat, in the Work?

Article No. 25, Tav-Shin-Mem-Het, 1987/88

Our sages said (*Masechet Avoda Zarah*, p 2), "In the future, the Creator brings a book of Torah and places it in His bosom. He says to those who engaged in it, 'Come, take your reward.' Promptly, idol-worshippers gather and come. The Creator says to them: 'In what did you engage?' The Creator says to them, 'All that you did, you did for yourselves.' They say to Him: 'Master of the world, give us in advance, and we will do.' The Creator says to them: 'Fools, he who toils on the eve of Shabbat [Sabbath], eats on Shabbat. He who did not toil on the eve of Shabbat, from where will he eat on Shabbat?'"

There are many explanations in the literal. But in the work, what is the toil on the eve of Shabbat, from which to have what to eat on Shabbat? We see that Shabbat is called a "gift," and not *Tzedakah* [almsgiving/charity/righteousness], as our sages said (*Beitza* 16), "To know that I the Lord sanctify you. The Creator said to Moses: 'Moses, I have a good gift in My treasury; its name is Shabbat. I want to give it to Israel; go tell them.'"

The Gemara brings evidence from here, that one who gives a gift to his friend should notify him. There are two things to understand here: 1) What is the reason that we should notify when giving a gift, whereas concerning *Tzedakah*, we learn the opposite, that *Tzedakah* should be in concealment, as it is written, "Giving in concealment subdues anger." 2) Why is Shabbat called "a gift," whereas faith is called *Tzedakah* [righteousness/charity], as it is written, "And he believed in the Lord and considered to Him as righteousness," and not a gift?

We should understand what is a gift and what is *Tzedakah*, in the work. Normally, one gives *Tzedakah* out of pity, and not out of love, as our sages said (*Baba Batra* 9), "One does not check with nourishments." It is so because *Tzedakah* is not given out of love, when we should check if we should really give the *Tzedakah* or not. In *Tzedakah*, the pity determines whether or not to give.

Since one who says he has no food—meaning nothing with which to sustain himself—evokes pity, they said there, "We do not check with nourishments," to see if he is an honest person or a crook. This is what he said there, "Rav Yehuda says, 'We check clothes and do not check with nourishments.'" RASHI interprets "clothes" as "He came naked and said, 'Cover me.'" Then, he is examined to see if he is not a crook, since clothing does not evoke any pity because a person can live without clothes, but he cannot live without food.

Conversely, a gift is something we give specifically to those we love. The value of the gift is measured by the measure of love for that person, and by the importance of that person. Normally, one who wants to show his love to another, expresses it by giving a gift. According to the value of the gift, so appears the measure of love.

However, there is another value to a gift. If the sender is an important person, the love cannot be measured according to the gift, since with an important person, even a small gift is valuable.

With an important person, the gift is measured by the importance and greatness of the giver.

Now we can understand the difference between *Tzedakah* and a gift. With a gift, when he wants to show his love for his friend or his teacher, or his parents or children, if the giver does not notify him that he has given him the gift, how will the receiver find out about the giver's love for him? This would make giving the gift pointless, in vain.

However, there is another condition about a gift. The thing he gives must be an accessory and not a necessity. Usually, we do not say, "I sent this poor man a gift of bread and fish for Shabbat." We also do not say, "I sent the groom a gold watch as a *Tzedakah*." Rather, a gift is specifically an accessory, and a *Tzedakah* is a necessity and not an accessory.

But sending him accessories, to which the other one has no necessity, why did he send it? It is in order to show him his love. It follows that if he does not notify him that he has sent him, what is the point of the gift? This is why our sages said, "He who gives a gift to his friend must notify him."

He does not have to notify him that he has sent him the gift, but also the value of the gift, since according to the value of the gift, so is the measure of the love revealed between them, since to the extent that the receiver is impressed by the gift, so is his measure of gratitude, and by this, the connection of love between them forms.

But with a *Tzedakah*, there is no matter of love, since *Tzedakah* concerns only the giver, and he has no connection to the receiver. There, it is to the contrary: If the receiver thanks the giver, then the giver is no longer giving *Tzedakah*, but there is room to grip onto the *Tzedakah*, which is *Lo Lishma* [not for Her sake] and receive gratitude from him. Hence, evidently, a *Tzedakah* must be in concealment, meaning only for the purpose of *Tzedakah*, and not that the poor will give him some pleasure in return.

Concerning giving in concealment as in the *Mitzva* [commandment/good deed] of *Tzedakah*, we should discern two manners: 1) The first is simple—the receiver of the *Tzedakah* does not know the identity of the giver. 2) The giver, too, does not know to whom he gives. This is giving in concealment, both on the part of the giver and on the part of the receiver.

Now we can understand the meaning of a gift and *Tzedakah* in the work. Faith means going above reason. This is regarded as not seeing, and it is called "in concealment." Faith is also called *Tzedakah* because the person giving the *Tzedakah* does not want the poor to give him anything in return. A person who has nothing, which is why he is poor, cannot give anything to the giver of the *Tzedakah*, but he could return him gratitude for the *Tzedakah*. This is why they said, "*Tzedakah* that is in concealment is real *Tzedakah*," since the poor one does not know whom to thank.

Therefore, one who takes upon himself the kingdom of heaven, called "faith in the Creator," should try to make it giving in concealment, so that the person will not know with his intellect, regarded as not knowing for whom he works, but he is rather working above reason. However, here the matter is to the contrary, since when the poor man receives *Tzedakah*, the receiver does not know who gave him the *Tzedakah*, but the giver does know.

However, there is another manner, too, where the giver also does not know to whom he gives. Conversely, with faith, which is called *Tzedakah*, it is as it is written, "And he believed in the Lord and considered to Him as *Tzedakah* [righteousness]" (Genesis 15:6). This is the complete opposite. *Malchut*, which is called "poor and meager," as it is written in *The Zohar*, that *Malchut* is called "Poor and meager because she has nothing of her own except that which her husband gives her." That is, *Malchut* has nothing of herself except what her husband gives her.

It follows that the person giving *Tzedakah* to the Creator, which is called "faith," does not know to whom he gives. But the Creator does know who is the giver, meaning from whom He received the *Tzedakah*. That is, the poor knows, and the giver, namely the person, does not know to whom he gives. This is called "the kingdom of heaven," and it was said about it, "and he believed in the Lord and considered it to Him as *Tzedakah*." In other words, the faith must be as *Tzedakah*, which is giving in concealment. Otherwise, it is not considered faith, but knowing, meaning knowing in the intellect.

Now we should interpret what the interpreters ask about the words, "and he believed in the Lord and considered it to Him as *Tzedakah*." The question is that we do not know who thought to whom. According to the rule we learned, "He alone does and will do all the deeds." Hence, the question is, What does a person do with his choice? If the Creator does everything, where is there room for choice, which is man's work?

Baal HaSulam said in the name of the Baal Shem Tov, that before the fact, a person should say, "If I am not for me, who is for me?" since everything depends on man's choice. But after the fact, he should say, "It is all under the Creator's guidance," and he must not say, "My strength and the might of my hand have gotten me success." Rather, even if he did not prevail, he would still do it because it was the Creator who did it. This is regarded as a person having to believe in Private Providence.

Therefore, we should make two discernments in faith in the Creator, which is called *Tzedakah*: 1) A person overcomes and takes upon himself the burden of the kingdom of heaven and makes *Tzedakah* to the Creator by believing above reason. This is called "giving in concealment." It is also called *Tzedakah* because no reward is requested from the poor when the *Tzedakah* is given to him. The poor does not know who gave him so it could be said that the giver of the *Tzedakah* to the poor can expect any reward, since the giver does not know to whom he gave. Here, with faith, when a person assumes the kingdom of heaven not in order to receive reward, it is like a poor man. Accordingly, this means that when Abraham believed in the Lord, he gave Him *Tzedakah*.

2) We should note that the Creator made a *Tzedakah* to Abraham. That is, after the work of overcoming, a person should say that the Creator "does and will do all the deeds." It follows that

the Creator gave Abraham the power to overcome above reason, which is called *Tzedakah*. This *Tzedakah*, for Abraham to have the strength to give the *Tzedakah*, is regarded as the Creator giving the *Tzedakah* to Abraham.

The words, "We do not know who considered to whom" mean that initially, Abraham thought that by believing, he is giving *Tzedakah* to the Creator. After the fact, he said that the Creator considered giving the power of faith so he could believe in a manner of *Tzedakah*. The Creator contemplated giving him the strength; hence, he had the strength to believe.

By this we will understand why faith is called *Tzedakah*, and *Tzedakah* is named after both. It follows that in the work, a "gift" means Torah. It is called *matanah* [gift], as it is written, "From Matanah to Nahaliel." Also, Shabbat is called a "gift," as was said that the Creator said, "I have a good gift in My treasury; its name is Shabbat; go tell them."

We should understand why Torah is called a "gift," and Shabbat is called a "gift," as well. It is known that the purpose of creation is to do good to His creations. For the purpose of *Dvekut* [adhesion], a *Tzimtzum* [restriction] was made, so the delight and pleasure illuminates only to vessels that have equivalence with the light, meaning vessels that work in order to bestow. This matter was done since there should be equivalence of form. Without it, the receiver becomes remote from the giver, to the point that the creatures that descended to this world due to disparity of form became removed from the root and do not know their origin. That is, the creatures must believe that they come from the Creator, but they do not know from where they come.

This is as it is written in the essay "Preface to the Wisdom of Kabbalah" (Item 10): "Thus, you find that this *Nefesh* [soul], the light of life that is dressed in the body, extends from His very essence, existence from existence. As it traverses the four worlds *ABYA*, it becomes increasingly distant from the light of His face until it comes into its designated *Kli* [vessel] called *Guf* [body]. This is considered that the *Kli* has completed its desirable form. And even if the light in it has so diminished that its origin becomes undetectable, through engagement in Torah and *Mitzvot* [commandments/good deeds] in order to bring contentment to the Maker, one cleanses one's *Kli*, called *Guf*, until it becomes worthy of receiving the abundance."

Thus, by observing Torah and *Mitzvot* in order to bestow, they receive *Kelim* [vessels] of bestowal, where there is a place capable of receiving the light called "His desire to do good to His creations." This is called a "gift." That is, faith is regarded as a person giving by overcoming the thoughts in the body and believing in the Creator. This is why it is considered that the person is giving, and why faith is called *Tzedakah*. But a gift is when a person takes what the Creator gives him. *Tzedakah* is the complete opposite—that a person gives *Tzedakah* to the Creator and the Creator is the receiver.

As we explained above, a gift is called "accessory." That is, the person can live without the gift, too. But a "*Tzedakah* for the poor" means precisely necessity, since without food it is impossible to live. For this reason, since it is impossible to be Jewish without faith, it follows that faith is regarded as "necessity." However, it is possible to be Jewish without Torah, although you would be considered "uneducated," meaning one who has not been rewarded with the Torah, called "the names of the Creator," where the delight and pleasure called "His desire to do good to His creations," is clothed.

Also, it is written, "A soul without knowledge is also not good." Our sages said, "There is no good but the Torah," and as it is written, "For I have given you a good lesson, My Torah [law]; do not leave it" (*Berachot* 5a). Nonetheless, he is already considered "Israel."

Now we can understand why the Torah is called a "gift." The Creator is the Giver, as it is written, "I have given you a good lesson, My Torah [law]; do not leave it." Also, it is regarded as accessory, meaning that it is possible to be Jewish without the Torah, too, as long as one is rewarded with faith, which is *Tzedakah*, for without faith it is impossible to be Jewish. For this reason, faith is called

Tzedakah, and Torah is regarded as the Creator being the Giver of the gift.

Also, Shabbat is called a "gift," as well, as our sages said, "Shabbat is a similitude of the next world (*The Zohar, Beresheet*), and as they also said, "Shabbat was given to Israel for *Kedusha* [holiness/sanctity], for pleasure, and for rest, but not for sorrow" (*Midrash Tanchuma*, Chapter 18:1).

Now we can understand what we asked, "What is the preparation on the eve of Shabbat in the work? Normally, only *Tzedakah* is asked for, and one does not check with food, but rather anyone who stretches his hand is given. We explained about this that faith is called assuming the burden of the kingdom of heaven, that anyone who stretches out his hand is given. It is as it is written (in the closing prayer), "You lend a hand to the transgressors, and Your right is stretched out to welcome the returning." This is because concerning necessity, our sages said (Sanhedrin 37), "Anyone who sustains one soul from Israel, it is as though he has sustained a whole world."

This is not so with a gift. Usually, people do not ask for gifts. Instead, when we love someone and want to express the love, so it becomes known to the other that we love him, so we send him gifts. Also, the value of the gift reflects the measure of love, meaning the value of the gift is as the measure of the love.

For this reason, when a person wants his friend to send him gifts, he must exert to do things that his friend will like, so he will love him. Love does its thing and by this he will receive gifts from his friend. However, it is not accepted to ask for a gift.

By this we will understand what we asked, "What is the trouble on the eve of Shabbat in the work?" It is that a person takes upon himself the kingdom of heaven. But for the kingdom of heaven, called *Tzedakah*, a person must ask the Creator because there was a *Tzimtzum* and concealment so we do not feel the Creator within reason, but must accept the faith above reason. And since the body disagrees to what the reason does not mandate, a person is in exile within self-love, and cannot understand how he can emerge from this exile.

This is called the "exile in Egypt." It was said about this, "I the Lord your God, who brought you out from the land of Egypt." Only the Creator Himself can change our nature and deliver us from self-love to love of the Creator, and only then can we observe, "And you shall love the Lord your God."

This request that a person makes, to be given the power of faith, is called *Tzedakah*. It is as we pray (written in the prayer, "As today..." that we say in the *Musaf* [supplemental prayer] of *Rosh Hashanah* after "Today You Strengthen Us"), "It was said, we shall have *Tzedakah* because we will observe and do all of this *Mitzva* before the Lord our God, as He has commanded us."

Also, Baal HaSulam said about "One *Mitzva*" or about "This *Mitzva*," that it pertains to the *Mitzva* of faith. Thus, it means that we say to the Creator that if we have the strength to do all of this *Mitzva*, that it will be *Tzedakah* on the part of the Creator if He gives us the power of faith above reason, which is called an "act," because it is above our reason, it is called an "act."

It follows that the work that a person should do and toil on the eve of Shabbat so as to have what to eat on Shabbat means that it is known what is customary in the world, that a person troubles himself only to obtain things that give him delight and pleasure. For example, we see that there are people who work two jobs, or work extra hours beyond what they have to work according to the days and hours that the state has determined. Each one earns a salary according to his hours and his skills. Yet, some work more than others. Clearly, by this he wants to obtain something he wants, and this is the reward that gives him the energy to work.

That is, according to the measure of reward that he expects, so is his energy to work. Our sages said that it is like the work and the meal. The meal is regarded as the reward. Therefore, they said, "He who did not toil on the eve of Shabbat," which is the time to prepare the ingredients of the meal, and did not prepare the ingredients of the meal, "from what will he eat?" as the ingredients are certainly labor and toil.

It therefore follows that since Shabbat is a gift, call a "meal," and it is customary that one who is having a meal invites only those he loves, the "ingredients of the meal" will mean preparations so as to be invited to the meal. This is so because from the perspective of the Creator, a person does not give to the Creator any help with the meal. Instead, what a person can do to prepare the meal is to have himself invited. He can do this in only one way: by doing good deeds that the Creator will like, so the Creator will love him.

As we say, "Who chooses His people Israel, with love." This means that the Creator chooses His people, Israel. But the question is, What is Israel? It is taking upon oneself faith. This is called "Israel," and all the preparation is the labor to become Israel.

What Is the Difference between Law and Judgment in the Work?

Article No. 26, Tav-Shin-Mem-Het, 1987/88

It is known that "law" means without intellect, meaning above reason. That is, there is no reasonable way to answer why this was done this way, or why it should be done this way, in the way and manner that the Torah requires of us.

For example, our sages said (*Minchot* 29b), "Rav Yehuda said, 'Rav said, 'When Moses went to heaven, he found the Creator sitting and tying crowns to the letters. He said to Him: 'Master of the world, who is holding You back?' (RASHI interprets that 'crowns' are like the tags [markings] in a book of Torah. 'Who is holding You back?' refers to what You wrote, that You must add tags to them). He told him, 'In a few generations time, there will be a man whose name is Akiva Ben Yosef. He will interpret myriad laws over each and every dot.' He said to Him: 'Master of the world, you have such a person, yet You are giving the Torah through me?' He replied, 'Be quiet! Such was My thought.' He said to Him: 'Master of the world,

You showed me his Torah [law], show me his reward.' He saw that his flesh was being weighed in a slaughterhouse. (RASHI interprets that this is the place where butchers weigh meat, as said in *Berachot*, p 61, that his flesh was combed with iron combs.) He said to Him: 'Master of the world, this is the Torah, and is this its reward?' He replied, 'Be quiet! Such was My thought.'"

We see Moses' above reason in two ways: 1) Above reason that the Creator gave to Moses, as it is written, "Moses will delight with the gift of his lot, the gift of the Torah that will come through him, which is certainly only the salvation of the Lord." A person does not know why he deserves such a great gift. That is, Moses saw that this was not according to his actions. In his view, the Torah should have been given through Rabbi Akiva and not through him. 2) Above reason in the opposite way: Moses asked, "This is the Torah, and is this its reward?" It seems to be a punishment. Above reason, he had to say that this was a reward and not a punishment, as Moses thought. This is called "the law of above reason," which the mind cannot attain.

It follows that when a person takes upon himself the burden of the kingdom of heaven, the body asks, "What will you get out of it?" There should be two answers to this: 1) *Lo Lishma* [not for Her sake]. That is, a person should make up for himself some answer that the body will understand with its reason that the goal is worthwhile. This is called *Lo Lishma* and it is called "within reason." As we explained (Essay No. 23, *Tav-Shin-Mem-Het*), we should discern five manners in *Lo Lishma*, and a person should sort out the *Lo Lishma* in the state that he is in, so the body will understand that it is worthwhile to work because of the *Lo Lishma*, that now it understands that it is worthwhile. In this manner, he will have fuel for work and he will always have a place to work.

However, a person should also try to begin to work and seek tactics by which to get to *Lishma* [for Her sake], since a person does not know what is *Lishma*. Its literal meaning is "to work for the sake of the Creator," and who does not know what is to work for the sake of the Creator? Still, before a person begins to engage in work in order to achieve this "for the sake of the Creator," he cannot know what "for the sake of the Creator" means, since in the work, what counts is the feeling, not the intellect.

For this reason, any person who wants to achieve *Lishma* must take time, part of his workday, meaning his *Lo Lishma*, and begin to work on *Lishma*. Then he will understand the meaning of "above reason," meaning that the body does not understand why it needs to work for the sake of the Creator. At that time, he also begins to understand what it means that a person must believe above reason. Conversely, in *Lo Lishma*, it is not so difficult to believe in the Creator since the body understands that it is worthwhile to observe Torah and *Mitzvot*, as it is written (Essay No. 23, *Tav-Shin-Mem-Het*) that there are five manners of *Lo Lishma*, and when the body finds something for which it is worthwhile to observe Torah and *Mitzvot* [commandments/good deeds], it is regarded as "working within reason." Since the body understands within reason that the matter is worthwhile, that he will gain more by being secular, meaning that his body will enjoy more than one who does not observe Torah and *Mitzvot*, for this reason, the *Lo Lishma* is called "within reason," meaning that the need for it makes sense.

But if he takes some of the time he has dedicated to Torah and work on the basis of *Lo Lishma*, for example half an hour a day, and begins to ponder whether it is worthwhile to work for the sake of the Creator, meaning not for his own benefit. Then, the body begins to ask the person Pharaoh's question, who said, "Who is the Lord that I should obey His voice?"

We should ask, How come before he began to think of working *Lishma*, he was content with faith in the Creator and the body did not ask those questions, whereas now that he is thinking only about walking on the path of bestowal, the body begins to ask such questions? The answer is that we see that when a person works for an employer, we should consider who is the employer and what is the salary that the employer pays. However, although he wants to know the employer, it does not matter. That is, even if he never sees the employer, but he is confident about the reward, a person agrees to work. Moreover, even if he is told that he will never see the employer, it will still not matter. Rather, what matters is the salary. This determines if the work is worthwhile.

But if a person is told, "There is an important person here who needs people to work for him. However, he does not pay anything for the work." In this case, he needs to see for whom he needs to work. That is, he wants to know if he is really an important person worth working for without any reward. However, if there are people who respect him and he sees that he will be honored, meaning that people who know the important person will respect him for his work because he is serving an important person, he can work even if he himself will never see him and will never be able to see if what they say is true so that he will grasp his greatness and importance.

This is also because this honor is not that the important person respects him, but he derives pleasure from people's respect for him because he is serving an important person. It follows that here it is enough that he sees the people who respect him, and therefore does not have such a great need to see the employer. Rather, he is content with knowing the people who pay his salary through their respect for him. That is, it is enough for him to see the people who pay his reward, which is called "respect."

Conversely, if he is in a place where there are no people who respect that important person, meaning he sees that according to the service that people give him, he sees that they appreciate him as one who is a little bit important, and only a handful of people regard him an important person, but those people are not important in the eyes of those who have little regard for him. In that state, a person faces a dilemma: Should he listen to those people who are not appreciated among the respected people?

That is, people of influence in the general public say that that person should be appreciated because of his importance, but only to a degree, not simply admire him above reason, meaning more than seems reasonable. But a person sees that the influential people are the majority and the most valued, and if he listens to them, meaning serve him according to their appreciation of him, these people will respect him.

Or, he should slightly obey those who are not influential, or even worse, that it is a disgrace to openly say that he has connected to these lowly people who say that he is an important person and worth serving devotedly. Since the rule is that the majority rule over the individual with their views, when a person begins to work in order to bestow and not accept any return, each time, the majority view awakens—perhaps it is not worthwhile to work and serve him with his heart and soul.

For this reason, Pharaoh's question awakens each time: "Who is the Lord that I should obey His voice?"

It follows that the reason that the "who" question appeared is the "what" question, which is the wicked's question. It is written about it, "A Wicked, what does he say? 'What is this work for you?'" That is, when a person wants to go against the general public, who say that they settle for working *Lo Lishma* because *Lishma* is for people who can go above reason, and we, the majority of Israel, settle for being able to observe Torah and *Mitzvot* with the aim to benefit ourselves, and doing everything with the aim to benefit the Creator is no business for us.

Yet, he does want to work in order to bestow and not receive at all. At that time the body asks, "Who is the Lord?" That is, are you sure that He is so important that it is worthwhile to work for Him? In other words, working for respect, meaning to work in order to be respected, does not apply here because the general public does not appreciate him because he is working in order to bestow. On the contrary, they degrade him and say about him that he is a fool.

For this reason, he must establish the importance of the Creator by himself. Here is where man's ascents and descents begin. Those two—the "who" and "what"—come to together and ask him their questions, and a person cannot always overcome them.

It follows that the main reason why a person begins to ask questions, and he is seemingly asking because he is ready to do the holy work and has no lowliness in himself, except it is hard for him to go with faith above reason, this is why he asks the "who" question. But in truth, the questions arise out of man's lowliness, since he is immersed in self-love and cannot overcome his self-love.

It is human nature that it is difficult for him to say that he is wrong, that he does not have a view about himself, but that he follows his heart, as our sages said, "A wicked is in the hands of his heart," as it is written, "And Haman said in his heart."

For this reason, it is better for him to say that if he knew the Creator, he would certainly serve the Creator. But since the mind does not understand the whole matter of faith above reason, it argues, "Who is the Lord that I should obey His voice?" But in truth, his will to receive claims that it only wants to understand if this is true, and wants an answer to the question, "Who is the Lord that I should obey His voice?" That is, when we say to the body that we need to work for the sake of the Creator and not for our own sake, this is why he asks the "Who is the Lord" question.

But when he worked with the intention *Lo Lishma*, he did not need to ask the "Who is the Lord" question, since the work *Lo Lishma* is within reason. Hence, the acceptance of faith is also within reason for him. That is, both the mind and the heart are built above reason, and both need the Creator's help in order to be rewarded with mind and heart.

It follows that "law" means that it is above reason, and the intention pertains to faith, and by faith above reason he becomes Israel. Conversely, before he was rewarded with faith above reason, he is regarded only as "sacred still," called "dust." That is, he still tastes in the spirituality that he attains the taste of dust. This is called "*Shechina* [Divinity] in the dust." This is so as long as he does not accept above reason. This is as we said above, that we must ask the Creator to give us the strength to be able to go above reason and not be enslaved to our reason.

Conversely, the Torah is called "judgment," which is specifically within reason. In other words, he must understand the Torah, called "the names of the Creator." However, it is impossible to attain the

Torah, called "within reason," before he is rewarded with "Israel," as it is written (Hagigah 13a), "Rabbi Ami said, 'One does not deliver words of Torah to idol-worshippers, as it was said, 'He did not do so to any nation, and they do not know the ordinances.'"

From this we see two things: 1) The Torah is called "judgment," as it is written, "and they do not know the ordinances." 2) It is forbidden to teach judgments, meaning Torah, to idol-worshippers.

The question is, Why is it forbidden to teach an idol-worshipper Torah if he wants to learn? It stands to reason that it should be to the contrary: By learning, there will be sanctification of the Creator. That is, even the idol-worshipper will acknowledge the importance of the Torah, so why the prohibition?

We should interpret this in the work. It means that idol-worshippers and Israel are in the same person. Before one is rewarded with the law, called "faith above reason," he is still not called "Israel," who can attain the Torah as "the names of the Creator," regarded as "within reason."

In the work, there is a rule that Baal HaSulam said, that where it is written "forbidden," it means "impossible." This is the meaning of the Torah being given specifically to Israel, since Israel is the quality of *Yashar-El* [straight to the Creator], which means that all his actions are for the sake of the Creator. This is called *Dvekut* [adhesion], "equivalence of form." When a person is rewarded with this law, then comes the time when he can be rewarded with the judgment called Torah. This is the meaning of the Torah being given only to Israel.

It therefore follows that "judgment" is the first nine *Sefirot*, which is regarded as the Torah. This is received within reason. It is as our sages said (*Baba Metzia* 59b), "Rabbi Yehoshua stood on his feet and said, 'She is not in heaven.' Rabbi Yirmiah said, 'For the Torah has already been given on Mount Sinai.'"

By this we will understand the side-locks, which are like the edges of the field. We must leave a side-lock, as the ARI wrote (*The Study of the Ten Sefirot*, Part 13), "*Malchut de Galgalta* is called *Pe'ah* [side-lock].

This is known from the words, 'You shall not reap the sides of your field. Leave them for the poor and for the stranger.' *Malchut* is the last of them, like the edge of the field that remains after the harvest. Likewise, after one shaves the hair of the head, which is like the harvesting of the field, one should leave the side-lock, which is as the *Malchut* of the hair. It follows that the *Pe'ah* is forever *Malchut*."

Accordingly, we see in the words of the ARI that he likens the reaping of the field to the shaving of the hair of the head. A person must not receive for himself the *Pe'ah*, which implies *Malchut*. Rather, both on the field and on the hair of the head, the *Pe'ah* must be kept, implying *Malchut*.

The meaning is that *Malchut* is regarded as faith above reason, when a person has no clue. This is the intimation that a person has no permission to receive into his reason, but that he must leave this to the Creator. That is, a person's hand does not reach there, and "hand" means "attainment," from the word "If a hand attains."

This is called "law." Conversely, the Torah, which pertains to the upper nine, is regarded as "judgment," which pertains specifically to man. That is, he must attain this within reason, as was said about the Torah, "She is not in heaven." This means that the field, except for the *Pe'ah* of the field, is called "the upper nine," regarded as the Torah, which pertains to man. But the *Pe'ah* of the field and the *Pe'ah* of the head imply *Malchut* and pertain only to the Creator, meaning above human reason. This is called "entirely for the Creator, and man's hand does not attain there at all."

The Torah is the opposite. It pertains specifically to people, to accept it within reason. This is the difference between Torah and *Mitzva* [commandment/good deed]. Concerning the *Mitzva*, we were not given the reasons for the *Mitzvot*. Rather, we accept the *Mitzvot* without any rhyme or reason, but as a constitution.

But the Torah, our sages said, is named after man. That is, the Torah pertains to man. The question is that once it is written, "He desires the Torah of the Lord," and another time, it is written, "He will contemplate His Torah day and night." They interpret, first it is called "the Torah of the Lord," and once he has learned it and has internalized it, it is called "his Torah." This is why Raba said, "The Torah is not his, for it is written, and he will contemplate His Torah day and night" (*Kidushin* 32b).

We see that the Torah is named after man. That is, it must come within reason. This is called "judgment," the opposite of "law," which is faith. However, this work of faith, which is regarded as *Tzedakah* [righteousness/charity] and not Torah, should be with joy, as it is written, "Serve the Lord with joy."

In other words, a person taking on himself the kingdom of heaven should be with joy. He must not look at the nature of humans, that it is hard for him to go against the intellect, and that instead, he wants to understand and to know what he wants. And since a person cannot immediately assume this work of acceptance of faith above reason, so it will give him joy, we must begin this work coercively, even though the body disagrees. This is regarded as a person having to "take upon himself the burden of the kingdom of heaven as an ox to the burden and as a donkey to the load."

However, one must know that he must achieve the degree of joy upon assumption of the kingdom of heaven. It is as we say after reading *Shema Israel* [Hear, O Israel], "And you will love the Lord." This means that although a person begins coercively, he must come to a state of joy, and then he will not feel "like an ox to the burden," which always wants to throw away the burden because it cannot stand it. Conversely, when he is glad about it, it cannot be said that he regards it as a burden.

Now we can interpret the meaning of the "red cow on which no burden has been placed." Since a red cow is called a "law," which is *Malchut*, it is written, "on which no burden has been placed." A "burden" means that he is still not in gladness and still cannot observe, "And you will love the Lord your God with all your heart and with all your soul."

What Is, "The Creator Does Not Tolerate the Proud," in the Work?

Article No. 27, Tav-Shin-Mem-Het, 1987/88

Our sages said (*Sotah* 5), "Any person in whom there is crassness, the Creator said, 'He and I cannot dwell in the world,' as was said, 'Whoever secretly slanders his neighbor, him I will destroy; one who has haughty eyes and a broad heart, him I cannot.' Do not read, 'him I cannot,' but rather 'with him I cannot.'" And about the words, "one who has haughty eyes and an arrogant heart," the *Metzudat David* interprets, "'Haughty eyes' means proud, and 'a broad heart' means one who covets and craves everything."

We should understand why the Creator did not say about the rest of the transgressions that He could not dwell with him in the world, and about pride, He cannot dwell with him. Also, we should understand what he said there, "Rabbi Yohanan said in the name of Rabbi Shimon Bar Yochai, 'Any person in whom there is crassness, it is as though he is idol-worshipping.' And Rabbi Yohanan himself said, 'as though he has become a heretic.'"

Thus, we should understand why pride is so grave. Also, we should understand what is written, "The Lord is high and the low will see," which means that a person should see the greatness of the Creator and his own lowliness. We can understand that a person should try to obtain the greatness of the Creator, since the purpose of man's work should be because "He is great and ruling." For this reason, to the extent that he appreciates the Creator, his work can be with his heart and soul. But for what purpose does he need to try to see his own lowliness? What will this add to him in the work?

First, we must know the purpose of creation, meaning what is the purpose for which we were born, so we may know what is the goal we must achieve, which will be our completion, and that before we have achieved this goal, we are incomplete. We learned that the purpose of creation is "His desire to do good to His creations." It follows that before the creatures come to a state where they feel happy in the world, they are regarded as incomplete because they have not found peace and quiet.

Yet, the question is, since the Creator created the creatures in order to give them delight and pleasure, and because of this, He has created a desire and yearning in the created beings to receive delight and pleasure, it follows that the Giver has a desire to give, and the receivers have a desire to receive. Thus, who is withholding them from achieving immediate wholeness? However, we were given work in Torah and *Mitzvot* [commandments/good deeds] by which we will be able to receive the delight and pleasure. Otherwise, we remain bare and denied of all the good that the Creator wants to give.

Even after a person engages in Torah and *Mitzvot*, not everyone is rewarded with receiving the good, as our sages said (*VaYikra Rabbah* 2:1), "A thousand people enter the Bible, a hundred of them emerge to the Mishnah, ten to the Talmud, and one to teach." It therefore follows that only one in a thousand can be rewarded with teaching, and "teaching" means wholeness. Otherwise, he is regarded as a "disciple who did not achieve teaching and instruction" (*Avoda Zarah* 19b). This is regarded as an "indecent judge." Our sages said about this (Sanhedrin 7b): "Rish Lakish said, 'Anyone who positions an indecent judge is as one who plants Ashera [tree used for idolatry] in Israel."

We see that it is not so easy to be rewarded with the delight and pleasure. Thus, the question is, Who is the obstructor? Here it seems as though there is no obstruction on the part of the Giver or on the part of the receiver. Clearly, the Creator, who created the creatures, has given them a desire to receive pleasure. This desire, which yearns to receive pleasures, cannot be revoked. Thus, what is the reason that we can receive it only through labor?

The answer is that it is known that in order to have equivalence of form, called *Dvekut* [adhesion], and to thereby prevent the issue of shame, a novelty was made—that the *Kelim* [vessels] that the Creator created in the creatures, which are desires to receive for oneself, are disqualified for the above-mentioned reason. Instead, a person must work to correct the vessels of reception so they work in order to bestow. This is the only prevention.

That is, no changes took place from the perspective of the Creator. However, from the perspective of the correction of creation, it is regarded as though he has no *Kelim* that are fit to receive the abundance. This matter was established in the upper worlds, and it is called *Tzimtzum* [restriction]. It is placed on the lower ones, so they cannot receive the delight and pleasure before they are rewarded with vessels of bestowal. It follows that what delays us from being able to receive the delight and pleasure is the will to receive for ourselves.

This means that there are two authorities: 1) the Creator, 2) the creatures, who must elicit from the authority of the Creator into their authority.

It follows that we should speak of two subjects here: Creator and creature. The difference between them is that the Creator is the giver, and the creature is the receiver. This means that the abundance imparted from the Creator must seemingly part from the Creator in order to enter the authority of the receiver, and this is considered separation. Yet, the *Tzimtzum* and concealment were primarily so the upper light would not part from the Creator. Rather, as we learned, the *Tzimtzum* was because *Malchut* wanted to adhere to the root, which is called "annulling her own authority," and to cling to the Creator, which is called "singular authority." This means that the authority of the receiver would be annulled and only the authority of the Creator would remain.

We see that what detains us from receiving the good is only our own authority—that we are unwilling to annul our authority, called "will to receive for ourselves." That is, everything that a person wants to receive is only into his own authority, as it is written, "Everything that a person has, he will give for his soul." A person is willing to give anything if only to keep his soul, meaning to feel his existence, but not the other way around.

That is, a person is told, "I will give you anything you want, and everything your soul desires, but first give me your soul." Then, the person asks, "To whom are you giving if not to his own authority?" meaning to his will to receive, meaning that he will have an authority of his own and he will receive everything into his own authority, otherwise a person cannot work. This derives from the nature that the Creator has imprinted in the creatures a desire to enjoy, which will befit the goal, which was the intention to do good to His creations.

Our sages said (*Masechet Berachot* 17), "Rabbi Alexandry said after he prayed, 'Lord of the world, it is revealed and known to You that our wish is to do Your will, and who detains? The leaven in the dough and the enslavement of *Malchuts* [plural of *Malchut*].'" RASHI interprets that "the leaven in the dough" is the evil inclination in our hearts, which makes us sour.

We should understand "after he prayed," as it is written, "said after he prayed." It means that after the prayer, he prayed another prayer. What did he pray for? that he must pray another prayer on top of the prayer he has already prayed. We should interpret that before he prayed, it was still not apparent to a person what he was missing. But after he has prayed, he is shown from above what is the real lack. That is, the prayer that a person prays for what he thinks he needs is only a *Segula* [remedy/power] where through this prayer, the Creator will send him from above an answer, to know what he needs and what to ask for.

This is as it is written (in the *Musaf* [supplement] prayer on *Rosh Hashanah*), "Be with the mouths of the messengers of Your people, the house of Israel, who are rising up to seek prayer and litany before You for Your people, the house of Israel. Teach them what to say; make them understand what they will speak; answer what they will ask." We see that there is a special prayer when we pray—that the Creator will send us knowledge to understand what we need, and for which to pray from the bottom of the hearts.

It is known that in the work, man is called "a whole world." Thus, when a person prays, that state is called "messenger of the public," for he is praying for the whole of Israel, of which one is a part. For this reason, there is a special prayer that one should pray, a prayer that the Creator will give him help form above to know the truth about what man is missing, and for this, ask the Creator's help.

By this we can interpret the words of Rabbi Alexandry, that after the prayer he would pray the main prayer, saying that he wants the Creator to help him with our obstructor, who does not let us come and receive the delight and pleasure the way the Creator wants it. This obstructor is called "the leaven in the dough and the enslavement of *Malchuts*," meaning the will to receive for oneself, which is man's authority, which is separated from the authority of the Creator, and comes from *Malchut*, who is regarded as the root of the will to receive for oneself and controls a person and does not let him out of her authority.

Malchut of *Kedusha* [holiness/sanctity] means (*The Study of the Ten Sefirot*, Part 2, "Answers," "Answer No. 39"), "The last discernment is called *Malchut*, since from her extends assertive governance and in complete control, such as 'the fear of *Malchut* [kingship].'" As we learned, *Malchut* is called "the will to receive." She received the delight and pleasure and then that *Malchut* made a *Tzimtzum*, not to receive unless with a correction called "in order to bestow." Under this control, all the *Partzufim* of *Kedusha* emerged.

It follows that it is only in this *Malchut*, who gave control so that no *Kedusha* would pour onto the vessels of reception except those who can aim to bestow and cancel their own authority. It follows that all the actions are only for the sake of the Creator, and for himself, he says that it is not worth living. By this he makes a singular authority in the world.

It follows that when he extends some pleasure, the intention in receiving the pleasure is not that it will enter his own authority, but the Creator's authority. That is, the pleasure he receives is for the sake of the Creator, and not for his own sake. Thus, there is only one authority here. This is called "singular authority." This awareness, to know what he really needs, comes after the prayer, once he has prayed to be notified what he really needs. At that time he prays an honest prayer that *Malchut*, meaning the enslavement of *Malchuts*, which is the opposite of *Kedusha*, namely the will to receive for himself, is the only obstructor from achieving the goal that a person should achieve.

But why do we need to pray for this and a person cannot overcome the vessels of reception for himself by himself? Our sages said about this, "Man's inclination overcomes him every day. Were it not for the Creator's help, he would not overcome it." It is not within man's power to exit the control of *Malchut*, for man was born in this nature and only the Creator Himself can deliver man from this control.

This is called "the exodus from Egypt," where only the Creator Himself delivered the people of Israel from Egypt, as it is written (in the Passover Haggadah [story]), "And the Lord took us out of Egypt with a mighty hand, not by an angel, not by a seraph [type of angel], and not by an emissary, but the Creator Himself." This means that since the Creator created man with a nature of wanting to receive for himself, only He can give man a second nature, which is the desire to bestow.

Accordingly, we see that we should make three discernments in man, since he was born after the cascading of the worlds, when *Klipot* [shells/peels] came out due to the breaking of the vessels that took place in the world of *Nekudim*. For this reason, in the work, we find in man himself, 1) People who have no connection to Torah and *Mitzvot*. These are called "a nation similar to an ass." They are simply asses, who have no notion of anything beyond beastly passions. 2) Those who do observe Torah and *Mitzvot*, but *Lo Lishma* [not for Her sake]. These are called "the nations of the world," as it is written in *The Zohar* about the verse, "The mercy of nations is a sin, for any good that they do, they do for themselves." This means that they do everything only for their own benefit. That is, all the good, called "acts of bestowal," is for their own benefit. This is called a "beast," which is a female, receiving. Conversely, "man" is called "male," as it is known that ZA, who is the giver, is called Adam [man]. In *Gematria*, Adam is the name MA, whereas *Malchut*, which is the receiver, is called BON, which in *Gematria* is *Behema* [beast], called "receiving."

As he writes in the "Introduction to The Study of the Ten Sefirot" (Item 31): "All flesh is hay, they are all as hay eating beasts, and all their mercy is as the bud of the field. Every mercy they do, they do for themselves, and even when they exert in Torah, every mercy they do, they do for themselves." From the words of *The Zohar*, we see that those who engage in Torah for their own benefit and not in order to bestow are as beasts, as it is written, "as hay eating beasts." We can call this, "the beast in man," since they already engage in Torah and *Mitzvot*, except it is *Lo Lishma*.

3) This is the "man in man," meaning those who work *Lishma* [for Her sake], which is because of the fear of the Creator and not for their own benefit. They are called "man," which is a male, as said above, that Adam [man] in *Gematria* is MA, who is ZA, the giver. This is as it is written (*Yevamot* 61a), "Rabbi Shimon Bar Yochai says, 'The graves of idol-worshippers are not defiled in a tent, as was said,

'And you, you are My flock, the flock of My pasture, you are man. You are called 'man,' and the idol-worshippers are not called 'man.'"

However, we should understand what is the quality of "man" that specifically Israel are called "man." We should interpret this as we explained about what our sages said (*Berachot* 6b) about the verse, "In the end, all his heard, fear God." The Gemara asks, "What is, 'for this is the whole of man?' Rabbi Elazar said, 'The whole world was created only for this.'"

This means that "fear God" is "the whole of man." In other words, "man" is one who has fear of the Creator, as Rabbi Elazar said, that the whole world was created only for this, for fear of heaven. However, we should understand why he says about "for this is the whole of man," that "the whole world was created only for this."

Our sages said (*Iruvin* 13), "It is better for man not to be created than to be created. But now that he is created, he should look into his actions." We should understand how it can be said that the Creator created man seemingly needlessly, meaning that it would be better if the Creator did not create him. Can it be said that when the Creator came to create man, He did not see through the end of time, and still created him? If so, how can it be said, "It is better for man not to be created than to be created"? Also, what is the advice that they gave, "Now that he is created, he should look into his actions"?

According to what Baal HaSulam interprets, we should interpret "it is better for man" to mean that "for man" means for him. That is, if a person wants to work only for his own benefit, it would be better if he were not created than if he were created. This is as our sages said (*Berachot* 17a), "Anyone who works *Lo Lishma*, it is better if he were not created."

However, we should understand the reason why in *Lo Lishma*, it is better if he were not created. The reason is the correction that took place, where even if the creatures receive delight and pleasure from the Creator, it will not be regarded as disparity of form and separation. For this reason, there was a correction that it is impossible to receive delight and pleasure unless in vessels of bestowal. That is, specifically when a person works only in order to bestow, His thought comes true, which is to do good to His creations—when he thinks only about the benefit of the Creator.

This means that when all of man's thoughts are about how he can bring contentment to the Creator, he comes to feel that by receiving the delight and pleasure he will be bringing contentment to his Maker, for this was the purpose of creation, and because of this, now he wants to receive delight and pleasure. And by this, the purpose of creation will come true.

Conversely, if he works *Lo Lishma*, but for his own sake, on this *Kli*, called "receiving for himself," there was a *Tzimtzum* and concealment. Naturally, he will never achieve the goal for which man was created. For this reason, if a person does not work *Lishma* then he was created in vain, meaning pointlessly. This is why our sages said, "He who learns *Lo Lishma*, it is better that he were not created than if he were created." This is the meaning of what our sages said, "It is better for man not to be created than to be created," meaning that if a person works for himself, it is better if he were not created.

By this we should interpret what we asked, "Can it be said about the work of the Creator that it would be better if He did not do the deed, meaning the creation of man, than if He did the deed of the creation of man? Do we have permission to slander the work of the Creator? And also, what does it mean that "now that he was created, he should look into his actions"?

Indeed, our sages come to open our eyes so we will see what we must do, meaning the purpose for which we were given the work in Torah and *Mitzvot*. For this reason, first they make us see that the fact that man was created and yearns to receive pleasures for his will to receive—which the Creator placed in our nature, meaning for ourselves—it would be better if it were not created. However, the Creator created man to do, and "doing" refers to the correction of the *Kelim* [vessels]—where we must place the aim to bestow over the will to receive. By this, man will be able to receive the delight and pleasure. This is the meaning of the words, "now that he was created." Hence, what should he do? "Look into his actions" and see that each and every thing he does is in order to bestow.

By this we will understand what we asked, why the Creator cannot dwell in one abode with one who is proud. It is known that equivalence of form connects one to the other, and disparity of form separates one from the other. Therefore, one who does not have equivalence of form becomes separated from Him. Hence, one who is proud means that he cannot annul his own authority and being. The "existence from absence" that was created is the authority of oneself, and the desire that the Creator will give him all the delight and pleasure into his own authority. This is called "will to receive for oneself."

It follows that anyone who is proud, the Creator says, "Know that this causes separation and remoteness. It follows that he and I cannot dwell in the world. Why? Because there is separation and remoteness." For this reason, they cannot be in the same world.

This is why Rabbi Shimon Bar Yochai says that any person in whom there is crassness, it is as though he is idol-worshipping. That is, a person must work for the sake of the Creator, yet he works for himself. This is called "idol-worship."

Rabbi Yohanan says that it is as though he has become a heretic. That is, it is as though he has denied the purpose of creation, which is to do good to His creations. One who has crassness can never achieve *Dvekut* [adhesion], which is equivalence of form. If he has no vessels of bestowal, he will never be able to receive the delight and pleasure. It follows that he has denied the purpose of creation, which is to do good to His creations, for without vessels of bestowal, man is in the dark. For this reason, they advise man to lower himself and annul his authority and give everything to the Creator.

By this will understand the question, Why we need to know our own lowliness, why is it not enough to know the greatness of the Creator, and what does it give us to know our own lowliness?

What Is, "The Creator Does Not Tolerate the Proud," in the Work?

The answer is that our lowliness means that we are powerless to annul ourselves before the Creator. Therefore, before we achieve the recognition of evil, we have no need to ask the Creator to help us because we think that we ourselves have knowledge and understanding, and what we understand, we have the power to do. We are unafraid of any force that can stop our spirit and purpose in life, and if we understand with our intellect that the Creator is important, we promptly do what befits intelligent people.

In the end, we see that when some small passion comes along, we surrender before it. Especially, when the work of dedicating ourselves to the benefit of the Creator comes along, and the body does not see what it will gain by this, a person immediately sees what weak heart he has, and he immediately wants to escape the campaign. Therefore, when he sees his own lowliness, this gives him the need for heaven's mercy, to be helped 1) not escape the campaign and have the ability to at least pray to the Creator, 2) that the Creator will truly help him emerge from the control of the body.

It follows that when a person is proud and has no desire to annul his authority before the Creator, and says that he has no lowliness in him, but he rather does what he wants, from this come to him all the bad qualities. The light of pleasure, which comes from above, illuminates as a slim light in order to sustain the world. As is known, it dresses in three qualities, called "envy," "lust," and "honor," and all three qualities are included in the quality of pride.

But seemingly, what is the connection between lust and pride? After all, lust is a beastly quality, so how is pride connected here? The thing is that pride is not necessarily between man and man. Primarily, it is between man and God. For this reason, when a person is proud with regard to the Creator and does not want to annul his own authority, this is the reason for the control of the will to receive for himself. But when a person annuls his authority before the singular authority, he is rewarded with eternal life.

What Is, His Guidance Is Concealed and Revealed?

Article No. 28, Tav-Shin-Mem-Het, 1987/88

Midrash Rabbah, Ruth (Chapter 2:11) asks, "One verse says, 'For the Lord will not abandon His people and will not leave His inheritance,' and another verse says, 'For the Lord will not abandon His people for the sake of His great name.' Rabbi Shmuel Bar Nachmani said, 'At times He does for the sake of His people and His inheritance, and at times He does for the sake of His great name.' Rabbi Ibi said, 'When Israel are worthy—for the sake of His people and His inheritance. When Israel are not worthy—for the sake of His great name. And our sages said, 'In the land of Israel, for the sake of His people and inheritance. Abroad, for the sake of His great name, as it was said, 'For My sake, for My sake I will do.''"

We should understand the meaning of "His great name," and the meaning of "His people and His inheritance." We should also understand the difference between "abroad," attributed to His great name, and "the land of Israel," which is "for the sake of His people and inheritance."

We are told to believe in His guidance—that He leads the world as good and doing good. We must believe that the purpose of creation was because He desires to do good to His creations. We must believe even though we suffer from what Providence sends us to feel. Nonetheless, we should believe that the punishments we suffer for not observing the *Mitzvot* [commandments/good deeds] of the Creator, which the Creator has commanded us, these punishments are not due to vengeance, as it occurs among flesh and blood, who punish because their honor was tarnished when their orders are disobeyed. Instead, here there is a matter of correction.

That is, the torments a person suffers for not observing the Creator's commandments is because the giving of Torah and *Mitzvot* was for man's sake. Through them, he is to receive *Kelim* [vessels] that can receive the delight and pleasure that the Creator has prepared for the creatures. For this reason, when a person does not observe Torah and *Mitzvot*, he is devoid of those *Kelim*. Hence, the Creator sends him suffering so he would take upon himself the Torah and *Mitzvot*. It is as Baal HaSulam said, that we must believe that the sin is the punishment and the punishment is the correction. This is the opposite of the common view.

It is as the Nahmanides says (presented in *The Study of the Ten Sefirot*, Part 1, *Histaklut Pnimit*, Item 1), "Nahmanides had already explained to us the matter of His uniqueness, as expressed in the words, 'One, Unique, and Unified.' There is a difference between 'One,' 'Unique,' and 'Unified': When He unites to act with one force, He is called 'Unified.' When He divides to act His act, each part of Him is called 'Unique.' When He is in a single evenness, He is called 'One.' Interpretation: Uniting to act with one force, when He works to bestow, as is fitting of His oneness, and His operations are unchanging. When He divides to act His act, meaning when His operations differ, and He seems to be doing good and bad, He is called 'Unique,' since all His different operations have a single outcome: doing good. We find that He is unique in every single act and does not change by His various actions. When He is in a single evenness, He is called 'One.' 'One' points to His essence." He also writes there, "'One' indicates a single evenness. 'Unique' implies that all those multiplicities are in Him as single as His essence. 'Unified' shows that although He performs many actions, one force performs all those, and they all return and unite in the form of 'Unique.'"

We see that all of Guidance is in the form of corrections. Although it is difficult to understand this, we must take upon ourselves faith in the sages, which is called "oral Torah [law]." That is, we must believe what they are telling us about what to do and what to believe, and we must follow their views blindly and without criticism because our reason cannot understand the ways of His Providence. Thus, everything must be in faith above reason, and specifically by this we are then rewarded with the delight and pleasure, since we are following the ways of the sages, who have determined for us in which way and manner to go, and not the way our intellect understands.

Specifically in this way of above reason, we are later rewarded with feeling in the organs that the Creator leads the world in a manner of good and doing good. At that time we do not have to believe because we can already feel this, and then we ourselves testify that the creation of the world was with the intention to do good to His creations.

We must believe that the Creator leads the world as *Elokim* [God], which is called *Teva* [nature], as it is written, the *Gematria* of "nature" is "God," which is the quality of judgment.

God is the quality of judgment, and *HaVaYaH* [the Lord] is the quality of mercy. Hence, the for the world in general, who do not believe in the Creator, they say that the guidance of the world follows the quality of nature, that nature determines the guidance of the world. However, they do not say that nature is God, but that it is nature, without any leader. We see that this nature, which the Creator created with the quality of judgment, has no mercy in the judgment, since nature has no intellect from which to ask for mercy so it does not punish us so harshly because we are so weak that we cannot follow its commandments.

The answer to this is "There is no mercy in the judgment." For example, if someone throws his friend in the water, and the water wants to drown him, he says to the water, "Is it my fault that my friend threw me into your domain? Therefore, I'm asking you to please have mercy on me, since I have a big family with many children and no one to take care of them. So please forgive me for entering your domain." The answer is "There is no mercy in the judgment" to those who break nature's laws, which is God, who is the quality of judgment. This is as it is written, "Judgment will puncture the mountain [justice should be done at all costs]." Only those who believe that nature is God, meaning that there is a leader to nature, through prayer, they can induce change in nature, since there is a landlord to nature, and therefore He can change nature.

It is written (*Taanit* 25a) that when Rabbi Hanina Ben Dosa saw on the eve of Shabbat [Sabbath] that his daughter was sad, he told her: "'My daughter, why are you sad?' She said to him: 'I swapped the jar of oil with the jar of vinegar, and I placed the vinegar in the candle. The candle will quench and it will be dark on Shabbat.' He replied, 'He who said to the oil, "Burn!" will tell the vinegar, "Burn!"'"

We see that one who believes that nature has a landlord can change nature. For this reason, those righteous for whom nature is regarded as God, meaning that the Creator is nature's landlord, through their prayer, the Creator changes nature because of them. This is why we pray to the Creator to help us change nature, meaning that even if as far as nature is concerned, all the doctors have given up on that person, and medicine gives him no chance of recovery, the Creator can still heal and change nature.

It is written (*Berachot* 10), "Even if a sharp sword is placed on his neck, he should not deny himself mercy." Although from the perspective of nature, there is a judgment that he will certainly die, a Jew believes that there is a leader to nature and that He has mercy, which is called *HaVaYaH*. Therefore, they said, "he should not deny himself mercy." This is the meaning of the words, "*HaVaYaH* is *Elokim*" [the Lord is God].

Conversely, those who say that nature is without a landlord and there is no one to lead it have no mercy in the judgment. Therefore, they have no complaints to nature because there is no one to be angry with, since it has no mind that you can speak to or ask for mercy.

This is similar to an old custom: Before the invention of road-signs as a means to put order in traffic, police officers would stand and streamline traffic. At that time, many people were angry and had grievances against the officers for not doing their job right, and that they were not noticing the line of cars. Sometimes, a person would approach the officer and ask for a favor, since he has a sick person at home, etc., or ask for some special treatment, and the officer would act on his own judgment. At that time everyone thought that the officers were not working properly. Many people were happy, and many were not.

But today, the streamliner of traffic has become inanimate, mindless. So, now each one accepts the verdict of the road-sign (traffic light), and no one gets angry with it or asks it for favors. For example, sometimes an ambulance drives with a sick person that must be rushed to the hospital on a life or death situation. He does not speak to the road-sign, which is similar to nature, "streamlining the conduct of creation," to let him through, since it is similar to nature, which is judgment, and there is no mercy in judgment.

Accordingly, we can understand that when the Creator wanted the physical world to exist and for the species to continue, and that generations will continue in succession and man will not be able to spoil the order of the existence of the world, for this reason, He has created the world as "nature." Since it is not revealed as orderly guidance and everyone thinks that there is no landlord to the world, and that man can do whatever he wants, since when they do not know that there is a landlord watching over the world, each one does as he pleases and they might spoil the world. What did He do? He revealed the reward and punishment. That is, anyone who wants to break nature's laws, which He did, will immediately be punished. And if they observe nature's laws they will be rewarded for their work. This is called "revealed reward and punishment."

For this reason, in the physical world, because of the correction called "equivalence of form," it is forbidden to receive for one's own sake. Rather, as it is written (*Avot*, Chapter 2:17), "All your actions will be for the sake of heaven." Since the greatest pleasure is when a person feels that he is standing in the King's palace and speaking with the King, and since any reception of pleasure must be for the sake of the Creator and not for one's own sake, it means that a person should aim—while receiving the pleasure—to receive because the Creator wants the creatures to enjoy. But for himself, he would relinquish the pleasure.

It is known that the greater the pleasure, the harder it is to relinquish it. For this reason, if the Creator were revealed and they would not have to believe in Him, it would be impossible for man to be able to aim in order to bestow, since a person is utterly unable to say that if the Creator did not want us near Him and to feel how we speak to Him, we would relinquish the pleasure of this meeting.

Hence, a concealment was made, so there would be room for choice. That is, we must believe that "The whole Earth is full of His glory." Before a person is rewarded with vessels of bestowal, a person cannot have permanent faith, as it is said in the "Introduction of The Book of Zohar." For this reason, there is a *Tzimtzum* [restriction] and concealment on spirituality. And in order not to have corruption in the world, the reward and punishment are revealed.

Conversely, if the reward and punishment in spirituality were revealed, there would not be any need to observe Torah and *Mitzvot* for the sake of the Creator. Instead, the reason mandating observing Torah and *Mitzvot* would remain in *Lo Lishma* [not for Her sake]. That is, where there are revealed reward and punishment, which is called "open Providence," there is no need to observe Torah and

Mitzvot because the Creator has commanded us to do so, and we want to do His will, and not because of reward and punishment.

Since we must observe Torah and *Mitzvot* because "He is great and ruling," it is a great privilege if we can do His will and observe His commandments. But if the reward and punishment were revealed, it would not matter to us who gives us the reward or punishment. It follows that if this were so, man would have no choice as to whether to achieve *Dvekut* [adhesion] with the Creator, since he would have no need for this because the reward and punishment would instruct man to keep the rules. The reward and punishment are as man's two legs, by which he walks and advances toward the goal to which his legs lead him, since from a place where he feels suffering, which is a punishment, he runs, and to a place where he feels he can derive delight and pleasure, he runs.

Naturally, at that time he has no need to know who is the landlord of the world, for what will it add to him to know that there is a leader to the world; he would only be interested in scrutinies of pleasure and suffering. Where one can derive more pleasure, in this he is immersed, and all his calculations in life are only about these matters. For this reason, the Creator hid Himself in the Torah, meaning that by engaging in Torah he can find Him, for otherwise He is hidden.

It follows that to the entire world, who have no connection to spirituality and He is hidden from them, He must lead the world with open Providence, meaning that the reward and punishment will be revealed. Naturally, they will not spoil the conducts of creation, for the Creator has created the world in nature, and they say that there is no landlord here, but only nature—which is seemingly inanimate—is the leader of the world.

And when there is no landlord to fear, each does as he pleases and they might spoil creation. (But because the Creator) leads (the whole world) in open Providence, naturally, they will observe every condition that nature stipulates, or nature will punish them. It follows that He can be hidden and everyone do His will, as He has arranged the world by nature, which is called "God," "the quality of judgment." It follows that He is hidden and the reward and punishment are revealed.

This is not so in spirituality, where He wants to be revealed to the lower ones. At that time Providence is covered, meaning that the reward and punishment are not revealed. Instead, one must believe that there are reward and punishment. Why are the reward and punishment concealed? It is because He wants them to search Him, meaning that the quality of "great and ruling" will compel them to engage in Torah and *Mitzvot*, and not the reward, but rather that everything will be *Lishma* [for Her sake], namely that the Creator is the reason for engaging in Torah and *Mitzvot* because this is His will.

Conversely, if we feel reward and punishment while observing the *Mitzvot*, this is called *Lo Lishma*, as it is written, "Crave His commandments" (Psalms 112:1). They interpreted, His commandments and not the reward for His commandments, but rather to observe because the Creator has commanded to do and a person wants to bring contentment to the Creator, and this is why he observes His commandments. It is as the RADAK says there: "Crave His commandments" is the positive *Mitzvot* [commandments to certain actions]. He does them willingly, out of love of the Creator, who commanded him to do them. For this reason, he says, "crave," meaning that he chases the *Mitzva* [sing. of *Mitzvot*] and exerts to do it with all his might, with his body and his wealth.

Accordingly, where we want the Creator Himself to be revealed to a person in the form of *Dvekut*, the reward and punishment are in concealed guidance. Otherwise, he will have no need to connect to Him. Instead, they would observe Torah and *Mitzvot* because of his own benefit, and from this they will derive satisfaction in their lives. But where it is impossible that they would be interested to know if there is a leader or not, which means that the world is governed only by corporeal things, it follows that the Creator is concealed there because they have no need to know if there is a landlord and a leader to the world. Instead, they say that the leader is nature, as though inanimate.

And what did the Creator do in order not to spoil nature's order? He placed a correction on nature, and that correction is called "revealed reward and punishment." This is a strict guarding that they will not spoil the nature that the Creator has created.

For this reason, we should say that where the Creator remains concealed, the reward and punishment are revealed. And where the Creator must be felt among the lower ones, the reward and punishment must be concealed from the lower ones.

Now we can interpret what we asked, What does it mean that they said about the verse, "For the Lord will not abandon His people," for two reasons: 1) for the sake of His people and His inheritance, 2) for the sake of His great name.

We asked, What is the difference between them? Our sages said (*Masechet Sanhedrin* 98) about the verse, "'For My sake, for My sake I will do,' Rabbi Alexandri said, 'Rabbi Yehoshua Ben Levi Rami, 'It is written, 'in its time' and it is written 'I will hasten it.' If they are rewarded, I will hasten it. If they are not rewarded, in its time.'" We should interpret the meaning of "I will hasten it." We learn that the creatures must come to be rewarded with the purpose of creation, which is to do good to His creations, and all of our work is to correct ourselves with vessels of bestowal, for only in those *Kelim* can the upper lights clothe, so there will be equivalence of form between the light and the *Kli*. This is the correction of the *Tzimtzum*, in order not to have the bread of shame. It follows that it is within man's power to correct this.

This is called "accelerating the achieving of the goal," which is to do good to His creations. We can do this only by annulling the authority, and only then is it possible to receive everything in order to bestow. For this reason, when the Creator imparts the abundance, He imparts to "His people and His inheritance." That is, everything is regarded as His, and the lower one has no authority of his own because he has annulled his own authority. For this reason, "He will not abandon," but He rather bestows upon "His people and His inheritance."

But if they are "not rewarded," meaning that they do not want to annul their authority and are unworthy of receiving the abundance, this is called "in its time." At that time the Creator works "for the sake of His great name," and the name of the Creator is The Good Who Does Good. For this reason, He bestows upon them because He is good and does good, which is called "His great name."

This is the meaning of what is written, "Our great sages say, 'In the land of Israel, for the sake of His people and His inheritance. Abroad, for the sake of His great name." What is the relation in the work between "the land of Israel" and "His people and His inheritance"? In the work, "the land of Israel" is when a person has already been rewarded with all his actions being *Yashar-El* [straight to the Creator], and he does not do anything for his own sake. It follows that "The Lord will not abandon." Instead, He bestows upon them delight and pleasure because they have vessels of bestowal. This is why they are called "His people and His inheritance," since they have no authority of their own.

Conversely, abroad, while they are still not in the land of Israel, when their actions are still not for the sake of the Creator, called *Yashar-El*, it is only by an awakening from above, regarded as "on the part of the upper one," whose purpose is His will to do good to His creations. This is called "in its time," and it is called "for the sake of His great name," where His great name is the name of the Creator, which is The Good Who Does Good. Also, "great" means *Hesed* [mercy], meaning that His manner is to bestow. For this reason, "The Lord will not abandon" only from the perspective of the awakening from above, since from the perspective of the lower ones, they are still not worthy of the Creator bestowing upon them delight and pleasure.

It therefore follows that in all the descents that a person suffers in the work, he must believe in reward and punishment although he does not see. Instead, he must believe that the Creator will not leave him even when he is in descent. Although it is a punishment when the Creator removes him from the work, since the fact that he feels no flavor in the work is only because the Creator has thrown him out, so that a person will not think that now he does not want to be a worker of the Creator, but it is the Creator who does not want him. He must believe that this is a punishment, but he must also believe that it is not out of vengeance, but that it is corrections by which he will be rewarded with ascending and achieving the desired goal.

How to Recognize One Who Serves God from One Who Does Not Serve Him

Article No. 29, Tav-Shin-Mem-Het, 1987/88

Our sages write in [*Masechet*] *Ketubot*: "Rabbi Hiya Bar Ashi said, 'Rav said, 'All infertile trees in the land of Israel are destined to bear fruit, as was said, 'For the tree has borne its fruit, the fig tree and the vine have yielded strength.''"

The MAHARSHA interprets that "Although it is an infertile tree, which by nature is unfit for yielding fruit, it will still bear fruit." We should understand what this teaches us in the work.

The *Sulam* [Baal HaSulam commentary on *The Zohar*], in its commentary on the "Essay about Letters" ("Introduction of The Book of Zohar," Item 23) writes, "It is known that God has made them one opposite the other. As there are four worlds ABYA *de* [of] *Kedusha* [holiness/sanctity], there are four worlds ABYA *de Tuma'a* [impurity] opposite them. Hence, in the world of *Assiya* there is no distinction between one who serves God and one who does not serve Him. Accordingly, how can we tell good from evil? However, there is one, very important scrutiny, which is that another god is barren and does not bear fruit. Hence, those who fail in him and walk by the path of ABYA *de Tuma'a*, their source dries out and they have no blessing of spiritual fruits. Thus, they wither away until they shut completely. The opposite is those who adhere to *Kedusha*. Their works are blessed, 'As a tree planted by streams of water, which yields its fruit in its season and its leaf does not wither; and in whatever he does, he prospers.' This is the only scrutiny in the world of *Assiya* to know if he is in *Kedusha* or to the contrary."

We should understand the meaning of "fruits" in spirituality. The word "fruits" is used to mean "profits," similar to saying, "I struck a big deal but it is yet to bear fruit." It means that he is still not making profit out of it. In work matters, we should interpret that when a person begins to take on the burden of Torah and *Mitzvot* [commandments/good deeds], the understanding he has about fear of heaven and the importance of the *Mitzvot*, and especially the importance of the Torah, when he is at the age of twenty or thirty, he does not know much about the work of the Creator, meaning what is fear of heaven and what is the feeling in Torah and *Mitzvot*.

Although he sees that he has already acquired the possession of several years of engagement in Torah and *Mitzvot*, he has not progressed in the understanding that he had since he became obliged to engage in Torah and *Mitzvot*. That is, he thought that as he grows up, he would probably have different intentions than when he first began the work of the Creator. However, he has remained in the same intention and he agrees to the general view that says about him, when they see that he observes Torah and *Mitzvot* in all its details and intricacies, they respect him and exalt him and honor him for his work in Torah and *Mitzvot*.

Therefore, he is in a state of "The whole world tells you that you are righteous." For this reason, he can never achieve wholeness, called "serving the Creator." He remains "a servant of himself."

How to Recognize One Who Serves God from One Who Does Not Serve Him

That is, all the work he does is for his own benefit. This is called "not serving Him." Instead, he is working for himself and not for the Creator.

In work matters, it is impossible to become a servant of the Creator before we come to a state of "not serving Him," for they are two degrees and it is impossible to rise to a higher level before one is on the lower level. Rather, first one enters the degree called "not serving Him." That is, a person must come to feel that as long as he is working for his own benefit, it is called "not serving Him."

Also, "not serving Him" does not mean that he sees that he is in a state of *Lo Lishma* [not for Her sake], which is called in the work, "not serving Him." He accepts the situation regardless of the excuses he has for this, since the reasons do not change the situation. Therefore, if he agrees to remain in that state, it is regarded as still not being in a state of "not serving Him."

When he sees that he is in a state of "not serving Him," he seeks advice to emerge from it, both by books and by authors. It pains him that he is in such lowliness and so immersed in self-love that he cannot emerge from this control, and he fears that he will stay this way forever. This is called being in a state of "not serving Him."

However, we should ask, How should one name the situation where he sees that he is in a state of "not serving Him"? That is, when a person comes to that state where he sees that he is immersed in self-love, and all the beastly lusts awaken in him—such that he has never dreamed of—in a state of "not serving Him," such thoughts and desires awaken that according to the work he has invested, which he exerted in order to be rewarded with *Kedusha* [holiness/sanctity] and for which he should have at least seen that although he has not been rewarded with *Kedusha*, he should have seen himself liberated from beastly lusts.

Otherwise, he asks, Our sages said, "The reward matches the pain," meaning that a person is rewarded according to the effort he has made. Yet, now he sees that he made the effort, but what reward did he receive? That he has become worse. Before he began the work of bestowal, he knew that he was a worker of the Creator. Although he knew even then that there are higher degrees, meaning those who work *Lishma* [for Her sake], he knew that work *Lishma* was meant for a chosen few. At that time he was certain that although he was not counted among the chosen few, he was regarded as a worker of the Creator like the rest of his environment. But now that he wants to work for the sake of the Creator, he is regressing. That is, he feels that he is worse than before. This brings up the question, Where is what our sages said, "The reward matches the pain"?

The truth is, as Baal HaSulam said, that because he has invested much effort to be rewarded with a little bit of *Kedusha*, by this he was rewarded with attaining the quality of truth. That is, he was rewarded from above with awareness of his true state—how the evil within him, meaning the will to receive for himself is so worldly and remote from the Creator. This means that before he began the work, he could not understand the lowliness of his state whatsoever.

Rather, as we said in previous articles, *The Zohar* interprets the verse, "if his sin is made known to him," that the Creator tells him that he has sinned, or the Torah notifies him that he has sinned. For himself, a person cannot see the evil in him, since a person is close to himself and is biased, and it is written that "bribe blinds the eyes of the wise," and the blind do not see. For this reason, a person cannot see the evil in him by himself. Instead, he is notified from above, which, in the words of *The Zohar*, is regarded as the Torah or the Creator notifying him. Both are made clear to us by one matter, meaning that it comes from above and not from himself, since recognition of evil is knowledge from above.

By this we can interpret what people ask: On one hand, our sages said (*Nida* 30b), "He is sworn, 'Be righteous and do not be wicked, and even if the whole world tells you that you are righteous, be wicked in your own eyes.'" They ask, But the Mishnah (*Avot*, Chapter 2) says, "Do not be wicked in your own eyes," so how come they say, "Be wicked in your own eyes"?

There are many answers to this. According to the above said, recognition of evil comes from above, and a person cannot come to the recognition of evil unless he has exerted in Torah and *Mitzvot* in order to come to work for the sake of the Creator. At that time he is shown from above the evil, and only then can he see that he is wicked. Naturally, in such a state, when he is shown from above that he is wicked, although judging by his actions, he seems righteous to the world, since no one can know what another has been shown from above.

It was said about this: "Even if the whole world tells you that you are righteous," since they do not know you, meaning your intentions, you should still know the truth. For this reason, they said, "Be wicked in your own eyes." "In your own eyes" means not as the world regards your externality. Rather, "in your own eyes" means the form of the intention, which none can see but you. This is called "in your own eyes." Then, you will see that you are wicked, as it is written, "Be wicked in your own eyes."

However, as said above, a person cannot see the truth, that he is wicked, until he has made great efforts in Torah and *Mitzvot* in order to achieve the truth. At that time he is shown from above the truth that he is in a state of "not serving Him." But by himself, without help from above, a person cannot see that he is wicked. This is the meaning of what is written, "Do not be wicked in your own eyes." This means that from his own perspective, a person cannot be wicked. Rather, this requires help from above.

For this reason, a person must ask the Creator to let him know the truth about his state in spirituality, where he is, meaning if he is among those who are called "servants of the Creator," or among those who are called "not serving Him." But by himself, a person cannot know. This is why they said, "Do not be wicked in your own eyes."

Now we will explain what we asked, How should one name the situation he is in, if he sees that he really is in a state of "not serving Him," meaning if he is not moving at all in the work but is regressing and his work has been in vain, without any profits? He should believe in what our sages said, "The reward is matches the pain," but he evidently sees that it would be better if he did not begin this work of bestowal in the first place. He sees that he is only descending in the work, and not ascending. Accordingly, the state of "not serving Him" should have been named "a descent."

However, according to what we said, that it is impossible to achieve a higher degree prior to attaining a lower one, regarded as "not serving Him," it follows that that state is not regarded as a "state of descent," but rather as a "state of ascent," for such is the way: The lower degree is the reason and the cause of the upper degree. Therefore, this descent, when he feels that he is in a state of descent, causes him to ascend to a higher degree.

That is, "the reward matches the pain." In other words, to the extent that he suffers from being in a state of "not serving Him," it causes him to seek counsel and advice to emerge from that state and ascend to a higher degree, called "serving the Creator." For this reason, that state is called "a time of ascent," and it is called "a state of progress toward the goal." However, even at a time of "not serving Him" there are ups and downs, and these descents are also regarded as ascents.

Explanation: A descent causes a person to see the state of the bad in him—to what he might come, meaning to what lowliness it might bring a person. That is, during an ascent, when a person has passion for Torah and prayer, and he thinks that now he is among the servants of the Creator and he no longer needs the Creator to help him out of his evil inclination since he feels good taste in the work, he looks at the times he was in descent and is ashamed of himself. It pains him very much if he remembers his descents.

But suddenly he falls "from the rooftop to the deep pit." That is, he feels from a state of thinking that he was already in heaven into seeing that he is already in a deep pit. Moreover, he does not remember how he fell into the pit and for what reason. Once he falls into the pit, he is there unconscious, meaning he does not feel how he has fallen into the pit. However, after some time he recovers and begins to feel that he is in the pit. The recovery time may take a minute, or an hour, or a day or two days, or a month, until he regains consciousness and sees the lowliness that he was in.

Afterward, he is given once more from above a desire and craving for the work. Once more, he is in a state of ascent, and this is the time that he can enjoy the descent. That is, during the ascent he can know the benefits from experiencing the descent, since according to what is said, the punishments given to a person are not as with a flesh and blood king, who avenges the person not following the king's orders. Rather, here there is a matter of correction. Thus, what benefit can he say that he has from the descents?

The answer is that the descent was not given to man so he would learn from the descent while he is in descent. During the descent he is unconscious. That is, he does not feel that he is in descent, since at that time there is no living being to feel some lack in vitality of *Kedusha*, since he has lost the awareness that there is spirituality in anyone in the world, and all his thoughts are only about life in self-love.

That is, since it is known that without life, it is impossible to live, therefore, each one chooses the right clothing from which to elicit life, which is called "pleasure," since there is no life without pleasure. When a person cannot find pleasure in his life, he immediately chooses death, which is called "committing suicide."

Therefore, during the descent, when he finds pleasure in some clothing, it does not matter to him what is the clothing, but how much pleasure he can derive from this clothing. This is called that at that time he does not think about spirituality, since the pleasure he receives makes him forget everything else, for he is completely preoccupied with continuing to obtain the pleasures in the dresses that suit his spirit at the time. In this he is immersed. At that time, he has no thoughts that there is such a reality called "service of the Creator," since a descent is called "death." That is, the little bit of spirituality when he was somewhat adhered to *Kedusha* has departed from him. For this reason, at that time he is regarded as "dead," without vitality of *Kedusha*.

However, afterward, he wakes up and begins to see that he is devoid of spiritual life. His awakening from the descent is called "the revival of the dead," when he begins to feel that he is deficient of life. Conversely, one who is dead does not feel that he is deficient of life so as to want to be awarded life.

Yet, the question is, Who revived him? The answer to this is "A King who puts to death and brings to life." And why do we need this? The answer is "and brings forth salvation." This means that by the Creator giving him a descent, called "putting to death," on the one hand, and on the other hand, by giving an ascent, called "and brings to life," by this comes salvation, as it is written, "and brings forth salvation."

Thus, when does one learn and profit from the descent? Certainly not during the descent, for then he is dead. However, afterward, when the Creator revives him, meaning gives him an ascent, this is the time to learn what happened to him during the descent, meaning in what lowliness he was, what he craved and what he expected—that if he were to have it, he would feel like a complete human being. At that time he sees that his entire life of being in descent was nothing short of the life of an animal.

Let us take, for example, when trash is thrown in the garbage. When the cats in the area feel that there is some leftovers of an animal that was thrown in the trash, they find it and eat it. With the strength from eating, each of them runs to its place to obtain other pleasures. If a person observes during the ascent, he understands that it is not worthwhile to occupy his mind and heart in beastly lusts. In his current eyes, it is complete trash. When he looks at such a life, it makes him so nauseous that he wants to vomit.

It follows that the great benefit from this descent is that he sees his own lowliness, to what state he might come, and that only the Creator has brought him out of that lowliness. This is the time to see the greatness of the Creator, that He can bring a person "out of the miry clay," where he could drown and remain forever in the hands of the *Sitra Achra* [other side], and only the Creator has brought him out of there.

Accordingly, we can see that during the ascent, a person should read everything that is written about the time of descent. From this reading he will know how to ask the Creator for his soul so He will not throw him once again into the trash. Also, he will know how to thank the Creator for raising him from the bottomless pit, as it was said, "A king who puts to death and brings to life, and brings forth salvation." That is, salvation grows out of the descents and ascents.

Thus, after he has completed the first stage, called "not serving Him," begins the time of being "a servant of the Creator." That is, once he has tried every advice and tactic to exit the state of "not serving Him," he receives help from above, as it is written in *The Zohar*, "He who comes to purify is aided," by giving him "a holy soul." By this he emerges from the governance of self-love and can work only in order to bestow.

Thus, how can a person come to be a servant of the Creator? By being rewarded with a soul from above. This is regarded that now he is bearing fruit. And what is the fruit? It is that he has been rewarded with a soul. This is the fruit. In other words, a person must know that before he was rewarded with fruits, called "a soul," he cannot be a servant of the Creator. Rather, he must be serving himself, which is called "not serving Him," for the above reason that a person cannot go against the nature in which he was born, which is self-love. Rather, only the Creator can make this miracle.

By this we should interpret what our sages said, "All infertile trees in the land of Israel are destined to bear fruit." That is, once a person has been rewarded with *Eretz Yashar-El* [Land of Israel], by being rewarded with a soul, everything becomes corrected, meaning even the quality of "infertile trees," which do not bear fruit. This refers to the time of "not serving Him"—that it also receives correction, as in "sins become to him as merits."

In other words, it is impossible to be a servant of the Creator before one feels that he is in a state of "not serving Him." That is, through the descents and ascents he had while in a state of self-love, these ascents and descents were stages and degrees so he would be able to climb up to the place of wholeness, and then everything enters *Kedusha* because all those things helped him achieve wholeness.

Now we can understand that "infertile trees," which are naturally unfit to bear fruit, will still bear fruit. That is, when a person is in *Lo Lishma*, that state is far from bearing fruit, meaning with being rewarded with understanding in work and Torah, regarded as being rewarded with entering the King's palace. But in a state of *Lo Lishma*, it is to the contrary: He moves himself away from *Dvekut* [adhesion] with the Creator. Still, after he has been rewarded with entering the land of Israel, all the *Lo Lishma*, called "infertile trees," will bear fruit, meaning that the upper light, called "a soul," will be on those *Kelim*, as well, since everything comes into *Kedusha*.

What to Look For in the Assembly of Friends

Article No. 30, Tav-Shin-Mem-Het, 1987-88

Our sages said (*Avot*, Chapter 1:6), "Make for yourself a rav [teacher], buy yourself a friend, and judge every person to the side of merit."

We should understand the attachment of "Judge every person to the side of merit" to "Buy yourself a friend." Also, it is written in the book *Matan Torah* (*The Giving of the Torah*, p 30), that the *Mitzva* [commandment/good deed], "Love your friend as yourself," is in order to achieve the love of the Creator, which is *Dvekut* [adhesion] with Him. He writes, "It is reasonable to think that the part of the Torah that deals with man's relationship with his friend is better capable of bringing one to the desired goal. This is because the work in *Mitzvot* [plural of *Mitzva*] between man and God is fixed and specific, and is not demanding, and one becomes easily accustomed to it, and everything that is done out of habit is no longer useful. But the *Mitzvot* between man and man are changing and irregular, and demands surround him wherever he turns. Hence, their cure is much more certain and their aim is closer."

This means that man must come to be rewarded with equivalence of form, meaning that all his thoughts and desires will be only for the benefit of the Creator and not for his own benefit. This stems from the correction of the *Tzimtzum* [restriction]. It means that from the perspective of the Creator, He created the worlds with the intention of wanting to do good to His creations. As our sages explain, the Creator said to the ministering angels that the creation of the world is like a king who has abundance, but no guests.

In other words, He has pleasure when the guests dine at His place, but to avoid shame, there was a correction that they must receive delight and pleasure with the aim of delighting the Creator. But the first degree is bestowing in order to bestow. One should enjoy while bestowing, just as the Creator enjoys. It is as our sages said (*The Zohar, VaYera*, Item 399), "There was no such joy before the Creator since the day the world was created as the joy that He is destined to rejoice with the righteous in the future."

We see that on the day when the world was created, there was great joy to the Creator. In other words, He had great joy in wanting to bestow. It follows that if a person performs acts of bestowal but feels no joy, there is no equivalence of form here. Although in the act he is bestowing and engaging in love of others, the act should be with joy, like the joy that the Creator has. Thus, the equivalence in joy is missing here.

Hence, there are two things that one must do: 1) Even though the body does not wish to work in bestowal, it must be forced. However, there is a rule that when a person does things coercively, he cannot be happy, since he would be happier if he did not have to do those deeds. Still, man must work coercively. This is called "coercing and subduing the evil in him." However, the joy that should come with each act of bestowal is missing here. When it comes to joy, one cannot force himself to be happy in a place where there is an act of coercion. Joy is a result of a person's enjoyment, and where there is pleasure, "coercion" is out of the picture. Hence, no joy or pleasure comes from coercion. 2) We say that we need joy for the work of the Creator, and as we said, joy is only a result of something that a person enjoys. Thus, since man can only perform acts of coercion, this is called "an action." An act is something to which the mind does not agree. It is considered that when one begins to coerce himself, he comes into a state of "He who comes to purify."

Thus, what else is missing? Only something that will evoke his gladness. We should interpret about that that this is given to him from above. This is called "He is aided." In what is the aid? *The Zohar* says, "In a holy soul." When one is rewarded with this, he has joy. It follows that when we say that one should work with joy, it means that through one's actions, he should evoke the awakening from above, for only by help from above can he enjoy while engaging in acts of bestowal.

Indeed, there is a question here: "Why is it necessary to perform acts of bestowal with joy?" The reason is simple: There is no equivalence of form here because when the Creator gives, He feels joy. But if when man gives and has no joy, the equivalence of form is absent.

However, there is an even graver issue here than equivalence of form. When a person is in a state of sadness, when he sees his life as pointless because wherever he looks, he sees only black—in corporeality as well as in spirituality—it is like a person who wears dark glasses. Wherever he looks, he sees only darkness.

In that state a person is considered heretical in regard to the Creator's guidance, since he cannot say that the Creator leads His world as The Good Who Does Good.

In that state, he is considered faithless. Thus, here the issue is no longer equivalence of form, but rather faithlessness, since he is in a state of heresy. It follows that man must always be in gladness and believe above reason that everything that the Creator does is done only in benevolence. But we should also believe that this is what we need—to believe above reason.

By our reason, it seems it would be better if the Creator treated us with open guidance. But Baal HaSulam said that we must not say that the Creator cannot give everything into the vessels of reception, called "within reason," meaning that the corporeal body, too, will understand that the Creator treats the whole world only with benevolence.

Why did He choose specifically the *Kelim* [vessels] of above reason? The Creator chose those *Kelim* because they are indeed the best, for by them we achieve the real wholeness, and then the verse, "And you will love the Lord your God with all your heart" will come true. Our sages said, "With both your inclinations—the good inclination and the evil inclination."

At that time, the body, too, feels the delight and pleasure that the Creator gives to the creatures and then there is no need to believe above reason. It follows that the main requirement is for man to be in gladness while doing the work of bestowal, when he does not see what self-reception—called "within reason"—would receive from it, since otherwise he is in a state of heresy.

It follows that one must perform the holy work above reason because these are the *Kelim* that are suitable for bringing man to wholeness. It was said earlier that only above reason can he take pleasure in the guidance of the Creator, which is in the form of benevolence. And this is called "right."

As Baal HaSulam said, one must try to walk on the right line, called "faith above reason," and picture that he has already been rewarded with complete faith in the Creator, that his organs already feel that the Creator leads the whole world in benevolence.

Thus, we should ask, "Why must we walk on the left line, too, if the right line is the most important? What is the purpose of the left line?" The answer is that it is to know our state within reason—the measure of our faith, how much Torah we have acquired, and how we feel the Creator during prayer, etc.

And then we come to feel that we are in utter lowliness, the lowest possible. This is the reason why, when we later shift to the right line, we have the work above reason. In other words, as the left line shows us our state within reason, here there is room to go above reason. But if we were always in the right line, it would not be regarded as right, but as a single line.

In other words, we would think that this is truly where we are, and we would think that we are truly within reason, in the perfect *Gadlut* [greatness/adulthood]. But in truth, only above reason are we in wholeness; hence, when we have the two lines, we can say that there is the matter of above reason, which is the right line.

It follows that the right line helps the left line because once he pictures himself already in gladness, enjoying the perfection of his work, when he shifts to the left line he sees that he is in a world of total darkness. That is, he sees and feels that he is still immersed in self-love and that he has no hope of exiting self-love.

Then there is room for prayer from the bottom of the heart. The state of the right was when he imagined being in a state that he pictured for himself the perfection of the work. In other words, he believed above reason in the commandment of faith in the teacher, who told him to go in that state, although his reason told him, "Why do you compare your situation to that of a person who has already been rewarded with complete faith when you know that you are in the lowest possible baseness that can ever be?" He feels that he is in a state of lowliness that is unbecoming to a person who wants to ever be a worker of the Creator.

And afterwards he moves to the right line, and the left gives him room to work in the right line. However, we must remember that anything that is a path of truth is hard to walk on without effort. Therefore, after those two lines he arrives at the middle line called "the Creator gives him the soul." And then he comes into complete faith, specifically through God's salvation. But by nature, man cannot achieve this by himself.

With all the above, we can understand the matter of the assembly of friends. When they gather, what should they discuss? First, the goal must be clear to everyone—this gathering must yield the result of love of friends, that each of the friends will be awakened to love the other, which is called "love of others." However, this is only a result. To beget this lovely offspring, actions must be taken to produce the love.

And concerning love, there are two forms: 1) Natural love, for which one does not have to exert. He should only be careful not to spoil nature. 2) One that comes by one doing good things to another. There is nature in that, too, since one who gives a present to another causes him to love him. Hence, when a group of people gathers and wishes to work together on love of friends, they must all help one another as much as they can.

And there are many discernments about that, since not everyone is the same, meaning that what one needs, the other does not. However, there is one thing in which all are equal: Each and every one of the friends needs high spirits. That is, when the friends are not in a good mood, they are not all the same in their needs. Rather, each has his own reason for being unhappy.

Therefore, each one must contemplate how he can bring about a good mood to the other. Thus, they should be careful and avoid discussing things that can bring sadness to the society, for by that one causes the others to feel bad. And then, after he goes home, he will ask himself, "What have I gained by going to the society? To know that I am in a state of lowliness and that I should regret it? It is as though I went to the society so they would bring me into a state of sadness. In that case, it was a waste of time. It would probably be better if I did not go to them." Then he probably says, "The next time I have to go to the society, I'll make up excuses to avoid them."

It therefore follows that each one should try to bring into the society a spirit of life and hopefulness, and infuse energy into the society. Thus, each of the friends will be able to tell himself, "Now I am starting a clean slate in the work." In other words, before he came to the society, he was disappointed with the progress in the work of the Creator, but now the society has filled him with life and hopefulness.

Thus, through society he obtained the confidence and strength to overcome because now he feels that he can achieve wholeness. And all his thoughts—that he was facing a high mountain that could not be conquered, and that these were truly formidable obstructions—now he feels that they are nothing. And he received it all from the power of the society because each and every one tried to instill a spirit of encouragement and the presence of a new atmosphere in the society.

But what can one do when he feels that he is in a state of sadness—both in terms of the corporeal state and the spiritual state—and the time when he must go to the society has come? And yet, our sages said, "A worry in a man's heart? Let him speak of it with others." In other words, he should tell his friends, and perhaps they can offer some help.

But if this is so, why do we say that everyone should bring high spirits into the society when one has none? Moreover, there is a rule that "one cannot give that which one does not have." Thus, what should he do to give something to the society that will give high spirits to the society?

Indeed, there is no other way but for man to walk on the right line. Thus, before he goes to the love of friends, he should read Baal HaSulam's essay (*Shamati*, No. 40) where he clarifies what is the right line, that this is the meaning of above reason. And he should draw strength from there so that when he comes to the society, each and every one will more or less be able to infuse a spirit of life, and by that, the whole of society will feel joy and strength, and confidence.

During the assembly, it is forbidden to evoke the left line. Only when one is alone is he permitted to use the left line, but not more than half an hour a day. But the essence of man's work is to go specifically by the right line, as is written (*Shamati*, No. 40). But two people together must not speak of the left, for only thus can they receive assistance from the society.

But the worst is when a person comes to the society and sees that the whole of society is in a state of decline, so how can he be strengthened by them? At that time, he must judge everyone to the side of merit.

Now we can understand what we asked about the proximity of "Buy yourself a friend" and "Judge every person to the side of merit." With the above written, we can understand that when one wishes to acquire something from the society, he should judge everyone to the side of merit. Then he can acquire from the friends so they will help him in the work, since he has someone from whom to receive. But when he sees that he is far above the whole of society, from whom will he receive? Our sages came and said about this, "Judge every person to the side of merit."

It follows that the main reason why a person needs to buy a friend and work in love of others is that thus he can be rewarded with the love of the Creator. But the friends should primarily speak together about the greatness of the Creator, because according to the greatness of the Creator that one assumes, to that extent he naturally annuls himself before the Creator. It is as we see in nature that the small one annuls before the great one, and this has nothing to do with spirituality. Rather, this conduct applies even among secular people.

In other words, the Creator made nature this way. Thus, the friends' discussions of the greatness of the Creator awaken a desire and yearning to annul before the Creator because he begins to feel longing and desire to bond with the Creator. And we should also remember that to the extent that the friends can appreciate the importance and greatness of the Creator, we should still go above reason, meaning that the Creator is higher than any greatness of the Creator that one can imagine.

We should say that we believe above reason that He leads the world in a benevolent guidance, and if one believes that the Creator wants only man's best, it makes a person love the Creator until he is rewarded with "And you will love the Lord your God with all your heart and with all your soul." And this is what a person must receive from the friends.

And in the matter of obtaining greatness, it should be obtained specifically through the society. It is as it is written in the book *Matan Torah* (*The Giving of the Torah*, p 141), where he speaks concerning the teacher and the student. It is the same with regard to the greatness of the Creator. He writes, "Obtaining the greatness depends entirely on the environment, and a single person cannot do a thing about it whatsoever. Yet, there are two conditions to obtaining the greatness: 1) Always listen and assume appreciation of the environment to the extent that they exaggerate. 2) The environment should be great, as it is written, 'In the multitude of people is the king's glory.'

"To receive the first condition, each student must feel that he is the smallest among all the friends. In that state, one can receive the appreciation of the greatness from everyone, since the great cannot receive from a smaller one, much less be impressed by his words. Rather, only the small is impressed by the appreciation of the great.

"And for the second condition, each student must extol the virtues of each friend and cherish him as though he were the greatest in the generation. Then the environment will affect him as a sufficiently great environment, since quality is more important than quantity."

However, what should a friend do if he needs help from his friends? We have said above that it is forbidden to speak of bad things that cause sadness at the assembly of friends. The answer is that one should tell a close friend, and that friend will speak to the society, but not at the time of the assembly of friends. In other words, he can speak to the whole of society together, but not during the regular assembly of friends. Instead, he can arrange for a special meeting in favor of the friend who needs assistance.

And regarding "Buy yourself a friend," we should interpret that "Buy" means that he must be paid, and through the payment he buys him. What does he pay him? We can say that payment is received in return for exertion. In other words, sometimes a person wishes to buy, for example, a nice closet, which is worth 2,000 dollars. He tells the seller, "Since I have no money to pay, but I heard that you are looking for an employee for two weeks, I will work for the amount that I have to pay you in return for the money for the closet," and the seller will probably agree. Thus, we see that the payment can be by exchange.

It is the same with love of friends. It is a great effort when one should judge the friends to the side of merit, and not everyone is ready for it.

Sometimes, it is even worse. At times, a person sees that his friend is disrespectful toward him. Even worse, he heard a slanderous rumor, meaning he heard from a friend that that friend, who is called so and so, said about him things that are not nice for friends to say about each other. Now he must subdue himself and judge him to the side of merit. This, indeed, is a great effort. It follows that through the exertion, he gives the payment, which is even more important than a payment of money.

However, if that person slanders him, where will his friend muster the strength to love him? He knows for certain that he hates him, or he would not slander him, so what is the point in subduing himself and judging him to the side of merit?

The answer is that love of friends that is built on the basis of love of others, by which they can achieve the love of the Creator, is the opposite of what is normally considered love of friends. In other words, love of others does not mean that the friends will love me. Rather, it is I who must love the friends. For this reason, it makes no difference if the friend slanders him and must certainly hate him. Instead, a person who wishes to acquire love of others needs the correction of loving the other.

Therefore, when a person makes the effort and judges him to the side of merit, it is a *Segula* [remedy/power/virtue], where by the toil that a person makes, which is called "an awakening from below," he is given strength from above to be able to love all the friends without exception.

This is called "Buy yourself a friend," that a person should make an effort to obtain love of others. And this is called "labor," since he must exert above reason. Reasonably thinking, "How is it possible to judge another person to the side of merit when his reason shows him his friend's true face, that he hates him?" What can he tell the body about that? Why should he submit himself before his friend?

The answer is that he wishes to achieve *Dvekut* [adhesion] with the Creator, called "equivalence of form," meaning not to think of his own benefit. Thus, why is subduing a difficult thing? The reason is that he must revoke his own worth, and the whole of the life that he wishes to live will be only with the consideration of his ability to work for others' benefit, beginning with love of others, between man and man, through the love of the Creator.

Hence, here is a place where he can say that anything he does is without any self-interest, since by reason, the friends are the ones who should love him, but he overcomes his reason, goes above reason, and says, "It is not worth living for myself." And although one is not always at a degree where he is able to say so, this is nonetheless the purpose of the work. Thus, he already has something to reply to the body.

It therefore follows that before each friend comes to the assembly of friends, he must contemplate what he can give to the society to uplift the spirit of life in it. In that, there is no difference between one who is unschooled or schooled, since the thought he thinks, though he may not know anything, he must pray to the Creator to help him and believe that the Creator hears the prayers.

What Is the Work of Man that Is Attributed to the Creator, in the Work?

Article No. 31, Tav-Shin-Mem-Het, 1987/88

It is written in *The Zohar* (*Ekev*, Item 1): "'And you shall eat and be satisfied, and bless the Lord your God.' This *Mitzva* [commandment] is to bless the Creator for all that he has eaten and drunk, and enjoyed in this world. If he does not bless, he is called 'a thief from the Creator.' Concerning the verse, 'He who robs his father and his mother,' the friends established that it relates to the Creator, since the blessings that a person blesses the Creator come to extend life from the source of life, which is *Bina*, to the holy name of the Creator."

We see here that two things are required: 1) Pleasure, which a person enjoys. 2) A person must bless on the pleasure he received. He says that otherwise, if a person does not bless, he is regarded as stealing from the Creator. He says that the reason is that through the blessing he extends abundance for the sake of the Creator.

We should understand why, if a person does not bless, abundance is not extended for the sake of the Creator. That is, if the Creator can give abundance, why does He need an awakening through the blessing?

He interprets there in the *Sulam* [Ladder Commentary] that his father is the Creator, and his mother is the *Shechina* [Divinity], and through the blessing, abundance is extended to the Creator and the *Shechina*. However, we should understand the importance of the blessing that extending the abundance from above causes. And if he does not bless, he robs the abundance that his father and mother should receive.

These words of our sages are also presented in the Talmud (*Berachot* 35b): "Anyone who enjoys this world without a blessing, it is as though he robs the Creator and the assembly of Israel, as it was said, 'He who steals from his father and his mother, and says, 'there is no crime,' is a friend of a pernicious man. His father is the Creator, as it was said, 'For He is your father, your Maker.' And his mother is the assembly of Israel, as it was said, 'Hear, my son, your father's instruction and do not forsake your mother's teaching.' What is, 'a friend of a pernicious man'? Rabbi Hanina Bar Papa said, 'He is a friend of Jeroboam, son of Nevat, who corrupted Israel to their Father in heaven.'"

This text is also difficult to understand. Is one who does not bless for a pleasure he enjoys a friend of Jeroboam, son of Nevat, who corrupted Israel to their Father in heaven? We should understand what is the gravity that we find in the blessing, and why it is worse than one who commits a transgression, that he deserves a punishment for the transgression he has committed, while here, it is as though the transgression of avoiding a blessing is akin to corrupting the entire world.

It is known that the whole world was created only for the fear of heaven, as our sages said (*Berachot* 6b), "Any person in whom there is fear of heaven, his words are heard, as it was said, 'In the end, all is heard, fear God.' He asks, 'What is, 'For this is the whole of man'? Rabbi Elazar said, 'The Creator said, 'The whole world was created only for this.''" RASHI interpreted "for this" as "to create this."

We should understand the meaning of "The whole world was created only for the fear of heaven." It seems like a contradiction to the known rule, that in the creation of the world, it is written (*Midrash Rabbah, Beresheet*) that the Creator said to the ministering angels that He wants to create the world, as it is similar to a king who has a tower filled abundantly but no guests. This is why He created man, to give him delight and pleasure.

Yet, here he says that the world was created only for the fear of heaven, as though the Creator needs to be feared and this is why He has created the world.

To understand this, we first need to understand what is called "world," and what is called "fear." According to the rule we learned, the reason for the creation of the worlds was to do good to His creations. For this reason, He created in the creatures a desire and yearning to receive delight and pleasure. This is called *Malchut de Ein Sof* [infinity/no end], since at that time, *Malchut* still did not put a stop on the expansion of the abundance, but received in the desire to delight herself.

However, afterward, once she received the light, we learned that *Malchut* craved equivalence of form because every branch wants to resemble its root. For this reason, she did not want to receive because of her own benefit, but in order to bring contentment to the Creator. In other words, because the Creator wants to do good to His creations, he wants to receive.

In the words of the ARI, this is called "*Tzimtzum* [restriction]," "concealment," and "hiding." In the book *Tree of Life*, he says that before the worlds were created, the upper light had filled the whole of reality, and there was no *Rosh* [head] or *Sof* [end], but everything was completely even. However, when He wished to emanate the emanations and create the creatures, He restricted Himself, leaving a vacant space. He says there, "And behold, after the aforementioned *Tzimtzum*, there was a place where the emanated, created, fashioned, and made could be."

We see that prior to the *Tzimtzum*, there was no matter of worlds, for *Olam* [world] comes from the words *He'elem* and *Hester* ["concealment" and "hiding"]. The concealment and hiding that took place then were as it is written, "In order to bring to light the perfection of His deeds." He explains there in *Ohr Pnimi* ["Inner Light," Baal HaSulam's commentary on the words of the ARI] that it means it is in order to have equivalence of form, called "receiving in order to bestow." Otherwise, they will not receive any abundance, so there will not be disparity of form called "separation," and *Malchut de Ein Sof* desired this.

Had there been disclosure of light in the vessels of reception, there would not be any room for work, so they could ever achieve equivalence of form. This is why there was the departure of the light, called "concealment and hiding." Afterward, according to the power to overcome, called "a *Masach* [screen] on the upper light," so they can receive in order to bestow, to that extent the light appears.

Since this *Kli* [vessel] comes from the lower one, meaning that the lower one must make the *Kli*, hence, the lower one is unable to receive all the light that was in the purpose of creation when the Creator placed the light in the *Kli* that He had made, called "will to receive." Rather, the light that illuminated in the vessels of reception is now received in portions, one at a time, called "bit by bit," since the *Kelim* [vessels] that the creatures make, which are called "in order to bestow," cannot do everything at once.

For this reason, many worlds emerged, meaning many *Masachim* [plural of *Masach*], where on the one hand, each *Masach* makes a concealment, and on the other hand through it, there is revelation. Yet, prior to the *Tzimtzum*, there was no place for the worlds, meaning that there was no place for the concealment simply because as it is written, "the upper light had filled the whole of reality."

It therefore follows that there are two actions in man: 1) He wants to receive everything for his own benefit, regarded as wanting to receive every delight and pleasure that he sees into the *Kli* called "receiving for himself." 2) He wants to bestow upon others.

According to the above, we should say that the act of wanting to receive for his own benefit comes to him from the Creator, meaning that the Creator imprinted in the creatures a *Kli* called "receiving in order to receive." A person does not need to work on this *Kli* or acquire it. Rather, it comes to him with the nature that the Creator created.

Conversely, an act that a person does in favor of another comes from the creatures, meaning that a person must make an effort to acquire this *Kli*, since the Creator did not intend that the creatures would give to Him, but rather that the Creator would give to the creatures. However, in order to avoid shame, the lower one made the *Tzimtzum* and the concealment so as not to receive any light except according to what it can receive in order to bestow. For this reason, since the lower one must perform this act by itself, the lower one must exert great efforts to acquire this *Kli*, as it is against the nature in which the creatures were created.

It follows that the question we asked, Which action that a person does do we attribute to the Creator, meaning that the Creator created it? It is that a person wanting to receive abundance for his own benefit comes directly from the Creator. But an act of bestowal we attribute to the creature. Hence, it is difficult for a person to acquire this *Kli* because it is against nature.

Accordingly, we can interpret what we asked about what our sages said, that the whole world was created for this, for the fear of heaven, as it is written, (Ecclesiastes 3:14), "And God made it that He would be feared." Yet, this contradicts what our sages said, that the creation of the world was in order to do good to His creations, and not in order to have fear, and this is why the world was created, as our sages said, that the whole world was created only for this, meaning for the fear of heaven, implying that the Creator needs to be feared, and this is why He has created the creatures.

As we explained, *Olam* [world] means *He'elem* and *Hester* ["concealment" and "hiding"]. This brings up the question, Why did the Creator create concealment and hiding when the reason for creating the world was to do good to His creations? However, there is a matter of correction here. In the book *Tree of Life*, the ARI refers to it as "In order to bring to light the perfection of His deeds, He restricted Himself." We see that the concealment and hiding, called *Tzimtzum*, was so they could receive the upper light and remain in *Dvekut*, called "equivalence of form."

In other words, although they receive delight and pleasure, since they are receiving in order to bestow, it is called "equivalence of form." This means that from the perspective of the desire and yearning they have for the upper abundance, they relinquish the reception of delight and pleasure. However, because the Creator derives delight and pleasure from their joy, as this was the purpose of creation, they receive, since the Creator wants them to enjoy and not because they want to receive pleasure for themselves.

That correction is specifically through the concealment and hiding, for then there is room for choice to say that without the aim to bestow, he does not want to receive. But if the light were revealed, as it was prior to the *Tzimtzum*, how could he say while the upper light fills the whole of reality, that there is room for choice, meaning that if he cannot aim to bestow, he will not receive? It would have been impossible, since we see that after all the restrictions that took place, it does not shine openly in this world.

The ARI says that only a slim light descended from the *Kedusha* [holiness/sanctity] to sustain the *Klipot* [shells/peels]. This means that all the pleasures in the corporeal world are but a slim light compared to the lights that exist in *Kedusha*. Yet, we see that when a person receives pleasure in the corporeal world, which is a tiny pleasure compared to spirituality, where the bulk of the pleasure is found, how difficult it is for him to say, "If I cannot aim to bestow,

I relinquish the pleasure." Thus, we can imagine that if the light were revealed, such as the light clothed in the commandment of *Tzitzit* [prayer shawl], how could a person say that he relinquishes the pleasure if he cannot aim to bestow?

Now we can understand that the word "world" means "concealment," and by this we can interpret what they said, "The world was created only for this," meaning for the fear of heaven. However, what does "fear of heaven" mean in the work of achieving the truth? It means as it is said in the "Introduction of The Book of Zohar" (Item 203), "Both the first fear and the second fear are not for his own benefit, but only for fear that he will decline in bringing contentment to his Maker."

By this we will understand what was written, "The whole world was created only for fear of heaven." This means that the whole matter of concealment, which is called "world," was created only in order to make it possible to achieve bestowal. That is, if there were no concealment, there would be no room for us to work in order to bestow.

Accordingly, the meaning of what we asked about what is written, that the world was created in order to do good to His creations, this refers to the purpose of creation, as was said, that the Creator said that it is like a king who has a tower filled abundantly. And then comes the correction of creation, which is to work in order to bestow, which is *Dvekut* [adhesion], equivalence of form, called "fear," and on this correction was the world made, meaning that there would be concealment and hiding.

It turns out that the world, which is concealment, was done so that He would be feared. This means that fear is for man's sake, so he would be able to work for the sake of the Creator. We should not say that the Creator needs to be feared, but that the fear is that a person fears he might not be able to work in order to bestow. This is why the concealment took place. This work pertains to man, who should make great efforts to acquire these *Kelim*, as it is

What Is the Work of Man that Is Attributed to the Creator, in the Work?

against nature because the Creator placed in the creatures a desire to receive delight and pleasure.

Now we can interpret what is written, "And God made it that He would be feared." That is, in order for a person to maintain the fear, called "kingdom of heaven," He had made a correction. As soon as a person leaves the kingdom of heaven, called "faith above reason," the Creator made it so that man will immediately descend from his state, where he thought about spirituality, and fall into the corporeal world, where there is no connection between them.

These falls cause man to keep himself from changing the order of the work of faith above reason. See in the "Introduction of The Book of Zohar": "The whole matter of fear is only for man's sake, and not that the Creator needs to be respected, such as a flesh and blood king. Instead, all that He has done is in man's favor, for these corrections that the Creator has performed will guide a person on the right path to lead him to the purpose of creation, namely for the creatures to receive delight and pleasure."

Now we will explain what we asked about the blessing, where it is written, "He who enjoys in this world without a blessing, is as Jeroboam, son of Nevat." We asked, Why is the transgression of enjoying without blessing so much graver than other transgressions? It is as though with other transgressions that a person performs, he is not as Jeroboam, son of Nevat, who was a sinner who made the public sin. But one who enjoys without a blessing is similar to Jeroboam, son of Nevat, who corrupted Israel to their Father in heaven?

In the work, we should interpret that when a person enjoys something and blesses for it, there is a matter of renewing the faith here. That is, when a person says the blessing, he must believe that the Creator has given him the pleasure, which falls into the category of "His desire to do good to His creations." Therefore, in corporeal pleasures, too, the pleasure that the Creator wants to give to the creatures is clothed, as well, since only the Creator sustains everything, as it is written, "And you sustain them all."

However, as long as a person is unfit to feel who is his provider, the Creator dresses in corporeal dresses, meaning that only in inferior dresses, which animals, too, can enjoy in these dresses, and the speaking can also feel pleasure in them.

In these corporeal pleasures, in which man feels delight and pleasure like animals, there is room for choice. That is, it is possible to say here that all the pleasures in these dresses are nature. That is, they say that there is no leader to nature, and from this it follows that all the secular people do not want to believe that there is a leader to nature, since they have clear proof within reason that it is as they say.

Some believers say that they are going above reason. That is, although it makes sense to say that everything is only nature, still, they are devout believers and have faith in the sages, who say that there is a Creator who leads the good. It follows that the fact that the Creator dresses in corporeal pleasures and they receive delight and pleasure is enough for them to lead a happy life, and they have no need to know if there is a leader to nature, for what will this add to our pleasures?

Instead, they want to increase the pleasures by increasing the dresses, such as more money, more respect, and more food and drink. The reason they have no need to search perhaps there is a leader to nature extends from the verse, "A slave in abandonment is content," as our sages said, that one does not want to take upon himself any enslavement from anyone. Rather, a person wants to be free and not be enslaved to any person. It follows that when a person seeks to find tactics to know that there is a leader to nature, if he takes upon himself the view that there is a leader, then he must follow the commandments of the leader and will have to say that there is reward and punishment. Thus, it is better to say that nature is without a leader. By this he can lead a life of abandonment.

It follows that the fact that the delight and pleasure in Torah and *Mitzvot* are hidden from us is deliberate, so there will be room for choice, since in Torah and *Mitzvot*, it cannot be said that there is no leader, for who is the Giver of the Torah and *Mitzvot*?

However, who awakens to choose and believe there is a leader to nature? When a person calculates that it is impossible that a person, who is the speaking level, will have the same level of life as animals, that is, they cannot accept that they do not have a more important role in life than animals, they begin to search for a purpose to their lives.

It is as our sages said about Abraham, who asked, "Is there a city without a leader? Promptly, the leader of the city appeared before him and said to him, 'I am the leader of the city.'" That is, he saw a city lit up, meaning he saw the world, which is called 'a city,' where everyone was suffering. He said about this, "Is there a city without a leader?" Certainly, nature does not afflict the world without a leader to nature. Thus, he began to search for the leader. Promptly, the leader appeared before him and said, "I am the landlord of the World."

We see that there must be an awakening by the lower one. He needs to want to know and feel that there is a leader to nature, and crave *Dvekut* with Him, and do whatever he can, although he sees that it is hard for him to see this within reason that nature's leader is good and does good, since he sees that he himself is devoid of delight and pleasure. Also, when he examines the world, he sees that the whole world is in suffering and poverty, both in corporeality and in spirituality. Yet, he must believe with faith above reason that the Creator leads the world and that He gives to the whole world only good.

It is as Baal HaSulam says (*Shamati*, Article No. 1), that one must believe above reason that the Creator leads the world in private Providence by way of "The Good Who Does Good." Although within reason he sees the opposite, he should know, "They have eyes and see not." As long as one has not been rewarded with entering the authority of the Creator and annuls his own authority, a person cannot see the truth.

Thus, we see that when a person enjoys in this world, meaning in the will to receive pleasure for himself, although this desire comes from the Creator, meaning that this was the only desire of the Creator—that the creatures will enjoy abundance—it follows that when a person enjoys, he does the will of the Creator.

Therefore, why does he need to bless the Creator? Was the intention of doing good to His creations because the Creator needs to be blessed? where blessing is about blessing the Giver that he will be blessed in everything he does.

We should ask, Does the Creator need to be given blessing and success? This applies only to the creatures, who are weak, and therefore need blessing and success in what they cannot obtain through their own work, for they are powerless. But how can you say this about the Creator?

Yet, as we learned, with respect to the correction of creation, there was the matter of *Tzimtzum* and concealment so the lower ones could receive and there would be no shame upon the reception of the pleasures.

In this regard, we can discern two things: 1) the act, meaning a person receives pleasure; 2) the intention, meaning the reason. That is, who makes him receive the pleasure, which is called "an act"? At that time a person contemplates so as to see who and what caused him pleasure, his enjoyment. He sees that any pleasure depends on the yearning for the matter. We attribute this to our nature, meaning that the Creator has given us a desire and yearning to receive pleasure from something from which we can derive pleasure. When a person calculates, he sees that this separates him from the Creator. That is, he sees that reception removes him from the work of the Creator because of the disparity of form. This, in turn, forces him to draw nearer to corporeality, and the main meaning of corporeality is that he takes upon himself to work for his own benefit. Man is called "corporeal," and not for the sake of the Creator, and the Creator is regarded as "spiritual."

What Is the Work of Man that Is Attributed to the Creator, in the Work?

For this reason, it is upon man to put an aim on the act of pleasure: 1) He should believe that this pleasure he is receiving comes from the Creator and from no other source. 2) He should intend to bestow, and say that since the Creator wants the creatures to receive pleasure, he is doing the Creator's will. Otherwise, if he cannot aim to benefit the Creator, he is willing to relinquish this pleasure.

However, one does not achieve this work at once. This is called "blessing the Creator." That is, through the work of bestowal, it is considered that a person gives the Creator *Kelim* [vessels] so He can bestow pleasure upon the person. Since the *Tzimtzum* was not to bestow into the vessels of reception, now it will be possible for the Creator to bestow, since the *Tzimtzum* has been removed from them because now he is receiving not for his own sake, but for the sake of the Creator.

For this reason, now we can say that a person who blesses, meaning that while receiving pleasure, he intends that his pleasure is that by doing the Creator's will, whose desire is to do good to His creations, this is regarded as blessing the work of the Creator. In other words, since the work of the Creator is to bestow upon the creatures, by aiming to bestow, there is power above to bestow unto the lower ones, since now the lower ones are not removed by the reception. On the contrary, now it is apparent that they are adhered to the Creator.

The proof of this is that the abundance can spread in the *Kelim* that are fit to receive, since the *Kelim* will remain in *Kedusha*. It follows that through the blessing, he causes the expansion of abundance to the lower ones.

By this we will understand what we asked, What is the gravity of the blessing? Apparently, he does more harm than other transgressions. But according to the above, the meaning of the blessing pertains to the qualification of the *Kelim*, so the Creator will be able to give to the lower ones delight and pleasure, and that abundance will not be detrimental to them. That is, they will not be pushed away by the reception of delight and pleasure from Him, due to disparity of form, as it is known that disparity of form causes moving away from the Creator.

It follows that one who does not bless for the pleasure, meaning he does not aim that it will be in order to bestow, causes the prevention of the abundance from above. It follows that it is as though he causes the Creator not to be able to carry out the purpose of creation, which is to do good to His creation.

As said above, there are two actions in man: 1) that which comes from the Creator, which is the desire and yearning for pleasures, 2) the act that we attribute to the creature, which is the intention to bestow. We attribute this to the lower one, who should aim in order to bestow.

It therefore follows that there are two conditions under which the *Kli* will be fit to receive the abundance and remain in *Dvekut* while receiving the abundance: the act and the aim. Also, there is partnership in building the wholeness of the *Kli*: 1) the Creator, 2) the creatures.

This is as it is written in *The Zohar* ("Introduction to The Book of Zohar," Item 67): "'And to say to Zion, 'You are My people.'' Do not pronounce 'You are My people [*Ami*]' with a *Patach* in the *Ayin*, but 'You are with Me [*Imi*],' with a *Hirik* in the *Ayin*, which means partnering with Me. As I made heaven and earth with My words, as it is written, 'By the word of the Lord the heavens were made,' you, with your words of wisdom, have made new heaven and earth. Happy are those who exert in Torah."

This means that through the Torah, whose light reforms him, they can achieve the degree of annulling their own authority, and everything a person does will all be in order to bestow contentment upon his Maker.

Accordingly, if a person does not give his part to the *Kli*, which is the second part, called "desire to bestow," he thereby causes the abundance that should come to the lower ones through the work of the lower one, by not giving the intention, the abundance delays because of him. In other words, by not giving the blessing, the connection of upper and lower is missing, since the upper one is the giver and the lower one is the receiver. Hence, there is disparity of form between them and they have no *Dvekut*, so how can the abundance come to the lower one?

Therefore, when there is a connector, meaning that the lower one also wants to be a giver like the upper one, the abundance can flow onto the lower one because of the connection that exists between them. Without this connection, it is as though he steals the nourishments that his father and mother should give to the children—that man steals and the children have nothing to sustain them.

In other words, if he enjoys and does not bless, it means that he did not give the intention for the sake of the Creator. Therefore, he has taken the pleasure, which is reception, and gave it to the *Sitra Achra* [other side], who take all the reception in order to receive, and this nourishes them. Had he aimed to bestow through the blessing, the *Kedusha* would have been nourished by this, meaning that through it, abundance would be added to the worlds of *Kedusha*. By acting without the aim, he has given strength to the *Klipot*.

We could ask, What does it mean that he corrupted the world, since he did not corrupt his self? Also, what is the connection between him and the entire world? We should interpret as our sages said (*Kidushin* 40b), "Rabbi Elazar Bar Rabbi Shimon says, 'Since the world is judged by its majority, and the individual is judged by its majority, if he performs one *Mitzva* [commandment/good deed], happy is he, for he has sentenced himself and the entire world to the side of merit. If he commits one transgression, woe unto him for he has sentenced himself and the entire world to the side of sin.'"

We therefore see that through his sin, one person robs the nourishments that should reach the entire world. For this reason, one who does not bless robs his father and his mother. That is, the abundance that they should give him, and what his father and mother should give to the entire world, he prevents this from them. It follows that he has corrupted the world to their Father in heaven.

This means the abundance and nourishment that their father in heaven should have given to the whole world, he robs this force that should have been received in order to add *Kedusha* throughout the world, and hands that power to the *Sitra Achra*. Every reception in order to receive that the lower ones perform adds power to the *Sitra Achra*, and every aim on an act that he intends in order to bestow causes addition of abundance in the *Kedusha*.

Now we can understand the gravity of "He who enjoys in this world and does not bless." As said above, it is the intention, for only through the blessing, abundance is added in all the worlds and abundance reaches the whole world.

Hence, if a person's intention is only to bring contentment to the Creator and not for his own benefit, he does not mind the amount of pleasure. He only looks at the amount of passion with which he wants to delight the Creator, since through the yearning to delight the Creator, he causes equivalence of form at the root of his soul. This, in turn, causes more abundance to be drawn, since the upper one wants to give more than the lower one wants to receive, and only vessels of bestowal are missing. It follows that by overcoming in bestowal, great abundance is extended. For this reason, we need not ask to have great lights, only try to have big vessels, which are vessels of bestowal.

It is as we interpreted, that our sages said, "Why is it written, 'For this is the whole of man'"? And he replies, "Rabbi said, 'The whole world was created only for this,'" meaning for fear of heaven, as it is written, "What does the Lord your God ask of you? Only fear." Fear is as he says in the *Sulam* [Ladder Commentary on *The Zohar*], that he is afraid he will not be able to bestow upon the Creator. "And this is the whole of man," meaning this is all that man should do, meaning offer Him vessels of bestowal. The rest, meaning the lights, the Creator gives. This is the meaning of "Everything is in the hands of heaven but the fear of heaven."

What Are the Two Actions During a Descent?

Article No. 32, Tav-Shin-Mem-Het, 1987/88

Our sages wrote in *Hulin* (p 7b), "Rabbi Hanina said, 'A person does not lift his finger from below unless he is called upon from above, as it was said, 'Man's steps are from the Lord, and how can man understand his way?'" We should understand what our sages tell us by this in the work, so we will know that a person does not lift his finger below unless he is called upon from above.

To explain this, we must always remember the purpose of creation and the correction of creation, which are two contradictory things. The purpose of creation is for the creatures to receive delight and pleasure from the Creator, as was said, that His desire is to do good to His creations. The correction of creation is the complete opposite—to do good to the Creator. This means that the purpose of creation is for the sake of the creatures, while the correction of creation is that the creatures will always think only about the benefit of the Creator. As long as the creatures have not achieved this degree—when they do not need anything for themselves and the only reason they want to live is to benefit the Creator through their actions—and they want to live for their own benefit, the creatures cannot receive the delight and pleasure that the Creator contemplated giving them.

In the work *Lishma* [for Her sake], reward and punishment are measured by the extent to which they want to bestow upon the Creator. That is, when they want to bestow upon the Creator, they consider it "reward." And when they see that all they want is their own benefit, and they are utterly unable to crave to work for the sake of the Creator, they regard this as a punishment.

It follows that when a person feels that he is in a state of descent, when he has no yearning or desire whatsoever to bestow upon the Creator, there are two manners in this: 1) He does not feel any suffering or pain from this state—from coming to a state of lowliness. Rather, he accepts the situation and begins to seek satisfaction in things that he had already determined were trash, unfit for human consumption. But now he sees that he cannot derive vitality from spiritual matters because the taste of spirituality has been flawed in him, so in the meantime he wants to live and derive satisfaction from corporeality. He says, "I'm waiting for a time when I can work without overcoming. That is, when I am given an awakening from above, I will return to work. In the meantime, I want to remain in the state I am in."

2) When he feels he is in a state of descent, he feels pain and deficiency at having fallen from a state where he thought he was rewarded with being like a man. That is, the nourishments that sustained him and from which he derived all his vitality were only from things that are not related to animals. He thought that soon he would be granted admission into the King's palace and would be rewarded with the flavors of Torah and *Mitzvot* [commandments/good deeds]. But without awareness or preparation, he sees that he is in a bottomless pit, which he never thought existed.

That is, after he has come to clear knowledge that he knows his purpose in life, now he sees himself in the company of cats, standing by garbage bins and eating the trash that people threw, since people cannot enjoy this, as it is unfit for human consumption. But now he himself is enjoying this trash, which he himself, when he was in a state of "man," said that such a life is trash. But now he himself is eating the waste that he threw. Hence, when he looks at his lowliness, it invokes in him pain and suffering at the state he has come to.

However, sometimes a person adds insult to injury. That is, not only has he come to a state of lowliness, but at that time he falls into despair and says that he cannot believe that the Creator hears the prayer of every mouth. Instead, at that time he says, "Since I've already been at the highest level several times, and since I have fallen into this state several times, I must conclude that this work is not for me. As I see it, this matter is endless and could continue for the rest of my life. Therefore, why should I afflict myself in vain thinking that perhaps the Creator will finally hear me? After all, every person learns from the past, from what has been registered in him and from what he has been through." This despair pushes him from the work and he wants to escape the campaign.

However, a person must believe two things, for only by this can he progress in the work: 1) All the descents that foreign thoughts he has in the work did not come from himself. Rather, they all come from the Creator. That is, the Creator sent him these states, and there is no other force in the world. It is as Baal HaSulam said, that a person must believe that there is no other force in the world, and everything comes from the Creator (see *Shamati*, No. 1, "There Is None Else Besides Him").

Indeed, we should understand why the Creator sends these states, since this is very unusual, for our sages said, "He who comes to purify is aided." But here we see the opposite: Where he should have been given help and to see that each day he is progressing, he sees that he is regressing. That is, each time, he sees how immersed he is in self-love. Instead of coming closer each day toward the desire to bestow, he sees each day that he is nearing self-love.

In other words, before he began the work of bestowal, he did not taste such flavors and pleasures in self-love. He thought that whenever he wanted, he could immediately revoke his will to receive for himself, and he could work without any reward for himself. But now, he sees that he cannot make even a single step without the permission of his receiver. He has come to a state that our sages describe as "A wicked is under the authority of his heart." Conversely, "a righteous, his heart is under his authority." "Heart" means desire. That is, he is in exile, the will to receive for himself has absolute control over him, and he is utterly powerless to go against his heart, which is called "will to receive." This is the meaning of the words, "A wicked is under the authority of his heart."

Yet, the question is, Who is considered "wicked," that we can say that he is under the authority of his heart? It is precisely when a person has come to a state where he sees that he condemns his Maker, when he cannot observe Torah and *Mitzvot* in order to bestow, and sees that he is immersed in self-love. When his heart tells him, "Do what I tell you," he mindlessly follows, and does not even have time to contemplate what he is doing. Our sages call this: "A person does not sin unless a spirit of folly has entered him." Only after the fact, he looks at himself and sees what folly he has done. Only then, in that state, he sees what our sages said, "A wicked is under the authority of his heart."

The answer to the question, Why did the Creator send him the states of lowliness? is so that a person will see the truth, meaning what the will to receive is willing to do in order to increase self-love, that it has no regard for anything, and whatever can bring it pleasure, it is willing to do.

It follows that the Creator helps him each time to see his real state. That is, it was concealed in his heart and he did not see his illness. Hence, the help of the Creator came and revealed to him the severity of the illness. In other words, we need not believe that the will to receive is a bad thing. Instead, now he sees it for himself. This is similar to a person seeing that something is wrong with him, and he goes to the hospital for tests and X-rays. The tests show him that he suffers from certain illnesses, such as a heart disease, and also in the lungs. The family members come to the hospital management with complaints saying, "We brought a person with a little fever, and not dangerous illnesses, and you, meaning your doctors and the X-ray, inflicted fatal diseases on our son."

It is likewise with us. Our will to receive was not so bad as to be dangerous. When we came to work here, we were told that pretty soon we would achieve the wholeness that we thought about the evil in us. But suddenly, after tests and examinations that you do, we see that the evil in us is very dangerous, that it can kill you and cause you to lose your spiritual life.

As it is in corporeality, we should thank the hospital for diagnosing the illnesses, meaning the evil in the body. Likewise, we should thank the Creator for revealing to us the danger of the evil in us, which is really mortal danger that could cost us our spiritual life. And certainly, we should thank the Creator for assisting us in discovering the illness we are suffering from, since previously, we thought that we were only slightly unwell, but the Creator revealed to us the truth. It follows that we did progress toward seeing the truth, meaning the real form of the evil in us.

By this we can interpret what we asked, What is the meaning of "A person does not lift his finger from below unless he is called upon from above," in the work? A "finger" means that a person sees within reason, as it is written, "Each and every one shows with his finger," or from the words, "pointing with the finger." "Lifting" means a lack from below. That is, a person who feels deficient, that his importance is low, meaning that he is far from the Creator, does not feel this awareness unless he is called upon from above.

There are two interpretations to "above": 1) "He is called upon from above" means that it came to him from private Providence. That is, it cannot be said that since he did not guard himself from "lifting" [the finger], meaning that he was not careful with guarding the body, we were given laws by which man should guard himself from harm, so the body will not suffer some damage, but he was not careful so his body received a flaw, which is called "lifting."

Yet, even if he did watch himself with a hundred types of care, it would not help at all because so it was sentenced about him "from above." It is as RASHI interpreted, "'called upon,' he is sentenced." That is, it is a sentence from above and it is not the person's fault. Yet, we could ask, Why was he sentenced to this from above?

2) "From above" means that it is of high importance. That is, the person received a flaw in his work that he did within reason, which is called "lifting his finger from below." In other words, now he sees that he is in a state of lowliness, meaning he sees that he is bare and destitute in matters of work on the path of truth.

This brings up the question, Did seeing his lowliness come to him for not observing Torah and Mitzvot, or is it the other way around—because he began work more enthusiastically, which brought him to a state of descent, called "lifting his finger from below"? We should say that it came because he put more effort into the work. According to the rule, a Mitzva [commandment/good deed] induces a Mitzva, he should have seen that he was in a state of "above," so why is he in a state of "below"?

The answer is that he is "called upon from above." That is, he has been sentenced from above to be admitted into a place of high importance. For this reason, he has been shown the real state of the evil in him, so he would know what to pray for. There is certainly a difference when we see in corporeality that a person comes to ask someone for a loan, to lend him money, or when someone comes to another to ask for a favor and speak on his behalf so he will not be thrown in prison, or when someone is sentenced to death, and he asks the one person who can save him from death. There are big differences among the pleas.

In spirituality, we understand these matters with regard to the Kli [vessel]. In spirituality, a prayer is regarded as a Kli. According to the rule, "There is no light without a Kli," there is a difference between a person praying to the Creator to help him so he can receive wholeness, meaning that in truth, he observes Torah and Mitzvot and engages in charity, but he understands from rumors he had heard that there is more wholeness than his observing of Torah and *Mitzvot*, both in quantity and quality. He believes in the verse, "There is not a righteous man on Earth who does good and did not sin," therefore he asks of the Creator to help him. It follows that he needs only one small thing.

For example, when someone comes to get a loan from someone, he is told that he can get it elsewhere, too. That is, we do not pay much attention when it comes to the lending. Therefore, normally, when a person refuses to lend, he leaves him.

This is not so when a person is sentenced to death, and there is one person who can save his life. If that person refuses to do him the favor of saving him, he will not leave him and say that he will go to another person to save him from death, since only the king himself can pardon him. For this reason, we do not leave the king, and we seek out every possibility for the king to give him the absolution.

Similarly, in spirituality, we need a real *Kli*, meaning a real need for the Creator to give us the filling. For this reason, when we are shown from above our true state, that we are truly bare and destitute, we can place the filling in that *Kli*, since a person has realized that he is lacking spiritual life, called "complete faith," and he has no grip on spirituality. In other words, he cannot say that he is doing something for the Creator, but it is all for his own benefit. This means that the entire structure of *Kedusha* [holiness/sanctity] is ruined in him, and everything he does is only lip-service. This is called a "real prayer," since he has no one to turn to, and only the Creator Himself can help him, as was said in the exodus from Egypt, that it was done by the Creator Himself, as it is written, "I the Lord your God, who brought you out from the land of Egypt."

This is similar to a person who was sentenced to death, and only the king can pardon him. It follows that when a person feels that he is in a state of "wicked," and "wicked in their lives are called 'dead,'" this is considered that he has been sentenced to death. However, when a person asks the Creator to give him his life as a present, this is considered that he has a *Kli* that can receive the filling, since the person is not asking the Creator for luxuries, but simply for his spiritual life.

Thus, on one hand, a person should say, "If I am not for me, who is for me?" That is, he should choose by himself. This means that anything he thinks that he can do, anything he thinks will help him emerge from self-love, he should do. On the other hand, a person should say that everything comes from above, as was said, "A person does not lift his finger from below unless he is called upon from above." Once a person has come to the recognition of the evil in him, which is risking his life, this is called an "act." But he should attribute this act to the Creator, too.

Afterward, he should pray for the action. That is, a person must attribute both the lack and the filling to the Creator. That is, once a person has begun the work of bestowal and worked devotedly to achieve the truth, the Creator sends him a sensation of his lack. A person can feel this only after he has made great efforts to achieve the quality of bestowal. At that time, he is notified that he is remote from *Dvekut* [adhesion] with the Creator, which is called "life." It is written about it, "And you who cling to the Lord your God are alive every one of you this day."

At that time, when he prays, it is regarded as a prayer for lack of life, and not as praying for things that one can live without. Instead, he simply asks for life, called "complete faith in the Creator."

What Is the Difference between General and Individual in the Work of the Creator?

Article No. 33, Tav-Shin-Mem-Het, 1987/88

Our sages wrote (*Makot* 24), "Habakkuk came and established them on one: As it was said, 'And a righteous lives by his faith.'" This means that the fact that we must observe all of the Torah and *Mitzvot* [commandments/good deeds] is in order to achieve this element, which is faith. That is, what is required of a person, that he must achieve wholeness, is to come to faith in the Creator. This means that once he has achieved faith, he is a complete person.

We must understand this matter. There is the matter that a person must engage in the correction of creation, since because man was created with a nature of wanting to receive for himself, which is opposite in form from the Creator, for the Creator is the giver and through disparity of form, man became separated from the Creator, so how does having faith help him if he is still separated from the Creator? Also, why did they say, "Habakkuk came and established them on one: 'And a righteous lives by his faith'"? which implies that if he has faith then he has wholeness.

The answer is that we must know that there is an important matter here, which is a key issue that requires much attention so that we can accept this as the gate by which man can be rewarded with complete faith. Otherwise, he will have only partial faith. It is written in the "Introduction to The Study of the Ten Sefirot" (Item 14): "Rather, it is partial faith. Thus, one allots oneself out of the measure of his faith in the Creator only one hour a day to practice Torah and work. ...The third does not neglect even a single moment. ...Thus, only the faith of the last one is whole." In order for a person to be rewarded with complete faith, he must first emerge from self-love, or he will not be able to be granted with complete faith. Otherwise, he will not be given from above the possibility to have complete faith.

However, this is for man's benefit. It is as it is written in the *Sulam* ("Introduction of The Book of Zohar," [with the *Sulam* (Ladder) Commentary], Item 138): "It is a law that the creature cannot receive disclosed evil from the Creator, for it is a flaw in the glory of the Creator for the creature to perceive Him as an evildoer, as it is unbecoming of the Complete Operator. Hence, when one feels bad, denial of the Creator's guidance lies upon him to that extent, and the Operator is concealed from him."

Therefore, before a person can receive the delight and pleasure from the Creator, he cannot achieve faith. The condition that must be met in order to be given the delight and pleasure is vessels of bestowal. On the vessels of reception, there was a correction not to use them, for by them one becomes distant from the Creator due to the disparity of form between them. It follows before faith, a person must be rewarded with the correction of the *Kelim* [vessels], called "correction of creation."

The Difference between General and Individual in the Work of the Creator

It is as Baal HaSulam wrote there: "Know that this is the whole difference between this world, before the correction, and the end of correction. Before the end of correction, *Malchut* is called 'the tree of good and evil,' since the *Malchut* is the guidance of the Creator in this world. As long as the receivers have not been completed so they can receive His whole benevolence, which He had contemplated in our favor in the thought of creation (meaning that while our vessels of reception have not been corrected to work in order to bestow, He cannot give us the delight and pleasure because it will all go to the *Klipot* [shells/peels]), the guidance must be in the form of good and bad, and reward and punishment. It is so because our vessels of reception are still tainted with self-reception, which is very restrictive in its quality, and also separates us from the Creator. Thus, the complete benefit, in the great measure He had contemplated for us, is absent."

Accordingly, we see that indeed, this element, which is faith, is the most important. We asked, How can it be said that faith is wholeness, since we also need the correction of creation, called "obtaining vessels of bestowal?" Otherwise, the abundance cannot come to the lower ones because of the disparity of form. The answer is that in general, we must observe Torah and *Mitzvot* in order to obtain vessels of bestowal. It is as our sages said, "I have created the evil inclination; I have created the Torah as a spice, for the light in it reforms him."

It follows that the first discernment in the order of the work is to reform the evil, called "will to receive for oneself," meaning that he will have the strength to use everything in order to bestow. However, we should discern here that in order to come to know that the will to receive is called "evil," we need Torah and *Mitzvot*. Before a person realizes that the receiver is called "evil," how can he be reformed? It is as we said in previous essays, that our sages said, "Why is the Torah called *Tushia* [gumption/resourcefulness]? It is because it *Mateshet* [drains/exhausts] man's strength." We asked, but they said, "If his head aches, let him engage in Torah. If his belly aches, let him engage in Torah, as was said, 'It is a healing to all his flesh'" (*Iruvin* 54).

According to what Baal HaSulam said, the Torah is called a "potion." That is, sometimes it is a potion of life, and sometimes it is a potion of death. He said that a medical potion heals those who are sick. But if a healthy person took medical potions he would become sick. That is, when the Torah comes to one who has a need, it can heal him. Accordingly, we should interpret that first a person must learn Torah, in order to see that he is sick.

This is why they said that the Torah exhausts a person's strength. That is, through the Torah, he can come to see that the "man" in him is weak and has no strength to overcome. At that time he sees that he is sick in spirituality. Through the Torah, he comes to the recognition of evil, as *The Zohar* says about the verse, "Or make his sin known to him," which means that the Torah notifies him that he has sinned.

If the Torah does not notify him, a person cannot know or feel that receiving for oneself is called "bad" due to the disparity of form between him and the Creator. Knowing that disparity of form causes separation has to come from above, through the Torah. Hence, we should say that the order is that 1) he observes Torah and *Mitzvot* in order to achieve recognition of evil, and 2) he observes Torah and *Mitzvot* because "the light in it reforms him." This is the time when he receives strength from above, called "desire to bestow," which is regarded as equivalence of form. 3) Faith, which is the meaning of "Habakkuk came and established them on one: 'A righteous lives by his faith.'" It follows that everything we do in Torah and *Mitzvot* in general is in order to achieve this element, which his faith. At that time he can receive complete faith. It follows that all of his work is only in order to achieve this.

However, before these three above discernments, there is a discernment that applies to the whole of Israel. This is the first discernment when a person's education in Torah and *Mitzvot* begins: It is that the whole world must know for what purpose they should observe the Torah and Mitzvot—to receive reward. And if they do not observe, they will suffer punishment. This is the common order, as Maimonides says, "When teaching children, women, and uneducated people, they are taught to work only out of fear and in order to receive reward. Until they gain knowledge and acquire much wisdom, they are taught that secret little by little" (Maimonides, *Hilchot Teshuva*, Chapter 10).

It follows that the order of the work is that 1) the whole of Israel are taught to observe Torah and Mitzvot with all its details and intricacies with an intention of self-love. They must not be taught that they must work *Lishma* [for Her sake], which is in order to bestow. Rather, they must work and toil only in order to receive for their own benefit.

We should know that work for self-love means to be rewarded with the next world by observing Torah and Mitzvot. If that person has real energy to work for self-benefit, he will be ready to do anything. That is, if he is energetic and wants to be rewarded with the next world, he will be willing to do work that is above reason, which a person's reason cannot understand. It is as it is written (Deuteronomy 12:30), "Beware, do not inquire after their gods, saying, 'How do these nations serve their gods, that I also may do likewise?' You shall not do so, for they even burn their sons and daughters in the fire to their gods."

RASHI brings the interpretation of our sages: "Including their fathers and mothers. Rabbi Akiva said, 'I saw a foreigner who tied his father before his dog and ate him.' The author of the book *Siftei Chachamim* interprets, 'He means to say idolatry. 'He ate him' means that he burned him in fire.'"

However, we must know that although a man is willing to work for his own benefit and do the hardest work if he believes that he will be guaranteed the next world, even if they are told to burn their sons and daughters and their parents, there are among them with energy and strength for this work, since they are still inside the *Kli* [vessel] of self-love. It follows that this is still not regarded as "above reason." In other words, we can understand that it is inherent in nature that a person is willing to do anything for the will to receive for himself.

We also find that during the ruin of the Temple, it is written (*Lamentations* 4:10), "Compassionate women cooked their own children; they became food for them." The Holy Alsheich interprets "food for them" to mean that "only they themselves ate their children's flesh. This is the meaning of 'for them,' only the mothers alone ate, and did not share it with their remaining children, even though they, too, were hungry."

This shows us what a person can do for self-love when there is no *Kedusha* [holiness/sanctity] but rather the ruin of *Kedusha*, and only the will to receive for themselves rules: "Compassionate women cooked their own children."

We have two examples: 1) For the will to receive, in return for burning children and parents, the next world, or in order to receive this world, for which "Compassionate women cooked their own children." It follows that a person can do anything in order to satisfy the will to receive—the nature in which man is born.

But when beginning to work on the path of the individual, meaning to be rewarded with *Dvekut* with the Creator, meaning when we must emerge from self-love, a person cannot do even the smallest work. That is, if a person is told, "Do the same thing you are doing, but place over it the aim to bestow upon the Creator without any reward. This is very hard to do because it is against nature, called "will to receive for oneself."

That is, the same work, meaning the same practical labor that a person does, without needing to add any effort but simply aim to do this for the sake of the Creator, leaves him powerless. It seems to him as though a high mountain stands in front of him and he cannot move the mountain one bit. He feels as though his whole world has been ruined, and all because it is against our nature.

In that state, when a person wants to reach the truth and do the work of the individual, he is notified from above that he is in a state of lowliness, since he sees that he cannot do anything for the sake of the Creator. That state is called "recognition of evil." This is called "the first state in the work of the individual," which is recognition of evil.

Afterward begins phase two, when he must observe Torah and *Mitzvot* so that the light in it will reform him, since through the light he will receive vessels of bestowal, meaning that he will have passion to bestow upon the Creator and from this he will enjoy.

After that comes phase three, which is complete faith, as was said above, that "Habakkuk came and established them on one: 'And a righteous lives by his faith.'" This is the element [also "individual"] that a person must achieve. When he has faith, he will be rewarded with the delight and pleasure in His providence, as The Good Who Does Good.

We could ask about what is written in the *Sulam* [Ladder Commentary on *The Zohar*]: "It is a law that the creature cannot receive disclosed evil from the Creator, for it is a flaw in the glory of the Creator for the creature to perceive Him as an evildoer. Hence, when one feels bad, the Operator is concealed from him." Why should the Creator mind if a person perceives him as an evildoer? Does the Creator seek respect from the created beings, to respect Him for His sake? He does not need things that pertain to flesh and blood.

Rather, it is for man's sake. The flaw that we speak of in spirituality, such as that he casts a flaw in *Kedusha*, the *Sitra Achra* [other side] is there at the root of the soul of a person who has caused the flaw above. That is, we must believe that the name of the Creator is The Good Who Does Good.

It follows that when a person feels that he is in a bad state, he cannot justify Providence and say that the Creator is behaving toward him as The Good Who Does Good. It follows that a person receives the flaw that he has flawed in the Holy Name, which is The Good Who Does Good. And when a person receives good from above, he is happy and can say wholeheartedly, "Blessed is He who said, 'Let there be the world.'"

But when a person feels bad, he cannot say, "Blessed is He who said, 'Let there be the world.'" Instead, a person says what Job said (Job 3), "And Job answered and said, 'Let the day on which I was born perish, and the night which said, 'A boy is conceived.' That day shall be darkness.'" For this reason, this is a correction because at that time, when a person does not believe that the Creator has caused him all the hardships, he does not slander the Creator.

By extension, in corporeality, we sometimes see a person whose son works for a salary that is not enough to sustain him. When he began to work, he was still a bachelor and the salary then was good. But now, he cannot sustain himself on this salary. The father speaks to his son: "Since you see that the employer is not giving you a raise, go look for a job that pays better." But the son replies, "I am already used to the employer and the coworkers; I cannot leave that place."

What does the father do? He goes to the employer and tells him of the situation with his son. The employer replies that he cannot give him a raise, but he can send him to where he will be better paid. At that time, the father asks of him: "Tell my son that you have no work for him, so he will go elsewhere. I spoke to him several times about leaving the job where he is not paid well and go where they pay a better salary, but I will tell you the truth, he told me that he likes you and his coworkers and this is why he does not want to leave this place. Therefore, if you fire him, he will have no choice but to go elsewhere. But I am asking you, don't tell him that I've been here and asked you not to let him work for you. Otherwise, he will say that he has a father who is cruel to his son. That is, he cannot understand that by trying to get him fired, it is for his best. That is, when he hears from his employer that I asked that he would be fired, what would he say, 'May the Lord bless my father, who is trying so hard only for my sake'? There is no doubt, he will be very angry at his father."

So it is in spirituality—that the Creator sends a person a state of descent. That is, from a situation where he received sustenance, although his father understood that it was not sufficient sustenance and he could earn more, the son did not understand it. For this reason, the Creator sends him a descent, which is akin to being fired from work. At that time, he is angry with the Creator for sending harm his way, since he knows that prior to this, he was in a state of ascent in spirituality, but the Creator threw him, so of course he is angry with the Creator. This is regarded as "He who doubts the *Shechina* [Divinity], his punishment is very grave." Therefore, when there is a correction that he does not find the evildoer, he has no one at whom to be angry. It follows that not knowing who is the one doing all these things is to his best.

He said there, "One who exerts not to part from faith in Him, although he tastes a bad taste in Providence, is rewarded. If he does not exert, he will be punished because he has parted from faith in Him. Thus, although He alone did, does, and will do all the deeds, this still remains hidden from those who feel good and bad."

We see that one who can exert and say that the Creator is sending him the bad, and it is for his best, he remains in faith, to the extent that he can say that the Creator has sent him the state he is in for his own benefit. This is not regarded as "doing harm." Thus, he remains in faith.

Conversely, if he cannot say that the Creator has sent him this for his sake, but that it is to his detriment, that state is called that the Creator does harm. For this reason, He must hide from him the Operator. This is regarded as losing the faith, and it is regarded as a punishment.

It follows that were it not for the ascents and descents, a person would not be able to feel that he is deficient. That is, he would not feel that he needs heaven's mercy, that it is not within man's power to emerge from self-love and make his wish only to bring contentment to his Maker. Rather, all his work can be only for his own sake, and in self-benefit, he has the power to do things that a person cannot imagine. Or, as it was at the time of the ruin of the Temple, when compassionate women cooked their own children, as they served their gods, burning their sons and daughters.

But to work for the Creator, meaning not wanting any return for their work, even merely an intention over the acts of reception, a person cannot do this. That is, if one wants to eat for the sake of the Creator and not for his own sake, although the act is reception of pleasure, what he should intend is out of his hands. Only the Creator can help here. This is the difference between the general work, which belongs to the general public, and the work of the individual.

What Are Day and Night in the Work?

Article No. 34, Tav-Shin-Mem-Het, 1987/88

It is written, "And God called the light, 'day,' and to the darkness, He called 'night.'" We should understand what this comes to teach us in the work, that He called the light "day," and to the darkness, He called "night." What does knowing this add to us? It appears that naming the light and the darkness was for the purpose of some correction. Thus, what do we understand better by Him naming them, which adds to us in the work of achieving *Dvekut* [adhesion] with the Creator?

Afterward, the verse says, "And there was evening and there was morning, one day." This, too, we should understand. After He said that darkness is called "night" and light is called "day," how did the two become one? After all, night is not day, so how can the two of them together be one day? That is, what makes them one day as though there is no difference between day and night?

Concerning "day" and "night," we see that the verse says (Psalms 19), "Day to day expresses speech; and night to night utters knowledge." In that regard, we see that it is written (in the Haggadah [Passover narrative], in the poem, "Then, Many Miracles"), "A day approaches that is neither day nor night. Exalted One, make known, for Yours is the day; Yours is also the night. You shine as the day, the darkness of the night." Thus, we should understand what are day and night, and what are light and darkness.

In order to understand all this, we must return to what we discussed several times—that we should always remember what is the purpose of creation and what is the correction of creation, so as to know what is required of us, meaning what state we should achieve so we can say that we have reached our destination.

It is known that the purpose of creation is to do good to His creations, as our sages said, that the Creator said about the purpose of creation that it is like a king who has a tower filled with abundance but no guests. For this reason, He has created man, so as to give him the delight and pleasure.

Thus, what does it mean that a person has achieved wholeness? It is precisely after a person has come to a state where he receives from the Creator delight and pleasure. This is regarded as achieving wholeness. If he has not come to a state of endless delight and pleasure, it is considered that he has not achieved wholeness. This is the purpose of creation.

Conversely, the correction of creation is that since it is the nature of creation that the branch wants to resemble its root, and since the Creator is the giver and the creature the receiver, there is no equivalence of form here. For this reason, in corporeality, too, we see the rule that when a person receives something from another, he is ashamed. It is as our sages said about the verse, "Chrome is vile for the sons of men," meaning that when a person needs other people, his face becomes as chrome.

For this reason, a correction of *Tzimtzum* [restriction] was made in the upper worlds, that the upper light does not reach *Kelim* [vessels] that receive for themselves. Rather, the light shines only to *Kelim* that have the correction of the *Masach* [screen] that raises *Ohr Hozer* [Reflected Light], meaning that it receives from the upper one because there is contentment to the upper one when He bestows upon the lower one.

In other words, the fact that he has great yearning to receive delight and pleasure still does not necessitate that he will receive delight and pleasure, since the pleasure is from having equivalence of form with the upper one, called *Dvekut* [adhesion]. In every possible way, he tries not to part due to disparity of form, and for this reason he does not receive although he yearns to receive delight and pleasure. But at the same time, he derives more pleasure from adhering to the Creator. Hence, he does not receive.

At that time, a person looks at two things: 1) He does not want to part from the Creator. In other words, even when he thinks that he has still not been rewarded with *Dvekut*, at least he does not want to be more separated than he currently is, since any reception for oneself makes a person farther from the Creator. For this reason, he does not want to receive for himself. 2) By doing what he is doing, distancing himself from reception, this causes him to adhere to the Creator. Although he still does not feel these discernments, he says that he believes in the sages who said that this is so. For this reason, he trusts them and is careful with self-reception.

Because of this, a person tries to do things that will bring him this force of wanting to do things that yield the power to be able to aim to place on every act the intention to bestow. At that time, he is fit to receive delight and pleasure, since now all his actions are for the sake of the Creator.

Accordingly, we can understand what is light and what is darkness. Light is when it shines for a person to walk in the path of the Creator. "The path of the Creator" means that he wants to walk in the way that the Creator walks, and His way is to bestow. When he has light and life by engaging in the work of bestowal and he does not care for his own benefit, this is called "light."

This is called a "time of ascent," meaning that the person has ascended in degree. That is, instead of serving a lowly, inferior person, now he is serving the Creator. This is called an "ascent in degree," for he is serving the King where he used to serve a simple man.

Clearly, the opposite of light is darkness. That is, a person finds no taste in the work of bestowal because he has begun to worry only about his own benefit once again. He finds no flavor in the work of bestowal or has any aspirations. Rather, he settles for satisfying only the passions that his body demands. This is called "a descent," since he wants to serve the body and not the Creator. This is called "darkness."

We should know that "day" indicates a complete thing, which consists of light and day, and darkness and night, as it is written, "And there was evening and there was morning, one day." We should understand how can it be said that evening and morning are one thing. That is, we do not say that evening and morning are both called "one night," but rather that the two are called "one day." What does it imply to us in the work, that specifically both are called "one day," as though there cannot be wholeness of a day without darkness.

The answer is that when a person says, "And God called the light 'day,' and to the darkness, He called 'night,'" it means that the person believes that God gave him both the light and the darkness. But why has He given him the darkness? It is possible to believe that He has given him the light, meaning that he says that the Creator wants to bring him closer, as our sages said, "He who comes to purify is aided." Hence, on the ascents that a person has, he can believe that they come from the Creator. But why are the descents?

When a person believes about the darkness, too, as it is written, "And God called ... and to the darkness, He called 'night,'" meaning that the darkness is also "night," which is part of the day, meaning that there cannot be a day without a night, then the darkness, which is called "night," comes to teach us that as there cannot be a day without a night, there cannot be light without darkness. Darkness is the *Kli* [vessel] and the light is the filling of the *Kli*, following the rule, "there is no light without a *Kli*."

In other words, it is impossible to appreciate His salvation without feeling the suffering and pain from the state one is in.

Between people, to the extent that one feels that his friend helped him in his distress, to that extent he feels the joy about the help he has received from his friend. That is, there is a difference between helping one's friend with accessories, which one can live without, and helping one's friend by saving him from death.

Since the help that comes from above is regarded as lights of *Kedusha* [holiness/sanctity], as *The Zohar* says, "He who comes to purify is aided," and *The Zohar* asks, With what is he aided? "With a holy soul." Yet, if a person does not appreciate the soul he has received from above because he thinks that it is not that important, the suffering that a person suffers from the states of descent makes him appreciate the help from above. Otherwise, he loses it and it all goes to the *Klipot* [shells/peels]. It follows that the darkness helps him, meaning that it gives him the possibility to know how to appreciate the importance of *Kedusha* so he does not lose it for lack of awareness.

Our sages say about this, "Who is a fool? He who loses what he is given," since he does not know or understand the importance of the nearness when the Creator brings a person near. That darkness is called a *Kli*, meaning a place where the abundance can be. It is as it is written, "Who will ascend up the mountain of the Lord, and who will rise?" That is, even when a person ascends but does not know how to maintain the value of the importance of nearing, the *Sitra Achra* [other side] takes it into his own authority. Therefore, the light must depart. This is why there is no resurrection, but each one must descend according to his degree.

Yet, there are several corrections about this: 1) The *Klipot* must not receive what he has. Therefore, they have nothing to receive from the person because he no longer has *Kedusha* for the *Sitra Achra* to receive from him. 2) Once a person has come to a descent and begins to recover and see the state he has come to, meaning after exerting so much work in order to be rewarded with some *Kedusha*, he suddenly sees that he is left bare and destitute. That is, he is in a state of lowliness that fits a person who did not exert and work in order to be regarded as "You are called 'man.'" Rather, he is much worse than an ordinary person, meaning that the will to receive for himself has become developed in him to an extent that he never dreamed would be, and the pain and sorrow he feels over it give him the need to appreciate and value the time when he is brought a little closer from above. Now he knows how to be careful and respect that state, and he guards himself from anything so as not to mix that state. At that time he knows that he should be afraid that a stranger might interfere.

It therefore follows that the descents are things that are called "corrections," which allow longevity when they are rewarded with some nearing on the part of the Creator. By this we can interpret the verse, "And God called the light, 'day,' and to the darkness, He called 'night.'" It means that if a person says that both light and darkness come from God, this is "And God called." At that time, both the light and the darkness make one day. That is, as there cannot be a complete day without evening and morning, so the light and darkness serve one role—both together are called "day."

By this we can interpret the words, "Blessed is our God, who has created us for His glory." We should understand how can we say, "Blessed is our God, who has created us for His glory," while we are immersed in self-love and our body is more content if we can say "Thank You very much" for creating us for our own glory. Thus, clearly, we are not telling the truth when we bless Him for creating for His glory. It is a total lie.

According to the above, when we believe that "He who comes to purify is aided," it follows that the Creator gives a person this power to be able to feel the importance of the matter, that when a person feels that he is serving the King, it is worth a fortune to him and he has no words to express its importance. Instead, he says, out of the pleasure and excitement that he feels, "Blessed is our God," for letting us feel the importance when we are serving the King, and for delivering us from the self-love in which we were immersed. It never occurred to us that we would ever be able to emerge from it. All of a sudden, we see that He has given us this feeling of finding flavor in being able to serve the King.

At that time we say, "Blessed is our God, who has created us for His glory." We bless Him for this gift that He has given us, which is the most important thing in the world, and we would not be able to obtain this by ourselves. Rather, it is a gift of God. This is why we bless Him for this. This is the meaning of the words, "Blessed is our God, who has created us for His glory."

However, before a person is rewarded with feeling flavor in His creating us for His glory, how can he say this? We should say that it is like all the blessings and thanks that we say for the future. It is as our sages said about the verse, "Then Moses will sing." *The Zohar* asks, "It did not say, 'sang,' in present tense, but rather 'will sing,' which is future tense. The answer is that the righteous sing about the future. That is, they believe that they will be rewarded with wholeness. For this reason, even before they are rewarded with wholeness, they already sing." Based on this, we say, "Blessed are you, our God, who has created us for His glory." The *Sulam* [*Sulam* (Ladder) Commentary on *The Zohar*] interprets the verse, "Day to day expresses speech; and night to night utters knowledge." These are its words: "Before the end of correction, meaning before we have qualified our vessels of reception to receive only in order to give contentment to our Maker and not to our own benefit, *Malchut* is called 'the tree of good and evil.' This is so because *Malchut* is the guidance of the world by people's actions. And since we are unfit to receive all the delight and pleasure ... we must accept the guidance of good and evil from the *Malchut*. This guidance qualifies us to ultimately correct our vessels of reception in order to bestow and to be rewarded with the delight and pleasure He had contemplated in our favor.

...

"Often, the guidance of good and evil causes us ascents and descents... This is why each ascent is considered a specific day, and similarly, each descent is considered a specific night.

"It is written, 'Day to day expresses speech.' ...At the end of correction, they will be rewarded with repentance from love... At that time, we will evidently see that all those punishments from the time of descents, which made us doubt the beginning, purified us and were the direct causes of all the happiness and goodness. Were it not for those terrible punishments, we would never have come to this delight and pleasure. Then these sins are inverted into actual merits."

The words "Day to day expresses speech" mean that all those nights, which are the descents, suffering, and punishments that stopped the *Dvekut* with the Creator until they became many days, one after the other, now that the nights and the darkness in between have also become merits and good deeds, the night shines as the day and the darkness as light; there are no more breaks between them.

Now we can understand what we asked about the meaning of the verse, "And God called the night, 'day,' and to the darkness, He called 'night.'" The meaning is as Baal HaSulam says, that as we see that "one day" is actually the connection of day and night. Likewise, it is impossible to have light without darkness. That is, the Creator has given us darkness so that through it, the light will appear. This is called "and God called." That is, the Creator has arranged for us the order of the work to be this way. Although we must believe that it could have been otherwise, since He is almighty, so why did He arrange for us specifically this order? We must say about this that we have no attainment in the Creator, to understand His thought. Rather, everything we learn is only by way of "By Your actions, we know You." In other words, by looking at the works of the Creator after He has created them, we begin to speak. But to say that He could have done things differently, our sages said about this, "One must not ask, 'What is above and what is below?'"

Accordingly, we can interpret what is written in the Haggadah: "A day approaches that is neither day nor night." This refers to the end of correction, when there is a day that does not consist of day and night, but is a day in and of itself. This will be done by "Exalted One, make known, for Yours is the day; Yours is also the night." It is so because at the end of correction it will be known to all that "Yours is the day; Yours is also the night." That is, since His will

What Are Day and Night in the Work?

is to do good to His creations, and good means day, so how can it be said that the Creator gives darkness? It is against His purpose! However, the darkness, too, meaning the night, is regarded as "day," even though the person feels cessations in *Dvekut* with the Creator, which are called "darkness" and "night."

But at the end of correction, when it is known that He has given the darkness, too, this is certainly light, as well. The proof of it is that then the sins become as merits. Thus, at that time we know that "Yours is the day; Yours is also the night," since both belong to You, meaning that both are You, meaning the Creator has given both as "day."

Conversely, before the end of the work, it is impossible to attribute the cessations that a person has in *Dvekut* with the Creator to the Creator, that He has sent him this, since this contradicts the purpose of creation. This is the meaning of the words, "The darkness of the night will shine as the light of the day." That is, since the sins have then become to him has merits, everything becomes day.

Now we can understand what are day and night in the work. A person should know that he must feel what is darkness, or he will not be able to enjoy the light, since in anything that a person wants to taste any flavor, whether it is worth using, he must learn one from the other, as it is written, "as the advantage of the light out of the darkness." Likewise, a person cannot enjoy rest unless he knows what is fatigue.

For this reason, a person must go through a process of ascents and descents. However, he must not be impressed by the descents. Instead, he should exert not to escape the campaign. For this reason, although during the work he must know that they are two things, at the end of the work he sees that light and darkness are as two legs that lead a person to the goal.

What Is the Help in the Work that One Should Ask of the Creator?

Article No. 35, Tav-Shin-Mem-Het, 1987/88

Our sages said (*Kidushin*), "Rabbi Yitzhak said, 'Man's inclination is renewed upon him every day.' Rabbi Shimon Ben Levi said, 'Man's inclination overcomes him every day and seeks to put him to death. Were it not for the help of the Creator, he would not overcome it, as was said, 'God will not leave him in its hand.'"" They also said (*Shabbat* 104), "He who comes to purify is aided."

We should understand what is the assistance that one should ask to be given from above. Clearly, where one feels weakness, there he needs reinforcement. It is like a child who has difficulties understanding, so his father tries to hire someone and pay him to help his son be on par with the rest of the children at school. Or, he knows that his son is not very virtuous, so he speaks to the overseer of the seminary to encourage him and strengthen him so he does not lose spirit over his virtues being unlike those of the rest of the children, and he always fails in them and feels inferior because of it.

What Is the Help in the Work that One Should Ask of the Creator?

Likewise, in the work of the Creator, we should say that where a person sees that he is weak, he needs to ask for help from above on that part, as our sages said, "He who comes to purify is aided." From the words of our sages, who said, "He who comes to purify," it seems as though all the weakness in the work is specifically on purity, that only this is out of man's hands and he needs help.

Yet, our sages promised that he who comes to purify and sees that he cannot overcome, they said about it that he should not be scared off and run from the campaign, nor should he pay attention to his inability to achieve purity. Instead, a person should believe that the Creator will help him.

However, we should also understand why the Creator did this, as this is unclear because there is a contradiction here. On one hand, we are told, "He who comes to purify." This means that the person must begin the work on purity. Yet, afterward, they said, "Were it not for the help of the Creator, he would not overcome it." This implies that man does not have the option of defeating his evil, as our sages said—without the help of the Creator, he would not overcome it.

This means that the Creator did not give man the strength to overcome the evil. Rather, it is precisely the Creator who gives him the power to overcome. Thus, what is the benefit from the fact that man must begin? Instead, he could say, "My work is worthless anyway. I cannot overcome, so why should I even begin the work? I'll wait until the Creator gives me from above the strength to overcome, and then I will begin to work. Why should I work for nothing?" The person understand that either the Creator gives him the strength to overcome the evil, or the Creator begins the work and finishes it, as we have already said in previous essays.

The answer is that since "There is no light without a *Kli* [vessel], no filling without a lack," a person must begin the work on purity because there is a known rule that we must not forget, that there is an order to the work, which is opposite from the view of landlords. Rather, it is the view of the Torah: The work on purity belongs specifically to those who study Torah, and those who study Torah are precisely those who want to achieve the level of the Torah. Our sages said about it: "The Torah exists only in he who puts himself to death over it."

The explanation of "puts himself to death over it" is that he annuls his self, which is self-love. He wants to achieve *Dvekut* [adhesion], which is equivalence of form. This is called "purity," when he purifies himself from the vessels of reception for himself. This is called "puts himself to death over it."

This is as it is written, "Purify our hearts to serve You in truth." The purity of the heart will be that our work will be in truth, meaning in order to bestow contentment upon his Maker. A lie means that a person says that he is working for the Creator, when in fact he is working for his own benefit and not for the sake of the Creator. "Learners of Torah" are those who understand that it is worthwhile to attain the Torah, since the Torah cannot be where there is separation, and self-benefit separates man from the Creator. Hence, they want to annul their own authority and be rewarded with *Dvekut* [adhesion] with the Creator, and with the Torah, which is called "the names of the Creator." She is also called "to do good to His creations," and this "doing good" is the Torah.

This is the wholeness that man must achieve because this was His thought. (We say so because "By Your actions we know You.") For this reason, they said that this is the purpose of creation, "to do good to His creations." As long as one has not achieved this, it is considered that he has not achieved completion.

However, we should understand why it is implied the help comes specifically on purity, why they do not talk about observing *Mitzvot* [commandments/good deeds] in general and the study of Torah in general, and no explicit emphasis on "Were it not for the help of the Creator."

On one hand, the words, "Man's inclination" imply that the inclination overcomes the observance of Torah and *Mitzvot* in general, and the Creator helps him. On the other hand, they say,

What Is the Help in the Work that One Should Ask of the Creator?

"He who comes to purify is aided." This means that he receives help precisely on purity.

In truth, man needs the Creator's help in all the things. However, we should determine in the work, between work of the general public and work of the individual. The work of the individual is that all their actions are only in order to bestow, and not for their own sake. This is truly against nature, for the Creator created creation to yearn to receive delight and pleasure, for the pleasure to be from satisfying their lack with delight and pleasure.

In the upper worlds, this is called "the world of Ein Sof [infinity/no end]." It means that the will to receive did not put an end on the abundance, such as to say, "I don't want to receive due to equivalence of form." There was still no such thing. Instead, we learn that afterward, this correction was done by the lower one: When the lower one wanted equivalence of form, there was a prohibition that it is forbidden to receive upper abundance in vessels of reception. Afterward, through special corrections, there was a matter that the light of pleasure will shine in vessels of reception, too.

There are many discernments in this. On one hand, The Zohar says that there is a "slim light," which is a thin light that shines within the Klipot [shells/peels]. Only because of the sin of the tree of knowledge, many sparks fell into the Klipot, and from them ABYA of Klipot were made. As a result, we discern three discernments in our work: 1) Mitzva [commandment/good deed], 2) permission/option, 3) transgression.

All of these three discernments apply in the act called "the practice of Mitzvot." Also, there is a discernment of Torah in this, "a practice," which is to know how to observe the Mitzvot. Also, there is Torah that is regarded as a practice, which is "the observing of Torah."

However, there is also the intention, namely what is the reason for observing Torah and Mitzvot, meaning what compels him to observe Torah and Mitzvot. This intention divides into two discernments: 1) for the sake of reward, called "reward and punishment." That is, the reward and punishment were said about the reward. In other words, if he observes Torah and *Mitzvot*, his reward will be that he receives in return for it good things. This, too, divides into two discernments: 1) reward in this world, that he will be happy, 2) that he will be happy in the next world.

Those two are called *Lo Lishma* [not for Her sake], since the reason he is observing Torah and *Mitzvot* is his own benefit. His exertion to engage in Torah and *Mitzvot* is in order to receive something good in return. That is, after his work, he will receive reward. Every single act that he does goes into his calculation, and afterward he is rewarded for every single act that he has done. Nothing is lost; everything is counted. He believes in the sages who said, "You can trust your landlord to pay for your work."

This is called *Lo Lishma*, as was said in *The Zohar* ("Introduction of The Book of Zohar," Item 190): "Fear is interpreted in three discernments, two of which do not contain a worthy root, and one is the root of fear. There is a person who fears the Creator so that his sons will live and not die, or fears a bodily punishment, or a punishment to one's money. Hence, he always fears Him. It follows that he does not place the fear he fears of the Creator as the root, for his own benefit is the root, and the fear is the result of it. Then there is a person who fears the Creator because he fears the punishment of that world and the punishment of Hell. Those two kinds of fear are not the essence of fear and its root. The fear that is the essence is that one should fear one's Master because He is great and ruling. That is, he should fear the Creator because He is great and rules over everything, and all the worlds He has created, upper and lower, are regarded as nothing before Him, for they do not add a thing to His essence."

Accordingly, we see that there is a huge difference between the general public and the individual. That is, "individual" means that this work does not belong to the general public, but to individuals who have the inclination to the truth, who yearn to achieve the degree where "All your actions are for the sake of the Creator," who want to serve the King because "He is great and ruling." And the only reward they want is to serve the King, meaning to observe Torah and *Mitzvot* because the greatness of the Creator commits them to observe Torah and *Mitzvot*, and not for their own sake.

It follows that among those people, who want to work only *Lishma* [for Her sake], there is also reward and punishment, because our sages said about them, too, that man must believe in reward and punishment. Thus, what is the difference between reward and punishment in *Lo Lishma*, and reward and punishment for people who want to walk in *Lishma*?

The answer is that we must understand what is "reward" and what is "punishment." Everyone knows that reward is a good thing and punishment is a bad thing. It follows that for people who work for their own benefit, "good" means that they receive for their work something that satisfies their will to receive, and they say that it is worthwhile to work in return for the good things he will receive. "Punishment" means simply that he says, "It is a shame that I did not engage in Torah and *Mitzvot* because I lost the reward and even suffered a punishment, meaning something that makes me suffer."

Conversely, those who want to work for the sake of the Creator regard the time when they have the strength to work to bestow and not receive for themselves as a "reward." And when they are immersed in self-love, they regard it as "punishment." However, the reward and punishment do not pertain to the reward, as with those who work *Lo Lishma*. In the work *Lishma*, which is against our nature, is called "purity." And since it is not within man's power, our sages said about this, "Were it not for the help of the Creator, he would not overcome it."

Conversely, in *Lo Lishma*, which is natural, there is no need to say, "Were it not for the help of the Creator, he would not overcome it," since *Lo Lishma* is not against nature. That is, it is the work of the general public, called "one line," who have no knowledge of anything but the reward of this world or the reward of the next world.

And since this pertains to self-love, meaning that they understand that it is worthwhile to relinquish pleasures in this world, which is a passing world, and in return to be able to eat "the wild ox and the whale," for this reason, many people who work in one line can afflict themselves in this world in order to be rewarded with pleasures in the next world, which is an eternal world. Hence, they do not need the help of the Creator, for they see that they themselves are the workers, and when they look at the general public, they feel superior.

But when those who want to work in order to bestow look at the general public, they feel that they are worse and lower than them, since they feel the evil in them, which is the will to receive for themselves, who is the ruler, and they cannot emerge from self-love. They always look at the how much work they have exerted in order to be able to work in order to bestow, and they are always shown how far they are inherently removed from it. They see that they are dirty in every way and need purification.

Since they walk in two lines, they see the truth. Hence, in order for such a person not to escape the campaign, he is told the truth, that it is not within our power to defeat the evil inclination. Instead, "Were it not for the help of the Creator, he would not overcome it."

This is why it was said in *The Zohar*, "He who comes to purify is aided." They did not merely say that he is given help, since specifically in purity, a person sees that he is unable to walk on the path where all your work is for the sake of the Creator. It follows that he does not have to believe above reason that "Were it not for the help of the Creator, he would not overcome it," since he sees the truth, that he is unable to emerge from self-love. For this reason, many times, a person falls into despair and needs great reinforcement to believe above reason that the Creator can help him emerge from self-love.

But those who walk on one line are completely opposite. A person sees within reason that he overcomes his evil inclination and does not need any help from the Creator in observing the Torah and *Mitzvot*. Rather, since our sages said, "Were it not for the help of the Creator, he would not overcome it," he believes above reason that the Creator helps him. Yet, within reason, he knows that he has the power to overcome his evil inclination and he is not like other people in the general public, who are lowly. He feels superior to them.

It therefore follows that concerning the help of the Creator, there is a big difference between those who walk on one line, and those who walk on two lines. Those who walk on one line see that they are doing everything and do not see that the Creator needs to give the help. Rather, they believe above reason that the Creator has helped them.

However, those who walk on two lines see that they cannot do a thing. They must make great efforts for the help that the Creator gives, and they must exert and say that the Creator can help them. Then, when they emerge from the control of the inclination, they see within reason that the Creator helped them, and otherwise, they would be forever governed by the inclination.

www.ingramcontent.com/pod-product-compliance
Lightning Source LLC
Chambersburg PA
CBHW051706160426
43209CB00004B/1041